I Am Providence

Lovecraft in front of his home at 598 Angell Street, Providence
(photo courtesy of Sean Donnelly)

I Am Providence

The Life and Times of H. P. Lovecraft: Volume 1

S. T. Joshi

Hippocampus Press

New York

Published by Hippocampus Press
P.O. Box 641, New York, NY 10156.
http://www.hippocampuspress.com

Hippocampus Press logo by Anastasia Damianakos.
Cover design by Barbara Briggs Silbert.

First Paperback Edition
1 3 5 7 9 8 6 4 2

ISBN 978-1-61498-051-3 (Volume 1)
ISBN 978-1-61498-053-7 (2 Volume Set)

The Library of Congress has cataloged the hardcover edition as follows:

Joshi, S. T., 1958-
I am Providence : the life and times of H.P. Lovecraft / S. T. Joshi. -- 1st ed.
p. cm.
Complete in 2 volumes.
In 1996, S. T. Joshi's H.P. Lovecraft: a life was published. The edition was abridged by more than 150,000 words. This new version I am Providence: the life and times of H.P. Lovecraft restores every word of Joshi's original manuscript. The text has been revised and updated in light of the new information on Lovecraft that has emerged since 1996--Provided by publisher.
Includes bibliographical references and index.
ISBN 978-0-9824296-7-9 (alk. paper)
1. Lovecraft, H. P. (Howard Phillips), 1890-1937. 2. Authors, American--20th century--Biography. 3. Fantasy fiction--Authorship. 4. Horror tales--Authorship. I. Title.
PS3523.O833Z72 2010
813'.52--dc22
[B]

2010028590

To
Kenneth W. Faig, Jr
Donald R. Burleson
and
David E. Schultz

PREFACE

I don't imagine that the publication of so large a biography of H. P. Lovecraft needs a defence today: his ascent into the canon of American literature with the publication of the Library of America edition of his *Tales* (2005), and, concurrently, his continued popularity among devotees of horror fiction, comics, films, and role-playing games suggest that Lovecraft will remain a compelling figure for decades to come. What may perhaps require some justification is my decision to issue this unabridged version of a biography that I wrote in 1993–95 and that was published in truncated form in 1996. In the nearly fifteen years since that time, a surprising amount of new information about Lovecraft—his life, his work, and his milieu—has emerged, necessitating some significant revisions in various portions of this book. Foremost in this regard must be cited Kenneth W. Faig, Jr, who with others has dug even deeper than before into Lovecraft's paternal and maternal ancestry. Other research by Steven J. Mariconda, David E. Schultz, T. R. Livesey, Robert H. Waugh, and any number of others has resulted in changes both large and small. I believe I have also benefited from the pertinent criticisms of a number of reviewers of the truncated edition.

A reader of the earlier version might ask: Exactly what is new about this edition aside from the bare addition of more than 150,000 words? In all humility I am now unable to answer this question in any detail. My pruning of the version I wrote in 1993–95—comprising more than 500,000 words—was on the level of both individual words, phrases, and sentences and some entire sections. One gauge of the kind and degree of omissions can be gauged by the number of footnotes in the trimmed and the full version; to choose a chapter at random, Chapter 14 in the earlier version had 75 footnotes; the current version has 98. In this version, therefore, I am even more determined to specify the documentary basis for my assertions.

In the past decade and a half, important publications by and about Lovecraft have made the biographer's life much simpler, at least in terms of citations. Far and away the most significant in this regard is Peter Cannon's exemplary compilation of memoirs of Lovecraft, *Lovecraft Remembered* (1998), a volume so close to definitive that it scarcely ever need be done over again. I have some small quibbles with Cannon's selections: for example, I wish he had not included the truncated version of Sonia Davis's memoir of her husband, successively edited by Winfield Townley Scott and August Derleth, and had included the first of Muriel Eddy's memoirs rather than a later one; as a result I have cited these (and a few other) items from sources other than *Lovecraft Remembered.*

The most radical development is the extensive publication of Lovecraft's letters, especially to important correspondents such as August Derleth, Robert E. Howard, and Donald Wandrei. And yet, because the Arkham House edition of *Selected Letters* (1965–76) is still the most widely available and convenient compendium of Lovecraft's letters, I have in general cited it even in cases where it has been superseded by these later editions.

I have not cited any specific editions of Lovecraft's fiction, essays, or poetry. In terms of the fiction, Barnes & Noble has issued for the first time a collection of all Lovecraft's original fiction (2008); but the first printing was marred by many typographical errors. As of this writing, I have received a promise from the in-house editor that these errors will be corrected (perhaps, however, not all at once), so that subsequent printings of the volume should be definitive. The book is, of course, not annotated, and readers interested in the background behind Lovecraft's stories might wish to consult my three Penguin editions (1999–2004), along with such volumes as *From the Pest Zone: Stories from New York* (2003).

Lovecraft's essays are now conveniently gathered in *Collected Essays* (2004–06; 5 vols.), and his poetry in *The Ancient Track: Complete Poetical Works* (2001).

I would like to repeat the many friends and colleagues who have, over the past thirty years, materially aided me in my research on Lovecraft. Among those who actually knew or corresponded with Lovecraft, I can thank Frank Belknap Long, J. Vernon Shea, Donald Wandrei, Robert Bloch, Mrs. Ethel Phillips Morrish, and Harry K. Brobst; sadly, all but the last of these are no more. Among students and scholars, I have learnt most about Lovecraft's life and work from the three individuals to whom this book is dedicated—Kenneth W. Faig, Jr, David E. Schultz, and Donald R. Burleson; but other individuals, such as Dirk W. Mosig, Steven J. Mariconda, Peter Cannon, J. Vernon Shea, George T. Wetzel, R. Boerem, Scott Connors, Richard L. Tierney, Matthew H. Onderdonk, Fritz Leiber, M. Eileen McNamara, Donovan K. Loucks, Stefan Dziemianowicz, T. E. D. Klein, Perry M. Grayson, Scott D. Briggs, Marc A. Michaud, Sam Moskowitz, Robert M. Price, A. Langley Searles, and Richard D. Squires should not be overlooked. I am most grateful to Donovan K. Loucks for assembling the photographs for this book

The John Hay Library of Brown University remains the chief repository of Lovecraft manuscript and printed material, and its Lovecraft Collection is now in the capable hands of Rosemary Cullen. She and her staff have allowed me unprecedented access to its bountiful documents.

As in so many of my recent projects, I am sincerely grateful to David E. Schultz for his customary care in the design of this book, and to Derrick Hussey for his courage and confidence in publishing it.

—S. T. JOSHI

Seattle, Washington
June 2009

CONTENTS

ABBREVIATIONS

AD	August Derleth
AEPG	Annie E. P. Gamwell
CAS	Clark Ashton Smith
DW	Donald Wandrei
EHP	E. Hoffmann Price
FBL	Frank Belknap Long
JFM	James F. Morton
JVS	J. Vernon Shea
LDC	Lillian D. Clark
MWM	Maurice W. Moe
REH	Robert E. Howard
RHB	R. H. Barlow
RK	Rheinhart Kleiner
CoC	*Crypt of Cthulhu*
LS	*Lovecraft Studies*
AHT	Arkham House transcripts of Lovecraft's letters
JHL	John Hay Library of Brown University, Providence

I Am Providence

1. Unmixed English Gentry

Only an intermittently diligent genealogist, Howard Phillips Lovecraft was unable to discover much about the paternal side of his ancestry beyond the notes collected by his great-aunt Sarah Allgood.[1] Subsequent genealogical research has failed to verify much of this information, especially regarding the Lovecrafts prior to their coming to America in the early nineteenth century. Moreover, some particulars of Lovecraft's reports concerning both his paternal and maternal ancestry have been proven definitively false. Some details may now be beyond recovery, but still much work remains for anyone wishing to reconstruct Lovecraft's ancestry.

According to the Allgood notes, the Lovecraft or Lovecroft name does not appear any earlier than 1450, when various heraldic charts reveal Lovecrofts in Devonshire near the Teign. Collateral lines, of course, can be traced to the Norman Conquest or even earlier. Lovecraft's own direct line does not emerge until 1560, with John Lovecraft. As he recounts it: "Well—*John* begat *Richard* who begat *William* who begat *George* who begat *Joseph* who begat *John* who begat *Thomas* who begat *Joseph* who begat *George* who begat *Winfield* who begat your antient Grandpa."[2]

Unfortunately, as Kenneth W. Faig, Jr, has recently pointed out, in reference to the Allgood notes, "the most charitable thing that can be said is that it appears to be largely the invention of the creator."[3] Faig and his collaborators A. Langley Searles and Chris Docherty, were unable to verify *any* of the male names of the Lovecraft line prior to Joseph Lovecraft (1775–1850), Lovecraft's great-grandfather. Some evidence exists as to the descent of Joseph from John Lovecraft (1742–1780), and John from Joseph [not Thomas] Lovecraft (1703–1781), but even this is conjectural. Faig goes on to remark, in regard to Lovecraft's repeated claims of his descent from a number of other collateral lines: "Lovecraft probably did not descend from any of the 'great' lines claimed by his charts—Fulford, Edgecombe, Chichester, Carew, Musgrave, and Reed are just a few of the lines probably not actually in Lovecraft's ancestry."[4]

It is, unfortunately, one of these collateral lines that Lovecraft (probably falsely) believed provided the one genuinely weird legend he could claim. The wife of George Lovecraft (Lovecraft's paternal grandfather) was Helen Allgood, and through her line Lovecraft thought he was related to the Musgraves of Eden Hall, Cumberland. A Musgrave was reputed to have stolen a drinking-glass from the fairies, who, after vain attempts to recover it, pronounced the following prophecy:

If the glass either break or fall,
Farewell to the luck of Eden Hall.

Lovecraft claimed that this glass was on display in the South Kensington Museum in London.[5] This was an informal name for the Victoria and Albert Museum, so renamed in 1899. The object—a 6¼" beaker of Syrian origin dating to the thirteenth century (presumably brought back by a Crusader)—is now in the Islamic Gallery there; it had been on loan from the Musgrave family since 1926, and had been purchased in 1959.[6] Longfellow paraphrased the legend as "The Luck of Edenhall."[7]

Late in life Lovecraft, given his strong astronomical interests, was pleased to discover a genuine man of science in his remote maternal ancestry. John Field or Feild (1520–1587), called "The Proto-Copernican of England", published an Ephemeris for 1557 in 1556 and another one for the years 1558, 1559, and 1560 in 1558; these two volumes contained the first account in English of the Copernican theory.[8] Unfortunately for Lovecraft, the relation of this John Field to a John Field (d. 1686) who was one of the original settlers of Providence, Rhode Island, and from whom Lovecraft actually was descended on the maternal side in a fairly direct line, is now in dispute. Lovecraft, unaware of the uncertainty of the matter, was understandably heartened by this discovery, for as an atheist he found his paternal line in particular "lousy with clergymen but short on straight thinkers,"[9] and said of his ancestry in general: "No philosophers—no artists—no writers—not a cursed soul I could possibly talk to without getting a pain in the neck."[10]

Lovecraft was much regaled by accounts (presumably preserved by Helen Allgood) of one Thomas Lovecraft (1745–1826), who apparently lived such a dissolute life that he was forced in 1823 to sell the ancestral estate, Minster Hall near Newton-Abbot. Lovecraft, a little surprisingly given his generally dim view of either sexual or monetary profligacy, found himself strangely attracted to this individual, boasting of owning a book with the inscription "Tho. Lovecraft, Gent. His Book, 1787"[11] and speaking almost approvingly of his dissipation of the estate. Again, it is regrettable that this connexion cannot be verified. Faig reports: "We have not been able to find any Thomas Lovecraft who married Letitia Edgecombe in 1766 and was proprietor of Minster Hall near Newton Abbot. Devon has no record of any estate called Minster Hall."[12] Lovecraft believed that it was Thomas Lovecraft's sixth child, Joseph Lovecraft, who decided in 1827 to emigrate, taking his wife Mary Fulford (actually Mary Full, 1782–1864) and their six children, John Full, William, Joseph, Jr, George, Aaron, and Mary, to Ontario, Canada. Finding no prospects there, he drifted down to the area around Rochester, New York, where he was established by at least 1831 as a cooper and carpenter. The details of this migration have not been confirmed, and some parts seem definitely erroneous; for example, Joseph and his children were still in England in 1828. The best one can say is that Joseph Lovecraft is found in the Rochester area around 1830–31.

Lovecraft was convinced that there were no Lovecrafts left in England, and this seems in the most literal sense of the term to be the case; but individuals with the name Lucraft or Luckraft are found in abundance as late as the end of the nineteenth century,[13] and many are listed in recent London telephone directories;[14] these seem to be either variant spellings or fairly closely related lines. Lovecraft himself, however, was never in touch with any relations in England. It is interesting to note that the 1840 U.S. census for Rochester gives the spelling of Joseph Lovecraft's sons John F. and William as "Lovecroft," and the 1840 U.S. census of Peru Township in Clinton County, New York, gives Joseph, Jr's last name as "Lucraft".[15]

Lovecraft's paternal grandfather was George Lovecraft, who was born in 1815.[16] In 1839 he married Helen Allgood (1820–1881) and lived much of his life in Rochester as a harness maker. Of his five children, two died in infancy; the other three were Emma Jane (1847–1925), Winfield Scott (1853–1898), and Mary Louise (1855–1916). Emma married Isaac Hill, principal of the Pelham, N.Y., high school;[17] Mary married Paul Mellon. Winfield married Sarah Susan Phillips and begat Howard Phillips Lovecraft. Several of these individuals—George Lovecraft, Helen Allgood Lovecraft, Emma Jane Hill, Mary Louise Mellon, among other relations—are buried in Woodlawn Cemetery in the Bronx.[18]

Lovecraft appears to have been much more industrious in tracking down his maternal ancestry, but again his conclusions are not always to be trusted. In 1915 he maintained that "The first Phillips of [his] branch came to Rhode Island from Lincolnshire in the latter part of the seventeenth century, and established himself in the western part of the colony";[19] at this point Lovecraft had no name for this first transplanted ancestor. By 1924 he was claiming descent from the Rev. George Phillips (d. 1644), who in 1630 left England on the *Arbella* and settled in Watertown, Massachusetts (the township directly west of Cambridge).[20] There is reason to doubt this; or, rather, to doubt Lovecraft's assertion that George was the father of Michael Phillips (1630?–1686?) of Newport, Rhode Island, from whom Lovecraft really is descended. In any event, Asaph Phillips (1764–1829), Michael's great-grandson (or, more likely, great-great-grandson), headed inland and settled around 1788 in Foster, in the west-central part of the state near the Connecticut border. Asaph and his wife Esther Whipple (collaterally related to Abraham Whipple, the Revolutionary war hero) had eight children, all of whom, incredibly, survived to adulthood. The sixth child, Jeremiah Phillips (1800–1848), built a water-powered grist mill on the Moosup River in Foster and was killed on November 20, 1848, when his flowing greatcoat got caught in the machinery, dragging him into it. As Jeremiah's wife Roby Rathbun Phillips had died earlier in 1848, their four children (a fifth, the first-born, had died in infancy) were left as orphans. They were Susan, James, Whipple, and Abbie. Whipple Van Buren Phillips (1833–1904) is Lovecraft's maternal grandfather.

Lovecraft mentions that Whipple attended the East Greenwich Academy (then called the Providence Conference Seminary),[21] but no date for his attendance has been established; probably it occurred prior to the death of his father, Jeremiah. In 1852 Whipple went to live with his uncle James Phillips (1794–1878) in Delavan, Illinois, a temperance town his relatives had founded; he returned the next year to Foster because (as his obituary declares) the climate did not suit him.[22] It was probably at this time that he engaged in what Lovecraft called a "brief career as a teacher in the country schools."[23] He married his first cousin, Robie Alzada Place (1827–1896),[24] on January 27, 1856, settling in a homestead in Foster built by Robie's father, Stephen Place. Their first child, Lillian Delora (1856–1932), was born less than three months later. There were four other children: Sarah Susan (1857–1921), Emeline (1859–1865), Edwin Everett (1864–1918), and Annie Emeline (1866–1941). Lovecraft's mother Sarah Susan was born, as her own mother had been, at the Place homestead.[25]

In 1855 Whipple purchased a general store in Foster and ran it for at least two years;[26] he then presumably sold the store and its goods, probably at a substantial profit, thereby commencing his career as entrepreneur and land speculator. At that time[27] he moved a few miles south of Foster to the town of Coffin's Corner, where he built "a mill, a house, an assembly hall, and several cottages for employees";[28] since he had purchased all the land there, he renamed the town Greene (in honour of the Rhode Island Revolutionary War hero Nathanael Greene). Many of these structures—including the house Whipple built for his family—were still standing in 1926, when Lovecraft and his aunt Annie visited them. It is remarkable to think of a twenty-four-year-old essentially owning an entire small town, but Whipple was clearly a bold and dynamic businessman, one who would gain and lose several fortunes in his crowded life.

Lovecraft states that his grandfather founded the Masonic Lodge at Greene, and this statement is confirmed by Henry W. Rugg's *History of Freemasonry in Rhode Island* (1895). Rugg writes:

> In the year 1869 Bro. Whipple D. [*sic*] Phillips and fifteen other brethren, nearly all members of Manchester Lodge, united in asking for a Dispensation authorizing the establishment of a new Lodge, to be called "Ionic Lodge." The petition was presented to Most Wor. Bro. Thomas A. Doyle, then Grand Master, who approved the same, and issued a Dispensation under date of January 15, 1870, authorizing and empowering the petitioners to form and open a new Lodge in the village of Greene, town of Coventry, to be designated Ionic Lodge, No. 12.

> Acting under the authority thus conferred, the first meeting of the brethren interested, was held March 19, 1870, with Bro. Whipple D. Phillips officiating as Master, Bro. Warren H. Tillinghast as S. W., and William R. Carter as J. W.[29]

Whipple Phillips held positions in other Masonic organisations in Rhode Island. In 1886, after the Lodge found itself crowded in its quarters, Whipple—although by then settled in Providence—leased to the Masons an edifice he had built and still owned, "Phillips Hall."[30]

Whipple at this time made his brief foray into Rhode Island politics, serving (according to his obituary) in the lower house of the state legislature from May 1870 to May 1872. But politics clearly did not suit him as well as business. Lovecraft tells the story of the ups and downs of his business dealings at the time: ". . . in 1870 [Whipple] was overtaken by sudden collapse financially—a thing he could have averted by disavowing responsibility for a signed note, but which as a gentleman he refused to evade. This moved the family to Providence, where a happy financial recovery took place . . ."[31] It may be possible to elaborate upon this incident somewhat. Casey B. Tyler, Lovecraft's maternal grandmother's cousin,[32] in his *Historical Reminiscences of Foster, Rhode Island* (1884–93) refers the fact that Whipple "at last fell prey to that noted demon, 'Hugog,' and lost much of his hard earnings." There is no telling who this Hugog is, but Tyler reports that he himself in 1869 lost $10,000 as a result of the "rascality of a pretended friend, called Hugog."[33] Perhaps the swindling of Tyler and Whipple's loss of money are related. In any event, Tyler had nothing good to say about Mr Hugog: "There has never been but one person from Foster who has been a disgrace and dishonor to the town and may his name never be mentioned and although possessed of much ill-gotten wealth, may he be forgiven and forgotten and his name sink in oblivion as not worthy to be remembered by future generations."[34] Tyler has apparently gotten his wish.

The Place homestead in Foster must have been sold at this time, as Lovecraft states that it passed out of the family in 1870.[35] The move to Providence probably occurred in 1874.[36] After several changes of residence Whipple settled around 1876 at 276 Broadway on the West Side of Providence—the western shore of the Providence River, site of the present business district—since his business offices were in this general area (principally at 5 Custom House Street near the river). The 1878 city directory lists him as owner of a "fringing machine" business, i.e. the manufacturing of fringes for curtains, bedspreads, and perhaps clothing. One curious sidelight is Whipple's travel to France for the Paris Universal Exposition of 1878 in connexion with his fringing business. He does not seem to have had good luck getting his name printed correctly, for the official report of the exhibition lists him as "Phillips (M. D.) & Co., Providence, R.I."[37] Lovecraft reports that his grandfather was "a man of culture & extensive travel" and makes note of "his acquaintance with all the wonders of Europe, which he had seen at first hand."[38]

Whipple's Paris jaunt was only the first (if indeed it was the first) of many such voyages to the Continent; his obituary reports that there was a "protracted business visit" to London and Liverpool in 1880.

By this time Whipple Phillips was clearly a man of substantial means, and aside from building the house at 194 Angell Street in 1880–81, he undertook what was to be his most ambitious business enterprise: the establishment of the Owyhee Land and Irrigation Company in Owyhee County in the southwest corner of Idaho, "which had for its object the damming of the Snake River & the irrigation of the surrounding farming & fruit-growing region."[39] Kenneth W. Faig, Jr, has performed a remarkable feat of excavation in supplying the details of his enterprise, and I can do no better than to summarise his findings.[40]

The company was incorporated in Providence as the Snake River Company as early as 1884, with Whipple as president and his nephew Jeremiah W. Phillips (son of his brother James W. Phillips) as secretary and treasurer. Initially the company dealt in "land and live stock" (as an advertisement in the 1888 Providence city directory states), but shortly thereafter Whipple shifted his attention to the building of a dam—not over the Snake River, as Lovecraft believed, but over its tributary, the Bruneau River. Lovecraft states that the company was reorganised in October 1889 as the Owyhee Land and Irrigation Company and incorporated as a Maine corporation;[41] in 1892 it was again reorganised as a Rhode Island corporation.

Work on the dam began in the autumn of 1887 and was completed by early 1890. Following his habit of naming towns, Whipple purchased the Henry Dorsey Ferry in 1887 and established a town near the ferry on the Snake River, naming it Grand View. (In the 1980 census this town, about thirty miles south of Boise, had a population of 366.) He also built a Grand View Hotel, to be managed by his son Edwin.

At this point disaster struck. On March 5, 1890, the dam was completely washed out by high waters, and the $70,000 spent in constructing it was lost. The *Owyhee Avalanche*, a paper published in nearby Silver City, made a sanguine prediction: "Mr. Phillips, the manager, is not the man to be disheartened by an accident of the kind above mentioned, and he will no doubt have a better dam than the one destroyed in the same place in less than two years." In the event, the *Avalanche* was only slightly optimistic: a new dam was begun in the summer of 1891 and completed by February 1893.

Whipple was, of course, by no means permanently at the site; indeed, he appears to have visited it only occasionally. We shall see that when he was not in Idaho, he was spending considerable time and effort (especially after April 1893) raising his then only grandchild, Howard Phillips Lovecraft. The *Avalanche* reports trips to Idaho by Whipple Phillips in June and October 1891 and July 1892. There must have been later trips also, for Lovecraft reports receiving letters from his grandfather postmarked Boise City, Mountain Home, and Grand View.[42] Oddly enough, the earliest known letter to Lovecraft from Whipple (June 19, 1894) is postmarked Omaha, Nebraska; a letter of February 20, 1899 is postmarked Grand View, while another of October 27, 1899 comes from Scranton, Pennsylvania.[43]

The Owyhee Land and Irrigation Company appears to have suffered some sort of financial difficulties around 1900; this is the last date the company is listed in the Providence city directory, and on March 12, 1901, the company was sold at a sheriff's sale in Silver City. Whipple Phillips was one of five purchasers, but the total property value of the company had been assessed on May 25, 1900, at only $9430, more than half of it a mining ditch. The final blow came in early 1904, when the dam was wiped out again. Lovecraft states that this second disaster "virtually wiped the Phillips family out financially & hastened my grandfather's death—age 70, of apoplexy."[44] Whipple Phillips died on March 28, 1904; after his death three other individuals bought out his interest in the Owyhee Land and Irrigation Company and renamed it the Grand View Irrigation Company, Ltd. I shall have more to say about this entire incident later.

The Owyhee project was clearly Whipple's principal business concern during his later years, although no doubt he had other interests in Providence and elsewhere, as his wide travels suggest. Arthur S. Koki, having gained access to the Phillips family papers, found some stationery listing Whipple as the proprietor of the Westminster Hotel at 317 Westminster Street in Providence, but there is no indication of the date or duration of his proprietorship.[45] In spite of the large sum of money that he lost in the Idaho venture, the picture that emerges of Whipple Phillips is that of an abundantly capable businessman—bold, innovative, and perhaps a little reckless—but also a man of wide culture and one who took great concern in the financial, intellectual, and personal well-being of his extended family. We shall see these latter traits well displayed in his nurturing of his young grandchild.

Of Whipple Phillips's wife Robie very little is known. Lovecraft states that she attended the Lapham Institute (cited by Lovecraft as "Lapham Seminary") in North Scituate, Rhode Island,[46] about fifteen miles northeast of Greene, but does not supply the date of her attendance. Lapham Institute was founded as Smithfield Institute in 1839 by the Rhode Island Association of Free Baptists,[47] and conceivably Robie Place could have been one of the first students to attend it. The mere fact that she went there suggests her strong religiosity, as does the fact that both she and her three surviving daughters joined the First Baptist Church in the 1880s; Robie and Susie, at least, remained on the rolls until their respective deaths.[48] Lovecraft describes his grandmother in an early letter as "a serene, quiet lady of the old school."[49]

Lovecraft's elder aunt, Lillian Delora Clark, attended the Wheaton Female Seminary (now Wheaton College) in Norton, Massachusetts, for at least the period

1871–73.[50] Norton is a small town in the southeastern part of the state, about ten miles from the Rhode Island border; it is not clear why Lillian and also Susie attended this college preparatory school rather than one more locally situated. Lovecraft states that she "also attended the State Normal School, and was for some time a teacher,"[51] but her attendance at the Normal School has not been confirmed. Lovecraft was proud of the artistic skills of both his aunt and his mother, and claimed that Lillian has "had canvases hung in exhibitions at the Providence Art Club."[52]

Lovecraft speaks little of his uncle, Edwin Everett Phillips, and it is clear that he was not close to him. We have seen that he briefly assisted his father in his Idaho enterprise, but he returned to Providence in 1889 and attempted—not very successfully, it appears—to go into business for himself. In 1894 he married Martha Helen Mathews; at some point they were divorced, then remarried in 1903. Throughout his life Edwin seems to have held various odd jobs—a manufacturer's representative, real estate and mortgage agent, rent collector, notary public, coin dealer[53]—and, probably in the early 1910s, established the Edwin E. Phillips Refrigeration Company. His one significant involvement with Lovecraft and his mother was, as we shall see, an unfortunate one.

Annie Emeline Phillips, Lovecraft's younger aunt, was nine years younger than Susie. Lovecraft remarks that she "was yet a very young lady when I first began to observe events about me. She was rather a favourite in the younger social set, & brought the principal touch of gayety to a rather conservative household."[54] I know nothing about her education.[55]

We can finally turn our attention to Sarah Susan Phillips, born on October 17, 1857, at the Place homestead in Foster. Regrettably little is known about her early years. A commonplace book she began keeping in her youth contains—aside from school lessons, genealogical information, and other matter—a touching tribute to her sister Emeline, who died of diphtheria in 1865, before her sixth birthday:

> Little Emma was a child of great promise, her budding intellect already began to awaken fond expectations in the minds of her friends, while her artless simplicity of manners and sweetness of temper not only doubly endeared her to her parents but won the hearts of all who knew her.
>
> She manifested much patience during her sickness although suffering severely from difficult breathing and once in her childlike manner said to her mother, "I wish I could stop breathing a little while just to rest." At another time she roused up and said "mother the bible is a guide to youth."[56]

Lovecraft states that she, like Lillian, attended Wheaton Female Seminary, but her attendance can only be confirmed for the school year 1871–72.[57] From this period up to the time of her marriage in 1889 the record is blank, aside from the fact that she is listed in the 1880 U.S. census as residing with her father at 276 Broadway. Clara Hess, a friend of the Lovecrafts, gives a description of Susie, probably dating from the late 1890s: "She was very pretty and attractive, with a beautiful and unusually white complexion—got, it is said, by eating arsenic, although whether there was any truth to this story I do not know. She was an intensely nervous person."[58] What to make of the arsenic story—and whether this had anything to do with Susie's later physical and psychological maladies—I have no idea. In a later piece Hess continues: "She had a peculiarly shaped nose which rather fascinated me, as it gave her a very inquiring expression. Howard looked very much like her."[59]

What little we know of Winfield Scott Lovecraft prior to his marriage derives from research conducted by Richard D. Squires of the Wallace Library at the Rochester Institute of Technology.[60] Winfield was born on October 26, 1853, probably at the home of George and Helen Lovecraft at 42 (later renumbered 67) Marshall Street in Rochester. His name, of course, derives from General Winfield Scott, and it is perhaps no accident that he was so named almost exactly a year after Scott, then the Whig candidate for president, visited Rochester (October 14, 1852). George Lovecraft was at the time a "traveling agent" for the Ellwanger & Barry Nursery, a major business in Rochester. The family attended services at the Grace Episcopal (now St Paul's) Church. These facts may be of some relevance to Winfield, since he was himself a salesman and as he was married at St Paul's Episcopal Church in Boston, even though his bride was a Baptist.

The family's address in 1859 is listed as 26 Griffith Street in Rochester, one street over from the Marshall Street address. (This house is no longer standing, although the Marshall Street house is.) There is no evidence as to the site of Winfield's early schooling; presumably it was in one of the elementary schools in Rochester. Around 1863 George Lovecraft left the area to investigate the possibility of the family's move to New York City, and for about a year Winfield lived with his mother, sisters, and uncle Joseph, Jr, at 106 Allen Street. The family did in fact move to New York around 1870, but Winfield stayed behind. From 1871 to 1873 he was employed as a blacksmith for the James Cunningham & Son carriage factory, Rochester's largest employer for many years. During this time Winfield boarded with another uncle, John Full Lovecraft, in a home on Marshall Street. By 1874 all traces of Winfield Scott Lovecraft disappear from the records in Rochester.

Lovecraft stated in 1915 that his father "was educated both privately, and at a military school, making modern languages his specialty";[61] but less than two years later he wrote that Winfield "was a lover of things military, and . . . in youth gave up an appointment to West Point only to please his mother."[62] Did, then, Winfield indeed attend any military academy at all? The location of this military school has not been traced, and Winfield clearly did not attend West Point, as a quick check of its registry of graduates establishes. It is possible that it may not have been a formal military academy (of which there were very few at the time) but a school that emphasised military training. In any event, it is likely to have been local—somewhere in New York State, perhaps close to the Rochester area—although according to Squires there does not seem to be any such school. Winfield's attendance (if it occurred at all) may have preceded his employment as a blacksmith, and the military school could have been the equivalent of a high school.

At some point Winfield moved to New York City, as this is given as his place of residence on his marriage certificate. He does not appear, however, in the city directories of Manhattan or Brooklyn (there were no city directories for Queens or the Bronx for the period of Winfield's presumable residence there). But one individual of some interest *is* found in the Manhattan city directory for much of the 1880s: Frederick A. Lovecraft (1850–1893), the son of George Lovecraft's older brother Aaron, and therefore Winfield's cousin. Is it possible that Winfield roomed or boarded with Frederick for some period prior to his marriage? Boarders were frequently overlooked in city directories (Lovecraft himself, boarding at 10 Barnes Street from 1926 to 1932, does not show up for any of these years in the Providence city directory), and I can imagine no other likely scenario for Winfield's New York residence.

It is believed that he became employed by Gorham & Co., Silversmiths, of Providence, a company founded in 1813 by Jabez Gorham[63] and for many years one of the major business concerns in the city. The testimony for this employment does not derive from any statement by Lovecraft, as far as I know, but from a remark by Lovecraft's wife Sonia in her 1948: "His father, Winfield Scott Lovecraft, had at one time been a traveling salesman for the Gorham Company, Silversmiths of the United States of America."[64] One would like to believe that Lovecraft told her this information. Arthur S. Koki, investigating the matter in the early 1960s, wrote: "Since the personnel records of the Gorham Company are not retained beyond forty years, it is difficult to determine when he was first employed there."[65] This may not be entirely accurate, as I have been informed that salesmen's records were kept at Gorham's New York office.[66] It is not clear how and when Winfield began work for Gorham (assuming that he actually did so), and why, even if he was working as a travelling salesman, he was listed as a resident of New York City at the time of his marriage on June 12, 1889. It may or may not be relevant that the 1889/90 Manhattan city directory lists Frederick A. Lovecraft as a "jeweler": is it possible that he somehow assisted Winfield in securing his position at Gorham? This is pure conjecture, but we have nothing else to go on.

Equally a mystery is how he met Sarah Susan Phillips and how they fell in love. Susie certainly does not appear to have been a "society girl" like her sister Annie, and Winfield was not a door-to-door salesman, so that he is not likely to have met her in this way; nor, if he had, would the social mores of the time have allowed them to fraternise. The Phillipses were, after all, part of the Providence aristocracy.

The fact that the wedding ceremony took place at St Paul's Episcopal Church in Boston may or may not be noteworthy. We have already seen that Winfield's family was Episcopal; and although there were many Episcopal churches in Providence where the ceremony could have taken place, the fact that Winfield planned to settle his family in the Boston area may have made St Paul's a logical site. Indeed, it might have been odd for a member of the Phillips family of Providence, so associated with the Baptist faith, to have been married in a local Episcopal church. I discount the possibility, therefore, that the marriage was somehow not approved by Susie's parents, for which no true evidence exists. Although she was thirty-one at the time of the marriage, Susie was the first of Whipple Phillips's daughters to be married; as she was still living under his roof, it is not likely that he would have allowed her to marry someone of whom he did not approve.

Lovecraft, so keen on racial purity, was fond of declaring that his "ancestry was that of unmixed English gentry";[67] and if one can include a Welsh (Morris) strain on his paternal side and an Irish (Casey) strain on his maternal, then the statement can pass. His maternal line is, indeed, far more distinguished than his paternal, and we find Rathbones, Mathewsons, Whipples, Places, Wilcoxes, Hazards, and other old New England lines behind Susie Lovecraft and her father Whipple Van Buren Phillips. What we do not find—as noted earlier and as Lovecraft frequently bemoaned—is much in the way of intellectual, artistic, or imaginative distinction. But if Lovecraft himself failed to inherit the business acumen of Whipple Phillips, he did somehow acquire the literary gifts that have resulted in a subsidiary fascination with his mother, father, grandfather, and the other members of his near and distant ancestry.

2. A GENUINE PAGAN (1890–1897)

In April 1636, Roger Williams left the Massachusetts-Bay colony and headed south, settling first on the east bank of the Seekonk River and later, when Massachusetts asserted territorial rights to this region, to the west bank. He named this site Providence. Williams's immediate reason for seeking new territory was, of course, religious freedom: his own Baptist beliefs did not sit well at all with the Puritan theocracy of the Massachusetts-Bay. Shortly afterward Rhode Island attracted two further religious dissidents from Massachusetts: Samuel Gorton, who arrived in Providence in 1640, and the Antinomian Anne Hutchinson (a collateral descendant of Lovecraft on the maternal side), who in 1638 established a colony called Pocasset at the northern end of Aquidneck Island in Narragansett Bay. The religious separatism present at the very birth of Rhode Island left a permanent legacy of political, economic, and social separatism in the state.[1]

Although Roger Williams had negotiated with the Indians for his plot of land at Providence, the native population of Rhode Island did not fare so well thereafter. King Philip's War (1675–76) was devastating to both sides, but particularly to the Indians (Narragansetts, Wampanoags, Sakonnets, and Nianticks), who were nearly wiped out, their pitiful remnants huddled together on a virtual reservation near Charlestown. The rebuilding of the white settlements that had been destroyed in Providence and elsewhere was slow but certain; from now on it would not be religious freedom or Indian warfare that would concern the white colonists, but economic development. In the eighteenth century the four Brown brothers (John, Joseph, Nicholas, and Moses) would be among the leading entrepreneurs in the Colonies. It is, however, a stain on Rhode Island's record that it was one of the leading slave-trading states both before and just after the Revolution, its many merchant vessels (some of them privateers) carting away hundreds of thousands of slaves from Africa. Relatively few ended up actually in Rhode Island; most that did so worked on large plantations in the southern part of the state.[2]

Much to the chagrin of Lovecraft's Tory sentiments, Rhode Island was a spearhead of the Revolution, and people here were more united in favour of independence than in the other colonies. Stephen Hopkins, provincial governor of Rhode Island for much of the period between 1755 and 1768—whose house (1707) at the corner of Benefit and Hopkins Street was a favourite of Lovecraft's—was one of the signers of the Declaration of Independence. Separatist to the end, however, Rhode Island refused to send delegates to the Constitutional Convention and was the last of the thirteen colonies to ratify the Federal Constitution.

Roger Williams had founded the Baptist church in Rhode Island—the first in America—in 1638. For more than two centuries the state remained largely Baptist—Brown University was founded in 1764 (as King's College) under Baptist auspices—but other sects came in over time. There were Quakers, Congregationalists, Unitarians, Episcopalians, Methodists, and other, smaller groups. A colony of Jews had been present since the seventeenth century, but their numbers were small and they were careful to assimilate with the Yankees. Roman Catholics only began to be prominent in the middle nineteenth century. Their numbers were augmented by successive waves of immigration: French Canadians during the Civil War (establishing themselves especially in the town of Woonsocket in the northeast corner of the state), Italians after 1890 (settling in the Federal Hill area of Providence's West Side), Portuguese shortly thereafter. It is disturbing, but sadly not surprising, to note the increasing social exclusiveness and scorn of foreigners developing among the old-time Yankees throughout the nineteenth century. The Know-Nothing Party, with its anti-foreign and anti-Catholic bias, dominated the state during the 1850s. Rhode Island remained politically conservative into the 1930s, and Lovecraft's entire family voted Republican throughout his lifetime. If Lovecraft voted at all, he also voted Republican almost uniformly until 1932. The state's leading paper, the *Providence Journal*, remains conservative to this day even though the state has been largely Democratic since the 1930s.

Newport, on the southern end of Aquidneck Island, gained early ascendancy in what became Rhode Island, and Providence did not overtake it until after the Revolutionary war. By 1890 Providence was the only city of any significant size in the state: its population was 132,146, making it the twenty-third largest city in the nation. Its principal topographic features are its seven hills and the Providence River, which divides at Fox Point and splits into the Seekonk River on the east and the Moshassuck River on the west. Between these two rivers is the East Side, the oldest and most exclusive part of the city, especially the lofty eminence of College Hill, which rises steeply on the east bank of the Moshassuck. Main, Benefit, Prospect, and Hope Streets successively ascend the hill and are the principal north-south thoroughfares, while Angell and Waterman Streets span the East Side in an east-west direction. The area west of the Moshassuck is the West Side—the downtown area and a newer residential district. To the north lies the suburb of Pawtucket, to the northwest North Providence, to the southwest Cranston, and to the east—on the other side of the Seekonk—the suburbs of Seekonk and East Providence.

Brown University lords it on the pinnacle of College Hill, and has lately been gobbling up more and more of the surrounding colonial area. This is the oldest part of the city in terms of the structures still surviving, although nothing dates before the middle of the eighteenth century. Lovecraft, ever (and justifiably) proud of the colonial antiquities in his native city, was fond of rattling them off for those of his correspondents less favourably situated:

> Colony House 1761, College Edifice 1770, Brick Schoolhouse 1769, Market House 1773, 1st Baptist Church with finest classic spire in America 1775, innumerable private houses and mansions from 1750 onward, St. John's and Round-Top Churches circa 1810, Golden Ball Inn 1783, old warehouses along the Great Salt River 1816, etc., etc., etc.[3]

Of these, the Golden Ball Inn (where Washington stayed) is no more, and Lovecraft bitterly lamented the destruction of the 1816 warehouses in 1929; but the others still stand. Lovecraft, in fact, would have been heartened at the tremendous restoration of the colonial houses on College Hill in the 1950s and onward, conducted under the aegis of the Providence Preservation Society (now housed in that 1769 schoolhouse at 24 Meeting Street). The restoration has caused Benefit Street in particular to be regarded as the finest mile of colonial architecture in America. At the very end of his life Lovecraft saw the opening of the John Brown house (1786) as a museum, and it is now the home of the Rhode Island Historical Society.

To the east of College Hill is a spacious array of residences dating no earlier than the middle nineteenth century but impressively built and with well-kept grounds and gardens. This, rather than the colonial area, is the true home of the Providence aristocracy and plutocracy. At the eastern edge of this area, running alongside the Seekonk River, is Blackstone Boulevard, whose luxurious homes are still the haven of old Yankee money. At the northern end of Blackstone Boulevard is found Butler Hospital for the Insane, opened in 1847 from a grant supplied by Nicholas Brown—of the illustrious mercantile family of the eighteenth and nineteenth centuries that in 1804 gave its name to Brown University—and Cyrus Butler, for whom it came to be named.[4] Juxtaposed to Butler Hospital on its north side is the vast expanse of Swan Point Cemetery—not perhaps quite as lavishly landscaped as Mt Auburn in Boston but one of the most topographically beautiful cemeteries in the country.

Howard Phillips Lovecraft was born at 9 A.M.[5] on August 20, 1890, at 194 (renumbered 454 in 1895/96) Angell Street on what was then the eastern edge of the East Side of Providence. Although a Providence Lying-in Hospital had opened in 1885,[6] Lovecraft was born "at the Phillips home,"[7] and he would remain passionately devoted to his birthplace, especially after having to move from it in 1904. Lovecraft notes in a late letter that the name "Howard" only became a given name, as opposed to a surname, around 1860, and that "by 1890 it was a fashion"; he goes on to supply other reasons for why he was given the name: 1) a boy in a neighbourhood family who were friends with the Phillipses was named Howard; 2) there was an ancestral connexion with Judge Daniel Howard of Howard Hill in Foster; 3) Clarke Howard Johnson was Whipple Phillips's best friend and executor of his will.[8]

In 1925 Lovecraft's aunt Lillian gave him some idea of what he did as a newborn infant, and he responded to her remarks: "So I threw my arms about, eh, as if excited at the prospect of entering a new world? How naive! I might have known it would only be a bore. Perhaps, though, I was merely dreaming of a weird tale—in which case the enthusiasm was more pardonable."[9] Neither Lovecraft's cynicism nor his interest in weird fiction developed quite this early, but both, as we shall see, were of early growth and long standing.

The sequence and details of the Lovecraft family's travels and residences in the period 1890–93 are very confused, as documentary evidence is lacking and Lovecraft's own testimony is not without obscurities and contradictions. In 1916 Lovecraft, after stating the fact of his birth in "the home of my mother's family," maintained that "my parents' actual residence at the time [was] Dorchester, Mass."[10] Dorchester is a suburb about four miles south of Boston. This residence in Dorchester has not been located; it will shortly be evident that these must have been rented quarters. For want of contradictory evidence, one must assume that Winfield and Susie Lovecraft took up residence in Dorchester as soon as they married on June 12, 1889, or after they returned from their honeymoon, if they went on one.

In another early letter (1915) Lovecraft states that "The Lovecrafts soon afterward [i.e., after his birth] took up their residence in Auburndale, Massachusetts."[11] Auburndale is now part of Newton, in the very far western edge of the metropolitan area of Boston, about ten miles from downtown Boston; in the 1890s it was likely a distinct community. It is at this point that confusion begins. What is the relationship between the Dorchester and Auburndale residences? What does "soon afterward" mean? In his 1916 letter he claims that "When I was two years old—or rather, a year & a half—my parents moved to Auburndale, Mass., sharing a house with the family of the well known poetess, Miss Louise Imogen Guiney . . ." But in a 1924 letter Lovecraft states that "At an early age—an age of very few months, in fact—the future master of literature emigrated to the Province of the Massachusetts-Bay, taking his parents along with him on account of a desire of his father's to transact business—commonplace thought—in the village of Boston."[12] Finally, in a late (1931) letter Lovecraft supplies a list of the states in which he has lived or travelled, and gives his first entry into Massachusetts as 1890.[13]

There is perhaps no actual contradiction in all this. My suspicion is that the Lovecrafts resumed their residence in Dorchester toward the end of 1890 and moved into the Auburndale area in 1892. There may even have been other temporary residences in the Boston metropolitan area. Indeed, Lovecraft states in 1934:

> My first memories are of the summer of 1892—just before my second birthday. We were then vacationing in Dudley, Mass., & I recall the house with its frightful

> attic water-tank & my rocking-horses at the head of the stairs. I recall also the plank walks laid to facilitate walking in rainy weather—& a wooded ravine, & a boy with a small rifle who let me pull the trigger while my mother held me.[14]

Dudley is in the west-central portion of Massachusetts, about fifteen miles south of Worcester and just north of the Connecticut border.

The crux of the matter is when (or if), and under what circumstances, the Lovecraft family lived with the poet Louise Imogen Guiney. Letters from Guiney to F. H. Day consulted by L. Sprague de Camp in the Library of Congress appear to allude to the Lovecrafts:

> [30 May 1892:] Two confounded heathen are coming to BOARD this summer. [14 June 1892:] There are two and a half of them, as I said atrocious Philistines, whom I hate with enthusiasm. [25 July 1892:] Our cursed inmates here, praise the Lord, go next month. [30 July 1892:] The unmentionables are gone, and we are our own mistresses again.[15]

But additional research by Kenneth W. Faig, Jr, has established that the "inmates" here referred to were some German guests, not the Lovecrafts.[16] Lovecraft himself states that "we stayed [at the Guineys'] during the winter of 1892–93";[17] and, pending further evidence, I think we are obliged to accept this statement provisionally. Winfield Scott Lovecraft's medical records (1893–98) list him as a resident of Auburndale,[18] and I suspect that the Lovecrafts may have resided with the Guineys for a short period of time until they found a place of their own (a rented house, no doubt), while they prepared to build a house there. Lovecraft makes clear that his parents had already bought a plot of land in Auburndale—he calls it a "home site"[19]—but that his father's illness in April 1893 "caused the sale of the property recently acquired there."[20] The sequence of Lovecraft's parents' residences seems, therefore, to be as follows:

> Dorchester, Mass. (12 June 1889?–mid-August? 1890)
> Providence, R.I. (mid-August? 1890–November? 1890)
> Dorchester, Mass. (November? 1890–winter? 1892)
> Dudley, Mass. (early June? 1892 [vacation, perhaps of only a few weeks])
> Auburndale, Mass. (Guiney residence) (winter 1892–93)
> Auburndale, Mass. (rented quarters) (February?–April 1893)

Lovecraft says that Guiney (1861–1920) "had been educated in Providence, where she met my mother years before."[21] There is some little mystery around this. Guiney was indeed educated at the Academy of the Sacred Heart at 736 Smith Street in the Elmhurst section of Providence, attending the school from the year it opened in 1872[22] until 1879;[23] but Susie, as we have seen, attended the Wheaton Seminary in Norton, Massachusetts, for at least the period 1871–72. Although Guiney scholar

Henry G. Fairbanks asserts that the Sacred Heart accepted Protestants as well as Catholics,[24] I think it is unlikely that Susie was actually sent there; nor is the academy especially close to the Phillips residence at 276 Broadway, being in the direction of North Providence. Faig, however, has now made the highly plausible conjecture that Susie's acquaintance with Guiney was facilitated, or even initiated, by a third party—the Banigan family. Joseph and Margaret Banigan were the Lovecrafts' next-door neighbours in Providence from the time Whipple Phillips built his residence at 194 (454) Angell Street around 1880, and at least two daughters of Joseph Banigan attended Sacred Heart Academy at the time when Guiney was attending the school. It is very likely that Susie's friendship with Guiney dates from this period.[25]

It is, of course, very possible that Lovecraft exaggerated the degree of his mother's acquaintance with Guiney; or perhaps his mother herself did so to her son. She may have stressed the Guiney connexion once she saw Lovecraft developing as a writer himself. The Lovecrafts were, indeed, very likely paying boarders at the Guiney residence, staying there only long enough to find their own rented quarters while preparing to build a house on the home site they had purchased.

Louise Imogen Guiney is of some interest in her own right. She was a literary prodigy of sorts, publishing her first book of poetry, *Songs at the Start* (1884), when she was twenty-three. Many other volumes of poetry and essays followed. She first moved to Auburndale with her mother after she graduated from the Sacred Heart in 1879; after a stay in England (1889–91), she returned to her home on Vista Avenue in Auburndale. At the time of the Lovecrafts' visit she was about thirty-one, four years younger than Mrs Lovecraft.

Lovecraft's memories of Auburndale—especially of the Guiney residence—are numerous and clear:

> I distinctly recall the quiet, shady suburb as I saw it in 1892—& it is a rather curious psychological fact that at this early age I was impressed most of all with the railway bridge & the four-tracked Boston & Albany road which extended beneath it. . . . Miss Guiney kept a most extraordinary collection of St. Bernard dogs, all named after authors and poets. A shaggy gentleman by the classic name of Brontë was my particular favourite & companion, being ever in attendance on my chariot as my mother wheeled that vehicle through the streets & avenues. Brontë would permit me to place my fist in his mouth without biting me, & would snarl protectingly if any stranger approached me.[26]

These St Bernards actually enjoyed a fleeting fame of their own. A *Chicago Sunday Tribune* article of December 3, 1893, notes: "With her great St. Bernard dog, her mother, and a small kit of books, she set up Postmaster at Auburndale. . . . The St. Bernard became chief deputy and was put in charge of the department of transportation."[27] This writer evidently did not know of the existence of several dogs. Guiney had portraits painted of these dogs, including Brontë, and hung them in her parlour.[28] Ironically, although—as Donald R. Burleson discovered in 1977—the Guiney home was long ago torn down and another one put up in its place, the original barn of the house still survives and the dogs are buried in the back yard; Brontë's grave is readily visible.

Another clear memory Lovecraft had was the tableau of the railway bridge, which in a 1930 letter he clearly dates to the winter of 1892–93: "I can see myself as a child of 2½ on the railway bridge at Auburndale, Mass., looking across and downward at the business part of the town, and feeling the imminence of some wonder which I could neither describe nor fully conceive—and there has never been a subsequent hour of my life when kindred sensations have been absent."[29] If Lovecraft is being exact about his age here, then this vista must have been seen in late 1892 or early 1893. His first literary stirrings can be dated to this period:

> At the age of two I was a rapid talker, familiar with the alphabet from my blocks & picture-books, & . . . absolutely *metre-mad!* I could not read, but would repeat any poem of simple sort with unfaltering cadence. Mother Goose was my principal classic, & Miss Guiney would continually make me repeat parts of it; not that my rendition was necessarily notable, but because my age lent uniqueness to the performance.[30]

Elsewhere Lovecraft states that it was his father who, with his taste for military matters, taught him to recite Thomas Buchanan Read's "Sheridan's Ride" at the Guiney residence, where Lovecraft declaimed it "in a manner that brought loud applause—and painful egotism." Guiney himself seems to have taken to the infant; she would repeatedly ask, "Whom do you love?" to which Lovecraft would pipe back: "Louise Imogen Guiney!"[31]

Lovecraft was clearly proud of his family's association with Guiney; as late as 1930 he is claiming that Guiney "now ranks among the really major figures of American literature."[32] This is only a slight exaggeration: after Guiney's death in 1920 at least two books about her were published—one by her friend Alice Brown (1921) and another by an English critic, E. M. Tenison (1923). Her letters were published in two volumes in 1926, and she had been praised by Andrew Lang, Edmund Gosse, and many other noted critics. A volume on Guiney by Sister Mary Adorita appeared in 1962, and a book on her for Twayne's United States Authors Series by Henry G. Fairbanks dates to 1973—sixteen years before one on Lovecraft appeared in the series. In a candid moment, however, Lovecraft gave his own assessment of Guiney's work:

> *It is said* that her "verses" mean something, but I have never taken the time and trouble to find out just what! Yet Dr. Oliver Wendell Holmes once predicted a bright future for her. She has written many books, and has an entrée to the best magazines, but I doubt if posterity will ever accord her a place even nearly approaching that of Dr. Holmes himself. . . . [H]e was a devotee of Pope, and has

> been called "the Modern Pope". But Miss Guiney followed vaguer literary deities, of whom the Miltonic spirit *Chaos* seems to be the leader.[33]

Lovecraft did not own her collected poetry (published in 1909 under the title *Happy Ending* and augmented in 1927), but did have a volume entitled *Three Heroines of New England Romance* (1895) containing a lengthy biographical essay by Guiney, "Martha Hilton." The book was probably acquired by his mother.

Lovecraft himself had a faint encounter with Oliver Wendell Holmes, one of many close brushes with established writers he would have throughout his life: "Oliver Wendell Holmes came not infrequently to this [Guiney's] menage, and on one occasion (unremembered by the passenger) is said to have ridden the future *Weird Tales* disciple on his venerable knee."[34] Holmes (1809–1894) was at this time very old, and was in fact a close friend of Guiney (her *Goose-Quill Papers* is dedicated to him); no doubt he failed to remember for very long his meeting with the future master of the weird tale. Holmes had had an earlier and more memorable association with a relative of Lovecraft's: Dr Franklin Chase Clark, Lovecraft's uncle, had taken a course under Holmes at the Harvard Medical School, and as late as 1935 Lovecraft had in his possession a letter by Holmes congratulating Dr Clark on an article in a medical journal.[35] Dr Clark was, however, not acquainted with the Lovecraft family at this time; he would marry Lillian D. Phillips only in 1902. It was in part this early association with Holmes that led Lovecraft to rank highly his weird novel, *Elsie Venner* (1861). Lovecraft also owned Holmes's *Autocrat of the Breakfast-Table* and his *Poetical Works.*

Lovecraft's early residences and travels were, of course, dictated by his father's business. His medical records list him as a "Commercial Traveller," and Lovecraft frequently affirms that his father's commercial interests kept him and his family in the Boston area during the period 1890–93. There is little reason to doubt Lovecraft when he says that "my image of him is but vague":[36] he lived with him for only the first two and a half years of his life, and perhaps less than that if his father's business trips took him very far afield for long periods of time, as there is some suggestion that they did.

The illness that struck Winfield Scott Lovecraft in April 1893 and forced him to remain in Butler Hospital in Providence until his death in July 1898 is worth examining in detail. The Butler Hospital medical record reads as follows:

> For a year past he has shown obscure symptoms of mental disease—doing and saying strange things at times; has, also, grown pale and thin in flesh. He continued his business, however, until Apr. 21, when he broke down completely while stopping in Chicago. He rushed from his room shouting that a chambermaid had insulted him, and that certain men were outraging his wife in the room above. He was extremely noisy and violent for two days, but was finally quieted by free use of

> the bromides, which made his removal here possible. We can get no history of specific disease.

Upon Winfield's death in 1898, the medical record diagnosed him as having "General Paralysis"; his death certificate listed the cause of death as "general paresis."[37] In 1898 (and, for that matter, today) these terms were virtually synonymous; Leland E. Hinsie and Robert Jean Campbell write in their *Psychiatric Dictionary* (4th ed., 1970): "Paresis, general . . . Also known as general paralysis of the insane (G.P.I.), dementia paralytica, Bayle's disease; the most malignant form of (tertiary) neurosyphilis consisting of direct invasion of the parenchyma of the brain producing a combination of both mental and neurologic symptoms."[38] What was not known in 1898—and would not be known until 1911, when the spirochete that causes syphilis was identified—was the connexion between "general paresis" and syphilis. Arthur S. Koki, who refused to believe that Winfield had syphilis, quotes Dr C. H. Jones, Administrator of Butler Health Center, as saying to him in 1960:

> . . . this term [general paresis] back in 1898 was a catch-all or waste-paper-basket term. It was found within the following decade that a substantial portion of the patients who displayed the general paresis symptoms did in fact have syphilis, but there are a number of other conditions which show the same set of symptoms. . . . Just sitting here I could name at least twenty other organic brain diseases.[39]

But M. Eileen McNamara, M.D., studying Winfield's medical record, concluded that the probability of Winfield's having tertiary syphilis is very strong:

> It is unlikely that he had a primary brain tumor such as a glioblastoma, or a brain metastasis, or his survival would have been shortened. If he had had a viral or bacterial meningitis, his survival would have been a matter of days. Tubercular meningitis is also rapidly fatal. The focal convulsions are also certain proof that WSL did not simply have manic-depression or schizophrenia. Winfield Scott Lovecraft almost certainly died of syphilis.[40]

Winfield displayed nearly all the symptoms of tertiary syphilis as identified by Hinsie and Campbell: "(1) simple dementia, the most common type, with deterioration of intellect, affect and social behavior; (2) paranoid form, with persecutory delusions; (3) expansive or manic form, with delusions of grandiosity; or (4) depressive form, often with absurd nihilistic delusions."[41] The medical record clearly bears out at least the first three of these symptoms: (1) on April 28, 1893 "the patient . . . broke out violently this morning—rushed up and down the ward shouting and attacked watchman"; (2) April 29, 1893: "says three men—one a negro—in the room above trying to do violence to his wife"; May 15, 1893: "believes his food is poisoned"; June 25, 1893: "looks upon the officers and attendants as enemies and accuses them of stealing his clothing, watch, bonds, &c."; (3) under the heading "Mental Condition": "boasts of his many friends; his business success, his family, and above all his great strength—asking writer to see how perfectly his muscles are developed". For the fourth symptom—depression—the record is not sufficiently detailed to make a conjecture.

If, then, it is admitted that Winfield had syphilis, the question is how he contracted it. This is, of course, at this point impossible to ascertain with certainty. McNamara reminds us that the "latent period between inoculation and the development of tertiary syphilis is ten to twenty years," so that Winfield "might have been infected as early as eighteen or as late as twenty-eight, well before his marriage at age thirty-five." It is, unfortunately, exactly this period of Winfield's life about which nothing is known. It is difficult to doubt that he contracted syphilis either from a prostitute or from some other sex partner prior to his marriage, either while attending the military academy or—despite Koki's scoffing of "that type of salesman who has become the butt of a thousand smoking car jokes"[42]—during his stint as a "Commercial Traveller," if indeed that began so early as the age of twenty-eight. It may be going too far to infer that Winfield was some sort of Casanova or *roué*, but the two recorded instances of his hallucination that his wife was being raped certainly point to some form of sexual obsession. I shall have more to say on the racist content of one of his hallucinations later.

One remarkable fact is that Winfield's cousin, Joshua Elliot Lovecraft (1845–1898), died of "general paralysis" on November 8, 1898, a few months after Winfield.[43] He had been committed to the state hospital in Rochester, New York, on April 10, 1896, dying after two and a half years. Richard D. Squires has unearthed Joshua's medical records and notes that some of his symptoms bear uncanny similarities to those of Winfield. In both cases there is mention of an "ataxic" gait (i.e., lack of coordination in locomotion), and, incredibly, the "alleged cause" of Joshua's illness is "business anxiety," exactly like Winfield. There seems little doubt that Joshua also died of syphilis. Although we know little of Joshua's life, hence cannot speak definitively on any relationship between him and Winfield, their similar fate is highly suggestive.

The nature of Winfield's ailment necessarily raises the question of his sexual relations with his wife. We of course have no grounds for any conjecture on the matter; they did, after all, conceive one son, and might presumably have conceived more had Winfield not fallen ill. The Phillips women tended to be prolific, although Susie's older sister Lillian produced no offspring and her younger sister Annie's two children died before reaching adulthood. Sonia H. Davis, Lovecraft's wife, made the following remarkable assertion in 1969: "In my opinion, the elder Lovecraft, having been a travelling salesman for the Gorham Silversmiths, and his wife being a 'touch-me-not,' took his sexual pleasures wherever he could find them; for H. P. never had a sister or a brother, and his mother, probably having been sex-starved against her will, lavished both her love and her hate on her only child."[44] I believe this is entirely a conjecture on Sonia's part; she obviously did not know Lovecraft's mother (she and Lovecraft first met six weeks after his mother's death), much less his father, and I doubt whether any of the above was something Lovecraft actually told her. It is likely both that Susie was a virgin prior to her marriage and that she remained celibate following her husband's death, but the fact that she and her husband conceived a son about six months after their marriage certainly suggests fairly normal sexual relations given their social position and the mores of the times, and especially in light of the frequent travelling her husband must have done.

The course of Winfield's illness makes horrifying reading. There are frequent references in the first few months of his stay to being "violent and noisy"; on April 29, 1893, he was given a small dose of morphine to quiet him. By August 29 he seemed to have made a recovery of sorts: "A few days ago patient was dressed and permitted to go about ward and into yard"; but he soon relapsed. Frequent convulsions—some occurring only on the left side of his body (which, as McNamara states, "indicat[es] a lesion of the right brain")—occur in November, but by December 15 there was "marked improvement."

At this point the entries in the medical record become quite infrequent, sometimes as many as six months passing before a notation is made. On May 29, 1894, he was allowed into the hall and airing-court even though he is "very noisy at times." By December 5 Winfield was said to be failing, with frequent convulsions; it was thought that he had only days to live, but then he began to rally. By May 10, 1895, his physical condition was said to have "improved much since last writing" even though "mentally, he has continued to become more demented." There is little change for a year and a half. On December 16, 1896, Winfield developed an ulcer on the penis, possibly from masturbation (the initial sign of syphilis is such an ulcer, but Winfield was long past this stage). His condition began to decline markedly by the spring of 1898, and blood and mucus are found in his stool. By May he developed constipation and required an enema every three days. On July 12 he developed a temperature of 103° and a pulse of 106, with frequent convulsions. On July 18 he "passe[d] from one convulsion into another," and he was pronounced dead the next day.

The trauma experienced by Susie Lovecraft over this excruciating period of five years—with doctors ignorant of how to treat Winfield's illness, and with periods of false hope where the patient seems to recover only to lapse into more serious physical and mental deterioration—can only be imagined. When Susie herself was admitted to Butler Hospital in 1919, her doctor, F. J. Farnell, "found disorder had been evidenced for fifteen years; that in all, abnormality had existed at least twenty-six years."[45] It is no accident that the onset of her "abnormality" dates to 1893.

It is of some interest that although Winfield is listed on his medical record as a resident of Auburndale, his wife's residence is given as 194 Angell Street. I do not know that much need be made of this; there has been speculation that Winfield and

Susie were somehow separated, and that she may have moved back to her father's home in Providence well before the date of April 1893 given by Lovecraft. It is, however, possible that the indication on the medical record refers merely to the fact that Susie (with Howard) had moved back to Providence immediately upon the onset of Winfield's illness; there would be no reason for remaining in Auburndale, and the home site that she and Winfield had purchased was quickly sold. We simply do not have enough information to make a hypothesis on this issue—certainly not enough to warrant the inference that Susie and Winfield had had some sort of falling out—and I think we must accept Lovecraft's testimony on the matter unless hard evidence to the contrary emerges.

I do not know that much attention has been paid to why Winfield was in Chicago at the time of his attack. I have been informed that the Gorham Company owned one-third of a silversmith firm in Chicago called Spaulding & Co.,[46] and it is conceivable that Winfield (if indeed he was working for Gorham) had been sent out there for a salesmen's meeting or something of the sort. He could not have gone there permanently, else his residence would not have been given on the medical record as Auburndale. Lovecraft makes no mention of this Chicago trip or any other trips by Winfield outside of the Boston area; perhaps, therefore, Winfield was somewhat more peripatetic than Lovecraft suggests.

The critical issue, of course, is what—if anything—Lovecraft himself knew of the nature and extent of his father's illness. He was two years and eight months old when his father was committed, and seven years and eleven months old when his father died. If he was already reciting poetry at two and a half, there is scarcely any question that he must at least have been aware that something peculiar had happened—why else would he and his mother have moved suddenly back from Auburndale to the maternal home in Providence?

It is obvious from Lovecraft's remarks about his father's illness that he was intentionally kept in the dark about its specific nature. One wonders, indeed, whether Susie herself knew all its particulars. Lovecraft's first known statement about his father's illness occurs in a letter of 1915: "In 1893 my father was seized with a complete paralytic stroke, due to insomnia and an overstrained nervous system, which took him to the hospital for the remaining five years of his life. He was never afterward conscious . . ."[47] It need hardly be said at this point that nearly every part of this utterance is false. When Lovecraft refers to a "complete paralytic stroke," he is either remembering some deliberate falsehood he was told (i.e., that his father was paralysed), or he is making a false inference from the medical record ("General Paralysis") or some account of it that he heard. The medical record does confirm that Winfield was overworked ("Has been actively engaged in business for several years and for the last two years has worked very hard"), and no doubt Lovecraft was told this also; and the remark about Winfield not being conscious may have been the excuse that was given for not visiting his father in the hospital. And yet, Lovecraft must have known something was not quite right here: he knew that Butler Hospital was not a place for the treatment of ordinary physical maladies but was in fact an insane asylum.

Lovecraft's later references to his father's illness are variations on the 1915 statement. In 1916 he states that "In April 1893 my father was stricken with a complete paralysis resulting from a brain overtaxed with study & business cares. He lived for five years at a hospital, but was never again able to move hand or foot, or to utter a sound."[48] This last statement is a remarkable elaboration, and I think that Lovecraft is again simply making his own inferences from the hints and outright deceptions he must have received about his father. I am certainly not criticising Lovecraft's mother for not elaborating upon the nature of her husband's illness: there are some things that one does not tell a three-year-old—or even an eight-year-old. Moreover, Lovecraft is under no obligation to be wholly candid about such a delicate matter even to close friends or correspondents.

I do not think that Lovecraft knew very much about his father's illness and death, but I think he wondered a great deal. One matter of transcendent importance is whether Lovecraft ever saw his father in Butler Hospital. He never says explicitly that he did not, but his late statement that "I was never in a hospital till 1924"[49] certainly suggests that he himself believed (or claimed to others) that he never did so. There has been speculation that Lovecraft did indeed visit his father in the hospital;[50] but there is absolutely no documentary evidence of this. I believe that this speculation is an inference from the fact that on two occasions—August 29, 1893, and May 29, 1894—Winfield was taken out into the "yard" and the "airing-court"; but there is no reason to believe that the three- or four-year-old Lovecraft, or his mother, or anyone at all, visited him at this or any other time.

Another highly significant but unresolvable issue is the provocative statement in the medical record that "For a year past he has shown obscure symptoms of mental disease—doing and saying strange things at times." This information must have been supplied to the doctors at Butler Hospital by whoever had accompanied Winfield at his admission, whether it be Susie herself or Whipple Phillips. The question becomes: To what degree was Lovecraft himself aware of his father's odd behaviour? If this behaviour had been manifesting itself as early as around April 1892, it would have predated the entire stay with the Guineys and have gone back to the family's days at Dorchester (if that is where they were at this time). If Winfield had been working "very hard" for the last two years (i.e., since about the beginning of 1891), then was the vacation in Dudley in the summer of 1892 a means of giving him some much-needed rest? Again, we can only conjecture.

Perhaps more important than all these matters is the image and tokens of his father which Lovecraft retained in maturity. There were, in the first place, some tangible relics: he reports inheriting his father's two-volume edition of *War and Peace*, adding wryly: "The fact that its text leaves are cut, plus the evidence supply'd by the fly-leaves that they were originally uncut, leads me to the conclusion that my father must have surviv'd a voyage thro' it; tho' it is possible that he merely amus'd himself of an evening by running a paper knife thro' it."[51] The bantering tone is very singular; almost all other references to his father are sombre or at best neutral.

Lovecraft retained his father's copy of James Stormonth's *Dictionary of the English Language* (1st edition 1871; Lovecraft's edition is a revised edition of 1885). This is of somewhat greater importance, for Lovecraft remarks that Stormonth was "a Cambridge man" and "esteemed as a conservative authority & used by my father."[52] This connects with Lovecraft's assertion of his father's preservation of his English heritage. Remarking that "In America, the Lovecraft line made some effort to keep from becoming nasally Yankeeised," he continues: ". . . my father was constantly warned not to fall into Americanisms of speech and provincial vulgarities of dress and mannerisms—so much so that he was generally regarded as an Englishman despite his birth in Rochester, N.Y. I can just recall his extremely precise and cultivated British voice . . ."[53] We need look no further for the source of Lovecraft's own Anglophilia—his pride in the British Empire, his use of British spelling variants, and his desire for close cultural and political ties between the United States and England. He notes that

> I suppose I heard people mentioning that my father was 'an Englishman' . . . My aunts remember that as early as the age of three I wanted a British officer's red uniform, and paraded around in a nondescript 'coat' of brilliant crimson, originally part of a less masculine costume, and in picturesque juxtaposition with the kilts which with me represented the twelfth Royal Highland Regiment. Rule, Britannia![54]

At about the age of six, "when my grandfather told me of the American Revolution, I shocked everyone by adopting a dissenting view . . . Grover Cleveland was grandpa's ruler, but Her Majesty, Victoria, Queen of Great Britain & Ireland & Empress of India commanded my allegiance. 'God Save the Queen!' was a stock phrase of mine."[55] It would be going too far to suggest that Lovecraft's father actually induced his son to take the British side in the American revolution; but it is clear that the maternal side of his family, proud Yankees as they were, did not share that view. Winfield Townley Scott reports that a "family friend" referred to Winfield as a "pompous Englishman."[56] This appears to be Ella Sweeney, a schoolteacher who knew the Lovecrafts from as early as their 1892 vacation in Dudley; the information was passed on to Scott by a friend of Sweeney's, Myra H. Blosser.[57] Even individuals beyond Lovecraft's immediate family appear to have found Winfield's English bearing a little trying.

It is poignant to hear Lovecraft tell of his one genuine memory of his father: "I can just remember my father—an immaculate figure in black coat & vest & grey striped trousers. I had a childish habit of slapping him on the knees & shouting 'Papa, you look just like a young man!' I don't know where I picked that phrase up; but I was vain & self-conscious, & given to repeating things which I saw tickled my elders."[58] This litany of his father's clothing—"his immaculate black morning-coat and vest, ascot tie, and striped grey trousers"—is found in an earlier letter, and Lovecraft adds touchingly: "I have myself worn some of his old ascots and wing collars, left all too immaculate by his early illness and death . . ."[59] The photograph of the Lovecraft family in 1892 shows Winfield wearing this attire, while Lovecraft himself appears to be wearing some of his father's clothing in the photograph of him printed on the cover of the September 1915 *United Amateur.*

Winfield Scott Lovecraft was buried on July 21, 1898, in the Phillips plot in Swan Point Cemetery, Providence. There is every reason to believe that young Howard attended this service, even though the very brief notice in the *Providence Journal* does not identify the attendees.[60] The mere fact that he was buried here is (as Faig has noted[61]) a testimony to Whipple Phillips's generosity of heart, and perhaps even an indication that Whipple paid for Winfield's medical expenses; Winfield's estate was valued at $10,000 upon his death,[62] a substantial sum (Whipple's own estate was valued at only $25,000), and it is unlikely that it could have been so great if it had been used for full-time hospital costs for more than five years.

The immediate effect of the hospitalisation of Winfield Scott Lovecraft was to bring the two-and-a-half-year-old Howard more closely than ever under the influence of his mother, his two aunts (both of whom, as yet unmarried, were still residing at 454 Angell Street), his grandmother Robie, and especially his grandfather Whipple. Naturally, his mother's influence was at the outset the dominant one. Lovecraft remarks that his mother was "permanently stricken with grief"[63] upon her husband's illness, although one wonders whether shame and loathing were intermixed with this emotion. We have already seen that the onset of Susie's own psychiatric trouble is likely to have begun at this time. The Providence city directory for 1896–99 anomalously lists Susie as "Miss Winfield S. Lovecraft"; it is unlikely that this error would have occurred four years running by mere accident.

For his part, Whipple Van Buren Phillips proved to be an entirely satisfactory replacement for the father Lovecraft never knew. Lovecraft's simple statement that at this time "my beloved grandfather . . . became the centre of my entire universe"[64] is all we need to know. Whipple cured his grandson of his fear of the dark by daring him at the age of five to walk through a sequence of dark rooms at 454 Angell Street;[65] he showed Lovecraft the art objects he brought from his travels to Europe; he wrote him letters when travelling on business; and he even recounted extemporaneous weird tales to the boy. I shall elaborate upon some of these points later; here I wish to give only one indication of how completely Whipple had replaced

Winfield in Lovecraft's consciousness. In 1920 Lovecraft had a dream that was the ultimate inspiration for his seminal tale, "The Call of Cthulhu" (1926). In the dream he has made a bas-relief and presents it to a museum curator, who asks him who he is. Lovecraft replies: "My name is Lovecraft—H. P. Lovecraft—grandson of Whipple V. Phillips."[66] He does not say "son of Winfield Scott Lovecraft." At the time of this dream Whipple Phillips had been dead for sixteen years.

And so, with Whipple virtually taking the place of his father, Howard and his mother seemed to lead a normal enough life; indeed, with Whipple's finances still robust, Lovecraft had an idyllic and rather spoiled early childhood. One of the first things that came to his notice was his immediate surroundings. Lovecraft frequently emphasised the quasi-rural nature of his birthplace, situated as it was at what was then the very edge of the developed part of town:

> . . . I was born in the year 1890 in a small town, & in a section of that town which during my childhood lay not more than four blocks (N. & E.) from the actually primal & open New England countryside, with rolling meadows, stone walls, cart-paths, brooks, deep woods, mystic ravines, lofty river-bluffs, planted fields, white antient farmhouses, barns, & byres, gnarled hillside orchards, great lone elms, & all the authentick marks of a rural milieu unchanged since the 17th & 18th centuries. . . . My house, tho' an urban one on a paved street, had spacious grounds & stood next to an open field with a stone wall . . . where great elms grew & my grandfather had corn & potatoes planted, & a *cow* pastured under the gardener's care.[67]

Lovecraft could not have had these memories much earlier than the age of three or four; in fact, he states in a late letter that "When I was 3 years old I felt a strange magic & fascination (not unmixed with a vague unease & perhaps a touch of mild *fear*) in the ancient houses of Providence's venerable hill . . ., with their fanlighted doorways, railed flights of steps, & stretches of brick sidewalk . . ."[68]

What is frequently ignored is that this return to Providence from Auburndale essentially allowed Lovecraft to grow up a native of Rhode Island rather than of Massachusetts, as he is very likely to have done otherwise; he himself emphasises this fact in an early letter, saying that the return to the Phillips household "caus[ed] me to grow up as a complete Rhode-Islander."[69] And yet, Lovecraft retained a passionate fondness for Massachusetts and its colonial heritage, finding wonder and pleasure in the towns of Marblehead, Salem, and Newburyport, and the wild rural terrain of the western part of the state. But the heritage of religious freedom in Rhode Island, and the contrasting early history of Puritan theocracy in its northeasterly neighbour, caused Massachusetts to become a sort of topographical and cultural "other"—attractive yet repulsive, familiar yet alien—in both his life and his work. It is not too early to stress that many more of Lovecraft's tales are set in Massachusetts than in Rhode Island; and in most of those set in the latter,

Lovecraft is careful to eliminate completely the horrors he has raised, whereas those in the Massachusetts tales linger and fester over the generations and centuries.

Lovecraft makes clear that his fondness for the antiquities of his native city were of very early growth:

> . . . how I used to drag my mother around on the ancient hill when I was 4 or 5! I hardly know what I was after, but the centuried houses with their fanlights & knockers & railed steps & small-paned windows had a strong & significant effect of some sort on me. This world, I felt, was a different one from the Victorian world of French roofs & plate glass & concrete sidewalks & open lawns that I was born into . . . It was a magic, secret world, & it had a *realness* beyond that of the home neighbourhood.[70]

Who can fail to recall the description of the young Charles Dexter Ward, whose "famous walks began" when he was a very small boy, "first with his impatiently dragged nurse, and then alone in dreamy meditation"? This combination of wonder and terror in Lovecraft's early appreciation of Providence makes me think of a letter of 1920 in which he attempts to specify the foundations of his character: ". . . I should describe mine own nature as tripartite, my interests consisting of three parallel and dissociated groups—(a) Love of the strange and the fantastic. (b) Love of the abstract truth and of scientific logick. (c) Love of the ancient and the permanent. Sundry combinations of these three strains will probably account for all my odd tastes and eccentricities."[71] This is really a remarkably apt summary, and we will see that all three of these traits emerged in the first eight or nine years of his life; but the emphasis must be laid on the idea of "combinations"—or, rather, the likelihood that the third trait (which, if Lovecraft's testimony is to be believed, seems to be of earliest development) led both directly and indirectly to the first.

In particular, what seems to have emerged at a remarkably early age in Lovecraft's consciousness is the notion of *time*—time as "some especial enemy of mine,"[72] one that he was always seeking to defeat, confound, or subvert. Occasionally Lovecraft tried to trace the origin of this feeling, and in a letter he enumerated certain possibilities: the illustrations in an unspecified book over which he pored at the age of two and a half or three, before he could read; the ancient houses and steeples of Providence; and the "fascinating isolation of the 18th century books in a black, windowless attic room"[73]—all appear to have played a part. Lovecraft states that his first acute realisation of time was

> when I saw newspapers bearing the heavily-inked date-line TUESDAY, JANUARY 1, 1895. *1895!!* To me the symbol *1894* had represented an eternity—the eternity of *the present* as distinguished from such things as 1066 or 1492 or 1642 or 1776—& the idea of personally outliving that eternity was absorbingly impressive to me . . . I shall never forget the sensation I derived from the

> idea of *moving through time* (if forward, why not backward?) which that '95 dateline gave me.[74]

Lovecraft frequently, in later years, yearned to move backward in time, and many of his stories carry out that wish, plunging their narrators not merely to the eighteenth century but into a prehistoric world hundreds of millions of years ago.

It was that "black, windowless attic room" at 454 Angell Street which proved to be the gateway to a remarkable intellectual development, one that very early on encompassed not only antiquarianism but weird fiction, belles lettres, and science. Lovecraft states frequently that he began reading at the age of four, and one of his earliest books appears to have been Grimm's *Fairy Tales.* We do not know what edition of Grimm he (or, rather, his family) owned; no doubt it was some bowdlerised version suitable for the very young. Nor do we know exactly what Lovecraft derived from Grimm; at one point he merely remarks that the fairy tales "were my truly representative diet, & I lived mostly in a mediaeval world of imagination."[75] Some of the Grimm tales are very peculiar: one, "The Story of the Youth Who Went Forth to Learn What Fear Was," tells of a young man who does not know what it is to be afraid, and so he goes to a haunted castle and phlegmatically fends off various supernatural forces; in the end he is still unable to feel fear. The imagery of this fairy tale may have stimulated Lovecraft, although one cannot know whether it was included in the edition he read.

The next year, at the age of five, Lovecraft discovered a seminal book in his aesthetic development: the *Arabian Nights.* There is some confusion as to which exact edition Lovecraft read. The copy found in his library—*The Arabian Nights Entertainments,* selected and edited by Andrew Lang (London: Longmans, Green, 1898)—was given to him by his mother; it bears the inscription in her handwriting: "Howard Phillips Lovecraft / From your Mother *Christmas 1898.*" Now clearly Lovecraft could not have read this edition—which Lang says he translated (and, very likely, bowdlerised) from the French translation of Galland—at the age of five. There were many competing editions of the *Arabian Nights* available at this time, not the least of which was, of course, Sir Richard Burton's landmark translation in sixteen volumes in 1885–86. Lovecraft certainly did not read this translation, either, as it is entirely unexpurgated and reveals, as few previous translations did, just how bawdy the *Arabian Nights* actually are. (Interestingly, in light of Lovecraft's later racial views, several tales speak with outrage about sexual encounters between black men and Islamic women.) My guess is that Lovecraft read one of the following three translations:

> *The Arabian Nights' Entertainments: Six Stories.* Edited by Samuel Eliot; translated by Jonathan Scott. Authorized for use in the Boston Public Schools. Boston: Lee & Shepard; New York: C. T. Dillington, 1880.

The Thousand and One Nights; or, The Arabian Nights' Entertainments. Chicago & New York: Bedford, Clarke & Co., 1885.

The Arabian Nights. Edited by Everett H. Hale; [translated by Edward William Lane]. Boston: Ginn & Co., 1888.

The Lane translation in particular went through many editions.

This matter is not of especial importance; what is significant is the book's effect upon Lovecraft:

> . . . how many dream-Arabs have the *Arabian Nights* bred! I ought to know, since at the age of 5 I was one of them! I had not then encountered Graeco-Roman myth, but found in Lang's *Arabian Nights* a gateway to glittering vistas of wonder and freedom. It was then that I invented for myself the name of Abdul Alhazred, and made my mother take me to all the Oriental curio shops and fit me up an Arabian corner in my room.[76]

There are at least two false statements here. First, I have already noted that it could not be *Lang's* edition of the *Arabian Nights* that Lovecraft read at this time. (Susie's presenting him the book for Christmas in 1898 was clearly a response to the fondness he had already exhibited for the work.) Second is the matter of the coining of the name Abdul Alhazred. In his most important formal autobiographical essay, "Some Notes on a Nonentity" (1933), written nearly two years after the letter just quoted (where he claims to have invented the name himself), he states that Abdul Alhazred was a name "some kindly elder had suggested to me as a typical Saracen name." Another letter clarifies the matter: "I can't quite recall where I did get *Abdul Alhazred.* There is a dim recollection which associates it with a certain elder—the family lawyer, as it happens, but I can't remember whether I asked him to make up an Arabic name for me, or whether I merely asked him to criticise a choice I had otherwise made."[77] The family lawyer was Albert A. Baker, who would be Lovecraft's legal guardian until 1911. His coinage (if indeed it was his) was a singularly infelicitous one from the point of view of Arabic grammar, since the result is a reduplicated article (Abd*ul Al*hazred). A more likely coinage would have been Abd el-Hazred, although this doesn't much have of a ring to it. In any event, the name stuck, as every reader of Lovecraft knows.

The *Arabian Nights* may not have definitively steered Lovecraft toward the realm of weird fiction, but it certainly did not impede his progress in that direction. It is frequently not noticed that a relatively small proportion of tales from the *Arabian Nights* are actually supernatural; even the celebrated story of Sindbad is largely a series of adventures on the high seas. There are, of course, tales of crypts, tombs, caves, deserted cities, and other elements that would form significant features in Lovecraft's imaginative landscape; but we are still in the realm of legend, where the supernatural is presented less as an appalling defiance of natural law than as a wonder to be accepted with relatively little fanfare.

What might have finally stacked the deck in favour of the weird for Lovecraft was his unexpected discovery of an edition of Coleridge's *Rime of the Ancient Mariner* illustrated by Gustave Doré, which he stumbled upon at the house of a friend of his family's at the age of six. The edition he saw is likely to have been the first American edition of the poem containing Doré's illustrations, *The Rime of the Ancient Mariner* (New York: Harper & Brothers, 1876), which went through many printings. Here is the impression the poem, and the pictures, made upon a young Lovecraft:

> . . . imagine a tall, stately Victorian library in a house sometimes visited with my mother or aunts. Marble mantel—thick bearskin rug—endless shelves of books. . . . A house of adults, so that a 6-year-old caller's interest strays most naturally to the shelves & great centre table & mantel. Fancy then the discovery of a great atlas-sized gift-book leaning against the mantel & having on the cover gilt letters reading "With Illustrations by Gustave Doré". The title didn't matter—for didn't I know the dark, supernal magic of the Doré pictures in our Dante & Milton at home? I open the book—& behold a hellish picture of a corpse-ship with ragged sails under a waning moon! I turn a page . . . . . God! A spectral, half-transparent ship on whose deck a corpse & a skeleton play at dice! By this time I am flat on the bearskin rug & ready to thumb through the whole book . . . of which I've never heard before. . . . . A sea full of rotting serpents, & death-fires dancing in the black air . . . . . troops of angels & daemons . . . . . crazed, dying, distorted forms . . . . . dead men rising in their putrescence & lifelessly manning the dank rigging of a fate-doomed barque . . . .[78]

Who could resist such a spell? If Lovecraft read this book at the age of six, it must have occurred between August 1896 and August 1897. He may have done so at the home of Whipple's cousin Theodore W. Phillips, who lived nearby at 256 (later numbered 612) Angell Street; but Lovecraft clearly identifies the location as a "friend's" house (by which he probably means a friend of his family), and it would seem odd to describe his great-uncle as such. In any event, if the *Ancient Mariner* was the principal *literary* influence in the early development of Lovecraft's taste for the weird, a searing personal event may have been as significant.

Lovecraft's paternal grandfather died in 1895, but Lovecraft gives no indication that this event affected him or his family in any way; indeed, he states that he never saw his paternal grandfather in person[79]—an indication, perhaps, of the degree to which the Lovecraft side of the family had become (or perhaps always remained) strangers to the Phillips side, especially after the illness and hospitalisation of Winfield Scott Lovecraft. But an event that occurred on January 26, 1896, did seriously affect the five-and-a-half-year-old boy: the death of his maternal grandmother, Robie Alzada Place Phillips.

It was, perhaps, not so much the loss of a family member—to whom Lovecraft does not appear to have been especially close—as its effect upon the remaining members of the family that so affected the young boy: ". . . the death of my grandmother plunged the household into a gloom from which it never fully recovered. The black attire of my mother & aunts terrified & repelled me to such an extent that I would surreptitiously pin bits of bright cloth or paper to their skirts for sheer relief. They had to make a careful survey of their attire before receiving callers or going out!" Seriocomically as Lovecraft narrates these events, twenty years after the fact, it is evident that they left a profound impression upon him. The aftermath was quite literally nightmarish:

> And then it was that my former high spirits received their damper. I began to have nightmares of the most hideous description, peopled with *things* which I called "night-gaunts"—a compound word of my own coinage. I used to draw them after waking (perhaps the idea of these figures came from an edition de luxe of *Paradise Lost* with illustrations by Doré, which I discovered one day in the east parlor). In dreams they were wont to whirl me through space at a sickening rate of speed, the while fretting & impelling me with their detestable tridents. It is fully fifteen years—aye, more—since I have seen a "night-gaunt", but even now, when half asleep & drifting vaguely along over a sea of childhood thoughts, I feel a thrill of fear . . . & instinctively *struggle to keep awake.* That was my own prayer back in '96—each night—to *keep awake* & ward off the night-gaunts![80]

And so begins Lovecraft's career as one of the great dreamers—or, to coin a term that must be coined for the phenomenon, nightmarers—of literary history. Even though it would be another ten years from the writing of this letter, and hence a full thirty years after these dreams, that he would utilise the night-gaunts in his work, it is already evident that his boyhood dreams contain many conceptual and imagistic kernels of his mature tales: the cosmic backdrop; the utterly outré nature of his malignant entities (in a late letter he describes them as "black, lean, rubbery things with bared, barbed tails, bat-wings, and *no faces at all*"[81]), so different from conventional demons, vampires, or ghosts; and the helpless passivity of the protagonist-victim, at the mercy of forces infinitely more powerful than himself. It would, of course, take a long time for Lovecraft to evolve his theory and practice of weird fiction; but with dreams like these at such an early age—and in the last year of his life he confessed that, of his subsequent nightmares, "even the worst is pallid beside the real 1896 product"[82]—his career as a writer of horror tales comes to seem like an inevitable destiny.

Lovecraft's family—in particular his mother—must, however, have been concerned for his physical and psychological health at the onset of his dreams, and at what may have been a general pattern of gloomy or depressed behaviour. Lovecraft speaks frequently in later years of a trip to western Rhode Island taken in 1896, but does not speak of its purpose or effect. It is difficult to deny that this trip to ancestral lands was, at least in part, an attempt by his family to rid him of his nightmares and his general malaise. Then, again, perhaps the entire family—bereaved husband Whipple, Robie's daughters Lillie, Susie, and Annie—were in need of solace. (The trip would not have been made for the purpose of burying Robie in Foster, for she was laid to rest in the Phillips plot at Swan Point Cemetery.)

Lovecraft reports visiting the homestead of James Wheaton Phillips (1830–1901), Whipple's older brother, on Johnson Road in Foster, spending two weeks there.[83] It is not entirely clear who accompanied him, but his mother must surely have come along, and perhaps both aunts as well. The ancient house, nestled against a hill and near a meadow with a winding brook flowing through it, must surely have encouraged both Lovecraft's yearning for the rural landscape and his burgeoning antiquarianism; but a still more remarkable event stimulated Lovecraft and effected perhaps his first concrete defeat of his personal enemy, Time:

> In 1896, when I was six years old, I was taken to visit in the Western Rhode Island region whence my maternal stock came; and there met an ancient gentlewoman—a Mrs. Wood, daughter to a rebel officer in the late unfortunate uprising against His Majesty's lawful authority—who was celebrating with proper pride her hundredth birthday. Mrs. Wood was born in the year 1796, and could walk and talk when Genl. Washington breath'd his last. And now, in 1896, I was conversing with her—with one who had talked to people in periwigs and three-cornered hats, and had studied from schoolbooks with the long s! Young as I was, the idea gave me a tremendous feeling of cosmic victory over Time . . .[84]

Such personal contact with an individual who was living in Lovecraft's beloved eighteenth century would not have had the obvious impact that it did if Lovecraft had not already become fascinated with the eighteenth century through the books in that "black, windowless attic room" at 454 Angell Street. And yet, it is not entirely clear at what precise age Lovecraft began to haunt that room; one must believe that it was perhaps around the age of five or six. In 1931 he maintained that "I think I am probably the only living person to whom the ancient 18th century idiom is actually a prose and poetic mother-tongue," and he explained how this came about:

> At home all the main bookcases in library, parlours, dining-room, and elsewhere were full of standard Victorian junk, most of the brown-leather old-timers . . . having been banished to a windowless third-story trunk-room which had sets of shelves. But what did I do? What, pray, but go with candles and kerosene lamp to that obscure and nighted aërial crypt—leaving the sunny downstairs 19th century flat, and boring my way back through the decades into the late 17th, 18th and early 19th century by means of innumerable crumbling and long-s'd tomes of

> every size and nature—*Spectator, Tatler, Guardian, Idler, Rambler,* Dryden, Pope, Thomson, Young, Tickell, Cooke's *Hesiod,* Ovid by Various Hands, Francis's Horace and Phaedrus, &c. &c. &c. . . .[85]

It's a wonder Lovecraft didn't burn the house down with that candle and kerosene lamp. Lovecraft added, "thank God I have 'em yet as the *main* items of my own modest collection"; true enough, his collection of books of or about the eighteenth century (some, of course, obtained in later years) is impressive. It is evident from the above list, and from the books in his library, that what especially attracted him in eighteenth-century literature was poetry and prose nonfiction; he remarked frequently that the early novelists appealed to him much less, noting at one point that the aspect of the eighteenth century represented by Fielding was "a side that Mr. Addison, Dr. Johnson, Mr. Cowper, Mr. Thomson, and all my best friends both hated and lamented."[86] No doubt the sexual frankness of Fielding, the buffoonery of Smollett, and the utter subversion of eighteenth-century rationalism represented by Sterne did not please either the young or the older Lovecraft at all.

This eighteenth-century predilection, especially in poetry, led indirectly to a literary and philosophical interest of still greater importance: classical antiquity. At the age of six[87] Lovecraft read Hawthorne's *Wonder-Book* (1852) and *Tanglewood Tales* (1853), and professed himself "enraptured by the Hellenic myths even in their Teutonised form" ("A Confession of Unfaith"). Lovecraft is here merely echoing Hawthorne's preface to *A Wonder-Book:* "In the present version [the myths] may have lost much of their aspect . . ., and have, perhaps assumed a Gothic or romantic guise."[88] These tales are narrated in a conversational manner, each myth being told by a college student, Eustace Bright, to a group of children. *A Wonder-Book* contains the myths of Perseus and Medusa, King Midas, Pandora, the Golden Apples of the Hesperides, Baucis and Philemon, and the Chimaera. *Tanglewood Tales* recounts the stories of the Minotaur, the Pygmies, the Dragon's Teeth, Circe's Palace, the Pomegranate Seeds, and the Golden Fleece. While most of the tales are originally Greek, it is likely that Hawthorne relied much on Ovid's *Metamorphoses* for descriptive details; he used it exclusively for the Baucis and Philemon story, which is found only there.

From Hawthorne Lovecraft naturally graduated to Thomas Bulfinch's *The Age of Fable* (1855), the first of three simplified rewritings of myths by Bulfinch; this, along with the other two—*The Age of Chivalry* (1858) and *Legends of Charlemagne* (1863)—constitute *Bulfinch's Mythology.* I see no evidence that Lovecraft ever read these latter two volumes, as he never expressed any interest whatever in the Middle Ages. The copy of *The Age of Fable* found in his library appears to date to 1898, so he must have read an earlier edition and obtained (or was given) this copy later.

There is no reason to wonder at Lovecraft's becoming captivated by Graeco-Roman myth upon reading Bulfinch; for his artless simplicity retains freshness and charm even after the lapse of more than a century and a half. His simple piety is wholly ingenuous: "The creation of the world is a problem naturally fitted to excite the liveliest interest of man, its inhabitant. The ancient pagans, not having the information on the subject which we derive from the pages of Scripture, had their own way of telling the story . . ."[89] Lovecraft no doubt shrugged this off with insouciance. Much of Bulfinch is similarly derived from Ovid's *Metamorphoses;* Bulfinch even copies Ovid's rhetorical device of switching to the present tense as a narrative approaches its climax.

Lovecraft finally came upon the *Metamorphoses* itself around this time, doing so in a way that felicitously united his burgeoning love of classical myth with his already existing fondness for eighteenth-century prosody. His grandfather's library had an edition of "Garth's Ovid"—that gorgeous 1717 translation of the *Metamorphoses* assembled by Sir Samuel Garth, taking some portions from previously published translations (Dryden had translated the entirety of books one and twelve and portions of others; Congreve had translated a portion of book ten) and commissioning poets both eminent (Pope, Addison, Gay, Nicholas Rowe) and obscure (Laurence Eusden, Arthur Maynwaring, Samuel Croxall, James Vernon, John Ozell) to fill in the remaining sections. Garth himself, a poet of no small distinction—Lovecraft owned a 1706 edition of his medical poem *The Dispensary* (1699)—translated book fourteen and a portion of book fifteen. The result is a riot of exquisite iambic pentameter couplets—thousands and thousands of lines in unending succession. It is not surprising that "The even decasyllabic rhythm seemed to strike some responsive chord in my brain, and I forthwith became wedded to that measure . . ."[90] The actual edition read by Lovecraft appears to be a two-volume edition simply titled *Ovid* (Harper & Brothers, 1837), of which volume 2 (the only one found in his library) contains the *Metamorphoses* and the *Epistles* (i.e., the *Heroides*).

Lovecraft's absorption of classical antiquity did not occur entirely through the medium of books. In a late letter he speaks of the multifarious influences, going back several years, that led him to the ancient world:

> . . . the chance circumstance that a child's reader which I devoured at the age of 6 had a very alluring selection about Rome & Pompeii—the equally chance circumstance that at 3 or 4 I was impressed by the great railway viaduct at Canton, between Providence & Boston, which has great masonry arches like a Roman aqueduct . . . & that my mother, in connexion with it, told me that arches were first extensively used by the Romans, & described the great aqueducts . . . which latter I soon saw in pictures—& so on, & so on.[91]

Whipple Phillips also assisted in fostering Lovecraft's love of Rome: "He had loved to muse amidst the ruins of the ancient city, & had brought from Italy a wealth of mosaics, . . . paintings, & other objets d'art whose theme was more often classically Roman than Italian. He always wore a pair of mosaics in his cuffs for buttons—one a view of the Coliseum (so *tiny* yet so *faithful*); the other of the Forum."[92] Whipple brought home from his travels pictures of Roman ruins and some Roman coins: "I cannot begin to suggest the feeling of *awe* and *anomalous familiarity* which those coins—the actual products of Roman engravers and mints, and actually passed from Roman hand to Roman hand twenty centuries ago—awaked in me."[93] The downstairs parlour of 454 Angell Street had a life-size Roman bust on a gilded pedestal. No doubt all this was part of the reason why Lovecraft always preferred the culture of Rome to that of Greece, although other philosophical, aesthetic, and temperamental factors eventually entered into it. Writing in 1931 to Robert E. Howard—that great champion of barbarism—he admitted: "I realise that the Romans were an extremely prosaic race; given to all the practical and utilitarian precepts I detest, and without any of the genius of the Greek or glamour of the Northern barbarian. And yet—I can't manage to think behind 450 A.D. except as a Roman!"[94]

In the short term the effect of reading Hawthorne, Bulfinch, and Garth's Ovid was that "My Bagdad name and affiliations disappeared at once, for the magic of silks and colours faded before that of fragrant templed groves, faun-peopled meadows in the twilight, and the blue, beckoning Mediterranean" ("A Confession of Unfaith"). A more important result is that Lovecraft became a writer.

It is not entirely clear what Lovecraft's first literary work was. He dates the commencement of his writing to the age of six, remarking: "My attempts at versification, of which I made the first at the age of six, now took on a crude, internally rhyming ballad metre, and I sang of the exploits of Gods and Heroes."[95] In context this appears to suggest that Lovecraft had begun to write verse prior to his discovery of classical antiquity, but that his fascination with the ancient world impelled him toward renewed poetic composition, this time on classical themes. None of this pre-classical verse survives, and the first poetical work we do have is the "second edition" of "The Poem of Ulysses; or, The Odyssey: Written for Young People." This elaborate little book contains a preface, a copyright notice, and an internal title page reading:

THE YOUNG FOLKS'
ULYSSES
or the *Odyssey* in plain
OLDEN *ENGLISH* VERSE
An *Epick* Poem Writ
by
Howard Lovecraft, Gent.

This is dated to November 8, 1897, in the preface, and I have to believe that the "first edition" dated to earlier in the year, prior to Lovecraft's seventh birthday on August 20, 1897.

On the copyright page Lovecraft writes: "Acknowledgements are due to Popes Odyssey and Bulfinch's Mythology and Harpers Half Hour Series." Then, helpfully, "Homer first writ the poem." Harper's Half-Hour Series was a series of small books of essays, poetry, plays, and other short works selling for a quarter—the idea being, presumably, that they could each be read in half an hour. There does not seem to have been any edition (even an abridged one) of Homer or of the *Odyssey,* and I suspect the work in question was Eugene Lawrence's *A Primer of Greek Literature* (1879), which may have had a summary of the *Odyssey.* In "A Confession of Unfaith" Lovecraft describes the volume as a "tiny book in the private library of my elder aunt" (i.e., Lillian D. Phillips). It is remarkable to think that Lovecraft had already read the whole of Pope's *Odyssey* by the age of seven (one cannot know whether a similar acknowledgment appeared in the "first edition"); but it becomes immediately obvious that Lovecraft in his 88-line poem could not possibly have been dependent upon Pope's 14,000-line translation either metrically or even in terms of the story line. Here is how Lovecraft's poem begins:

> The nighte was darke! O readers, Hark!
> And see Ulysses' fleet!
> From trumpets sound back homeward bound
> He hopes his spouse to greet.

This is certainly not Pope; what, in fact, does it remind one of? How about this?

> And through the drifts the snowy clifts
> Did send a dismal sheen:
> Nor shapes of men nor beasts we ken—
> The lee was all between.[96]

It's our old friend the *Ancient Mariner.* Indeed, Lovecraft has done Coleridge one better by internally rhyming every iambic heptameter line (Coleridge sometimes becomes lax and does only every other one, or sometimes none at all), and he abandons Coleridge's stanzaic divisions. Lovecraft, in his surprisingly frequent discussions of "The Poem of Ulysses" in essays and letters, never suggests Coleridge as the metrical model of the work. In 1926 Lovecraft remarked that "My 6-year-old 'verse' was pretty bad, and I had recited enough poetry to know that it was so"; he goes on to say that what helped him to improve his prosody was a very careful study of Abner Alden's *The Reader* (1797), of which he had a third edition (1808), and which he declares "was so utterly and absolutely the very thing I had been looking for, that I attacked it with almost savage violence."[97] After a month or so, Lovecraft asserts, he produced "The Poem of Ulysses."

If nothing else, the work is a remarkable example of concision: in 88 lines Lovecraft has compressed the 12,000 lines of Homer's *Odyssey.* Even Bulfinch's prose account takes up thirty pages in the Modern Library edition. Lovecraft achieves this compression by deftly omitting relatively inessential portions of the story—in particular, the entire first four books (the Adventures of Telemachos) and, perhaps surprisingly, book eleven (the descent into Hades)—and, more importantly, by retelling the entire story in *chronological sequence,* from Odysseus' sailing from Troy to his final return home to Ithaca, rather than in the elaborately convoluted way in which Homer's Odysseus narrates his adventures. Much later Lovecraft made this distinction between order of occurrence and order of narration a pillar of his technique of weird fiction, and it is remarkable that he had gained a practical knowledge of it so early. Perhaps the Harper's Half-Hour Series had performed the feat for him in this instance, but nevertheless Lovecraft's utilisation of it is striking.

"The Poem of Ulysses" is a delight. There are only a small number of grammatical errors ("it's" for "its"; false archaisms such as "storme" and "darke"), some dubious rhymes (storme/harme), and one actually false rhyme (first/nurse), but otherwise it is charming from beginning to end. Consider Ulysses' defeat of the Cyclops:

By crafty ruse he can confuse
The stupid giant's mind
Puts out his eye with dreadful cry
And leaves the wretch behind.

Or his wrath at Circe for turning his men into pigs:

Unhappy he his men to see
Engaged in swinish bliss.
He drew his sword and spake harsh word
To Circe standing there
"My men set free", in wrath quoth he
"Thy damage quick repair"!!!

And if Lovecraft genuinely saw an internal rhyme in "He'll ne'er roam far from Ithaca," it may give us some idea of his New England pronunciation.

Perhaps the most interesting thing about "The Poem of Ulysses" is a sort of catalogue or notice for "Providence Classics" of the Providence Press Co. appended to the poem. The list is as follows:

MYTHOLOGY FOR THE YOUNG ---------------- 25¢
ULYSSES FOR YOUNG FOLKS IN VERSE ---------5¢
AN OLD EGYPTIAN MYTH PREPARED
SPECIALLY FOR SMALL CHILDREN ---------5¢

SOON TO BE PUBLISHED

THE YOUNG FOLKS ILIAD IN VERSE -------------5¢
THE ÆNEID ---5¢
OVIDS METAMORPHOSES ------------------------- 25¢

This suggests that "Mythology for the Young" and "An Old Egyptian Myth . . ." have already been written; they do not, so far as is known, survive. There is another, more extensive catalogue at the end of *Poemata Minora, Volume II* (1902), which lists all three of the "Soon to Be Published" works cited above. The first two have apparently perished; they too are likely to have been paraphrased from Bulfinch. And, of course, one must keep in mind that Lovecraft might have read Pope's translation of the former and Dryden's of the latter. Of "Ovid's Metamorphoses" I shall have more to say later.

The fact that "Mythology for the Young" is priced at 25¢ suggests that it was a fairly substantial document; it appears to be Lovecraft's first prose work, perhaps a sort of paraphrase of some of Bulfinch. Chapter 34 of *The Age of Fable* has a relatively brief discussion of some Egyptian myths, mostly the myth of Isis and Osiris, and I suspect that this is where Lovecraft derived the source material for "An Old Egyptian Myth . . ." At 5¢, it is likely to have been a very short work. The 1902 catalogue lists something called "Egyptian Myths" at 25¢, probably an expansion of the original work.

The elaborate "publishing" efforts involved in "The Poem of Ulysses"—illustrations, title and copyright pages, catalogue, price—certainly suggest that Lovecraft, so early as the age of seven, is determined to make a career of writing. A "P.S." after the preface notes: "The later works may be much better than this because the author will have more practice." Lovecraft had not yet learnt the use of the hectograph, so if he "sold" copies of "The Poem of Ulysses" (and he may well have done so to members of his family, who would no doubt have provided encouragement), he would presumably have written out a fresh copy for each sale.

Classical antiquity was, however, more than a literary experience for Lovecraft; it was both a personal and even a quasi-religious one. He speaks warmly of going to the museum of the Rhode Island School of Design (the college situated at the foot of College Hill, mostly along Benefit Street) in 1897–99 (the museum had in fact only opened in 1897[98]); at that time the museum was, as Lovecraft notes, housed in the "awkward & inadequate basement of the main building" at 11 Waterman Street (destroyed to make way for the bus tunnel of 1914), but nevertheless it

> . . . was an enchanted world for me—a true magick grotto where unfolded before me the glory that was Greece & the grandeur that was Rome. I have since seen many other museums of art, & am now sojourning but a five-cent fare from the next-greatest in the world [i.e., the Metropolitan Museum in New York]; yet I vow that none has ever moved me so much, or given me so close & vivid a sense of contact with the ancient world, as that modest basement on Waterman St. hill with its meagre plaster casts![99]

No doubt his mother or his grandfather took him there. Elsewhere Lovecraft says that "Before long I was fairly familiar with the principal classical art museums of Providence and Boston"[100] (by which he presumably refers to the Museum of Fine Arts in Boston and the Fogg Museum at Harvard) and that he had begun a collection of small plaster casts of Greek sculptures. The result was an infatuation with the classical world and then a kind of religious epiphany. Let Lovecraft tell it in his own inimitable way:

> When about seven or eight I was a genuine pagan, so intoxicated with the beauty of Greece that I acquired a half-sincere belief in the old gods and Nature-spirits. I have in literal truth built altars to Pan, Apollo, Diana, and Athena, and have watched for dryads and satyrs in the woods and fields at dusk. Once I firmly thought I beheld some of these sylvan creatures dancing under autumnal oaks; a kind of "religious experience" as true in its way as the subjective ecstasies of any Christian. If a Christian tell me he has *felt* the reality of his Jesus or Jahveh, I can reply that I have *seen* the hoofed Pan and the sisters of the Hesperian Phaëthusa. ("A Confession of Unfaith")

This certainly puts the lie to Bulfinch, who solemnly declared at the very beginning of *The Age of Fable:* "The religions of ancient Greece and Rome are extinct. The so-called divinities of Olympus have not a single worshipper among living men."[101]

In writing the above passage Lovecraft was clearly wishing to show that his scepticism and anticlericalism were of very early origin; but he may be guilty of some exaggeration. Earlier in this essay he reports that "I was instructed in the legends of the Bible and of Saint Nicholas at the age of about two, and gave to both a passive acceptance not especially distinguished either for its critical keenness or its enthusiastic comprehension." He then declares that just before the age of five he was told that Santa Claus does not exist, and that he thereupon countered with the query as to "why God is not equally a myth." "Not long afterwards," he continues, he was placed in a Sunday school at the First Baptist Church, but became so pestiferous an iconoclast that he was allowed to discontinue attendance. Elsewhere, however, he declares that this incident occurred at the age of twelve.[102] When we examine Lovecraft's philosophical development, the likelihood is that the Sunday school incident indeed took place at the age of twelve, and not at five. But clearly there was an earlier Sunday school stint for Lovecraft, and here his growing attachment for Rome did seem to get him into a little trouble:

> When Rome was presented to me from . . . [an] unfavourable angle—the Sunday-School horror of Nero and the persecution of Christians—I could never quite sympathise in the least with the teachers. I felt that one good Roman pagan was worth any six dozen of the cringing scum riff-raff who took up with a fanatical foreign belief, and was frankly sorry that the Syrian superstition was not stamped out. . . . When it came to the repressive measures of Marcus Aurelius and Diocletianus, I was in complete sympathy with the government and had not a shred of use for the Christian herd. To try to get me to identify myself with that herd seemed in my mind ridiculous.[103]

This leads to the charming admission that "at seven I sported the adopted name of L. VALERIUS MESSALA & tortured imaginary Christians in amphitheatres."[104]

By the age of seven Lovecraft had already begun to read—Grimm's *Fairy Tales* at four, the *Arabian Nights* at five, and classical antiquity at six or seven—gone through two pseudonyms (Abdul Alhazred and L. Valerius Messala), begun to write poetry and prose nonfiction, and gained what would prove to be a lifelong love of England and of the past. But his imaginative appetite was not complete; for he claims that in the winter of 1896 yet another interest emerged: the theatre. The first play he saw was "one of Denman Thompson's minor efforts,"[105] *The Sunshine of Paradise Alley,* which featured a slum scene that fascinated him. Shortly thereafter he was enjoying the "well-made" plays of Henry Arthur Jones and Arthur Wing Pinero;[106] but the next year his taste was improved by seeing his first Shakespearean play, *Cymbeline,* at the Providence Opera House. Lovecraft's memory was good enough in 1916 to remember that the Christmas matinee he attended in 1897 was on a Saturday.[107] He set up a little toy theatre in his room, hand-painted the scenery, and played *Cymbeline* for weeks. Lovecraft's interest in drama continued sporadically for at least the next fifteen to twenty years; around 1910 he saw Robert Mantell's company perform *King John* in Providence, with the young Fritz Leiber, Sr, as Faulconbridge.[108] Lovecraft was also a very early enthusiast of film, and throughout his life we will find selected films influencing some of his most significant writing.

From the age of three onward—while his father was slowly deteriorating both physically and mentally in Butler Hospital—the young Howard Phillips Lovecraft was encountering one intellectual and imaginative stimulus after the other: first the colonial antiquities of Providence, then Grimm's *Fairy Tales,* then the *Arabian Nights,* then Coleridge's *Ancient Mariner,* then eighteenth-century belles-lettres, then the theatre and Shakespeare, and finally Hawthorne, Bulfinch, and the classical world. It is a remarkable sequence, and many of these stimuli would be of lifelong duration. But there remained one further influence that would definitively turn Lovecraft into the man and writer we know: "Then I struck EDGAR ALLAN POE!! It was my downfall, and at the age of eight I saw the blue firmament of Argos and Sicily darkened by the miasmal exhalations of the tomb!"[109]

3. Black Woods & Unfathomed Caves (1898–1902)

The history of what Lovecraft called weird fiction up to 1898 is a fascinating one, and Lovecraft himself has written perhaps the ablest historical account of it in "Supernatural Horror in Literature" (1927). The use of the "supernatural" in Western literature can, of course, be traced back to the *Iliad* with the intervention of the gods in the affairs of men; but Lovecraft is correct in maintaining that weird fiction as such can only be a product of an age that has ceased to believe generally in the existence of the supernatural. The ghost in *Hamlet* inspires fear and awe not by what he says or does but by his mere existence: he represents a defiance or contravention of what we have understood to be the unvarying laws of Nature. It is, therefore, not surprising that the first canonical work of supernatural fiction was written by a prototype of the eighteenth-century English Enlightenment, one who had no awareness that the story he wrote down in two months based on a dream of a mediaeval castle would assist in subverting the rationalism he otherwise so cherished.

And yet, it is not often realised that when Horace Walpole published *The Castle of Otranto* from his press at Strawberry Hill on Christmas Day 1764, there was no *immediate* literary sea-change. Although Clara Reeve's *The Old English Baron* (1777) was a direct imitation (and, in part, a rebuke) of Walpole's little novel, it required the added impetus of German Romanticism actually to launch the "Gothic" movement in literature in the 1790s. It was then that Ann Radcliffe published *The Romance of the Forest* (1791), *The Mysteries of Udolpho* (1794), *The Italian* (1797), and other of her novels, becoming for a time the most popular writer in the English-speaking world. It was also then that twenty-year-old Matthew Gregory Lewis published *The Monk* (1796); a little later Charles Robert Maturin published the first of his novels, *The Fatal Revenge* (1807), and culminated the Gothic tradition with *Melmoth the Wanderer* (1820). Walpole, Radcliffe, Lewis, and Maturin are only the dominant figures of the English Gothic, and they were surrounded by dozens of imitators, parodists, and hacks—a phenomenon very similar to the horror "boom" of the 1980s. Frederick S. Frank's definitive treatment of Gothic fiction lists a total of 422 novels up to 1820, most of them having long ago attained merciful oblivion.[1] (The eccentric William Beckford's *Vathek* [1786] is in a somewhat separate class, owing more to the Arabian tale and Johnson's *Rasselas* than to Walpole.)

In "Supernatural Horror in Literature" Lovecraft, although deriving much of his information on the Gothic tradition from Edith Birkhead's landmark study,

The Tale of Terror (1921), nevertheless ably identifies the "novel dramatic paraphernalia" which Walpole and his successors introduced, and which

> consisted first of all of the Gothic castle, with its awesome antiquity, vast distances and ramblings, deserted or ruined wings, damp corridors, unwholesome hidden catacombs, and galaxy of ghosts and appalling legends, as a nucleus of suspense and daemoniac fright. In addition, it included the tyrannical and malevolent nobleman as villain; the saintly, long-persecuted, and generally insipid heroine who undergoes the major terrors and serves as a point of view and focus for the reader's sympathies; the valorous and immaculate hero, always of high birth but often in humble disguise; the convention of high-sounding foreign names, mostly Italian, for the characters; and the infinite array of stage properties which includes strange lights, damp trap-doors, extinguished lamps, mouldy hidden manuscripts, creaking hinges, shaking arras, and the like.

This very description displays Lovecraft's awareness that the Gothic "stage properties" had very quickly devolved into hackneyed and standardised tropes that had lost all symbolic value and were more capable of raising a smirk than a shiver. Jane Austen did exactly that in *Northanger Abbey* (1818). By 1820—in spite of the novelty of Mary Shelley's *Frankenstein* (1818), in which science was shown to be as productive of horrors as mediaeval superstition—a new direction was required; and, appropriately, it came from a new country.

Charles Brockden Brown had attempted to establish Radcliffian romance on American soil with *Wieland* (1798) and later novels, but with indifferent success. As early as 1829 William Hazlitt raised a point concerning Brown, and by extension all American Gothic writing, that has some bearing on Lovecraft:

> . . . no ghost, we will venture to say, was ever seen in North America. They do not walk in broad day; and the night of ignorance and superstition which favours their appearance, was long past before the United States lifted up their head beyond the Atlantic wave. . . . In this orderly and undramatic state of security and freedom from natural foes, Mr Brown has provided one of his heroes with a demon to torment him, and fixed him at his back;—but what is to keep him there? Not any prejudice or lurking superstition on the part of the American reader: for the lack of such, the writer is obliged to make up by incessant rodomontade, and face-making.[2]

Hazlitt may have been somewhat sanguine about the rationality of the American mind, but he points to a real dilemma: if the secret of the "kick" (as Lovecraft would have called it) provided by Gothicism is the evocation of the supernatural in a mediaeval age, how could the supernatural be manifested in a country that had no mediaeval age?

It was Edgar Allan Poe (1809–1849) who produced one solution to this problem, not so much by setting his tales back on the Old Continent but by creating a very meticulously described but ultimately imprecise never-never-land that shifted the focus of horror from topography to the human mind. It is often forgotten how *close* Poe is to the final stages of Gothicism; his first important tale, "Metzengerstein," was published in 1832, only twelve years after *Melmoth;* and whether or not we accept G. R. Thompson's belief that it is actually a parody of Gothic conventions,[3] it is very clear that much of the imagery derives from English and German Gothic, particularly E. T. A. Hoffmann. Recall Poe's celebrated defence of the originality of his tales against those critics who claimed that it was too Germanic: "If in many of my productions terror has been the thesis, I maintain that terror is not of Germany, but of the soul."[4] This single sentence pinpoints the revolutionary shift of emphasis effected by the body of Poe's work; Lovecraft elaborates upon the notion:

> Before Poe the bulk of weird writers had worked largely in the dark; without an understanding of the psychological basis of the horror appeal, and hampered by more or less or conformity to certain empty literary conventions such as the happy ending, virtue rewarded, and in general a hollow moral didacticism . . . Poe, on the other hand, perceived the essential impersonality of the real artist; and knew that the function of creative fiction is merely to express and interpret events and sensations as they are, regardless of how they tend or what they prove—good or evil, attractive or repulsive, stimulating or depressing—with the author always acting as a vivid and detached chronicler rather than as a teacher, sympathiser, or vendor of opinion.

The shift from external to internal horror was by no means universal, and is not universal even in Poe's work: many of his tales are definitely supernatural, and in some tales it is impossible to determine whether a given horrific effect is supernatural or psychological (when the protagonist of "The Black Cat" sees on the wall of his house, "as if graven in *bas relief* upon the white surface, the figure of a gigantic *cat,"*[5] is the apparition real or is he merely hallucinating?). But Poe's work was a model for many writers aside from Lovecraft, in its richly complex style, its emphasis on abnormal psychology, and—perhaps most important of all—its theoretical and practical proof that horror works best in short compass. In all subsequent horror literature from Poe's time to the present, the issue of whether there can even be such a thing as a "horror novel" (as opposed to a suspense or mainstream novel with horrific or supernatural interludes) has not been satisfactorily answered or even dealt with.

It is difficult to detect Poe's immediate influence on the weird literature that followed him, since what Lovecraft called the "aftermath of Gothic fiction" lingered in both England and the United States until almost the end of the century, with such writers as Frederick Marryat (*The Phantom Ship* [1839]), Edward Bulwer-Lytton ("The Haunted and the Haunters" [1859], *A Strange Story* [1862]), Wilkie Collins, and many others. Shortly after Poe, the Irishman Joseph

Sheridan Le Fanu (1814–1873), evidently uninfluenced by Poe, produced work startlingly like his, especially in such short stories as "Green Tea" and "Carmilla"; his novels, the best of which is *Uncle Silas* (1864), are more in the traditional Gothic vein. By the turn of the century Le Fanu's work had fallen into obscurity; Lovecraft never read much of it and did not like what he did read. He did, however, assiduously read Nathaniel Hawthorne's short stories and novels, calling *The House of the Seven Gables* "New England's greatest contribution to weird literature"; but Hawthorne was working in an older tradition. And yet, his work was suggestive to Lovecraft in offering yet another solution to the problem posed by Hazlitt, in that it drew upon the dark heritage of New England Puritanism so as to create a universe that, in the words of Maurice Lévy, "has a *historical profundity*"[6] that much other American weird fiction lacks.

The latter quarter of the nineteenth century saw an enormous outpouring of horror literature; as Lovecraft remarked in a letter, "The Victorians went in strongly for weird fiction—Bulwer-Lytton, Dickens, Wilkie Collins, Harrison Ainsworth, Mrs. Oliphant, George W. M. Reynolds, H. Rider Haggard, R. L. Stevenson & countless others turned out reams of it."[7] Prefaced by Stevenson's *The Strange Case of Dr. Jekyll and Mr. Hyde* (1886), the decade of the 1890s was remarkably fertile in what later came to be regarded as classics of the form, although Lovecraft did not become aware of many of them until much later.

In the United States, Ambrose Bierce (1842–1914?), whose first story, "The Haunted Valley," dates to so early as 1871, produced two landmark collections, *Tales of Soldiers and Civilians* (1891) and *Can Such Things Be?* (1893), which carried on Poe's interest in psychological horror, augmented by a delightful lacing of cynicism and misanthropy; Lovecraft, however, did not discover Bierce's work until 1919. He came upon the early weird work of Robert W. Chambers (1865–1933) at a still later date, but relished such eccentric volumes as *The King in Yellow* (1895), *The Maker of Moons* (1896), and other collections of tales. Chambers abandoned the weird and went on to become one of the best-selling writers of the first three decades of the new century with an appalling array of shopgirl romances, causing Lovecraft to refer to him as a "fallen Titan."[8] Henry James's *The Turn of the Screw* (1898) was regarded as a brilliant but eccentric anomaly in the work of a writer already well established as a profound social commentator.

In England, Arthur Machen (1863–1947) established his reputation with *The Great God Pan and The Inmost Light* (1894), *The Three Impostors* (1895), *The House of Souls* (1906), *The Hill of Dreams* (1907), and other works. Lovecraft did not encounter him until 1923. Bram Stoker (1847–1912) published *Dracula* in 1897, although it took some time for that novel to achieve eminence as the prototypical vampire novel. The enormously significant work of M. R. James (1862–

1936), Lord Dunsany (1878–1957), and Algernon Blackwood (1869–1951), all of whom began publishing in the first decade of the twentieth century, was discovered by Lovecraft between 1919 and 1925.

Weird fiction, then, was, if by no means a dominant voice (it never has been such), at least a significant presence in the final decade of the nineteenth century; and yet, I have elsewhere maintained[9] that the weird was not considered a genre at this time, and may not have been so considered for many years thereafter. Even Poe did not fancy himself as working exclusively in a weird vein, and he in fact did not do so, writing many humorous and satiric tales as well as the first detective stories. As he huffily declared in his preface to *Tales of the Grotesque and Arabesque* (1840): "Let us admit, for the moment, that the 'phantasy-pieces' now given *are* Germanic, or what not. Then Germanism is 'the vein' for the time being. To morrow I may be anything but German, as yesterday I was everything else."[10] Similarly, it cannot be asserted that the work of Le Fanu, Stoker, Machen, Blackwood, or Dunsany is wholly weird, or was so regarded by their authors; and certainly only a very small proportion of Hawthorne's or Stevenson's work is weird.

It may be observed that no mention has been made of periodicals devoted to weird fiction; there were none, and there would be none until the establishment of *Weird Tales* in 1923. Poe published in the standard periodicals of his day (*Graham's Magazine, Godey's Lady's Book, Southern Literary Messenger*), some of which he edited; Bierce was widely published in magazines and newspapers. In other words, the weird was not automatically banned from mainstream magazines as it would be in the early twentieth century in America; indeed, Machen, Blackwood, and Dunsany continued to publish in mainstream magazines in England through the 1950s. The establishment of the Munsey magazines in the 1890s gave an impetus of sorts to the field, as they published much weird, detective, and speculative fiction; but, since they were scorned (justifiably, for the most part) as cheap "popular" reading for the masses, they initiated that tendency—which the pulp magazines of the 1920s only solidified—of ghettoising all the genres and banishing them from standard magazines. I shall later have more to say about this phenomenon.

The fact (and I believe it is a fact) that the weird was not a recognisable or discrete genre or mode of writing at the turn of the century, and for some time thereafter, is important in understanding Lovecraft's place in the field, for I maintain that he was among the first to regard himself as predominantly a "weird writer." One telltale sign of this state of affairs is the nearly total lack of historical or literary criticism of weird fiction prior to 1917, when Dorothy Scarborough published *The Supernatural in Modern English Fiction,* a thematically exhaustive but critically undistinguished work that nevertheless is a landmark for its mere existence. Even the Gothic tradition failed to secure a critic before Birkhead's *The Tale of Terror* (1921). (Charles L. Eastlake's *History of the Gothic Revival* [1872] is exclusively concerned with neo-Gothic architecture, not literature. Edward Yardley's *The Supernatural in Romantic Fiction* [1880] is a rather cursory thematic study of supernatural motifs used in literature from the Middle Ages to the Romantic period.) This is what makes "Supernatural Horror in Literature" still more impressive as a watershed in literary criticism.

Lovecraft dates his first work of prose fiction to 1897[11] and elsewhere identifies it as "The Noble Eavesdropper"; about all we know of it is that it concerned "a boy who overheard some horrible conclave of subterranean beings in a cave."[12] As the work does not survive, it would perhaps be idle to point to any literary sources for it; but the influence of the *Arabian Nights* (the cave of Ali Baba and other stories involving caves) might be conjectured. A still more likely source, perhaps, would be his grandfather Whipple, the only member of his family who appears to have enjoyed the weird. As Lovecraft states in a late letter:

> I never heard *oral* weird tales except from my grandfather—who, observing my tastes in reading, used to devise all sorts of impromptu original yarns about black woods, unfathomed caves, winged horrors (like the "night-gaunts" of my dreams, about which I used to tell him), old witches with sinister cauldrons, & "deep, low, moaning sounds". He obviously drew most of his imagery from the early gothic romances—Radcliffe, Lewis, Maturin, &c.—which he seemed to like better than Poe or other later fantaisistes.[13]

Here are some of the components (unfathomed caves, deep, low, moaning sounds) of the imagery of "The Noble Eavesdropper." But Lovecraft admits that this is the only tale he wrote prior to his reading of Poe.

Given the state of the field of weird fiction in 1898, and given Lovecraft's age, it is not surprising that the tales of Poe would have been the first weird literature he stumbled upon. The Gothic novels were far too long for absorption by most youths, even one so devoted to the eighteenth century as Lovecraft. Many of them had, moreover, by this time become very difficult to obtain (in the 1920s Lovecraft was disconcerted to find that even the New York Public Library did not own a copy of *Melmoth the Wanderer*). As for more modern writers, in 1921 Lovecraft would lament that "nine persons out of ten *never heard of* Ambrose Bierce, the greatest story writer except Poe whom America ever produced" (*In Defence of Dagon*). This may be somewhat of an exaggeration, but Bierce was by 1898 probably known widely only in the San Francisco literary circle in which he had established himself; in any case, his tales would probably have been considered too gruesome to give to an eight-year-old. The other writers I have mentioned here were either too recent or, again, too "adult" to be given to a young boy.

Poe was, by the turn of the century, slowly gaining a place of eminence in American literature, although he still had to face posthumous attacks such as that of Henry James, who in 1876 made the celebrated remark: "With all due respect to the very original genius of the author of the 'Tales of Mystery,' it seems to me that to take him with more than a certain degree of seriousness is to lack seriousness one's self. An enthusiasm for Poe is the mark of a decidedly primitive stage of reflection."[14] Poe's championing by Baudelaire, Mallarmé, and other Continental writers had slowly impelled reconsideration of his work by English and American critics. The English scholar John H. Ingram wrote the first biography, the two-volume *Edgar Allan Poe: His Life, Letters and Opinions* (1880); it was followed in 1885 by George E. Woodberry's *Edgar Allan Poe* for the American Men of Letters series, later expanded as *The Life of Edgar Allan Poe* (1909). Lovecraft later acquired Ingram's work and Woodberry's 1885 volume.

I am not sure which exact volume or edition of Poe was read by Lovecraft in 1898. In his library are found the Raven Edition (5 vols., 1903) and one volume (*Essays and Philosophy*) of the Cameo Edition (10 vols., 1904), but of course these could not have been what he read in 1898. It is highly unlikely that his family had the first collected edition (Griswold's, 4 vols., 1850–56), as Lovecraft would surely have retained it; the same could be said for other early editions: Ingram's (4 vols., 1874–75), Richard Henry Stoddard's (6 vols., 1884), Edmund Clarence Stedman and Woodberry's (10 vols., 1894–95). The landmark critical edition by James A. Harrison (17 vols., 1902), which would not be superseded until T. O. Mabbott's edition of 1969–78, would have been a jewel in Lovecraft's or his family's library. One can only assume that he read some one-volume selection of tales, possibly a children's or young adult's edition, of which there were already many by this time.

It is, in fact, a little difficult to discern any clear-cut Poe influence in the first several of Lovecraft's juvenile stories. He claims that his first story, written in 1897 (not named, but surely "The Noble Eavesdropper"), was "pre-Poe,"[15] implying that the subsequent tales were inspired by Poe; but I cannot see anything of Poe in "The Little Glass Bottle," "The Secret Cave; or, John Lees Adventure," "The Mystery of the Grave-yard; or, A Dead Man's Revenge," or "The Mysterious Ship." The first of these was described by Lovecraft as "a juvenile attempt at humour";[16] that is about as charitable an assessment as one can make.

"The Little Glass Bottle" tells of a ship commanded by a Captain William Jones which comes upon a bottle with a message in it (perhaps one is to infer the influence of Poe's "MS. Found in a Bottle" here). This note—written in a very wild and hasty hand on Lovecraft's autograph manuscript (a crude but effective attempt at realism)—announces the writer as John Jones (no relation to the captain, one imagines) and says that there is a treasure to be found on the spot marked with an asterisk on the reverse of the note (here we find a crude map of the Indian Ocean, with a nebulous land mass labelled "Austrailia" at the bottom left). This note is dated January 1, 1864.

Captain Jones decides that "it would pay to go" to the spot, and the crew do so. There they find another note from John Jones: "Dear Searcher excuse me for the practical joke I have played on you but it serves you right to find nothing for your foolish act . . ." But John kindly defrays their expenses with an iron box containing "$25.0.00," whatever that is. It is after reading this note (which, for some reason, is dated December 3, 1880) that Captain Jones delivers the one funny line in the entire story: "I'd like to kick his head off."

None of these early stories is dated, with the exception of "The Mysterious Ship" (clearly dated to 1902), but they must have been written during the period 1898–1902, perhaps more toward the earlier than the later end of that spectrum. Lovecraft almost never speaks of "The Secret Cave"; it is easily the slightest of the juvenile tales. Mrs Lee instructs her son, ten-year-old John, and daughter, two-year-old Alice, to be "good children" while both parents are "going off for the day"; but immediately upon their departure John and Alice go down to the cellar and begin "to rummage among the rubbish." Alice leans against a wall and it suddenly gives way behind her; a passage is discovered. John and Alice enter the passage, coming successively upon a large empty box, a small, very heavy box that is not opened, and a boat with oars. The passage comes to an abrupt end; John pulls away "the obstacle" and finds a torrent of water rushing in. John is a good swimmer, but little Alice is not, and she drowns. John manages to struggle into the boat, clinging to the body of his sister and the small box. Suddenly he realises that "he could shut off the water"; he does so, although how he does it—and why he did not think of it earlier—is never explained. "It was very gruesome & uncanny absolutely dark his candle being put out by the flood & a dead body lying near." Finally he reaches the cellar. Later it is discovered that the box contains a solid gold chunk worth $10,000—"enough to pay for any thing but the death of his sister."

I have no idea of the purpose of this unpleasantly gruesome little story. Lovecraft apparently wrote it with great haste, making many grammatical errors and occasionally even failing to capitalise the proper noun "Alice." "They" is frequently rendered as "the." I shall not speculate on the existence of a sister in the story: the tale does not seem especially autobiographical, so one cannot infer that Lovecraft was somehow wanting a sister. Again, no discernible influence from Poe or anyone else can be found.

Of "The Mystery of the Grave-yard"—which contains not only a subtitle ("or, 'A Dead Man's Revenge'") but a sub-subtitle ("A Detective story")—rather more may be said. This is the longest of Lovecraft's juvenile stories, and at the end of the autograph manuscript he has noted (obviously at a much later date): "Evidently written in late 1898 or early 1899." The fact that it is labelled a detective story should not lead us to think it is influenced by Poe's "The Murders in the Rue Morgue" or any of his other detective stories, although no doubt Lovecraft read them; he also (as I shall discuss later) read the early Sherlock Holmes stories and could conceivably have read them at this early date. But even the most cursory glance at this wild, histrionic, and rather engaging story should allow us to point to its predominant source: the dime novel.

The first dime novel was published in 1860, when the firm later known as Beadle & Adams reprinted, in a 128-page paper-covered volume 6 × 4 inches in dimensions, Ann Sophia Winterbotham Stephens's *Malaeska: The Indian Wife of the White Hunter*. The fact that it was a reprint was critical, for it allowed the firm to claim that here was a "dollar book for a dime."[17] Beadle & Adams was the leading publisher of dime novels until it folded in 1898, having been driven out of business by the bold and innovative publishing practices of Street & Smith, which entered the dime novel market in 1889. Frank Tousey was a lesser publisher of dime novels.

It should not be assumed that dime novels were merely action thrillers, although many of them were; there were westerns (Deadwood Dick from Beadle & Adams; Diamond Dick from Street & Smith), detective or espionage stories (Nick Carter from Street & Smith; Old King Brady from Frank Tousey), tales of high school and college life (Frank Merriwell from Street & Smith), and even pious tales of moral uprightness (Horatio Alger, Jr, wrote prolifically for Street & Smith in the 1890s).[18] Their principal feature was their price, their format (paper covers, 128 pages or less), and, in general, their action-packed narrative style. The leading dime novel series were, of course, priced at 10¢, although there was a wide array of smaller books, called "nickel libraries," at 5¢ aimed at younger readers.

It is one of the great paradoxes of Lovecraft's entire literary career that he could, on the one hand, absorb the highest aesthetic fruits of Western culture—Greek and Latin literature, Shakespeare, the poetry of Keats and Shelley—and at the same time go slumming in the cheapest dregs of popular fiction. Throughout his life Lovecraft vigorously defended the *literary* value of the weird tale (unlike some modern critics who misguidedly vaunt both the good and the bad, the aesthetically polished and the mechanically hackneyed, as representative of "popular culture"—as if literary merit is determined by what masses of half-literate people like to read), and he adamantly (and rightly) refused to consider the weird work found in dime novels and pulp magazines as genuine literature; but this did not prevent him from voraciously lapping up these lesser products. Lovecraft knew that he was reading trash, but he read it anyway.

It has become fashionable to find literary—as opposed to sociological—value in dime novels by maintaining that they (and popular fiction generally) were read by all classes of society; Edmund Pearson, writing in 1929, already initiated this tendency by concluding his study with accounts by eminent literati of the day (Booth Tarkington, Samuel Hopkins Adams, Marc Connelly, William Lyon

Phelps) who read and enjoyed dime novels in their youth. But the brute fact is that the dime and nickel novels were read primarily by the young, the poor, and the ill-educated. The literary formulae they inculcated—thrilling action at all cost and in spite of all probability and verisimilitude; "cliffhanger" conclusions to chapters; stereotyped character portrayal; stilted dialogue; a highly stylised and mechanical structure—were the worst possible influences on anyone wishing to write serious literature, and were all repudiated by Lovecraft by the time he developed a critical awareness of the distinction between good and bad writing. By then, however, he had already read so much of this material—and its descendants, the pulp magazines—that, as he himself correctly detected, his own style became, in small part, insidiously corrupted by their example.

Lovecraft does not go out of his way to mention to his correspondents that he read dime novels, but every now and then the confession slips through. In 1935 he writes: "If I had kept all the nickel novels—Pluck & Luck, Brave & Bold, Frank Reade, Jesse James, Nick Carter, Old King Brady, &c.—which I surreptitiously read 35 years ago . . ., I could probably get a young fortune for 'em today!"[19] This comment, if interpreted literally, would date Lovecraft's reading of dime or nickel novels to 1900, but in fact it must have occurred earlier. *Pluck and Luck* (Tousey) began publication in 1898; *Brave and Bold* (Street & Smith) in 1903; Frank Reade made his debut in the *Frank Reade Library* (Tousey, 1892–98) and then continued in the *Frank Reade Weekly* beginning in 1903; *Jesse James Stories* (Street & Smith) began in 1901; the first Nick Carter stories appeared in the *New York Weekly* (Street & Smith) in 1886, and the *Nick Carter Detective Weekly* began in 1891; Old King Brady was featured first in the *New York Detective Library* (Tousey, 1885–99), then (along with his son, Young King Brady) in *Secret Service* (1899–1912).

Old King Brady may be the most interesting of the lot for our purposes, since the hero of "The Mystery of the Grave-yard" is one King John, described as "a famous western detective." Old King Brady was not a Western character, but he was a detective. Most of the early Old King Brady novels were written by Francis Worcester Doughty; many appear—like "The Mystery of the Grave-yard"—to have contained suggestions of the supernatural.[20] If Lovecraft continued to read *Secret Service,* we may find a connexion with some books in his library: La Fayette Charles Baker's *History of the United States Secret Service* (1868) and William Pittenger's *Capturing a Locomotive: A History of the Secret Service During the Late War* (1885). Perhaps he read these at this time also. Moreover, Beadle had a series detective, Prince John (written by Joseph E. Badger, Jr), in the early 1890s. I do not know whether King John—even in terms of his name—is some sort of fusion of Old King Brady and Prince John, but he is certainly a dime novel detective.

And "The Mystery of the Grave-yard" is a miniature dime novel, pure and simple. The fact is trumpeted even in its subtitle, which copies the "or . . ." subtitles of all the early dime and nickel novels. The action is nothing if not fast-paced. In twelve relatively short chapters (some as little as 50 words in length) we read the following lurid story:

Joseph Burns has died. The rector, Mr Dobson, is instructed by Burns's will to drop a ball in his tomb at a spot marked "A." He does so and disappears. A man named Bell announces himself at the residence of Dobson's daughter, saying that he will restore her father for the sum of £10,000. The daughter, thinking fast, calls the police and cries, "Send King John!" King John, arriving in a flash, finds that Bell has jumped out the window. He chases Bell to the train station, but unfortunately Bell gets on a train as it is pulling out of the station; still more regrettably (and implausibly), there is no telegraph service between the town of Mainville, where the action is taking place, and the "large city" of Kent, where the train is headed. King John rushes to a hackney cab office and says to a black hackman that he will give him two dollars (even though pounds were mentioned before) if he can get him to Kent in fifteen minutes. Bell arrives in Kent, meets with his band of desperadoes (which includes a woman named Lindy), and is about to depart with them on a ship with King John dramatically arrives, declaring: "John Bell, I arrest you in the Queen's name!" At the trial, it is revealed that Dobson had fallen down a trap-door at the spot marked "A" and had been kept in a "brilliantly lighted, and palatial apartment" until he rescues himself by making a wax impression of the key to the door and makes a dramatic entrance at the trial. Bell is sent to prison for life; Miss Dobson, "by the way," has become Mrs King John.

There is much of interest in this story. In the first place, at the very beginning there is a hint of supernaturalism in the sudden disappearance of Dobson, although it should be obvious to even a casual reader that this is only the result of some sort of trickery. In later years Lovecraft chided Ann Radcliffe in particular for suggesting the supernatural only to explain it by implausible natural means; in his own mature fiction he was careful never to make that mistake.

In this tale Lovecraft is learning, clumsily, to maintain several narrative threads at once. This is somewhat crudely displayed by the successive openings of chapters four, five, and six: "Now let us return to the Dobson Mansion"; "Now let us return to the station house"; "Now let us return To the Dobson Mansion again." The plot is actually quite complex, and one must wait till almost the last chapter for all the subsidiary mysteries to be cleared up.

It should already be evident from the synopsis that the tale is histrionic and sensational. At the end of chapter three a man shouts, "Oh! Terrors! Come To the Graveyard!" At the end of chapter eight (soberly marked "Long" at the right margin—it is a full 200 words in length) there is a dramatic one-sentence paragraph—

"It was King John"—as he suddenly appears at the wharf to foil the escape of the miscreants. Italics are used liberally throughout the story, and when Dobson dramatically appears at the trial, we are made aware of "The *figure of Mr Dobson Himself*" (the last word printed in very large letters with triple underscoring).

Perhaps the most interesting feature is the use of the "negro hackman." He speaks in classic (or hackneyed) black dialect: "'I doan' see how I'm ter git there', said the negro 'I hab'n't got a decent pair of hosses an' I hab—'" This sort of dialect was much used in dime novels, and Lovecraft would of course elaborate upon it greatly in his later work.

The 1902 catalogue of works (found at the end of *Poemata Minora, Volume II*) lists the following works of fiction: "The Mysterious Ship" (25¢), "The Noble Eavesdropper" (10¢), "The Haunted House" (10¢), "The Secret of the Grave" (25¢), and "John, the Detective" (10¢). It is interesting to note that "The Noble Eavesdropper" is still extant (and for sale) at this time, and still more interesting to note the absence of "The Little Glass Bottle" and "The Secret Cave"; has Lovecraft already "repudiated" these stories, as he would successively do in later years with many of his earlier works? If so, it is remarkable that he has not yet repudiated "The Noble Eavesdropper," which one would imagine was even cruder, being his first story.

"The Secret of the Grave" is something of a mystery, and I suspect that it is simply a variant title (or slip of the pen) for "The Mystery of the Grave-yard." In a 1931 letter Lovecraft writes: "I do . . . have copies of some 8-year-old junk which my mother saved—'The Mysterious Ship' & 'The Secret of the Grave.'"[21] The fact that "The Secret of the Grave" is listed at 25¢ suggests that it is a relatively lengthy work; and "The Mystery of the Grave-yard" is Lovecraft's longest surviving juvenile tale, far longer than "The Mysterious Ship."

"John, the Detective" is presumably another tale about King John. "The Haunted House" may perhaps be Lovecraft's first authentically supernatural tale, although if it were in the dime or nickel novel tradition it may have only hinted at the supernatural but explained it away. Indeed, it is interesting to note that of all these tales, only "The Noble Eavesdropper" can genuinely be assumed to be a horror tale; "The Little Glass Bottle" is a humorous story, "The Secret Cave" is a sort of grim domestic tale, and "The Mystery of the Grave-yard," "The Mysterious Ship," and presumably "John, the Detective" are mystery or suspense stories with only a faintly horrific atmosphere.

"The Mysterious Ship" is the latest of the surviving juvenilia, and by far the most disappointing. This little story—consisting of nine very brief chapters, some as short as 25 words and none longer than 75 words—is so dry and clipped that it led L. Sprague de Camp to think it "an outline rather than a story."[22] This seems unlikely given the elaborate "publishing" procedures Lovecraft has undertaken for this work. In the first place, we here encounter Lovecraft's first surviving *typescript,* a text of twelve pages enclosed in a little booklet. This could not have been typed on the 1906 Remington that served Lovecraft for the rest of his life, but must have been some similar behemoth belonging to his grandfather or perhaps even his father. Moreover, there is a sort of gauze cloth cover with a drawing of a ship in pen on it, and another drawing of a ship on the back cover. The imprint on the title page is "The Royal Press. 1902."

It is obvious, then, that Lovecraft is aiming for a sort of dramatic terseness in this narrative; but the result is mere boredom and even confusion as to what exactly happens. The tale is unambiguously non-supernatural: we are never expected to believe that the disappearance of random individuals shortly after the docking of a "strange brig" at various ports is anything but a species of kidnapping. This ship goes all over the world—a place (presumably in the United States) called Ruralville, Madagascar, Florida—and for some reason deposits its kidnapped individuals at the North Pole. At this point Lovecraft feels it "necessary to relate a geographical fact," namely that "At the N. Pole there exists a vast continent composed of volcanic soil, a portion of which is open to explorers. It is called 'No-Mans Land.'" I have no idea whether Lovecraft actually believes this (if so, he cannot have read the several books he owned on the North Pole very carefully) or is merely inventing it for the sake of the story; if the latter, then it is a rare instance of Lovecraft failing to adhere to scientific truth in the presentation of a tale. In any event, the mystery is solved and all the kidnapped individuals go to their respective homes and are showered with honours.

A strange document that has recently come to light is what appears to be a revised or elaborated version of "The Mysterious Ship." This item was collected by August Derleth and transcribed along with several other now otherwise lost juvenile items, mostly astronomical treatises. This version of the story fleshes out each chapter to about 75 to 100 words each, so that the total is about 1000 words, more than twice the length of the original. Derleth dated this version to 1898, but this cannot be correct, as it cannot possibly predate the shorter version.[23]

What is so disappointing about either version of "The Mysterious Ship" is the utter lack of progress it reveals from Lovecraft's earlier juvenilia. If "The Mystery of the Grave-yard" is at least entertaining as a blood-and-thunder dime novel, "The Mysterious Ship" is simply tiresome and silly. It actually represents a regression in terms of plot development and narrative skill. How Lovecraft could have written the very able "The Beast in the Cave" three years later is a complete mystery. And yet, given that Lovecraft priced "The Mysterious Ship" at 25¢, one must believe that he actually saw some merit in the tale, at least at the time.

There must have been many more very early stories than those enumerated above. Late in life Lovecraft admitted to being enthralled with W. Clark Russell's

The Frozen Pirate (1887): "I read it in extreme youth—when 8 or 9—& was utterly fascinated by it . . . writing several yarns of my own under its influence."[24] *The Frozen Pirate* is a wild, improbable story of a man, Paul Rodney, who comes upon a ship in the ice floes near Antarctica whose crew are all frozen; one becomes unfrozen by the heat of a campfire lit by Rodney and discovers that he has been frozen for forty-eight years. At some point, and for no apparent reason, he ages forty-eight years in a few days and dies. Even this novel, be it noted, is not explicitly supernatural; it is more in the tradition of the scientific romance or extravaganza, in that there is at least a thin—even if grotesquely implausible—scientific rationale behind the events of the tale. It is possible, then, that Lovecraft's own tales inspired by *The Frozen Pirate* were similarly not definitively supernatural.

Aside from discovering Poe and giving his fledgling fictional career a boost, Lovecraft also found himself in 1898 fascinated with science. This is the third component of what he described as his tripartite nature: love of the strange and fantastic, love of the ancient and permanent, and love of abstract truth and scientific logic. It is perhaps not unusual that it would be the last to emerge in his young mind, and it is still remarkable that it emerged so early and was embraced so vigorously. Lovecraft gives an engaging account of his discovery:

> The science of chemistry . . . first captivated me in the Year of Our Lord 1898—in a rather peculiar way. With the insatiable curiosity of early childhood, I used to spend hours poring over the pictures in the back of Webster's *Unabridged Dictionary*—absorbing a miscellaneous variety of ideas. After familiarising myself with antiquities, mediaeval dress & armour, birds, animals, reptiles, fishes, flags of all nations, heraldry, &c., &c., I lit upon the section devoted to "Philosophical & Scientific Instruments", & was veritably hypnotised with it. Chemical apparatus especially attracted me, & I resolved (before knowing a thing about the science!) to have a laboratory. Being a "spoiled child" I had but to ask, & it was mine. I was given a cellar room of good size, & provided by my elder aunt (who had studied chemistry at boarding school) with some simple apparatus & a copy of "The Young Chemist"—a beginner's manual by Prof. John Howard Appleton of Brown—a personal acquaintance. . . . The laboratory "work"—or play—seemed delightful, & despite a few mishaps, explosions, & broken instruments, I got along splendidly.[25]

A later account states that "my father [was] no more"[26] by the time he became interested in chemistry, so that this must date to after July 1898. This account also identifies the Webster's dictionary as the edition of 1864, an edition he retained in his own library. As with his enthusiasm for the *Arabian Nights,* his chemical tastes led his family to indulge the boy in whatever tools he needed. *The Young Chemist* (1876) also remained in his library to the end of his life. Lovecraft identifies Appleton as a professor of chemistry at Brown and "a friend of ours."[27] Appleton (1844–1930) graduated from Brown in 1863 and then taught at the university from that time until his retirement in 1914. It is difficult to know which member of Lovecraft's family he was actually friends with; it is likely that the medical doctor Franklin Chase Clark (Class of 1869) encountered Appleton at Brown, and although he would not marry Lillian Phillips (the "elder aunt" mentioned above) until 1902, he perhaps was already acquainted with her and her family.

In any event, the immediate result was a spate of literary work. Lovecraft began the *Scientific Gazette* on March 4, 1899. This first issue—a single sheet—still survives, although it is now nearly indecipherable; it contains an amusing report: "There was a great explosion in the Providence Laboratory this afternoon. While experimenting some potassium blew up causing great damage to everyone." Incredibly, this magazine was initially a *daily,* but "it soon degenerated into a weekly."[28] No subsequent issues survive until the New Issue Vol. I, No. 1 (May 12, 1902), and I shall postpone discussion of it until the next chapter.

Lovecraft also wrote a number of chemical treatises, which are also by now almost illegible. There was a six-volume series with the general title *Chemistry* (as announced in the catalogue of works in the *Poemata Minora, Volume II*), of which four volumes survive: *Chemistry* (10¢); *Chemistry, Magic, & Electricity* (5¢); *Chemistry III* (5¢ [this price remains after 25¢, 20¢, 19¢, and 10¢ were all crossed out]); and *Chemistry IV* (15¢ [25¢ crossed out]). These volumes discuss such things as argon, gunpowder, a carbon cell battery, gases, acids, tellurium, lithium, explosives, "explosive experiments" (see the mention of the "explosion" above), and the like. There is also a small work called *A Good Anaesthetic* (5¢). Judging by the handwriting, these works probably all date to around 1899. Non-extant works (as listed in the 1902 catalogue) include *Iron Working* (5¢), *Acids* (5¢), *Explosives* (5¢), and *Static Electricity* (10¢).

It appears that Lovecraft's early scientific interests engendered some practical experimentation, if the following account—related to W. Paul Cook by one of Lovecraft's neighbours—dates to this period. It is one of the most delightful and celebrated anecdotes about Lovecraft that has come down to us; let Cook tell it in his own inimitable way:

> That section [of Providence, in which Lovecraft lived] was then open fields, rather swampy here and there, with very few houses. One day this neighbor, Mrs. Winslow Church, noticed that someone had started a grass fire that had burned over quite an area and was approaching her property. She went out to investigate and found the little Lovecraft boy. She scolded him for setting such a big fire and maybe endangering other peoples' property. He said very positively, "I wasn't setting a *big* fire. I wanted to make a fire one foot by one foot." That is the little story in the words in which it came to me. It means little except that it shows a passion

> for exactitude (in keeping with him as we knew him later)—but it is a story of Lovecraft.[29]

This anecdote is, as I say, not dated; but the mention of "open fields" suggests that it occurred while Lovecraft was at 454 Angell Street, since the area was already being built up during his early teenage years. A Winslow Church is listed in the Providence city directories as living at 292 Wayland Avenue all throughout Lovecraft's youth; this would be about five blocks from 454 Angell Street.

Another rather anomalous discovery Lovecraft made at this time was anatomy—or, rather, the specific facts of anatomy relating to sex. Here is his account of it:

> In the matter of the justly celebrated "facts of life" I didn't wait for oral information, but exhausted the entire subject in the medical section of the family library (to which I had access, although I wasn't especially loquacious about this side of my reading) when I was 8 years old—through Quain's Anatomy (fully illustrated & diagrammed), Dunglison's Physiology, &c. &c. This was because of curiosity & perplexity concerning the strange reticences & embarrassments of adult speech, & the oddly inexplicable allusions & situations in standard literature. The result was the very opposite of what parents generally fear—for instead of giving me an abnormal & precocious interest in sex (as *unsatisfied* curiosity might have done), it virtually killed my interest in the subject. The whole matter was reduced to prosaic mechanism—a mechanism which I rather despised or at least thought non-glamourous because of its purely animal nature & separation from such things as intellect & beauty—& all the drama was taken out of it.[30]

This is an intensely interesting statement. First, when Lovecraft says that he did not wait for "oral information," he is suggesting (perhaps without even knowing it) that his mother would certainly not have told him the "facts of life"—at least not at the age of eight, and perhaps not at any age. Perhaps even his grandfather might not have done so. It is remarkable to note that Lovecraft was already so keenly aware of the "strange reticences & embarrassments of adult speech" at this time that he sensed something was not being told him; we shall see that at least up to the age of eight, and perhaps beyond, he was a solitary child who largely spent time in the company of adults. And as one who was already a prolific reader (and a reader of material rarely given to the very young), he may have become early aware of anomalies in some of his books also (perhaps his edition of the *Arabian Nights* had, after all, included some of the bawdier stories!). And as for his declaration that his knowledge of the matter killed his interest in sex: this is certainly an impression Lovecraft consistently conveyed to his friends, correspondents, and even his wife. He does not seem to have had any romantic involvements in high school or at any time prior to about 1918 (and even this one is, as we shall see, a matter of inference). It took three years for Sonia Greene to convince Lovecraft to marry her; the impetus was clearly on her side. There has been much speculation on Lovecraft's sex life, but I do not believe there are sufficient grounds for much of an opinion beyond the testimony given by Lovecraft himself—and his wife.

In any event, Lovecraft's initial enthusiasm for chemistry and physiology would lead to further interests in geography, geology, astronomy, anthropology, psychology, and other sciences that he would study over a lifetime. He may have remained a layman in all these branches of knowledge, although his absorption of many of them—especially astronomy—was prodigious for a literary man; but they helped to lay strong foundations for his philosophical thought and would provide the backbone for some of his most powerful works of fiction.

Lovecraft reports that he began learning Latin around 1898.[31] Elsewhere he says that "My grandfather had previously [i.e., previous to his entering high school] taught me a great deal of Latin,"[32] which suggests that he had begun the study of Latin independently prior to his attendance at the Slater Avenue School in the fall of 1898. Indeed, I am not sure that Lovecraft was taught Latin at all at Slater Avenue, for among the first courses he took at Hope Street High School in 1904–05 was "Latin (First Book),"[33] suggesting that his formal training in Latin began only then. It was natural for a boy so enthralled with the classical world to learn Latin, although to have begun it so early—and, evidently, to have mastered it in a few years, without much formal instruction—was an incredible feat even at a time when knowledge of Latin was far commoner than it is now.

Lovecraft's collection of Latin texts—almost all derived, surely, from his grandfather's library—was an entirely adequate one. It included most of the standard poets (Horace, Juvenal, Lucretius, Martial, Ovid, Persius, Vergil) and prose writers (Caesar, Cicero [selected orations only], Livy [selections], Nepos, Sallust), although many of these are simplified school texts with interlinear translations, a technique upon which classicists now look with horror. Of course, he had a wide array of translations, including some classic ones: Dryden's Virgil, Murphy's Tacitus, Francis's Horace, and the like. One work, Alfred Gudeman's two-volume *Latin Literature of the Empire* (1898–99), contains many handwritten interlineations, including the charming note on the *Pervigilium Veneris:* "Mr Parnell hath made a very elegant translation of this poem, tho' he ascribes it to the classic age and to Catullus."[34] Lovecraft also had a sound collection of reference works on classical literature, history, and antiquities. Some of them were a little out of date even in his day—he had Ethan Allan Andrews's *Latin-English Lexicon* (1854) rather than Lewis and Short's *A Latin Dictionary* (1879), which remained the standard work until the publication of the *Oxford Latin Dictionary*—but they were sound enough for his purposes.

We will find that the poetry of Virgil, Horace, and Juvenal left a lasting impression upon Lovecraft, and that the Epicurean philosophy embodied in Lucretius was a central influence in his early thought. One remarkable instance of the classical influence on Lovecraft's juvenile writing is the piece entitled "Ovid's Metamorphoses."

This 116-line work is nothing less than a literal pentameter verse translation of the first 88 lines of Ovid's *Metamorphoses.* The date of composition of this piece is, unfortunately, in doubt. We have seen that in the catalogue of works appended to "The Poem of Ulysses" (1897) this work is listed as "Soon to Be Published"; in the catalogue appended to *Poemata Minora, Volume II* (1902) it appears, anomalously, in a list of "Works by H. Lovecraft in Prose." In both catalogues, however, it is priced at 25¢, so that I am led to believe that the item was simply placed erroneously in the 1902 catalogue. The handwriting of the autograph manuscript is, moreover, consistent with other of Lovecraft's juvenilia, so that I am inclined to date this work to 1900–1902.

The first thing to note about this translation is how different it is from Dryden's (he translated the first book of the *Metamorphoses* in "Garth's Ovid"). Here is the Latin:

> In nova fert animus mutatas dicere formas
> corpora: di, coeptis (nam vos mutastis et illas)[35]
> adspirate meis primaque ab origine mundi
> ad mea perpetuum deducite tempora carmen.

Here is Dryden's:

> Of bodies changed to various forms, I sing:
> Ye gods, from whom these miracles did spring,
> Inspire my numbers with celestial heat,
> Till I my long laborious work complete;
> And add perpetual tenor to my rhymes,
> Deduced from Nature's birth to Caesar's times.[36]

Here now is Lovecraft's:

> I tell of forms transmuted into new;
> And since, ye Gods, these deeds were wrought by you,
> Smile on my task, and lead my ceaseless lay
> From Earth's beginning to the present day.

The differences are clear: Lovecraft attempts a more literal, line-for-line translation (in spite of Dryden's archaic use of "deduced" for *deducite* [to bring down]), adhering as closely to the Latin as he can. Lovecraft has two subdivisions in his essay, with the headings "The Creation of the World" (ll. 5–84) and "The Creation of Man" (ll. 85–116). There are, admittedly, similar divisions and headings in Dryden, but his first one ("The Golden Age") appears just where Lovecraft's poem leaves off.

On the whole, Lovecraft's is a highly felicitous rendition. The opening—in which Ovid, clearly imitating Lucretius, presents the spectacle of the *rudis indigestaque moles* ("a raw unfinish'd mass") of elements slowly brought to order by "kind Nature & a God" (*deus et melior . . . natura* in Ovid)—displays a cosmic scope not unlike Lovecraft's later fiction, even though in later years he scorned the idea of vaunting the human race as some special creation of Nature:

> Though animals of less exalted birth,
> With drooping glances eye the lowly earth,
> The man is bid to lift his lofty face;
> Enjoy the blue, & view the starry space.
> Terrestrial matter, rough & undefin'd,
> Thus chang'd, gave rise to stately humankind.

And yet, perhaps even here there is a connexion with some of his later views. In arguing in 1920 with Rheinhart Kleiner about the role of eroticism in human affairs, he declared with conscious bombast: "The primal savage or ape merely looks about his native forest to find a mate; the exalted Aryan should lift his eyes to the worlds of space and consider his relation to infinity!!"[37]

There is one other remarkable thing about "Ovid's Metamorphoses," and that is the possibility that it may be a fragment. The autograph manuscript covers 5 sheets, and the text proceeds to the very bottom of the fifth sheet. Could Lovecraft have translated more of Ovid's text, and could this portion have been lost? I think the probability is strong: this item, priced at 25¢, is currently not much longer than "The Poem of Ulysses," priced at 5¢. Perhaps it is not unreasonable to think that Lovecraft might have translated the entire first book of Ovid (779 lines in Latin, hence perhaps about 1000 lines in a translation). The translation as it stands admittedly ends at a clear break in the Latin text, as at line 89 Ovid is about to begin the account of the four ages of man; but I still believe there was once more to this work than we have.

The year 1898 was certainly an eventful one for Lovecraft: he discovered Poe and science, and began learning Latin; he first began attendance at school; and he had his first nervous breakdown. In a late letter he refers to it as a "near-breakdown";[38] I have no idea what it means. Another "near-breakdown" occurred in 1900. There certainly does not seem to have been anything physically wrong with the boy, and there is no record of his admission into a hospital. The history and nature of Lovecraft's early nervous condition are very vexed issues, largely because we have only his words on the matter, most of them written many years after the fact.

Lovecraft reports that "I didn't inherit a very good set of nerves, since near relatives on both sides of my ancestry were prone to headaches, nerve-exhaustion, and breakdowns." He goes on to cite the case of his grandfather (who had "frightful blind headaches"), his mother (who "could run him a close second"), and his father, whom at the time of the writing of this letter (1931) Lovecraft still believed to be affected by "paralysis" from overstrain. Then he adds: "My own headaches and nervous irritability and exhaustion-tendency began as early as my existence itself—I, too, was an early bottle baby with unexplained miseries and meagre nutriment-assimilative capacities . . ."[39] (As Kenneth Faig wryly remarks, "So, in addition to all her other worries, Susie had her infant's colic."[40]) Early weaning was common practice at the turn of the century and for a long time thereafter; but Lovecraft's remark suggests that his weaning occurred even earlier than was the custom.

In an earlier letter Lovecraft stated that "As an infant, I had been restless & prone to cry." He refers to the effect of his maternal grandmother in correcting "my increasingly boorish deportment—for my nervousness made me a very restless & uncontrollable child."[41] One remarkable admission Lovecraft made late in life was as follows: "My own nervous state in childhood once produced a tendency inclining toward chorea, although not quite attaining that level. My face was full of unconscious & involuntary motions now & then—& the more I was urged to stop them, the more frequent they became."[42] Lovecraft does not exactly date these chorea-like attacks, but context suggests that they occurred before the age of ten. All this led J. Vernon Shea to suspect that Lovecraft might actually have had chorea minor, a nervous ailment that "manifests itself in uncontrollable facial tics and grimaces" but gradually dissipates by puberty.[43] Certainty on the matter is, of course, impossible, but I think the probability of this conjecture is strong. And although Lovecraft maintains in the above letter that "in time the tendency died down" and that his entrance into high school "caused me to reform," I shall have occasion to refer to possible recurrences of these chorea-like symptoms at various periods in Lovecraft's life, even into maturity.

If, then, it is true that Lovecraft suffered some sort of "near-breakdown" in 1898, it seems very likely that the death of his father on July 19, 1898, had much to do with it. We have already seen how a cloud of gloom hung over the household upon the death of Robie Phillips in January 1896 (Lovecraft notes that his family was still in mourning during the winter of that year[44]); and the long-expected but still shocking and tragic death of Winfield can only have been traumatic for the entire family and especially for a boy not yet eight. I have already conjectured that Lovecraft probably attended his father's funeral and burial in Swan Point Cemetery two days later. The effect on his mother of her husband's death—and, indeed, of his increasingly worsening condition over the last year or two of his life—can only be imagined. It may be well, then, to summarise the relations between Lovecraft and his mother up to this time, as best we can piece them together.

There is no question but that his mother both spoiled Lovecraft and was overprotective of him. This latter trait appears to have developed even before Winfield's hospitalisation in 1893. Winfield Townley Scott tells the following story:

> On their summer vacations at Dudley, Massachusetts . . ., Mrs. Lovecraft refused to eat her dinner in the dining room, not to leave her sleeping son alone for an hour one floor above. When a diminutive teacher-friend, Miss Ella Sweeney, took the rather rangy youngster to walk, holding his hand, she was enjoined by Howard's mother to stoop a little lest she pull the boy's arm from its socket. When Howard pedaled his tricycle along Angell Street, his mother trooped beside him, a guarding hand upon his shoulder.[45]

Scott derived this information from Ella Sweeney (via her friend Myra H. Blosser), a Providence woman who became associate superintendent of schools and who met the Lovecrafts in Dudley. The mention of "summer vacations" (plural) is apparently an error copied by Scott from Blosser's letter to him.[46] Lovecraft admits that "My array of toys, books, and other youthful pleasures was virtually unlimited"[47] at this time; whatever he wanted, he seems to have got. We have already seen how his mother was dragged to all the curio-shops in Providence to satisfy Lovecraft's early enthusiasm for the *Arabian Nights,* and how he instantly got a chemistry set when his interest turned in that direction. Another instance of how far his family would go to indulge the boy occurred about this time: "When I was very small, my kingdom was the lot next my birthplace, 454 Angell St. Here were trees, shrubs, and grasses, and here when I was between four and five the coachman built me an immense summer-house all mine own—a somewhat crude yet vastly pleasing affair, with a staircase leading to a flat roof . . ."[48] This helped to foster Lovecraft's interest in railroads, as I shall note later.

At this point it may be well to mention a remarkable bit of testimony provided by Lovecraft's wife. In her 1948 memoir Sonia H. Davis states the following:

> It was . . . at that time the fashion for mothers to start "hope-chests" for their daughters even before they were born, so that when Mrs. Winfield Scott Lovecraft was expecting her first child she had hoped it would be a girl; nor was this curtailed at the birth of her boy. So this hope-chest was gradually growing; some day to be given to Howard's wife. . . . As a baby Howard looked like a beautiful little girl. He had, at the tender age of three years, a head of flaxen curls of which any girl would have been proud. . . . These he wore until he was about six. When at last he protested and wanted them cut off, his mother had taken him to the barber's and cried bitterly as the "cruel" shears separated them from his head.[49]

I suppose one must accept this statement for the most part, although I think rather too much has been made of it—and also of the apparent fact that Susie dressed her son in frocks at an early age. The celebrated 1892 photograph of Lovecraft and his parents shows him with the curls and the frock, as does another picture probably taken around the same time.[50] Lovecraft remarks on the curls himself, saying that it was this "golden mane" that partly led Louise Imogen Guiney to name him "Little Sunshine."[51] But another photograph of Lovecraft, probably taken at the age of seven or eight,[52] shows him as a perfectly normal boy with short hair and boy's attire. In fact, it cannot be ascertained when Susie ceased to dress Lovecraft in frocks; even if she had persisted up to the age of four, it would not have been especially unusual.

There are two other pieces of evidence one can adduce here, although their purport is not entirely clear. R. H. Barlow, in his jottings about Lovecraft (mostly taken down in 1934 but some made evidently later), writes: "Mrs. Gamwell's stories of how HPL for a while insisted 'I'm a little girl' . . ."[53] Annie Gamwell could not have made this observation later than early 1897, as that was when she married and moved out of 454 Angell Street; and the context of Barlow's remark (he adds the detail of how Lovecraft would spout Tennyson from the table-top) could date the event to as early as 1893. Then there is a letter from Whipple Phillips to Lovecraft, dated June 19, 1894: "I will tell you more about what I have seen when I get home if you are a good boy and *wear trousers*."[54] Whipple has underscored the last two words. The implication is, I suppose, that Lovecraft at this time was not fond of wearing trousers.

In spite of the above, I see little evidence of gender confusion in Lovecraft's later life; if anything, he displayed quick and unwavering prejudice against homosexuals. Susie may have wanted a girl, and may have attempted to preserve the illusion for some years, but Lovecraft even in youth was headstrong and made it early evident that he was a boy with a boy's normal interests. It was, after all, he who wanted his flowing curls cut off at the age of six.

In addition to being oversolicitous of her son, Susie also attempted to mould him in ways he found either irritating or repugnant. Around 1898 she tried to enrol him in a children's dancing class; Lovecraft "abhorred the thought" and, fresh from an initial study of Latin, responded with a line from Cicero: *"Nemo fere saltat sobrius, nisi forte insanit!"* ("Scarcely any sober person dances, unless by chance he is insane").[55] Evidently Lovecraft had developed a certain skill in getting his own way, for—like his initial Sunday school attendance (perhaps the previous year), which he was allowed to forego—he evidently escaped the dancing lessons. But what he did not escape were violin lessons, which lasted a full two years, between the ages of seven and nine.

These lessons were, however, initially at his own insistence:

> My rhythmic tendencies led me into a love of melody, and I was forever whistling & humming in defiance of convention & good breeding. I was so exact in time & tune, & showed such a semi-professional precision & flourish in my crude attempts, that my plea for a violin was granted when I was seven years of age, & I was placed under the instruction of the best violin teacher for children in the city—Mrs. Wilhelm

> Nauck. For two years I made such progress that Mrs. Nauck was enthusiastic, & declared that I should adopt music as a career—BUT, all this time the tedium of practising had been wearing shockingly on my always sensitive nervous system. My "career" extended until 1899, its summit being a public recital at which I played a solo from Mozart before an audience of considerable size. Soon after that, my ambition & taste alike collapsed like a house of cards . . . I began to detest classical music, because it had meant so much painful labour to me; & I positively *loathed* the violin! Our physician, knowing my temperament, advised an immediate discontinuance of music lessons, which speedily ensued.[56]

Lovecraft's later accounts of this episode do not differ greatly in details. One interesting elaboration occurs in a letter of 1934:

> . . . I had a very irregular heart action—badly affected by physical exertion—& such acute kidney trouble that a local practitioner would have operated for stone in the bladder had not a Boston specialist given a sounder diagnosis & traced it to the nervous system. That was when I was 9, & reduced to a very irritable state of pressure of violin lessons. On the specialist's advice those lessons were stopped . . .[57]

Now it appears that this specialist, and not the family doctor, was the one who stopped the violin lessons.

It may be worth engaging in some idle speculation as to what the "solo" was that Lovecraft performed in front of a sizeable audience. Mozart wrote no works for *unaccompanied* violin—such as Bach's six spectacularly difficult sonatas and partitas, BWV 1001–06—so that one assumes he played one of Mozart's sonatas for violin and piano; Mrs Nauck presumably accompanied him on the piano. If this assumption is correct, then we may be limited to some of Mozart's very early—and very easy—sonatas, e.g. K. 6–15 (where the keyboard part is actually substantially more difficult than the violin part). Even among this group we can eliminate some of the harder sonatas (K. 11–15) as being well beyond the capabilities of a young violinist of two years' experience, as these works involve relatively advanced techniques (rapid string-crossings, triple- or even quadruple-stops, rapid succession of trills, tremolos, shifts into second or third position, etc.) that Lovecraft is not likely to have learnt. Indeed, Lovecraft may have played only one movement (probably the slow movement or the minuet, since even the allegros of the early sonatas are demanding to a very inexperienced player) of the sonata in C, K. 6, in D, K. 7, or in B-flat, K. 8. Lovecraft's description of a "solo *from* Mozart" implies that only part of a work was performed.

One does not wish to minimise Lovecraft's accomplishment, however. Most violinists of his age are nowadays not given any works in the standard repertoire to play, but are rather trained on workbooks involving scales, arpeggios, and the like. Probably Lovecraft used these as well (and they are very likely what led him to loathe practising, as they are indeed quite dull and repetitious), but to perform any work of Mozart at the age of nine bespeaks considerable natural ability. A moot question is whether Lovecraft actually learnt to read music: he may have and later forgot; if he did not, he could still have played the Mozart piece by having the proper fingerings "coded" to the proper strings.[58]

One would like to date Lovecraft's second "near-breakdown" to the termination of his violin lessons, but he clearly asserts that the first occurred in 1898 and the second in 1900. In any event, Lovecraft manifestly continued to be under considerable nervous strain; a situation in part relieved and in part augmented by his first attempt at school attendance, in which he was withdrawn after a year's term (1898–99). Indeed, his casual remark in 1929 that "I spent the summer of 1899 with my mother"[59] in Westminster, Massachusetts, must lead one to speculate on the purpose of such a trip, and to wonder whether health reasons were a factor. Faig suspects that the vacation may have been taken to relieve the stress of Lovecraft's father's death;[60] but this had occurred a full year before, and even if that event had caused Lovecraft's "near-breakdown" of 1898, he seemed well enough to begin school in the fall of that year. I am therefore inclined to connect the trip with the trauma of his first year of school and also of his violin lessons, which probably ended in the summer of 1899.

Westminster, incidentally, strikes me as an odd place for Lovecraft and his mother to spend a vacation. It is in north central Massachusetts, near Fitchburg, and not at all near Dudley, where the Lovecrafts had vacationed in 1892. Perhaps they had relatives there. We know almost nothing about this trip; thirty years later, when revisiting the spot, he wrote: ". . . we looked up Moses Wood's 'Harvard Cottage' . . . Wood is dead, & so is old Mrs. Marshall who kept the gaol at the foot of the hill, but Wood's widow is still living. . . . It was certainly interesting to leap back 30 years & recall the summer of 1899 when I was so bored with rusticity that I longed for the sight of a town!"[61] That last remark is telling: for all Lovecraft's yearning to be a country squire, he was really a city boy. As a *permanent* residence, he wanted something between the vacancy of unspoilt Nature and the cacophonic phantasmagoria of New York City—something very like Providence, in fact.

From all that has gone before it will be evident that Lovecraft led a comparatively solitary young childhood, with only his adult family members as his companions. Many of his childhood activities—reading, writing, scientific work, practising music, even attending the theatre—are primarily or exclusively solitary, and we do not hear of any boyhood friends until his entrance into grade school. All his letters discussing his childhood stress his relative isolation and loneliness:

> Amongst my few playmates [at the age of five] I was very unpopular, since I would insist on playing out events in history, or acting according to consistent plots.[62]

> You will notice that I have made no reference to childish friends & playmates—I had none! The children I knew disliked me, & I disliked them. I was used to adult company & conversation, & despite the fact that I felt shamefully dull beside my elders, I had nothing in common with the infant train. Their romping & shouting puzzled me. I hated mere play & dancing about—in my relaxations I always desired *plot.*[63]

One confirmation of this comes from the recollections of Lovecraft's second cousin Ethel M. Phillips (1888–1987), later Mrs Ethel Phillips Morrish. Ethel, two years older than Lovecraft, was living with her parents Jeremiah W. Phillips (the son of Whipple's brother James Wheaton Phillips) and his wife Abby in various suburbs of Providence (Johnston, Cranston) during the 1890s, and was sent over to play with young Howard. She confessed in an interview conducted in 1977 that she did not much care for her cousin, finding him eccentric and aloof. She became very irritated because Lovecraft did not apparently know how a swing worked. But she does have a delightful image of Lovecraft, at about the age of four, turning the pages of some monstrously huge book in a very solemn and adult manner.[64]

Lovecraft provides one remarkable glimpse of some of the solitary games he played as a young boy:

> My favourite toys were *very small* ones, which would permit of their arrangement in widely extensive scenes. My mode of play was to devote an entire table-top to a scene, which I would proceed to develop as a broad landscape . . . helped by occasional trays of earth or clay. I had all sorts of *toy villages* with small wooden or cardboard houses, & by combining several of them would often construct *cities* of considerable extent & intricacy. . . . Toy trees—of which I had an infinite number—were used with varying effect to form parts of the landscape . . . even *forests* (or the suggested edges of forests). Certain kinds of blocks made walls & hedges, & I also used blocks in constructing large public buildings. . . . My people were mainly of the lead-soldier type & magnitude—frankly too large for the buildings which they presumably tenanted, but as small as I could get. I accepted some as they were, but had my mother modify many in costume with the aid of knife & paint-brush. Much piquancy was added to my scenes by special toy buildings like windmills, castles, &c.

No doubt Lovecraft once again pestered his mother into both procuring these toys from various shops and helping him to decorate them. But there was more to it than just a static landscape; with his inveterate feel for plot, and his already developing sense of time, history, and pageantry, Lovecraft would actually act out historical scenarios with his miniature cities:

> I was always as consistent—geographically & chronologically—in setting my landscapes as my infant store of information would allow. Naturally, the majority of scenes would be of the 18th century; although my parallel fascination with rail-

> ways & street-cars led me to construct large numbers of contemporary landscapes with intricate systems of tin trackage. I had a magnificent repertoire of cars & railway accessories—signals, tunnels, stations, &c—though this system was admittedly too large in scale for my villages. My mode of play was to construct some scene as fancy—incited by some story or picture—dictated, & then to act out its life for long periods—sometimes a fortnight—making up events of a highly melodramatic cast as I went. These events would sometimes cover only a brief span—a war or plague or merely a spirited pageant of travel & commerce & incident leading nowhere—but would sometimes involve long aeons, with visible changes in the landscape & buildings. Cities would fall & be forgotten, & new cities would spring up. Forests would fall or be cut down, & rivers (I had some fine *bridges*) would change their beds. History, of course, would suffer in this process; but my data . . . was of a distinctly juvenile kind & extent. Sometimes I would try to depict actual historic events & scenes—Roman, 18th century, or modern—& sometimes I would make everything up. Horror-plots were frequent, though (oddly enough) I never attempted to construct fantastic or extra-terrestrial scenes. I was too much of an innate realist to care for fantasy in its purest form. Well—I got a great kick out of all this. In about a week or two I'd get fed up on a scene & substitute a new one, though now & then I'd be so attached to one that I'd retain it longer—starting a fresh scene on another table with materials not forming scene #1. There was a kind of intoxication in being lord of a visible world (albeit a miniature one) & determining the flow of its events. I kept this up till I was 11 or 12, despite the parallel growth of literary & scientific interests.[65]

Lovecraft does not give an explicit date for the commencement of this fascinating exercise, but one imagines it dates to his seventh or eighth birthday.

Although Lovecraft may have been solitary, he was by no means devoted merely to indoor activities. The year 1900 saw the commencement of his career as bicyclist, something he would keep up for more than a decade. He tells the story piquantly:

> Good old 1900—will I ever forget it? My mother gave me my first bicycle on Aug. 20 of that memorable year—my tenth birthday—and I found myself able to *ride* it without lessons . . . although *I couldn't get off.* I just rode around and around until pride vanished and I confest my technical limitation—slowing up and letting my grandfather hold the wheel still whilst I clamber'd down with the aid of the horse-block. But before the year's end I was master of my steed—burning up all the roads for miles around.[66]

Late in life he referred to himself as a "veritable bike-centaur" at this time.[67]

Lovecraft's attendance at the Slater Avenue School (located at the northeast corner of Slater Avenue and University Avenue, where St Dunstan's Prep School now stands) changed all this, at least to some degree. I am not entirely clear on the exact period or duration of Lovecraft's attendance, as his records from the school (which was abandoned as early as 1917[68]) do not seem to survive. Lovecraft says that he entered the Slater Avenue School for the first time in 1898, adding: "Hitherto it had been deemed unwise to subject so irritable & sensitive a child to discipline of any sort. I entered the highest grade of primary school, but soon found the instruction quite useless, since I had picked up most of the material before."[69] By the "highest grade of primary school" Lovecraft presumably means the fourth or perhaps even the fifth grade, one or two grades higher than the level expected of a boy of his age. In an earlier letter he notes: "About this time I tried attendance at school, but was unable to endure the routine."[70] In other words, it appears that Lovecraft's initial stint at Slater Avenue lasted only for the school year 1898–99.

In any event, it was at this time that Lovecraft finally began developing some playmates outside of his immediate family. His friendship with Chester Pierce Munroe (one year older than Lovecraft), Harold Bateman Munroe (one year younger), and Stuart Coleman can be dated to this time. These friendships seem to have developed over the next several years, and I shall discuss them in greater detail in the next chapter.

Lovecraft does not seem to have returned to Slater Avenue until the 1902–03 school year. What he did during the interim in regard to schooling is not easy to ascertain; at a later period he received private tutoring, but apparently not in the period 1899–1902. I suspect that Lovecraft was, as before, left to satisfy his intellectual curiosity in his own way: his family could hardly have failed to see that the boy was naturally bookish and did not need much incentive to investigate any subject that caught his fancy. One extremely odd remark which Lovecraft made in passing is that he frequented the Providence Athletic Association in 1899–1900, where he took shower-baths for the first time.[71] I have no idea what he could have been doing here: Lovecraft certainly never displayed any interest in sports, either as a participant or as a spectator. Could his mother have urged him to use the gym simply to get him out of the cloistered confines of that "black, windowless attic room" and make him a somewhat more "normal" nine-year-old boy? The impetus could also have come from Whipple, who perhaps wished his grandson to develop more "normal" or "masculine" interests, or may have simply felt that a little exercise was a good thing for a boy too exclusively given to intellectual pursuits. But this athletic experience did not, apparently, last very long, for as Lovecraft notes in a late letter: "My family kept me away from gymnasiums after I had a fainting fit in one at the age of 9."[72]

If Lovecraft was by no means idle as a reader—he even remarks that his mother urged him around 1899 (perhaps during their summer in Westminster) to read, of all things, *Little Women,* which "bored me to death"[73]—he continued to experiment as a writer. Fiction, poetry, and scientific treatises emerged from his pen; and he now even ventured on some historical works. The 1902 catalogue lists two lost items, "Early Rhode Island" and "An Historical Account of Last Year's War with SPAIN." The latter, at any rate, must date to 1899, and the former probably also dates to around that time. Lovecraft's interest in the antiquities of his native city and state began, as we have seen, from as early as the age of three; and there seems little doubt that he began absorbing the history of his state through books from an early period. "Early Rhode Island" was priced at 25¢, suggesting that it was a substantial work. Among the books in his library that might have served as sources for it are Alice Earle's *In Old Narragansett: Romances and Realities* (1898), James Davis Knowles's *Memoir of Roger Williams, the Founder of the State of Rhode-Island* (1834), and two volumes of the Rhode Island Historical Society Collections: John Callendar's *An Historical Discourse on the Civil and Religious Affairs of the Colony of Rhode-Island* (1838) and William Reed Staples's *Annals of the Town of Providence, from Its First Settlement to the Organization of the City Government, in June, 1832* (1843). Some of these works may seem a little weighty for a nine-year-old, but I would not wish to discount Lovecraft's ability to comprehend any of them. If "Early Rhode Island" dates to as late as 1902, then Lovecraft may also have benefited from a landmark three-volume work compiled by Edward Field, *State of Rhode Island and Providence Plantations at the End of the Century* (1902).

Of the treatise on the Spanish-American war much might be said, in spite of the fact that we have absolutely no idea of its contents. The work is significant if only because it is the first clear indication we have of Lovecraft's interest in contemporary politics.

H. P. Lovecraft was born in the entirely undistinguished administration of the Republican Benjamin Harrison—whose birthday, oddly enough, he shared. His year of birth coincides with the emergence of the Populist movement in the South and West, which initially dominated the Democratic party and later formed its own party. In part as a result of its influence, the Democrat Grover Cleveland won the election of 1892. We have already seen Lovecraft's declaration at the age of six that he did not own allegiance to President Cleveland, as the rest of his family (grudgingly, no doubt, since they were almost certainly Republicans) did, but to Queen Victoria. His entire family (the male members, at any rate) would surely have voted for McKinley against William Jennings Bryan in the election of 1896.

Part of the backlash against Cleveland and the Democrats—aside from an economic crisis in 1893–96 that hit working people very hard—was Cleveland's unwillingness to intervene in Cuba's revolution against Spain in 1895, a cause many Americans supported. McKinley himself was reluctant to become entangled in the matter, but he had no option after the battleship *Maine* was blown up in Havana harbour on February 15, 1898, with the loss of 260 Americans. Although Spain was willing to yield to American ultimatums, public pressure forced McKinley to go to war. It was not much of a contest. The war was over in ten weeks (May–July 1898), and was highlighted by Theodore Roosevelt's leading of the Rough Riders into battle. The Americans demanded the independence of Cuba (which then became a U.S. protectorate in 1901) and the cession of Puerto Rico and Guam; McKinley also decided at this time to annex the Philippines. It was, of course, partly this military triumph that allowed the McKinley-Roosevelt ticket to prevail over the hapless Bryan in 1900.

I have no doubt that Lovecraft, who was probably already engaging in imitations of historical battles with his toy figures on tabletops, found the easy triumph of the American forces over Spain inspiring. For all his Anglophilia, he always took pride in American political and cultural victories over the rest of the world (except England). His treatise is not likely to have delved much into the political or diplomatic background of the war, but would probably have been a stirring narrative of the principal battles. And yet, if the words "historical account" in its title are to be taken literally, perhaps Lovecraft did engage in some historical description of Spanish influence in the Caribbean or perhaps in the whole of the Americas, a subject he found compelling in later life.

If Lovecraft is accurate in stating that he discovered Russell's *The Frozen Pirate* at the age of eight or nine, then that melodramatic novel—along, perhaps, with the scarcely less melodramatic but more artistically finished *Narrative of Arthur Gordon Pym* by Edgar Allan Poe—may have helped to inspire his interest in geography, particularly the Antarctic, an interest that led not merely to several works of fiction both early and late but several works of nonfiction as well.

Lovecraft is unclear on when he became interested in geography in general and Antarctica in particular: in two letters (1916, 1935) he dates his interest to 1900,[74] while in two others (1915, 1926) he dates it to the age of twelve, or 1902.[75] I am inclined to accept the earlier date, for in the 1916 letter he goes on to say: "The Borchgrevink expedition, which had just made a new record in South Polar achievement, greatly stimulated this study." The Norwegian Carsten Egeberg Borchgrevink's great achievement was to have established the first camp on actual Antarctic soil. He had sailed from England in August 1898, established the camp in February 1899, stayed all through the long Antarctic night (May–July 1899), walked on the Ross Ice Shelf on February 19, 1900, and returned to England by the summer of 1900.[76] In his 1935 letter Lovecraft explains: "I think it was the newspaper accounts of Borchgrevingk's [*sic*] second expedition of 1900 . . . which first captured my attention & interest."

It is not surprising that Lovecraft's interest would have been aroused by the Borchgrevink expedition, for this was the first important Antarctic voyage since the 1840s. It is also for this reason that the three lost treatises on Antarctic exploration which Lovecraft wrote around this time—"Voyages of Capt. Ross, R.N." (1902),

"Wilkes's Explorations" (1902), and "Antarctic Atlas" (1903)[77]—discuss those 1840s expeditions: there were no others in recent memory he could have written about. In fact, I am wondering whether the dates of writing supplied (in 1936) by Lovecraft are entirely accurate: I would like to date them to an even earlier period, say 1900, for reasons I shall supply presently.

The history of Antarctic exploration can rightly be said to begin with Captain James Cook, who attempted in 1772–74 to reach the South Pole but had to turn back because of the ice fields. It was on the second of his journeys (1774) that he stumbled upon Easter Island when heading north. Edward Bransfield of England actually sighted the Antarctic continent on January 30, 1820, and Alexander I Island (a large island off the coast of what is now called the Antarctic Peninsula) was discovered by Fabian von Bellingshausen on January 29, 1821; because of the heavy ice field in which it is embedded, it was not known to be an island until 1940, thereby creating considerable controversy over who had actually discovered the continent of Antarctica.

In the late 1830s three separate expeditions did much to chart various portions of Antarctica. The American Charles Wilkes (1798–1877) went to the Antarctic, bizarrely enough, to test the hollow earth theory proposed in 1818 by John Cleves Symmes (a theory Lovecraft attacked in a letter to the *Providence Journal* of 1906). An expedition mounted in 1829 by Symmes and Jeremiah N. Reynolds was a failure, but some years later Reynolds managed to persuade Wilkes, then only a lieutenant in the U.S. Navy, to lead another voyage. Wilkes's expedition—with six ships, eighty-three officers, and 345 crewmen—got under way on August 18, 1838, reaching the Antarctic zone in March 1839. One group attempted to enter the frozen Weddell Sea on the eastern side of the Antarctic Peninsula, but could not get very far because of the ice. Another group, after wintering in Sydney, skirted the western coast of the Antarctic, actually sighting land on January 19, 1840 (Edgar Allan Poe's thirty-first birthday, incidentally). By January 30 Wilkes had seen enough of the land mass to be certain that an actual continent was involved, not merely a series of islands or a huge frozen sea, and he made a momentous pronouncement: "Now that all were convinced of its existence, I gave the land the name of the Antarctic Continent." Wilkes returned to Sydney on March 11, 1840.

The Englishman James Clark Ross (1800–1862) left England on September 25, 1839, for the purpose of exploring the huge ice shelf that now bears his name. In doing so, he discovered the small island at the mouth of the ice shelf now called Ross Island, and named the two enormous volcanoes there (Mt Erebus and Mt Terror) after his two ships, the *Erebus* and *Terror*. Dr Joseph Hooker, one of the ship's doctors, gives a vivid impression of the first sight of Mt Erebus: "This was a sight so surpassing everything that can be imagined . . . that it really caused a feeling of awe to steal over us at the consideration of our own comparative insignificance and helplessness, and at the same time, an indescribable feeling of the greatness of the Creator in the works of His hand."[78] Lovecraft would certainly have echoed the first half of that utterance, but demurred about the second half. In any event, Ross made two further expeditions (1841–43), but they accomplished little. His great achievement was the discovery of the Ross Ice Shelf, "the grim barrier which in later years would prove to be the gateway to Antarctica."[79] It is interesting to note that Ross did not believe the Antarctic continent to be a single land mass—a view in which Lovecraft persisted until it was finally disproven in the 1930s.

There was, at this time, yet another Antarctic expedition, this one conducted by the Frenchman Jules Dumont d'Urville (1837–40), which covered some of the same territory as Wilkes; in fact, the two expeditions encountered each other by accident, and in a not very friendly manner, on January 29, 1840. I do not know why Lovecraft did not bother to write a treatise about d'Urville; perhaps his prejudice toward Anglo-Saxons led him to minimise the French explorer's accomplishment.

Lovecraft reports that by 1902 "I had read virtually everything in fact or fiction concerning the Antarctic, & was breathlessly awaiting news of the first Scott expedition."[80] This latter remark must refer to the expedition by Robert Scott on the *Discovery* that left New Zealand in August 1901, the high point of which was an attempt by Scott, Ernest Shackleton, and Edward Wilson to traverse the Ross Ice Shelf beginning on November 2, 1902; the team, ill-equipped for so arduous a journey, was forced to turn back on December 30 and almost died on the return trip.

As for having read everything ever written on the Antarctic, I don't imagine Lovecraft means the accounts left by the explorers themselves, some of which are enormous and not likely to have been available to him: Captain James Cook's *Voyage towards the South Pole* (1777), James Weddell's *A Voyage towards the South Pole* (1825), Charles Wilkes's *Narrative of the Exploring Expedition, by Authority of Congress, During the Years 1838–1842* (1845), James Clark Ross's *A Voyage of Discovery and Research in the Southern and Antarctic Regions* (1847), F. A. Cook's *Through the First Antarctic Night* (1900) (Cook was a member of Adrien de Gerlache's expedition of 1898–99); C. E. Borchgrevink's *First on the Antarctic Continent* (1901). Then again, perhaps Lovecraft did read some of these. In terms of treatises on the subject, there is only one found in his library: Karl Fricker's *The Antarctic Regions* (1900) (Prescott Holmes's *The Story of Exploration and Adventure in the Frozen Sea* [1896] deals with the north pole) aside from such fictional treatments as Frank Cowan's *Revi-Lona* (1879), James De Mille's *A Strange Manuscript Found in a Copper Cylinder* (1888), and Frank Mackenzie Savile's *Beyond the Great South Wall: The Secret of the Antarctic* (1899), as well as Poe and W. Clark Russell, of course.

I want to date Lovecraft's three lost treatises to around 1900, since it would seem odd for Lovecraft not to have chosen to write up the Borchgrevink and Scott expeditions, so fresh as they would have been in his mind, rather than the expeditions of the 1840s, some of whose discoveries had been superseded by the work of these later explorers. His correspondent C. L. Moore actually saw a copy of "Wilkes's Explorations" in late 1936,[81] although it was not found among his papers after his death a few months later. "Antarctic Atlas" must have been an interesting work, and presumably consisted largely of a map of the continent; but so little exploration of the land mass had been done by this time that large parts of it were utterly unknown and unnamed.

In addition to "composing 'learned' treatises on the real facts" of Antarctic discovery, Lovecraft admitted to writing "many fanciful tales about the Antarctic Continent" in youth.[82] Aside from those inspired by *The Frozen Pirate,* we have no information on what these are. The fact that they—like the treatises—do not appear on the catalogue of works appended to *Poemata Minora, Volume II* (1902) need not indicate that they were written after that date, since we have already noted that some extant works written earlier do not appear on the list. Suffice it to say that Lovecraft found the Antarctic a fascinating land for fictional composition precisely because so little was then—and for many years later—known of it. One might imagine almost anything existing in that bleak world of ice and death.

Lovecraft reports in "A Confession of Unfaith" that "my pompous 'book' called *Poemata Minora,* written when I was eleven, was dedicated 'To the Gods, Heroes, and Ideals of the Ancients', and harped in disillusioned, world-weary tones on the sorrow of the pagan robbed of his antique pantheon." I wonder whether Lovecraft has temporarily forgotten that there were two volumes of *Poemata Minora,* only the second of which survives; this second volume does in fact bear the dedication Lovecraft mentions, but the preface is dated to September 1902, meaning that the completed book dates to just past his twelfth birthday. Perhaps the poems themselves were written just before August 20, 1902. In a 1929 letter he dates Volume I of *Poemata Minora* to 1900, but later in the letter refers to its "publication" as occurring in 1901.[83]

Poemata Minora, Volume II is Lovecraft's most finished and aesthetically satisfying juvenile work. The five poems bear comparison with any of his later verse, although this is an indication not so much of the merit of these early poems as of the mediocrity of his later ones. It is telling that he allowed three of them—"Ode to Selene or Diana," "To the Old Pagan Religion," and "To Pan"—to appear (albeit with different titles and under pseudonyms) in the amateur paper the *Tryout* for April 1919. The other two—"On the Ruin of Rome" and "On the Vanity of Human Ambition"—could as well have been chosen.

The imprint of this book is "The Providence Press" and the price is 25¢. The preface reads as follows:

I submit to the publick these idle lines, hoping they will please.

They form a sort of series with my *Odyssey, Iliad, Æneid,* and the like.

THE AUTHOR

454 Angell St.
Prov. R.I. Sep. 1902.

That second statement is a little ambiguous, for in the catalogue appended to the volume the three works cited in the preface are listed in the category "Works for Children," while "The Hermit," "The Argonauts," and the two volumes of *Poemata Minora* are listed in the category "Other Verses." This leads me to think that those first three works are paraphrases of actual ancient works while the others are poems or poem-cycles inspired by classical themes. In other words, "The Argonauts" (15¢) may not in fact be a paraphrase of Apollonius Rhodius' *Argonautica* (a work with which Lovecraft was never very familiar), but a loose take-off on the voyage of the Argonauts, perhaps derived solely or largely from Bulfinch. "The Hermit" (25¢) may not be a classically inspired work at all; its price suggests that it was substantial.

The poems in *Poemata Minora* reveal considerable originality, and few can be traced to any specific works of classical poetry. Lovecraft was endlessly fond of citing the fourth and final stanza of "Ode to Selene or Diana" as prototypical of his disharmony with the modern age:

Take heed, *Diana,* of my humble plea.
Convey me where my happiness may last.
Draw me against the tide of time's rough sea
And let my spirit rest amid the past.

But the third stanza is more significant as a sociological commentary:

The modern world, with all it's care & pain,
The smoky streets, the hideous clanging mills,
Fade 'neath thy beams, *Selene* and again
We dream like shepherds on *Chaldaea's* hills.

I'm not sure where Lovecraft heard any "hideous clanging mills": it is true that his native state had pioneered the use of mills for manufacturing, but that was far in the past. And yet, the "plea" is nonetheless sincere for all that.

"To the Old Pagan Religion" begins boldly:

Olympian Gods! How can I let ye go
And pin my faith to this new *Christian* creed?
Can I resign the deities I know
For him who on a cross for man did bleed?

This reminds me of a remark in "A Confession of Unfaith": "In this period [c. 1899] I read much in Egyptian, Hindoo, and Teutonic mythology, and tried experiments in pretending to believe each one, to see which might contain the greatest truth. I had, it will be noted, immediately adopted the method and manner of science!" The apparent upshot of this informal course in comparative religion was both a renewed faith in the Graeco-Roman religion—it was so much prettier than the gloomy Christian faith practised by his Baptist family—and a still more pronounced rejection of Christianity, something his studies in astronomy beginning later in the year only augmented. But at the moment it was not secularism so much as wistful pathos at the passing of the ancient pantheon that seemed to affect him:

How in my weakness can my hopes depend
On one lone God, though mighty be his pow'r?
Why can *Jove's* host no more assistance lend,
To soothe my pains, and cheer my troubled hour?

I have no doubt that Lovecraft actually felt the "pains" he cites here; to someone so imbued with the spirit of classicism—and so isolated from his fellows that he fails to observe that that spirit is an anomaly—the awareness that Jove and his minions are no longer living objects of faith might well have been a cause of genuine anguish.

"On the Ruin of Rome" is a more conventional lament on the passing of the Roman empire. It is made distinctive only by a curious sort of dactylic pentameter line that is perhaps an attempt to imitate the dactylic hexameter of ancient epic poetry:

How dost thou lie, *O Rome,* neath the foot of the *Teuton*
Slaves are thy men, and bent to the will of the conqueror:
Whither hath gone, great city, the race that gave law to all nations,
Knew not defeat, but gave it to all who attack'd thee?

"To Pan" is a pleasing little lyric in quatrains (with an odd couplet thrown in before the last stanza) telling of seeing Pan playing on his pipes—perhaps an echo of the vision of fauns and dryads Lovecraft claimed to have had at the age of seven. "On the Vanity of Human Ambition" is a ten-line poem that betrays the influence of three separate authors: Samuel Johnson (the title of whose *The Vanity of Human Wishes* has been adapted here), Ovid (whose tale of Apollo and Daphne from *Metamorphoses* 1.452–567 is condensed in the first two lines), and Juvenal (whose *mens sana in corpore sano* is echoed in the final two lines: "True bliss, methinks, a man can only find / In virtuous life, & cultivated mind"). Otherwise the poem is a conventional attack on greed and the dissatisfaction that inevitably results from the attainment of some long-sought prize. It is the only poem in the book written in heroic couplets.

Something should be said about the illustrations in *Poemata Minora.* Each poem bears an illustration in pencil with accompanying Latin mottos. The illustrations are for the most part unremarkable, and the Latin occasionally erroneous but on the whole clever and pertinent. The illustration for "To the Old Pagan Religion" shows a figure (a pagan, one supposes, although he looks more like an Arab) bowing before an altar to Zeus, with a Latin tag noting how the Emperors Constantine and Theodosius suppressed the pagan religion. The illustration for "On the Vanity of Human Ambition" is a little more disturbing: it shows an obviously Jewish figure (there are Hebrew letters next to him) with the Latin inscription: "HIC.HOMO. EST.AVARISSIMVS.ET.TVRPISSIMVS.IUDAEVS" ("This man is a most greedy and filthy Jew"). Consider the inscription on the illustration for "On the Ruin of Rome": "ROMA.REGINA.ORBIS.TERRARVM. DECEDEBAT. CVM.ROMANI.SVCCEDEBANTVR.A.GENTIBVS.INFERIORIBVS" ("Rome, queen of the world, declined when the Romans were succeeded by inferior peoples"). The poem indeed refers to "we, base *Italians,*" and it is interesting to note—in light of Lovecraft's later vaunting of the Teuton—that the Teuton is here blamed for the destruction of Rome. It would be another three years before Lovecraft wrote an explicitly racist poem, and his early racial views should be discussed at that time.

Poemata Minora, Volume II is a pleasing little product, fully worth the 25¢ Lovecraft was charging. Volume I is likely to have been equally substantial, as an advertisement in Volume II offers it for 25¢ also. But this volume is the final product of Lovecraft's classicism. Although he would continue to draw upon the ancients for aesthetic and even philosophical inspiration, a new interest would for a time eclipse all others and impel an overhauling of his entire world view. For it was in the winter of 1902–03 that Lovecraft discovered astronomy.

4. What of Unknown Africa? (1902–1908)

The most poignant sensations of my existence are those of 1896, when I discovered the Hellenic world, and of 1902, when I discovered the myriad suns and worlds of infinite space. Sometimes I think the latter event the greater, for the grandeur of that growing conception of the universe still excites a thrill hardly to be duplicated. I made of astronomy my principal scientific study, obtaining larger and larger telescopes, collecting astronomical books to the number of 61, and writing copiously on the subject in the form of special and monthly articles in the local press. ("A Confession of Unfaith")

This remark, made around 1921, is a sufficient indication of the degree to which the discovery of astronomy affected Lovecraft's entire world view. I shall pursue the philosophical ramifications of his astronomical studies later; here it is worth pursuing in detail how he came upon the science and what immediate literary products it engendered. In the winter of 1902 Lovecraft was attending the Slater Avenue School, but his statements lead one to believe that he stumbled upon astronomy largely of his own accord. The majority of his astronomy volumes were inherited from his maternal grandmother Robie Phillips's collection,[1] and he notes that the first *new* astronomy book he purchased was in February 1903: Charles Augustus Young's *Lessons in Astronomy Including Uranography* (rev. ed. 1903)[2] (his library also contains the first edition of this book [1893], presumably an inheritance from his grandmother). Of the sixty-one books he claims to have had in his library in 1921, only about thirty-five were found after his death, when his library was catalogued; and some of these are rather old and elementary school manuals: George F. Chambers's *The Story of the Stars, Simply Told for General Readers* (1895), Thomas Dick's *The Practical Astronomer* (1846), a 30th edition of Joseph Guy's *Elements of Astronomy* (1871), Simon Newcomb's *Popular Astronomy* (1880), John A. Westwood Oliver's *Astronomy for Amateurs* (1888), Joel Dorman Steele's *A Fourteen Weeks Course in Descriptive Astronomy* (1873), and the like. These books are too old to have been used at Slater Avenue or at Hope Street High School (Lovecraft did not, in any event, take astronomy courses at Hope Street, even though they were offered), and some at least must have come from Robie's library. Of course, Lovecraft, ever the ardent used-bookstore hunter, could have picked up some of these titles on various book-hunting expeditions throughout his life.

As with so many of his other early interests, Lovecraft's family was very obliging in supply the materials necessary for his pursuit of astronomy. His first telescope, acquired in February 1903, was a 99¢ affair from a mail-order house, Kirtland Brothers & Co. in New York City. In July of that year, however, he acquired a 2¼-inch telescope from Kirtland for $16.50, plus a tripod made by a local craftsman for $8.00. Then in the summer of 1906 (and recall that this was *after* the financial crash following the death of Whipple Phillips in 1904) Lovecraft obtained a Bardon 3" from Montgomery Ward & Co.—for $50.00. "It came on a pillar-&-claw table stand, but I shifted it to the old tripod . . ."[3] He retained this telescope to the end of his life, and it is now in the possession of the August Derleth Society.

Lovecraft's initial concerns as an astronomer were not very ambitious. In a 1918 letter to Alfred Galpin he states that began a survey of the heavens after securing his second telescope, and was content merely to familiarise himself with the solar system and constellations:

> My observations . . . were confined mostly to the moon and the planet Venus. You will ask, why the latter, since its markings are doubtful even in the largest instruments? I answer—this very MYSTERY was what attracted me. In boyish egotism I fancied I might light upon something with my poor 2¼ inch telescope which had eluded the users of the 40-inch Yerkes telescope!! And to tell the truth, I think the moon interested me more than anything else—the very nearest object. I used to sit night after night absorbing the minutest details of the lunar surface, till today I can tell you of every peak and crater as though they were the topographical features of my own neighbourhood. I was highly angry at Nature for withholding from my gaze the other side of our satellite![4]

He did, however, manage to see Borelli's comet in August 1903—the first comet he observed.[5]

Lovecraft's interests were, in their way, not wholly dissimilar from those of the professional astronomers of his day. He discovered astronomy just before the time when it was beginning to transform itself into astrophysics and enter the realm of philosophy with Einstein's formulation of the theory of relativity in 1905. The eighth planet of the solar system, Neptune, had been discovered in 1846, and in 1902 the discovery of Pluto was still almost thirty years away. Pierre Simon de Laplace had articulated the nebular hypothesis in *Système du monde* (1796), and it was not seriously questioned as an account of the formation of the solar system until very early in the twentieth century. The great eighteenth-century astronomer Sir William Herschel (1738–1822) was still regarded as the greatest astronomer in Western history; he had discovered Uranus in 1781. His work in the discovery of nebulae, double stars, and the like was carried on by his son, John Herschel (1792–1871), who discovered the Magellanic Clouds around 1835.[6] In other words, the heavens were still being charted and the basic features of novae, nebulae, and the Milky Way were still not fully understood.[7]

As with his previous intellectual interests, Lovecraft's discovery of astronomy led eventually to writing—in this case, to an unprecedented quantity of writing. He does not seem to have commenced astronomical writing until the late summer of 1903, but when he did, he did so with gusto. Perhaps one of his earliest pieces is "My Opinion as to the Lunar Canals,"[8] a brief discourse on the curiously regular canals on the moon, similar to the more celebrated Martian canals. (A date of 1903 has been written on the text, but it is not in Lovecraft's handwriting.) Lovecraft conjectures that they were "matter volcanically ejected from the moon's interior in past ages" and that they are, accordingly, "but natural curiosities." He then launches into a bold attack on some illustrious astronomical contemporaries: "As to Prof. Pickering's theory—i.e.—That they are streaks of vegetation, I have but to say that any intelligent astronomer would consider it unworthy of notice, as our satellite is wanting in both water and atmosphere, the two essentials for life either animal or vegetable. Of course Lowell's theory (that they are artificial) is perfectly ridiculous." Lovecraft later had an amusing encounter with Percival Lowell.

Among the treatises Lovecraft produced around this time is "The Science Library," a nine-volume series probably written in 1903 or 1904. The list of volumes are as follows: 1. Naked Eye Selenography; 2. The Telescope; 3. Galileo; 4. Herschel (revised); 5. On Saturn and His Ring; 6. Selections from author's "Astronomy"; 7. The Moon, Part I; 8. The Moon, Part II; 9. On Optics. Of these, nos. 1, 2, and 5 survive. My guess is that no. 4 does not refer to Sir William Herschel but rather to the planet Uranus, which Lovecraft through much of his early astronomical work refers to as Herschel, even though this designation had not been in common use since the eighteenth century.

The surviving items are all about 3 × 4 inches in dimensions and eight pages long (four sheets folded in half); they combine Lovecraft's astronomical and antiquarian interests by being written in archaic English, with the long s. The hand lettering attempts to imitate print (including italics), although the lines are not very even or straight. They are all profusely illustrated, and the one on the telescope contains a number of fairly complicated diagrams explaining the construction of telescopes by Galileo, Huygens, Herschel, and others. This volume also contains an advertisement for one R. L. Allen at 33 Eddy Street (on the West Side, just across the Providence River), who is selling telescopes ranging from $40.00 to $200. Perhaps this is the local craftsman who made Lovecraft's tripod. The title of the treatise on Saturn identifies only one ring around that planet, but the text itself makes clear that Lovecraft is aware of at least three rings, the third of which is "actually *transparent*." The volume on naked-eye selenography contains, on its last page (the back cover), a list of the nine volumes in "The Science Library" and a sort of coupon:

ENCLOSED FIND ____ ¢ FOR WHICH SEND ME NOS. ________ OF THE SCIENCE LIBRARY——

Of the three surviving specimens, the first is priced at 1 gr. (groat?) and .05, the second at 1 gr., and the third (a bargain) at .005; perhaps this is the case because this volume is taken from the author's *Astronomy*.

One item that survives only in a transcript prepared by Arkham House is "The Moon." This substantial item was written on November 26, 1903, and may perhaps be a version of Volumes 7 and 8 of "The Science Library"; this copy is a 7th edition prepared in 1906. The preface to the first edition declares: "The author's object in bringing this little work before the public is to acquaint all with the principal facts concerning our moon. The ignorance displayed by otherwise educated persons is apalling, [*sic*] but I hope that this volume will do at least *something* to remove the clouds that have hitherto shrouded moon-study."

Astronomy and the *Monthly Almanack* survive in nine issues, from August 1903 to February 1904; sometimes they are combined with each other. These issues are not of compelling interest, consisting largely of data on the moon's phases for that month, planetary aspects, drawings of the planets, and the like. The issue for November 1903 features an article, "Annual of Astronomy '03":

> The Year 1903 has been quite good for astronomy, many clear nights prevailing. The most important discovery was that of a comet on Jn. 21., by Prof. Borelly. The comet was visible to the naked eye from Jul. 17 to Aug. 2nd inclusive., and had a tail, which, however, was not visible to the unassisted eye. . . . During it's visibility it travelled from Cygnus to Urs. Maj. A lunar eclipse that was nearly total occured on Apl. 11. 11 digits was the maximum totality. The dark part was hardly visible.

And so on. All issues are, again, profusely illustrated.

The *Planet* survived for only one issue (August 29, 1903). In appearance this looks like most of Lovecraft's other juvenile scientific periodicals, being about 4 × 7 inches in dimensions and written in two long vertical columns per page. Amusingly enough, this periodical combines scientific information with dime-novel sensationalism, as the titles of the articles are frequently followed by exclamation marks: "Jupiter Visible!" "Venus Has Gone!" "Telescopes!" A "Notice!" informs us of what we might have suspected: "This number is only an experiment, possibly no more will be issued."

A good many of these periodicals were reproduced using a process called the hectograph (or hektograph). This was a sheet of gelatin in a pan rendered hard by glycerine. A master page is prepared either in written form by the use of special hectograph inks or in typed form using hectograph typewriter ribbon; artwork of all sorts could also be drawn upon it. The surface of the pan would then be moistened and the master page pressed down upon it; this page would then be removed and sheets of paper would be pressed upon the gelatin surface, which had now picked up whatever writing or art had been on the master. The surface would be good for up to 50 copies, at which time the impression would begin to fade. Different colours could also be used.[9] Lovecraft must have had more than one such pan, since no more than one page could be hectographed in a day, as the inks must be given time to settle to the bottom. Although the hectograph was a relatively inexpensive reproductive process, the sheer quantity of work Lovecraft was running off must have come to no small expense—inks, carbon paper, gelatin, pans, and the like. No doubt his mother and grandfather were happy to foot the bill, given the precocity and enthusiasm Lovecraft must have exhibited.

We can now finally come to the most significant of Lovecraft's astronomical periodicals, the *Rhode Island Journal of Astronomy.* Even Lovecraft, with his seemingly boundless energy, must have had difficulty writing his other juvenile treatises and periodicals while the weekly deadline of the *Rhode Island Journal* continually impended. The journal, of which sixty-nine issues survive, was issued weekly on Sundays beginning on August 2, 1903; this schedule was kept up quite regularly until January 31, 1904 (the end of Volume I). The surviving issues resume on April 16, 1905 (the beginning of Volume III), continuing weekly until November 12, 1905 (the last page of which was written on November 23). Beginning in January 1906, the journal becomes a monthly, until it is abandoned with the issue of April 1907. There are two anomalously late issues, January and February 1909. Lovecraft states that the journal "was printed in editions of 15 to 25 on the hectograph" ("Autobiography of Howard Phillips Lovecraft").[10] At the moment I wish to study only the issues of 1903–04.

An average issue would contain a number of different columns, features, and charts, along with news notes, advertisements (both for works by Lovecraft and items from his collection and for others, including Kirtland Brothers and the ubiquitous R. L. Allen), and fillers. They make wholly entertaining reading. Consider the first part of a serial, "How to Become Familiar with the Constellations," beginning with the issue of January 10, 1904:

> Familiarity with the constellations is an utmost requisite for astronomers.
>
> There are many treatises that take up the subject in a masterful manner, but they are beyond the reach of many, so this article had better be read carefully by those who wish to gain a knowledge of the constellations.

Lovecraft then instructs the reader how to identify the pole star, appending four diagrams to the article. It continues for three more issues, and would have continued for more if Lovecraft had not suspended the journal at this point for more than a year.

The issue for September 20, 1903, announces that "NUMEROUS SERIALS are now appearing in this paper in a form less complete than the original MS. Those who desire to be fully informed must apply at office [i.e., 454 Angell Street], where (,if they can decipher the writing,) they may read the original & complete MS." The serials are enumerated as follows:

Title	*No. Pages*
The Telescope	12
The Moon	12
On Venus	10
Atlas Wld.	7 maps
Practical Geom.	34
ASTRONOMY	60
Solar System	27

Those last three certainly seem like substantial items. The treatises on "Astronomy" and "Practical Geometry" seem particularly impressive, especially given that Lovecraft had probably not taken geometry at Slater Avenue and would not do so at Hope Street until his second year there (1906–07).

The issue for November 1, 1903, makes an interesting announcement: "The Ladd Observatory Visited by a Correspondent Last Night." The correspondent, of course, is Lovecraft. The Ladd Observatory, situated on Doyle Avenue off Hope Street, is a charming small observatory operated by Brown University; the fact that a thirteen-year-old boy who was not even attending school at the time was allowed to use this facility is a testament to the degree of expertise Lovecraft had gained in astronomy, largely on his own. He states that "The late Prof. Upton of Brown, a friend of the family, gave me the freedom of the college observatory, (Ladd Observatory) & I came & went there at will on my bicycle."[11] He goes on to say that the perpetual craning of his neck to look through the telescope there caused him "much pain" and "resulted in a permanent curvature perceptible today to a closer observer." Winslow Upton (1853–1914) was a respected astronomer whose *Star Atlas* (1896), and probably other volumes, Lovecraft owned. One wonders whether he was a friend of Dr Franklin Chase Clark, who had married Lovecraft's aunt Lillian in 1902. It is not clear when Lovecraft first visited Ladd; he states in 1926 that he was to have met Prof. Upton there in April or May of 1903, but that the worst cold of his life prevented it.[12] Probably, therefore, he did go to Ladd sometime that summer. He may have seen Borelli's comet in August at Ladd or with his own telescope. In any event, on this October 31 visit Lovecraft was bold enough to find fault with the telescope: "The telescope is a 12 in. equatorial, but does not perform in the manner that a glass of it's size should. Chromatic aberration is the principal defect. every lunar crater and every bright object is surrounded by a violet halo." He adds, however, in extenuation: "The observatory has an excellent time system, with 3 siderial clocks, 1 chronograph, 1 telegraph, and 2 transits. The library is excellent, containing all the standard works on astronomy, besides having current issues of all the periodicals of the Science."

The issue of 27 December 1903, announces:

> For the past few nights a course of Lectures has been given by this office on the solar system.
>
> It was illustrated by a dozen lantern slides which were made by Mr. Edwards of the Ladd Observatory. The slides are:
>
> 1: The Solar System.
> 2: Sun-spots.
> 3: Total Solar Eclipse.
> 4: Venus: 2 views.
> 5: Full Moon.
> 6: Gibbous Moon. (*Defective*)
> 7: Mars.
> 8: Jupiter.
> 9: Saturn.
> 10: Comet of 1811.
> 11: Ærolite falling.
> 12: Lunar Scenery.
>
> The Lectures are given at the office of this paper and the admission is free.

The audience no doubt consisted of his immediate family and probably some of his Slater Avenue friends. Ever the perfectionist, Lovecraft cannot help pointing out that one of the slides made by John Edwards—whom Lovecraft elsewhere describes as "an affable little cockney from England"[13]—was defective; it must have been a mortifying interruption of his lecture.

Incredibly, while producing the *Rhode Island Journal of Astronomy* every Sunday, issuing other occasional weekly or monthly magazines, and writing separate treatises, Lovecraft resumed his chemical journal, the *Scientific Gazette.* As I have mentioned, after the first issue (March 4, 1899) we have no issue until May 12, 1902 (labelled Vol. XCI, No. III [New Issue Vol. I, No. 1]). This issue declares: "The Scientific Gazette, so long discontinued, has been resumed. It is better printed, on better paper, &c &c the price is raised [to 2¢], but is subject to reduction at any time[.] The *Sunday Gazette* has discontinued." This three-page issue is largely concerned with the causes of volcanism, although there is one odd note: over a picture of a chemical retort is written the bold notice, "KEEP THIS RETORT!" Perhaps this was intended to serve as a coupon of some sort, something that we find occasionally in the *Rhode Island Journal.* It is difficult to know for how long the journal had been discontinued prior to this issue; in the final extant issue (January 1909) Lovecraft announces that he is returning to the "plan of 1899–1902." In any event, we again have no more issues for more than a year, but by the issue of August 16, 1903 (two weeks after the commencement of the *Rhode Island Journal of Astronomy*), Lovecraft was ready to resume this journal as a weekly, doing so quite regularly until January 31, 1904, with sundry extra issues. Counting the issues for 1899 and 1902, there are a total of thirty-two surviving numbers. No doubt this was printed on the hectograph like the *Rhode Island Journal.* (Of the very earliest issues, of 1899 and following, Lovecraft states that he "made four carbon copies for 'circulation.'"[14])

The journal strayed from its chemical focus pretty early on in the 1903 sequence, discussing such matters as Venus' rotation, how to construct a camera obscura, perpetual motion, telescopes (a series taken over from the *Rhode Island Journal* and later to return there), microscopy, and the like. When the journal was resurrected in October 1906 (for which see below), ads in the *Rhode Island Journal* declare that it is "A popular epitome of general science"; it had become that long ago.

These scientific interests also manifested themselves in fictional composition. Lovecraft admits to being a "Verne enthusiast" and that "many of my tales showed the literary influence of the immortal Jules". He goes on to say: "I wrote one story about that side of the moon which is forever turned away from us—using, for fictional purposes, the Hansen theory that air and water still exist there as the result of an abnormal centre of gravity in the moon. I hardly need add that the theory is really exploded—I was even aware of that fact at the time—but I desired to compose a 'thriller.'"[15] This would presumably qualify, if it survived, as Lovecraft's first authentic tale of science fiction; and the fact that he labelled it a "thriller" evidently means that he was still under the influence of the dime novels of the day, which he—with that bewildering catholicity of taste he displayed throughout his life—was no doubt still reading.

I have mentioned that Lovecraft was writing most of these scientific treatises and journals while not in school. He attended the Slater Avenue school in 1898–99, but was then withdrawn; he resumed schooling there for the 1902–03 school year, and was withdrawn again. He adds that "In 1903–04 I had private tutors."[16] We know of one such tutor, A. P. May, although Lovecraft did not have a very high opinion of him. There is an unwontedly sarcastic ad for this person in the January 3, 1904, issue of the *Rhode Island Journal,* proclaiming May as a "10th rate Private Tutor" who is offering "Low Grade Instruction at High Rates"; the ad concludes: "HIRE ME. I CAN'T DO THE WORK BUT I NEED THE MONEY." Perhaps May was teaching Lovecraft things he already knew. Years later he spoke of May a little more charitably, if condescendingly, as "my odd, shy private tutor Arthur P. May—a theological student whom I loved to shock with my pagan materialism . . ."[17] In any case, it is not surprising that the flood of scientific periodicals began during the summer of 1903, when he probably had much time to himself.

We actually do not know much of what Lovecraft did in school during this second stint at Slater Avenue, since the school records do not survive. There was a class photograph taken at the end of the term,[18] but it has not turned up and is not likely to do so. All we know about this school year comes from Lovecraft himself. He observes that when he resumed attendance in 1902, his attitude was very different from what it had been in 1898: he had learnt in the interim that childhood was customarily regarded as a sort of golden age, and so he resolutely set about ensuring that this would be the case. Actually, he did not need much encouragement; for it was in this year of Slater Avenue that he developed two of his earliest but strongest friendships—with Chester and Harold Munroe, who lived about four blocks away from him at 66 Patterson Avenue (corner of Patterson and Angell Streets).[19] Other friends were Ronald Upham, two years younger than Lovecraft,[20] who lived at 21 Adelphi Avenue[21] (about three blocks from 454 Angell Street), and Stuart Coleman,[22] who had known him from his earlier Slater Avenue session. Another friend Lovecraft mentions only by the first name Ken; subsequent research has identified him as one Kenneth Tanner.[23] Twenty-five years later Lovecraft could still rattle off names of other classmates: "Reginald & Percival Miller, Tom Leeman & Sidney Sherman, 'Goo-Goo' [Stuart] Coleman & Dan Fairchild the teacher's pet, 'Monk' McCurdy the rough guy whose voice had changed . . . old days, old days!"[24] Lovecraft also reports being friendly with three brothers named Banigan who were neighbours of his, although it is not clear whether they went to school with him.[25] I suspect that these brothers were the sons of John J. Banigan, who from 1898 through at least 1908 lived at 468 Angell Street—not quite "next-door neighbours," as Lovecraft states, but perhaps two or three houses down from 454. These brothers were the grandsons of Joseph and Mary Banigan, who, I have conjectured (following the research of Kenneth W. Faig, Jr), represent the connecting link between Lovecraft's mother and Louise Imogen Guiney.

It is difficult to know which of the Munroe brothers Lovecraft felt closest to. In a 1921 letter he mentions Harold as "my best friend of my youth,"[26] but consider the following passage from a 1915 essay:

> Visitors at the Slater Avenue Primary and Grammar School in Providence, examining the desks and walls of the building, or the fence and the long bench in the boys' yard, may today discern among the multitude of names unlawfully carved by generations of youthful irrepressibles frequent repetitions of the initials "C. P. M. & H. P. L.", which the vicissitudes of sixteen years have failed completely to efface. The two friends whose initials are thus early associated have not been separated in spirit during the ensuing years . . . ("Introducing Mr. Chester Pierce Munroe," *Conservative*, April 1915)

Elsewhere Lovecraft remarks: ". . . Chester Pierce Munroe & I claimed the proud joint distinction of being the worst boys in Slater Ave. School . . . We were not so actively destructive as merely antinomian in an arrogant & sardonic way—the protest of individuality against capricious, arbitrary, & excessively detailed authority."[27] This comment at least is confirmed by another letter: "At school I was considered a bad boy, for I would never submit to discipline. When censured by my teacher for disregard of rules, I used to point out to her the essential emptiness of conventionality, in such a satirical way, that her patience must have been quite severely strained; but withal she was remarkably kind, considering my intractable disposition."[28] Lovecraft certainly got an early start as a moral relativist.

This "disregard of rules" came to the fore during the graduation ceremony for Lovecraft's class in June 1903. He was asked to make a speech for the occasion—which may or may not suggest that he was the valedictorian and therefore ranked first in his class—but had initially refused to do so; then, while the ceremony was actually in progress, he changed his mind. Approaching Abbie A. Hathaway, his teacher, he announced boldly that he wished to make the speech after all, and she acquiesced and duly had him announced. Lovecraft had, in the interim, written a hasty biography of Sir William Herschel, the astronomer; and as he mounted the podium he declaimed in "my best Georgian mode of speech":

> "Ladies and gentlemen: I had not thought to trespass upon your time and patience today, but when the Muse impels, it becomes a man but ill to stifle her demand. When I speak of the Muse, I do not mean to say that I am about to inflict my bad verses upon you—far be that from my intention. My Muse this day is Clio, who presides over affairs of history; and my subject, a very revered one to me, is the career of one who rose from the most unfortunate condition of insignificance to the utmost height of deserved eminence—Sir William Herschel, who from an Hanoverian peasant became the greatest astronomer of England, and therefore of the World!"

He adds:

> I think these are nearly the words I used. I kept them long in memory (through egotism) though I have not a copy beside me now. If this version be incorrect, it is because there are not enough long words present. . . . Much to my concern, this offering elicited smiles, rather than attention, from the adult part of my audience; but after I had done, I received a round of applause which well compensated for my trouble, and sent me off the platform with the self-satisfied glow of a triumphant Garrick.[29]

That Lovecraft was a smart-aleck would be a considerable understatement.

But school was the least significant of Lovecraft's and his friends' concerns; they were primarily interested—as all boys of that age, however precocious, are—in playing. And play they did. This was the heyday of the Providence Detective Agency, which Lovecraft describes in 1918 as follows:

> As to "Sherlock Holmes"—I used to be infatuated with him! I read every Sherlock Holmes story published, and even organised a *detective agency* when I was thirteen, arrogating to myself the proud pseudonym of S.H. This P.D.A. [Providence Detective Agency]—whose members ranged between nine & fourteen in years, was a most wonderful thing—how many murders & robberies we unravelled! Our headquarters were in a deserted house just out of the thickly settled area, and we there enacted, and "solved", many a gruesome tragedy. I still remember my labours in producing artificial "bloodstains on the floor!!!"[30]

In a 1931 letter he elaborates:

> Our force had very rigid regulations and carried in its pockets a standard working equipment of police whistle, magnifying glass, electric flashlight, handcuffs, (sometimes plain twine, but "handcuffs" for all that!) tin badge, (I have mine still!!) tape measure, (for footprints) revolver, (mine was the real thing, but Inspector Munro [*sic*] (aet 12) had a water squirt-pistol while Inspector Upham (aet 10) worried along with a cap-pistol) and copies of all newspaper accounts of desperate criminals at large—plus a paper called "The Detective", which printed pictures and descriptions of outstanding "wanted" malefactors! Did our pockets bulge and sag with this equipment? I'll say they did!! We also had elaborately prepared "credentials"—certificates attesting our good standing in the agency. Mere scandals we scorned. Nothing short of bank robbers and murderers were good enough for us. We shadowed many desperate-looking customers, and diligently compared their physiognomies with the "mugs" in "The Detective", yet never made a full-fledged arrest. Ah, me—the good old days![31]

How engaging it is to see Lovecraft, for perhaps the first (and last) time in his life, behaving like a "normal" boy!

These accounts are full of interest. First let us consider the Sherlock Holmes connexion. If Lovecraft is correct in saying that he read every Holmes story published up to that time (circa 1903), then this would include the novels *A Study in Scarlet* (1888), *The Sign of Four* (1890), and *The Hound of the Baskervilles* (1902), and the collections *The Adventures of Sherlock Holmes* (1892) and *The Memoirs of Sherlock Holmes* (1894); the tales that would make up *The Return of Sherlock Holmes* (1905) had begun appearing in the United States in *Collier's Weekly* beginning with the issue of September 26, 1903, so Lovecraft probably read at least some of these. Indeed, the resurrection of Holmes in these tales (he had, let us recall, been killed off in the last story in *Memoirs,* "The Final Problem") perhaps gave Lovecraft and his pals the impetus to imitate him. Lovecraft later states that he read no more Holmes stories aside from the works mentioned above and "an odd (& rather mediocre) pair or series of tales appearing about '08";[32] which leads one to suspect that his interest in Holmes—and detective fiction—died at the end of his high school years. Indeed, he declares that "I had a vilely narrow taste at 16 or 17—phantasy or nothing!"[33] Probably it is just as well for literature that this was the case.

The Conan Doyle stories were, clearly, not the only detective stories he read at this time; no doubt he continued to read the dime and nickel novels, which were light on abstract detection but heavy on the sort of "bloodstains on the floor" and other sensational imagery Lovecraft seemed at this time to delight in. Some of the early Munsey magazines, which he may already have been reading in 1903, carried detective, mystery, and suspense fiction as well.

Lovecraft did some actual detective writing at this time. He writes in 1916 that "I used to write detective stories very often, the works of A. Conan Doyle being my model so far as plot was concerned," and then goes on to describe one such work:

> One long-destroyed tale was of twin brothers—one murders the other, but conceals the body, and tries to *live the life of both*—appearing in one place as himself, and elsewhere as his victim. (Resemblance had been remarkable.) He meets sudden death (lightning) when posing as the dead man—is identified by a scar, and the secret is finally revealed in his diary. This, I think, antedates my 11th year.[34]

This tale does not seem to me especially influenced by Doyle. If Lovecraft is accurate in the dating of this tale, it would predate "The Mysterious Ship," and sounds rather more entertaining than that specimen.

The mention of *The Detective* is of interest. This is clearly a reference to the magazine published from 1885 to 1922; its subtitle is: "Official Journal of the Police Authorities and Sheriffs of the United States," and it no doubt carried the images of any number of redoubtable suspected criminals who needed to be brought to justice. It is difficult to imagine that Lovecraft's family, or that of any of his friends, actually subscribed to the monthly magazine; possibly the boys consulted copies at the Providence Public Library.

Among the enthusiasms which Lovecraft and his boyhood friends shared was railroads. I have noted that the coachman at 454 Angell Street built a summer-house for Lovecraft when the latter was about five. Lovecraft named this building "The Engine House" and himself built "a splendid engine . . . by mounting a sort of queer boiler on a tiny express-waggon." Then, when the coachmen left (probably around 1900) and the stable vacated of its horses and carriage, the stable itself became his playground, with "its immense carriage room, its neat-looking 'office', and its vast upstairs, with the colossal (almost scareful) expanse of the grain loft, and the little three-room apartment where the coachmen and his wife had lived."[35]

Some odd literary works were produced as a result of this interest in railroads. First there is a single issue of a magazine called the *Railroad Review* (December 1901), a three-page item full of Lovecraft's usual profusion of illustrations. Much more interesting is a 106-line poem dated to 1901 whose title on the cover reads: *An Account in Verse of the Marvellous Adventures of H. Lovecraft, Esq. Whilst*

Travelling on the W. & B. Branch of the N.Y.N.H. & H.R.R. in Jany. 1901 in One of Those Most Modern of Devices, to Wit: An Electric Train. Like "The Poem of Ulysses," this work bears an alternate title in its interior: "H. Lovecraft's Attempted Journey betwixt Providence & Fall River on the N.Y.N.H. & H.R.R."

This poem is notable for being the first—and, as it happens, one of the best—instances of Lovecraft's *humorous* verse. A little historical background for this piece is useful. The New York, New Haven, and Hartford Railroad (N.Y.N.H. & H.R.R.) had by 1893 become the principal operator of all railroads in the state of Rhode Island.[36] The first electric street cars in Providence had begun running in 1892,[37] and the extension of this service to the outlying localities of Warren, Bristol (the W. & B. Branch), and Fall River appears to have occurred in 1900.[38] With his fascination for railroads, Lovecraft not surprisingly became one of the first patrons of the new service; and the result is a delightfully witty poem on a very modern theme.

The poem begins:

Long, long ago, in prehistoric times
Began the subject of these ill-form'd rhymes,
When some craz'd mind, which engines did disdain,
Conceiv'd a plan for an electric train.

Lovecraft mentions that the trains were "by Osgood Bradley built," and that "One winter's morn, when all man kind did shiver, / I took a train, directed toward Fall-River." As the train labours up steep College Hill, it leaps off its track and crashes into "the front of Leonard's Groc'ry store!" Order is eventually restored, and the train is set on its course again. But at a junction one part of the train seeks to go toward Wickenden Street, while another yearns to go to South Main (at right angles to Wickenden); "The motor-car in dizzy fashion tips." Once again things are put to right, and the conductor comes around to collect the fares. "Quoth one old man, 'Take what ye will from me', / 'But in my damage suit I'll take from thee!'" This is one of the best poetic jokes Lovecraft ever made in his undistinguished career as a versifier. The train groans up Brook Street, but cannot quite make it up the hill; as it starts to slide back, "We're tow'd to safety by a one-horse hack." Soon it crosses a bridge "(This bridge was in the middle ages made)," and the car seeks to make a bold turn: "The monstrous car our bodies threats to mangle, / For this strange curve resembles a right angle." Finally the train begins to pick up speed, passing through various rural communities where "the rustics in confusion gape." Coming to Barrington, the passengers learn that "Warren's ceased to give us pow'r" and the car must be pulled by a locomotive. After yet another delay, "With crippled motors, and the wires dead," Lovecraft leaves the car and finds

A willing yokel with an ox-drawn cart
Who when with most of my spare change I part,

Consents to take me where I wish to go,
If I demur not at his progress slow.

In this way Lovecraft finally reaches Fall River, where he spends the night in a hotel. "Next day *by boat* safe homeward I return'd," only to learn that the trolley, though bound for Fall River, had ended up in Bristol.

All this is great fun, and I don't know that we need draw any overwhelmingly serious messages from it: the fact that Lovecraft had to take an ox-cart to Fall River may connect with his belief in the supremacy of the past over the present, but it certainly seems as if he had developed a great fondness for railroads, trolleys, and other forms of modernity in transport. How autobiographical the poem is cannot, of course, now be ascertained; no doubt Lovecraft really did take a ride on the trolley, and probably it did encounter tedious delays, breakdowns, and perhaps even some minor accidents or mishaps; but the comic exaggeration of the poem is clearly evident.

Lovecraft's and his friends' railroad enthusiasms gradually expanded or metamorphosed in a more military direction, and the railroad station in his backyard became "a little village":

> Many new roads and garden spots were made, and the whole was protected from the Indians (who dwelt somewhere to the north) by a large and impregnable fort with massive earthworks. The boy who suggested that fort and supervised its construction was deeply interested in military things . . . My new village was called "New Anvik", after the Alaskan village of "Anvik", which about that time became known to me through the boys' book *Snow-Shoes and Sledges,* by Kirk Munroe.[39]

Elsewhere Lovecraft admits to reading Munroe's *Rick Dale: A Story of the Northwest Coast* (1896) and *The Fur-Seal's Tooth: A Story of Alaskan Adventure* (1894).[40] *Snow-Shoes and Sledges* (1895) is in fact a sequel to *The Fur-Seal's Tooth.* Kirk Munroe (1850–1930) was a prolific author of boys' adventure novels: he published at least thirty-seven books, mostly between the years 1887 and 1905. Many of them have as their locales various exciting places in the United States (especially the Florida Everglades, Alaska, California, and Texas) or, in a few instances, overseas (China, Japan, the West Indies). I do not imagine he was related to Chester and Harold Munroe.

In discussing Lovecraft's boyhood pastimes it is impossible to pass over the Blackstone Military Band. Lovecraft's violin lessons may have been a disaster, but this was something altogether different. Here's how he tells it:

> When, at the age of 11, I was a member of the Blackstone Military Band, (whose youthful members were all virtuosi on what was called the "zobo"—a brass horn with a membrane at one end, which would transform humming to a delightfully brassy impressiveness!) my almost unique ability to keep time was rewarded by my

> promotion to the post of drummer. That was a difficult thing, insomuch as I was also a star zobo soloist; but the obstacle was surmounted by the discovery of a small papier-mache zobo at the toy store, which I could grip with my teeth without using my hands. Thus my hands were free for drumming—whilst one foot worked a mechanical triangle-beater and the other worked the cymbals—or rather, a wire (adapted from a second triangle-beater) which crashed down on a single horizontal cymbal and made exactly the right cacophony . . . Had jazz-bands been known at that remote aera, I would certainly have qualified as an ideal general-utility-man—capable of working rattles, cow-bells, and everything that two hands, two feet, and one mouth could handle.[41]

I don't think I can add much to this. The zobo appears to have been a sort of combined harmonica and kazoo. Lovecraft himself elsewhere describes it as "a brass horn with a membrane at the mouthpieces, which would make the human voice sound like the tones of a band instrument," although he goes on to say that it could also be made out of cardboard.[42] Recall the delightful passage in "Waste Paper" (1923), Lovecraft's parody of T. S. Eliot's *The Waste Land:*

> I used to sit on the stairs of the house where I was born
> After we left it but before it was sold
> And play on a zobo with two other boys.
> We called ourselves the Blackstone Military Band

Lovecraft always regretted his insensitivity to classical music, but he also found tremendous nostalgic relish in recalling the popular songs of his boyhood—and recall them he did. It was, let us remember, because he was "forever whistling & humming in defiance of convention & good breeding"[43] that led to his abortive violin lessons. It becomes clear that what he was whistling were the barbershop tunes of the day. In a 1934 letter he writes down the lyrics of "Bedelia," the big hit of 1903—"a veritable knockout—a stampede—lasting well into 1904."[44] He continues: "But by the fall of '04 it was played out as a serious offering. After that—like 'On the Banks of the Wabash'—it became a typical back number, for humorous or parodic use. 'You're the Flower of My Heart, Sweet Adeline' (Spring '04) was its principal immediate successor in popular favour—& then in '05 the new riot—'In the Shade of the Old Apple Tree' appeared." We shall presently see where this led.

All this may seem to give the impression that Lovecraft, in spite of his precociousness, his early health problems, his solitude as a very young boy, and his unsettled nervous condition, was evolving into a relatively "normal" youth with vigorous teenage enthusiasms (except sports and girls, in which he never took any interest). He also seems to have been the leader of his "gang" of boys. But how normal, really, was he? The later testimony of Stuart Coleman is striking: ". . . from the age of 8 to 18, I saw quite a bit of him as we went to schools together and I was many times at his home. I won't say I knew him 'well' as I doubt if any of his contemporaries at that time did. He was definitely not a normal child and his companions were few."[45]

Winfield Townley Scott, who was in touch with some of Lovecraft's boyhood friends in the 1940s, adds another anecdote that he learned from Clarence Horace Philbrick, who graduated from Hope Street High School in 1909 and therefore must have been in school with Lovecraft for at least a few years:

> Clarence H. Philbrick told me that he and others in high school with Lovecraft made attempts at friendliness but always were rebuffed by a chill disinterest or a shyness that seemed like it; they finally quit the attempts. Lovecraft later did have a few local friends, and loyal ones; the sort who failed to understand him and yet were impressed by his extraordinary range of interests, by his phenomenally exact memory, and by the brilliance of his talk; who found, when they gave him affection, the depth of goodwill and charm to which his later literary friends have testified.[46]

Lovecraft was slow to make friends, but once he made them he remained firm and devoted. This is a pattern that persisted throughout his life, and in fact he became still more forthcoming with his time, knowledge, and friendship by means of correspondence, writing enormous treatises to perfect strangers when they had asked him a few simple questions or made some simple requests.

Clara Hess, the same age as Lovecraft, supplies a telling and poignant memory of Lovecraft's devotion to astronomy around this time:

> Howard used to go out into the fields in back of my home to study the stars. One early fall evening several of the children in the vicinity assembled to watch him from a distance. Feeling sorry for his loneliness I went up to him and asked him about his telescope and was permitted to look through it. But his language was so technical that I could not understand it and I returned to my group and left him to his lonely study of the heavens.[47]

This is certainly touching, but one should not conclude that Lovecraft's "loneliness" was inveterate or even that he necessarily found in it anything to regret: intellectual interests were always dominant in his temperament, and he was willing to sacrifice conventional gregariousness for its sake.

One does not wish to belabour this point, nor to deny Lovecraft's own frequent admissions that his youth was an idyllic time of carefree play and pleasurable intellectual stimulation. I also do not know what overwhelming virtues there are in being "normal," whatever criteria one cares to apply to that word.

But Lovecraft's days of innocence came to an abrupt end. Whipple Phillips's Owyhee Land and Irrigation Company had suffered another serious setback when a drainage ditch was washed out by floods in the spring of 1904; Whipple, now an old man of seventy, cracked under the strain, suffering a stroke and dying on March 28, 1904. This blow was bad enough, but there was still worse to come:

> His death brought financial disaster besides its more serious grief. . . . [W]ith his passing, the rest of the board [of the Owyhee Land and Irrigation Company] lost their initiative & courage. The corporation was unwisely dissolved at a time when my grandfather would have *persevered*—with the result that others reaped the wealth which should have gone to its stockholders. My mother & I were forced to vacate the beautiful estate at 454 Angell Street, & to enter the less spacious abode at 598, three squares eastward.[48]

This was probably the most traumatic event Lovecraft experienced prior to the death of his mother in 1921. By 1904 he and his mother were living alone with his widowed grandfather at 454 Angell Street, as both of his aunts and his uncle had married. With Whipple gone, it would have been both financially and practically absurd to have maintained the huge house at Angell and Elmgrove just for the two of them, and the residence at 598 Angell Street was no doubt chosen because of its propinquity. It was, however, a duplex (the address is 598–600 Angell Street), and Lovecraft and his mother occupied only the western side of the smallish house. One would imagine that these quarters—which Lovecraft describes as five rooms and an attic[49]—would, in literal terms, still be adequate for a boy and his mother; but psychologically the loss of his birthplace, to one so endowed with a sense of place, was shattering.

I am not sure who was occupying the eastern side of the house in 1904; in 1911 the Providence house directory lists three members of the Metcalf family: Jennie T., a widow, and two boarders (perhaps her sons), Houghton and Henry K., the latter a clerk. Lovecraft never mentions these people to my knowledge, and I suspect he avoided them where possible.

The death of Whipple Phillips was, of course, the most severe financial blow to the family up to that time, but even the young boy Lovecraft had been noticing the gradual cutbacks in amenities since at least 1900. At the time of his birth the Phillips household had four servants, three horses,[50] and a coachman to tend them. One by one Lovecraft saw all these go. The coachman probably left around 1900, when the horses and carriage were dispensed with. Lovecraft supplies an amusing but poignant recollection of him and of another servant:

> I sadly missed Kelly, the coachman, who was an indisputable authority on all matters pertaining to Hibernian dialect, and who had the forbearance to listen placidly to my laudation of Mother England. By the time of his departure I had acquired a beautiful brogue, which I occasionally aired for the amusement of myself and those about me—particularly Miss Norah ______ (last name forgotten!) who presided over the culinary department.[51]

Then the servants began to depart. Twenty years later Lovecraft still remembered their names: Norah, Delia, Svea, Jennie, Bridget, and Delilah.[52] These are six, so perhaps some had been replaced by others. Delilah (who at a later date worked for Lovecraft's aunt Lillian) was black. Lovecraft claims that Bridget Mullaney (presumably an Irishwoman) was the last servant to go;[53] the U.S. census for 1900, however, lists only one live-in servant at 454 Angell Street, Maggie Corcoran. Lovecraft makes clear that the financial decline well predated Whipple's death:

> Money as a definite conception was wholly absent from my horizon. Rather was I a simple, unplaced entity like the carefree figures moving through the Hellenick myths. But actual decline did set in when I was about ten years old; so that I saw a steady dropping of servants, horses, and other adjuncts of domestick management. Even before my grandfather's death a sense of peril and falling-off was strong within me, so that I felt a kinship to Poe's gloomy heroes with their broken fortunes.[54]

To compound the tragedy, Lovecraft's beloved black cat, Nigger-Man, disappeared sometime in 1904. This was the only pet Lovecraft ever owned in his life, in spite of his almost idolatrous adoration of the felidae. Its name, it need hardly be pointed out, was not regarded as offensive at the time—or at least not as offensive as it would be now. It is not clear when Lovecraft was first given this pet; conceivably he could have received it as early as when he and his mother moved back to 454 Angell Street in 1893. Late in life he rhapsodised about the creature:

> What a boy he was! I watched him grow from a tiny black handful to one of the most fascinating & understanding creatures I've ever seen. He used to talk in a genuine language of varied intonation—a special tone for every different meaning. There was even a special "prrr'p" for the smell of roast chestnuts, on which he doted. He used to play ball with me—kicking a large rubber sphere back at me from half across the room with all four feet as he lay on the floor. And on summer evenings in the twilight he would prove his kinship to the elfin things of shadow by racing across the lawn on nameless errands, darting into the blackness of the shrubbery now & then, & occasionally leaping at me from ambush & then bounding away again into invisibility before I could catch him.[55]

Nigger-Man's loss perhaps symbolised the loss of his birthplace as no other event could.

To see exactly what an impact the death of his grandfather, the loss of the family fortune (whatever of it was left by this time—Whipple had left an estate only valued at $25,000, of which $5000 went to Susie and $2500 to Lovecraft[56]), and the move from his birthplace had on the thirteen-year-old boy, we must read a remarkable letter of 1934:

> . . . for the first time I knew what a congested, servantless home—with another family in the same house—was. . . . I felt that I had lost my entire adjustment to

> the cosmos—for what indeed was HPL without the remembered rooms & hallways & hangings & staircases & statuary & paintings . . . & yard & walks & cherry-trees & fountain & ivy-grown arch & stable & gardens & all the rest? How could an old man of 14 (& I surely felt that way!) readjust his existence to a skimpy flat & new household programme & inferior outdoor setting in which almost nothing familiar remained? It seemed like a damned futile business to keep on living. No more tutors—high school next September which would probably be a devilish bore, since one couldn't be as free & easy in high school as one had been during brief snatches at the neighbourly Slater Ave. school. . . . Oh, hell! Why not slough off consciousness altogether?

Was Lovecraft actually contemplating suicide? It certainly seems so—and, incidentally, this seems virtually the *only* time in Lovecraft's entire life (idle speculation by later critics notwithstanding) when he seriously thought of self-extinction. His letter goes on to state, with a certain wry relish, that "the *method* was the only trouble": poisons were hard to get, bullets were messy and unreliable, hanging was disgraceful, daggers were tricky, falls from a cliff were completely out of the question in view of the "probable state of the remains," and so on and so on. Then he thought of the Barrington River—far to the east of Providence, on the border between Rhode Island and Massachusetts—and went riding there on his bicycle frequently in the summer of 1904, pondering its weed-grown depths and wondering what it might be like to rest placidly at its bottom. What stopped him? Let us read on:

> And yet certain elements—notably scientific curiosity & a sense of world drama—held me back. Much in the universe baffled me, yet I knew I could pry the answers out of books if I lived & studied longer. Geology, for example. Just *how* did these ancient sediments & stratifications get crystallised & upheaved into granite peaks? Geography—just *what* would Scott & Shackleton & Borchgrevink find in the great white antarctic on their next expeditions . . . which I could—if I wished—live to see described? And as to history—as I contemplated an exit without further knowledge I became uncomfortably conscious of what I didn't know. Tantalising gaps existed everywhere. When did people stop speaking Latin & begin to talk Italian & Spanish & French? What on earth ever happened in the black Middle Ages in those parts of the world other than Britain & France (whose story I knew)? What of the vast gulfs of space outside all familiar lands—desert reaches hinted of by Sir John Mandeville & Marco Polo . . . Tartary, Thibet . . . What of unknown Africa?[57]

This is a defining moment in the life of H. P. Lovecraft. How prototypical that it was not family ties, religious beliefs, or even—so far as the evidence of the above letter indicates—the urge to write that kept him from suicide, but scientific curiosity. Lovecraft may never have finished high school, may never have attained a degree from Brown University, and may have been eternally ashamed of his lack of formal schooling; but he was one of the most prodigious autodidacts in modern history, and he continued not merely to add to his store of knowledge to the end of his life but to revise his world view in light of that knowledge. This, perhaps, is what we ought most to admire about him.

In the short term the dreaded commencement of high school proved—to both Lovecraft's and his family's surprise—a delight. Hope Street English and Classical High School, at the corner of Hope and Olney Streets (the building, opened in 1898, was on the southeast corner; the present building, on the southwest corner, was opened in 1938), was a good mile from Lovecraft's 598 Angell Street home, but there was no closer public high school to which he could have gone. I suspect that Lovecraft rode his bicycle most of the time—he reports that the period 1900–1913 was the heyday of his bicycle-riding[58]—perhaps skirting the large property housing the Dexter Asylum (a home for the indigent), which obtruded along his path. (This area is now the Aldrich-Dexter Field, owned by the athletic department of Brown University; Dexter Asylum was torn down long ago.) The trip was not insignificant, as is perhaps reflected in the fair number of times during his first term of 1904–05 that Lovecraft reported late (seventeen times in four quarters); his twenty-seven absences are no doubt the result of his always precarious nervous condition. But Lovecraft on the whole had a very nice time:

> Knowing of my ungovernable temperament, & of my lawless conduct at Slater Avenue, most of my friends (if friends they may be called) predicted disaster for me, when my will should conflict with the authority of Hope Street's masculine teachers. But a disappointment of the happier sort occurred. The Hope Street preceptors quickly *understood* my disposition as "Abbie" [i.e., Abbie Hathaway, his teacher at the Slater Avenue School] never understood it; & by *removing all restraint,* made me apparently their comrade & equal; so that I ceased to think of discipline, but merely comported myself as a gentleman among gentlemen.[59]

Since there are no independent accounts of Lovecraft's high school years, we have to accept this statement at face value.

Things were not always entirely harmonious between Lovecraft and his teachers, however. He notes several occasions in which he had various academic disputes: one professor did not like Lovecraft's method in solving algebraic problems, even though the solutions were correct; another doubted Lovecraft's assertion that there were *two* native races of Europe, Caucasian and Mongolian, until Lovecraft reminded him that the Lapps were Mongol. But the most celebrated encounter was with a "fat old lady English teacher" named Mrs Blake. Let Lovecraft tell it in his inimitable way:

> I had handed in a theme entitled "Can the Moon Be Reached by Man"? And something about it (gawd knows what) led her to question its originality. She said it sounded like a magazine article. Well—chance was with me that day, for I had

> the ammunition to stage a peach of a tableau. Did I deny the magazine-article charge? Not so! Instead, I calmly informed the lady that the theme was indeed a verbatim parallel of an article which had appeared in a rural weekly only a few days before. I felt sure, I said, that no one could possibly object to the parallelism! Indeed, I added—as the good soul's bewilderment became almost apoplectic—I would be glad to show her the printed article in question! Then, reaching in my pocket, I produced a badly printed cutting from a Rhode Island village paper (which would accept almost anything sent to it). Sure enough—here was the self-same article. And mixed were the emotions of the honest Mrs. Blake when she perused the heading—CAN THE MOON BE REACHED BY MAN? BY H. P. LOVECRAFT.[60]

This, of course, was an article he had published in the *Pawtuxet Valley Gleaner* for October 12, 1906. Once again, as in several of his Slater Avenue antics, Lovecraft comes off as a show-off and smart-aleck, and it is perhaps not surprising that his teachers—unsuccessfully, at least as he recounts it—attempted now and again to put him in his place.

It is worth studying in detail what courses Lovecraft actually took during his three years at Hope Street. His transcript fortunately survives, and it is full of interesting and suggestive information. The school year lasted for 39 weeks, and most of the courses Lovecraft took covered an entire year; occasionally he took courses lasting only one term, either 19 or 20 weeks. (In the following enumeration, classes are for 39 weeks save where listed.) Numerical grades were issued; an 80 represented a Certificate grade, 70 a passing grade. During the 1904–05 year, Lovecraft took Elementary Algebra, Botany, English, Ancient History, and Latin. These are the grades Lovecraft received:

Elementary Algebra	74
Botany	85
English	77
Ancient History	82
Latin	87

There is not much that is unusual here, except the surprisingly low grade Lovecraft received in English. Lovecraft was absent 18 days and tardy 17 days during this year.

Lovecraft returned to Hope High in September 1905, but his transcript states that he left on November 7 of that year, not returning until September 10, 1906 (presumably the beginning of the 1906–07 school year). This is no doubt the period of his "near-breakdown" of 1906. There is not much evidence as to the nature of this illness. The final page of the *Rhode Island Journal of Astronomy* for November 12, 1905, declares: "The stress of events has delayed the R.I. JOURNAL for 11 days, it being published on NOV. 23, 1905 instead of NOV. 12, 1905. The next issue we hope to have out promptly on DEC. 3, 1905." No such issue evidently appeared, and the next one we have is dated January 1906. But the magazine continues regularly on a monthly schedule until January 1907, and is in fact rather more sizeable and substantial than the previous weekly issues. It is surely peculiar that Lovecraft does *not* admit to a "near-breakdown" in 1904, when he faced the trauma of Whipple Phillips's death and the move from 454 Angell Street; the 1906 breakdown does not appear to have been as serious as its two predecessors (1898 and 1900), even if it did mean his withdrawal from high school for nearly a year.

When Lovecraft returned for the 1906–07 school year he received the following grades:

Intermediate Algebra (20 weeks)	75
Drawing (19 weeks)	85
English (19 weeks)	90
Plane Geometry	92
Greek Texts (19 weeks)	85
Latin Grammar (19 weeks)	85
Latin Texts (20 weeks)	85
Physics	95

The ominous thing here is the continuing low marks for algebra, for which more below. For all Lovecraft's later laments on his inability to draw, his marks in drawing were respectable. High marks in physics were also to be expected, and he is now also applying himself more in English. He is recorded as being absent 6 days and tardy 25 days during the first term, the only period for which such information is available.

In his final year at Hope High (1907–08) Lovecraft took only the following:

Intermediate Algebra (10 weeks)	85
Chemistry	95
Physics	95

Here the interesting thing is his retaking Algebra, Lovecraft himself remarks: "The first year I barely passed in algebra, but was so little satisfied with what I had accomplished, that I voluntarily repeated the last half of the term."[61] There is a slight inaccuracy here, since it was not the Elementary Algebra of his first year that he retook, but the Intermediate Algebra of the second year; and he does seem to have finally achieved a better grade this time. Elsewhere he states that it was "only a supreme effort of the will that gained for me the highest marks in Algebra and Geometry at school."[62]

The transcript states that Lovecraft left on June 10, 1908, presumably at the end of the term, since he is recorded as having attended the full 39 weeks of chemistry and physics. (No record of days absent or tardy is given.) But Lovecraft clearly did not receive a diploma, and indeed it is evident that he has only finished the eleventh grade—or perhaps not even that, since he anomalously took only two full courses during this third year. He would surely have required at least another full year of schooling to qualify for graduation.

Lovecraft, aside from finding the teachers more or less congenial, had the usual scrapes with his classmates. He had been called "Lovey" at Slater Avenue, but by the time he became well-established at Hope Street he was nicknamed "Professor" because of his published astronomical articles.[63] He admits to having an "ungovernable temper" and being "decidedly pugnacious":

> Any affront—especially any reflection on my truthfulness or honour as an 18th century gentleman—roused in me a tremendous fury, & I would always start a fight if an immediate retraction were not furnished. Being of scant physical strength, I did not fare well in these encounters; though I would never ask for their termination. I thought it disgraceful, even in defeat, not to maintain a wholly "you-go-to-hell" attitude until the victor ceased pummelling of his own accord. . . . Occasionally I won fights—aided by my habit of assuming a dramatically ferocious aspect frightening to the nervous . . . the "by God, I'll kill you!" stuff.[64]

Evidently he managed to survive these encounters. One wonders if he ever tangled with "Monk" McCurdy, the seventeen-year-old bully at Slater Avenue.

The sense of foreboding Lovecraft mentions as preceding his grandfather's death is evident in his juvenile scientific work—or, rather, in the absence of such work. Both the *Rhode Island Journal of Astronomy* and the *Scientific Gazette* come to an abrupt end with the issues of January 31, 1904; the last issue of *Astronomy* (now combined with the *Monthly Almanack*) dates to February 1904. Note that this is more than a month *before* Whipple's death. Lovecraft states that the *Scientific Gazette* and the *Rhode Island Journal* both resumed as monthlies, the first in May 1904 and the second in August 1904, but that both were stopped after a few weeks;[65] these issues do not survive. Advertisements for the *Scientific Gazette* appear in the *Rhode Island Journal* throughout the summer of 1905, until in the issue of September 17, 1905, it is announced as discontinued. We have, therefore, clearly lost several issues of the *Scientific Gazette,* as we have none between January 31, 1904, and the final issue of January 1909.

And yet, Lovecraft clearly retained his interest in chemistry and, even if he had given up chemical writing, continued conducting experiments in chemistry and obtaining new instruments. Among the latter were a spectroscope (which Lovecraft still owned in 1918) and a spinthariscope for the detection of radioactivity; Lovecraft notes in a letter that it contained "a minute quantity of radio-active matter."[66] He goes on to relate a "physical memorial" of his chemical interests: ". . . the third finger of my right hand—whose palm side is permanently scarred by a mighty phosphorus burn sustained in 1907. At the time, the loss of the finger seemed likely, but the skill of my uncle [F. C. Clark]—a physician—saved it."

As for the *Rhode Island Journal of Astronomy,* the later issues (beginning on April 16, 1905) are not appreciably different from their predecessors. Lovecraft was now experimenting with using various colours in the magazine, the only result of which is that some of the issues are extremely difficult to read; by the issue of May 14, 1905, Lovecraft declared that no more colour will be used. Some of Lovecraft's crochets begin to appear, as in the article on "Astronomical Cranks" (June 11, 1905), hurling abuse on those (mostly leaders of eccentric religious sects) who refuse to accept the Copernican theory. A lengthy serial on "How to Make and Use a Telescope" (evidently adapted from a similar series in the *Scientific Gazette* in 1903) appears all through the summer, along with articles on the history of the telescope, ancient astronomy, the sighting of Jupiter's seventh satellite, and much else besides.

These issues provide some indication of who exactly was reading the *Rhode Island Journal of Astronomy.* It is scarcely to be doubted that members of his own family had done so at the outset; now that only his mother remained in the house with him, perhaps Lovecraft concentrated on selling copies (still priced at 1¢ per copy, 25¢ for six months, and 50¢ for a year) to his friends and to relatives living in the vicinity. A startling "Notice!!" in the issue of October 8, 1905, states: "Subscribers residing outside of Providence will receive their papers in a bunch once a month by mail." This notice would not have been necessary unless there were at least a handful of such subscribers. Perhaps one can suspect Lovecraft's aunt Annie, now living in Cambridge, Massachusetts, with her husband; and there may have been other relatives.

Still more startling is a notice in the issue of October 22, 1905: "Since we have started, others are constantly copying, there is a new paper just out that is a direct copy. PAY NO ATTENTION to these but to the GENUINE." Lovecraft's schoolmates at Hope Street were apparently offering him the sincerest form of flattery, but Lovecraft did not appreciate it. The later issues of his journal bear a stamped notice, "ORIGINAL COPY," to ensure the genuineness of the paper.

One of Lovecraft's imitators was Chester Pierce Munroe, although he wisely did not emulate Lovecraft in the realm of science. the *Rhode Island Journal of Astronomy* for April 30, 1905, announces the establishment of the *East Side News,* C. P. Munroe, Editor. The price is the same as for Lovecraft's journal (1¢ per issue, 25¢

for six months, 50¢ for a year). This magazine—described by Lovecraft in the issue of May 21, 1905, as "a very superior sort of paper, . . . which, besides local news, contains much of general interest"—suffered considerably greater vicissitudes in issuance than Lovecraft's. The paper was suspended for the summer of 1905, but resumed in September when the Munroe family returned from vacation. Shortly thereafter the paper is renamed the *Providence Times;* Lovecraft "personally recommends the 'TIMES' as the best paper of it's kind published anywhere" (September 17, 1905). But by October 8, 1905, there is the following announcement: "PROVIDENCE TIMES! BIG NOTICE! We have not been able to continue this paper and have *failed!* We hope sometime to resume it, or the East Side News." This was probably written by Chester. The paper did in fact resume in early 1906, but by July it had sold out to the *Blackstone News,* a paper begun by Chester's brother Harold in May 1905. It is not clear how long this paper continued to run.

One new enthusiasm that emerged around the fall of 1905 was meteorology. This interest had initially developed toward the end of 1903, as notices in the *Scientific Gazette* suggest. The issue of January 24, 1904, announced a new "Climatological Station" that "belongs to the publishers [*sic*] of this paper"; it had "6 circular windows with shutters, in case of severe storm. The instruments have not all arrived yet . . . Although the station is not, as yet, fully equipped, it *can* do much practice-work, for the storm glass is very accurate, and the wet-bulb thermometer, which was made by the observer works to perfection." We can probably connect this with another surviving juvenile item, a "Providence Observatory Forecast" for April 5, 1904, made on the 4th. This is a single sheet giving a prediction of the weather for the next day ("no clouds will cross the sky—excepting a few sunset strata").

Whipple's death halted this work for at least a few months, but then we learn in the *Rhode Island Journal* for September 3, 1905, that Lovecraft has entered a contest by a New York lawyer, F. R. Fast, for the best weather forecasts. He adds smugly that his "forecasts have been right 1/3 more times than the local weather station since October [1904?]." There is no announcement that he won the prize, so presumably he did not. But Lovecraft went on to state that daily forecasts would be issued after October 15 for 50¢ a year. There seems to have been some hiatus in the forecasts (probably in November and December 1905, which is likely to have been the time of the onset of his "near-breakdown" of 1906), for the January 1906 issue of the *Rhode Island Journal* states that the forecasts will now resume. In February we learn that a great many new instruments have now been added to the meteorological observatory, including a barometer, a maximum and minimum thermometer, a dry bulb thermometer, a wet thermometer, a rain gauge, a hair hygrometer, a storm-glass, and other things. The April 1906 issue informs us that Lovecraft has "just constructed a new wind-vane for the station. It was Finished on March 28, and works finely." But in May 1906 it is announced that "Of late many accidents have happened to the instruments at our station, so the records are badly broken." These were evidently repaired, and later such things as a quadrant, sundial, and magnetic compass were added. A small pamphlet dating to this period—*Third Annual Report of the Prov. Meteorological Station* (dated January 16, 1907)[67]—clearly suggests that there were two previous annual reports, now non-extant.

Lovecraft was also continuing to add to his astronomical collection as well: his 3" telescope was obtained on September 14, 1906, and somewhat earlier he acquired a 12" celestial globe and a Barritt-Serviss Planet Finder. The generosity of Lovecraft's family—for these items could only have come from his mother or aunts or uncle—even in their relatively straitened circumstances cannot be overstressed.

Still another activity in which Lovecraft engaged was amateur printing. This, too, had begun as early as 1902, as an ad in the *Rhode Island Journal* for January 3, 1904, has a notice for a "Providence Printing Co. / Card & Job Work at Low Rates / Estab. 1902." Not much is heard of this until 1905, when another ad (April 30, 1905) states: "We have re-opened at our old location with a new press, type, and outfit. We now do *card work only* but we do it in a way much superior to that which we used last year. ALL COLOURS SAME RATES." In the issue of October 22, 1905, we learn that the Providence Printing Co. has "re-opened with new double cylinder rotary press! Jobs done also hecto. work." The issue of November 12, 1905 informs us that H. P. Lovecraft, Printer, successor of the Prov. Printing Co., is now equipped with three presses and five new styles of type. Cards only 5¢ per dozen. A very professional-looking printed card is affixed to the last page of the *Rhode Island Journal* for January 1906:

H. P. LOVECRAFT
CARD & JOB PRINTER
Established 1902 598, Angell St.

Best quality work of any kind (up to size 3 × 5) done promptly, and at lowest rates.
NEW "EXCELSIOR" PRESS & ALL KINDS OF TYPE.
CARDS ONLY 5¢ PER DOZEN.
Trial order solicited.

It would seem likely, given Lovecraft's vigorous ad campaign, that he was actually receiving offers for small-scale printing from friends and family. But by April 1906 Lovecraft "permanently discontinued" his card printing owing to "the stress of the R.I. Journal," whatever that may have been; he referred patrons to Mr Reginald Miller, 7 Irving Avenue, and offered all his presses, types, and supplies for sale.

Lovecraft, then, was making a game effort to resume his normal life and writing after his grandfather's death and the move to 598 Angell Street. And perhaps his friends lent their assistance. One of the first things they did was to re-establish "New Anvik" in the vacant lot next door:

> This was my aesthetic masterpiece, for besides a little village of painted huts erected by myself and Chester and Harold Munroe, there was a landscape garden, all of mine own handiwork. I chopped down certain trees and preserved others, laid out paths and gardens, and set at the proper points shrubbery and ornamental urns taken from the old home. My paths were of gravel, bordered with stones, and here and there a bit of stone wall or an impressive cairn of my own making added to the picture. Between two trees I made a rustic bench, later duplicating it betwixt two other trees. A large grassy space I levelled and transformed into a Georgian lawn, with a sundial in the centre. Other parts were uneven, and I sought to catch certain sylvan or bower-like effects. The whole was drained by a system of channels terminating in a cess-pool of my own excavation. Such was the paradise of my adolescent years, and amidst such scenes were many of my early works written.[68]

Lovecraft kept this up till the age of seventeen, when he realised "with horror" that he was growing too old for such an enterprise; he turned it over to a younger boy who lived across the lot from him.

The Providence Detective Agency was similarly revived in 1905 or thereabouts. In the *Rhode Island Journal of Astronomy* for May 7, 1905, appears this announcement: "The Providence Detective Agency has again opened for business. Rates etc. same as before. All civil or criminal cases quickly attended to. Low Prices. H. P. Lovecraft, C. P. Munroe, Detectives." Then, however, in the issue of May 21, 1905, there appear two *separate* ads, one for "H. P. Lovecraft, Priv. Detec., Formerly with the P.D.A.," and a similar one for Chester Munroe. Was there some sort of schism? If so, it does not appear to have been of long duration, for the very next issue (May 28, 1905) lists something called the "East Side Detective Agency / Organised—May 1905" ("Best on the East Side"); no names are mentioned, but surely Lovecraft and Munroe had teamed up again. An amusing announcement in the *Rhode Island Journal* for June 1906 states that the P.D.A. has resumed: "It is the same as before. Beware of imitators. Carter & Brady, Mgrs." Are these two new boys? Hardly: Lovecraft and Chester Munroe have clearly adopted as pseudonyms the names of two of the most illustrious of the dime-novel detectives, Nick Carter and Old King Brady. But, as with the rank imitators of the *Rhode Island Journal*, the P.D.A. apparently spawned its share of copycats; the July 1906 issue declares huffily that "a cheap agency is trying to compete with us. BEWARE!!!" As no more such notices appear, we can be confident that the temerity of these imitators was roundly upbraided.

The Blackstone Orchestra likewise resumed. the *Rhode Island Journal of As-*

tronomy for April 16, 1905, prints an ad listing H. P. Lovecraft and C. P. Munroe as the leaders ("Fine music cheap"). The ads continue to appear as late as October 1906. In January 1906 we learn of its "New Repertoire—Tenor & Baritone Solos" as well as "Phonograph Concerts." Can it be that Lovecraft was actually attempting to sing? It certainly seems that way; consider a letter of 1918:

> Something over a decade ago I conceived the idea of displacing Sig. Caruso as the world's greatest lyric vocalist, and accordingly inflicted some weird and wondrous ululations upon a perfectly innocent Edison blank. My mother actually liked the results—mothers are not always unbiased critics—but I saw to it that an accident soon removed the incriminating evidence. Later I tried something less ambitious; a simple, touching, plaintive, ballad sort of thing a la John McCormack. This was a better success, but reminded me so much of the wail of a dying fox-terrier that I very carelessly happened to drop it soon after it was made.[69]

Much as we might like to have such recordings—there is much doubt as to what Lovecraft's voice actually sounded like—it is clear that they do not survive. Since Lovecraft in a 1933 letter rattles off many of the hit songs of 1906—"When the Whippoorwill Sings, Marguerite," "When the Mocking-Bird Is Singing in the Wildwood," "I'll Be Waiting in the Gloaming, Genevieve," "In the Golden Autumn Time, My Sweet Elaine"—we can imagine that these were the songs he both performed in public and recorded on the phonograph. Indeed, he adds in this letter: ". . . weren't the Blackstone Military Band's voices changing? . . . From bad to worse, as an impartial outsider might have observed with uncharitable accuracy. But how we howled & bellowed those damned old barber-shop tunes!"[70]

This period was also the heyday of the Great Meadow Country Clubhouse. Lovecraft and his pals would ride on bicycles along the Taunton Pike (now State Road 44) to the rural village of Rehoboth, about eight miles from Providence just across the state line into Massachusetts. Here they found a small wooden hut with stone chimney and built an addition to it—"larger than the hut itself"[71]—where they could conduct whatever games they fancied. The hut and chimney had been built by an old Civil War veteran named James Kay, who probably also assisted them in building the addition.[72] When Lovecraft and Harold Munroe returned to this site in 1921, they found very little changed: "Tables stood about as of yore, pictures we knew still adorned the walls with unbroken glass. Not an inch of tar paper was ripped off, & in the cement hearth we found still embedded the small pebbles we stamped in when it was new & wet—pebbles arranged to form the initials G. M. C. C."[73] I saw those pebbles myself about twenty-five years ago, although on a more recent trip I found them almost entirely scattered. Now, of course, only the stone chimney remains, and even that is disintegrating. In its day it must have been a sight. Lovecraft dates this entire episode to the ages of about sixteen to eighteen and mentions Ronald Upham, Stuart Coleman, and Kenneth

Tanner as part of the gang along with the Munroes. One wonders how they stumbled upon Rehoboth as the locale of their adventures; perhaps one of the other boys had relations nearby.

Also at this time Lovecraft himself developed an interest in firearms. Recall that during the initial creation of the Providence Detective Agency he himself, unlike the other boys, sported a real revolver. Lovecraft evidently amassed a fairly impressive collection of rifles, revolvers, and other firearms: "After 1904 I had a long succession of 22-calibre rifles, & became a fair shot till my eyes played hell with my accuracy."[74] At this point Lovecraft seemed to lose interest, and ads like the following begin to appear in the *Rhode Island Journal:* "Wanted to Trade / Sharp 50-70 breech loading rifle carbine, new, for Astronomical goods" (May 7, 1905). A later issue (October 8, 1905) states that this rifle was originally purchased for $12.00 and is now going for $2.50. Also advertised for trade is a Stevens $5.00 Diamond Model .22 caliber target pistol, "only shot 2 or 3 times" (May 14, 1905). Even with Whipple Phillips's fortune gone, whatever Lovecraft wanted, he got.

Rifle-shooting was, however, the only sport that might remotely be said to have interested Lovecraft. Other team or individual sports he shunned with disdain as unfit for an intelligent person. Harold W. Munro (another high-school friend of Lovecraft's, not to be confused with Harold Bateman Munroe) recounts that he and Lovecraft had frequent arguments in high school over the merits of athletics: "On one occasion I confidently observed that athletics develop better bodies which in turn develop better brains. Without a moment of hesitation Howard beamingly cited one of Hope's foremost athletes whose classroom performances varied between disappointing and pathetic." One wonders whether this anecdote can be connected with another one told by Munro: "Henry G. Marsh, Hope quarterback and third baseman, lived opposite Howard on Angell Street. Buoyed by school spirit, Henry once ventured to sell Howard a ticket to a championship game. There were no recriminations but the venture fell very flat. Henry never tried again. Howard and athletics just did not mix."[75] This attitude persisted throughout Lovecraft's life: nothing would inspire his scorn or disgust more quickly than an offer to play cards or do crossword puzzles or watch a sporting event.

Interestingly, Lovecraft began to guide Chester and Harold Munroe into more academic interests, enlisting them as assistants and even colleagues in some of his own intellectual work. The *Rhode Island Journal* for March 1906 states that a meteorological sub-station has been opened by Harold at his home at 66 Patterson Street. Three months later we hear of the establishment of a Providence Astronomical Society. This society had apparently been formed as early as 1904, although there is no mention of it in earlier issues of the *Rhode Island Journal;* but consider the following notice (attached to the April 1907 issue and surely printed by Lovecraft):

PROV. ASTRONOMICAL SCY.

ESTAB. 1904 H. P. LOVECRAFT, PRES'T.

An organisation designed to encourage the study of the heavens. All persons interested in Astronomy should at once join, as this society affords valuable instruction and cooperation. All business transacted by mail, so those far from Providence may join. Persons unfamiliar with the science are taught. Members are required only to send in monthly reports. ALL FREE

Write for directions and membership certificate NOW
598, Angell St., Providence, R.I., U.S.A.

In June 1906 one of the Munroes is noted as assisting Lovecraft in giving a lecture on the sun at the East Side Historical Club by showing lantern slides. In the July 1906 issue we are told that the society is flourishing and gaining members, and all members are now urged to keep an astronomical and meteorological diary. More lectures were given on December 7, 1906, and January 4, 1907, the latter with 50 slides ("A large number attended"). I do not imagine that the East Side Historical Club was anything but a group of Lovecraft's high school friends; we shall see later that they continued to meet in this fashion for several years.

Rather different was the lecture Lovecraft gave to the Boys' Club of the First Baptist Church on January 25, 1907.[76] This was clearly a formal organisation, although I am not convinced that Lovecraft was a member: if the contretemps with his Sunday school class (for which see below) dates to 1902, it is not likely that he would have been invited back anytime soon. But the mere fact that he gave the lecture may indicate that he had achieved a certain celebrity as an astronomical authority; for he had already become widely published in the local papers by this time.

The death of Lovecraft's grandfather roughly coincided with the emergence of two new elderly male figures in his personal and intellectual life: his uncles, Dr Franklin Chase Clark (1847–1915) and Edward Francis Gamwell (1869–1936).

Lovecraft became acquainted with Gamwell in 1895, when the latter began courting his aunt Annie Emeline Phillips.[77] Edward and Annie married on January 3, 1897, with the six-year-old Lovecraft serving as usher.[78] Annie went to live with Edward in Cambridge, Massachusetts, where Edward was the city editor of the *Cambridge Chronicle* (1896–1901), then the *Cambridge Tribune* (1901–12), and then the *Boston Budget and Beacon* (1913–15).[79] It appears, however, that Annie and Edward visited Providence frequently, especially after the birth on April 23, 1898, of Phillips Gamwell, Lovecraft's only first cousin on the maternal side.

(A second child, Marion Roby Gamwell, lived for only five days in February 1900.) Lovecraft reports that his uncle Edward was one of his favourite subjects of mimicry when the latter would call on Annie at 454 Angell Street.[80] Gamwell taught Lovecraft to recite the Greek alphabet at the age of six, and Lovecraft even maintains that it was his uncle's extensive editorial capacities that incited him to start the *Rhode Island Journal of Astronomy*.[81]

Lovecraft was much closer to Dr Clark than to Gamwell, and indeed the former became after Whipple's death exactly the sort of father replacement Whipple himself had been. Franklin Chase Clark had received an A.B. from Brown University in 1869, as Edward F. Gamwell would in 1894, had attended Harvard Medical School in 1869–70 (where he is likely to have studied with Oliver Wendell Holmes), and had gone on to attain his M.D. at the College of Physicians and Surgeons in New York. He also obtained an M.A. from Columbia College.[82] He married Lillian Delora Phillips on April 10, 1902, presumably in Providence, as he was both residing and operating a medical practice at 80 Olney Street at the time. Lovecraft does not mention being involved with the wedding, but he probably served in some capacity. One imagines that Lillian left 454 Angell Street at that time and moved in with her husband. Kenneth W. Faig says of Clark: "He was a prolific writer on medicine, natural history, local history and genealogy and was elected a member of the Rhode Island Historical Society in 1905."[83]

In spite of Clark's scientific background, it was in the area of belles lettres that he exerted the greatest influence on the young Lovecraft. Clark had translated Homer, Virgil, Lucretius, and Statius into English verse (Lovecraft retained Clark's unpublished translations of the *Georgics* and *Aeneid* of Virgil to the end of his life,[84] but it is not clear what subsequently happened to them), and Lovecraft reports that he "did much to correct & purify my faulty style," specifically in verse but also in prose. He goes on to say: "I regarded, & still regard, his level as unattainable by myself; but I was so desirous of his approbation, that I would labour hours with my work to win a word of praise from his lips. I hung upon his conversation as Boswell hung upon Dr. Johnson's; yet was ever oppressed by a sense of hopeless inferiority."[85] We can perhaps see Clark's influence so early as the accomplished classical verses in *Poemata Minora, Volume II* (1902).

One hopes, however, that Clark did not have any influence on the only surviving poem by Lovecraft between *Poemata Minora* and the several poems written in 1912: "De Triumpho Naturae: The Triumph of Nature over Northern Ignorance" (July 1905). This poem, dedicated to William Benjamin Smith, author of *The Color Line: A Brief in Behalf of the Unborn* (1905), is the first explicitly racist document Lovecraft ever produced; but it was not to be the last. In twenty-four lines Lovecraft paraphrases several central arguments out of Smith's book: that the Civil War was a tragic mistake; that freeing blacks and granting them civil and political rights is folly; and that in so doing the abolitionists have actually ensured the extinction of the black race in America:

> The savage black, the ape-resembling beast,
> Hath held too long his Saturnalian feast.
> From out the land, by act of far'way Heav'n,
> To ling'ring death his numbers shall be driv'n.
> Against God's will the Yankee freed the slave
> And in the act consign'd him to the grave.

Let us ignore the highly disingenuous appeals to God, in whom Lovecraft had long ceased to believe. How does he imagine that "God's will" will ensure the destruction of blacks? The argument here expressed is a little cryptic, and in fact cannot be understood without recourse to Smith's book. Smith maintains that the inherent biological inferiority of blacks, their physiological and psychological weaknesses, will cause them to perish over time. Smith quotes at length a Professor W. B. Willcox who states:

> "The medical evidence available points to the conclusion that they are more than ever afflicted with the scourges of disease, such as typhoid fever and consumption, and with the physical ills entailed by sexual vice. I have argued elsewhere to show that both in the North and in the South crime among the Negroes is rapidly increasing. Whether the race as a whole is as happy, as joyous, as confident of the future, or thoughtless of it, as it was before the war, you, my hearers, know far better than I. I can only say that in my studies I have found not one expression of dissent from the opinion that the joyous buuyancy of the race is passing away; that they feel upon them a burden of responsibility to which they are unequal; that the lower classes of Negroes are resentful, and that the better classes [are] not certain or sanguine of the outcome. If this judgment be true, I can only say that it is perhaps the most fatal source of race as of national decay and death."[86]

This allows Smith to conclude, in a passage Lovecraft clearly copied in his poem:

> But what a weird light is now cast upon the War between the States, its cause, and its ultimate result! Aside from questions of political theory, the North sought to free to Negro, the South to hold him in bondage. As a slave he had led a protected, indeed a hothouse, existence and had flourished marvellously. His high-hearted champions shed torrents of blood and treasure to shatter the walls of his prison-house, to dispel the pent-up, stifling gloom of his dungeon, and to pour in upon him the free air and light of heaven. But the sum of liberty is no sooner arisen with burning breath than, lo! smitten by the breeze and the beam, he withers and dies![87]

All that can be said in defence of "De Triumpho Naturae" is that it is a little less virulent than Smith.

The whole issue of Lovecraft's racism is one I shall have to treat throughout this book; it is an issue that cannot be dodged, but it is also one that we must attempt to discuss—difficult as it may be—without yielding to emotionalism and by placing Lovecraft's views in the context of the prevailing intellectual currents of the time. It is not likely that at the age of fifteen Lovecraft had formulated clear views on the matter of race, and his attitudes were surely influenced by his environment and upbringing. Recall Winfield Scott Lovecraft's hallucinations regarding a "negro" who was molesting his wife; it is conceivable that he could have passed on his prejudice against blacks even to his two-year-old son. Lovecraft's most virulently prejudiced letters were written to his aunt Lillian in the 1920s, who in all likelihood shared his sentiments, as probably did most of the other members of his family.

Lovecraft himself supplies a highly illuminating account of his early views on the subject when he notes his reaction to entering Hope Street High School in 1904:

> But Hope Street is near enough to the "North End" to have a considerable *Jewish* attendance. It was there that I formed my ineradicable aversion to the Semitic race. The Jews were brilliant in their classes—calculatingly and schemingly brilliant—but their ideals were sordid and their manners coarse. I became rather well known as an anti-Semite before I had been at Hope Street many days.[88]

Lovecraft appears to make that last utterance with some pride. This whole passage is considerably embarrassing to those who wish to exculpate Lovecraft on the ground that he never took any direct actions against the racial or ethnic groups he despised but merely confined his remarks to paper. It is not clear, of course, exactly what he did to earn the reputation of an anti-Semite in high school, but clearly some sort of overt demonstration, if only verbal, is suggested.

Lovecraft's racism manifested itself in many different forms, but here I wish to consider specifically his prejudice against blacks. To the end of his life Lovecraft retained a belief in the *biological* (as opposed to the cultural) inferiority of blacks, and maintained that a strict colour line must be enforced in order to prevent miscegenation. This view began to emerge in the late eighteenth century—both Jefferson and Voltaire were convinced of the black's biological inferiority—and gained ground throughout the nineteenth century. Robert Chambers's *Vestiges of Creation* (1843), which Lovecraft had in his library, put forth a pre-Darwinian evolutionary hypothesis that maintained that the human race had passed through various stages, from the lowest (blacks) to the highest (Caucasians). In 1858 Abraham Lincoln stated that "there is a physical difference between the white and black races which I believe will for ever forbid the two races living together on terms of social and political equality." Theodore Roosevelt in a 1906 letter declared: "I entirely agree with you that as a race and in the mass they are altogether inferior to whites."

Henry James in 1907 referred to a "group of tatterdemalion darkies [who] lounged and sunned themselves within range."[89]

I do not cite these passages in extenuation of Lovecraft but to demonstrate how widely, in 1905, such views were prevalent even among the intellectual classes. New Englanders were particularly hostile to foreigners and blacks, for a variety of reasons, largely economic and social. The Immigration Restriction League was founded in Boston in 1894, and John Fiske—whose anthropological work Lovecraft later admired—was its first president. In Providence, as in most other large cities, there was a clearly defined "Negro" district; in Lovecraft's boyhood it was the area north of Olney Street. In a letter reminiscing about his boyhood he speaks of "the dark stretch of Cole's Woods to the north, with niggerville beyond, whence would troop [to Slater Avenue] Clarence Parnell & Asa Morse, & the ash-cart Brannons, & the white-trash Taylors whose father tended the furnace at Slater Ave. & East Manning St. schools . . ."[90]

The curious thing is that Lovecraft's offensive little poem was written at exactly the time when a new generation of African American intellectuals and political leaders was emerging to challenge these stereotypes of black inferiority. W. E. B. Du Bois's landmark collection of essays, *The Souls of Black Folk* (1903), made a sensation when it was published, although obviously not to Lovecraft. Paul Laurence Dunbar's poetry (*Lyrics of Lowly Life,* 1896) and novels (*The Sport of the Gods,* 1902) were winning high praise from William Dean Howells and other critics. African American writers would, of course, continue to work in obscurity until the 1920s and the heyday of the Harlem Renaissance, when Zora Neale Hurston, Claude McKay, Jean Toomer, and Langston Hughes would make their mark. Lovecraft never read any of this literature, even though he was in New York at the height of this movement.

What he did read, naturally, was the racist white literature of the time, whether it be Southern nostalgia writers as Thomas Nelson Page (who propagated the view, shared by Lovecraft and William Benjamin Smith, of the black slave's "idyllic" life on the plantation), actual negrophobes such as Thomas Dixon, Jr, or writers like Frank Norris and Jack London who axiomatically accepted the inferiority of "primitive" peoples and the moral rightness of whites to dominate them. Lovecraft later admitted to having read both the novel (*The Clansman,* 1905) and the play (*The Clansman: An American Drama,* 1905) by Dixon on which *The Birth of a Nation* was based,[91] and he may have read them when they first appeared. Dixon's *The Leopard's Spots* (1902), another viciously anti-black novel, was in his library. Lovecraft's sympathy for the Southern cause in the Civil War was of very long standing and would persist throughout his life. He states that he and Harold Munroe were "Confederates in sympathy, & used to act out all the battles of the War in Blackstone Park."[92] As early as 1902 he wrote a brief poem in defence of the Confederacy—"C. S. A. 1861–1865: To the Starry Cross of the SOUTH"—and placed it on the desk of Abbie A. Hathaway of the Slater Avenue School, whose father had fought in the Union army.[93]

The scientific refutation of racism was only beginning at the turn of the century, led by the pioneering work of Franz Boas (1858–1942) and others under his direction. If it is excusable for a fifteen-year-old not to have paid much attention to this work in 1905, it would be much less excusable for a forty-year-old not to have done so in 1930; it is exactly here, as I shall discuss later, that Lovecraft deserves censure.

"De Triumpho Naturae" appears to be an isolated example of this ugly strain in Lovecraft's early thought and writing; in other regards he continued to pursue abstract intellectual endeavour. A more significant literary product of 1905—one for which Franklin Chase Clark probably provided impetus and guidance—was *A Manual of Roman Antiquities.* This was first announced, under the title *A Handbook of Roman Antiquities,* as "Soon to Appear" in the *Rhode Island Journal of Astronomy* for July 30, 1905. Here is the description:

> A handbook of Roman Antiquities by H. P. Lovecraft. To which is added, the biographies of certain great Romans, including Romulus, L. Tarquinius, L. Quntius [*sic*] Cincinnatus, M. Tullius Cicero, C. Iulius Caesar, C. Octavius, M. Ulpius Trajanus, T. Flavius Sabinus Vespasianus, Flav. Anicius Justinianus, and many others, extending from A.V.C. 1 to 1353 (B.C. 753 to A.D. 600). price 50 cts.

The *Rhode Island Journal* for August 13, 1905, declares that the volume is now ready and that "The work will be issued on the hecto. by subscription." Regrettably, the "Lives of Great Romans" was not able to be included, but instead there is other, unspecified matter "invaluable to small students of Roman History or Literature." At 50¢ this was very likely the most substantial—at least the lengthiest—single work Lovecraft had produced up to this time; it is unfortunate that it does not survive. The proposed list of biographies is a good selection of celebrated figures from the Republic as well as some of the leading emperors. Lovecraft no doubt delighted in using Roman years (A.V.C. = "Ab Urbe Condita," from the founding of the city) rather than the parvenu calendar imposed by the Christians.

This work very likely gave Lovecraft much-needed practice in sustained prose composition; certainly his prose needed work, if "The Mysterious Ship" was the best he could do in 1902. I am not sure that Clark was much inclined toward the weird tale, but if he did nothing more than to urge Lovecraft to read fewer dime novels and read more standard literature, it would have been a benefit. Something remarkable certainly seems to have happened in the three years subsequent to the writing of "The Mysterious Ship," and it is highly unfortunate that we have no tales from this period, including those stories written under the influence of Verne, which probably date to this time. In any event, we find ourselves wholly unprepared for the surprising competence and maturity of the tale entitled "The Beast in the Cave."

The first draft of this tale was written prior to the move from 454 Angell Street in the spring of 1904,[94] and the finished version dates to April 21, 1905. Lovecraft reports having spent "days of boning at the library"[95] (i.e., the Providence Public Library) in researching the locale of the tale, Mammoth Cave in Kentucky. It would take Lovecraft quite some time to learn the wisdom of basing a tale's locale on first-hand, rather than second-hand, information.

"The Beast in the Cave" deals with a man who is slowly facing the realisation that he is lost in Mammoth Cave and may never be found. He wavers between resignation at his fate and a desire for self-preservation; but when he begins shouting to call attention to himself, he summons not the guide who had led his tour group but an anomalous, shambling beast whom he cannot see in the blackness of the cave but can only hear. In attempting to protect himself from the creature he hurls rocks at it, and appears to have fatally injured it. Fleeing from the scene, he comes upon the guide and leads him back to the site of his encounter with the beast. The "beast" turns out to be a man who has been lost in the cave for years.

The tale is admirably well-told and suspenseful, although not many will have failed to guess the conclusion before it is hyperbolically announced ("The creature I had killed, the strange beast of the unfathomed cave was, or had at one time been, a **MAN**!!!"). What is most interesting about the tale is its detailed portrayal of the narrator-protagonist, who in the first person recounts his fluctuating mental state as he experiences the anomalous phenomena. At the outset he—like Lovecraft—maintains that, in spite of his dire condition, and because he is "indoctrinated . . . by a life of philosophical study," "I derived no small measure of satisfaction from my unimpassioned demeanour." And yet, this phlegmatic exterior gives way as the darkness of the cave, and the creature's propinquity, begin to oppress him: "My disordered fancy conjured up hideous and fearsome shapes from the sinister darkness that surrounded me, and that actually seemed to *press* upon my body." Later he confesses that "groundless, superstitious fear had entered my brain." Like many of Lovecraft's later protagonists, outward rationalism collapses in the face of the unknown.

The climax of the tale is deftly foretold in the fourth paragraph, well before he has encountered the "beast":

> I remembered the accounts which I had heard of the colony of consumptives, who, taking their residence in this gigantic grotto to find health from the apparently salubrious air of the underground world, with its steady, uniform temperature, pure air, and peaceful quiet, had found, instead, death in strange and ghastly form. I had seen the sad remains of their ill-made cottages as I passed them by with the party, and had wondered what unnatural influence a long sojourn in this immense and silent cavern would exert upon one as healthy and as vigorous as I.

This sort of foreshadowing would become very common in Lovecraft's later tales, where the conclusion is virtually announced at the outset and the principal element of suspense comes to reside in seeing how exactly that conclusion is to be reached. In the present instance, however, this foreshadowing serves to establish a queer bond between the narrator and the "beast" that other aspects of the tale are seeking to repudiate. The very title of the story suggests that the victim has renounced his humanity by virtue of his isolated condition, and the tale continually refers to him as a "wild beast," "animal," "creature," and at one point even a *"thing."* And yet, the narrator is aware of anomalies. "Certainly, the conduct of the creature was exceedingly strange," for the entity sometimes walks on two feet, sometimes on four. When the figure is dimly seen, the narrator takes it for "an anthropoid ape of large proportions"; but closer examination reveals physiological peculiarities that no normal ape could possibly bear. In effect, the tale suggests that the narrator himself, although "healthy and vigorous," might have been reduced to the "beast's" status if he had not been rescued; indeed, when he is rescued, he begins "gibbering" as if he were an animal himself.

In spite of Lovecraft's later dismissal of it as "ineffably pompous and Johnsonese,"[96] "The Beast in the Cave" is a remarkable story for a fourteen-year-old and represents a quantum leap over the crudeness of "The Mysterious Ship." Lovecraft is right to declare that in it "I first wrote a story worth reading."[97] I do not know if any significant literary influence can be adduced. Perhaps we can think of this tale as a sort of mirror-image of Poe's "The Murders in the Rue Morgue": in that story what are taken to be the actions of a man turn out to have been performed by an ape, whereas here what is initially taken for an ape proves to be a man. I do not wish to belabour this point, but I must again note that this tale is also not supernatural. The style is indeed very antiquated, especially for a tale that appears to be set in the present day, and is also a trifle overwrought ("That nevermore should I behold the blessed light of day, or scan the pleasant hills and dales of the beautiful world outside, my reason could no longer entertain the slightest unbelief"). "The Beast in the Cave" is, however, the first tale of Lovecraft's that actually bears a recognisable resemblance to his later work; he had found his idiom, and it would now only be a matter of refining it.

"The Alchemist" (1908) is still more of an advance in style and technique. Antoine, last of the Comtes de C——, tells the tale of his life and ancestry. This ancient aristocratic line has occupied a lofty castle in France surrounded by a dense forest; but a deadly curse seems to weigh upon it. Antoine finally learns the apparent cause when he comes of age and reads a paper handed down through the generations. In the thirteenth century an ancient man, Michel ("usually designated by the surname of Mauvais, the Evil, on account of his sinister reputation"), dwelt on the estate together with his son Charles, nicknamed Le Sorcier. These two practised the black arts, and it was rumoured that they were seeking the elixir of life. Many disappearances of children were attributed to them. When Godfrey, the young son of Henri the Comte, is missing, Henri accosts Michel and kills him in a rage; just then Godfrey is found, and Charles, who learns of the deed, pronounces a curse:

> May ne'er a noble of thy murd'rous line
> Survive to reach a greater age than thine!

He thrusts a vial in the face of Henri, who dies instantly. From that time on no comte of the line lives beyond the age of thirty-two, the age of Henri when he died. This curse continues for hundreds of years, and Antoine has no recourse but to believe that he will suffer a similar fate. Wandering alone over his deserted and cobweb-festooned castle, he comes upon a hidden cellar and encounters a hideous-looking man "clad in a skull-cap and long mediaeval tunic of dark colour." This man tells of how Charles Le Sorcier killed Henri and also Godfrey when the latter reached Henri's age; but Antoine wonders how the curse could have been continued thereafter, "when Charles Le Sorcier must in the course of Nature have died." As the man attacks Antoine, the latter hurls a torch at him, setting him afire. Just before he expires, however, he reveals the truth:

> "Fool," he shrieked, "can you not guess my secret? Have you no brain whereby you may recognise the will which has through six centuries fulfilled the dreadful curse upon your house? Have I not told you of the great elixir of eternal life? Know you not how the secret of Alchemy was solved? I tell you, it is I! I! *I! that have lived for six hundred years to maintain my revenge,* FOR I AM CHARLES LE SORCIER!"

This conclusion, too, will not be a surprise to any attentive reader, for again Lovecraft has anticipated it well in advance. The remarkable thing about "The Alchemist," however, is its atmosphere. If the murder of Michel Mauvais occurred in the thirteenth century and Charles Le Sorcier has lived for six hundred years, then the tale must actually have been set in the nineteenth century; and it is one of Lovecraft's minor triumphs to have created a convincing aura of mediaeval antiquity in this tale. The narrator at one point even remarks that "Isolated as I was, modern science made no impression upon me, and I laboured as in the Middle Ages."

As with "The Beast in the Cave," the narrator's emotions are really at the heart of the tale. This tale, much more than its predecessor, betrays the influence of Poe in the narrator's obsessive interest in his own psychological state; indeed, many details in the story make us think of Lovecraft's remark that he himself "felt a kinship to Poe's gloomy heroes with their broken fortunes." Antoine is of a lofty and ancient line; but "poverty but little above the level of dire want, together with a pride of name that forbids its alleviation by the pursuits of commercial life, have prevented the scions of our line from maintaining their estates in pristine splendour." As a result, Antoine—an only child—spends his years alone, "poring over the ancient tomes that filled the shadow-haunted library of the chateau, and in roaming without aim or purpose through the perpetual dusk of the spectral wood"; he is kept away from the "peasant children" who dwell nearby. All this can be seen as a deliberately distorted, but still recognisable, reflexion of Lovecraft's own childhood and upbringing.

"The Alchemist" is, at last, the first extant tale by Lovecraft to be avowedly supernatural. And yet, even here the supernaturalism is manifested from a somewhat unexpected direction. All along we have been led to believe that the supernatural element of the tale is the curse that causes the Comtes to die around the age of thirty-two; but in fact these deaths are now seen to be mere murders. It is the murderer, Charles Le Sorcier, who is the supernatural component, for it is he who has unnaturally prolonged his life through sorcery and "will" so as to exact revenge for his father's death. The conclusion of the story reveals that Lovecraft is still overly given to histrionics; he would, in fact, find it one of the hardest faults to correct in his entire career.

The last page of the autograph manuscript of "The Beast in the Cave" bears the following notation:

Tales of Terror
I. The Beast in the Cave
By H. P. Lovecraft
(Period—Modern)

It is interesting to note that Lovecraft was already at this time thinking of assembling a collection of his tales; we do not know what other tales, if any, were to make up the volume. The autograph manuscript of "The Alchemist" does not survive, so we do not know whether it formed part of this volume. It may well have, for if "The Beast in the Cave" is a "modern" story, then "The Alchemist" could have formed part of a putative subsection of "ancient" tales, even though, as I have noted, the central action of the story occurs in the nineteenth century.

It is, however, highly significant that, so far as we can tell, "The Beast in the Cave" is the first work for which Lovecraft did not undertake the elaborate "publishing" procedures which we have seen for all his other juvenilia: there is no price affixed, no invented imprint, and no attached catalogue of works. This story becomes, therefore, the first exemplar of that abstract and disinterested self-expression which was to become the pillar of Lovecraft's later aesthetic theory.

We have only hints of what further tales Lovecraft wrote in the next three years, for he declares that in 1908 he destroyed all but two of the stories he had been writing over the past five years.[98] Late in life Lovecraft discovered a composition book bearing the title of one lost story dating to 1905: "Gone—But Whither?" He remarks wryly: "I'll bet it was a hell-raiser! The title expresses the fate of the tale itself."[99] Then there was something called "The Picture" (1907), which in his Commonplace Book he describes as concerning a "painting of ultimate horror". Elsewhere he says of it:

> I had a man in a Paris garret paint a mysterious canvas embodying the quintessential essence of all horror. He is found clawed & mangled one morning before his easel. The picture is destroyed, as in a titanic struggle—but in one corner of the frame a bit of canvas remains . . . & on it the coroner finds to his horror the painted counterpart of the sort of claw which evidently killed the artist.[100]

Perhaps one can dimly infer the influence of Poe's "The Oval Portrait," in which a painter, in painting a portrait of his wife, insidiously sucks the life out of the woman and transfers it into the portrait.

For one other tale we know its subject but not its title. "The idea of a Roman settlement in America is something which occurred to me years ago—in fact, I began a story with that theme (only it was about Central America & not U.S.) in 1906 or 1907, tho' I never finish'd it."[101] This story would have been fascinating, for it combined two of the traits that he claimed to make up the core of his personality—love of the ancient and love of the weird. Actually, it is not likely to have been supernatural, hence would probably not—even if finished—have formed part of the contents of the prospective *Tales of Terror* volume. It seems instead to have been an historical fantasy about a voyage by a Roman trireme across the Atlantic to South America and encounters between the Romans and the Mayans of the region. No doubt Lovecraft was already fascinated by the mystery-shrouded ancient civilisations of central and south America, as he would be for the rest of his life.

By 1908, the time of the fourth "near-breakdown" of his young life, Lovecraft had decided that he was not a fiction-writer and resolved instead to devote himself to science and belles-lettres. At that time, in spite of the promise shown by "The Beast in the Cave" and "The Alchemist," his decision would not have been entirely unwarranted. It is not likely that either of his surviving tales—or any others, for that matter—were actually submitted to magazines or book publishers; if they had been, they would probably have been rejected, largely on account of their antiquated style. But Lovecraft had by this time already amassed an impressive record of publications on science, and it would have been a reasonable conjecture that he would have continued to pursue such a course to become a professional writer in this field.

Lovecraft first broke into true print with a letter (dated May 27, 1906) printed in the *Providence Sunday Journal* for June 3. This letter, titled (surely by the editor) "No Transit of Mars," points out an elementary fallacy—there can be no transit of Mars over the sun, since Mars is outside the earth's orbit—in a letter to the editor published on May 27. The letter in question was by an astrologer, one Thomas Hines, Jr, of Central Falls, R.I., and bears the title "Hard Times Coming"; his remark was: "According to the transit of Mars and Saturn, I judge that Providence and Boston will suffer from great fires this summer."[102] Hines went on to predict such things as the deaths of Pope Pius X (d. 1914) and the Czar Nicholas II of Russia (d. 1918) and earthquakes in New England. This was too much for Lovecraft to bear, and he prefaces his factual correction with the scornful: "Passing over the fact that astrology is but a pseudo-science, not entitled to intelligent consideration . . ."

On July 16, 1906, Lovecraft wrote a letter to the *Scientific American* on the subject of finding planets in the solar system beyond Neptune. Much to his delight, it was published in the issue of August 25, 1906, under the title "Trans-Neptunian Planets." This letter does not seem to have been written in response to any article in the *Scientific American,* but merely proposes that the observatories of the world team up to locate planets of the solar system beyond Neptune, as had been suspected by many astronomers; if they "band together and minutely photograph the ecliptic, as is done in asteroid hunting, the bodies might be revealed on their plates." Curiously, Lovecraft discounts the possibility that mathematical calculations alone could locate such planets, even though it was in fact such calculations that largely impelled the discovery of Pluto in 1930.

Lovecraft was not finished with his letter campaign in the cause of science. The *Providence Sunday Journal* for August 12, 1906, published, under the title "The Earth Not Hollow," a letter he had written six days earlier concerning the hollow-earth theory as advanced in a book, William Reed's *The Phantom of the Poles* (1906), that had served as the basis of an article in the *Journal* for August 5. Lovecraft systematically destroys the arguments for the theory as expressed in the book (or, rather, in the article, as he admits not having read the book itself): the compression of the earth is not due to apertures at the poles but the centrifugal force; the Auroras are not burning volcanoes; there are no "open Polar seas," as whatever land masses are around both poles appear to be bound by frozen seas; surface gravity of the earth is not greater at the poles but at the equator; and so on.

This letter, which appears to have been printed complete, is considerably longer than the previous two (which may or may not have been abridged), being nine full paragraphs and totalling about 500 words. There could well be more such letters in the *Journal* and elsewhere, as I discovered "The Earth Not Hollow" by accident while looking for something else.

Around this time, however, Lovecraft simultaneously began to write two astronomy columns for local papers, the *Pawtuxet Valley Gleaner* and the *Providence Tribune* (morning, evening, and Sunday editions). The *Gleaner* articles begin on July 27, 1906, and after a hiatus of a month progress weekly until the end of the year. The *Tribune* articles commence on August 1, 1906, and proceed monthly until June 1, 1908.

The *Pawtuxet Valley Gleaner* was a weekly based in Phenix, R.I., a community now incorporated into the city of West Warwick, well to the west and south of Providence. The paper had been started in 1876 by John H. Campbell and Reuben Capron; sometime thereafter Campbell became sole proprietor, being both the editor and publisher.[103] Lovecraft described it as a "country paper" and stated that the Phillipses had taken the paper when they were at Greene.[104] Elsewhere he elaborated:

> This rural paper was the oracle of that section of the country from which my mother's family had originally come, & was taken for old times' sake in our household. The name "Phillips" is a magic word in Western Rhode Island, & the *Gleaner* was more than willing to print & feature anything from Whipple V. Phillips' grandson. Only the failure of the *Gleaner* put an end to my activity in its columns.[105]

This raises the question of just how long Lovecraft contributed to the paper. In this letter he maintains that "During 1906, 1907, & 1908 I flooded the *Pawtuxet Valley Gleaner* with my prose articles"; but no issues subsequent to December 28, 1906, seem to survive. There was a competing paper by this time, the *Pawtuxet Valley Daily Times,* and various notices in that paper suggest that the *Gleaner* did in fact continue publication through at least 1907. Since Lovecraft wrote the above remark in 1916 and was therefore writing of events that had occurred less than a decade previously, one must accept his statement that the paper continued into 1908 and that he contributed to it until the end.

Given that Lovecraft was still producing the *Rhode Island Journal of Astronomy* at the time, it was natural that he would draw from that hectographed monthly for the articles in the *Gleaner.* In one remarkable instance—"Is There Life on the Moon?" (*Gleaner,* September 14, 1906)—he reached back a year to a series of that title published in the *Rhode Island Journal* for September 3, 10, and 17, 1905. "Can the Moon Be Reached by Man?" (*Gleaner,* October 12, 1906) had appeared in the *Rhode Island Journal* as a series from April to July 1906. "The Moon" (*Gleaner,* October 19, 1906), the longest of the *Gleaner* articles, was a serial that started in the *Rhode Island Journal* in August 1906 and was not finished there until January 1907. A note in the October 1906 issue states that the entire serial "can be had complete in book form, bound in pasteboard for 50¢," which shows that it was already finished at that time.

The *Gleaner* articles do more than merely provide information on the astronomical phenomena for the month; they are among the first of several attempts by Lovecraft over the years to educate the public on the fundamentals of astronomy. In the present instance, Lovecraft chose provocative queries about Mars, the moon, and the solar system which he believed (probably rightly) the public would find stimulating. He tentatively endorsed as "not only possible, but even probable" Percival Lowell's belief that the Martian canals have been made artificially and are for purposes of irrigation; returning to the question of lunar canals, he now accepted Pickering's theory that they are deep furrows full of hoar frost; he discounted the theory of Vulcan (a supposed intra-Mercurial planet)[106] but reiterated his *Scientific American* letter in stating that trans-Neptunian planets ought to be sought by means of celestial photography. On the critical question of "Can the Moon Be Reached by Man?," Lovecraft maintained that all other difficulties—lack of air, absence of gravity, extreme cold—could all be overcome; the big sticking point was "motive power," i.e., getting a satellite off the earth. He considered three possibilities:

> (a) To fire an inhabited projectile from an immense cannon.
> (b) To interpose between the earth and the selected vehicle a screen, consisting of some material impervious to gravity.
> (c) To send off a projectile by electrical repulsion.

Of these, Lovecraft believed the third the most likely; but he doubted whether such a journey would occur "within the lifetime of anyone who now reads these pages."

The articles for the *Providence Tribune* tend to be less interesting only because they rather mechanically deal with the purportedly noteworthy celestial phenomena of each month, becoming somewhat repetitive in the process. They are distinguished, however, for the fact that they constitute one of the few occasions when illustrations by Lovecraft were published: of the twenty articles, sixteen were accompanied by hand-drawn star charts; in one anomalous instance (the *Evening Tribune* for March 3, 1908), only the illustration, not the article, was published (the article and the illustration appeared in the *Morning Tribune* the previous day).

Lovecraft stated that it was one of these articles that almost caused great awkwardness on one occasion—the occasion in 1907 when he was introduced by Winslow Upton to Percival Lowell when the astronomer was lecturing at Sayles Hall at Brown University. Lovecraft goes on:

> With the egotism of my 17 years, I feared that Lowell had read what I had written! I tried to be as non-committal as possible in speaking, and fortunately discovered that the eminent observer was more disposed to ask me about my telescope, studies, etc., than to discuss Mars. Prof. Upton soon led him away to the platform, and I congratulated myself that a disaster had been averted![107]

There are several troubling features in this seemingly innocuous account. First, there is no mention of Lowell's speculations on the canals or possible inhabitants of Mars in the *Tribune* articles; secondly, although Lovecraft in this letter declares that "I never had, have not, and never will have the slightest belief in Lowell's speculations," we have just seen that he had explicitly approved them as "probable" in a *Pawtuxet Valley Gleaner* article. One wonders, then, about the exact nature of Lovecraft's meeting with Lowell.

My feeling is that a purchase Lovecraft made at this time with his own money—a rebuilt 1906 Remington typewriter[108]—was connected with these published astronomy articles. The typewriter was not used not for preparing his hectographed scientific journals (for they remain handwritten to the very end) nor even, apparently, the fiction he was writing (no typescripts from this period survive), so that the preparation of the astronomy columns—the only things he was submitting to a publisher at this time—would be the only logical purpose for securing a typewriter. It was the only typewriter Lovecraft would ever own in his life.

Lovecraft also stated that he wrote a lengthy treatise, *A Brief Course in Astronomy—Descriptive, Practical, and Observational; for Beginners and General Readers,* in 1906: "it got as far as the typed and hand-illustrated stage (circa one hundred fifty pages), though no copy survives."[109] Not only does no copy survive, but there does not appear to be any mention of it in any issues of the *Rhode Island Journal* for 1906 or 1907. This strikes me as very odd. In a 1918 letter Lovecraft said that in 1906 "I set about writing a book—a complete treatise on astronomy,"[110] but does not explicitly say that he finished it; one must assume, however, that he did. Only one part of this work—clearly the most substantial scientific work he had ever written or ever would write—is extant: a separate treatise titled "Celestial Objects for All," whose preface declares that "The greater part of this work is also printed in 'A Brief Course in Astronomy' by the same author."

The quotation from "A Confession of Unfaith" with which I opened this chapter suggests how radically the study of astronomy affected Lovecraft's entire philosophical conception of the universe. Indeed, it is around the period of 1906 that we can definitively date his philosophical awakening. Previous to that there had only been his various conflicts with church authorities in Sunday school. His first attendance, if it truly dates to the age of five or seven, saw him taking sides with the Romans against the Christians, but only because of his fondness for Roman history and culture and not out of any specifically anticlerical bias. By the age of nine, as he declares, he was conducting a sort of experimental course in comparative religion, pretending to believe in various faiths to see whether they convinced him; evidently none did. This led to his final Sunday school encounter:

> How well I recall my tilts with Sunday-School teachers during my last period of compulsory attendance! I was 12 years of age, and the despair of the institution. None of the answers of my pious preceptors would satisfy me, and my demands that they cease taking things for granted quite upset them. Close reasoning was something new in their little world of Semitic mythology. At last I saw that they were hopelessly bound to unfounded dogmata and traditions, and thenceforward

> ceased to treat them seriously. Sunday-School became to me simply a place wherein to have a little harmless fun spoofing the pious mossbacks. My mother observed this, and no longer sought to enforce my attendance.[111]

I would give much to have been able to attend one of these sessions. They presumably occurred at the First Baptist Church, where his mother was still on the rolls. It is not clear to me why she insisted on his attendance after a presumable lapse of years and after the previous episode was such a signal failure; perhaps she was becoming concerned about his isolation—no doubt he was already deep in astronomy at this time—and perhaps she even found his atheism and scepticism, which he is likely to have voiced openly, dismaying.

But years of astronomical study triggered the "cosmicism" that would form so central a pillar of both his philosophical and aesthetic thought:

> By my thirteenth birthday I was thoroughly impressed with man's impermanence and insignificance, and by my seventeenth, about which time I did some particularly detailed writing on the subject, I had formed in all essential particulars my present pessimistic cosmic views. The futility of all existence began to impress and oppress me; and my references to human progress, formerly hopeful, began to decline in enthusiasm. ("A Confession of Unfaith")

There is no explicit account here of *why* Lovecraft developed these "pessimistic cosmic views" from the study of astronomy; a later remark in this essay—"My attitude has always been cosmic, and I looked on man as if from another planet. He was merely an interesting species presented for study and classification"—is suggestive, but no more. Having sloughed off any belief in deity as scientifically unjustified (recall his later statement that "A mere knowledge of the approximate dimensions of the visible universe is enough to destroy forever the notion of a personal godhead whose whole care is expended upon puny mankind"[112]), Lovecraft was left with the awareness that mankind was (probably) alone in the universe—at least, we have no way to establish contact with extraterrestrial races—and that the *quantitative* insignificance of the planet and all its inhabitants, both spatially and temporally, carried with it the corollary of a *qualitative* insignificance. I shall have more to say about the validity of this view, but it is best to wait until it is more fully developed in Lovecraft's mind.

A rather remarkable consequence of Lovecraft's philosophical interests was a reformist instinct that led him to attempt to educate the masses—or, at least, one member of them:

> I came across a superficially bright Swedish boy in the Public Library—he worked in the "stack" where the books are kept—and invited him to the house to broaden his mentality (I was fifteen and he was about the same, though he was smaller and seemed younger.) I thought I had uncovered a mute inglorious Milton (he pro-

> fessed a great interest in my work), and despite maternal protest entertained him frequently in my library. I believed in equality then, and reproved him when he called my mother "Ma'am"—I said that a future scientist should not talk like a servant! But ere long he uncovered qualities which did not appeal to me, and I was forced to abandon him to his plebeian fate.[113]

This account is full of interest. We know who this boy was: he was Arthur Fredlund, who lived at 1048 Eddy Street on the West Side of Providence, just across the Providence River. The degree to which Lovecraft took Fredlund under his wing is suggested by an ad that appears in the back cover of the *Rhode Island Journal of Astronomy* for September 1906: this declares that Fredlund has (no doubt with Lovecraft's aid) revived and become the editor of the *Scientific Gazette,* which had been defunct since September 1905. That Lovecraft would have allowed Fredlund to take over the earliest of his scientific periodicals must have meant that he saw great things in the boy. What "qualities" he revealed that did not appeal to Lovecraft we do not know, as there is no other account of this incident.

The fact that Lovecraft's mother objected to Fredlund's coming to their house—whereas she presumably did not object to other of Lovecraft's friends, as Stuart Coleman's lack of any mention of "maternal objections" to his coming over implies—seems indicative of Susie's social snobbery. Lovecraft, of course, as a member of the Providence Yankee aristocracy, was not devoid of class consciousness himself, as his reference to the "white-trash Taylors" who attended Slater Avenue reveals. Throughout his life he believed alternately, and sometimes simultaneously, in an aristocracy of class and breeding and an aristocracy of intellect; very gradually the latter took over more and more, but he never renounced the former. At this time we can see how scientific enthusiasm and the pleasure of having a disciple who "professed a great interest" in his work caused his intellectual aristocracy to come to the fore; perhaps, indeed, the "qualities" that revealed Fredlund to be a "plebeian" made Lovecraft believe that the aristocracy of breeding was not wholly to be despised.

In 1908 Lovecraft stood at the threshold of adulthood: he was doing reasonably well at Hope Street High School, he had become prodigiously learned in chemistry, geography, astronomy, and meteorology, and he was accomplished in belles lettres as a Latinist, poet, and fiction writer. He seemed destined for a career as an academician of some sort; perhaps he would be a sort of transatlantic version of those later Oxford dons who wrote detective stories, teaching astronomy at a university while writing horror tales in his spare time. In any event, the future for so precocious and accomplished a young man seemed assured.

What derailed that future—and what ensured that Lovecraft would never lead a "normal" life—was his fourth "near-breakdown," clearly the most serious of his life. In some ways he never recovered from it.

5. Barbarian and Alien (1908–1914)

Lovecraft is very reticent about the causes or sources of what we can only regard as a full-fledged nervous breakdown in the summer of 1908. Beyond the mere fact of its occurrence, we know little. Consider four statements, made from 1915 to 1935:

> In 1908 I should have entered Brown University, but the broken state of my health rendered the idea absurd. I was and am a prey to intense headaches, insomnia, and general nervous weakness which prevents my continuous application to any thing.[1]

> In 1908 I was about to enter Brown University, when my health completely gave way—causing the necessary abandonment of my college career.[2]

> . . . after all, high-school was a mistake. I liked it, but the strain was too keen for my health, and I suffered a nervous collapse in 1908 immediately after graduating, which prevented altogether my attending college.[3]

> My health did not permit me to go to the university—indeed, the steady application to high-school gave me a sort of breakdown.[4]

In the first, second, and fourth of these statements Lovecraft is a little disingenuous, even tendentious: he implies that his entry into Brown University was a matter of course, but in fact he *never* graduated from high school, and certainly would have required at least another year of schooling before he could have done so. The third statement, which states that he actually did graduate, is one of the few instances I have found where Lovecraft plainly lies about himself.

Since we are generally left in the dark about the nature of this breakdown, we can work only on conjecture. We have two pieces of external evidence. One comes from Harry Brobst, who spoke to a woman who had gone to high school with Lovecraft: "She . . . described these terrible tics that he had—he'd be sitting in his seat and he'd suddenly up and jump—I think they referred to them as seizures. The family took him out of high school, and then whatever education he got presumably was done by private tutors, whatever that meant. She said, oh, yes, she remembered him. I guess he scared the student body half to death."[5] This certainly is a remarkable account, and it suggests that Lovecraft's chorea minor (if indeed he was afflicted with that disease) had not entirely worn off even by this time. Brobst, a Ph.D. in psychology who was trained as a psychiatric nurse, considers the possibility of "chorea-like symptoms" and also conjectures that a hysteroid seizure—a purely psychological ailment without any organic basis—may have been involved. Whether these seizures were the actual cause of his removal from high school is something that cannot now be settled.

The other piece of evidence comes from Harold W. Munro, who writes of an accident suffered by Lovecraft:

> . . . a new house was going up, which of course intrigued the youth of the neighborhood, especially after the carpenters had left for the day. There were many inspections and generous samplings from open kegs of nails. Ladders were still the only means of going up or down. The more challenging upper floors were the favourites. The mystery of it also appealed to little Howard, who never ran with the pack but waited until near darkness when the field was clear for his solo visitations. Then came news that a boy, the Lovecraft boy, had fallen (nobody ever knew how far) and landed on his head. As excitement of the fall was subsiding, word followed that day and night the injured head was kept "packed in ice."[6]

Munro does not date this incident (which he himself did not see but only heard about from a girl "a little younger than Howard" who later became Munro's wife), but he tells it directly after writing: "Lovecraft did not graduate from Hope Street or anywhere else. He wanted credits to enter Brown University but long before the rest of us graduated failing health had compelled him to drop out." Munro, therefore, implicitly links this incident with his withdrawal from high school.

Lovecraft's breakdown—whether purely mental or nervous or a combination of mental and physical factors—was, clearly, something related to his schoolwork, the same sort of thing that may have caused his milder breakdown of 1906; and yet, even "steady application" in only three classes (all he was taking in his third year at Hope Street) would not seem sufficient to induce so severe a collapse. Note, however, what three courses he was taking: chemistry, physics, and algebra. He was receiving the highest marks in the first two; in algebra he was repeating a part of the course he had taken the previous year. My feeling, therefore, is that Lovecraft's relative failure to master algebra made him gradually awaken to the realisation that he could never do serious professional work in either chemistry or astronomy, and that therefore a career in these two fields was an impossibility. This would have been a shattering conception, requiring a complete revaluation of his career goals. Consider this remark, made in 1931:

> In studies I was not bad—except for mathematics, which repelled and exhausted me. I passed in these subjects—but just about that. Or rather, it was *algebra* which formed the bugbear. Geometry was not so bad. But the whole thing disappointed me bitterly, for I was then intending to pursue *astronomy* as a career, and of course advanced astronomy is simply a mass of mathematics. That was the first major setback I ever received—the first time I was ever brought up short against a con-

> sciousness of my own limitations. It was clear to me that I hadn't brains enough to be an astronomer—and that was a pill I couldn't swallow with equanimity.[7]

Again, Lovecraft does not connect this with his breakdown of 1908, but I think the implication of a connexion is strong. I repeat that this is a conjecture, but until further evidence is forthcoming, it may be the best we have.

One more small piece of evidence comes from Lovecraft's wife, who reports that Lovecraft told her that his sexual instincts were at their greatest at the age of nineteen.[8] It is conceivable that sex frustration—for I do not imagine Lovecraft actually acted upon his urges at this time—may have been a contributory cause of his breakdown; but for one whose sexuality was, in general, so sluggish as Lovecraft's, I am not convinced that this was a significant factor.

Lovecraft provides a stark picture of what this breakdown meant in terms of his psychological outlook:

> Many times in my youth I was so exhausted by the sheer burden of consciousness & mental & physical activity that I had to drop out of school for a greater or lesser period & take a complete rest free from all responsibilities; & when I was 18 I suffered such a breakdown that I had to forego college. In those days I could hardly bear to see or speak to anyone, & liked to shut out the world by pulling down dark shades & using artificial light.[9]

As a result, the period 1908–13 is a virtual blank in the life of H. P. Lovecraft. It is the only time in his life when we do not have a significant amount of information on what he was doing from day to day, who his friends and associates were, and what he was writing. It is also the only time of his life when the term "eccentric recluse"—which many have used with careless ignorance in reference to his entire life—can rightly be applied to him. Accordingly, we know the merest scraps of his life and activities, mostly from random remarks made in letters years later.

Lovecraft doggedly attempted to maintain his scientific interests, although it seems a little pathetic that he revived his juvenile periodicals, the *Scientific Gazette* and the *Rhode Island Journal of Astronomy*, in early 1909, the latter after two years', the former after four years' hiatus (not counting the apparently brief revival by Arthur Fredlund). The sole issue of the *Gazette* for this period (January 1909) has an interesting ad:

> INTERNATIONAL
> CORRESPONDENCE
> SCHOOLS
> Established 1891
> T. J. Foster, President.
>
> ———
>
> 14 Courses in
> General and Industrial Chemistry.
>
> ———
>
> Reasonable Rates.
> All apparatus & Chemicals
> furnished at low prices
>
> ———
>
> COMPLETE COURSE
> $161.00
> All textbooks free.
>
> Scranton, Pa. U.S.A.

This is no doubt the correspondence course Lovecraft admits to taking "for a time."[10] There is no indication of how long he took the course. As to where he learned of this organisation, I shall have more to say presently. That Lovecraft's mother was willing to pay out $161 for such a thing suggests that she was still allowing him the freedom to pursue his interests; perhaps she thought this course might lead to a job, although that likelihood was surely remote. Once again, however, it was the more technical or tedious parts of the science that caused him difficulty:

> Between 1909 & 1912 I tried to perfect myself as a chemist, conquering inorganic chemistry & qualitative analysis with ease, since they had been favourite pastimes of my youth. But in the midst of *organic* chemistry, with its frightfully dull theoretical problems, & involved cases of isomerism of hydrocarbon radicals—the benzene ring—&c., &c., &c.—I found myself so wretched bored that I positively could not study for more than fifteen minutes without acquiring an excruciating headache which prostrated me completely for the rest of the day.[11]

One significant work did come out of this, however: *A Brief Course in Inorganic Chemistry,* written in 1910 and deemed by Lovecraft a "bulky manuscript."[12] This work, so far as I know, does not survive, and we know nothing of its contents.

The two issues of the *Rhode Island Journal of Astronomy* (January and February 1909) are not especially revealing. Incredibly, Lovecraft picks up the serialisation of "The Moon," suspended after the April 1907 issue—as if readers had been avidly awaiting its continuation! The second issue is rather sad: the first page presents four news articles, but the second page never got beyond the writing of the masthead; the rest of the page is blank aside from two vertical lines to separate the columns. Perhaps Lovecraft realised the absurdity of maintaining what was really a boy's undertaking: he was eighteen and a half years old by this time.

Lovecraft did attempt a more ambitious astronomical project, but it was not designed for publication. This is an astronomical notebook, once in the possession of David H. Keller and later in the Grill-Binkin collection of Lovecraftiana. The notebook bears the title "Astronomical Observations Made by H. P. Lovecraft, 598 Angell St., Providence, R.I., U.S.A., Years 1909 / 1910 / 1911 / 1912 / 1913 / 1914 / 1915."[13] Keller[14] reports that the book contains at least 100 pages of writing; page 99 has the following:

Principal Astronomical Work

1. To keep track of all celestial phenomena month by month, as positions of planets, phases of the moon, Sign of Sun, occultations, Meteor Showers, unusual phenomena (record) also new discoveries.
2. To keep up a working knowledge of the constellations and their seasons.

3. To observe all planets, etc. with a large telescope when they are favourably situated (at 7 h 30" in winter, abt. 9 h in summer, supplemented by morning observations)
4. To observe opera or field glass objects among the stars with a low power instruments, recording results.
5. To keep a careful record of each night's work.
6. To contribute a monthly astronomical article of about 7p. Ms. or 4p. Type to the Providence Evening News[15] (begun Jan. 1, 1914.)

This sounds like an impressive agenda, but Lovecraft did not maintain it consistently; in fact, Keller reports that for the years 1911 and 1913 there are no observations at all. Otherwise what we have are things like an eclipse of the moon on June 3, 1909, a "lengthy description" of Halley's Comet on May 26, 1910, a partial eclipse of the moon on March 11–12, 1914, and a long discussion of Delavan's Comet on September 16–17, 1914. I have not been able to consult this document myself and am reliant on Keller's account of it; but it does not seem to offer much evidence that Lovecraft was doing anything either to relieve his reclusiveness or to find a useful position in the outside world. It is, once again, a sort of retreat into his young adulthood.

Later in life Lovecraft knew that, in spite of his lack of university education, he should have received training in some sort of clerical or other white-collar position that would at least have allowed him to secure employment rather than moping about at home:

> I made the mistake in youth of not realising that literary endeavour does not always mean an income. I ought to have trained myself for some routine clerical work (like Charles Lamb's or Hawthorne's) affording a dependable stipend yet leaving my mind free enough for a certain amount of creative activity—but in the absence of immediate need I was too damned a fool to look ahead. I seemed to think that sufficient money for ordinary needs was something which everyone had as a matter of course—and if I ran short, I "could always sell a story or poem or something". Well—my calculations were inaccurate![16]

And so Lovecraft condemned himself to a life of ever-increasing poverty.

What was his mother doing in this entire situation? It is a little hard to say. Recall her own medical record at Butler Hospital (now destroyed) as paraphrased by Winfield Townley Scott: "a woman of narrow interests who received, with a traumatic psychosis, an awareness of approaching bankruptcy."[17] This assessment was made in 1919, but the condition must have been developing for years, at the very least since the death of Susie's own father, Whipple Phillips. Although she had high praise for her son ("a poet of the highest order"), Scott rightly conjectures: "However she adored him, there may have been a subconscious criticism of Howard, so brilliant but so economically useless." No doubt her disappointment with her son's inability to finish high school, go to college, and support himself did not help this situation any.

Lovecraft, in speaking of the steady economic decline of the family, notes "several sharp jogs downward, as when an uncle lost a lot of dough for my mother and me in 1911."[18] Faig is almost certainly correct in identifying this uncle as Susie's brother Edwin E. Phillips.[19] Edwin had difficulty even maintaining his own economic position, as his chequered employment record indicates. We do not, of course, know how Edwin lost money for Susie and Howard, but one suspects that bad investments—which not only failed to yield interest but also dissolved the capital—might have been a factor.

The effect of all this on Susie, and on her view of her son, can only be conjectured. Lovecraft's wife, although she never knew Susie, makes a plausible claim that Susie "lavished both her love and her hate on her only child";[20] this comment may receive confirmation from the following disturbing anecdote related by Clara Hess, which I believe dates to around this time if not a little earlier:

> . . . when she [Susie] moved into the little downstairs flat in the house on Angell Street around the corner from Butler Avenue I met her often on the Butler Avenue cars, and one day after many urgent invitations I went in to call upon her. She was considered then to be getting rather odd. My call was pleasant enough but the house had a strange and shutup air and the atmosphere seemed weird and Mrs. Lovecraft talked continuously of her unfortunate son who was so hideous that he hid from everyone and did not like to walk upon the streets where people could gaze at him.
>
> When I protested that she was exaggerating and that he should not feel that way, she looked at me with a rather pitiful look as though I did not understand about it. I remember that I was glad to get out in the fresh air and sunshine and that I did not repeat my visit.[21]

This is one of the most notorious pieces of evidence regarding Lovecraft and his mother, and I see no reason why we should not accept it. The reference to "hideous" is presumably to his physical appearance, and this is why I want to date the anecdote to Lovecraft's late teens or early twenties: as a younger boy he is so normal-looking that no one—even a mother who was getting a little "odd"—could have deemed him hideous; but by the age of eighteen or twenty he had perhaps reached his full height of five feet eleven inches, and had probably developed that long, prognathous jaw which he himself in later years considered a physical defect. Harold W. Munro testifies that as early as his high school years Lovecraft was bothered by ingrown facial hairs; but when Munro speaks of "mean red cuts" on Lovecraft's face he evidently believes these to have been the product of a dull razor.[22] In fact, as Lovecraft attests, these cuts came from his using a needle and tweezers to pull out the ingrown hairs.[23] This recurring ailment—which did not subside until Lovecraft was well into his thirties—may also have had a negative effect on his perception of his appearance. As late as February 1921, only a few months before his mother's death, Lovecraft writes to his mother of a new suit that "made me appear as nearly respectable as my face permits."[24]

I am of course not trying to defend this remark by Lovecraft's mother—surely no mother ought ever to say such a thing about her son, no matter how ugly he in fact is—and it may also be that her comment has a somewhat broader implication. It is often conjectured that she was transferring to her son the hatred and disgust she felt at her husband after he was stricken with syphilis, and I think this is very likely. Susie, of course, is not likely to have known the exact nature or causes of her husband's ailment—the doctors themselves did not—but she must have sensed that something relating to sex had afflicted him; and now that her own son was developing into an adult male with burgeoning sexual instincts, she may have suspected that he would turn out very much like her husband—especially if Lovecraft was at this time wearing his father's clothing. In any case, I do not think we have any grounds to deny that she made the "hideous" remark; Lovecraft himself once (and only once) admitted to his wife that his mother's attitude to him was (and this is his word) "devastating,"[25] and we need look no further for the reasons for that than this single comment.

Both Clara Hess and Harold W. Munro give evidence that Lovecraft did indeed avoid human contact in his post–high school period. Hess, when asked by August Derleth to elaborate upon her remarks, wrote: "Sometimes I would see Howard when walking up Angell Street, but he would not speak and would stare ahead with his coat collar turned up and chin down."[26] Munro states: "Very much an introvert, he darted about like a sleuth, hunched over, always with books or papers clutched under his arm, peering straight ahead recognizing nobody."[27]

We have the merest scraps of information as to what Lovecraft was actually doing during this entire period. One highly suggestive datum is his admission that he visited Moosup Valley, and specifically the Stephen Place house in Foster (birthplace of his mother and grandmother), in 1908.[28] This visit can scarcely have been purely recreational, since his previous trip, in 1896, is likely to have occurred after his grandmother's death. His mother accompanied him, as there is a photograph of her (probably taken by Lovecraft himself) standing in front of the house.[29] Once again it seems as if Lovecraft required some sort of renewal of ancestral ties to help him out of a difficult psychological trauma; but in this case the visit seems to have accomplished little.

The record for 1909 (aside from his astronomical observations and the correspondence courses) is entirely blank. For 1910 we know that he saw Halley's

Comet, but probably not at Ladd Observatory. In 1918 he states: "I no more visit the Ladd Observatory or various other attractions of Brown University. Once I expected to utilise them as a regularly entered student, and some day perhaps control some of them as a faculty member. But having known them with this 'inside' attitude, I am today unwilling to visit them as a casual outsider and non-university barbarian and alien."[30] This sense of alienation presumably began soon after his collapse in 1908, and he probably saw Halley's with his own telescope. He mentions that he missed seeing a bright comet earlier that year "by being flat in bed with a hellish case of measles!"[31] Elsewhere he states that he lost fifty-four pounds during this bout with the measles and nearly died.[32] The year 1910 was, however, the period of his most frequent attendance of stage plays, and he reports seeing many Shakespeare productions at the Providence Opera House.[33] He also visited Cambridge, Massachusetts—probably to see his aunt Annie Gamwell and his twelve-year-old cousin Phillips.[34] He also took a balloon ride in Brockton, Massachusetts—a city about equidistant between Providence and Boston.[35] These visits suggest that he was not at least a total hermit; indeed, perhaps Phillips Gamwell accompanied him on the balloon-ride. He celebrated his twenty-first birthday—August 20, 1911—by riding the electric trolley cars all day:

> Though in poor health, I attempted an all-day electric-car trip as a celebration—riding westward through the picturesque countryside of my maternal ancestors, eating lunch at Putnam, Conn., going north to Webster, Mass., (near which my first actual *memories* begin), then turning northeast to Worcester, keeping on to Boston, & finally returning home at night after a virtually record-breaking circuit.[36]

Perhaps this too was a sort of reversion to his childhood: no doubt he recalled his ride of 1900 or 1901, which led to the writing of his amusing "Attempted Journey" poem.

Also in 1911 (probably toward the end of the year) he saw President Willam Howard Taft on a campaign stop in Providence.[37] In later years he expressed great admiration for Theodore Roosevelt, and one would imagine that he would have voted for (or at least supported) Roosevelt, who had had a falling out with his protégé Taft and ran furiously against him on the Bull Moose ticket from the fall of 1911 onward. Although Lovecraft admits to seeing Roosevelt at the Providence Opera House in August 1912,[38] just two or three months before the election, he makes a startling revelation late in life: "As for Woodrow Wilson—he is a hard bird to analyse. I was for him in 1912 because I thought he represented a civilised form of government as distinguished from the frankly thieving plutocracy of the Taft die-hards and from the blindly rebellious Bull Moosers. His vacillating policy toward Mexico, however, alienated me almost at once."[39] Lovecraft thereby ended up on the winning side of the 1912 election: since Taft and Roosevelt split the Republican vote, the Democrat Wilson captured the presidency. The reference to

Mexico relates to the Mexican Civil War, which would embroil the United States into Mexican politics sporadically for the next three years. It is unclear from the above remark whether Lovecraft actually voted in the 1912 election, as he was eligible to do.

On August 12, 1912, Lovecraft made his one and only will. I shall have more to say about this document at a later time, but in its essentials it spells out what is to be done with his estate and effects upon his death: they will go to his mother, Sarah S. Lovecraft or, in the case of her predeceasing him, to his aunts Lillie D. Clark (two-thirds) and Annie E. Gamwell (one-third) or, if they predecease him, to their descendants. The witnesses to the will were Addison P. Munroe (father of Harold and Chester), Chester P. Munroe, and Albert A. Baker, Lovecraft's lawyer who, up to his majority, had been his guardian.

This brings up the issue of Lovecraft's continued association with his friends. The evidence is a little ambiguous. No doubt Lovecraft felt a certain sense of failure and defeat as he saw his high school friends marry, find jobs, and in general take on the responsibilities of adult life. Harold Munroe married, moved to East Providence, and became deputy sheriff.[40] Chester Munroe, as we shall see presently, went to North Carolina. Stuart Coleman at some point joined the army, rising at least to the rank of Major. Ronald Upham became a salesman.[41] One schoolmate whose compositions Lovecraft used to correct later published at least one article in the *New York Tribune*.[42] All this led him to state in 1916: "Of my non-university education, I never cease to be ashamed; but I know, at least, that I could not have done differently. I busied myself at home with chemistry, literature, & the like . . . I shunned all human society, deeming myself too much of a failure in life to be seen socially by those who had known me in youth, & had foolishly expected such great things of me."[43]

But consider this remarkable testimony from Addison P. Munroe, whom Winfield Townley Scott interviewed:

> He lived but a few houses distant from our own home and was quite frequently over here with our sons. I remember that we had a room fixed up in our basement for the boys to use as a club room, which was a popular place with Howard. The club, so called, consisted of about a half-dozen of the neighborhood boys, around twenty years of age, and when they had a so-called "banquet," improvised and usually self-cooked, Howard was always the speaker of the evening and my boys always said he delivered addresses that were gems.[44]

This appears to be East Side Historical Club, still meeting even after the boys had graduated from high school. If Munroe is right about the boys' age, then these sessions would have occurred exactly at the time (1910) when Lovecraft was maintaining that he "shunned all human society," in particular his friends. Harold W. Munro (who was presumably not a member of the club) remarks that "After Hope

Street days I never talked with Howard, but saw him several times";[45] but Munro does not appear to have been one of Lovecraft's close friends. In any event, there seems no reason to doubt that Addison P. Munroe was right about both the nature and the date of these meetings. He continues:

> Occasionally I would have an opportunity to talk with him and he always surprised me with the maturity and logic of his talk. I remember one time in particular, when I was a member of the R.I. Senate, 1911–1914, we had several important measures before that body; Howard, being over here one evening, started to discuss some of these measures, and I was astounded by the knowledge he displayed in regard to measures that ordinarily would be of no interest to a young fellow of twenty. In fact he knew more about them than 75 per cent of the Senators who would finally vote on them.[46]

Munroe is not likely to be mistaken about his own term of office in the Rhode Island Senate, so I am confident that his recollections here are accurate. Lovecraft's knowledge of Rhode Island politics no doubt derived, in part, from the fact that—probably at this time—he read the entire run of the *Providence Gazette and Country-Journal* (1762–1825) at the Providence Public Library.[47] No doubt he also read the *Providence Journal* (or, more likely, the *Evening Bulletin,* the paper to which he subscribed in later years) regularly.

That Lovecraft did not sever all ties with at least one of the Munroes is made clear by the existence of two curious if lacklustre poems, "Verses Designed to Be Sent by a Friend of the Author to His Brother-in-Law on New-Year's Day" and "To Mr. Munroe, on His Instructive and Entertaining Account of Switzerland." The first poem is undated, but probably dates to around 1914; the manuscript of the second is dated 1 January 1914. The "friend of the author" in the first poem is a Munroe, but I do not know which one. Lovecraft elsewhere states ("Introducing Mr. Chester Pierce Munroe") that the treatise on Switzerland was written by Chester, although he does not state its purpose; perhaps it was part of some college course. One couplet unintentionally betrays Lovecraft's hermitry during this period: "Th' untravell'd student, close within his doors, / The lofty peak and crystal lake explores." Lovecraft—who would not set foot outside of the three states of Rhode Island, Massachusetts, and Connecticut until 1921,[48] who would not sleep under a roof other than his own between 1901 and 1920,[49] and who (largely for economic reasons) never left the North American continent—must have found the idea of visiting Switzerland as fantastic as visiting Antarctica.

Lovecraft gives a picture of his literary production during this "empty" period:

> Chemical writing—plus a little historical and antiquarian research—filled my years of feebleness till about 1911, when I had a reaction toward literature. I then gave my prose style the greatest overhauling it has ever had; purging it at once of

> some vile journalese and some absurd Johnsonianism. Little by little I felt that I was forging the instrument I ought to have forged a decade ago—a decent style capable of expressing what I wished tosay. But I still wrote verse and persisted in the delusion that I was a poet.[50]

The curious thing about this is that we have very few examples of his expository prose between "The Alchemist" (1908)—or the last astronomy column for the Providence *Tribune,* "Solar Eclipse Feature of June Heavens" (June 1, 1908), whichever was later—and the beginning of his astronomy column for the *Providence Evening News* on January 1, 1914. There is a curious letter to the editor of the *Providence Sunday Journal* for August 3, 1913, complaining of the inadequate seating for band concerts at Roger Williams Park (the letter suggests that Lovecraft was a frequent attendant of these concerts) and recommending, a trifle implausibly, that the city build a huge auditorium resembling the Dionysiac Theatre in Athens. And there are a few other letters that I shall mention presently.

What we do have are a series of poems presumably written "about 1911" or sometime thereafter. Few of these are at all distinguished, but one is of consuming biographical interest: "The Members of the Men's Club of the First Universalist Church of Providence, R.I., to Its President, About to Leave for Florida on Account of His Health."

There is no clear way of dating this poem, and it may have been written as early as 1910 or as late as 1914; but what is remarkable about it is its mere existence, indicating that Lovecraft was a member of this men's club. The First Universalist Society had been established in Providence since 1821, and had initially set up a chapel at Westminster and Union Streets in what is now downtown Providence. A new church was built in 1872 at the corner of Greene and Washington Streets[51] (at the western end of downtown Providence, near the Providence Public Library), and this must have been where Lovecraft went when he participated in the men's club. I can only sense the hand of Lovecraft's mother in this entire enterprise: having failed on at least two occasions to inculcate standard Sunday school training in him as a boy, she perhaps felt that a less rigidly doctrinal church would be more to his liking. Actually, in all likelihood it was a means of preventing Lovecraft from becoming wholly withdrawn from society—in effect, a way of getting him out of the house every now and then. The poem sings the praises of the unnamed founder and president of the club:

> The club's foundations by your hands were laid;
> Beneath your rule its guiding laws were made;
> Your efforts caus'd the social band to gain
> The pow'r at once to teach and entertain.
> With careful thought, its policy you fix'd,
> The grave and gay in just proportion mix'd;

Nor let its frequent meetings know a dearth
Of lofty learning, or diverting mirth.

This does not tell us very precisely what this club's purpose and functions were, but those are things we are not likely ever to know.

The other poems written around this time similarly concern themselves with local affairs, and unfortunately their one clear thematic link is racism. "Providence in 2000 A.D." is Lovecraft's first published poem, appearing in the *Evening Bulletin* for March 4, 1912. It is actually quite funny, although much of the humour would not be very well received today. The parenthetical prose paragraph that prefaces the poem—"(It is announced in the *Providence Journal* that the Italians desire to alter the name of Atwell's Avenue to 'Columbus Avenue')"—tells the whole story: Lovecraft ridicules the idea that the Italians of the Federal Hill area have any right to change the Yankee-bestowed name of the principal thoroughfare of their own district. (The street was not in fact renamed.) The satire is quite devastating, telling of an Englishman who, in the year 2000, returns to Rhode Island, the land of his forbears, and finds everything foreignised. He disembarks at the port in Narragansett Bay: "I left the ship, and with astonish'd eyes / Survey'd a city fill'd with foreign cries." He finds that Fox Point has been changed by the Portuguese to Sao Miguel's Cape; that the Irish have changed South Main Street to O'Murphy's Avenue; that the Jews have changed Market Square to Goldstein's Court and Turk's Head to Finklestein's Cross-ways. Finally he reaches the Italian district:

I next climb'd on a car northwestward bound,
And soon 'mid swarthy men myself I found
On La Collina Federale's brow,
Near Il Passagio di Colombo.

He finds that the entire town of Pawtucket has been renamed New Dublin Town, and Woonsocket has become Nouvelle Paris. In Olneyville he has the following experience: "In what was once called 'Olneyville' I saw / A street sign painted: "Wsjzxypq$?&%$ ladislaw." Fleeing in horror back to the wharf, he finds a "shrivell'd form" who declares himself a "monstrous prodigy": "Last of my kind, a lone unhappy man, / My name is Smith! I'm an American!" The fact that the *Evening Bulletin* published this thing must have meant that others aside from Lovecraft found it funny. At least he does not discriminate against anyone in this poem: *all* the ethnic minorities of Providence—Italians, Portuguese, Jews, Poles, Irish, French-Canadians—are skewered.

Other poems of this period are much nastier, but were fortunately not published at the time. "New-England Fallen" (April 1912) is a wretched 152-line spasm headed predictably with an epigraph from Juvenal's third satire (on the mongrelisation of Rome) and speaking of some mythical time when hard-working, pious Anglo-Saxon yeomen established the dominant culture of New England—

> Oft to the village drove good Farmer John,
> To stock his larder, and supply his barn.
> 'Mid shady streets he sought the village store,
> And hail'd the rustics cluster'd 'round the door.

—only to have "foreign boors" infiltrate the society and corrupt it from within:

> The village rings with ribald foreign cries;
> Around the wine-shops loaf with bleary eyes
> A vicious crew, that mock the name of "man",
> Yet dare to call themselves "American".

This is surely close to the nadir of Lovecraft's poetic output—not only for the ignorant racism involved, but for its array of trite, hackneyed imagery and nauseating sentimentality in depicting the blissful life of the stolid yeoman farmer. Perhaps only the notorious "On the Creation of Niggers" (1912) exceeds this specimen in vileness. This is the entire poem:

> When, long ago, the Gods created Earth,
> In Jove's fair image Man was shap'd at birth.
> The beasts for lesser parts were next design'd;
> Yet were they too remote from humankind.
> To fill this gap, and join the rest to man,
> Th' Olympian host conceiv'd a clever plan.
> A beast they wrought, in semi-human figure,
> Fill'd it with vice, and call'd the thing a NIGGER.

The only thing that can be said for this is that it at least does not, like "De Triumpho Naturae" or "New-England Fallen," hypocritically convey its racism by appealing to the Christian imagery in which Lovecraft did not believe. No publication has been found for this poem, and one can only hope there is none. The text survives, however, in a hectographed copy, which suggests that Lovecraft may at least have passed this poem around to friends or family; it is likely that they approved—or at least did not object—to his sentiments.

"On a New-England Village Seen by Moonlight" is dated to September 7, 1913, on the manuscript; it was not published until 1915. Its introductory paragraph is all one needs to read: "(The peaceful old villages of New England are fast losing their original Yankee inhabitants and their agricultural atmosphere, being now the seats of manufacturing industries peopled by Southern European and Western Asiatic immigrants of low grade.)" This poem, in eight quatrains, returns to the theme of "New-England Fallen" but lays somewhat more emphasis on the loss of agriculture and its ways of life and the dominance of machinery than on the incursion of foreigners, although to Lovecraft the two phenomena worked together.

A somewhat more innocuous poem is "Quinsnicket Park," which Lovecraft dates to 1913.[52] Quinsnicket Park (now called Lincoln Woods Park) is situated four miles north of Providence and was one of Lovecraft's favourite sylvan retreats; throughout his life he would walk there and read or write in the open air. His 117-line paean to this rustic haven is trite, wooden, and mechanical, but contains at least this interesting passage:

> In yonder reedy pool we half expect
> Some timid Nymph or Satyr to detect:
> Our raptur'd eyes for fleeing Naiads scan,
> And ears are strain'd to hear the pipes of Pan.

One thinks of Lovecraft's mystical vision of "the hoofed Pan and the sisters of the Hesperian Phaëthusa" at the age of seven, although that is more likely to have occurred at Blackstone Park on the banks of the Seekonk rather than in Quinsnicket.

We do not know much else about Lovecraft's specific activities during these years. It is likely that he sequestered himself in his study and read enormous quantities of books, whether it be science or belles lettres; it was probably at this time that he laid the foundations for that later erudition in so many fields which astounded his colleagues. No doubt he continued to read weird fiction also. He states in 1925 that he read Conan Doyle's *The Lost World* "fifteen or more years ago,"[53] but actually he could not have read it any earlier than 1912, when it was published; and he probably did read it on that occasion.

One specific type of fiction we know he read in great quantities was the early pulp magazines. In the only extant issue of the *Rhode Island Journal of Science & Astronomy* (September 27, 1903) makes reference to an article by E. G. Dodge entitled "Can Men Visit the Moon?" in the October issue of *Munsey's Magazine,* which if nothing else indicates that Lovecraft was reading the journal at least as early as this. It is a point of debate whether the various magazines founded by Frank A. Munsey are or are not pulps; for our purposes it will suffice to say that they were significant forerunners of the pulp magazines and form a natural chain of continuity in popular magazine fiction from the dime and nickel novels of the later nineteenth century to the genuine pulps of the 1920s. As avid a dime novel reader as Lovecraft appears to have been, it is in no way surprising that he would ultimately find the Munsey magazines a compelling if guilty pleasure. What he did not know at the time was that they would radically transform his life and his career—largely, but not uniformly, for the better.

There is no evidence of how long Lovecraft had read *Munsey's* prior to the October 1903 issue (which, as with most popular magazines, was on the stands well before the cover date), nor how long he continued to read it. But there is no gainsaying the following letter to the *All-Story Weekly* for March 7, 1914:

> Having read every number of your magazine since its beginning in January, 1905, I feel in some measure privileged to write a few words of approbation and criticism concerning its contents.
>
> In the present age of vulgar taste and sordid realism it is a relief to peruse a publication such as *The All-Story,* which has ever been and still remains under the influence of the imaginative school of Poe and Verne.

Elsewhere Lovecraft stated that that first issue, January 1905, was available on the newsstands as early as November 1904.[54] The *All-Story* was a companion magazine to the *Argosy,* which Munsey had changed to an all-fiction magazine in October 1896.[55] It went through many permutations of title, changing to a weekly on March 7, 1914, and then combining with the *Cavalier* (which had commenced in October 1908) to become the *All-Story Cavalier Weekly* on May 16, 1914. Lovecraft of course read the *Argosy* also, as we shall presently see, although it is difficult to know how early he began reading it. Lovecraft in 1916 admitted a little sheepishly that "In 1913 I had formed the reprehensible habit of picking up cheap magazines like *The Argosy* to divert my mind from the tedium of reality,"[56] but it is now evident that this is, at the very least, an equivocation as far as the *All-Story* is concerned. It is quite conceivable that Lovecraft read the *Argosy* from as early as 1905 or even before, but at the moment this will have to remain a conjecture. One further bit of evidence is the fact that full-page advertisements for the International Correspondence Schools of Scranton, Pennsylvania, regularly appear in the *Argosy,* and it is very likely from this source that Lovecraft learned of this organisation and used its services around 1909. In 1935 he reports reading the *Popular Magazine* (Street & Smith's rival to the *Argosy*) "25 or 30 years ago,"[57] hence about the period 1905–10; but it is not clear how long or how regularly he read this periodical, which on the whole did not feature as much weird material as the Munseys.

One other interesting—indeed, almost alarming—fact is that Lovecraft read the entire run of the *Railroad Man's Magazine* (1906–19),[58] a staggering quantity of fiction and articles about railroads. This was the first specialised Munsey pulp, and the image of Lovecraft reading 150 monthly issues of this magazine is somewhat unnerving. Perhaps the very fact that he had to give up his "New Anvik" at the age of seventeen compelled him to satisfy his enthusiasm for railroads through print.

What was the fascination of these magazines for Lovecraft? The letter quoted above supplies a part of the answer: they contained a significant amount of horror, fantasy, mystery, and science fiction, material that was already ceasing to appear in the standard "slick" or literary magazines of the day. As Lovecraft noted in 1932:

"In general . . . the Munsey publications did more to publish weird fiction than any other magazine enterprise of the early 20th century."[59] Elsewhere he remarks that he "first began to notice"[60] the *Black Cat* (1895–1922) around 1904, and that that magazine and the *All-Story* "were the first source of *contemporary* weird material I ever stumbled on."[61] To one who had nurtured himself on Poe, W. Clark Russell, and other nineteenth-century authors, the notion that weird fiction was being written in his own day must have been both stimulating and, perhaps, inspiring.

And yet, I have refrained from mentioning Lovecraft's prodigious reading of the Munsey pulps until now because, unlike the dime and nickel novels, they do not appear to have influenced the two surviving tales of the 1903–08 period, "The Beast in the Cave" and "The Alchemist." The influence of Poe, the Gothics, and the Augustan essayists (in prose style) seems dominant there, a somewhat anomalous fact given Lovecraft's obvious enthusiasm for the Munseys. In any event, we now know another thing Lovecraft continued to do during his "blank" period of 1908–13: he may have had a nervous breakdown, but he never missed an issue of the *All-Story*.

Lovecraft's first published letter to the Munsey magazines—discovered only recently—appeared in the *Argosy* for November 1911.[62] The letter-column of the *Argosy*—entitled "The Log-Book"—had only been established in the February 1911 issue, and letters were initially slow to come in; but by the end of the year many letters (identified only by the initials of the writer and his or her city of residence) were being published, with running commentary by the editor. In the November 1911 issue the editor announces: "And now comes H. P. L., of Providence, Rhode Island," and goes on to quote some actual portions of Lovecraft's letter: his favourite writer is Albert Payson Terhune (at this time an author of historical novels and tales, not yet the creator of Lassie); he disapproves of the slang in some stories, and prefers tales set in the past or in some other exciting locale rather than those set in the present. All this is entirely typical of Lovecraft, although his lack of critical acumen in praising Terhune, who was no better than a competent hack writer, is painfully evident. An undated poetic paean to Terhune—"To Mr. Terhune, on His Historical Fiction"—may date to this time. It is, in fact, in the form of a letter to the editor of the *Argosy*, although perhaps it was not actually submitted to the magazine; in any event, it did not appear there.

Lovecraft's next letter, appearing in the February 8, 1913, issue of the *All-Story Cavalier*, is a comment on Irvin S. Cobb's magnificent tale of a half-man, half-fish hybrid, "Fishhead," of which Lovecraft says: "It is the belief of the writer that very few short stories of equal merit have been published anywhere during recent years." I believe that this powerful tale lodged in Lovecraft's mind and would form a significant influence on one of his major stories, as I shall have occasion to note later.

In the fall of that year Lovecraft's letter-writing campaign shifts back to the *Argosy;* but at the moment I wish to return to the letter of 1914 that I have already quoted, a letter of close to 2000 words, taking up nearly two full printed pages. It is a sort of grand summation of everything he liked in the magazine and an encapsulation of what he thought it stood for. Scorning the plea of one G. W. F. of Dundee, Scotland, for more "probable" stories, Lovecraft declaims:

> If, in fact, man is unable to create living beings out of inorganic matter, to hypnotise beasts of the forest to do his will, to swing from tree to tree with the apes of the African jungle, to restore to life the mummified corpses of the Pharaohs and the Incas, or to explore the atmosphere of Venus and the deserts of Mars, permit us, at least, in fancy, to witness these miracles, and to satisfy that craving for the unknown, the weird, and the impossible which exists in every active human brain.

That last statement is certainly a little sanguine: if everyone had a craving for the unknown, then weird fiction would not be as unrecognised a literary mode as it is. But the catalogue presented above is not only a series of synopses of some of the celebrated tales published in the *All-Story* but, in several instances, a selection of plot-elements that Lovecraft himself would use in his own later work (and, for all we know, had already used in the destroyed tales of 1903–08).

There follow paeans to many of the *All-Story*'s most popular writers. Who is first to be named? "At or near the head of your list of writers Edgar Rice Burroughs undoubtedly stands." Lovecraft goes on to single out *Tarzan of the Apes* (October 1912), *The Gods of Mars* (January–May 1913), and *Warlord of Mars* (December 1913–March 1914), although it is typical that while praising these stories he takes care to point out astronomical and other factual errors in the works. Later in life Lovecraft seemed embarrassed at his juvenile (or not so juvenile: he was twenty-three when he wrote this letter) fondness for Burroughs, and he sought to distance himself from the creator of Tarzan. In 1929, when urging a correspondent not to yield to the temptations of the market and write hackwork, he lumps Burroughs with Edgar A. Guest and Harold Bell Wright as examples of the fact that "the veriest idiot and ignoramus can sometimes bring down fame on a luck-shot."[63] Not long thereafter, in saying that "I shall sooner or later get around to the interplanetary field myself," he adds explicitly: "you may depend upon it that I shall not choose Edmond Hamilton, Ray Cummings, or Edgar Rice Burroughs as my model!"[64] This gives no indication of how much he had enjoyed the John Carter Martian novels fifteen years before.

In his letter Lovecraft goes on to praise many other writers, few of whom are of any note—William Patterson White, Lee Robinet, William Tillinghast Eldridge, William Loren Curtiss, Donald Francis McGrew, and others. A later letter (published in the *All-Story Cavalier Weekly* for August 15, 1914) praises George Allan England, Albert Payson Terhune, and Zane Grey. What is remarkable is that most of these writers did not even write weird fiction: Zane Grey, of course, was the legendary Western writer; Terhune, as just noted, became famous for dog stories; McGrew was an adventure writer whose "red-blooded" stories met with Lovecraft's thunderous approval; and Lovecraft even liked the many humorous tales in the magazine. This means that Lovecraft read each issue—sometimes 192 pages, sometimes 240 pages—from cover to cover, month after month or even (when it changed to a weekly) week after week. This is an appalling amount of popular fiction for anyone to read, and in fact it contravened the purpose of the magazines, whereby each member of the family would read only those stories or those types of stories that were of interest to him or her.[65] One begins to develop the impression that Lovecraft was compulsive in whatever he did: his discovery of classical antiquity led him to write a paraphrase of the *Odyssey, Iliad,* and other works; his discovery of chemistry led him to launch a *daily* scientific paper; his discovery of astronomy led him to publish a weekly paper for years; and now his discovery of pulp fiction caused him to be a voracious reader of both the good and the bad, both the work that appealed to his special tastes and the work that did not.

It is possible that the *All-Story* published this long letter in its issue of March 7, 1914, because Lovecraft himself had become, after a fashion, a celebrity in the entire Munsey chain. This had come about in a very odd way. Lovecraft, reading everything the *Argosy* put in front of him, found some material less appealing to his fastidious taste than others. Consider a comment in his long letter:

> "The Souls of Men," by Martha M. Stanley, was a distinctly disagreeable tale, but "Pilgrims in Love," by De Lysle Ferrée Cass, is contemptibly disgusting, unspeakably nauseating. Mr. G. W. S., of Chicago, has written that Cass "diplomatically handles a very difficult subject—Oriental love."
>
> We do not care for subjects so near allied to vulgarity, however "diplomatically" they may be "handled." Of such "Oriental love" we may speak in the words of the lazy but ingenious schoolboy, who when asked by his tutor to describe the reign of Caligula, replied, "that the less said about it, the better."

This gives some idea of the trend of Lovecraft's thinking at this time: rousing action plots by Edgar Rice Burroughs he did not consider "vulgar," but anything that suggested anything even remotely off-colour earned the puritanical Lovecraft's quick and vicious condemnation. I have not read the Cass story,[66] but it is quite possible that it did explore sexual situations somewhat more daringly than was customary in the standard literature of the day; one gets the impression, however, that no such work, however artistic, would have met with Lovecraft's favour.

It is, then, no surprise that a very popular *Argosy* writer named Fred Jackson would be blasted by Lovecraft in the issue for September 1913. Jackson had become an *Argosy* staple, and two of his short novels had appeared complete in recent issues, "The First Law" in April 1913 and "The Third Act" in June 1913. This really was an unprecedented amount of space to give to a single author, and the subject-matter of these works was not of a kind to sit well with Lovecraft. "The First Law" is an unbelievably sappy, melodramatic, and verbose story of an opera singer; here is a sample:

> She struggled against him fiercely, her whole being outraged, but he was by far the stronger. He held her fast, and his lips touched her ear, her throat, her chin, and eyes, and at last crushed her mouth until she gasped for breath.
>
> Then he drew back and she lay passive in his arms, trembling, terrified at the madness that possessed her. It was as though he had awakened some sleeping demon—a creature unknown to her, a creature thirsty for his kisses, aching for his embrace.[67]

Jackson would probably have made a good Harlequin romance writer today.

What is frequently overlooked is that Lovecraft's tirade was not inspired merely by the unwonted dominance of Jackson in the pages of *Argosy* but by a letter purportedly attacking him in the July 1913 issue. This letter—by one F. V. Bennett of Hanover, Illinois—is, however, so illiterate that Lovecraft believed it to be a sort of self-parody designed indirectly to praise Jackson:

> do you know why I stoped taking *The Cavalier* It was Fred Jackson to mutch of him I should Say Now I have to Pay for THE ARGOSY when he takes up Nearly half of It . . . I shall not Subscribe for THE ARGOSY again If you Publish Jackson's Stories so often for I don't Read them any more Just Cant stand them and I see you are to Publish another Book Length Novel by Jackson in June supose you won't Like this Letter.

Lovecraft could well be excused for thinking as he did, especially since the editor added the wry note: "Oh, no, you are mistaken—I do like this letter."

Lovecraft's own letter in the September 1913 issue could hardly be taken as a self-parody. He begins by quoting Thomas Tickell's preface to Addison's *Cato* ("Too long hath love engross'd Britannia's stage, / And sunk to softness all our tragic rage"), and goes on to express his opinion that Bennett's letter "is in reality a sly attempt at augmenting the fame of your contributor, Fred Jackson." He continues: "To the eye of a disinterested observer it appears as though an effort were being made forcibly to obtrude Mr. Jackson upon the reading public by an unexampled campaign of advertising, and by the selection for publication in the Log-Book of those letters wherein he receives the greatest amount of adulation." There is something to be said for this, too: "The Log-Book" of the previous several issues had been filled with praise for Jackson, many of them from men, curiously enough. Of course, Lovecraft overlooks the possibility that Jackson really was popular with *Argosy* readers; or, rather, overlooks the undoubted fact that most of the magazine's readers had very lax literary standards and were only interested in cheap entertainment. Lovecraft, indeed, does not claim that Jackson's novels "are wholly wanting in merit," noting a little dryly that "There is a numerous set of people whose chief literary delight is obtained in the following of imaginary nymphs and swains through the labyrinthine paths of amorous adventure"; but he strenuously objects to the dominance of such work in the *Argosy.* And it is a fact, maintains Lovecraft, that Jackson is simply a bad writer:

> Apart from the mere choice of subject, let me venture to describe the Jacksonine type of tale as trivial, effeminate, and, in places, coarse.
>
> . . .
>
> Into the breasts of his characters, and appearing to dominate them to the exclusion of reason, he places the delicate passions and emotions proper to negroes or anthropoid apes.
>
> His literary style is feeble, and often excessively familiar. He abounds in "split" infinitives, and occasionally falls into the use of outlandish words, as, for instance, "live-in-able," instead of "habitable."

The remark about "negroes or anthropoid apes" is only what one would expect from someone who the previous year had written "On the Creation of Niggers."

The response to this letter is not likely to have been predicted either by Lovecraft or by Matthew White, Jr, editor of the *Argosy.* The November 1913 issue contained several more letters on Jackson: one by the redoubtable F. V. Bennett, just as illiterate as its predecessor and evidently unaware that Lovecraft had ranked him as a Jackson supporter ("H. P. Lovecraft Is Right he gets My Meaning give us a Rest from Jackson Stuff"); one, by "E. F. W. C." of Paris, Kentucky, attacking Bennett but not alluding to Lovecraft; and two others specifically supporting Jackson and attacking both Lovecraft and Bennett. One of these, by T. P. Crean of Syracuse, New York, claims: "I am still puzzling over H. P. Lovecraft's letter. I can understand how the brilliant F. V. Bennett cannot go Jackson's stories. But Mr. Lovecraft, from his letter, should be able to tell a good story when he reads one. I am personally of the opinion that this letter was merely to display to THE ARGOSY world his vocabulary . . ." This is a refrain that would frequently be rung in the entire controversy. The affair, however, might not have taken the peculiar turn it did had not the other letter, by John Russell of Tampa, Florida, been written *in verse.* This is a whimsical four-stanza piece which begins:

> Does Mr. Lovecraft think it wise
> With such long words to criticize
> An author whom we greatly prize?
> That's Freddie Jackson.

Lovecraft describes it as "a piece of tetrameter verse . . . which had in it so much native wit, that I resolved to answer it."[68] Sure enough, he responded in the January

1914 issue with a verse epistle of his own in what he fancied was the manner of Pope's *Dunciad.* In fact, it is a very clever poem, and reveals that penchant for stinging satire which would be one of the few virtues of his poetic output.

The manuscript of the poem is headed "Ad Criticos" ("To [my] critics") (with the subtitle "Liber Primus," probably added at a later date as Lovecraft continued to add to the cycle); in the published version it is titled "Lovecraft Comes Back: Ad Criticos." It opens thunderously:

> What vig'rous protests now assail my eyes?
> See Jackson's satellites in anger rise!
> His ardent readers, steep'd in tales of love,
> Sincere devotion to their leader prove;
> In brave defence of sickly gallantry,
> They damn the critic, and beleaguer me.

The pun on "ardent" is very good. Lovecraft praises Russell for his cleverness and wit, and then proceeds to take his other enemies to task. To T. P. Crean he replies:

> In truth, my words are not beyond the reach
> Of him who understands the English speech;
> But Crean, I fear, by reading Jackson long,
> Hath lost the pow'r to read his mother tongue.

Lovecraft concludes the poem by comparing the present time to "Charles the Second's vulgar age," when "Gross Wycherley and Dryden soil'd the stage."

But before Lovecraft's verse letter was printed, he was ferociously assailed in the December 1913 issue. Some of the titles which the editor affixed to the letters give some idea of the outrage Lovecraft had provoked: "Challenge to Lovecraft" (G. E. Bonner, Springfield, Ohio); "Virginia *vs.* Providence" (Miss E. E. Blankenship, Richmond, Virginia); "Elmira *vs.* Providence" (Elizabeth E. Loop, Elmira, New York); "Bomb for Lovecraft" (F. W. Saunders, Coalgate, Oklahoma). Miss Blankenship wrote: "I think you are very ungenerous in your attitude, Mr. Lovecraft. Your words 'erratic [*sic*] fiction' I fail to acknowledge. Instead I find pages filled with innocence, sweetness, loveliness, and fascination." G. E. Bonner, praising Jackson's two recent novels, wrote: ". . . when a man gets weary of reading that kind of a story I think the trouble is with the man himself and not with the author." Elizabeth E. Loop found Lovecraft's polysyllables tiresome and confusing, concluding: "I am an admirer of Mr. Jackson's stories, but this letter of Mr. Lovecraft's filled me with a distaste for our friend from Providence."

Saunders' "Bomb for Lovecraft" was the longest attack, but it has little substance; and in the process he reveals his own ignorance. He maintains: "It seems to me that Mr. L. is inconsistent, in that he charges Fred Jackson with a number of faults, among them being the use of outlandish words. In this respect, I think Mr. L. is equally at fault, if it be a fault." Complaining, like Elizabeth Loop, of Lovecraft's long words, he states that he cannot find such words as "Josh-Billingsgate" and "Hanoverian" in his dictionary: "If any of the readers have a dictionary with these expressions, please tear the leaf out and send it to me so that I may 'study up' on 'em."

Two letters did take Lovecraft's side, however; they were each headed "Agrees with Lovecraft." One, by A. Missbaum of Paris, France, expressed sentiments very similar to Lovecraft's: ". . . I entirely agree . . . with H. P. Lovecraft . . . Yes, Fred Jackson is rotten. Give us less love stories (unless they are live ones) and more scientific mystery tales." The other letter, by H. F. B. of Los Angeles, complains merely that Jackson is given too much space in the magazine while other "excellent first-class writers" are given short shrift.

In a "Liber Secundus" published in the February 1914 *Argosy* Lovecraft takes potshots at these new opponents. The tone of this poem is much sharper than that of its predecessor. Lovecraft was, of course, in a position of overwhelming intellectual superiority to most of his victims, and sometimes it seems as if he is shooting fish in a barrel; but the satire is nonetheless withering for all that. To F. W. Saunders and his dictionary-hunting, Lovecraft advises: "Too much upon your lexicon you lean, / For *proper names* in such are seldom seen." And as for the flocks of women who attacked him:

> Now fairer forms from out the ranks emerge;
> The Amazons in reckless fury charge.
> Good Madam Loop, like Crean of Syracuse,
> Protests unkindly 'gainst the words I use:
> Whoe'er this lady's firm esteem would seek,
> In monosyllables must ever speak.

He could hardly have passed up Miss Blankenship's error of "erratic" for "erotic":

> Exactitude the fair one hardly heeds,
> Since she "erratic" for "erotic" reads,
> But unimportant 'tis, for by my troth,
> Jackson's erratic and erotic both!

In this issue Lovecraft begins to gather both friends and enemies—mostly the latter. One of the staunchest of the former is no other than F. V. Bennett, who had unwittingly begun the controversy. Now becoming literate (or having his letter corrected of spelling mistakes and of erroneous or absent punctuation), he writes, "well, shake, H.P.L.," and claims that "we started the ball that called a halt to the rush of Jackson soft stuff." This remark is confirmed by a note by Bob Davis in the issue: "I can promise that you won't get too much Jackson in 1914 . . ." This does not mean, of course, that readers would get *no* Jackson: another short novel, "Ambushed" (a mystery story with a romance element), had already appeared in the October 1913 issue, and "Winged Feet" was published in February 1914; but after this there was nothing until "The Marriage Auction" in January 1915. Thereafter, however, Jackson returns with a vengeance: "Red Robin" appeared in July 1915, "The Diamond Necklace" in October and November 1915, "Where's the Woman?" from October 6 to November 3, 1917, and "A Woman's Prey" in November 24, 1917; "Young Blood" appeared serially in *Munsey's* beginning in October 1917. In this sense it could hardly be said that Lovecraft and his supporters had helped to effect any sort of change in the *Argosy's* editorial policy; the fact is that, as various editor's notes make clear, Jackson finally ceased to appear in the Munsey magazines because he decided to take up the writing of plays, and in later years gained considerable success at this new career.

In a lengthy response in the February 1914 issue, headed "Replies to Lovecraft," T. P. Crean maintains that "I admire very much his use of the English language and his poetic ability" but goes on to say that

> He tells Mr. Russell, one of Mr. Jackson's defenders, that his (Russell's) poem was worthy of a better cause. In the same sense it strikes me that Mr. Lovecraft's extensive vocabulary and easily adapted rimes should be employed other than roasting an author, who, although he may have a few defects in a story, produces a tale that is interesting from start to finish, which is all that a reader of a fiction magazine can ask for.

Amusingly, he concludes with "Ta-ta, Lovey," unwittingly exhuming the derogatory nickname Lovecraft had endured at the Slater Avenue School.

In the March 1914 issue there is a curious interruption in the controversy. There are, of course, any number of letters attacking Lovecraft. Clifford D. Ennis of Buffalo, New York, makes a now familiar argument: "If Mr. Lovecraft wishes to display his vocabulary I wish, for the sake of Mr. Jackson's many admirers, he would exhibit it in praising, not criticizing." W. J. Thompson of Winnipeg, Canada, claims: "Unlike our friend, 'The Rhode Island Scholar and Critic' (H. P. Lovecraft), I did not expect to get five dollars' worth of reading for fifteen cents. Bring on Jackson as often as you can." H. M. Fisher of Atlanta makes a snide reference to "Mr. H. P. Lovecraft's 'bee-u-ti-ful' poem," adding:

> Mr. Lovecraft must feel better since he got rid of his "Mary had a little lamb" effort.
>
> However, if a man can be judged by the stories he writes, Mr. Jackson, to use the vernacular of the day, is "some" man. I consider him one of the best writers THE ARGOSY has on its staff, and I feel certain that Mr. Lovecraft had better thank his stars that his disposition is expressed in letter form and not personally.

> Congratulate Mr. Jackson for me, please, on his stories, from one who has possibly more books *on* his book-case than Mr. Lovecraft has perused in his career, although they may not be "high-brow" caliber.

But the principal item in "The Log-Book" is a long (prose) letter by Lovecraft entitled "Correction for Lovecraft." Here he cites two lines of his first verse epistle as printed in the *Argosy* for January 1914: "Think not, good rimester, that I sought to *shew* / In my last letter, merely what I *knew*." Lovecraft had, of course, written "know," but the copy editor, no doubt puzzled by Lovecraft's British usage, made the alteration in the belief that "shew" was pronounced "shoe." This brought down Lovecraft's wrath: ". . . three faults remain: (1) The rime is destroyed. (2) The sense of 'know' is changed from present to past, and (3) 'shew' remains unaltered and inharmonious with the general spelling of the verse." This letter brought a devastating response from John Russell in the May 1914 issue:

> Lovecraft has dropped from rime to prose,
> To shew that what he knew, he knows.
> I say that really to my view
> 'Twas little that he ever knew.

In April 1914 Lovecraft was attacked from several different directions. Ira B. Forrest (Messick, Virginia) unwittingly made perhaps the most acute analysis of Lovecraft's position when he noted: "Possible [*sic*] Mr. Lovecraft is a grouchy old bachelor and dislikes sentiment in any form." E. P. Rahs also notes perspicaciously: "Be considerate and remember the magazine is not published for any one of us exclusively"; he concludes: "Give us more Jackson and less Lovecraft." Russell responded with a pungent verse:

> Say! Lovecraft in his last epistle
> Has jumped upon a Scottish thistle.
> I hold no brief for Jackson
> (His stories give me satisfaction).
> He scoffed at everything romantic;
> He talks about an am'rous pest
> Well, take the Author's proven best.
> Dickens and Fenny, Shakespeare, Scott,
> You'll find the same in all the lot;
> Where there's a tale, there's love, of course;
> Sometimes it's better, sometimes worse.

Lovecraft no doubt violently objected to that last conception and would strive as far as possible to exemplify his disagreement with it in his own tales. F. W. Saunders also attempted to respond in verse, with a poem entitled "Ruat Caelum" ("Let the heavens shake"), written in heroic couplets clearly meant to mimic and parody Lovecraft's:

> With humbled horn, and hide with fat well filled,
> I waddle forth to meet this chieftain skilled
> In martial notes. Then on doth pout [*sic*] my feet
> To battleground, upon fair Angell Street.

This entire long poem is really rather clever, if at times a bit incoherent.

Something strange now happens: no more replies by Lovecraft are published in the *Argosy* until October 1914. There are two further books of Lovecraft's "Ad Criticos" in manuscript: did he not submit them for publication? or were they not accepted? The latter seems unlikely, since an editorial note at the end of "Correction for Lovecraft" declares: "You are always welcome in the Log-Book." Whatever the situation, Lovecraft's "Liber Tertius" first addresses Russell—

> "Behold," he cries, "through classic pages move
> The sweet delusions of idyllic love."
> Russell, 'tis true. Give proper love its own,
> But let us not be fed on love alone!

—and then Rahs, whose name he cannot resist punning:

> But what shrill shoutings now offend my ear?
> Methinks, some rough and raucous Rahs I hear.
> No brutal force my new opponent lacks;
> He bluntly yells, I should receive the axe!

He also takes note of Saunders's poem—"His verse is modell'd after Pope's (or mine)."

But when Lovecraft was writing this response, he did not know that the April 14, 1914, issue of the *All-Story Weekly* would contain a bombshell from an S. P. N. (Kennett Square, Pennsylvania) who blasted Lovecraft's own long letter in the March 7 issue.

> I have become acquainted with that gentleman before. He seems to be a born knocker and an egoist of the worst type. His vanity is awful. His assumed eloquence and literary powers are disgusting.
>
> This is the first time I have seen him in the *All-Story* and I don't wish to see him again.

This goes on for half a column ("Wait till he starts firing some of his rotten poetry at you. Oh, my!"). Lovecraft does not seem ever to have made a public response to this bit of venom.

By summer the controversy is beginning to die down. An editorial note in the May 1914 issue declares that "The same old warfare over Jackson is going on, in prose and verse," and this issue does indeed contain (aside from Russell's verse, already cited) a number of other poems attacking Lovecraft. J. C. Cummings of Chicago writes in blundering verse:

> I think, indeed, he has no sense
> When he has no *love* for Jackson,
> For, unlike the bard of Providence,
> His *craft* brings satisfaction.

Here is Richard Forster of Rothwell, Wyoming:

> I think, indeed, it would be best
> To let poor Jackson have a rest,
> And Lovecraft try his bitter spite
> On some other poor luckless wight.

Mrs W. S. Ritter of Cleveland objects to "the amount of space given this person Lovecraft when two or three *interesting* letters might have been printed in the space so used." But the most vicious response is a prose letter by Jack E. Brown of Kellogg, Idaho: "I get sore at people like H. P. L. I will pay his fifteen cents a month if he will quit reading the ARGOSY. . . . I am a cow-puncher, and certainly would like to loosen up my .44-six on that man Lovecraft." Lovecraft had no defenders in this issue, although H. R. G. of Cedar Rapids, Nebraska, writes ambiguously: "The Log-Book has become very interesting lately on account of the comments on H. P. Lovecraft." But with Lovecraft himself not replying (or, at least, with his replies not being printed), the debate had little to feed itself upon. The unpublished "Liber Quartus" of "Ad Criticos" does address Russell's acid lines in the May issue:

> He shuns politeness in his spleenful scrawl,
> And swears my stock of learning is but small.
> In well-turn'd lines, with sickly venom writ,
> He counts my failings to display his wit.

Clearly Russell's squib got under his skin. As for J. C. Cummings, he "gains distinction and eternal fame / From neatly playing on a hated name"; and Lovecraft devastatingly points out the clumsiness in Forster's attempt at verse:

> In true trochaic rage the bard begins,
> When, lo! an odd iambus intervenes.
> Some eight lines down, he strikes the ballad form,

> But soon a dactyl swells the shapeless swarm:
> The fifteenth line assumes heroic length,
> And stands apart in solitary strength.

This is an entirely valid criticism, for unlike free verse Forster's poem attempted to adhere to regular metre but simply failed to do so. Lovecraft then unleashes an argument that he would use over and over again in regard to free verse:

> As for the rest, what man among us knows
> If it be verse, or merely rhyming prose?
> On Forster's sense I waste but little care,
> For why discuss a thing that is not there?

In June Russell comes back with a poem entitled "Love Versus Lovecraft," responding to Lovecraft's "Liber Secundus." He puts forth an interesting speculation:

> If by mischance some fair, false maid
> Has havoc with his feelings played,
> He should in silence bear the pain
> And from his jeers at love refrain.
> Perchance he thinks in his smart way
> That woman is of meaner clay;
> That love is but a thing of jest,
> He stands, a cynic, self-confessed.

C. M. Turner's letter is headed "Lovecraft in Irons" and states: ". . . I think Mr. Jackson's stories are the very best you publish, Mr. Lovecraft to the contrary notwithstanding, and I sincerely trust that you will not listen to the unjust criticism of Mr. Lovecraft and his ilk . . . So, please put Mr. Lovecraft in 'irons,' and place Mr. Fred Jackson in the position of first mate and let the good old ARGOSY sail on." The issue contains many other defences of Jackson (spurred, probably, by the editor's challenge in the April 1914 issue for Jackson fans to write letters in support of their favourite: "People are much more likely to object to a thing than to admit that it pleases them. It is up to the Jackson fans"), but with fewer specific attacks on Lovecraft.

The July 1914 issue contains only a few letters of interest. Ed. Ellisen of Stratford, Ontario, declares: "Please tell that Mr. H. P. Lovecraft if he does any more kicking to come up here in Canada to do it, as there are places up here to put him in." E. M. W. of Fallon, California, utters a complaint that would gain force in the coming months: ". . . I do not approve of the way Messrs. Lovecraft and Russell use the Log-Book as a medium in which to vent their sarcasm at each other."

In August and September there is very little on the matter: letters in praise of Jackson continue to appear, but neither Lovecraft nor Russell is specifically mentioned. G. E. Bonner returns, crowing about how many more defenders Jackson has than attackers, but he directs his remarks to "friend Bennett" and not to Lovecraft.

The controversy comes to an end in the October 1914 issue. An entire section of "The Log-Book" bears the heading "Fred Jackson, Pro and Con"; inevitably, the "Jackson Boosters" outnumber the "Jackson Knockers." None of the former addresses Lovecraft specifically, but of the latter the loyal F. V. Bennett stands up for his mentor and attacks his principal opponent: "As for the writers who attack Mr. Lovecraft, I don't agree with them, as Mr. Lovecraft is of the same mind about such trash. As for John Russell Potery, [*sic*] it's—well in the same class with Jackson." But the most interesting item is a poem headed "The Critics' Farewell" and bearing both Lovecraft's and Russell's names. They did not actually collaborate on the poem; rather, Lovecraft wrote the first part (headed "The End of the Jackson War") and Russell wrote the second (headed "Our Apology to E. M. W."). Lovecraft's, naturally, is in heroic couplets, and Russell's is in very racy short and irregular anapaests. Lovecraft notes that this truce was made at the insistence of an editor at the *Argosy* who "intimated that the poet's war must soon end, since correspondents were complaining of the prominence of our verses in their beloved magazine."[69] Lovecraft identifies this editor as T. N. Metcalf. We know that Matthew White, Jr, was editor of the *Argosy* proper, and Metcalf is known to have been a sub-editor of the *All-Story* under Robert H. Davis;[70] perhaps Metcalf was in charge of the Log-Book. In any event, Lovecraft's section of the poem concludes:

> So do we now, conjoin'd in lasting peace,
> Lay down our pens, and mutual slander cease.
> What sound is this? 'Tis but a joyous yell
> From thankful thousands, as we say farewell.

The December 1914 Log-Book has an editorial heading, "Fred Jackson's Coming Back!," with several paeans to that author. Stanley H. Watson of Stockton, Manitoba, writes: "I hope by this time some one has squelched Mr. Lovecraft for running down Jackson. He must be one of those smart Alecs who could write better himself."

There are some other items among Lovecraft's papers that relate to the Jackson controversy, although they do not appear to have been published. There are two poems, "I. Frustra Praemunitus" ("Fortified in vain") and "II. De Scriptore Mulieroso" ("On an effeminate writer"). Both are responses to John Russell's "Love Versus Lovecraft" poem (June 1914); they were evidently written at that time, but again Lovecraft either did not submit them or the editor declined to publish them. The first poem ironically seeks to reassure Russell that, even if Lovecraft attacks Jackson's "Winged Feet," it will simply allow Russell—"The *Argosy's* crown'd Laureate"—to shine all the more with some response of his own. The second takes up the charge that Lovecraft is merely a man who has been disappointed in love and turned into a cynic—an accusation we have already seen many other Jackson defenders make. Two other poems, "Sors Poetae" and "'The Poetical Punch' Pushed from His Pedestal," seem generally related to the controversy—the first mentions Jackson explicitly and the other is a satire on love stories—but these were perhaps never submitted.

It is worth reflecting on what the whole *Argosy/All-Story* battle over Fred Jackson meant to Lovecraft. In a sense we owe thanks to Mr Jackson (or perhaps F. V. Bennett) for making the rest of Lovecraft's career possible, for there is no telling how long he would have continued to vegetate in the increasingly hothouse atmosphere of 598 Angell Street. Lovecraft had no job, was only toying with chemistry and astronomy, was living with a mother who was steadily losing her mental stability, was writing random undistinguished bits of verse about his native region, and was devouring the Munsey magazines but had no thought of contributing any fiction to them or to any other market. But Jackson's work so irritated Lovecraft that he emerged from his hermitry at least to the extent of bombarding letters to the magazines in question. While it was John Russell who initiated the habit of writing in verse, Lovecraft found it in a golden opportunity to adapt his beloved Augustan satire against a very modern target, as he would do again later in 1914. He probably did not even think it especially odd that he was using the *Dunciad* as a model; recall that he would later assert, with some plausibility, that "I am probably the only living person to whom the ancient 18th century idiom is actually a prose and poetic mother-tongue."[71] On the other hand, Matthew White, Jr (or T. N. Metcalf) probably found Lovecraft's work interesting precisely because it was so quaintly old-fashioned, as well as being rousingly controversial.

Lovecraft seems to have responded reasonably well to the abuse with which he was bombarded, although it is evident that at least a few items—especially by Russell—irritated and perhaps even wounded him. Possibly he ceased to submit his work to the *Argosy* after the first few items because he felt the cause was hopeless: it was obvious that he was not changing very many people's minds and was only annoying many loyal readers. Some of the responses to Lovecraft are surprisingly bitter and hostile, suggesting—whimsically, one hopes—that physical violence be done to the opponent of the beloved Fred Jackson.

The curious thing about the responses to Lovecraft is that many readers took offence at his mere voicing of criticism of Jackson, as if such a thing were in itself somehow off-limits. Some of these comments were on target—those that maintain that the *Argosy* was not published exclusively for one reader's benefit, or that no one is under the obligation to read the magazine—but many readers expressed indignation at the mere levelling of criticism of any kind. The slang terms used to designate this adverse criticism—to "knock" or "kick"—are inherently pejorative, and were interpreted as a sort of personal failing, as if Lovecraft were a misanthrope who could not say anything good about anyone.

One also wonders whether Lovecraft would have engendered the response that he did had he attacked any other writer but Fred Jackson. It certainly appears as if Jackson had a very loyal following both in the *Cavalier* and in the *Argosy;* and I repeat my amazement at the number of men who seemed genuinely to enjoy his love stories. Here again some of the personal attacks are interesting: Lovecraft as the crusty bachelor, as one who has been jilted and is therefore hostile to any expressions of tender emotion, as a cynic who scorns the romantic element in life. Some of these accusations are, indeed, on the mark, but they are irrelevant to the issue of the actual merits of Jackson as a writer; and here Lovecraft is correct in declaring Jackson to be sentimental, stylistically careless, and catering rather calculatingly to the expectations of his audience. But Jackson's defenders were on the whole so pathetically ill-educated that they could not even begin to make the fundamental critical distinction between a story they happened to like and a story that had genuine literary substance. Of course, Jackson's attackers were by and large not much better in this regard.

The ramifications of this entire episode, for Lovecraft, go far beyond the exchange of abuse on a mediocre and insignificant writer. It was, perhaps, the first occasion when he encountered opinions differing radically from his own and coming from a group of people very different (and, quite honestly, quite inferior) in education, culture, and socioeconomic status from his. Although he does not seem to have had much respect for many of his opponents—except, again, Russell—and indeed seems to have had a fairly easy time dynamiting their positions, he would later find such differences of opinion among his friends, colleagues, and correspondents invaluable in shaking him out of his certitudes and broadening his perspective.

The principal immediate benefit of the *Argosy* experience was, of course, his discovery of—or, rather, by—the world of amateur journalism. Edward F. Daas, then Official Editor of the United Amateur Press Association, noticed the poetic battle between Lovecraft and Russell and invited both to join the organisation. Both did so, Lovecraft officially enrolling on April 6, 1914. In a few years he would be transformed both as a writer and as a human being.

6. A Renewed Will to Live (1914–1917 [1])

The world of amateur journalism which Lovecraft entered in April 1914 with wide-eyed curiosity was a peculiar if fascinating institution. The papers produced by the members exhibited the widest possible range in content, format, style, and quality; in general they were quite inferior to the "little magazines" of their day but considerably superior (both in typography and in actual literary content) to the science fiction and fantasy "fanzines" of a later period, although few were so focused on a single topic as the fanzines were. Lovecraft himself gives a potted history of amateur journalism in *United Amateur Press Association: Exponent of Amateur Journalism,* a recruiting pamphlet he wrote early in his term as First Vice-President of the United Amateur Press Association (UAPA), August 1915–July 1916. Here he notes that amateur journalism as a formal institution began around 1866, with a short-lived society being formed by the publisher Charles Scribner and others around 1869. This society collapsed in 1874, but in 1876 the National Amateur Press Association (NAPA) definitively took form; it continues to exist today. In 1895 the UAPA was formed by William H. Greenfield (at that time only fourteen years old[1]) and others who (as Lovecraft believed) wished for an organisation more devoted to serious intellectual endeavour; it was this branch that Lovecraft initially joined. There still exists an alumni association of amateur journalists, The Fossils, who continue to issue a paper, the *Fossil,* on an irregular basis.

By general consensus, the high-water mark of the original amateur journalism movement was the decade of 1885–95, later deemed the "Halcyon Days." It was immortalised, after a fashion, in Truman J. Spencer's anthology, *Cyclopaedia of the Literature of Amateur Journalism* (1891). Not many of the prominent figures of that time were still active during Lovecraft's early days, although a few of them—notably Ernest A. Edkins and James F. Morton—eventually became close friends of Lovecraft. But the period 1916–21 in the UAPA can be thought of as another period when literary quality was at a relatively high level, and Lovecraft can take much of the credit for it. It is, however, a sad fact that no one aside from Lovecraft himself has ever emerged from amateurdom to general literary recognition. This is not to say that others do not deserve to do so: the poetry of Samuel Loveman and Rheinhart Kleiner, the fiction of Edith Miniter (much of it professionally published), and the critical work of Edkins, Morton, and Edward H. Cole need fear no comparison with their analogues in the standard literature of the day. It is, unfortunately, unlikely that much of this work will ever be revived or even taken note of except in connexion with Lovecraft himself.

Amateur journalism was rather more hierarchical and organised than the fantasy fandom movement of the 1930s and following: nearly every issue of the *United Amateur* and the *National Amateur* (the "official organs" of their respective associations) contained detailed membership lists, arranged by state and sometimes by city, and both organisations had an extensive array of officers and departments. They were, in addition, much larger in scope and rather differently organised than the amateur press associations of today: whereas members of the latter send copies of their self-published journals to an Official Editor for distribution to each member, old-time amateur journalists would themselves mail issues of their papers to members of their own choice—and Lovecraft notes (in the "Encouraging Recruits" section of "Finale" [*Badger,* June 1915]) that members occasionally exercised unfortunate prejudices in determining who would receive their papers. These papers were in many instances highly distinguished: at a time when typesetting, printing, paper, and mailing costs were relatively low, such products as W. Paul Cook's *Vagrant,* John Milton Samples's *Silver Clarion,* Lovecraft's own *Conservative,* and the two official organs are as polished in appearance—if not always in contents—as many of the little magazines of their day, and somewhat superior to such things as the *Fantasy Fan* or the *Phantagraph.* Other journals were, of course, very humbly produced, utilising mimeograph, ditto, and other elementary reproduction procedures. In a few anomalous cases, members would simply type or even handwrite sheets of paper and send them on a designated round of circulation.

It is not the case that all, or even the majority, of amateur journalists were young. The members of the UAPA were regularly designated by number and age group: "a" stood for members under 16, "b" for members 16 to 21, and "c" for members over 21 (Lovecraft's number was 1945c). The last category was significantly in the majority. The NAPA in its earlier days was perhaps more youth-oriented: in 1920 Lovecraft makes note of a NAPA convention in 1915 in which the Fossils sought to drive out from amateurdom anyone over twenty;[2] the attempt was unsuccessful, but bespeaks the prejudice toward youth prevailing among the founders of amateur journalism.

And yet, the young were perhaps always the driving forces of amateurdom, lending to it their enthusiasm and energy. In his 1920 essay, *Looking Backward,* Lovecraft, poring over some old amateur journals lent to him by a friend, refers to a semi-professional journal entitled *Young Nova Scotia* that contained "the usual melange of verses, fictional thrillers, puzzles, jests, philately, numismatics, curiosities, and bits of general information." This sounds uncannily like Lovecraft's own juvenile periodicals, especially when he takes note of the advertisements in *Young Nova Scotia* for "such things as chromos, stamps, acquaintance cards, popular songs, lovers' garlands, and printing materials." Lovecraft frequently remarks how the *Rhode Island Journal of Astronomy* and the *Scientific Gazette* were entirely in the spirit of amateur journalism, even though he knew nothing about the institution at the time.

It was not required of amateur journalists of Lovecraft's day—as it is of members of today's amateur press associations—that they produce their own journals. Indeed, no more than a fraction of the members were editors of their own papers, and some of these papers were extremely irregular. In most cases members would send contributions directly to editors of existing amateur journals or to two "Manuscript Bureaux," one for the eastern part of the country, one for the western part; the managers of these bureaux would then dole out the manuscripts to journals in need of material. Individuals with printing apparatus were greatly in demand; indeed, NAPA was originally an organisation not for disinterested *littérateurs* to excel in the art of self-expression but for youthful printers to practise the art of typography. The expense really was very nominal: Lovecraft reports that in 1915 a 5" × 7" paper at 250 copies would cost only 55 or 60 cents a page, while a 7" × 10" paper would cost $1.60 per page.[3] Most journals averaged 4, 8, or 12 pages, although a few ran to as many as 60 or 70 pages.

The literature produced by members varied widely in both content and quality: poetry, essays, fiction, reviews, news items, polemics, and every other form of writing that can fit into a small compass. If it is generally true that most of this material is the work of tyros—"amateurs" in the pejorative sense—then it only means that amateur journalism was performing a perfectly sound if humble function as a proving-ground for writers. Some amateurs did in fact go on to publish professionally. And yet, Lovecraft was all too correct when, late in life, he summed up the general qualitative level of amateur work: "God, what crap!"[4]

In *Looking Backward* Lovecraft reported an old-time amateur's division of members into three types: the literati, the plodders, and the politicians. To Lovecraft the third group was always the most pernicious, and yet it was exactly the elaborate political system of organised amateurdom that fostered the type. Each association held an annual convention—NAPA in early July, UAPA in late July—at which the officers for the next official year were elected. These officers (for the UAPA) included President; First and Second Vice-President; Treasurer; Official Editor; and three members of the Board of Directors. Other officers—Historian, Laureate Recorder, the two Manuscript Managers, and, for a time, a Third and Fourth Vice-President—were appointed by the President, as were the members of the Departments of Criticism (Public and Private), the Supervisor of Amendments, the Official Publisher, and the Secretary. The functions of most of these offices is self-explanatory: the Laureate Recorder was in charge of conducting laureateship awards for best poems, stories, essays, and editorials each year; the Chairman of the Department of Public Criticism would write a critique of amateur journals for that season in each issue of the official organ; the Department of Private Criticism would privately assist cruder members in improving their work. With this elaborate hierarchy, it was no surprise that some members became interested only in attaining eminence in the organisation by holding office, and that intensely bitter, personal, and vituperative election campaigns were held to ensure the victory of a given individual or faction. Lovecraft writes of these people:

> They sought office for its own sake; and their ideals and triumphs were of tinsel only. They had no issues to champion, and their standard of success was merely the ability to sway those about them. Office to them was not an opportunity to serve, but a mere prize to be captured for its own intrinsic value as an advertisement of cunning and popularity. The politicians saw in amateurdom an easy field for the exercise of cheap subtlety on a small scale . . . (*Looking Backward*)

The subtlety was cheap and the scale was small because the number of individuals involved in amateurdom was always relatively modest. The November 1918 *United Amateur* lists only 247 active members; the November 1917 *National Amateur* lists 227 (many individuals belonged to both associations). It is exactly for this reason that both the politicians—and, indeed, Lovecraft, even though his goals were loftier and his capabilities far superior—could achieve eminence in this field: they did not have a great deal of competition.

Amateur journalism was exactly the right thing for Lovecraft at this critical juncture in his life. For the next ten years he devoted himself with unflagging energy to the amateur cause, and for the rest of his life he maintained some contact with it. For someone so unworldly, so sequestered, and—because of his failure to graduate from high school and become a scientist—so diffident as to his own abilities, the tiny world of amateur journalism was a place where he could shine. Lovecraft realised the beneficial effects of amateurdom when he wrote in 1921:

> . . . Amateur Journalism has provided me with the very world in which I live. Of a nervous and reserved temperament, and cursed with an aspiration which far exceeds my endowments, I am a typical misfit in the larger world of endeavour, and singularly unable to derive enjoyment from ordinary miscellaneous activities. In 1914, when the kindly hand of amateurdom was first extended to me, I was as close to the state of vegetation as any animal well can be—perhaps I might best have been compared to the lowly potato in its secluded and subterranean quiescence. With the advent of the United I obtained a renewed will to live; a renewed sense of existence as other than a superfluous weight; and found a sphere in which I could feel that my efforts were not wholly futile. For the first time I could imagine that my clumsy gropings after art were a little more than faint cries lost in the unlistening void. ("What Amateurdom and I Have Done for Each Other")[5]

To this analysis there is really very little to add, although a wealth of detail is necessary to flesh out the picture and to pinpoint exactly how this transformation occurred. As for what Lovecraft did for amateurdom, that too is a long story, and one worth studying carefully.

In 1914, when Lovecraft entered amateur journalism, he found two schisms that were creating much bad blood and using up valuable energy. The first was, of course, the split between the National and United Amateur Press Associations, which had occurred when the latter was founded in 1895. Perhaps schism is not quite the correct term here, for ostensible reason for the establishment of the UAPA was the desire of certain members to devote themselves more concentratedly to literature and less to fraternal good cheer and mutual back-patting. As I have mentioned, a good many members belonged to both associations; Lovecraft, in spite of labelling himself repeatedly and ostentatiously a loyal "United man," joined the National himself as early as 1917, and would later serve as interim president.

The other split—a schism in the full and proper sense of the word—was one within the United itself, with the result that the very name of the organisation was (as a few hostile NAPA members gleefully pointed out) a cause for embarrassment. Lovecraft addresses this matter in two essays, "The Pseudo-United" (1920) and "A Matter of Uniteds" (1927). (The former was published anonymously in the *United Amateur* for May 1920, but Lovecraft was credited as the author when the piece won the Editorial Laureateship for that year.) In 1912 occurred a hotly contested election at the UAPA convention in La Grande, Oregon; the result was that both of the two candidates for president, Helene E. Hoffman and Harry Shepherd, declared themselves the winner. Lovecraft states in his earlier article that "it was determined to the satisfaction of all impartial observers that . . . Miss Hoffman was safely and lawfully elected"; in his later piece, either because at that time he had become less passionately devoted to his own side and was attempting to reconcile the two factions or because he had gained more accurate information on the matter, he declares more neutrally that "the final vote [was] so close and so dependent on a technically accurate interpretation of the voting status of many members that no one can say even now with absolute finality which side gained the legal victory." What actually happened was that, although Hoffman had received 56 proxy votes and Shepherd 48 (with 9 others going to other candidates), a complicated technicality awarded the presidency to Shepherd.[6]

In his various remarks Lovecraft never points out that it was the Hoffman faction that refused to accept the verdict of the UAPA directors (who confirmed the election of Shepherd) and withdrew. Indeed, if all one knows of the controversy comes from Lovecraft, one would think it was the Shepherd group that was the rebel organisation; but in fact the amateur world to this day regards the Hoffman group as the rebels and the discontents, even though many acknowledge their literary and numerical superiority.

In any event, the Hoffman supporters established their own association, retaining the title United Amateur Press Association, while the group around Shepherd called itself the United Amateur Press Association of America. Lovecraft joined the former because he had been recruited by Edward F. Daas of that faction; probably he did not at the time even know of the existence of the other, as it was largely centred on Seattle. This latter really was the smaller and less consequential group (it had only 149 members in September 1919, and that was a considerable increase over the figure of some years before), even though it doggedly published its own *United Amateur* for years, largely through the financial and editorial support of J. F. Roy Erford. From 1917 to 1919 this faction had no official editor and was essentially quiescent; in 1917 Lovecraft wrote, a little sanguinely, that it "seems to have disappeared beneath the horizon of adversity" ("Editorially," *United Amateur,* July 1917), and he urged its remaining members to join his United. Not many appear to have done so. In late 1919 the group revived after a fashion, and it was exactly some members' hostility to another of Lovecraft's overtures at amalgamation that led to the writing of "The Pseudo-United." Now deciding to hold nothing back, Lovecraft presents a devastating portrayal of the intellectual backwardness of this group: "Its cultural tone has steadily declined, until today the majority of its members are of extreme crudity—mostly superficial near-Bolsheviki and soulful plumbers and truck-drivers who are still at the moralising stage. Their little schoolboy compositions on 'Individualism', 'The Fulfilment of Life', 'The Will', 'Giving Power to the Best', and so on, are really touching." Let it pass that Lovecraft himself would become a near-Bolshevik ten or fifteen years after writing this.

It is somewhat ironic that the "pseudo-United" actually outlasted Lovecraft's United; the latter essentially collapsed from disorganisation and apathy around 1926, while the other United carried on until 1939. But for all practical purposes it was a moribund association, and when Lovecraft was persuaded to resume amateur activity in the 1930s he saw no option but to work for the NAPA.

The United's split with the National was something Lovecraft vigorously supported and never wished to see healed. His contempt for the older group—which he fancied (perhaps rightly) to be a haven of old-timers resting on their laurels, men and women who looked back fondly to their lost youth as amateur printers and typographers, and politicians devoted to furthering their own causes and gaining transient and meaningless power in an insignificant arena—is unremitting. In "Consolidation's Autopsy" (published in the *Lake Breeze* for April 1915 under the not very accurate pseudonym "El Imparcial") he dynamites the position of those Nationalites who are seeking some sort of rapport with the United. Dismissing the National as "an inactive Old Men's Home," he writes:

> The National has never more ingenuously confessed its fundamental failing than when referring affectionately to "the small boy with a printing press". This is the much-vaunted grandeur of the National. Not literary, not educational, grandeur, but a record of mere juvenile typographical achievement; a development of the small-boy ideal. While this may be eminently laudable in its way, it is not the kind of grandeur that our United is seeking, and we would certainly hesitate before bartering our own literary traditions for any print-shop record like the National's.

There are several interesting things here. First, that "small-boy ideal" was something Lovecraft himself would have found very congenial during his own youth when he was diligently hectographing the *Rhode Island Journal of Astronomy* and other periodicals; and the fact that he now scorns this ideal may bespeak his realisation that, as a man of twenty-five, he must move on toward some higher literary goal. Indeed, perhaps the vehemence of his response rests precisely in his awareness that he himself had a somewhat arrested adolescence and was anomalously long in separating himself from boyhood interests. Second, Lovecraft may perhaps be exaggerating the degree to which the United was at this time literarily superior to the National. In the late teens the National had some very fine papers—notably W. Paul Cook's *Vagrant,* to which Lovecraft himself would contribute a number of tales and poems—which the United would have had difficulty matching. It is true that the *United Amateur,* especially under Lovecraft's editorship, evolved into a much more substantial and interesting literary organ than the *National Amateur,* which tended to remain a dry chronicle of official business—convention reports, membership lists, financial statements, and the like. But ultimately the literary distinction between the two associations was one of degree and not of kind.

Lovecraft was always ready to defend his association from attacks by the other. In "A Reply to *The Lingerer*" (*Tryout,* June 1917) he is quick to rebut the Rev. Graeme Davis, who would become Official Editor of the NAPA for the 1917–18 term and who in his amateur journal, the *Lingerer,* alliteratively accused the United of "permanent puerility and immutable immaturity." To this Lovecraft responded, correctly, that "all amateurdom is more or less homogeneously tinctured with a certain delicious callowness," so that "it ill becomes the pot to call the kettle black."

And yet, it was only a few months after this that Lovecraft joined the NAPA; but he did so, he reports, for the overall good of amateurdom. On November 8, 1917, he wrote to Rheinhart Kleiner:

> At the repeated solicitation of many persons who declared that my aloofness from the National was a barrier to inter-associational harmony, I sent in an application for membership about a week ago. My connexion, however, will be purely nominal; as I gave the Nationalites very clearly to understand. I have time and

> strength only for my own association, yet was willing to have my name on the National's list if it would help any.[7]

The "many persons" referred to here may have included several NAPA members who had by this time become close friends of Lovecraft: Edward H. Cole, Charles W. Smith (editor of the long-running amateur journal, the *Tryout*), and W. Paul Cook (whose allegiance for years wavered between the NAPA and the "other" United). For several years Lovecraft contented himself with sending occasional contributions to NAPA journals; only in the exceptional circumstances of the winter of 1922–23 did he consent to become actual interim president of the association he had for scorned for so long, fulfilling his obligations admirably.

It was only in 1925, when his own association was in its long death-agony, that Lovecraft even considered an offer—this time made by C. W. Smith—for the consolidation of the UAPA and NAPA. Even here, however, he held out a hope against hope for the revival of his own association: "It may be that the new board, by crusading far afield for youthful, energetic, and superior membership, will be able to inaugurate a new era of active writing, criticism, stimulation, and discussion in the traditional United manner . . ." ("Editorial," *United Amateur,* July 1925). But it was all a pipe-dream.

But that was eleven years in the future. In 1914 Lovecraft entered a thriving if unfocused organisation of heterogeneous membership but substantial promise. As he plunged into amateur activity, contributing essays and poems (later stories) to amateur journals, becoming involved in heated controversies, and in general taking stock of the little world he had stumbled upon, he gradually formulated a belief—one that he gained remarkably early and maintained to the end of his life—that amateur journalism was an ideal vehicle for the effecting of two important goals: first, abstract self-expression without thought of remuneration; and second, education, especially for those who had not had the benefit of formal schooling. The first became a cardinal tenet in Lovecraft's later aesthetic theory, and its development during his amateur period may be the most important contribution of amateur journalism to his literary outlook. It is not, of course, likely that amateurdom actually originated this idea in Lovecraft's mind; indeed, Lovecraft would not have responded so vigorously to amateurdom if he had not already held this view of literature as an elegant diversion. His statement of 1923—"A gentleman shouldn't write all his images down for a plebeian rabble to stare at. If he writes at all, it shou'd be in private letters to other gentlemen of sensitiveness and discrimination"[8]—could, if shorn if its tongue-in-cheek snobbery, apply to the whole of his writing career.

Lovecraft very much stressed the *amateur* in amateur journalism. In public he vigorously denied that "amateur" was equivalent to "tyro" or "bungler" (even though privately he knew there were many such in amateurdom), preferring to maintain: "Our amateurs write purely for love of their art, without the stultifying influence of commercialism. Many of them are prominent professional authors in the outside world, but their professionalism never creeps into their association work. The atmosphere is wholly fraternal, and courtesy takes the place of currency" (*United Amateur Press Association: Exponent of Amateur Journalism*). This was, of course, more wishful thinking than fact; but Lovecraft tried his best to make it a reality. His proposal in 1916—whether jocular or not—to retitle the UAPA "The United Association for the Cultivation of Letters" ("Editorial," *Providence Amateur,* February 1916) gives sufficient indication of the direction of his thought. His most idealistic utterance comes in "For What Does the United Stand?" (*United Amateur,* May 1920):

> . . . the United now aims at the development of its adherents in the direction of purely artistic literary perception and expression; to be effected by the encouragement of writing, the giving of constructive criticism, and the cultivation of correspondence friendships among scholars and aspirants capable of stimulating and aiding one another's efforts. It aims at the revival of the uncommercial spirit; the real creative thought which modern conditions have done their worst to suppress and eradicate. It seeks to banish mediocrity as a goal and standard; to place before its members the classical and the universal and to draw their minds from the commonplace to the beautiful.

A noble utterance, but again largely wish-fulfilment—or, rather, a poignant testimonial to all that amateurdom meant for Lovecraft himself. Gone were the days when he would charge anywhere from a penny to a half-dollar for his hectographed magazines or treatises or stories; art for art's sake (although he would not so term it until a little later) was now the desideratum.

Lovecraft never tired of attacking the commercial spirit, whether in the amateur world or outside it. A hilarious broadside is "The Proposed Authors' Union" (*Conservative,* October 1916), in which the attempt by "a certain class of American professional authors" to form a union and join the American Federation of Labor is viciously derided. He remarks archly that "the professions of the average modern author and of the day-labourer are remarkably alike":

> Both types shew a certain rough vigour of technique which contrasts very strikingly with the polish of more formal times, and both seem equally pervaded with that spirit of progress and enlightenment which manifests itself in destructiveness. The modern author destroys the English language, whilst the modern strike-loving labourer destroys public and private property.

And how is one to adjudicate pay for poets, since some (like Thomas Gray) spend seven years on a poem only 128 lines long, while "speedy labourers" like Coleridge and Southey can collaborate on an entire verse drama in an evening? What about possible violence against scabs? Would it manifest itself in the form of "stoning or of satire"? And so on.

At the same time that Lovecraft was hailing the non-mercenary spirit of amateurdom, he was regarding the amateur world as a practice arena for professional publication. This is not a paradox because what he meant by "professional publication" was not hackwork but publication in distinguished magazines or with reputed book publishers. In so doing one is not buckling down to produce insincere pseudo-literature simply for money but allowing the polished products of one's "self-expression" to achieve a worthy audience. "The normal goal of the amateur writer is the outside world of letters, and the United should certainly be able to provide improved facilities for the progress of its members into the professional field" ("Department of Public Criticism," *United Amateur,* August 1916).

The means to achieve these lofty goals in amateurdom was education. It is surely plausible to believe that Lovecraft's own failures in formal education caused him to espouse this goal as fervently as he did; in effect, it was his own way of fulfilling the promise of that nickname "Professor" which he probably acknowledged secretly, or even openly, in high school. Consider the wording of "For What Does the United Stand?":

> The United aims to assist those whom other forms of literary influence cannot reach. The non-university man, the dwellers in different places, the recluse, the invalid, the very young, the elderly; all these are included within our scope. And beside our novices stand persons of mature cultivation and experience, ready to assist for the sheer joy of assisting. In no other society does wealth or previous learning count for so little. . . . It is an university, stripped of every artificiality and conventionality, and thrown open to all without distinction. Here may every man shine according to his genius, and here may the small as well as the great writer know the bliss of appreciation and the glory of recognised achievement.

This all sounds very well, but Lovecraft regarded it as axiomatic that he was one of the "great" writers in this little realm, one of the "persons of mature cultivation and experience" who would raise his lessers to whatever heights they could achieve. This was not arrogance on Lovecraft's part but plain truth; he really was one of the leading figures of amateurdom at this time, and his reputation has remained high in this small field. This ideal of amateurdom as a sort of informal university was something Lovecraft found compelling and attempted—ultimately in vain—to bring about.

Lovecraft was by no means alone in holding this view of amateur journalism; one of the reasons he became so enthusiastic about the UAPA was his awareness that others had the same vision. In *United Amateur Press Association: Exponent of Amateur Journalism* he cites an article by Maurice W. Moe, "Amateur Journalism and the English Teacher," published in the high school edition of the *English*

Journal for February 1915. This article was an address delivered at a meeting of the National Council of Teachers of English (then and now the leading organisation for high school teachers) at Chicago on November 27, 1914, and recommended the formation of amateur press clubs in high schools—Moe himself had organised such a group in Appleton High School in Appleton, Wisconsin. Moe speaks of the virtues of amateurdom in much the same tones as Lovecraft: "Every endeavor is made to promote a friendly spirit and a love of writing among the members, through correspondence and mutual criticism and even through a bureau of private criticism conducted by professionals, who give their services without charge."[9] Lovecraft maintained that Moe's address "created so much enthusiasm for the *United,* that scores of instructors have subsequently joined our ranks, many of them forming school clubs on the model of the original club at Appleton."

Lovecraft tirelessly promoted this idea; at one point (in "Finale," *Badger,* June 1915) he declared explicitly and personally his regret that such a thing had not been available at Hope Street High School. Speaking of himself in the third person, Lovecraft wrote:

> He himself published an amateur paper from 1903 to 1907 in absolute ignorance of his organised contemporaries, and placed before the indifferent and uncritical readers of rural newspapers and cheap magazines those immature literary efforts of his which might have received a far warmer welcome and a far sounder criticism in the congenial atmosphere of the United. Had he found a copy of the *United Amateur* at the high-school or library, he would certainly have been enjoying the privileges of amateur journalism for more than a decade instead of being at this moment a raw recruit.

This was written in connexion with Lovecraft's support for two proposals made by Paul J. Campbell: the first would transform the *United Amateur* into a monthly magazine that would feature both literary works as well as official business; the second would make an aggressive effort to bring amateurdom to the attention of high schools and colleges. The first of these proposals was formalised into an amendment to be voted upon by the membership at the UAPA convention in July 1915. It passed, and in August 1915 the *United Amateur* began monthly publication, continuing until January 1917, when—probably because of lack of funds—it reverted to its customary bi-monthly schedule. But throughout this whole period the official organ did substantially increase its proportion of literary as opposed to official matter, and would continue to do so in later years under the official editorship of Verna McGeoch, Anne Tillery Renshaw, and Lovecraft himself. As for attracting high school students, Lovecraft during his term as President of the UAPA (August 1917–July 1918) won approval for the creation of a third and fourth Vice-President to assist in recruiting at, respectively, colleges and high schools. The fourth Vice-President during Lovecraft's term was his friend Alfred

Galpin, then at Appleton High School. It is not clear how much these two offices contributed to increasing United membership; as apathy set in among the members in the early 1920s, these positions—as well as even the second Vice-President for a time—disappeared.

Another proposal Lovecraft backed was the formation of a Department of Instruction, "which may teach in an easy and gradual manner the basic principles of grammar, rhetoric, and versification, as well as direct the aspirant to a well-graded and selected course of reading in the works of the best authors" ("New Department Proposed: Instruction for the Recruit," *Lake Breeze,* June 1915). Interestingly, Lovecraft excluded himself from consideration for such a department by maintaining that "all amateurs not engaged in the educational profession should be debarred *ipso facto* from participation in the activities of such a department, however great their general scholarship." This may not have been quite as altruistic as it sounds: earlier in this essay he noted that both critical bureaux (the Departments of Public and Private Criticism) were overwhelmed with requests for revisory services, and it is conceivable that part of Lovecraft's motive for proposing the Department of Instruction was to relieve himself of some of the burdens of this task. In June 1916 he wrote: "I am now struggling with reams of crude MSS. for the forthcoming paper of credentials; in fact, I have before me the entire contents of both MSS. Bureaus for revision."[10]

This idea does not appear to have met with much enthusiasm. By August 1916 Lovecraft announced that he had "learned that under present conditions such a department is not perfectly feasible" ("Department of Public Criticism," *United Amateur,* August 1916); he did not explain this remark, but perhaps lack of money to set up the department was a factor. The UAPA was chronically short of funds and frequently required donations from members in addition to their $1.00 dues for printing the *United Amateur* and other purposes. Lovecraft, in spite of his declining financial situation, would frequently contribute to this "Official Organ Fund." In any event, he now proposed that each of the "cultivated" members take one or more of the "cruder" members under his or her wing and tutor them privately. So far as I can tell, this idea too fell flat.

By this time, however, Lovecraft had acquired a more concrete vehicle for pushing his literary agenda. His first prose contribution to the UAPA was a short essay, "A Task for Amateur Journalists" (*New Member,* July 1914), in which he urged the amateur world to assist in preserving the language from "pernicious" corruptions. This is, of course, a theme Lovecraft would sound throughout his life: as one who had raised himself to regard eighteenth-century prose as the norm, any modern prose—especially the occasionally slovenly and colloquial prose of amateurs less well-educated than he—could only be offensive. A few months thereafter Lovecraft obtained a forum whereby he could more materially keep amateurs linguistically in line: around October 1914 he was appointed by President Dora M. Hepner to take over the chairmanship of the Department of Public Criticism, presumably because the previous chairman, Ada P. Campbell, retired or withdrew. It was the first office Lovecraft held, and he made the most of it.

The office entailed Lovecraft's writing a lengthy article for the *United Amateur* criticising in detail each and every amateur journal that was submitted for review. His first article appeared in the November 1914 issue, and over the next five years Lovecraft wrote twenty more. These pieces must be read to gain some idea of his devotion to the amateur cause. Here is a representative passage:

> *Aurora* for April is a delightful individual leaflet by Mrs. Ida C. Haughton, exclusively devoted to poetical matters. The first poem, "Aurora", is truly exquisite as a verbal picture of the summer dawn, though rather rough-hewn metrically. Most open to criticism of all the features of this piece, is the dissimilarity of the separate stanzas. In a stanzaic poem the method of rhyming should be identical in every stanza, yet Mrs. Haughton has here wavered between couplets and alternate rhymes. In the opening stanza we behold first a quatrain, then a quadruple rhyme. In the second we find couplets only. In the third a quatrain is followed by an arrangement in which two rhyming lines enclose a couplet, while in the final stanza the couplet again reigns supreme. The metre also lacks uniformity, veering from iambic to anapaestic form. These defects are, of course, merely technical, not affecting the beautiful thought and imagery of the poem; yet the sentiment would seem even more pleasing were it adorned with the garb of metrical regularity. "On the Banks of the Old Wegee" is a sentimental poem of considerable merit, which suffers, however, from the same faults that affect "Aurora". Most of these defects might have been obviated when the stanzas were composed, by a careful counting of syllables in each line, and a constant consultation of some one, definite plan of rhyming. ("Department of Public Criticism," *United Amateur,* September 1915)

Plodding and schoolmasterly as this is, it is exactly the sort of criticism the amateurs needed. It would have been futile to present a lofty dissection of the philosophical substance of their work when many were struggling to achieve the barest minimum of grammatical correctness in prose and verse. Lovecraft is tireless in the patient, careful advice he gives: he always attempts to find some merit in the work under consideration, but he never lets a technical flaw go by.

Naturally, Lovecraft had his biases. As early as January 1915 Lovecraft took note of Leo Fritter's complaint (not addressed toward Lovecraft himself) that "some authorised amateur critics deal far too roughly with the half-formed products of the young author." Lovecraft was not guilty of this exact charge; rather, his flaws as an official critic (at least in his early phase) were political and social prejudices and an unwillingness to realise that not everyone wished a return to "tasteful Georgian models" ("Department of Public Criticism," *United Amateur,* August

1916). Slang and colloquialism particularly offended him. In writing of William J. Dowdell's *Dowdell's Bearcat,* he noted:

> While the general style of the paper is fluent and pleasing, we believe that "Bruno" might gain much force of expression through the exercise of a little more care and dignity in his prose. For instance, many colloquial contractions like "don't", "won't", or "can't" might be eliminated, while such slang phrases as "neck of the woods", "make good", "somewhat off", or "bunch of yellow-backs" were better omitted. ("Department of Public Criticism," *United Amateur,* May 1915)

Poor Dowdell faced another barrage when, in the *Cleveland Sun,* he introduced a sports page:

> Of "The Best Sport Page in Amateurdom" we find it difficult to speak or write. . . . We learn with interest that a former United member named "Handsome Harry" has now graduated from literature to *left field,* and has, through sheer genius, risen from the lowly level of the ambitious author, to the exalted eminence of the *classy slugger.* . . . Speaking without levity, we cannot but censure Mr. Dowdell's introduction of the ringside or ballfield spirit into an Association purporting to promote culture and lettered skill. ("Department of Public Criticism," *United Amateur,* September 1916)

"Too many of our authors," writes Lovecraft in 1916, "are contaminated with modern theories which cause them to abandon grace, dignity, and precision, and to cultivate the lowest forms of slang" ("Department of Public Criticism," *United Amateur,* August 1916).

Lovecraft summed up his early views on this issue in "The Dignity of Journalism"—published, perhaps with some irony, in *Dowdell's Bearcat* for July 1915. Opening with a lofty and Johnsonian dictum—"It is a particular weakness of the modern American press, that it seems unable to use advantageously the language of the nation"—Lovecraft lashed out at the use of slang in amateurdom, doing so in a manner that remarkably fuses intellectual and social snobbery:

> The idea that slang-infested literature is more readable and pleasing than that which conforms to refined taste is nearly parallel to that of the Italian peasant immigrant, who fondly considers his soiled but flaming kerchief and other greasy but gaudy apparel far more beautiful than the spotless white linen and plain, neat suit of the American for whom he works. While good English may in unskilful hands sometimes become monotonous, this defect cannot justify the introduction of a dialect gathered from thieves, ploughboys, and chimney sweeps.

But Lovecraft did present other arguments that are a little sounder. In rebutting the charge that "the slang of today is the classic language of tomorrow," he keenly advised the interested reader to examine "any one of the numerous dictionaries of slang and Americanisms" wherein are contained words that, though once common, had now fallen completely out of usage. Lovecraft himself owned at least one such volume: John Russell Bartlett's *Dictionary of Americanisms* (1877), which the author had inscribed and presented to F. C. Clark.

Another frequent target was simplified spelling. We may find Lovecraft's comments on this subject somewhat heavy-handed—akin to using a sledgehammer to crack a nut—but simple spelling was being advocated by a great many distinguished critics and grammarians of the day, including Brander Matthews, whom Lovecraft skewered at the conclusion of his witty satiric poem, "The Simple Speller's Tale" (*Conservative,* April 1915): "Yet why on us your angry hand or wrath use? / We do but ape Professor B——— M———!" This poem really is a delight, telling of how the protagonist, seeking a way to avert other amateurs' criticism "because I could not spell," goes past a madhouse and hears a man "Who had from too much study lost his mind":

"Aha!" quoth he, "the men that made our tongue
Were arrant rogues, and I shall have them hung.
For long-establish'd customs what care we?
Come, let us tear down etymology.
Let spelling fly, and naught but sound remain;
The world is mad, and I alone am sane!"

Lovecraft delivers a learned lecture on the history of simplified spelling in "The Simple Spelling Mania" (*United Co-operative,* December 1918), starting from Sir Thomas Smith's "radical and artificial scheme of phonetic spelling" in the Elizabethan period, "which defied every law of conservatism and natural growth," through other attempts in the seventeenth, eighteenth, and nineteenth centuries. Curiously, his historical survey ends around 1805, thereby failing to take much note of the vigorous campaigns for "spelling reform" undertaken in his own time, including such things as the new alphabet proposed by George Bernard Shaw and the simplified spelling utilised by Robert Bridges. Lovecraft ends with the plea: "Are there not enough sound critics in amateurdom to conduct a systematic campaign, both by example and precept, against 'simplified' spelling?"

Lovecraft's main thrust in this debate—aside from his desire to "conserve" the traditions of English usage—is that the etymological system of orthography enshrined in Samuel Johnson's dictionary (1755; Lovecraft owned a 12th edition [1802]) should be maintained because it has now become so uniform and widespread throughout the English-speaking world; Johnsonian orthography was conveyed to America, as Lovecraft notes, through the *New England Primer* (1760), of the first edition of which he had three ancestral copies. This danger to the English language appears to have passed, and Lovecraft has ended up on the right side of the argument; although he would look askance at the encroachments of "advertising English" and the bastardised forms—*nite, thru,* and the like—propagated in its name.

The degree to which Lovecraft was devoted to the literary standards of the eighteenth century is no more evident than in "The Case for Classicism" (*United Co-operative,* June 1919), in which he took to task one Prof. Philip B. McDonald—Chairman of the Department of Private Criticism and identified as Assistant Professor of Engineering English (whatever that is) at the University of Colorado—for belittling the relevance of classic authors in developing effective style and rhetoric. Although Lovecraft claimed that "It is not my purpose here to engage in any extensive battle of ancient and modern books, such as that fought in Saint-James's Library and veraciously chronicled by Dean Swift," such a battle of the books was exactly what Lovecraft conducted here: ". . . I cannot refrain from insisting on the permanent paramountcy of classical literature as opposed to the superficial productions of this disturbed and degenerate age." As if this were not enough, Lovecraft continued: "The literary genius of Greece and Rome, developed under peculiarly favourable circumstances, may fairly be said to have completed the art and science of expression. Unhurried and profound, the classical author achieved a standard of simplicity, moderation, and elegance of taste, which all succeeding time has been powerless to excel or even to equal."

This utterance is quite remarkable. Many who read the masterworks of Latin and Greek literature find them so perfect of their kind that reactions like the above are not uncommon. Indeed, taken in a very literal sense, Lovecraft's statement is fundamentally true. But to say that the ancients "completed the art and science of expression" means that there is nothing left for subsequent writers to do but to imitate; and Lovecraft in fact went on to say that "those modern periods have been most cultivated, in which the models of antiquity have been most faithfully followed." What Lovecraft ignores here is that even in the eighteenth century it was the adaptation of classical models to the contemporary world that produced the most viable literature of the period. The brilliance of Johnson's *London* or Pope's *Dunciad* stems not from their aping of the forms of Roman verse satire but from their application of these forms to vivify very modern concerns. Lovecraft, indeed, attempted to do something similar in his own poetry—using eighteenth-century forms in writing poems about World War I, for example—but, as we shall later see, his efforts were on the whole quite unsuccessful.

Lovecraft was, however, correct in refuting McDonald's claim that "the classical style is too restrained, and lacking in humanity"; he added, a little impishly, "So far as restraint goes, a malicious commentator might easily use Prof. McDonald's own bare and staccato prose style as an illustration of inconsistency betwixt precept and practice." It should again be emphasised that Lovecraft was so intent on rebutting McDonald precisely because he felt McDonald's recommendation to abandon classicism would set a bad precedent and undo much of his own work in weaning the amateur world away from informality, slang, and colloquialism: "I am an advocate of the highest classical standard in amateur journalism, and shall continue to bend all my energies toward its maintenance."

With attitudes like these, it is not surprising that Lovecraft was, throughout the course of his amateur career, forced to defend himself against those who felt that his criticism was both too harsh and misguided. In "A Criticism of Amateur Journals," published in Lovecraft's own amateur journal, the *Conservative* (July 1918), Philip B. McDonald noted that "it is more important to be interesting than to be correct." In "Amateur Criticism," an article in the very same issue, Lovecraft attempted to blast this position: "We may pardon a *dull* writer, since his Boeotian offences arise from the incurable mediocrity of his genius; but can we thus excuse the *careless* scribbler whose worst blunders could be corrected by an extra hour of attention or research?" This really evades the question of whether there is a place for slang or colloquialism in writing, since it is a truism that elementary errors of grammar and syntax ought to be corrected if a piece is written in an orthodox style. This leads, in any event, to a discussion of "the element of individual taste and personal preferences in official criticism":

> . . . it would be foolish to insist that the reviewer suppress all honest convictions of his own; foolish because such suppression is an impossibility. It is, however, to be expected that such an one will differentiate between personal and general dicta, nor fail to state all sides of any matter involving more than one point of view. This course *The Conservative* sought to follow during his tenure of the critical chairmanship . . .

This answer did not seem to satisfy everyone, for in 1921 the controversy arose again, this time from John Clinton Pryor (editor of *Pine Cones*) and, of all people, Lovecraft's close friend W. Paul Cook. Even though Lovecraft had by this time ceased to be an official critic (his last stint as Chairman of the Department of Public Criticism ended in July 1919), something in Pryor's and Cook's remarks touched a raw nerve, and Lovecraft felt obliged to respond with one of the most vitriolic articles of his entire literary career, "Lucubrations Lovecraftian" (*United Co-operative,* April 1921). One section in particular, entitled "Criticism Again!," attempts a direct rebuttal of attacks against the severity of official criticism. It opens with towering cynicism:

> It would be futile for the United's Department of Public Criticism to reply to most of the querulous complaints levelled against it. In nine cases out of ten the circumstances are very simple—one mediocre and egotistical author plus one honest review equals one plaintive plea that the bureau, or part of it, is engaged in a diabolical plot to suppress incipient genius. The complainer, as a type, is one who candidly opposes any attempt at genuine constructive criticism, but who expects

> the department to mince along as a medium of flattery. He feels that his dollar dues entitle him to a certain amount of praise irrespective of merit.

And yet, Lovecraft acknowledged that "there is another sort of complaint which must be received very differently—a calm, balanced sort prompted by intelligent difference in opinion, and connected only subconsciously with personal feelings anent reviews"; and he claimed—outwardly at least—that the criticism of Pryor and Cook was of this latter variety. But his treatment of it is nonetheless harsh. The essence of both articles[11] was, as Lovecraft states it, that "personal opinions on various subjects have been expressed on various subjects in the official critical reviews" and that this practice is "harmful," in that "it causes the views of individuals to be published as the official views of the United as a body."

Lovecraft's response is similar to, but more pointed than, that of his earlier article, "Amateur Criticism." He announces with emphasis: *"Official criticism is 'official' only so far as it concerns the relation of the work criticised to the artistic standards recognised as universal."* Again, *"no personal opinions are given the stamp of officialdom, because officialdom does not extend beyond art."* It is actually preferable for a critic to state his or her position on a literary or philosophical or political subject in the course of a review rather than to suppress it, for it will inevitably emerge in the very tenor of the critic's remarks. "Seldom have our critics failed to separate general and personal views"; and this statement can apply to virtually all of Lovecraft's own official reviews.

The tone of Lovecraft's rebuttal is so sharp precisely because he placed so much value in the Department of Public Criticism as a tool for the educational improvement of amateur writing. Lovecraft himself certainly felt so during the three terms he was Chairman of the department (1915–16, 1916–17, and 1918–19), and he very likely inculcated his views to the two other chairmen who served between 1915 and 1922 (Rheinhart Kleiner [1917–18] and Alfred Galpin [1919–22]), since both were close friends of his. (Lovecraft in fact quietly took over the position when Kleiner fell ill and was unable to fulfil his duties, so that the unsigned articles for January, March, and May 1918 are by Lovecraft.) The fact that both these individuals shared many of Lovecraft's strict views on the "dignity of journalism" may have caused resentment from those members who did not.

Beginning sometime in 1914 Lovecraft made an attempt to practise his educational ideal very close to home, by assisting in the formation of a Providence Amateur Press Club. The impetus for this club came from one Victor L. Basinet, who on the suggestion of Edward H. Cole (a Boston amateur journalist associated with the NAPA) formed an amateur press club among some working-class people in the "North End" of Providence who were attending night classes at a local high school.[12] Cole—who was very likely already in touch with Lovecraft—probably urged the group to gain assistance from the UAPA's only Rhode Island member; and Lovecraft, thinking that this attempt to "uplift the masses" might succeed better than the incident with Arthur Fredlund eight years earlier, gave considerable assistance. The group met at the end of each month,[13] and no doubt Lovecraft attended these meetings as often as he could.

Most of the members were Irish; among them was a particularly feisty young man, about a year and a half older than Lovecraft, named John T. Dunn (1889–1983). In the first issue of the *Providence Amateur* (June 1915) Basinet is listed as President, Eugene M. Kern as Vice President, Caroline Miller as Secretary-Treasurer, Lovecraft as Literary Director, and Dunn as Official Editor; other members listed are Edmund L. Shehan, Fred A. Byland, Mildred Metcalf, and Peter J. MacManus.

The poem that opens the issue, Lovecraft's "To the Members of the United Amateur Press Ass'n from the Providence Amateur Press Club," gives some idea of who these people were. Basinet at this point seems to have been the guiding force ("By his bright genius all the club was made"); his radical political views are treated with studied politeness ("With fearless mien he scorns oppressive laws, / And stands a champion of the people's cause"), although elsewhere Lovecraft alluded to the fact that Basinet was a socialist,[14] which could hardly have sat well with him at this time. Dunn was rabidly anti-English, and he and Lovecraft sparred with each other on this issue in letters for at least two years. In his poem Lovecraft alluded to arguments over historical matters ("Skill'd in dispute, with none he fears to vie, / But picks up L———'s faults in history"); although Dunn himself later confessed that Lovecraft "knew . . . his history,"[15] at least as far as the Irish question was concerned. As for the other members, we learn that Edmund L. Shehan was a movie buff but evidently found some films objectionable on moral grounds; Caroline Miller was a writer of heart-rending love stories; one Reilly (not listed in the staff list of the first issue) was a writer of unspecified prose work; and "the quiet" Fred A. Byland wrote prose of "forceful logic" and "pleasing style." We are reliant on Lovecraft's (no doubt flattering) portraits of these individuals, since very few of them actually had any contributions published in the two issues of the *Providence Amateur*.

The first issue, indeed, appears to have been written entirely by Lovecraft and Dunn, although only three of the six pieces are signed. The poem is signed by Lovecraft; there follows an article, "Our Candidate" (probably by Lovecraft), supporting Leo Fritter for President of the UAPA at the next election (Fritter in fact won the election); "Exchanges" (what in later amateur press circles would be termed "mailing comments"), brief remarks on other amateur journals received by the club (probably by Lovecraft); an "Editorial" (signed "J. T. D.") declaring that the Providence Amateur Press Club is emphatically part of the UAPA as opposed to the NAPA, and (in contradistinction to the "other" United) part of "the association of which Miss Hepner is now President"; "On Acknowledgements" (signed "J. T. D."), on Dunn's failure to receive many amateur publications even though he is a member; and "For Historian—Ira A. Cole" (probably by Lovecraft), supporting Cole's candidacy for that office.

It is by no means an insignificant issue. The last page declares that it has been printed at the Lincoln Press, Cambridge. There is considerable evidence (see below) that the printer was fellow-amateur Albert A. ("Sandy") Sandusky, and it is likely that Cole had recommended Sandusky to the club. Lovecraft elsewhere made note of "some unauthorised omissions made by the printer" ("Department of Public Criticism," *United Amateur,* September 1915), so presumably more contributions (perhaps by other members) were to have been included. The "Office of Publication" of the *Providence Amateur* is given as 83 Commodore Street in Providence (Dunn's residence), and one imagines that the monthly meetings of the group, with Lovecraft in attendance, occurred here at least on some occasions.

Basinet seems to have severed his connexion with the club shortly after the first issue. Lovecraft wrote to Dunn in July 1915 that Basinet was about to issue his own paper, the *Rebel,*[16] but no such paper appears to have been published. Indeed, a later remark by Lovecraft to Dunn—that Basinet is "about to revisit Providence"[17]—indicates that Basinet had moved out of the city altogether; he had in fact gone to Brooklyn. As a result, the leadership of the club fell almost entirely to Lovecraft and Dunn.

The second issue of the *Providence Amateur* (February 1916) is more substantial than the first, although the typographical accuracy is very poor. It was also printed by the Lincoln Press, but one hopes that Lovecraft was not in charge of the proofreading. It opens with a weighty poem, "Death," by Edmund L. Shehan. There follows a curious article by Peter J. MacManus, "The Irish and the Fairies," in which the author recounts what he believes to have been a sighting of fairies when he was seven years old and living in Connacht. Part of this article is likely to have been revised, or even written, by Lovecraft; the following sentence almost certainly came from his pen: "I observed in the field adjoining ours what appeared to be a graceful procession of about twelve young maidens, all draped in robes whose hue rivalled that of the fleecy clouds in the azure vault above." Lovecraft has added an "Editor's Note" in which he regards MacManus as a sort of quaint *naïf* from some primitive age: "The Irish of today, as startlingly shewn by Mr. MacManus, have as vital and as real a belief in the various Aryan personifications of Nature as had the Greeks of the Homeric period." MacManus, however, is deadly serious and really believes what he writes ("let no man doubt the existence of fairies on the Green Isle"). Lovecraft may have dealt with him kindly because the incident perhaps recalled his own fancied sighting of Greek deities at exactly the same age.

John T. Dunn follows with a humorous poem, "A Post-Christmas Lament"; Edmund L. Shehan then adds an interesting brief piece, "The Making of a Motion Picture," on visiting the Eastern Film Company in Providence; Lovecraft then supplies a four-page "Editorial" lamenting the paucity of good prose in amateurdom and urging more members to issue their own journals; the issue concludes with two of Lovecraft's poems, "To Charlie of the Comics" (unsigned) and "The Bride of the Sea" (as by "Lewis Theobald, Jr."). In this issue Lovecraft is listed as Official Editor and his address is given as the office of publication.

Dunn, interviewed by L. Sprague de Camp in 1975, provides some fascinating glimpses of Lovecraft's personal comportment at the meetings of the club:

> Dunn found Lovecraft . . . odd or even eccentric. At gatherings, Lovecraft sat stiffly staring forward, except when he turned his head towards someone who spoke to him. He spoke in a low monotone.
>
> "He sat—he usually sat like that, looking straight ahead, see? Then he'd answer a question, and go back again," said Father Dunn. "I can see him now . . . and he looked straight ahead; and . . . he didn't emphasize things. He nodded sometimes to emphasize a word or an expression.
>
> "I liked the fellow," he continued. "I didn't have anything against him at all, see? Only we did disagree; but I hope we disagreed like gentlemen, see?"
>
> . . .
>
> Lovecraft's voice was high-pitched but not what one would call shrill; Dunn said it was about like his own. Lovecraft had great self-control, never losing his temper no matter how heated the argument. "He—ah—I never saw him show any temper, see? But when he wrote, he wrote very vigorously; there's no doubt about that, see . . .? And he never got excited like I would get excited."[18]

Dunn and Lovecraft certainly did have some epistolary fireworks, as I shall discuss later.

Lovecraft washed his hands of the club shortly after the appearance of the second issue, although he continued to keep in touch with Dunn for another year or so. In a mid-1915 letter he spoke of hoping to aid one "Mr. Wright" (Hubert A. Wright) form a similar club in Pawtucket, but this never came about. The club itself had definitely folded by the fall of 1916, for a poem by Lovecraft, "Providence Amateur Press Club (Deceased) to the Athenaeum Club of Journalism"—evidently unpublished in his lifetime but dated November 24, 1916—speaks gloomily of the collapse of the group:

> What can we say, who on Rhode Island's shore
> Were once a club, but are a club no more;

Whose puny petals ne'er to bloom unclos'd,
Nor on Pierus' sacred slopes repos'd:
Who stand apart, disorganis'd and weak,
With naught save one *Conservative* to speak?

So ended Lovecraft's second attempt to uplift the masses.

I have made frequent reference to the *Conservative.* This was, of course, Lovecraft's own amateur journal, and the first periodical he edited since the demise of the *Rhode Island Journal of Astronomy* in February 1909. Although Lovecraft was on the editorial board of several other amateur journals, the *Conservative* was the only one of which he was the sole editor. Thirteen issues appeared from 1915 to 1923, broken down as follows:

Volume I: April 1915, July 1915, October 1915, January 1916
Volume II: April 1916, July 1916, October 1916, January 1917
Volume III: July 1917
Volume IV: July 1918
Volume V: July 1919
No. 12: March 1923
No. 13: July 1923

The issues range from 4 to 28 pages. The first three issues were written almost entirely by Lovecraft, but thereafter his contributions decline considerably except for occasional poems and—beginning with the October 1916 issue—a regular editorial column entitled "In the Editor's Study." The first issue is 8 unnumbered pages and contains one poem, six articles, and some random notes on amateur affairs, all written by Lovecraft. I shall examine the content of these and other issues presently; right now I wish to concern myself with mechanical matters of printing and distribution. Lovecraft reported that 210 copies of the first issue were printed[19] and were already sent out by mid-March. No printer is listed for the issue, so it was probably printed locally. There is, in fact, a curious note directly below the masthead on the first page: "*The Conservative* desires to apologise for any errors in proofreading which may be found in this issue. Circumstances necessitated a change of printer at the last moment, and an already great delay rendered haste a prime essential." I am not sure what this means, especially since the issue clearly appeared at least a week or two before the cover date. Lovecraft probably sent out copies to every member of the UAPA.

The next four issues were printed by The Lincoln Press. Lovecraft wrote to Dunn on October 25, 1915: "*The Conservative* was promised to me today, but it has not yet arrived. I hope Sandusky will have it soon enough for me to send out during the month for which it is dated."[20] This makes it clear that the printer for these issues (as well as for the two issues of the *Providence Amateur*) was Albert A. Sandusky, an amateur in Cambridge, Massachusetts, whom Lovecraft later met on several occasions. Probably Lovecraft's disgust with the "stupid printer" ("Amateur Notes," *Conservative,* July 1915) of the first issue, and the relative success of Sandusky's printing of the first *Providence Amateur,* persuaded Lovecraft to use him as his regular printer. Sandusky's typographical and printing work was generally good; Lovecraft (or Sandusky) now adopted a two-column format except for poems whose lines could not be so accommodated.

On August 15, 1916, Lovecraft reported to Dunn that "Sandusky cannot print *The Conservative* any more, so I am now in quest of a suitable typographical artist."[21] In this same letter Lovecraft stated: "The July number, sadly overdue, has been expressed to me, but is delayed in transit. If I do not receive it soon, I shall have to ask Sandusky to have the package traced." This suggests that Sandusky printed the July 1916 issue, even though it does not bear any notice for the Lincoln Press and the issue has a very different typeface and design from those of its predecessors. This four-page issue, containing only a single article by Henry Clapham McGavack, reverts to the single-column format.

The next three issues are clearly printed by the same printer. Lovecraft noted to Dunn on November 13, 1916, that "*The Conservative* for October is in the hands of a local printer, and has been promised for delivery today."[22] Lovecraft went on to say that this issue, "the largest ever published," cost him $30.00. This rate is considerably higher than what Lovecraft was citing in his recruiting pamphlet for papers of this size (5" × 7"). By "largest" Lovecraft presumably meant cumulative wordage, for it is only 12 pages whereas the issue for October 1915 had been 16.

In September 1917 Lovecraft wrote to Kleiner that he had decided to have the *Conservative* printed in future by W. Paul Cook of Athol, Massachusetts, whom he had just met: "His low rates are a philanthropic favour to amateurdom, & are based upon a complete sacrifice of personal profit. He is so anxious to establish a revival of amateur journalism, that he is doing the work absolutely at cost."[23] Lovecraft then cited Cook's rates:

300 copies 5 × 7 = $0.85 per page
300 copies 6 × 9 = $1.05 per page
300 copies 7 × 10 = $1.25 per page

It would be nearly a year, however, before Lovecraft took advantage of Cook's cheap rates. The next *Conservative,* July 1918, is 8 pages in a 5" × 7" format, which means it must have cost Lovecraft only $6.80. Cook may have printed only this issue and that of July 1919; the last, and possibly the second to last, were printed by Charles A. A. Parker.

Although Lovecraft, in the "Editorial" for the first issue, declared with "trembling humility" that he was "thrusting upon an unsuspecting public this first issue of what purports to be a paper" and concluded the editorial by wistfully saying that "he may never perpetrate another number of this modest magazine," it is clear that he welcomed the prospect of editing his own paper rather than merely contributing random pieces to other amateur journals or appearing in the official organ. In particular, what this allowed him to do—aside from promoting his own vision of amateurdom as a haven for literary excellence and a tool for humanist education—was to express his own opinions fearlessly. He did just that. The "Editorial" in the July 1915 issue contains his statement of editorial policy:

> That the arts of literature and literary criticism will receive prime attention from *The Conservative* seems very probable. The increasing use among us of slovenly prose and lame metre, supported and sustained by the light reviewers of the amateur press, demands an active opponent, even though a lone one, and the profound reverence of *The Conservative* for the polished writers of a more correct age, fits him for a task to which his mediocre talent might not otherwise recommend him.
>
> . . .
>
> Outside the domain of pure literature, *The Conservative* will ever be found an enthusiastic champion of total abstinence and prohibition; of moderate, healthy militarism as contrasted with dangerous and unpatriotic peace-preaching; of Pan-Saxonism, or the domination by the English and kindred races over the lesser divisions of mankind; and of constitutional representative government, as opposed to the pernicious and contemptible false schemes of anarchy and socialism.

A mighty tall agenda. I have already touched on some of the controversies over literature in which Lovecraft engaged; his political debates—both in published works and in private correspondence—were no less vigorous, and I shall treat them in due course. We will find that some of Lovecraft's early opinions are quite repugnant, and many of them are uttered in a cocksure, dogmatic manner greatly in contrast with his later views. Nevertheless, it was evident to all amateurs that the editor of the *Conservative* was an intellectual force to be dealt with. Rheinhart Kleiner gives some idea of how the first issue of the journal was received:

> . . . many were immediately aware that a brilliant new talent had made itself known. The entire contents of the issue, both prose and verse, were the work of the editor, who obviously knew exactly what he wished to say, and no less exactly how to say it. *The Conservative* took a unique place among the valuable publications of its time, and held that place with ease through the period of seven or eight years during which it made occasional pronouncements. Its critical pronouncements

> were relished by some and resented by others, but there was no doubt of the respect in which they were held by all.[24]

Kleiner, in referring to the controversies stirred up by Lovecraft's articles and poems, goes on to say: "Those of his opponents who were able to withdraw from such encounters with dignity and prestige unimpaired were somewhat few." But we shall find that Lovecraft did not always get the better of an argument.

Lovecraft's official career in amateur journalism was augmented by his election in July 1915 as First Vice-President of the UAPA. Leo Fritter (whom Lovecraft supported as a proponent of his literary agenda in "For President—Leo Fritter" in the April 1915 *Conservative*) renewed his appointment as Chairman of the Department of Public Criticism, a position he would hold until July 1917. Part of his responsibility as First Vice-President was to be the head of the Recruiting Committee, for which he wrote the pamphlet *United Amateur Press Association: Exponent of Amateur Journalism.* This, the second separate publication by Lovecraft (for the first, *The Crime of Crimes* [1915], see the next chapter), appears to have been issued in late 1915. In "Report of First Vice-President" (*United Amateur,* November 1915) he wrote that the "long-promised recruiting booklet is now in press at Columbus, O., having been financed jointly by President Fritter and the undersigned." I would have thought that, since the item was an official publication, it would have been printed by the then Official Printer (E. E. Ericson of Elroy, Wisconsin), but evidently Fritter decided to have it printed locally. Lovecraft went on to add a little smugly: "The text is of dignified nature, offering a sharp contrast to the sensational advertising of some of the inferior associations." The reference can scarcely be to anything but the NAPA.

Other official duties fell upon Lovecraft. In the second "Report of First Vice-President" (*United Amateur,* January 1916) he notes working on a "paper of credentials"; that is, a journal collecting pieces by new or prospective members establishing their literary capability. (Lovecraft's own credential, "The Alchemist," did not appear until the November 1916 *United Amateur.*) By June Lovecraft was declaring that he was still "struggling with with reams of crude MSS. for the forthcoming paper of credentials."[25] (There is a certain paradox in this: why would the mss. need revision, since their very purpose was to verify a potential member's literary ability?) I am not sure that this paper—which was to have been edited by Mrs E. L. Whitehead[26]—ever appeared. There is a much later journal, the *Credential* (April 1920), for which Lovecraft is listed as assistant editor, but Anne Tillery Renshaw is the editor. In the spring of 1916 Lovecraft was offered the official editorship of the UAPA upon the resignation of Edward F. Daas; he declined on the grounds of "ill health,"[27] and the task fell to George S. Schilling.

For the next term (1916–17) Lovecraft had no official function except Chairman of the Department of Public Criticism. Schilling, as a member of the Ohio National Guard, was summoned to duty in Mexico and was therefore unavailable as Official Editor. Paul J. Campbell, running for President, wished Lovecraft to run as Official Editor, but again Lovecraft declined on account of ill health. He also refused to accept another term as First Vice-President, urging instead his young protégé David H. Whittier.[28] Whittier was in fact elected to the office but withdrew by October for some reson, being replaced by Ira A. Cole. Lovecraft was nevertheless on the ballot for President and Official Editor at the UAPA convention in July; presumably because most members knew that he was not a declared candidate, Lovecraft lost to Campbell for President by a vote of 38-2, and lost to Andrew F. Lockhart for Official Editor by a vote of 28-1.

Late in 1916 Campbell appointed Lovecraft Chairman of the Year Book Committee, and for the next several months he was occupied with the compilation of a "biographical directory of United members"[29] for 1916–17. The "other" United actually did issue a yearbook for 1914, published by W. Paul Cook and consisting largely of laureate-award-winning items and lists of officers.[30] Perhaps in order not to be outdone by its rival, the UAPA decided to do one of its own. There had been talk of a yearbook for 1915–16, but I do not believe it was ever published. In the January 1917 *Conservative,* in the brief article "A Request," Lovecraft urged members to send him information on their amateur careers. By November 1917 ("President's Message," *United Amateur*) Lovecraft announced that the yearbook—which contained a revised version of his recruiting pamphlet, *United Amateur Press Association: Exponent of Amateur Journalism*—was complete in "sixty-three closely typed manuscript pages" (which probably means single-spaced pages, Lovecraft's customary manner of typing at the time), but he expressed concern that there was not enough money in the Year Book Fund actually to publish the volume. The yearbook, so far as I know, never appeared, and it is very likely that lack of funds—which would have to have come from contributions by UAPA members—was the cause of its non-issuance.

In July 1917, however, the *United Amateur* listed Lovecraft as Official Editor. This came about in a somewhat peculiar way. The Official Editor of the 1916–17 term, Andrew F. Lockhart of Milbank, South Dakota, was a vigorous temperance advocate, achieving notable success in his efforts in 1915 and 1916. But in May 1917 he suffered, according to Lovecraft, "defeat at the hands of his enemies—the vice & liquor interests of South Dakota—and has been sent to the Federal Prison at Ft. Leavenworth, Kansas, after a farcially unfair trial."[31] The UAPA membership lists indicate that Lockhart remained at Leavenworth through 1919. President Paul J. Campbell appointed Lovecraft Official Editor for the final issue of the term (July 1917); Lovecraft stated his intention of "planning an issue which will be long remembered in amateurdom, though I am not certain that I shall succeed."[32]

Whether it was a long-remembered issue or not, the July 1917 issue was certainly full of Lovecraft's own work. It contained five substantial pieces by him: an editorial (pretentiously entitled "Editorially"); a lengthy "Department of Public Criticism" article; a section of "News Notes" (brief notes about amateurs, customarily written by the Official Editor); an article on Eleanor J. Barnhart in a column entitled "Little Journeys to the Homes of Prominent Amateurs"; and the poem "Ode for July Fourth, 1917." The editorial, in countering the attacks of Graeme Davis, resoundingly asserts the literary supremacy of the UAPA over the NAPA:

> As the United Amateur Press Association concludes its twenty-second year of existence, its members may well pause to consider the commanding position it now occupies in the world of amateur letters. Beginning as an obscure competitor to an association big with pride of achievement and hoary with years and traditions, our United has forged to the front rank with a steady certainty which speaks well for its equal loftiness and liberality of ideals.

As this was being written, however, Lovecraft was anticipating a still greater distinction in the association. "I am named as candidate for the Presidency next year, and Campbell informs me that my election is very probable."[33] True enough, Lovecraft was elected President at the UAPA convention in late July, and most of the other elected or appointed officials were those who were as eager to promote his literary programme as he: Wesley H. Porter, First Vice-President; Winifred Virginia Jordan, Second Vice-President; Verna McGeoch, Official Editor; W. Paul Cook, Official Publisher; and Rheinhart Kleiner, Chairman of the Department of Public Criticism. Although Lovecraft had declared in June 1916 that "I shall never give up my place on the Department of Public Criticism till some future President refuses to appoint me,"[34] the burdens of the presidency clearly made a continuance of this office impossible, and the meticulous Kleiner was a logical choice. For the next five years Lovecraft and his associates essentially controlled the UAPA, and the result really was a very significant raising of the literary tone. For a time it looked as if Lovecraft's goals for amateurdom would be grandly fulfilled.

During this whole period Lovecraft had recommenced the writing of monthly astronomy articles, this time for the *Providence Evening News.* The first one appears in the issue for January 1, 1914, hence actually predates his entry into amateur journalism. I do not know how Lovecraft got this assignment, which lasted until May 1918 and is by far his most extensive astronomical series; he stated in 1916 that the series in the *Tribune* was "transferred"[35] to the *Evening News,* but the former had ceased in 1908, and there was moreover no connexion between the two papers. As for its termination, Lovecraft made the cryptic remark that "a change of management produced a demand for a changed style to which I refused to accede."[36] Elsewhere he was more forthright: ". . . the request of its editor for me to make my articles 'so simple that a child might understand them' caused me to withdraw from the field."[37] I have no doubt that Lovecraft was paid for each of the fifty-three articles he published, even if the pay is likely to have been insignificant.

The *Evening News* articles become tedious and repetitious if read all at once, for they are in large part merely accounts of the notable celestial phenomena for the month: the phases of the moon, the constellations visible in the morning or evening sky, any eclipses, meteor showers, or other events of note, and the like. After a year, of course, many of the same phenomena will recur. Nevertheless, Lovecraft gradually made attempts to loosen up a little and to introduce other sidelights along the way. In particular, he took it upon himself to explain the origin of the Greek or Roman names for the constellations, and this naturally allows him to recount, sometimes at considerable length, the myths behind such names as Castor and Pollux, Argo Navis (recall his lost juvenile work, "The Argonauts"), and many others. His early reading of Bulfinch and other mythographers held in him good stead here. Consider his charming elucidation of "dog days" (*dies caniculares*):

> The traditions surrounding the Dies Caniculares are very interesting and very ancient. In Egyptian times the appearance of Sirius in the morning twilight, preceding the rising of the Nile, counselled the farmers to sow their grain. From this important function, the star acquired a religious significance, and was the object of much worship. Seven ruined temples have been discovered which were so built that the beams of Sirius, heliacally rising, should strike the great altars. Even the name "Sirius" is thought by some students to be derived from "Osiris", the name of the greatest of the Egyptian gods. In Asia, the heliacal rising of Sirius was regarded as the source of the extreme heat of late summer, a belief to which Virgil more than once alludes; whilst among the Romans a dog was each year sacrificed to the star at this season. ("The August Sky," August 1, 1914)

What becomes even more charming is his increasingly frequent citation of poems by himself or by others. The entirety of his poem "On Receiving a Picture of Swans" is quoted in the article for August 1916; a recasting of part of "The Poet's Nightmare" appears in the article for May 1917; there are poetry extracts by Lovecraft—evidently original to these articles—in October and November 1916. Needless to say, Lovecraft does not acknowledge himself as the author of these poems, referring instead to "a recent bard" or "the following lines."

In the fall of 1914, however, as Lovecraft was steadily writing article after article for the *News,* a rude interruption occurred. An article entitled "Astrology and the European War" by one J. F. Hartmann appeared in the issue for September 4, 1914—only three days after Lovecraft's astronomy column for that month, and in the exact place in the newspaper (the centre of the last page) occupied by his column. Joachim Friedrich Hartmann (1848–1930) was, one imagines, of German ancestry, but was born in Pennsylvania. He came to Providence no later than 1912, and through his life held such occupations as masseur, shoe store clerk, and Santa Claus.[38] In 1914 he was residing at 77 Aborn Street in downtown Providence. Hartmann's article begins resoundingly:

> The vulgar prejudice against the noble science of astrology by otherwise learned men is greatly to be deplored.
>
> Almost every author on astronomy, mythology, anthropology and philosophy; school teachers, professors of universities and the clergy, while willfully ignorant of astrology, yet never tire loading it with slurs and abuse, ridicule and misrepresentation; ever insinuating that astrologers must either be fools or knaves.

Hartmann went on to attack both scientists and the clergy for their hostility to astronomy, then transcribed certain predictions for the rest of the year, culled from *Raphael's Ephemeris,* published the previous year. Given the state of international relations in Europe in 1913, the predictions are not especially remarkable: "The influences operating in King George's horoscope are very unfavourable"; "The kaiser is under very adverse directions, and danger both to health and person is indicated"; and so on.

This was just the sort of thing to make Lovecraft see red. Writing to Maurice W. Moe in early December 1914, he noted: "Recently a quack named Hartmann, a devotee of the pseudo-science of Astrology, commenced to disseminate the usual pernicious fallacies of that occult art through the columns of *The News,* so that in the interests of true Astronomy I was forced into a campaign of invective and satire."[39]

Lovecraft began with a straightforward but somewhat intemperate response entitled (probably by Lovecraft rather than the editor of the *News*) "Science versus Charlatanry," published in the issue for September 9. In all honesty, the response is not especially effective, merely asserting without much argument "the utter absurdity of the idea that our daily affairs can be governed by the mere apparent motions of infinitely distant bodies whose seeming arrangements and configurations, on which the calculations of judicial astrology are based, arise only from perspective as seen from our particular place in the universe." Lovecraft does keenly point out the dubious nature of the *Raphael* predictions: "War in the Balkans, unrest in Russia, and revolutions in Central or South America are among the events most successfully predicted." And he cannot help referring to his very first appearance in print, when the "learned astrologer of Central Falls, R.I." who spoke of a "transit of Mars" also asserted that Pope Pius X (1835–1914) would die in 1906.

But Lovecraft had underestimated his foe. Hartmann responded with a direct rebuttal to Lovecraft's letter in the issue for October 7, addressing Lovecraft's points systematically and actually scoring a few telling blows. Lovecraft had asserted that astrology had been "exploded over 200 years ago"; Hartmann hurls the rejoinder: "No one ever heard the explosion; where and when did it occur?" The thrust of Hartmann's response, however, is that Lovecraft and other astronomers had not truly examined astrology: "If they really feel 'obliged' to disprove astrology, why don't they try it, and in a manner becoming the scientific method." As for the many astrological predictions that had not come true, Hartmann responded:

> But just think of all the astronomers who have made mistakes. Then astronomy must be a superstition. There is no science but its votaries have made mistakes. Then all the sciences must be false.
>
> Think of all the mistakes in calculation made by bookkeepers and bank clerks. Then what a wretched pseudo-science must be arithmetic.
>
> What a poor rule that won't work both ways!

Sophistical as some of this is, it required a stronger and more systematic attack than Lovecraft had given it in his initial letter. He was not slow to take up the challenge.

Three days later, on October 10, a letter by Lovecraft appeared under the title "The Falsity of Astrology." This letter is still more intemperate than the first, opening with the assertion that "the ordinary modern astrologer is merely a mountebank who seeks to defraud the ignorant by means of crude gibberish which he knows to be untrue" but maintaining that Hartmann was of that more troublesome class "who actually believe in their own ridiculous teachings, and who can therefore invest their fallacious arguments with the convincing force of genuine though misplaced enthusiasm." While asserting that Hartmann had said little new in his response, Lovecraft's own letter does little to flesh out his argument. He added an amusing personal note: "The baleful effect of Astrology upon the reputation of Astronomy is far too patent for Mr. Hartmann to argue away. I was not long ago asked by a man who had seen my astronomical articles, 'if I did not cast horoscopes or calculate nativities'! It is not pleasant for a serious student of the heavens to be taken for a petty fortune-teller." I would give much to have been present at this encounter. The one important point Lovecraft here asserts—important more for his own philosophical development rather than for the present controversy—is an appeal to anthropology:

> Astrology is the legacy of prehistoric ignorance. Since our primitive ancestors saw that the motion of the sun through the Zodiac influenced their affairs by the change of season which it causes, or that the movements and phases of the moon affected their nocturnal pursuits by the alternative presence and absence of moonlight, they must have believed themselves under the direct control of these bodies. . . . In time, the ancients came to seek explanations for all the phenomena of earthin the phenomena of the heavens, and arbitrarily to assign a celestial cuase for every terrestrial occurrence.

We shall see this exact argument used as a significant weapon in Lovecraft's dismissal of the metaphysical claims of religion.

But before Hartmann could respond to this latest attack, Lovecraft struck back in a different manner. He explained in a letter: ". . . eventually the stupid persistence of the modern Nostradamus forced me to adopt ridicule as my weapon. I thereupon went back to my beloved age of Queen Anne for a precedent, and decided to emulate Dean Swift's famous attacks on the astrologer Partridge, conducted under the nom de plume of Isaac Bickerstaffe (or Bickerstaff—I have seen it spelled both ways)."[40] The result is an article in the issue for October 13 entitled "Astrology and the Future" (true to the *News*'s typographical standards, the first word in the headline was misprinted "Astrologh") by "Isaac Bickerstaffe, Jr." This really is an exquisite—if rather broad and obvious—piece of satire. Lovecraft does not follow Swift in exact particulars—Swift's *tour de force* had been to predict the death of Partridge, and then to follow up with a very convincing account of Partridge's death, after which the poor devil had a very difficult time proving that he was still alive—but merely maintains that, by its own principles, astrology ought to be able to predict events far in the future rather than merely a year or so in advance. Consider the following: "The crossed transit of Jupiter and Uranus over the alternately radical sun and moon on March 9, 2448, is certain evidence that the American monarch will be overthrown in that year as a result of a popular uprising led by Gen. José Francisco Artmano and a new republic established; the capital being moved from Mexico City back to Washington." Note the reference to a "transit" of a superior planet, which is of course impossible; similarly a later reference to the "sextile opposition of Vulcan in Gemini," even though Lovecraft asserted frequently in his astronomy columns that the existence of the conjectured intra-Mercurial planet Vulcan had been definitively disproven. But this is not the worst:

> Last and most terrible of all, the collusive quaternary trine of Mars, Mercury, Vulcan, and Saturn, in the 13th progressed house of the sign Cancer on Feb. 26, 4954, stands out as plainly as the handwriting on the wall to shew us the awful day on which this earth will finally and infallibly perish through a sudden and unexpected explosion of volcanic gases in the interior.

Hartmann battled gamely on, however. The October 22 issue contains the lengthiest of his pieces, a long and sober article entitled "The Science of Astrology" in which he systematically lays down the "principles" of astrological science in a relatively orderly manner. He made no allusion either to Lovecraft's "Falsity of Astrology" or to the Bickerstaffe squib.

In turn, Lovecraft parried with "Delavan's Comet and Astrology," a Bickerstaffe article printed in the October 26 issue, which takes up where its predecessor left off, making the following proclamation: ". . . the computed alternating back eccentric transit of the future projection of Delavan's comet around the progressed quartile square of the prolonged inclination of the retrograde orbit of Saturn clears up the perplexing situation in a moment, renders the whole matter most simple and obvious, and restores to man that hope without which the heart would sicken and break." In short, Delavan's comet will strike the earth fifty-six years prior to the explosion of our planet, and will take all the inhabitants of the globe on its tail to dwell "for evermore . . . in peace and plenty" on Venus. Humanity is saved! But not everyone will emerge unscathed:

> I find to my extreme regret that several fragments from the terrestrial explosion of 4954 will strike the planet Venus, there creating much damage, and causing grave injuries to Señor Nostradamo Artmano, a lineal descendant of our talented Prof. Hartmann. Señor Artmano, a wise astrologer, will be hit in the cranial region by a large volume of astronomy, blown from the Providence Public Library, and his mind will be so affected by the concussion that he will no longer be able to appreciate the divine precepts of astrology.

Crude, but effective.

This second parody seems to have stunned Hartmann for a time, for it was not until the issue of December 14 that he finally came back. He now sounds extremely resentful against Lovecraft for what he believes (not entirely unjustly) are his "false statements, angry contempt, abusive language, and vulgar personalities." But the most exquisite passage in his lengthy tirade is the following:

> Two recent articles in these columns, by an enemy falsely posing as an astrologer, are real "gibberish," the kind which our critic does not criticise.
>
> Real astrologers never write such ridiculous parodies upon their own sacred science, which Mr. Lovecraft calls a "base superstition."

It is pitifully obvious that Hartmann, although recognising that the Bickerstaffe articles are parodies, has not deduced that they are also the work of his enemy.

Lovecraft responded more soberly with "The Fall of Astrology" in the December 17 issue, elaborating the anthropological argument and maintaining that "The downfall of astrology was the inevitable result of intellectual progress; of new discoveries in science, improved methods of reasoning, more intelligent examination of history, and more discriminating investigation of the prophecies of astrologers."

But Lovecraft couldn't help piling it on. A final letter by Isaac Bickerstaffe, Jr, printed without title in the December 21 issue, parodies the vagueness and obviousness of some astrological predictions, giving some glimpses of what can be expected in the first six months of 1915: January ("Conjunction of Mercury and Mars on first indicates prosperous and disastrous year"); March ("Entrance of Sun into sign Aries shews that spring will begin on the 21st"); May ("Superior Conjunction of Mercury on 1st shews that weather will be much warmer than January"); June ("Summer will probably commence this month"); and so on. Of course, he expresses sorrow and disappointment at the base attacks on him by

"Prof. Hartmann," asserting: "How can we astrologers hope successfully to promulgate our glorious science, if we have such bitter dissensions amongst ourselves?"

Hartmann evidently decided to give up at this point. Amusingly enough, however, in the issue for December 23 he published an article on "Santa Claus and the Christmas Tree: Their Origin and Meaning"; but as this article was inoffensive to Lovecraft's scientific principles, it did not earn a rebuttal.

Lovecraft did not quite let Hartmann off the hook, however. He continued to jab at him, usually without mentioning him, in later astronomical columns in the *News.* In October 1914, at the height of the controversy, Lovecraft wrote huffily:

> It is with regret that the writer notes at the present time a rather virulent epidemic of astrological quackery in this city. Belief in the fortune-telling power of the stars and planets is of course superstition of the grossest sort, and a most incongruous feature of this enlightened age; yet astrology is a plague which has proved most difficult to eradicate, and only too many persons of indifferent education are still the dupes of its absurd pretensions. ("The November Sky," October 31, 1914)

As late as May 1915, in recounting the origin of the name Coma Berenices, Lovecraft makes reference to "Conon, the court astrologer [of Egypt], a sage no doubt almost as wise as our star-gazing contemporary Mr. Hartmann" ("The May Sky," April 30, 1915).

I do not know that much need be made of the Lovecraft-Hartmann feud. In some particulars it resembles the *Argosy* controversy, although on the whole John Russell was a more formidable opponent than Hartmann; but the latter was by no means a pushover, and his vigorous defence of his views clearly took Lovecraft aback. Lovecraft really gained the victory by the Bickerstaffe pieces rather than by his formal rebuttals, which are not as strong and convincing as one would like. But perhaps they showed Lovecraft that satire could be effective in both prose and verse: over the years he would write a number of charmingly vituperative prose sketches that occupy a perhaps minor but nonetheless distinctive place in his corpus.

The March 1917 astronomy article for the *News* begins rather awkwardly: "To many readers of these monthly chronicles of the heavens, certain technical terms used in describing the apparent motions of the planets have doubtless seemed obscure and meaningless. It is accordingly the writer's design to attempt an explanation of those which most frequently occur in articles of this sort." This was a somewhat belated attempt to convey systematic instruction to the layman, and one would have expected such a thing to have occurred at the very commencement of the series. Perhaps readers had actually written to the paper complaining of the unexplained use of technical terms; indeed, it may have been complaints of this kind that led the editor, a year later, to demand that Lovecraft simplify his language, although after the above article he does not appear to have made much effort to do so.

Two years earlier Lovecraft was given a chance to begin a series more auspiciously, and he took full advantage of it. A series of fourteen articles entitled "Mysteries of the Heavens Revealed by Astronomy" appeared in the *Asheville* (N.C.) *Gazette-News* from February to May 1915, although part of the thirteenth and the fourteenth article have not come to light. What we have, however, is a systematic and elementary treatise on all phases of astronomy for the complete novice. As Lovecraft announced at the head of the first article:

> The series beginning with this article is designed for persons having no previous knowledge of astronomy. Only the simplest and most interesting parts of the subject have here been included. It is hoped that this series may help in a small way to diffuse a knowledge of the heavens amongst the readers of *The Gazette-News,* to destroy in their minds the pernicious and contemptible superstition of judicial astrology, and to lead at least a few of them to a more particular study of astronomical science. ("The Sky and Its Contents," February 16, 1915)

The allusion to the J. F. Hartmann controversy, then concluded only a few months previously, is of note, as is the almost desperate attempt to avoid any of the technicalities of the subject; in the *Providence Evening News* article of September 1915 he would speak of the benefits of astronomical knowledge "disencumbered of its dull mathematical complexities," a bittersweet reference to the principal cause of his own failure to become a professional astronomer. "Mysteries of the Heavens" is, then, a good example of what Lovecraft might have done had he decided to become merely a popular science writer. Mildly interesting as the series is, it is good for the sake of literature that he did not so limit his horizons.

But how did Lovecraft arrange to write an astronomy series for a newspaper in Asheville, North Carolina? The solution appears in Lovecraft's early article "Introducing Mr. Chester Pierce Munroe" (1915), where we are told that Lovecraft's boyhood friend has now "established himself at the Grove Park Inn, Asheville." I have little doubt that Chester, wishing to give his friend some remunerative work (Lovecraft is almost certain to have been paid for the series), spoke with the editor of the *Gazette-News,* perhaps even offering him some of Lovecraft's *Providence Evening News* articles as samples.

The result is an orderly and workmanlike series discussing, in sequence, the solar system (including specific discussions of the sun and each of the planets), comets and meteors, the stars, clusters and nebulae, the constellations, and telescopes and observatories. Some of the articles were split into two or more parts and were not always published in sequence: in one anomalous instance, the first part of "The Outer Planets" was followed by the first part of "Comets and Meteors," followed by two segments of "The Stars," followed by the second parts, respectively, of "The Outer Planets" and "Comets and Meteors." A segment was published every three to six days in the paper. The last surviving article, "Telescopes and Observatories," appeared in two parts in the issues for May 11 and 17, 1915, and the second part ends with "(TO BE CONTINUED)" prominently displayed; but some issues subsequent to May 17 appear to be no longer extant, so that we have either lost the end of this article (the thirteenth) or—if "Telescopes and Observatories" concluded here—the fourteenth. My feeling is that there should be another segment of the thirteenth article in addition to an entire fourteenth article, since this final segment only broaches the topic of observatories, concluding after a single lengthy paragraph on the subject.

There is not much one can say about the *Asheville Gazette-News* save that they are competent pieces of popular science. Naturally, Lovecraft harps on some of his favourite topics, especially cosmicism. In speaking of the possibility that the farthest known star may be 578,000 light-years away, he notes:

> Our intellects cannot adequately imagine such a quantity as this. . . . Yet is it not improbable that all the great universe unfolded to our eyes is but an illimitable heven studded with an infinite number of other and perhaps vastly larger clustes? To what mean and ridiculous proportions is thus reduced our tiny globe, with its vain, pompous inhabitants and arrogant, quarrelsome nations! ("[The Stars, Part II]," March 23, 1915)

As with the later *Evening News* articles, Lovecraft gradually introduced larger cosmological conceptions such as the nebular hypothesis and entropy, something I shall discuss in the context of his philosophical development. Otherwise the *Gazette-News* articles are dry and undistinguished. Toward the end of his life Lovecraft dug up the articles from his files; "their obsoleteness completely bowled me over."[41] If anything, they—and the amateur journalism work—show that Lovecraft had still not realised where his true literary strengths lay: it would be two years before he would recommence the writing of fiction.

Sean Donnelly

Lovecraft's birthplace at 454 Angell Street, Providence
(demolished; formerly numbered 194 Angell Street)

Sean Donnelly

Sarah Susan Phillips Lovecraft, Winfield Scott Lovecraft,
and Howard Phillips Lovecraft (1892)

Brown University Library

Whipple Van Buren Phillips,
Lovecraft's maternal grandfather

Brown University Library

Annie E. P. Gamwell,
Lovecraft's younger aunt

Brown University Library

Lovecraft as a boy

Donovan K. Loucks

Lovecraft's home from 1904 to 1924
at 598 Angell Street, Providence

7. Metrical Mechanic (1914–1917 [II])

If Lovecraft's views on prose style were conservative and old-fashioned, in poetry they were still more so, both in precept and in practice. We have seen that the prose of his teenage years bears a self-consciously antiquated cast, and is in some ways *more* archaistic than even some of his juvenile verse, which (as in the "Attempted Journey") at least features some contemporaneousness in subject.

The interesting thing is that, right from the beginning, Lovecraft was aware that his poetry had relatively little intrinsic merit aside from academic correctness in metre and rhyme. Writing in 1914 to Maurice W. Moe, a high-school English teacher and one of his earliest amateur colleagues, he stated in defence of his inveterate use of the heroic couplet: "Take the form away, and nothing remains. I have no real poetic ability, and all that saves my verse from utter worthlessness is the care which I bestow on its metrical construction."[1] He goes on to say:

> Now I am perfectly aware that this is no more than downright perverted taste. I know as well as any man that the beauties of poetry lie not in the tinsel of flowing metre, or the veneer of epigrammatical couplets; but in the real richness of images, delicacy of imagination, and keenness of perception, which are independent of outward form or superficial brilliancy; yet I were false and hypocritical, should I not admit my actual preference for the old resounding decasyllabics. Verily, I ought to be wearing a powdered wig and knee-breeches.

That last remark is telling, as we shall see in a moment. What the above comment generally reveals is Lovecraft's keenness as a critic of poetry but his utter inability to exemplify its fundamental principles in his own work. One wonders why he wrote the 250 to 300 poems he did over his career, most of them in the eighteenth-century mode. In 1918, after supplying an exhaustive list of the amateur publications of his poetry, he adds an entirely sound summation: "What a mess of mediocre & miserable junk. He hath sharp eyes indeed, who can discover any trace of merit in so worthless an array of bad verse."[2] Lovecraft seems to have derived a sort of masochistic thrill in flagellating himself over the wretchedness of his own poetry.

In 1929 Lovecraft articulated perhaps the soundest evaluation of his verse-writing career that it is possible to give:

> In my metrical novitiate I was, alas, a chronic & inveterate mimic; allowing my antiquarian tendencies to get the better of my abstract poetic feeling. As a result, the whole purpose of my writing soon became distorted—till at length I wrote only as a means of re-creating around me the atmosphere of my 18th century favourites. Self-

> expression as such sank out of sight, & my sole test of excellence was the degree with which I approached the style of Mr. Pope, Dr. Young, Mr. Thomson, Mr. Addison, Mr. Tickell, Mr. Parnell, Dr. Goldsmith, Dr. Johnson, & so on. My verse lost every vestige of originality & sincerity, its only core being to reproduce the typical forms & sentiments of the Georgian scene amidst which it was supposed to be produced. Language, vocabulary, ideas, imagery—everything succumbed to my own intense purpose of thinking & dreaming myself back into that world of periwigs & long s's which for some odd reason seemed to me the normal world.[3]

To this analysis very little need be added. What it demonstrates is that Lovecraft utilised poetry not for *aesthetic* but for *psychological* ends: as a means of tricking himself into believing that the eighteenth century still existed—or, at the very least, that he was a product of the eighteenth century who had somehow been transported into an alien and repulsive era. And if the "sole test of excellence" of Lovecraft's verse was its success in duplicating the style of the great Georgian poets, then it must flatly be declared that his poetry is a resounding failure.

Lovecraft did, indeed, have an enviable array of works by late seventeenth- and eighteenth-century poets in his library, beginning with Samuel Butler's *Hudibras,* the poetical works of Dryden (including his translation of Virgil's *Aeneid*), Samuel Garth's *Dispensary* (1699), and, of course, Milton, and moving on to the poetical works of Joseph Addison, James Beattie, Robert Bloomfield (*The Farmer's Boy*), Thomas Chatterton, William Collins, William Cowper, George Crabbe, Erasmus Darwin (*The Botanick Garden*), William Falconer (*The Shipwreck*), Oliver Goldsmith, Thomas Gray, "Ossian" (James Macpherson), Alexander Pope, Matthew Prior, William Shenstone, Robert Tannahill, James Thomson, "Peter Pindar" (John Wolcot), and Edward Young, along with several anthologies of eighteenth-century poetry. He also had the poems of the early American poet John Trumbull and was familiar with the work of Joel Barlow,[4] although he did not own it. This list does not include some of the authors cited in the above letter (Thomas Tickell, Thomas Parnell), but no doubt Lovecraft read these and still other poets at the Providence Public Library or elsewhere. In other words, Lovecraft was, for a layman, a near-authority on eighteenth-century poetry.

It should not be thought that Lovecraft was striving to imitate specific eighteenth-century poems in his own metrical work; such similarities are uncommon and imprecise. He early stated that he had "made a close study of Pope's Dunciad,"[5] but we need not have been told of the fact after reading "Ad Criticos"; although perhaps that poem, with its unusually direct attacks on various individuals, owes more to Dryden's "Mac Flecknoe" than it does to Pope. In fact, much of Lovecraft's poetry is really more similar to the casual occasional poetry of Dryden than it is to Pope, whose compact and scintillating poetical rhetoric Lovecraft could not hope to match. His many seasonal poems may perhaps owe something to Thomson's *The Seasons,* but again Lovecraft never succeeded in the use of seemingly conventional descriptions of seasons for the conveying of moral or philosophical messages that gives such substance to Thomson's work. The one case of clear imitation that I have found (and even this may be unconscious) is the first stanza of "Sunset" (1917):

> The cloudless day is richer at its close;
> A golden glory settles on the lea;
> Soft, stealing shadows hint of cool repose
> To mellowing landscape, and to calming sea.

No reader can fail to recall the opening of Gray's *Elegy:*

> The Curfew tolls the knell of parting day,
> The lowing herd wind slowly o'er the lea,
> The plowman homeward plods his weary way,
> And leaves the world to darkness and to me.[6]

"Sunset," incidentally, was reprinted in, of all places, the *Presbyterian Advocate* for April 18, 1918—one of the earliest instances where his work appeared outside the narrow confines of amateurdom.

Lovecraft's poetry falls into a number of groupings differentiated generally by subject-matter. The bulk of his verse must fall under the broad rubric of occasional poetry; within this class there are such things as poems to friends and associates, seasonal poems, poems on amateur affairs, imitations of classical poetry (especially Ovid's *Metamorphoses*), and other miscellaneous verse. There is, at least up to about 1919, a large array of political or patriotic verse, almost entirely worthless. There is also a small group of mediocre philosophical or didactic verse. Satiric poetry bulks large in Lovecraft's early period, and this is perhaps the most consistently meritorious of his early metrical output. Weird verse does not become extensive until 1917—the precise time when Lovecraft resumed the writing of weird fiction—so shall be considered later. These categories of course overlap: some of the satiric poetry is directed toward colleagues or individuals in the amateur circle, or is on political subjects. The poetry of 1914–17 exemplifies nearly all the above types with the exception of the weird verse.

Of the occasional poetry in general it is difficult to speak kindly. In many instances one quite is literally at a loss to wonder what Lovecraft was attempting to accomplish with such verse. These poems appear frequently to have served merely as the equivalents of letters. Indeed, Lovecraft once confessed that "In youth I scarcely did any letter-writing—thanking anybody for a present was so much of an ordeal that I would rather have written a two-hundred-fifty-line pastoral or a twenty-page treatise on the rings of Saturn."[7] Thankfully for us, the following was not 250 lines, but it served the same purpose:

Dear Madam (laugh not at the formal way
Of one who celebrates your natal day):
Receive the tribute of a stilted bard,
Rememb'ring not his style, but his regard.
Increasing joy, and added talent true,
Each bright auspicious birthday brings to you;

May they grow many, yet appear but few!

This poem—"To an Accomplished Young Gentlewoman on Her Birthday, Decr. 2, 1914"—is of course an acrostic. I do not know who Dorrie M. is. This poem was not published, so far as I know, in Lovecraft's lifetime. In any event, poems of this sort are lamentably common in Lovecraft's early work, many of them much longer and more tedious than this. "To the Rev. James Pyke" (*United Official Quarterly,* November 1914) is a poem to a neighbour, a retired Congregational minister, who (as Lovecraft writes in a brief note following the poem) "declines absolutely to have his works published. He has written verse since early boyhood, and has in manuscript enough lyrics, dramas, epics, sacred poems, and the like to fill about ten good-sized volumes." At least as regards publication, one wishes Lovecraft had exercised restraint of this sort.

There are any number of poems on amateur matters. Lovecraft was keen on giving encouragement to individual amateurs or amateur press clubs, especially if the latter consisted of younger members. "To the Members of the Pin-Feathers on the Merits of Their Organisation, and on Their New Publication, *The Pin-feather,*" appeared in the first issue of the *Pin-Feather* (November 1914). The Pin-Feathers appear to have been a women's amateur press club ("Hail! learned ladies, banded to protect / The lib'ral arts from undeserv'd neglect"); I know nothing more about them. An evidently unpublished poem, "To 'The Scribblers'" (1915), pays tribute to a club apparently under the supervision of Edward F. Daas, as Lovecraft makes mention of Milwaukee, Daas's place of residence. "To Samuel Loveman, Esquire, on His Poetry and Drama, Writ in the Elizabethan Style" (*Dowdell's Bearcat,* December 1915), is a tribute to an old-time amateur with whom Lovecraft was not at this time acquainted. Later Loveman would become one of Lovecraft's closest friends.

Of the seasonal poems very little can be said. There are poems on almost every month of the year, as well as each of the individual seasons; but all are trite, mechanical, and quite without genuine feeling. One recently discovered poem, "New England," appeared in the *Providence Evening News* for December 18, 1914, along with John Russell's "Florida" (reprinted from the *Tampa Times*) under the general heading "Heat and Cold"; it shows, at least, that Lovecraft continued to keep in touch with his *All-Story* nemesis. The poem itself—aside from the use of a very long iambic line—is entirely undistinguished. A somewhat later poem, "Spring" (*Tryout,* April 1919), had a curious genesis, as the subtitle reveals: "Paraphrased from the Prose of Clifford Raymond, Esq., in the *Chicago Tribune.*" I have not attempted to find the article by Raymond in the *Tribune;* but this poem makes us think of what Lovecraft wrote in an early letter: "Impromptu verse, or 'poetry' to order, is easy only when approached in the coolly *prosaic* spirit. Given something to say, a *metrical mechanic* like myself can easily hammer the matter into technically correct verse, substituting formal poetic diction for real inspiration of thought."[8] One early poem, "A Mississippi Autumn" (*Ole Miss',* December 1915), was actually signed "Howard Phillips Lovecraft, Metrical Mechanic." Lovecraft in his letter goes on to say that the ten-line poem "On Receiving a Picture of Swans" (*Conservative,* January 1916) was written in about ten minutes.

One heroic work—in more ways than one—that requires some consideration is "Old Christmas" (*Tryout,* December 1918; written in late 1917[9]), a 332-line monstrosity that is Lovecraft's single longest poem. Actually, if one can accept the premise of this poem—a re-creation of a typical Christmas night in the England of Queen Anne's time—then one can derive considerable enjoyment from its resolutely wholesome and cheerful couplets. Occasionally Lovecraft's desire to maintain sprightliness to the bitter end leads him astray, as when he depicts the family gathered in the old manor house:

> Here sport a merry train of young and old;
> Aunts, uncles, cousins, kindred shy and bold;
> The ample supper ev'ry care dispels,
> And each glad guest in happy concord dwells.

This could only have been written by one who has not attended many family gatherings. Nevertheless, the sheer geniality of the poem eventually wins one over if one can endure the antiquated diction. At times self-parodic humour enters in ("Assist, gay gastronomic Muse, whilst I / In noble strains sing pork and Christmas pie!"); and even when Lovecraft pays an obligatory tribute—which he clearly did not feel—to Christianity ("An age still newer blends the heathen glee / With the glad rites of Christ's Nativity"), he gently dynamites it by depicting the guests anxious to begin the feast ("Th' impatient throng half grudge the pious space / That the good Squire consumes in saying grace"). The pun on "consumes" is very nice.

Years later this poem received some very welcome praise from a Canadian associate of Lovecraft's, John Ravenor Bullen, who had spent much time in England. Commenting on the work when Lovecraft submitted it in 1921 to the Anglo-American correspondence group called the Transatlantic Circulator, Bullen remarked that the poem was "English in every respect" and went on to say about Lovecraft's poetry generally:

> May I point out that poets of each period have forged their lines in the temper and accent of their age, whereas Mr Lovecraft purposefully "plates over" his poetical works with "the impenetrable rococo" of his predecessors' days, thereby running geat risks. But it may be that his discerning eyes perceive that many modern methods are mongrel and ephemeral. His devotion to Queen Anne style may make his compositions seem artificial, rhetorical descriptions to contemporary critics, but the ever-growing charm of eloquence (to which assonance, alliteration, onomatopoeic sound and rhythm, and tone colour contribute their entrancing effect) displayed in the poem under analysis, proclaims Mr Lovecraft a genuine poet, and "Old Christmas" an example of poetical architecture well-equipped to stand the test of time.[10]

This is, indeed, a very charitable assessment, but on the whole it is an accurate one. In later years Lovecraft produced some of his most unaffectedly delightful verse by writing original Christmas poems to friends and family; these poems, brief and humble as they are meant to be, contain some of his most heart-warming metrical work.

It should already be evident that the bulk of Lovecraft's poetry was published in the amateur press; and in many instances it appears that he was anxious to keep various magazines well supplied with copy to fill up a page. Lack of contributions was a constant problem in amateur circles, and Lovecraft was determined to counteract it as best he could. Hence he wrote "On the Cowboys of the West" for his colleague Ira A. Cole's paper, the *Plainsman* (December 1915). Naturally, Lovecraft had no first-hand acquaintance with any cowboys, and all he knew of them came from what Cole had presumably told him in correspondence; so he allowed himself to imagine that in them (as the subtitle of the poem states) "Is Embodied the Nature-Worshipping Spirit of Classical Antiquity." Cole, interestingly enough, agreed with Lovecraft's poetical assessment; writing in a note following the poem:

> Of a certainty, Mr. Lovecraft has described with a beautiful exactitude the fearless, carefree men who were my boyhood companions. . . . I can think of no better comparison, no more appropriate name than the poet has given them. "Children"—yes, they were children; they were young gods, they were heroes. . . . Only such fellows as I, who were boys among them, are left to tell their story, and as spokesman between their time and the present I feel it a great honor that words of mine should inspire so worthy poet [*sic*] as Howard P. Lovecraft to the writing of lines like the above.[11]

This sort of writing to order may account for some anomalies in the poetry, especially those instances where thoughts and conceptions quite alien to Lovecraft are expressed with apparent sincerity. In some instances this is sheer hypocrisy (as in "Lines on the 25th. Anniversary of the *Providence Evening News,* 1892–1917," where he champions that paper as "the people's friend" and as "The chosen mouthpiece of Democracy," even though he never believed in democracy); in other instances one may perhaps take a milder view. "Wisdom" (*Silver Clarion,* November 1918) contains an introductory note: "The 28th or 'Gold-Miner's' Chapter of Job, paraphrased from a literal translation of the original Hebrew text, supplied by Dr. S. Hall Young." Sure enough, this is a verse paraphrase of chapter 28 of the Book of Job, contrasting the value of gold, silver, and precious gems and the value of wisdom; it concludes:

> Then did He see and search, and then proclaim
> The truth supreme, that He alone could frame:
> "Behold," He cries unto the mortal throng,
> "This is the Wisdom ye have sought so long:
> To reverence the Lord, and leave the paths of wrong!"

This is not something Lovecraft the atheist would have written of his own accord. But in fact he seems to have developed a half-patronising fondness for John Milton Samples, whose simple piety as editor of the *Silver Clarion* somehow affected him. Lovecraft wrote an evaluation of the magazine, entitled "Comment" (*Silver Clarion,* June 1918), in which he remarks that the paper is "an able and consistent exponent of that literary mildness and wholesomeness which in the professional world are exemplified by the *Youth's Companion* and the better grade of religious publications." A number of Lovecraft's more "wholesome" poems appeared in this paper.

Among the more delightful of Lovecraft's occasional poems are those that focon books and writers. Here he is in his element, for in his early years books were his life and his life was books. "The Bookstall" (*United Official Quarterly,* January 1916), dedicated to Rheinhart Kleiner, is one of the earliest and best of these. Casting off the modern age, Lovecraft's "fancy beckons me to nobler days":

> Say, waking Muse, where ages best unfold,
> And tales of times forgotten most are told;
> Where weary pedants, dryer than the dust,
> Like some lov'd incense scent their letter'd must;
> Where crumbling tomes upon the groaning shelves
> Cast their lost centuries about ourselves.

Lovecraft uses this poem to cite some of the curiouser books in his own library: "With Wittie's aid to count the Zodiac host" (referring to Robert Wittie's *Ouronoskopia; or, A Survey of the Heavens* [1681], at this time the oldest book he owned), "O'er Mather's prosy page, half dreaming, pore" (referring to his ancestral copy of the first edition of Cotton Mather's *Magnalia Christi Americana* [1702]), and, most delightful of all, "Go smell the drugs in Garth's Dispensary!" (referring to his copy of Sir Samuel Garth's *The Dispensary* [1699]). That last line is worth nearly all his other archaistic verse put together. And how can we not be touched by the little paean to the cat?

Upon the floor, in Sol's enfeebled blaze,
The coal-black puss with youthful ardour plays;
Yet what more ancient symbol may we scan
Than puss, the age-long satellite of Man?
Egyptian days a feline worship knew,
And Roman consuls heard the plaintive mew:
The glossy mite can win a scholar's glance,
Whilst sages pause to watch a kitten prance.

If Lovecraft had written more of this sort of thing, he could have deflected Winfield Townley Scott's severe but quite justified branding of his poetry as "eighteenth-century rubbish."[12]

Another poem of this sort is "To Mr. Kleiner, on Receiving from Him the Poetical Works of Addison, Gay, and Somerville" (dated on the manuscript April 10, 1918), evidently not published in Lovecraft's lifetime. Although he had by this time been corresponding with Kleiner for three years, Lovecraft still felt obligated to write a thank-you note in verse for so welcome and appropriate a gift. (The book was not found among Lovecraft's effects upon his death, hence is not listed in my compilation of his library.) There is another delightful image of ancient authors languishing in a dingy bookstall:

The shadowy cave, within whose depths are mass'd
The ling'ring relicts of a lustrous past:
Where drowse the ancients, free from modern strife,
That crusty pedants fain would wake to life!

Lovecraft goes on to describe, in a very felicitous way, the respective poetical merits of Joseph Addison, John Gay, and William Somerville.

Two facets of Lovecraft's poetry that must be passed over in merciful brevity are his classical imitations and his philosophical poetry. Lovecraft seemed endlessly fond of producing flaccid imitations of Ovid's *Metamorphoses*—one of his first poetic loves, let us recall—including such things as "Hylas and Myrrha: A Tale" (*Tryout,* May 1919), "Myrrha and Strephon" (*Tryout,* July 1919), and several others. Of the early philosophical poetry, only two are notable. "Inspiration" (*Conservative,* October 1916) is a delicate two-stanza poem on literary inspiration coming to a writer at an unexpected moment. It is of importance largely because it is the very first piece of *professionally* published poetry by Lovecraft outside of local newspaper appearances: it was reprinted in the *National Magazine* of Boston in November 1916. Lovecraft had a number of poems printed in this magazine over the next several years; I do not know what remuneration he received for them, but he clearly states that it was a professional magazine and he must have received at least a token payment. "Brotherhood" (*Tryout,* December 1916) is a genuinely meritorious poem and a surprising one for Lovecraft at this stage of his career to have written. We have already seen many instances of his social snobbery, so that it is no surprise that this poem begins:

> In prideful scorn I watch'd the farmer stride
> With step uncouth o'er road and mossy lane;
> How could I help but distantly deride
> The churlish, callous'd, coarse-clad country swain?

The narrator determines that he is "no kin to such as he"; but then he is taken aback to observe the farmer delicately avoiding stepping on the flowers in his path, and concludes:

> And while I gaz'd, my spirit swell'd apace;
> With the crude swain I own'd the human tie;
> The tend'rest impulse of a noble race
> Had prov'd the boor a finer man than I!

How sincere Lovecraft is in this poem is another matter; it would take him a long time to renounce distinctions of class and breeding, and in some ways—even as a socialist—he never did so. But "Brotherhood" is a poignant poem nonetheless.

As the years passed, it became evident to Lovecraft's readers in the amateur press (as it was always evident to Lovecraft himself) that in his poetry he was a self-consciously antiquated fossil with admirable technical skill but no real poetical feeling. Even W. Paul Cook, who so ardently encouraged Lovecraft the fiction-writer, said of his poetry in 1919: "I cannot fully appreciate Mr. Lovecraft as a poet . . . To me, most of his verse is too formal, too artificial, too stilted in phraseology and form."[13] Eventually Lovecraft began to poke fun at himself on this score; one of the most delightful of such specimens is "On the Death of a Rhyming Critic" (*Toledo Amateur,* July 1917). The satire here is emphatically double-edged. Speaking of the death of one Macer, the narrator of the poem remarks in tripping octosyllabics (the metre of choice of Samuel Butler and Swift, and also of Rheinhart Kleiner and John Russell):

> A curious fellow in his time,
> Fond of old books and prone to rhyme—
> A scribbling pedant, of the sort
> That scorn the age, and write for sport.
> A little wit he sometimes had,

But half of what he wrote was bad;
In metre he was very fair;
Of rhetoric he had his share—
But of the past so much he'd prate,
That he was always out of date!

This and a later passage ("His numbers smooth enough would roll, / But after all—he had no soul!") show once again that Lovecraft was fully cognisant of his own deficiencies as a poet; but toward the end of the poem things take an unexpected turn. Lovecraft now plays upon his skill as a corrector of bad poetry—he had probably already by this time commenced his occupation as literary revisionist, as I shall explore later—by having the poem's narrator stumble incompetently toward the end. He must write an elegy on Macer for the *Morning Sun;* but who will help him with it? The poem literally disintegrates:

So many strugglers he befriended,
That rougher bards on him depended:
His death will still more pens than his—
I wonder where the fellow is!
He's in a better land—or worse—
(I wonder who'll revise this verse?)

A later poem, "The Dead Bookworm" (*United Amateur,* September 1919), deals somewhat with the same subject. Here the subject of mock-eulogy is someone simply named Bookworm—a "Temp'rance crank—confounded ass!," and one who "never seemed to thrive / I guess he was but half alive."

Well, now it's over! (Hello, Jack!
Enjoy your trip? I'm glad you're back!)
Yes—Bookworm's dead—what's that? Go slow!
Thought he was dead a year ago?

And so on. The sprightliness and colloquialism of this poem are highly unusual for Lovecraft, and may bespeak the influence of the *vers de société* of Rheinhart Kleiner, an unjustly forgotten master of this light form.

Lovecraft was as willing to parody others as himself. An amateur poet named James Laurence Crowley particularly irked Lovecraft, who roundly condemned him in the "Department of Public Criticism" (*United Amateur,* April 1916): "'My Dear, Sweet Southern Blossom' . . . is a saccharine and sentimental piece of verse reminiscent of the popular ballads which flourished ten or more years ago. Triteness is the cardinal defect, for each gentle image is what our discerning private critic Mr. Moe would call a 'rubber-stamp' phrase." Not content with delivering such an Olympian pronouncement, Lovecraft parodied him in a poem entitled "My Lost Love," written in late spring 1916:[14]

When the evening shadows come
Then my fancies they do roam
Round the dear old rustic cottage by the lane,
Where in days that are no more
Liv'd the maid I did adore,
Liv'd my own beloved sweetheart, darling Jane!

(Chorus)
O my dearest, sweetest pride,
Thou couldst never be my bride,
For the angels snatch'd you up one summer day;
Yet my heart is ever true,
And I love you yes I do,
And I'll mourn for you until I pine away!
I—pine—a—way— (by 1st Tenor).

No doubt this is the sort of stuff Lovecraft and his pals used to caterwaul in high school. Lovecraft did not in fact publish this poem, but he did write several poems under the obviously parodic name "Ames Dorrance Rowley," one of which—"Laeta; a Lament" (*Tryout,* February 1918)—is another parody, although a little more restrained than the above. A few years later Lovecraft expressed some regret at treating Crowley in this fashion, and he ended up revising Crowley's verse, probably without pay.[15]

In other instances Lovecraft did not so much write parodies as mere responses to verses by others. To Olive G. Owen's "The Modern Business Man to His Love" (*Tryout,* October 1916) Lovecraft countered with "The Nymph's Reply to the Modern Business Man" (*Tryout,* February 1917):

Your silks and sapphires rouse my heart,
But I can penetrate your art—
My seventh husband fool'd my taste
With shoddy silks and stones of paste!

Rheinhart Kleiner's "To Mary of the Movies" (*Piper,* September 1915) inspired Lovecraft's "To Charlie of the Comics." Kleiner's "To a Movie Star" brought forth Lovecraft's "To Mistress Sophia Simple, Queen of the Cinema"; both were published in the *United Amateur* for November 1919. I shall study both these poems a little later.

This brings us to Lovecraft's satiric poetry, which not only ranges over a very wide array of subject-matter but is clearly the only facet of his poetry aside from his weird verse that is of any account. Kleiner made this point in "A Note on Howard P. Lovecraft's Verse" (*United Amateur,* March 1919), the first critical article on Lovecraft:

> Many who cannot read his longer and more ambitious productions find Mr. Lovecraft's light or humorous verse decidedly refreshing. As a satirist along familiar lines, particularly those laid down by Butler, Swift and Pope, he is most himself—paradoxical as it seems. In reading his satires one cannot help but feel the zest with which the author has composed them. They are admirable for the way in which they reveal the depth and intensity of Mr. Lovecraft's convictions, while the wit, irony, sarcasm and humour to be found in them serve as an indication of his powers as a controversialist. The almost relentless ferocity of his satires is constantly relieved by an attendant broad humour which has the merit of causing the reader to chuckle more than once in the perusal of some attack levelled against the particular person or policy which may have incurred Mr. Lovecraft's displeasure.[16]

This analysis is exactly on target. Lovecraft himself remarked in 1921: "Whatever merriment I have is always derived from the satirical principle . . ."[17]

Fellow-amateurs were frequently an object of attack, since they left themselves open to ridicule on so many fronts. One of the first of his victims was one W. E. Griffin, who contributed a light-hearted article to the *Blarney-Stone* for May–June 1914 entitled "My Favorite Pastime—Flirting." Lovecraft, with his puritanical views about women and sex, was not about to let this go unpunished. He first wrote a short poem, "On a Modern Lothario" (*Blarney-Stone,* July–August 1914), attacking Griffin ("A dozen faces must he daily see / Red with the blush of maiden modesty"), then decided to make a pun on Griffin's name in a much longer poem, "Gryphus in Asinum Mutatus; or, How a Griffin Became an Ass." This poem bears the subtitle "(after the manner of Ovid's *Metamorphoses*)" and is one of the few instances where Lovecraft used Ovid in a skilful and original way. I am not sure whether any real event is related in the poem—which speaks of a griffin who sets his eyes on the virgin goddess Diana but is turned by her into an ass—but the satire is sharp. The poem is undated, but was probably written late 1914; it remained in manuscript, so far as I know, so perhaps Lovecraft considered the satire a little too pungent for publication.

Literary faults or literary modernism (much the same thing to Lovecraft) are also the target of many satires. When Charles D. Isaacson in his amateur journal *In a Minor Key* championed Walt Whitman as the "Greatest American Thinker," Lovecraft responded with a sizzling rebuttal in prose entitled "In a Major Key" (*Conservative,* July 1915) in which he included an untitled poem on Whitman:

> Behold great *Whitman,* whose licentious line
> Delights the rake, and warms the souls of swine;

Whose fever'd fancy shuns the measur'd place,
And copies Ovid's filth without his grace.

And so on. Whitman was the perfect anathema for Lovecraft at this time, not only in his scornful abandonment of traditional metre but in his frank discussions of both homosexual and heterosexual sex. It is not clear to me how much of Whitman Lovecraft actually read: he owned a volume of *Selections from Whitman,* but it dates to 1927. In any case, Lovecraft says in "In a Major Key" that the squib on Whitman was "written several years ago as part of an essay on the modern poets." I would give much to have this work, which I take to be a mixture of prose and verse; as it is, the only other piece that can be attributed to it is a satire on Browning quoted by Lovecraft in a letter:

Thy lyrics, gifted Browning, charm the ear,
And ev'ry mark of classic polish bear.
With subtile raptures they enchain the heart;
To soul and mind a mystic thrill impart:
Yet would their rhythmic magic be more keen,
If we could but discover what they mean![18]

This is a little more on the mark than the polemic on Whitman.

Isaacson, incidentally, was not about to take Lovecraft's attack on Whitman lying down, and he delivered a crushing rebuttal directed against Lovecraft's entire antiquated literary style:

> Mr. Lovecraft writes couplets in good rhyme against Whitman.
> I am impelled to inquire if Mr. Lovecraft ever really read Whitman.
> . . .
> I have said that Mr. Lovecraft's writings smell of the library. They are literary. They are of the play-world. Everything is so unreal about everything in the Conservative's writings.
> If only Mr. Lovecraft would come out into the open and breathe deeply of the ozone I am sure he would open himself.[19]

Toward the end of 1914 Maurice W. Moe urged Lovecraft to abandon the heroic couplet and attempt other metrical forms. Lovecraft replied:

> I have written in iambic octosyllabics like those of Swift, in decasyllabic quatrains, as in Gray's *Elegy,* in the old ballad metre of Chevy-Chase, in blank verse like Young's and Thomson's, and even in anapaests like those in Beattie's *Hermit,* but only in the formal couplet of Dryden and Pope can I really express myself. Once I privately tried imitations of modern poets, but turned away in distaste.[20]

Some of these metrical experiments do not appear to survive, and in other cases Lovecraft seems to be referring to his very early juvenile verse. "Ode to Selene or

Diana" and "To the Old Pagan Religion" (from *Poemata Minora, Volume II,* 1902) are written in decasyllabic quatrains; by the "old ballad metre of Chevy-Chase" Lovecraft is perhaps referring to "On the Ruin of Rome"; "Frustra Praemunitus" (an apparently unpublished satire on John Russell) is in iambic octosyllabics; but I find no surviving instances prior to December 1914 of blank verse or of anapaests. Nor do I know what the "imitations of modern poets" could be: it cannot be the aforementioned "essay" on modern poets, since the poems on Browning and Whitman are not written in the manner of Browning or Whitman but are Popean satires on them.

In any event, this discussion with Moe seems ultimately to have led to the writing of a series of four poems under the general title "Perverted Poesie; or, Modern Metre." The four poems are: "The Introduction"; "The Bride of the Sea"; "The Peace Advocate"; and "A Summer Sunset and Evening." These poems appeared together only in the *O-Wash-Ta-Nong* for December 1937; the second and third appeared separately in 1916 and 1917, respectively. I am not clear whether all four were conceived as a unit, and if so, when. "The Bride of the Sea" is quoted in a letter to Rheinhart Kleiner of September 30, 1915,[21] with the following heading:

Unda
Or, The Bride of the Sea.

Respectfully Dedicated without Permission to
MAURICE WINTER MOE, Esq.

A Dull, Dark, Drear, Dactylic Delirium in Sixteen Silly,
Senseless, Sickly Stanzas

($5000.00 Reward for the Apprehension, Alive or Dead, of the Person or Persons who can prove that This is the Work of

HOWARD PHILLIPS LOVECRAFT

The poem as quoted in this letter—as well as in its first appearance, in the *Providence Amateur* for February 1916—does not include an "Epilogue" in heroic couplets found at the conclusion of the *O-Wash-Ta-Nong* appearance; without the epilogue (and without the bombastic and self-parodic subtitle, which also was omitted from the *Providence Amateur* appearance), it actually becomes difficult to tell that this poem is in fact a parody of the Romantic ballad of the Byron or Thomas Moore type. "A Summer Sunset and Evening" is subtitled "In the Metre (though Perchance not the Manner) of the 'Poly-Olbion' of MIKE DRAYTON,

ESQ."—hardly a parody of a "modern" form, since the *Poly-Olbion* of Michael Drayton (1563–1631) is an Elizabethan geographical poem. "The Peace Advocate" is not a parody at all but merely a satire on pacifism. But "The Introduction" attempts to link the three following poems together:

> Wise Doctor Moe prescribeth
> That I should change my Rhyming;
> So let him, pray, peruse each Lay,
> None with the other chiming.
>
> As for my lov'd Heroicks,
> Destroy 'em if you can, Sir!
> *These* silly Strains and wild Refrains
> Are but your Victim's Answer.

One curious specimen of this type is "Nathicana," which was probably written no later than 1920 although first published only in W. Paul Cook's much-delayed final issue of the *Vagrant* (Spring 1927). Lovecraft later stated that the poem was a "*joke* concocted by Galpin & myself in the old days—a parody on those stylistic excesses which really have no basic meaning."[22] The fact that the poem is a collaboration accounts for the pseudonym, Albert Frederick Willie, which Lovecraft in the same letter explains as "a Galpinian synthesis—Al(bert) fred(erick)—& 'Willie' is a variant of Willy, which is Galpin's mother's maiden name." It is now difficult to know which parts were written by which collaborator, but in its overall effect the poem proves to be a parody of Poe with his sonorous repetition:

> And here in the swirl of the vapours
> I saw the divine Nathicana;
> The garlanded, white Nathicana;
> The slender, black-hair'd Nathicana;
> The sloe-ey'd, red-lipp'd Nathicana;
> The silver-voic'd, sweet Nathicana;
> The pale-rob'd, belov'd Nathicana.

Taken out of context this indeed sounds absurd; but there is actually something to be said for the view of a later colleague (Donald Wandrei) who noted: "It is a rare and curious kind of literary freak, a satire too good, so that, instead of parodying, it possesses, the original."[23]

Lovecraft ordinarily chose to satirise literary trends he did not care for not by parody but by simple condemnation. Occasionally these can be amusing. "The State of Poetry" (*Conservative,* October 1915) is an attack on bad (but not necessarily modern) poetry which has some clever bits. False rhymes are skewered wittily:

How might we praise the lines so soft and sweet,
Were they not lame in their poetic feet!
Just as the reader's heart bursts into flame,
The fire is quenched by rhyming "gain" with "name",
And ecstasy becomes no easy task
When fields of "grass" in Sol's bright radiance "bask"!

Lovecraft's repeated strictures on the subject in the "Department of Public Criticism" had apparently gone for naught. "The Magazine Poet" (*United Amateur,* October 1915) is an amusing squib on hack writing:

The modern bard restrains poetic rage,
To fit his couplets to a quarter-page.
Who now regards his skill, or taste, or strength,
When verse is writ and printed for its length?
His soaring sentiment he needs must pinch,
And sing his Amaryllis by the inch.

But Lovecraft's greatest poem in this regard is "Amissa Minerva" (*Toledo Amateur,* May 1919). Steven J. Mariconda has written a thorough commentary on this poem, and has illuminated many of its distinctive features.[24] After supplying a highly encapsulated history of poetry from Homer to Swinburne, Lovecraft launches upon a systematic attack on modern poetry, mentioning Amy Lowell, Edgar Lee Masters, Carl Sandburg, and others by name. (One "Gould" is unidentified; it could perhaps be John Gould Fletcher, although why Lovecraft would refer to him by his middle name is a mystery.) Here is an excerpt:

Yet see on ev'ry hand the antic train
That swarm uncheck'd, and gibber o'er the plain.
Here Librist, Cubist, Spectrist forms arise;
With foetid vapours cloud the crystal skies;
Or led by transient madness, rend the air
With shrieks of bliss and whinings of despair.

The subject-matter of modern poetry offends Lovecraft ("Exempt from wit, each dullard pours his ink / In odes to bathtubs, or the kitchen sink") as much as its abandonment of traditional rhyme and metre. The former point is the subject of a poem (not published in Lovecraft's lifetime) included in the Kleicomolo correspondence cycle, "Ad Balneum" ("To the Bathtub").[25]

Actually, Lovecraft's first exposure to poetic radicalism had occurred some years before. "I have lately been amusing myself by a perusal of some of the 'Imagism' nonsense of the day," he wrote in August 1916.[26] "As a species of pathological phenomena it is interesting." This provides a sufficient indication of Lovecraft's attitude toward free verse in general and Imagism in particular. I am not sure what works Lovecraft read at this time; perhaps he read some of the three anthologies entitled *Some Imagist Poets,* which appeared between 1915 and 1917 and which Lovecraft might have found at the Providence Public Library. He continues in his letter:

> There is absolutely no artistic principle in their effusions; ugliness replaces beauty, and chaos supplies the vacant chair of sense. Some of the stuff, though, would mean something if neatly arranged and read as prose. Of the major portion no criticism is necessary, or even possible. It is the product of hopelessly decayed taste, and arouses a feeling of sympathetic sadness, rather than of mere contempt.

These arguments are repeated in "The Vers Libre Epidemic" (*Conservative,* January 1917). Here Lovecraft distinguishes between two forms of radicalism, one of mere form, the other of thought and ideals. For the first, Lovecraft cites a fellow-amateur, Anne Tillery Renshaw, whom he admired greatly for her energies toward the amateur cause but whose poetic theories he found every opportunity to rebut. He frequently remarks that, for all the metrical novelty of her poetry, it very often lapses in spite of itself into fairly orthodox forms. In "Metrical Regularity" (*Conservative,* July 1915) Lovecraft paraphrases her theory ("the truly inspired bard must chant forth his feelings independently of form or language, permitting each changing impulse to alter the rhythm of his lay, and blindly resigning his reason to the 'fine frenzy' of his mood") as expressed in an article in her amateur journal, *Ole Miss',* for May 1915; to which Lovecraft makes the pointed response: "The 'language of the heart' must be clarified and made intelligible to other hearts, else its purport will forever be confined to its creator." This single sentence could serve as an adequate indictment of the entire tendency of twentieth-century poetry.

The second, more disturbing type of radicalism—of both thought and ideals—is treated more harshly. In "The Vers Libre Epidemic" this school is said to be represented by "Amy Lowell at her worst": "a motley horde of hysterical and half-witted rhapsodists whose basic principle is the recording of their momentary moods and psychopathic phenomena in whatever amorphous and meaningless phrases may come to their tongues or pens at the moment of inspirational (or epileptic) seizure." This is fine polemic, but not very good reasoned argument. Lovecraft, however, goes on to assert: "The type of impression they receive and record is abnormal, and cannot be transmitted to persons of normal psychology; wherefore there is no true art or even the rudiments of artistic impulse in their effusions. These radicals are animated by mental or emotional processes other than poetic." This allows Lovecraft to conclude: "They are not in any sense poets, and their work, being wholly alien to poetry, cannot be cited as an indication of poetical decadence." This is a clever rhetorical ploy, but that is all, and Lovecraft was probably aware of it. His contention that Imagism or free verse in general was not the vanguard of the future may have been a case of wishful thinking, even though the major poets of the day were still on the whole metrically orthodox. Lovecraft would carry on the battle against avant-garde poetry for the rest of his life, although one imagines that by the thirties he was beginning to feel that the struggle was hopeless. But this did not alter his devotion to conservative poetry, although in his later arguments he modified his position considerably and advocated the view that poetry must speak straightforwardly, but elegantly and coherently, in the language of its own day.

Curiously, Lovecraft himself was accused of being lax—not in metre, but in rhyme—by Rheinhart Kleiner. In the May 1915 issue of his amateur journal, the *Piper,* Kleiner noted that Lovecraft in his critical utterances "is inclined to be a little too lenient, perhaps, in the case of 'allowable' rhymes, using the standards of another day, in fact, as his authority"; he continued, in reference to "The Simple Speller's Tale": ". . . the word 'art' is rhymed with 'shot.' This could not be considered 'allowable' even by a very liberal interpretation of the poet's own theory."[27]

Lovecraft was not about to take this sitting down, although as a friend of Kleiner's he did not wish to deal with him harshly. Lovecraft was aware that the "allowable rhyme"—the use of such rhymes as *sky* and *company,* or *love* and *grove*—was a hallmark of the poetry of Dryden and his successors, and that the absolute uniformity of rhyming sounds stressed by Kleiner emerged only in the poetical generation of Samuel Johnson, Oliver Goldsmith, and the whole nineteenth century. This is the burden of "The Allowable Rhyme" (*Conservative,* October 1915), which like "The Simple Spelling Mania" presents a history of the subject and correctly stresses the fact that Dryden's reformation of English metre made his use of the allowable rhyme far more pardonable than that of his predecessors. Lovecraft concludes with an obviously personal plea for leniency: "But exceptions should and must be made in the case of a few who have somehow absorbed the atmosphere of other days, and who long in their hearts for the stately sound of the old classic cadences." Truly, "I am certainly a relic of the 18th century both in prose and in verse."[28]

I have noted Lovecraft's use of the pseudonym "Ames Dorrance Rowley" to parody the work of James Laurence Crowley, at least in the one instance of "Laeta; a Lament." (Oddly enough, the three other poems published under this pseudonym—"To Maj.-Gen. Omar Bundy, U.S.A."; "The Last Pagan Speaks" [= "To the Old Pagan Religion"]; "The Volunteer"—are in no way parodies of Crowley.) The whole issue of Lovecraft's use of pseudonyms is a very large one: so far we have seen him use the pseudonym "Isaac Bickerstaffe, Jr." for the attacks on the astrologer J. F. Hartmann and "El Imparcial" for some articles on amateur journalism, but Lovecraft's pseudonyms are otherwise almost entirely restricted to poetry. A total of about twenty pseudonyms have been identified, and there may even be one or two more lurking in the amateur press. Only a few, however, were used with any regularity: Humphry Littlewit, Esq.; Henry Paget-Lowe; Ward Phillips; Edward Softly; and, most frequent of all, Lewis Theobald, Jun. Some of these names are scarcely very concealing of Lovecraft's identity. The Lewis Theobald pseudonym, of course, derives from the hapless Shakespearean scholar whom Pope pilloried in the first version (1728) of *The Dunciad.*

In some cases Lovecraft used pseudonyms merely because he was contributing poetry so voluminously to the amateur press—especially to C. W. Smith's *Tryout*—that he perhaps did not wish to create the impression that he was hogging more space than he deserved. In other instances, he may have genuinely wished to disguise his identity because of the anomalous content of the poem involved: hence the curiously religious poem "Wisdom" appeared under the name Archibald Maynwaring, a name that only someone well-versed in eighteenth-century poetry—and familiar with Lovecraft's fondness for it—could trace to the minor Augustan poet Arthur Mainwaring, who translated a portion of the *Metamorphoses* for "Garth's Ovid." But it becomes very difficult to characterise some of Lovecraft's pseudonyms, especially those under which a large number of works were published, and Lovecraft evidently used them merely as the spirit moved him and without much thought of creating any sort of genuine persona for the pseudonyms in question.[29] I shall have occasion to comment on specific pseudonyms as they are coined for later works.

Many of Lovecraft's early poems were on political subjects. Political events of the period 1914–17 offered abundant opportunities for his polemical pen, given his early attitudes on race, social class, and militarism. Lovecraft could of course not know that his entry into amateur journalism in April 1914 would occur only four months before the outbreak of World War I; but once the war did commence, and once he saw that his country was not about to enter it anytime soon to stand with his beloved England, Lovecraft's ire was stirred. For prose attacks on world affairs his chosen vehicle was the *Conservative;* his verses on world affairs were scattered far and wide throughout amateurdom.

One event prior to the war that earned Lovecraft's notice, at least to the point of writing a sharp little satire, was the Mexican Civil War. Lovecraft reports that the poem "To General Villa" (*Blarney-Stone,* November–December 1914) was written in the summer "for the purpose of defying those who had charged the author with pedantry and pomposity" ("Department of Public Criticism," *United Amateur,* March 1915). To be sure, aside from an opening "'Tis," the poem is modern, even colloquial in tone ("You can't read a word; your name you can't write, / But ¡Santa Maria! you know how to fight"). Lovecraft goes on to say that the last stanza has been rendered "sadly out of date" by "changes of time and revolutions":

So while crafty old Huerta, half drunk with bad brandy,
Still clings to his throne, 'cross the far Rio Grande,
'Tis to you our friend Bryan would lend his assistance:
Si, General Villa, you'll do—at a distance.

What he means is that Victoriano Huerta, who had assumed the presidency upon the assassination of Francisco I. Madero in February 1913, had been overthrown on July 15, 1914, setting up a struggle for power between Pancho Villa and Venustiano Carranza. President Wilson did in fact briefly "lend assistance" to Villa, but after Villa lost the battle of Celaya in 1915 Wilson chose to recognise Carranza instead. In response, Villa actually invaded New Mexico in early March 1916. Some months later, to compound the insult in Lovecraft's eye, a man named Henry F. Thomas published a poem, "A Prayer for Peace and Justice," in the *Providence Evening News* for June 23, 1916, in which, Lovecraft claims, "he called it a 'shame' for America to prepare for defence against the Mexican bandits."[30] One has to assume that Lovecraft is correct in his understanding of the thrust of the work, since it is otherwise merely a sappy little poem urging pacifism and arbitration ("But let us build—not to destroy, / And thus create world-lasting joy") and making no mention of any specific enemies whom it would be wrong to fight. Lovecraft could not endure such folly, so he responded with "The Beauties of Peace" (*Providence Evening News,* June 27, 1916):

Let blood-mad Villa drench the Texan plain;
Let sly Carranza ev'ry right profane;
To savage hordes a cordial hand extend,
And greet th' invader as a welcome friend:
What tho' he slew your brothers yesternight?
We must be pious—and 'tis wrong to fight!

This becomes a sort of litany throughout the first three years of World War I, prior to American intervention in the summer of 1917. Lovecraft could simply not abide Americans not standing with their English brethren to battle the Huns, and it must have infuriated him not merely that the government failed to intervene in the European war but that American public opinion was resolutely against such intervention. Even the sinking of the British liner *Lusitania* on May 7, 1915—resulting in the loss of 128 Americans in its death toll of more than 1200—only began a slow change in people's minds against Germany. The incident led Lovecraft to write a thunderous polemic in verse, "The Crime of Crimes: Lusitania, 1915":

Craz'd with the Belgian blood so lately shed,
The bestial Prussian seeks the ocean's bed;

In Neptune's realm the wretched coward lurks,
And on the world his wonted evil works.

And on and on. There is no question of Lovecraft's burning sincerity in this poem; but the antiquated metre and diction he has used here makes it difficult to take the poem seriously, and it gains an unintentional air of frivolity, almost of self-parody. This could be said for much of Lovecraft's political verse.

"The Crime of Crimes" has the distinction of being Lovecraft's first separately published work. It appeared in a Welsh amateur journal, *Interesting Items,* for July 1915, and apparently at about the same time was issued as a four-page pamphlet by the editor of *Interesting Items,* Arthur Harris of Llandudno, Wales. This item is now one of the rarest of Lovecraft's publications; only three copies are known to exist. I do not know how Lovecraft came in touch with Harris; perhaps he sent him the first issue of the *Conservative.* In any event, he stayed sporadically in touch with Harris for the rest of his life.

The *Lusitania* incident led to President Wilson's celebrated utterance, "There is such a thing as a man being too proud to fight," something that made Lovecraft see red and which he threw back in Wilson's teeth at every opportunity, especially in poems. Lovecraft published an array of anti-pacifist poems ("Pacifist War Song—1917," *Tryout,* March 1917; "The Peace Advocate," *Tryout,* May 1917) and articles ("The Renaissance of Manhood," *Conservative,* October 1915), along with any number of truly awful poems expressing loyalty to England ("1914," *Interesting Items,* March 1915; "An American to Mother England," *Poesy,* January 1916; "The Rose of England," *Scot,* October 1916; "Britannia Victura," *Inspiration,* April 1917; "An American to the British Flag," *Little Budget,* December 1917). It is not surprising that Lovecraft wrote a poem to the mediocre American poet Alan Seeger, who joined the French Foreign Legion at the outset of the war and died in July 1916. Seeger's "A Message to America" is almost as bad as Lovecraft's poetry:

You have the grit and the guts, I know;
You are ready to answer blow for blow
You are virile, combative, stubborn, hard,
But your honor ends with your own back-yard . . .[31]

Lovecraft's "To Alan Seeger" (*Tryout,* July 1918) goes like this:

But while thou sleepest in an honour'd grave
Beneath the Gallic sod thou bledst to save,
May thy soul's vision scan the ravag'd plain,
And tell thee that thou didst not fall in vain . . .

Years later Lovecraft, in the story "Herbert West—Reanimator" (1921–22), maintained that Herbert West and his sidekick were two "of the many Americans to precede the government itself into the gigantic struggle" by joining the Canadian army.

Lovecraft's immediate reaction to the war, however, was a curious one. He did not care what the actual causes of the war were, or who was to blame; his prime concern was in stopping what he saw was a suicidal racial civil war between the two sides of "Anglo-Saxondom." It is here that Lovecraft's racism comes fully to the forefront:

> High above such national crimes as the Servian plots against Austria or the German disregard of Belgian neutrality, high above such sad matters as the destruction of innocent lives and property, looms the supremest of all crimes, an offence not only against conventional morality but against Nature itself; the violation of race.
>
> In the unnatural racial alignment of the various warring powers we behold a defiance of anthropological principles that cannot but bode ill for the future of the world.

This is from "The Crime of the Century," one of the salvos in Lovecraft's first issue (April 1915) of the *Conservative.* What makes the war so appalling for Lovecraft is that England and Germany (as well as Belgium, Holland, Austria, Scandinavia, and Switzerland) are all part of the Teutonic race, and therefore should on no account be battling each other. Political enemies though they may be, England and Germany are racially one:

> The Teuton is the summit of evolution. That we may consider intelligently his place in history we must cast aside the popular nomenclature which would confuse the names "Teuton" and "German", and view him not nationally but racially, identifying his fundamental stock with the tall, pale, blue-eyed, yellow-haired, long-headed "Xanthochroi" as described by Huxley, amongst whom the class of languages we call "Teutonic" arose, and who today constitute the majority of the Teutonic-speaking population of our globe.
>
> Though some ethnologists have declared that the Teuton is the only true Aryan, and that the languages and institutions of the other nominally Aryan races were derived alone from his superior speech and customs; it is nevertheless not necessary for us to accept this daring theory in order to appreciate his vast superiority to the rest of mankind.

We have already seen Lovecraft's prejudice against blacks manifest so early as the age of fourteen; whence did these ideas of Teutonic superiority arise? The above passage itself suggests one source: Thomas Henry Huxley. Huxley's work cannot carelessly be branded as racist, and he was very circumspect when it came to notions of racial superiority or inferiority; but in "The Crime of the Century" Lovecraft has made explicit reference to two essays by Huxley, "On the Methods and Results of Ethnology" (1865) and "On the Aryan Question" (1890), both included in *Man's Place in Nature and Other Anthropological Essays* (1894). In the former essay Huxley coins the term "Xanthochroi" (races that are yellow-haired and pale in complexion), applying it to the inhabitants of northern Europe, ultimate descendants of the "Nordic" barbarians. Along with the Melanochroi (pale-complexioned but dark-haired) who occupy the Mediterranean lands and the Middle East, the Xanthochroi were and are the pinnacle of civilisation: "It is needless to remark upon the civilization of these two great stocks. With them has originated everything that is highest in science, in art, in law, in politics, and in mechanical inventions. In their hands, at the present moment, lies the order of the social world, and to them its progress is committed."[32]

Although Lovecraft's statements make it evident that he was appealing to evolutionary theories in his vaunting of the Teuton, it had been fashionable for nearly a century to praise Teutons, Anglo-Saxons, Nordics, or Aryans (all these terms being extremely nebulous and frequently interchangeable in their application) as the summit of civilisation. English and American historians in particular—beginning with Sir Francis Palgrave's *Rise and Progress of the English Commonwealth* (1832), and continuing on through such distinguished scholars as Edward A. Freeman, J. R. Green, Francis Parkman, William H. Prescott, and John Fiske—became enamoured of the idea that the virtues of the English (hence the American) and German political systems owed their existence to the Teuton or Anglo-Saxon.[33] Lovecraft read many of these writers and had their books in his library. With authorities like these, it is not surprising that he would echo their racial theories, even if in a particularly strident and pompous manner.

There is a certain paradox in Lovecraft's praising the Teuton given his strong classical predilections. How can he account for the fact that, as he saw it, civilisation collapsed for centuries after the barbarian invasions of Rome? In "The Crime of the Century" Lovecraft tries to make the best of it by saying that the Teutons at least prevented the decline from being even worse than it was: "As the power of the Roman empire declined, the Teuton sent down into Italy, Gaul, and Spain the revivifying elements which saved those countries from complete destruction." This is certainly not the view of Lovecraft's old friends Hume and Gibbon, who regarded the barbarian invasions as an unmitigated disaster for civilisation. In this instance, at least, racial prejudice has overcome Lovecraft's allegiance both to the Georgians and to the ancients.

If Teutons or Aryans or Anglo-Saxons are the pinnacle of civilisation, then by necessity other races are below them, sometimes vastly below. Accordingly, in Lovecraft's view, these other races ought to allow themselves to be ruled by their betters for their own benefit and for the benefit of civilisation. In discussing whether the U.S. should maintain control of the Philippines, Lovecraft declares: "It is difficult to be patient with the political idiots who advocate the relinquishment of the archipelago by the United States, either now or at any future time. The mongrel natives, in whose blood the Malay strain predominates, are not and never will be racially capable of maintaining a civilised condition by themselves." And later in the same article:

> Of the question raised regarding the treatment of the Indian by the white man in America it is best to admit in the words of Sir Roger de Coverly, 'that much might be said on both sides'. Whilst the driving back of the aborigines has indeed been ruthless and high-handed, it seems the destiny of the Anglo-Saxon to sweep inferior races from his path wherever he goes. There are few who love the Indian so deeply that they would wish this continent restored to its original condition, peopled by savage nomads instead of civilised colonists. ("Department of Public Criticism," *United Amateur,* June 1916)

Lovecraft, to be sure, was not one of those few.

The question again arises as to the sources for Lovecraft's views. The anthropology of Huxley and others is a clear influence, and I have no doubt that his family played its role. Lovecraft, as a member of the New England Protestant aristocracy, would have come to such views as a matter of course, and he is only distinctive in expressing them in his early years with a certain vehemence and dogmatism. L. Sprague de Camp has maintained[34] that Lovecraft was significantly influenced by Houston Stewart Chamberlain's *Foundations of the Nineteenth Century,* published in German in 1899 and translated into English in 1911. But there is not a single reference to Chamberlain in any documents by Lovecraft that I have seen; and even a cursory examination of the specific tenets of Chamberlain's racism shows that Lovecraft's beliefs are very different. Chamberlain, according to one scholar, "set himself to reconcile Christianity, the religion of humility and forgiveness, with aggressive German nationalism,"[35] something Lovecraft never concerned himself to do; indeed, as we shall see, Lovecraft's anti-Christianity only gained force as he encountered Nietzsche around 1918. Chamberlain also praised the Teutonic barbarians who overthrow Rome, as being the bearers of "true Christianity" (i.e., a "strong" Christianity shorn of its elements of pity and tolerance), a view Lovecraft could never adopt given the belief he maintained to the end of his life that "To me the Roman Empire will always seem the central incident of human history."[36] In these and other ways did Lovecraft's racism differ fundamentally from Chamberlain's, so that any influence of the latter seems remote, especially given the total absence of documentary evidence that Lovecraft was even familiar with Chamberlain.

A somewhat more likely source is Madison Grant's *The Passing of the Great Race,* which was a best-seller upon its emergence in December 1916.[37] And yet, there are also significant differences between Grant's views and Lovecraft's. Grant's basic notion is that Europe is populated by three races, the Nordic, the Alpine, and the Mediterranean; this does not correspond to analogous comments by Lovecraft, and in any event all the quotations from Lovecraft's works I have made here were written prior to the appearance of Grant's book, so that it is clear that Lovecraft's views were already well established by this time. We do not have much information on what other racist tracts Lovecraft may have read—we only know of his reading of William Benjamin Smith's *The Color Line* (1905) because of the dedication of "De Triumpho Naturae" to it—but it is clear that a variety of factors (familial influence, reading of specific volumes, and the general beliefs of his community and his class) led to these views. And it cannot be overemphasised that many of them were modified in the course of time.

Later in 1915 the issue of blacks was raised again. We have already seen how Lovecraft attacked Charles D. Isaacson's championing of Walt Whitman in his amateur paper, *In a Minor Key*. The bulk of Isaacson's paper, however, was a plea for racial tolerance, especially for African Americans. He is particularly harsh on D. W. Griffith's *The Birth of a Nation,* asserting that it presented a false view of the relations between blacks and whites after the Civil War and that it incited racial hatred.

Lovecraft, in "In a Major Key" (*Conservative,* July 1915), makes the astounding claim that "Mr. Isaacson's views on racial prejudice . . . are too subjective to be impartial" (had Lovecraft known Freud at this time, he would have been able to refer to this as "projection"). In regard to *The Birth of a Nation,* Lovecraft states that he has not yet seen the film (he would do so later[38]), but says that he has read both the novel (*The Clansman,* 1905) by Thomas Dixon, Jr, and the dramatic adaptation of the novel on which the film was based. He then launches into a predictable paean to the Ku Klux Klan, "that noble but much maligned band of Southerners who saved half of our country from destruction at the close of the Civil War." It is certainly uncanny that Lovecraft's remarks were made at exactly the time when the Klan was being revived in the South by William J. Simmons, although it was not a force to be reckoned with until the 1920s. It can be pointed out here that Lovecraft is strangely silent on the thousands of lynchings of blacks throughout the early decades of the century; but he never mentions the KKK again until very late in life, and then he repudiates it. In any event, he attempts in "In a Major Key" to account for Isaacson's plea for racial tolerance:

> He has perhaps resented the more or less open aversion to the children of Israel which has ever pervaded Christendom, yet a man of his perspicuity should be able to distinguish this illiberal feeling, a religious and social animosity of one white race toward another white and equally intellectual race, from the natural and scientifically just sentiment which keeps the African black from contaminating the Caucasian population of the United States. The negro is fundamentally the biological inferior of all White and even Mongolian races, and the Northern people must occasionally be reminded of the danger which they incur in admitting him too freely to the privileges of society and government.

The best that can be said of this is that Lovecraft's remarks on Jews are relatively tolerant; we shall find that later remarks are less so. Ugly and ignorant as the above is, this view of blacks as biologically inferior—which we have seen to be common in the late nineteenth and early twentieth centuries—is one that Lovecraft in essence never renounced, in spite of massive evidence to the contrary that emerged in the course of the 1920s and 1930s.

As, however, with the pestiferous astrologer J. F. Hartmann, Lovecraft underestimated his opponent. The responses by both Isaacson and James Ferdinand Morton in the second issue of *In a Minor Key* (undated, but published in late 1915) are so devastating that they are worth quoting at length. In "Concerning the Conservative" Isaacson, keenly pointing out that "There comes a musty smell as of old books with the reading of the Conservative," goes on to say:

> . . . although I am confident he will not be able to realize it until he is shown very carefully—
>
> He is against free speech.
> He is against freedom of thought.
> He is against the liberty of the press.
> He is against tolerance of color, creed and equality.
> He is in favor of monarchy.
>
> Despite his repeated abeisance [*sic*] to the intellectuality and spirituality of the Jew, he continually attempts to place him apart—explaining away the ideas of an individual by his religion. It is unseemly for a man who boasts of his land and his ancestry that he should still cling to the Tory notion and defy the best spirit of America by refusing to acknowledge the nationality of an American, born here of American-born parents, a citizen, loyal, broad, [*sic*] eager to serve his nation, because of opposing creeds![39]

The reference to being against free speech applies to Lovecraft's outrageous remark that the publication of an article by Isaacson entitled "The Greater Courage" urging refusal to serve in the military "is a crime which in a native American of Aryan blood would be deserving of severe legal punishment." Lovecraft contrasts "Mr. Isaacson and his hyphenated fellow-pacifists" with "the real American people," leading to Isaacson's observation that he is as "real" an American as Lovecraft.

Morton's response is still more overwhelming. James Ferdinand Morton (1870–1941) was, as Lovecraft admits in a letter of the time,[40] a remarkable individual. He had gained a simultaneous B.A. and M.A. from Harvard in 1892 and became a vigorous advocate of black equality, free speech, the single tax, and secularism. He wrote many pamphlets on these subjects, most of them published either by himself or by The Truth Seeker Co.; among them are *The Rights of Periodicals* (1905?), *The Curse of Race Prejudice* (1906?), and many others.[41] He had been President of the NAPA in 1896–97 and would later become President of the

Thomas Paine Natural History Association and Vice President of the Esperanto Association of North America. He would end his career (1925–41) as Curator of the Paterson (New Jersey) Museum. All this activity earned him an entry in *Who's Who in America,* a distinction Lovecraft never achieved.

In "'Conservatism' Gone Mad" Morton begins by stating presciently that "I presume that Mr. H. P. Lovecraft . . . is a rather young man, who will at some future day smile at the amusing dogmatism with which he now assumes to lay down the law." There then follows a broadside on Lovecraft's racism:

> It is not surprising to find a "conservative" of Mr. Lovecraft's type unashamed to advocate the base passion of race prejudice. Here again dogmatism is made to do duty for argument. As an enemy of democracy, Mr. Lovecraft holds that a mere accident of birth should determine for all time the social status of an individual; that the color of the skin should count for more than the quality of the brain or the character. That he gives no reasons for the reactionary assertions is not surprising. Race prejudice is not defensible by reason. . . . Lovecraft has no scientific warrant for the pretence that race prejudice is more "a gift of Nature" or an essential factor in social evolution than any other prejudice whatever. It is the product of specific historic causes, and does not strike its roots deep in the foundations of human nature. Like other vices it can be readily overcome by individuals capable of rising to a rational view of existence.

Taking up the notion that Isaacson should be muzzled for uttering unpatriotic sentiments, Morton counters: "One who is not even loyal to the Bill of Rights contained in our National Constitution is hardly in a position to set himself up as an authority on patriotism." In conclusion, Morton makes another wise prediction:

> From the sample afforded in the paper under discussion it is evident that Mr. Lovecraft needs to serve a long and humble apprenticeship before he will become qualified to sit in the master's seat and to thunder forth *ex cathedra* judgments. The one thing in his favor is his evident sincerity. Let him once come to realize the value of appreciating the many points of view shared by persons as sincere as he, and better informed in certain particulars, and he will become less narrow and intolerant. His vigor of style, when wedded to clearer conceptions based on a wider comprehension, will make him a writer of power.[42]

It is passages like this that led Lovecraft ultimately to make peace with Morton, who would then become one of his closest friends.

But that was several years in the future. At the moment Lovecraft had in mind no thought but a towering rebuttal. But the interesting thing is that no genuine rebuttal ever appeared. Lovecraft even anticipated Isaacson's rejoinder in the October 1915 *Conservative,* remarking in "The Conservative and His Critics" that if "the predicted reprisal" comes, "it will find its object, as usual, not unwilling to deliver blow for blow." In a letter he says of Isaacson: "He will call me superficial, crude, barbaric in thought, imperfect in education, offensively arrogant and bigoted, filled with venomous prejudice, wanting in good taste, etc. etc. etc. But what I can and will say in reply is also violent and comprehensive."[43] But for all his bluster, when the double attack by Isaacson and Morton came, Lovecraft remained strangely quiet. In the October 1915 *Conservative* he had already delivered another broadside against Isaacson ("Gems from *In a Minor Key*"), but this must have been written before the Isaacson-Morton response. All we get afterward is a thinly veiled allusion to Isaacson in a section of "In the Editor's Study" (*Conservative,* October 1916) entitled "The Symphonic Ideal": ". . . his [Lovecraft's] whole literary style was condemned a year ago by a learned Jew, who with Semitic shrewdness declared that these pages, with their reverence for the storied past, savour of the 'play world.'" But this, of course, is directed toward Isaacson's attack on Lovecraft's literary work, not his political or racial views.

What Lovecraft did do was write a magnificent poem, "The Isaacsonio-Mortoniad," around September 1915;[44] but he did not allow it to be published in an amateur journal, and there is no evidence that he even showed it to anyone.[45] It is a splendid verse satire, as scintillating as some of the "Ad Criticos" pieces. Lovecraft naturally picks apart every little error made by Isaacson—his misspelling of "obeisance" as "abeisance"; his attribution of the phrase "Honi soit qui mal y pense" to the French court—and attempts systematically to refute his notions of political equality: "'All men are equal! Let us have no kings!' / (How tritely thus the well-worn sentence rings.)," and his remark that "Anything which incites to prejudice of any sort should be restrained" (a foreshadowing of current debates over political correctness):

> Whilst the brave Semite loud of freedom cants.
> Against this freedom he, forgetful, rants:
> Eternal licence for himself he pleads,
> Yet seeks restraint for his opponents' deeds;
> With the same force that at oppression rails,
> He'd bar *The Jeffersonian* from the mails!

Turning to Morton, who by this time he had learned was an evangelical atheist, Lovecraft treats him with much greater respect:

> Sound now the trumpets, and awake the drums,
> For matchless Morton in his chariot comes!
> The Dean of Darkness, wrecker of the church,
> Crowing with scorn from his exalted perch!

The conclusion is somewhat amusing. The poem ends, "Tho' like a bull at us he plunges one day, / Tomorrow he'll be goring Billy Sunday!" Evidently Lovecraft was unaware that Morton had done just that: a pamphlet published by The Truth

Seeker Co. in 1915 entitled *The Case of Billy Sunday* contained a lengthy broadside by Morton, "Open Letter to the Clergy." Later Morton renounced his atheism and converted to the Baha'i faith.

Lovecraft claimed to be more charmed than offended by Morton's attack ("The raging blast, sent earthward to destroy, / Is watch'd and study'd with artistic joy"), but he must have been taken aback by it and was unable to discount it as easily as he might have wished. Beyond this poem, which lay in manuscript for seventy years before being posthumously published, Lovecraft said no more on the Isaacson-Morton controversy. Regrettably, however, the whole incident does not seem to have affected his own racial views in any particular.

A side-issue of the war that began to exercise Lovecraft's attention in 1915 was the Irish question. This issue was understandably raised in a heated letter-exchange with John T. Dunn. Lovecraft's correspondence with Dunn (1915–17) covers the most critical period in modern Irish history. Since the later nineteenth century, Irish politicians and voters had been split into three main factions: those who (like Lord Dunsany in the early part of the twentieth century) supported union with England, with Irish representation (in relatively small numbers) in the British Parliament; those who supported Home Rule, or the establishment of a separate Irish parliament that would have power over many aspects of local life but would still be subordinate to the British Crown; and those who wanted outright independence from England. Lovecraft was naturally at one end of this extreme, Dunn at the other.

Irish and English politicians had been moving toward Home Rule throughout the later nineteenth century, and a Home Rule Act was finally passed in September 1914, with the six counties of Ulster, which were vehemently Unionist, being exempted from its conditions; but the war caused a suspension of its operation. The war itself proved a great strain in Anglo-Irish relations, as the more radical groups—including Sinn Féin, the Irish Republican Brotherhood (later to become the Irish Republican Army), and the Irish Volunteers—pressed for immediate independence from England.

When Lovecraft took up the whole issue with Dunn, he did not help matters any by very painstakingly drawing a fluttering Union Jack at the head of his first extant letter to him (July 20, 1915). But aside from this bit of malicious humour, Lovecraft makes a good case for moderation:

> You take a stand as an Irishman by descent, and enumerate all the past mistakes of England in the government of Ireland. Can you not see that past experience has mellowed the judgment of England in these matters? Can you not see that every effort is being made to give justice to the Irish? That the land is being transferred from absentee landlords to the Irish people? That effective Home Rule will be in force before long?[46]

When Lovecraft goes on to say that "I believe that you are more hostile to England than the Irish still in Ireland," he is quite correct; Lovecraft knew that Irish-Americans were in fact more radical than their compatriots in Ireland. The Fenian movement had had its origins amongst the Irish immigrants in New York and Chicago in the 1850s,[47] as a means of combating anti-Irish prejudice stirred up by the Know-Nothing party (a party that, incidentally, was very strong in Rhode Island at the time[48]).

What concerned Lovecraft most about Ireland was its neutrality during the war, a stance that he saw might lead insidiously to Irish tolerance or even support for Germany and the establishment of a hostile wedge at England's very doorstep. Lovecraft was also deeply offended by Irish-Americans who openly sided not only with Ireland in its quest for independence but also with Germany itself, or at least were hostile to the Allied cause. The April 1916 *Conservative* contains a vicious verse satire, "Ye Ballade of Patrick von Flynn; or, The Hibernio-German-American England-Hater." All that can be said of this piece is that it is crude but effective. Written entirely in a parodic Irish dialect, it tells of a band of Irish-Americans who join some German-Americans in lambasting England. As the two groups begin to mingle and drink together ("Thin all began to fraternise; McNulty and von Bohn— / O'Donovan and Munsterberg, von Bulow an' Malone"), the Irishman experiences a strange transition:

> Ochone! Ochone! Where am Oi now? What conflict am Oi in?
> Do Oi belong in Dublin town or back in Ould Berlin?
> A week ago me son was borrn; his christ'nin's not far off;
> Oi wonther will I call him Mike, or Friedrich Wilhelm Hoff?

But aside from things like this, Lovecraft does get in a few good jabs concerning the United States' supposed lack of neutrality ("They all denounc'd the Prisident an' currs'd the Yankee laws / Fer bein' too un-noothral loike to hilp the German cause"). Lovecraft had the bad taste to send the poem to Dunn, noting with incredible naiveté, "I sincerely hope you will take no personal offence at the 'Ballade of Patrick von Flynn' . . ."[49] Dunn's response, as recorded by Lovecraft, is what one might have expected: "I . . . am scarcely surprised that the 'von Flynn' ballad proved less than pleasing."[50]

"Ye Ballade of Patrick von Flynn" was published at the exact time that the Easter Rebellion of 1916 occurred. This movement, which sought to take over the government of Dublin on Easter Sunday with the aid of arms sent by Germany, was organised by a small and confused band of politicians, revolutionaries, and poets including Padraic Pearse, Joseph Plunkett, Sir Roger Casement, and others. By and large it had no popular support and was a spectacular failure: the German transport ship carrying arms was intercepted by the British navy, and the rebellion itself was put down within a week by the British army, with much loss of life on both sides (450 revolutionaries and civilians, more than 100 British soldiers) and with the principal revolutionaries executed for treason.

Lovecraft does not actually say much to Dunn about the rebellion, save to note that in his latest *Conservative* (presumably the April 1916 issue containing "Ye Ballade") "I have felt impelled to retaliate upon those who call my race 'murderers' when seeking only to quell sedition."[51] He continues to argue with Dunn as to why Ireland should—at least for the duration of the war—remain allied with England. In October 1916 Lovecraft published "Old England and the 'Hyphen'" in the *Conservative,* taking up again the issue of the Irish-Americans and other "hyphenates" using the United States as a base for launching anti-English propaganda:

> The Prussian propagandists and Irish irresponsibles, failing in their clumsy efforts to use the United States as a tool of vengeance upon the Mistress of the Seas, have seized with ingenious and unexpected eagerness on a current slogan coined to counteract their own traitorous machinations, and have begun to fling the trite demand "America first" in the face of every American who is unable to share their puerile hatred of the British Empire.

England, Lovecraft argues, is not really a foreign country, "nor is a true love of America possible without a corresponding love for the British race and ideals that created America." I shall return to this essay—and its emphatic rejection of the notion of the "melting pot"—at a later point.

Lovecraft was heartened when in late September President Wilson sent a "pretty stinging telegram"[52] to Jeremiah A. O'Leary, a radical Irish-American attempting to prevent American support of Britain. Wilson, in the final stages of his re-election campaign, had declared, in response to O'Leary's vow not to vote for him: "I would feel deeply mortified to have you or anybody like you vote for me. Since you have access to many disloyal Americans, and I have not, I will ask you to convey this message to them."[53] This certainly shows Wilson's increasingly open support of the Allied cause, although Lovecraft could not have been pleased when Wilson won re-election in November largely on the basis of the campaign slogan "He kept us out of war."

By early 1917 Lovecraft acceded to Dunn's wish to declare a "truce, armistice, or permanent peace"[54] regarding their discussion of the Irish question; but the matter inevitably flared up again a few months later. When, in late February 1917, the United States intercepted a telegram from Germany to Mexico promising Texas, New Mexico, and Arizona if Mexico were to enter the war, American invention became inevitable. Wilson appeared before Congress to declare war against Germany on April 2, 1917; the Senate approved the war resolution two days later, the House two days after that. A draft bill was signed on May 18, and the draft was to begin on June 5.

In early July Lovecraft expressed puzzlement at Dunn's "present war attitude,"[55] going on to say: "It is my honest opinion that your opinions have been perverted by a long devotion to a biased and partisan press." The correspondence abruptly ends here. What happened? Lovecraft explains in a letter written in the next year: "[Dunn] took the war very badly, & wrote treasonable letters by the score. When the draft came, he refused to register, & was arrested by government agents. In July he was drafted, but refused to respond to the summons—hence was court-martialled & sentenced to 20 years in the Atlanta Federal Prison—where he still languishes, I presume. I am done with Dunn!"[56] Dunn in fact spent only about two years in prison, and was released shortly after the end of the war. He went on to become a priest of the Catholic church, remaining in a diocese in Ohio for more than forty years until his death in 1983. Incredibly, he paralleled Bertrand Russell in protesting both World War I and the Vietnam War![57]

Rather more significant for our purposes is not Dunn's adventures with the draft but Lovecraft's; for he announces to Dunn on May 16, 1917: ". . . I have lately tried to assume my share of the present responsibility by applying, despite my invalid condition, for enlistment in the National Guard. My attempt met with ultimate failure, for I am really too feeble for military service; but I have at least done my best to prove that my consistent opposition to pacifism is not a matter of words only."[58] What has not been observed by commentators is that Lovecraft's entire episode with the Rhode Island National Guard (R.I.N.G.) occurred *before* Wilson's signing of the draft bill (May 18, 1917), and well before the institution of the draft itself. Lovecraft must have felt that, with the declaration of war in April, it was now appropriate for him to attempt to enter the hostilities himself as a matter of patriotic duty.

It is difficult to conceive of Lovecraft making this decision. In 1915, anticipating what he thinks will be Charles D. Isaacson's accusation of why he is not himself serving in the war given his militarism, he observes: "I shall not stoop to explain that I am an invalid who would certainly be fighting under the Union Jack if able . . ."[59] This is a refrain that can be found throughout Lovecraft's letters and essays of the period. Consider now his most detailed account of his attempt at enlistment in the R.I.N.G.:

> Some time ago, impressed by my entire uselessness in the world, I resolved to attempt enlistment despite my almost invalid condition. I argued that if I chose a regiment soon to depart for France; my sheer nervous force, which is not inconsiderable, might sustain me till a bullet or piece of shrapnel could more conclusively & effectively dispose of me. Accordingly I presented myself at the recruiting station of the R.I. National Guard & applied for entry into whichever unit should first proceed to the front. On account of my lack of technical or special training, I was told that I could not enter the Field Artillery, which leaves first; but was given a blank of application for the Coast Artillery, which will go after a short preliminary period of defence service at one of the forts of Narragansett Bay. The ques-

> tions asked me were childishly inadequate, & so far as physical requirements are concerned, would have admitted a chronic invalid. The only diseases brought into discussion were specific ailments from which I had never suffered, & of some of which I had scarcely ever heard. The medical examination related only to major organic troubles, of which I have none, & I soon found myself (as I thought) a duly enrolled private in the 9th Co. R.I.N.G.![60]

This tells us a number of important things. First, if he had actually become a member of the R.I.N.G., Lovecraft would probably not have been sent overseas into actual combat, but instead would have been merely stationed near home (a later letter declares that the 9th Coast Artillery was stationed at Fort Standish in Boston Harbour[61]) in an auxiliary capacity. Second, Lovecraft took an actual physical examination which, however cursory, revealed no major physical ailments. He elaborates elsewhere: "The Guard examination . . . was conducted in an office whose privacy was absolute, & whose floor & temperature were both suitable. The physician who conducted this examination, Maj. Augustus W. Calder, has just been rejected himself by the Federal surgeons as physically unfit."[62] This examination, if it survives, has not come to light, but its results make one much inclined to think that Lovecraft's "ailments" were largely "nervous" or, to put it bluntly, psychosomatic.

If Lovecraft passed the examination, how was it that he was not serving in the R.I.N.G.? Let him tell the story:

> As you may have deduced, I embarked upon this desperate venture without informing my mother; & as you may also have deduced, the sensation created at home was far from slight. In fact, my mother was almost prostrated with the news, since she knew that only by rare chance could a weakling like myself survive the rigorous routine of camp life. Her activities soon brought my military career to a close for the present. It required but a few words from our family physician regarding my nervous condition to annul the enlistment, though the army surgeon declared that such an annulment was highly unusual & almost against the regulations of the service. . . . my final status is that of a man "Rejected for physical disability."[63]

This account too is full of interest. One wonders what exactly Susie and Lovecraft's physician told the R.I.N.G. officials. Some have speculated that the latter might have revealed the fact of Winfield Lovecraft's paretic condition. The connexion between paresis and syphilis had been established in 1911, and it is likely that both Susie and the physician now had a pretty good idea of the true cause of Winfield's death. But the physical examination had presumably indicated that Lovecraft himself was not afflicted with paresis or syphilis, so it is not clear what effect the information about Winfield would have had. I think it is safer to concur with Lovecraft's own testimony and assume that the physician's account of Lovecraft's "nervous condition" caused the annulment.

Psychologically, Lovecraft confessed to a feeling of depression and disappointment. "I am told that a week of camp life and its hardships would probably wreck my constitution forever; but who can tell until it is attempted? And besides, what is the life or health of one weakling, when thousands of sturdy and useful young men are to be killed, crippled, and disfigured in a few months?"[64] I am not sure what we are to make of these frequent expressions of a wish for—or at least a lack of concern about—self-destruction. A little later he writes:

> I am feeling desolate and lonely indeed as a civilian. Practically all my personal acquaintances are now in some branch of the service, mostly Plattsburg or R.I.N.G. Yesterday one of my closest friends entered the Medical . . . Corps of the regular army. The physical tests for this corps are very light, and in spite of my previous rejection for Coast Artillery I would try to enter, were it not for the almost frantic attitude of my mother; who makes me promise every time I leave the house that I will not make another attempt at enlistment! But it is disheartening to be the one non-combatant among a profusion of proud recruits.[65]

Here was one more indication, for Lovecraft, of his being left behind in life: having failed to finish high school and enter college, he had seen his boyhood friends go on to gain good jobs in journalism, trade, and law enforcement. Now he saw them go off to war while he remained behind to write for the amateur press.

Lovecraft did in fact register for the draft on June 5; indeed, he was legally obliged to do so. He gave his occupation as "Writer." "I am told that it is possible I may be used even though I fail to pass the physical test for active military service."[66] Clearly Lovecraft was not so used. His draft record, if it survives, has also not come to light.

Another sociopolitical interest that emerged in the earliest part of Lovecraft's amateur journalism phase was temperance. This had, indeed, been an enthusiasm of remarkably early development. He announces in 1916: "It was in the sombre period of 1896 [after the death of his maternal grandmother] that I discovered an old copy of John B. Gough's *Sunshine* [*sic*] *& Shadow* & read & re-read it, backward and forward. From that time to this, I have never been at a loss for something to say against liquor!"[67] Gough (1817–1886) is an interesting case in himself. A small-time actor, he found himself falling increasingly under the influence of alcohol until he met a member of the so-called Washingtonian Movement (a temperance organisation emerging in the 1840s and employing George Washington as a sort of moral symbol of upright living) and took a pledge of abstinence in 1842. In spite of several relapses in the next few years, he ultimately became a complete teetotaller and spent the rest of his life delivering hundreds of lectures across the country to enthralled audiences.[68] His *Sunlight and Shadow; or, Gleanings from My Life Work* was published in 1880. The mere fact that this volume was in the

Phillips family library indicates that one member of the family at least was sympathetic to the temperance cause. Indeed, we may not have to look far, for the town of Delavan, Illinois, was founded by Lovecraft's maternal ancestors as a temperance town. We have seen that Whipple Phillips spent at least a year there as a young man in the 1850s.

Lovecraft himself did not get a chance to say anything in public on the subject until about 1915. About this time he discovered in the amateur world an ardent colleague in the fight against the demon rum—Andrew Francis Lockhart of Milbank, South Dakota. An article entitled "More *Chain Lightning*" (*United Official Quarterly*, October 1915) is a paean to Lockhart's efforts in the cause of temperance. *Chain Lightning* was a professional magazine edited by Lockhart which, according to Lovecraft, "last April succeeded in ridding the city of Milbank of its licenced saloons, and in securing the conviction of illicit retailers and resort proprietors."

Lovecraft was aware of the difficulty of the task: "The practical difficulty in enforcing Prohibition is admittedly great, but no man of virtue can do otherwise than work toward the final downfall of Rum." He realised the money, power, and influence of the liquor interests, and the unpopularity of abstinence among a broad cross-section of the populace who think that a social drink now and then is not a bad thing. Indeed, he took particular offence at an insidious advertising campaign launched by "a notorious beer-brewing corporation of St. Louis" in which the founding fathers were all portrayed as moderate drinkers. Lovecraft noted huffily that these ads are being published "by supposedly respectable newspapers, including those of the very highest class, such as the Providence *Daily Journal* and *Evening Bulletin*."

This remark itself points to the fact that the temperance movement was quite unpopular in Rhode Island, for a variety of reasons. A prohibition amendment to the state constitution was passed in 1885 but was repealed four years later. Rhode Island did not, in fact, ratify the Eighteenth Amendment.[69] It is true that the Baptists—the denomination of many of Lovecraft's maternal ancestors—had long been proponents of abstinence; but the modern temperance cause was really an outgrowth of the Progressive movement of the 1890s, and gained ground particularly in the first decade and a half of the new century. It is not at all surprising that Lovecraft would have become converted to temperance, for the movement had strong class- and race-conscious overtones; as one historian notes, it was led by "old stock, Protestant middle-class Americans"[70] who were repelled by what they considered the excessive drinking habits of immigrants, particularly Germans and Italians. Lovecraft unwittingly confirms this bias in his account of a Prohibition lecture given by an Episcopal clergyman in Providence in October 1916:

> . . . scarcely less interesting than the speaker were the dregs of humanity who clustered closest about him. I may say truly, that I have never before seen so many human derelicts all at once, gathered in one spot. I beheld modifications of human

> physiognomy which would have startled even a Hogarth, and abnormal types of gait and bodily carriage which proclaim with startling vividness man's kinship to the jungle apes. And even in the open air the stench of whiskey was appalling. To this fiendish poison, I am certain, the greater part of the squalor I saw was due. Many of these vermin were obviously not foreigners—I counted at least five American countenances in which a certain vanished decency half showed through the red whiskey bloating.[71]

The implication of that last sentence is that even "Americans" could sink to the level of "foreigners" under the influence of liquor. We have already seen Lovecraft referring to the foreigners in New England who "Around the wine-shops loaf with bleary eyes" ("New-England Fallen"); and he would not fail to stress the imbibing habits of the Irish in "Ye Ballade of Patrick von Flynn" (1916).

Lovecraft never missed an opportunity to champion the cause or to excoriate its opponents. His detestation of Woodrow Wilson was only augmented when the president's new Secretary of State, Robert Lansing, reversed the policy of William Jennings Bryan and reintroduced the serving of wine at state dinners. In a stinging diatribe, "Liquor and Its Friends" (*Conservative,* October 1915), Lovecraft acidly cites Mrs Lansing's remark, "Mr. Lansing and I are not extremists in the advocacy of Temperance," and defends the moral character of Bryan against his "wine-bibbing, time-serving, vice-sanctioning successor." He ominously sees in the incident "a conscious disregard for natural law and moral rectitude; a hideous disregard which will eventually wreck civilisation."

"A Remarkable Document" (*Conservative,* July 1917) praises a temperance article by Booth Tarkington published in the *American Magazine* for January 1917 and reprinted in the professional temperance magazine, the *National Enquirer,* for April 12. There are some interesting philosophical ruminations in this article which I shall discuss later.

Lovecraft found in poetry another means of advocating the cause. His first such foray was "The Power of Wine: A Satire," first published in the *Providence Evening News* for January 13, 1915, reprinted in the *Tryout* for April 1916, and then in the *National Enquirer* for March 28, 1918. Some of the satiric touches here are moderately effective:

> The youthful Tom, with Dionysiac might,
> Waylaid and robb'd an aged Jew last night,
> Whilst reeling Dick, with Bacchic ire possess'd,
> Shot down his best beloved friend in jest.

I don't know that there is a more sympathetic reference to Jews in all Lovecraft's early work than in that second line. Toward the end of the poem the imagery becomes fantastic and horrifying:

Shriek with delight, and writhe in ghoulish mirth;
With every draught another sin hath birth;
Beat your black wings, and prance with cloven feet;
With hideous rites the friends of Chaos greet!
Minions of Hell, your fiendish tones combine,
And chant in chorus of the Pow'r of Wine!

Rather less successful is "Temperance Song," published in the *Dixie Booster* for Spring 1916. This poem, in five stanzas with a chorus, was meant to be sung to the tune of "The Bonnie Blue Flag"; the first stanza will be sufficient:

We are a band of brothers
Who fight the demon Rum,
With all our strength until at length
A better time shall come.

That internal rhyme in the third line makes us think a little incongruously of "The Poem of Ulysses." Some poems that presumably date to around this time but which were apparently not published carry on the diatribe, their only virtue being their ingenious inclusion of the chemical compound for various types of alcohol within the metrical scheme. Here is the third stanza of "The Decline and Fall of a Man of the World":

$C_{17}H_{19}N$
　　　　$O_3 + H_2O$
The hapless youth took now and then,
　　　　And knew De Quincey's woe.

"The Road to Ruin" exists in a two-stanza and a one-stanza version, both expatiating on what happened when "Young Cyril / . . . first partook with curious mind / Of C_2H_6O."

Prohibition was ratified on January 15, 1919, and was deemed to go into effect in a year. On July 1, 1919, however, the government banned the manufacture and sale of liquor, and this appears to have been the occasion of Lovecraft's "Monody on the Late King Alcohol," published in the *Tryout* for August 1919. It does little but replay the message of "The Power of Wine" ("Less are the jokes, the nonsense, and the laughter— / And less the headaches of the morning after!").

One has to wonder why Lovecraft became so obsessed with temperance. He himself was fond of declaring that "I have never tasted intoxicating liquor, and never intend to";[72] in later years, while continuing to be theoretically in favour of Prohibition, he began to doubt its effectiveness and accepted its repeal in 1933 with cynical resignation. There is clearly a philosophical aspect to his stance, as when he states that "I can't see that it [liquor] does much save to coarsen, animalise, and degrade,"[73] and I shall have more to say about this a little later. But when Lovecraft remarks that "I am nauseated by even the distant stink of any alcoholic liquor,"[74] one is reminded of his extreme aversion to fish and cannot help wondering whether some event in infancy or boyhood triggered this severe physiological and psychological response. We know nothing of the drinking habits of Lovecraft's immediate family; even for his father, whatever other sins he may have committed, we have no evidence of any inclination toward imbibing. It would, therefore, be irresponsible and unjust to make any conjectures on the subject. What must be said is that the cause of temperance is the only aspect of social reform for which Lovecraft showed any enthusiasm in his earlier years—an enthusiasm seemingly out of keeping with the "cosmic" philosophy he had already evolved, which led him outwardly to maintain a perfect indifference to the fate of the "flyspeck-inhabiting lice"[75] on this terraqueous globe.

I have already noted that among the great benefits Lovecraft claimed to derive from amateurdom was the association of sympathetic and like-minded (or contrary-minded) individuals. For one who had been a virtual recluse during the 1908–13 period, amateur journalism allowed Lovecraft a gradual exposure to human society—initially in an indirect manner (via correspondence or discussions in amateur papers), then by direct contact. It would take several years for him to become comfortable as even a limited member of human society, but the transformation did indeed take place; and some of his early amateur associates remained for the rest of his life his closest friends.

Curiously, Lovecraft does not seem to have become close to Edward F. Daas, who recruited him into the amateur world. He noted that Daas withdrew from active participation in amateurdom around February 1916,[76] but he had returned by no later than the autumn of 1918,[77] and he visited Lovecraft in June 1920.[78] He and Lovecraft did not have much in common intellectually, as Lovecraft confesses ("our tastes are not especially similar"[79]). Lovecraft did, however, establish a fairly regular correspondence with his old *Argosy* opponent John Russell, although his letters to Russell have not come to light. Russell did not join the UAPA immediately when contacted by Daas; but Lovecraft ushered him into the association in "Introducing Mr. John Russell" (*Conservative,* July 1915).

It is not surprising that Lovecraft managed to convince his old boyhood chum Chester Pierce Munroe to join the UAPA. Averring in "Introducing Mr. Chester Pierce Munroe" (*Conservative,* April 1915) that Chester "was always of literary tastes," Lovecraft noted that Chester wrote several short stories as a youth "and in later years became the author of more than one unpublished novel." Chester's credential, the poem "Thoughts," appeared in the *Blarney-Stone* for March–April

1915, and random other poems—"To Flavia" in the *United Amateur* (May 1916), "To Chloris" in *Amateur Special* (July 1916) (also in the *Providence Evening News* for January 2, 1917), "Twilight" in Lovecraft's own *Conservative* (October 1916)—appeared from time to time. "To Flavia" had an unfortunate typographical error: the last line, which should have begun "Small maid . . .," read instead "Swell maid . . ." Chester also wrote a poem entitled "My Friend—H. L.: A Poet of the Old School," which appeared in the *Tryout* for March 1917. It is, frankly, a pretty poor excuse for a poem, and at that was probably revised by Lovecraft. It concludes, rather touchingly:

> The world too little knows you yet
>   But I do, friend of mine!
> And when your name they shall have met
>   Your skill will widely shine.
>
> When that bright time shall come at last,
>   I shall be proud to know
> The great H. L., atop Fame's mast,
>   My friend of long ago![80]

I do not know how long Chester remained in the UAPA: he is on the membership list until at least July 1920. He never issued his own paper.

Perhaps the three closest colleagues in Lovecraft's early amateur period were Maurice W. Moe, Edward H. Cole, and Rheinhart Kleiner. Moe (1882–1940) was a high school teacher at Appleton High School in Appleton, Wisconsin (later at the West Division High School in Milwaukee) and one of the giants of the amateur world at the time, even though he held relatively few offices. His religious orthodoxy was a constant source of friction with Lovecraft, and it may have helped to develop and refine Lovecraft's own hostility to religion. None of the withering polemics on religion to which Lovecraft treated Moe in his letters seem to have had any effect on their recipient.

Edward H. Cole (1892–1966) was also a well-respected amateur, but he was a staunch supporter of the NAPA and inflexibly hostile to the UAPA. He was Official Editor of the NAPA for 1911–12 and President for 1912–13. His journal, the *Olympian,* is one of the jewels of amateur literature in both content and typography, even though it lapsed after 1917 and would not resume for two decades. It was, as we have seen, Cole who urged John T. Dunn, who was forming the Providence Amateur Press Club, to get in touch with Lovecraft. Perhaps Cole's influence led Dunn momentarily to consider joining the NAPA, something Lovecraft squelched immediately: ". . . I am sorry that you admit even the possibility of the local club's being National in name. . . . Since I am so wholly a United man, I could not continue to support *The Providence Amateur* if it should affiliate itself with the National."[81]

Cole was one of the first amateurs, aside from the members of the Providence Amateur Press Club, whom Lovecraft met. He resided in various Boston suburbs and attended a meeting of the club in North Providence in late November 1914.[82] Also in 1914—possibly before his meeting with Cole—Lovecraft met the amateur William B. Stoddard at the Crown Hotel in Providence.[83] Not much is known about these encounters, but Cole became a close correspondent of Lovecraft—Stoddard did not, perhaps because he attacked the first issue of the *Conservative*[84]—and, in later years, Lovecraft would always look up Cole when he went to Boston. In spite of his prejudice against the UAPA, Cole in 1917 married Helene E. Hoffman (who had been President of the UAPA in the 1913–14 term, the period when Lovecraft joined) and persuaded himself to appear on the UAPA membership list. Lovecraft's early letters to Cole are very stiff and formal, but eventually he unwinds and becomes less self-conscious. When Cole's son E. Sherman Cole was born in 1919, Lovecraft wrote some delightfully owlish letters to him.

Rheinhart Kleiner (1892–1949) of Brooklyn came in touch with Lovecraft when he received the first issue of the *Conservative* in late March 1915. An immediate and voluble correspondence sprang up, and Kleiner of course sent Lovecraft copies of his own sporadic amateur paper, the *Piper*. The two first met on July 1, 1916, when Kleiner and some others—including Lovecraft's recent nemeses Charles D. Isaacson and W. E. Griffin—were passing through Providence on the way to the NAPA convention in Boston.[85] Thereafter—especially when Lovecraft himself lived in Brooklyn in 1924–26—he and Kleiner would form a strong bond of friendship.

In the summer of 1916 Moe suggested to Lovecraft that a rotating correspondence cycle be formed among UAPA members. Lovecraft, already a voluminous correspondent, readily assented to the plan and suggested Kleiner as a third member. Moe suggested a fourth—Ira A. Cole, an amateur in Bazine, Kansas, and editor of the *Plainsman*. Cole (no relation to Edward H. Cole) was a somewhat peculiar individual whom Lovecraft described in 1922 as follows:

> Ira A. Cole was a strange and brilliant character—an utterly illiterate ranchman and ex-cowboy of Western Kansas who possessed a streak of brilliant poetic genius. . . . His imagination was the most weird and active I have ever seen in any human being. But in the end that very streak of overdeveloped imagination and emotionalism was his aesthetic undoing. Worked upon by a hectic and freakish "Pentecostal" revivalist, he "got religion" and became an absolutely impossible fanatic in his eccentric sect. He even reached the hallucination stage—he fancied strange voices spoke gospel messages through his tongue—in languages he did not understand. He is a Pentecostal preacher and small farmer now, living in Boulder, Colorado.[86]

But that was several years in the future. Lovecraft published Cole's poems, "The Dream of a Golden Age" and "In Vita Elysium," in the *Conservative* for July 1915 and July 1917, respectively. The correspondence cycle started up, under the name (invented by Moe) Kleicomolo, derived from the first syllables of the last names of each member. (There is some debate in modern Lovecraft studies as to how to pronounce this coinage; I say Klei-co-MO-lo while others say Klei-CO-mo-lo.) Each member would write a letter addressed to the other three, in doing so leaving out his own syllable from the compound (hence Lovecraft would address the others as "Dear Kleicomo"; Kleiner as "Dear Comolo"; and so on). The idea at the outset was to rescue letter-writing as an art form from oblivion; whether or not the group succeeded, it certainly gave an impetus to Lovecraft's own letter-writing and to the development of his philosophical thought. I shall study the substance of Lovecraft's remarks a little later; at the moment we can turn our attention to an unsigned article entitled "The Kleicomolo" published in the *United Amateur* for March 1919. Some have thought this the work of Lovecraft, but the style does not strike me as at all Lovecraftian. My feeling is that it was written by Kleiner. The author of the article, after giving potted biographies of the four members, goes on to describe the precise working of the correspondence cycle:

> Klei writes to Co, who adds his instalment and sends the whole to Mo. Mo does the same and sends it to Lo, and Lo completes the articles and sends it back to Klei, who takes out his letter, writes another, and starts the packet around again. With the admission of Gal [Alfred Galpin] and the gradual warming up of the writers to the opportunity, the time required for a whole circuit has gradually increased until now it takes from six to ten months, although prompt attention to the letter upon its arrival would cut that down to two or three months. One of the members [Moe?] was desirous of keeping a complete copy of the correspondence, and began by copying the letters as they went through his hands. This task soon became so great as to be impracticable, and the rest elected him librarian and promised to send him carbon copies of their instalments. It is not at all unlikely that the future may see the best parts of the *Kleicomolo* given to the public as a book.[87]

Such a book would be a consummation devoutly to be wished, but it is not clear what has happened to the sections of the Kleicomolo correspondence aside from Lovecraft's. If, as I believe, Moe was the librarian, he appears to have turned over only Lovecraft's segments to August Derleth and Donald Wandrei for publication in the *Selected Letters.* Even the whereabouts of the originals of these are not known. In any event, Lovecraft's career as letter-writer had emphatically begun.

A more distant colleague, Andrew Francis Lockhart, is of some interest in having written the first genuine article on Lovecraft. A long-running but intermittent series of articles entitled "Little Journeys to the Homes of Prominent Amateurs" was revived when Lockhart wrote a biographical piece on Lovecraft for the

September 1915 issue of the *United Amateur.* It is a testimonial to Lovecraft's renown after only a year and a half in amateurdom that he was chosen to be the first subject for this series. Lockhart, of course, did not visit Lovecraft but clearly corresponded extensively with him. The article is a little sentimental and somewhat of a panegyric, but perhaps that is to be expected: "Just why he holds a firm grip on my heart-strings is something of a mystery to me. Perhaps it is because of his wholesome ideals; perhaps it is because he is a recluse, content to nose among books of ancient lore; perhaps it's because of his physical afflictions; his love of things beautiful in Life, his ardent advocacy of temperance, cleanliness and purity—I don't know."[88] This passage itself reveals how Lovecraft is already fashioning a precise image of himself: the recluse buried in books; the man of frail health and therefore not suited to the turmoil of the outside world. What these "physical afflictions" could have been is a mystery: the article later notes that, just as he was about to enter college, "his feeble health gave way, and since then he has been physically incapacitated and rendered almost an invalid." Whether this is the case or not, it is clearly what Lovecraft wanted Lockhart (and the whole UAPA) to believe.

Lovecraft's photograph was printed on the cover of this issue of the *United Amateur.* He repaid Lockhart the favour by writing a biography of him (under his "El Imparcial" pseudonym) as the second instalment of the "Little Journeys" series in the *United Amateur* for October 1915. The fifth article in the series, published in July 1917, was signed "El Imparcial" and discusses the young amateur Eleanor J. Barnhart. Lovecraft expected great things of Barnhart, especially as he thought her one of the best fiction-writers in amateurdom, but she evidently dropped out shortly after the writing of this piece.

In the meantime changes of some significance were occurring in Lovecraft's family life. He had been living alone with his mother at 598 Angell Street since 1904: with his grandfather Whipple Phillips dead, his younger aunt Annie married and living in Cambridge, Massachusetts, and his elder aunt Lillian married and living in Providence but some distance away, the atmosphere of 598 might well have become somewhat claustrophobic. I have already noted Clara Hess describing the "strange and shutup air" of the house at about this time. Then, on April 26, 1915, after thirteen years of marriage to Lillian, Lovecraft's uncle Franklin Chase Clark died at the age of sixty-seven.

It is difficult to know how close Lovecraft was to Clark beyond his teenage years. After Whipple Phillips's death in 1904, Clark would have been the only adult male whom Lovecraft could have regarded as a father-figure. His other uncle by marriage, Edward Francis Gamwell, was much younger than Dr Clark and was in any case living in another state. As for Edwin E. Phillips, it is evident from Lovecraft's silence about him that he did not care much for his uncle. We can certainly not gauge Lovecraft's emotions about Dr Clark from his "Elegy on Franklin Chase Clark, M.D.," which appeared in the *Providence Evening News* three days after his death, for a more wooden, lifeless, and mechanical poem would be difficult to find. Not a particle of genuine feeling can be found in this piece; what we find instead is some obnoxious class consciousness in sharp contrast to the later "Brotherhood":

> Say not that in the void beyond Death's door
> The mighty and the lowly are the same;
> Can boorish dust, in life but little more,
> Equality with mental essence claim?

About a year and a half later, on the very last day of 1916, Lovecraft's cousin Phillips Gamwell died of tuberculosis at the age of eighteen. Phillips, the only one of Annie E. Phillips Gamwell's and Edward F. Gamwell's children to survive beyond infancy, was the only male member of Lovecraft's family of his own generation. Lovecraft's various references to him make it clear that he was very fond of Phillips, even though he could only have seen him when he visited Cambridge or when Phillips came down to Providence. Lovecraft observes that Phillips, when he was twelve years old (i.e., in 1910), had "blossomed out as a piquant letter-writer eager to discuss the various literary and scientific topics broached during our occasional personal coversations,"[89] and Lovecraft attributes his fondness for letter-writing to four or five years' correspondence with Phillips. Lovecraft also remarks attempting to tutor Phillips in mathematics in 1915, finding that he had no better command of the subject than his pupil.[90] The next year Lovecraft, Phillips, and Annie Gamwell explored Trinity Church in Newport.[91] Lovecraft also gave Phillips his stamp-collection at about this time.[92]

Annie had taken her son to Roswell, Colorado, in October 1916 for his health, but his tuberculosis had obviously advanced too far and he died there on December 31, 1916. Lovecraft's "Elegy on Phillips Gamwell, Esq.," published in the *Providence Evening News* for January 5, 1917, is as uninspired as his tribute to Dr Clark: "Such was the youth, whose stainless mind and heart / Combin'd the best of Nature and of Art . . ." After Phillips's death, Annie returned to Providence, apparently living with her brother Edwin until his death on November 14, 1918 (and it is remarkable that Lovecraft says almost nothing about this event in any letters of the period or later), then probably in various rented quarters until early 1919, when she moved in with Lovecraft at 598 Angell Street.

Lovecraft, so far as I can tell, was not actually *doing* much during this period aside from writing; but he had discovered one entertaining form of relaxation—moviegoing. His enthusiasm for the drama had waned by around 1910, which roughly coincided with the emergence of film as a popular, if not an aesthetically distinguished, form of entertainment. By 1910 there were already 5000 nickelodeons throughout the country, even if these were regarded largely as entertainment for the working classes.[93] Lovecraft reports that the first cinema shows in Providence were in March 1906; and, even though he "knew too much of literature & drama not to recognise the utter & unrelieved hokum of the moving picture," he attended them anyway—"in the same spirit that I had read Nick Carter, Old King Brady, & Frank Reade in nickel-novel form."[94] One develops the idea that watching films may have occupied some, perhaps much, of the "blank" years of 1908–13, as a letter of 1915 suggests: "As you surmise, I am a devotee of the motion picture, since I can attend shows at any time, whereas my ill health seldom permits me to make definite engagements or purchase real theatre tickets in advance. Some modern films are really worth seeing, though when I first knew moving pictures their only value was to destroy time."[95] And yet, Lovecraft was willing at this time to entertain the possibility that film might eventually evolve into an aesthetically viable medium: "The moving picture has infinite possibilities for literary and artistic good when rightly presented, and having achieved a permanent place, seems destined eventually to convey the liberal arts to multitudes hitherto denied their enjoyment" ("Department of Public Criticism," *United Amateur,* May 1915). Nearly a century later we are perhaps still waiting for this eventuality to occur.

When Rheinhart Kleiner wrote "To Mary of the Movies" in the *Piper* for September 1915, Lovecraft immediately responded with "To Charlie of the Comics" (*Providence Amateur,* February 1916). It is no surprise that the two poets chose to pay tribute to Mary Pickford and Charlie Chaplin, as they were the first true "stars" of the film industry. Lovecraft's undistinguished poem is notable only for its relative modernity of subject and style and its use of octosyllabic quatrains:

> I've seen you as an artist rare,
> With brush and paint-smear'd palette;
> I've seen you fan the empty air
> With ill-intention'd mallet.
> I've watch'd you woo a winsome fay
> (You must a dream to her be),
> But ne'er have caught you in a play
> Without that cane and derby!

The poem ends with an outrageous "rouse us / trousers" rhyme, which, as Lovecraft admitted to the metrical purist Kleiner, "is not meant to be perfect—merely *allowable.*"[96]

Lovecraft clearly had a fondness for Chaplin, remarking: "Chaplin is infinitely amusing—too good for the rather vulgar films he used to appear in—and I hope he will in future be an exponent of more refined comedy."[97] Douglas Fairbanks "doubtless has much less of actual genius," but Lovecraft enjoyed his films "because there is a certain wholesomeness present, which the Chaplin type sometimes lacks."[98]

But Lovecraft's doubt as to the aesthetic substance of film is evident in "To Mistress Sophia Simple, Queen of the Cinema," dated to August 1917 on the manuscript but not published until the November 1919 *United Amateur,* when it appeared along with the poem that inspired it, Kleiner's "To a Movie Star." This exquisite little satire in quatrains skewers the insipid film heroine very effectively:

> Your eyes, we vow, surpass the stars;
> Your mouth is like the bow of Cupid;
> Your rose-ting'd cheeks no wrinkle mars—
> Yet why are you so sweetly stupid?

This leads us to a rather peculiar episode that occurred in January 1917. Fay's Theatre, located at the corner of Union and Washington Streets in downtown Providence, offered a prize of $25 for the best review of a film that Lovecraft calls *The Image-Maker of Thebes,* but whose title as listed in reference works is simply *The Image Maker;* it was shown (according to newspaper advertisements) on January 22–24, 1917. Lovecraft, having nothing better to do, went to see the film and participated in the contest. The five-reel film—about a modern-day couple in Florida who eventually realise that they are reincarnated counterparts of ancient Egyptians—was even worse than he expected: "a rough-hewn amateurish affair dealing with reincarnation in a pitifully feeble & hackneyed manner, containing not the slightest subtlety or technical skill in plot, directing, or acting."[99] Lovecraft, now giving up hope of winning the contest, wrote a sizzling four-page review "in my customary U.A.P.A. manner—which would, in colloquial parlance, be designated as a 'roast'!" To his amazement, he won the contest!

It would be a delight to have this review—the only movie review Lovecraft ever wrote, so far as I can tell—but efforts made by Marc A. Michaud and myself in 1977 to locate the files of Fay's Theatre (which had been torn down in 1951) proved unavailing. *The Image-Maker* was directed by Edgar Moore and starred Valda Valkyrien, the Baroness Dewitz. Although today a very obscure film (no copy appears to survive), it was actually well received in its day; but a representative review—from the *New York Dramatic Mirror*—may give some hint as to why Lovecraft himself found the film not at all to his taste: "'The Image Maker' will satisfy that multitude which likes Romance—spelt with a capital R—in motion pictures. . . . There are thrilling adventures frequently enough in both narratives to satisfy even the most blasé and the happily ended love affair will be liked. . . . This is the kind of a picture the crowd likes and an exhibitor will make no mistake in booking it."[100]

This episode is of interest only because Lovecraft's later comments on film are increasingly critical. As we have seen, he by no means lacked an appreciation of the artistic potential of film; but shortly after winning the Fay's Theatre award he remarked to Dunn:

> Save for a few Triangle, Paramount & Vitagraph pictures, everything I have seen is absolute trash—though some are quite harmless & amusing. Worst of all are the *serials*—whose authors are probably the same poor creatures that wrote the "dime novels" of yesterday. I have yet to see a serial film worth the time wasted in looking at it—or dozing over it. The technique could be surpassed by most ten year old children.[101]

In 1921 he remarked to his mother that "In matters of scenery the moving picture can of course leave the stage far behind; though this hardly atones for the lack of sound and colour."[102] Even with the advent of sound pictures in 1927, Lovecraft's low opinion of film persisted, and certain early horror films based upon some of his favourite literary works incited his especial ire. With rare exceptions, Lovecraft did not care for the surprising number of films he saw in the course of his life.

For three years Lovecraft had written reams of essays, poems, and reviews of amateur papers. Would he ever resume the fiction writing that had showed such promise up to 1908? In 1915 Lovecraft wrote to the amateur G. W. Macauley: "I wish that I could write fiction, but it seems almost an impossibility."[103] Macauley claims that he "violently disagreed"—not because he had actually seen any of Lovecraft's fiction but because, having sent a story to Lovecraft for comment, he had received such an acute and elaborate analysis that he became convinced that Lovecraft had the short-story writing faculty within him. Criticism of fiction and fiction-writing are, of course, two different things, but in Lovecraft's case one cannot help feeling that the frequency with which he remarks on the failings of stories published in the amateur press points to a growing urge to prove that he can do better. Fiction was, of course, always the weakest point in the amateur press, not only because it is generally harder to master than standard essay-writing but because the space limitations in amateur papers did not allow the publication of much beyond sketches or vignettes.

One comment in particular, discussing a story by William T. Harrington, is highly illuminating in showing a key shift of Lovecraft's preferences:

> In this tale, Mr. Harrington exhibits at least a strong ambition to write, and such energy, if well directed, may eventually make of him one of our leading authors of fiction. Just now, however, we must protest against his taste in subject and technique. His models are obviously not of the classical order, and his ideas of probability are far from unexceptionable. In developing the power of narration, it is generally best . . . to discard the thought of elaborate plots and thrilling climaxes, and to begin instead with the plain and simple description of actual incidents with which the author is familiar. . . . Meanwhile, above all things he should read clas-

> sic fiction, abstaining entirely from the *Wild West Weeklies* and the like. ("Department of Public Criticism," *United Amateur,* March 1915)

So the "elaborate plots and thrilling climaxes" of the dime novels are now *verboten!* Even though Lovecraft was at this time still reading the *Argosy, All-Story,* and other early pulp magazines, he instead encouraged Harrington to read Scott, Cooper, and Poe. There are, certainly, plenty of thrills in these authors, but they are of a "classic" variety that Lovecraft could approve. About a year later he gave a lengthy criticism of the imaginatively titled "A Story" by David H. Whittier, a teenager whom Lovecraft had lauded in "The Youth of Today" (*Conservative,* October 1915). In particular, the use of coincidence offends him: "In an artistically constructed tale, the various situations all develop naturally out of that original cause which in the end brings about the climax . . ." Lovecraft could not, however, help adding tartly that "such . . . coincidences in stories are by no means uncommon among even the most prominent and widely advertised professional fiction-blacksmiths of the day" ("Department of Public Criticism," *United Amateur,* June 1916).

Lovecraft finally allowed his credential, "The Alchemist," to be printed in the *United Amateur* for November 1916, two and a half years after he had entered amateurdom. It was to be expected that he would himself attack it in the "Department of Public Criticism" (*United Amateur,* May 1917):

> *The United Amateur* for November is heavily burdened with a sombre and sinister short story from our own pen, entitled "The Alchemist". This is our long unpublished credential to the United, and constitutes the first and only piece of fiction we have ever laid before a critical and discerning public; wherefore we must needs beg all the charitable indulgence the Association can extend to an humble though ambitious tyro.

The single word "ambitious" may suggest Lovecraft's desire to write more fiction if this one specimen, however much he may deprecate it himself, receives favourable notice. It appears to have done just that, but even so it would still be more than half a year before Lovecraft would break his self-imposed nine-year ban on fiction-writing. That he finally did so, writing "The Tomb" and "Dagon" in quick succession in the summer of 1917, can be attributed in large part to the encouragement of a new associate, W. Paul Cook of Athol, Massachusetts, who would be a significant presence throughout the rest of Lovecraft's life.

8. Dreamers and Visionaries (1917–1919 [II])

W. Paul Cook (1881–1948), who also appeared in the amateur press as Willis Tete Crossman, had long been a giant in the amateur world. Cook was unmistakably a New Englander: he had been born in Vermont; he was, as Lovecraft was fond of pointing out, a direct descendant of the colonial governor Benning Wentworth of New Hampshire; and he resided for much of his adult life in Athol, Massachusetts. One of his earliest amateur journals was the *Monadnock Monthly*, named for the mountain in New Hampshire near his home in Athol. For years he was the head of the printing department of the *Athol Transcript*, and his access to printing equipment and his devotion to the amateur cause permitted him to be a remarkable philanthropist in printing amateur journals virtually at cost. We have seen that he began printing the *Conservative* in 1917. During his term as President of the UAPA Lovecraft appointed Cook Official Printer, a position he held for three consecutive years (1917–20) and again for three more years in 1922–25. Curiously, at the same time he served as Official Editor of the NAPA (1918–19) and its President (1919–20).[1]

After his first meeting with Cook in September 1917 (which I shall discuss in greater detail later) Lovecraft summed him up as follows: "Though not overwhelmingly bookish, he has a keen mind, dry humour, & an infinite & quite encyclopaedic knowledge of the events & personages of amateur journalism past & present."[2] What he does not say here is that Cook had a strong taste in weird fiction; indeed, Lovecraft would later admit that Cook's "library was the most remarkable collection of fantastic & other material that I have ever seen assembled in one place,"[3] and he would frequently borrow many rare books to which he himself did not have access. It is scarcely to be doubted that Cook, during his visit with Lovecraft, discussed this topic of mutual interest. Whether at this time he convinced Lovecraft to let him print his other juvenile tale, "The Beast in the Cave," is not clear; at any rate, that story appeared in Cook's *Vagrant* (a NAPA paper) for June 1918.

Lovecraft makes it very clear that Cook's encouragement was instrumental in his resumption of weird writing:

> In 1908, when I was 18, I was disgusted by my lack of technical experience [in fiction-writing]; & *burned all my stories (of which the number was infinite) but two;* resolving (amusing thought!) to turn to verse in the future. Then, years later, I published these two yarns in an amateur paper; where they were so well received that I began to consider resumption. Finally an amateur editor & critic named

> W. Paul Cook . . . egged me on to the point of actual resumption, & "The Tomb"—with all its stiffness—was the result. Next came "Dagon" . . .[4]

The chronology here is a little confused: "The Beast in the Cave" was published well after Lovecraft resumed fiction-writing in the summer of 1917. In any event, Lovecraft—although he apparently did not know it at the time—had found his *métier.* "The Tomb" was written in June 1917, "Dagon" in July.[5] One instance of the encouragement Cook provided was an effusive article entitled "Howard P. Lovecraft's Fiction," prefacing his printing of "Dagon" in the *Vagrant* for November 1919:

> Howard P. Lovecraft is widely and favorably known throughout the amateur journalistic world as a poet, and in a lesser degree as an editorial and essay writer. As a story-writer he is practically unknown, partly because of the scarcity of publications large enough to accommodate much prose, and partly because he does not consider himself a competent story-teller. His first story to appear in the amateur press was "The Alchemist," published in the *United Amateur.* This story was enough to stamp him as a pupil of Poe in its unnatural, mystical and actually morbid outlook, without a hint of the bright outdoors or of real life. His second story, "The Beast in the Cave," published in the *Vagrant,* was far inferior in every respect, even in being given a modern setting, which may be counted as against it in Mr. Lovecraft's case. The outstanding feature of this really slight effort was the skill with which an atmosphere was created.
>
> In "Dagon," in this issue of the *Vagrant,* Mr. Lovecraft steps into his own as a writer of fiction. In reading this story, two or three names of short-story writers are immediately called to mind. First of all, of course, Poe; and Mr. Lovecraft, I believe, would be the first to acknowledge his allegiance to our American master. Second, Maupassant; and I am quite sure that Mr. Lovecraft would deny any kinship with the great Frenchman.
>
> Mr. Lovecraft with "Dagon" is not through as a contributor of fiction to the amateur press. He will never be as voluminous a fiction writer as a poet, but we may confidently expect to see him advance even beyond the high mark he has set in "Dagon."
>
> I cannot fully appreciate Mr. Lovecraft as a poet . . . But I can and do appreciate him as a story-writer. He is at this day the only amateur story-writer worthy of more than a polite passing notice.[6]

Almost everything in this statement is correct, except perhaps Cook's suspicion of an influence of Guy de Maupassant, whom Lovecraft had probably not read at this time, although he would later find much of Maupassant's weird work compelling. This remarkable paean—I know of nothing quite like it in the amateur press, even including Lovecraft's various "introductions" of his friends and colleagues into amateurdom—could only have heartened Lovecraft, who required the approbation of friends to overcome his ingrained diffidence over the quality of his fictional work. In this case, the approbation was entirely justified.

It is worth pondering the general influence of Poe on Lovecraft's early tales, since Poe certainly looms large over the bulk of Lovecraft's fiction up to at least 1923. We have seen that, for all his enthusiasm for Poe when he first discovered him in 1898, Lovecraft's juvenile fiction bears relatively few similarities to Poe's work. This changes abruptly with "The Tomb," which makes no secret of its borrowings from Poe. And yet, even "The Tomb" and "The Outsider" (1921), Lovecraft's most obviously Poe-esque tales, are far from being mere pastiches; but that Lovecraft found in Poe a model both in style and in overall short-story construction is evident. Many of Lovecraft's early tales—and, for that matter, even later ones—open with that ponderous enunciation of a general truth which the story itself purports to instantiate: recall Poe's memorable opening of "Berenice," "Misery is manifold. The wretchedness of earth is multiform."[7] Poe himself may well have derived this pseudo-nonfictional opening from the eighteenth-century essayists, by whom he was influenced scarcely less than Lovecraft was; and we will see that both Poe and Lovecraft utilised it in order to create a sort of "hoax-like" atmosphere whereby the story actually passes for a factual account.

Late in life Lovecraft actually disputed that his style was directly derived from Poe. In remarking on a story by Richard F. Searight which some thought to be influenced by Lovecraft, he states:

> . . . I can't see this in any marked degree. Rather would I say that you have simply chosen the same general cast of language which I prefer—but which hundreds of others, long before I was born, have preferred. Many think I have derived this style exclusively from Poe—which (despite the strong influence of Poe on me) is another typical mistake of uninformed modernism. This style is no especial attribute of Poe, but is simply *the major traditional way of handling English narrative prose.* If I picked it up through any especial influence, that influence is probably the practice of the 18th century rather than Poe . . .[8]

I think there is a certain amount of posturing here. It is true enough that Lovecraft's fictional style is a sort of amalgam of the eighteenth-century essayists and Poe; and by the time he wrote the above (1935) he had indeed gotten well away from any direct stylistic imitation of Poe. But the fact is that the idiom Lovecraft evolved in his early tales—dense, a little overheated, laced with archaic and recondite terms, almost wholly lacking in "realistic" character portrayal, and almost entirely given over to exposition and narration, with a near-complete absence of dialogue—is clearly derived from Poe and is *not* the "major traditional way of handling English narrative prose," as the very different work of Hawthorne, Thackeray, or Joseph Conrad will amply testify.

Lovecraft elsewhere is a little more honest in assessing the Poe influence on himself: "Since Poe affected me most of all horror-writers, I can never feel that a tale starts out right unless it has something of his manner. I could never plunge into a thing abruptly, as the popular writers do. To my mind it is necessary to establish a setting & avenue of approach before the main show can adequately begin."[9] This is exactly a reference to that quasi-nonfictional opening that both Poe and Lovecraft felt was essential to set the stage for the events to follow. So much, indeed, did Lovecraft customarily acknowledge the Poe influence that he would go to the opposite extreme, as in his famous lament of 1929: "There are my 'Poe' pieces & my 'Dunsany' pieces—but alas—where are any 'Lovecraft' pieces?"[10]

The most obvious stylistic feature common to both Poe and Lovecraft is the use of adjectives. In Lovecraft's case this has been derisively termed "adjectivitis," as if there is some canonical number of adjectives per square inch that are permissible and that the slightest excess is cause for frenzied condemnation. But this sort of criticism is merely a holdover from an outmoded and superficial realism that vaunted the barebones style of a Hemingway or a Sherwood Anderson as the sole acceptable model for English prose. We have seen that Lovecraft was predominantly influenced by the "Asianic" style of Johnson and Gibbon as opposed to the "Attic" style of Swift and Addison; and few nowadays—especially now that the Thomas Pynchons and Gore Vidals of the world have restored richness of texture to modern English fiction—will condemn Lovecraft without a hearing for the use of such a style.

The specific object of this criticism, however, is the use of words that transparently suggest or are meant to inspire horror. Edmund Wilson speaks for many when he declares pontifically:

> One of Lovecraft's worst faults is his incessant effort to work up the expectations of the reader by sprinkling his stories with such adjectives as "horrible," "terrible," "frightful," "awesome," "eerie," "weird," "forbidden," "unhallowed," "unholy," "blasphemous," "hellish" and "infernal." Surely one of the primary rules for writing an effective tale of horror is never to use any of these words . . .[11]

If Wilson's dictum were followed literally, there would scarcely be any horror stories in existence today. Firstly, Lovecraft clearly derived this stylistic device from Poe. Consider "A Descent into the Maelström": "To the right and left, as far as the eye could reach, there lay outstretched, like ramparts of the world, lines of horridly black and beetling cliff, whose character of gloom was but the more forcibly illustrated by the surf which reared high up against it its white and ghastly crest, howling and shrieking for ever."[12] It is only in Lovecraft's inferior work that this device becomes overused or hackneyed. Secondly, it has incredibly escaped most observers that such a technique, especially in first-person narration, serves as a critical indication of the protagonist's state of mind, becoming therefore an element in character portrayal.

Nevertheless, I think a case could be made that Lovecraft spent the better part of his fictional career in attempting to escape—or, at best, master or refine—the stylistic influence of Poe, as his frequent remarks in the last decade of his life on the need for simplicity of expression and his exemplification of this principle in the evolution of his later "scientific" manner suggest.

If in style and texture Lovecraft owes much to Poe, he owes scarcely less to Poe's theory and practice of story-construction. I do not at the moment wish to examine Lovecraft's theory of weird fiction, as it does not seem to have taken shape until about 1921; but, right from the beginning, Lovecraft intuitively adopted many of the principles of short-story technique that (as he himself points out in "Supernatural Horror in Literature") Poe virtually invented and exemplified in his work—"such things as the maintenance of a single mood and achievement of a single impression in a tale, and the rigorous paring down of incidents to such as have a direct bearing on the plot and will figure prominently in the climax." This "paring down" applies both to word-choice and to overall structure, and we will find that all Lovecraft's tales—even those that might be classified as short novels—adhere to this principle.

There is, then, no question of the general influence of Poe upon Lovecraft's early work, and I shall point to the influence of specific works by Poe in my analysis of Lovecraft's stories; but a more recent influence on Lovecraft's actual commencement of fiction-writing in 1917 may be worth examining. In Lovecraft's library are two volumes on short-story writing: *Facts, Thought, and Imagination: A Book on Writing* by Henry Seidel Canby, Frederick Erastus Pierce, and W. H. Durham (1917), and *Writing the Short-Story* by J. Berg Esenwein (1909), of which Lovecraft had the 1918 printing. The fact that he apparently acquired these two volumes at the very outset of his fiction-writing career suggests that he wished some theoretical and practical advice on a literary mode he had not attempted in nearly a decade.

The book by Canby, Pierce, and Durham is a rather abstract study of the components of the short story and what it seeks to accomplish. Perhaps most interesting for our purposes is the chapter on "Imagination" by W. H. Durham. Maintaining that any story that "does more than merely thrill or amuse the reader" has behind it "the effort to convey effectively some kind of idea," Durham emphasises that "Any writer of fiction who takes his work at all seriously is attempting to record his impression of life," and that a story must therefore be true to life.[13] It is important to realise that this volume is not stressing realism in the narrow sense, a point brought home by its inclusion of H. G. Wells's "The Story of the Last Trump" as one of several examples of the model short story; this book, therefore, may have helped to plant a seed in Lovecraft's mind that the weird tale could be a serious form of expression and not merely a potboiler—entertaining though that may be—of the sort found in the Munsey magazines.

Esenwein's treatise is more of a nuts-and-bolts practical guide to writing and selling the short story, complete with recommendations on how to type the manuscript, how to write a cover letter, what markets are suitable for various types of work, and other mundane details. Its orientation is much less aesthetically refined than the Canby volume, but it nevertheless stresses the fundamental way in which the short story differs from the novel: *"A short-story produces a singleness of effect denied to the novel."*[14] This principle is manifestly derived from Poe, and Esenwein makes no secret of the fact, going on to cite the canonical passage in Poe's essay-review of Hawthorne where it is first enunciated. Esenwein goes on to list seven characteristics of the short story: 1. A Single Predominating Incident. 2. A Single Preeminent Character. 3. Imagination. 4. Plot. 5. Compression. 6. Organization. 7. Unity of Impression.[15] There is nothing remarkable here, and this too is ultimately derived from Poe; Lovecraft adhered to many of these conceptions, but they are so general that he is likely to have derived them independently merely through an analytical study of Poe's stories.

One influence that some very recent research has rendered much more problematical is that of the Munsey magazines. It is certainly likely that Lovecraft continued to read some of these magazines after his contretemps in the *Argosy* in 1913–14; but some of the "evidence" that has hitherto been advanced on this point has now been shown to be invalid. Lovecraft frequently remarks that he preserved the issue of the *All-Story* containing A. Merritt's spectacular novelette, "The Moon Pool" (June 22, 1918), so that he probably read this magazine at least up to this date and perhaps up to the time it consolidated with the *Argosy* (July 24, 1920). But the belief that he read the *Argosy* itself as late as 1919 or 1920 has long been based upon letters Lovecraft purportedly published in that magazine under the pseudonym "Augustus T. Swift." Two such letters have been discovered, in the issues for November 15, 1919, and May 22, 1920. But these letters are almost certain to be spurious.

At this time the *Argosy* letter column was no longer supplying complete addresses of letter-writers but merely the city of origin; both these letters are, to be sure, written from Providence, but a quick check of the Providence city directory for 1919–20 reveals an actual individual named Augustus T. Swift, a teacher, living at 122 Rochambeau Avenue. These letters have a superficially Lovecraftian tone to them (there is one complaint about too much "hugging and kissing" in some stories), but other features are highly peculiar, both in phraseology and in actual content. The second letter in particular, commenting on a whaling story by a writer named Reynolds, declares: "Being a native of New Bedford, Massachusetts, and having heard whale-ship talk from infancy, I followed the detailed descriptions of polar scenes with unusual interest." Lovecraft a native of New Bedford, Massachusetts? I don't think so.

The question arises as to how these letters were attributed to Lovecraft to begin with. The "culprit" is Larry Farsaci, editor of the fanzine *Golden Atom*. In the issue for December 1940 Farsaci—who was a well-known collector of early pulp magazines—reprinted these two letters along with a genuine letter by Lovecraft (from the *All-Story* of August 15, 1914). Elsewhere in the issue he gave a list of Lovecraft's pseudonyms, derived largely from a list printed earlier by R. H. Barlow, but with Augustus T. Swift added and with the note: "This last is your ed's belief."[16] From here, the Augustus T. Swift "pseudonym" was picked up by many subsequent scholars and bibliographers who, if they had actually seen the letters in question, should have known better. Contrived "explanations" for the "pseudonym" have also appeared ("Augustus" standing for the Augustan age; "Swift" standing either for the boy's writer Tom Swift or for Jonathan Swift). But the existence of a real Augustus T. Swift can, I think, put this entire episode to rest.

Some consequences follow from the exposure of the spuriousness of these letters. There is now no concrete evidence that Lovecraft read the *Argosy* subsequent to 1914. Much of A. Merritt's work, which Lovecraft did indeed enjoy, appeared here, although some of it much later (e.g., *The Dwellers in the Mirage* was serialised in 1932, *Creep, Shadow!* in 1934); *The Metal Monster,* serialised in 1920, was not read by Lovecraft until 1934. The influence of Merritt on Lovecraft, and of Lovecraft on Merritt, is a fascinating subject that needs to be addressed later. Moreover, the two Augustus T. Swift letters effusively praise Francis Stevens (the pseudonym of Gertrude Bennett), although they believe the author to be a man. Stevens's *The Citadel of Fear* (serialised 1918) and *Claimed* (serialised 1920) are indeed quite striking works that Lovecraft might conceivably have enjoyed; but we shall now need other evidence to testify to his fondness for them. (Still more awkwardly, both these novels have been reprinted in paperback with blurbs from the Swift letters attributed to Lovecraft!)

I am still not certain why Lovecraft chose to resume fiction-writing at this exact time. Is it perhaps because his poetry was being showered with abuse in the amateur press for being antiquated and void of feeling? If Lovecraft expected his fiction to be better received, he was on the whole to be disappointed. His own colleagues certainly sang his praises in brief critical notices of his tales; but many amateurs, stolidly unreceptive to the weird, found his tales even less bearable than his poems. Is there a connexion with his failed attempt to enlist, which occurred only a month or so before he wrote "The Tomb"? One does not wish to engage in armchair psychoanalysis with so little evidence at hand; suffice it to say that literature is fortunate for Lovecraft's ultimate realisation that fiction, and not poetry or essays, was his chosen medium. His first several tales show remarkable promise, and they are the vanguard for the great work of the last decade of his life.

In "The Tomb" a first-person narrator tells of his lonely and secluded life: "My name is Jervas Dudley, and from earliest childhood I have been a dreamer and a visionary." We become immediately suspicious of his account, since he admits to telling it within the confines of an insane asylum; but he believes that his story will vindicate him and his belief that "there is no sharp distinction betwixt the real and the unreal." Dudley discovers, in a wooded hollow near his home, a tomb that houses the remains of a family, the Hydes, that dwelt in a mansion nearby. This mansion had been struck by lightning and burned to the ground, although only one member of the family had perished in the flame. The tomb exercises an unholy fascination upon Dudley, and he haunts it for hours at a time. It is locked, but the door is "fastened *ajar* in a queerly sinister way by means of heavy iron chains and padlocks, according to a gruesome fashion of half a century ago." Dudley resolves to enter this tomb at any cost, but he is too young and weak to break open the lock (he is only ten years old at this time).

Gradually Dudley begins to display various odd traits, in particular a knowledge of very ancient things that he could not possibly have learnt from books. One night, as he is lying on a bower outside the tomb, he seems to hear voices from within: "Every shade of New England dialect, from the uncouth syllables of the Puritan colonists to the precise rhetoric of fifty years ago, seemed represented in that shadowy colloquy . . ." He does not say what the colloquy was about, but upon returning home he goes directly to a rotting chest in the attic and finds a key to unlock the tomb.

Dudley spends much time in the tomb. But now another peculiar change takes place in him: hitherto a sequestered recluse, he begins to show signs of "ribald revelry" as he returns from the tomb. In one instance he declaims, "in palpably liquorish accents," a drinking song of Georgian cast, but one "never recorded in a book." He also develops a fear of thunderstorms.

Dudley's parents, worried about his increasingly odd behaviour, now hire a "spy" to follow his actions. On one occasion Dudley thinks that this spy has seen him coming out of the tomb, but the spy tells his parents that Dudley had spent the night on the bower outside the tomb. Dudley, now convinced that he is under some sort of supernatural protection, frequents the tomb without fear or circumspection. One night, as thunder is in the air, he goes to the tomb and sees the mansion as it was in its heyday. A party is under way, and guests in powdered wigs are brought in by carriage. But a peal of thunder interrupts the "swinish revelry" and a fire breaks out. Dudley flees, but finds himself being restrained by two men. They maintain that Dudley had spent the entire night outside the tomb, and point to the rusted and unopened lock as evidence. Dudley is put away in a madhouse. A servant, "for whom I bore a fondness in infancy," goes to the tomb, breaks it open, and finds a porcelain miniature with the initials "J. H."; the picture could be of Dudley's twin. "On a slab in an alcove he found an old but empty coffin whose tarnished plate bears the single word *'Jervas'*. In that coffin and in that vault they have promised me I shall be buried."

Lovecraft gives an interesting account of the genesis of the story:

> . . . one June day in 1917 I was walking through Swan Point Cemetery with my aunt and saw a crumbling tombstone with a skull and crossbones dimly traced upon its slaty surface; the date, 1711, still plainly visible. It set me thinking. Here was a link with my favourite aera of periwigs—the body of a man who had worn a full-bottom'd wig and had perhaps read the original sheets of *The Spectator*. Here lay a man who had lived in Mr. Addison's day, and who might easily have seen Mr. Dryden had he been in the right part of London at the right time! Why could I not talk with him, and enter more intimately into the life of my chosen age? What had left his body, that it could no longer converse with me? I looked long at that grave, and the night after I returned home I began my first story of the new series—"The Tomb". . .[17]

Donovan K. Loucks has identified this tombstone as the grave of one Simon Smith (1662–1711), a distant ancestor of Lillian D. Clark.

"The Tomb" is, as it turns out, quite anomalous in Lovecraft's fictional work for a variety of reasons. In the first place, there is some doubt as to whether the horror is external or internal, supernatural or psychological: is Jervas Dudley possessed by the spirit of his ancestor and lookalike, Jervas Hyde, or has he imagined the entire thing? The supernatural explanation must, I think, in the end be accepted, especially because of Dudley's possession of knowledge about the past (e.g., that Squire Brewster was not dead when he was interred in 1711) and about the mansion that he could not otherwise have known: "On one occasion I startled a villager by leading him confidently to a shallow sub-cellar, of whose existence I seemed to know in spite of the fact that it had been unseen and forgotten for many generations." The fundamental idea is that the spirit of Jervas Hyde, who was burned to death in the fire that consumed his house, has reached across the centuries to seize a body who will at last fill his empty coffin in the tomb of the Hydes.

But how to account for the unbroken lock on the tomb and the fact that Dudley's spy claims to have seen him not in the tomb but on the bower outside it? Was Dudley (as he believes) being protected by a "supernatural agency"? But if he had actually entered the tomb, how did the lock remain unbroken and rusted? The servant at the end really does have to break it open. Perhaps Dudley's body did in fact spend those nights on the bower but his spirit entered the tomb.

The other thing that makes "The Tomb" peculiar for Lovecraft is the degree of psychological analysis which Dudley's character undergoes. The influence of Poe and his "typical protagonist . . . a dark, handsome, proud, melancholy, intellectual, highly sensitive, capricious, introspective, isolated, and sometimes slightly mad gentleman of ancient family and opulent circumstances" (as Lovecraft wrote in "Supernatural Horror in Literature") is very evident in this regard. Lovecraft echoes "Berenice" ("Our line has been called a race of visionaries"[18]) in his opening sentence. This literary influence should make us cautious in reading autobiographical traits in the narrator of "The Tomb." When he says that he was "wealthy beyond the necessity of a commercial life," we may see this as wish-fulfilment on Lovecraft's part, but the narrator's need to be independently wealthy is crucial to the development of the tale. Lovecraft, too, may have been "temperamentally unfitted for the formal studies and social recreations of my acquaintances," but it is important that the narrator have these traits also. Nevertheless, in a broad sense the narrator reflects Lovecraft's own absorption in the Georgian age, and the sense of dislocation from his own time that this absorption brought about.

But there is much more probing of the narrator's psyche than this. Jervas Dudley is much more introspective, and much more concerned with analysing his own emotional state, than most of Lovecraft's other characters are. But again, the demands of the plot necessitate such self-scrutiny, for it is by the anomalous departures from his normal state of mind that we can gauge the insidious incursion of the soul of Jervas Hyde. Some of his reflexions are very poignant: "I was no longer a young man, though but twenty-one years had chilled my bodily frame." We *care* about this character as we do for few others in Lovecraft's corpus.

Although Lovecraft makes clear that the setting of the tale is New England, "The Tomb" contains so little topographical description that it could really be set almost anywhere. It is, of course, essential that the tale be situated in a region that has been settled for several centuries, so that the spectral hand of the distant past can reach forward into the present; but one wonders whether a setting in England—where several of Lovecraft's other early tales take place—might not have served a little better, since the contrast between the narrator's sober present-day demeanour and his vivacious behaviour when possessed by Hyde might better have been achieved with an English background. The narrator in fact remarks that in his transformed state he "covered the flyleaves of my books with facile impromptu epigrams which brought up suggestions of Gay, Prior, and the sprightliest of the Augustan wits and rimesters."

This brings us to what has come to be called "The Drinking Song from 'The Tomb.'" This four-stanza song, inserted bodily into the story—a technique Lovecraft probably derived not so much from the Gothics (whose poetical interruptions are scarcely integral to the work) as from Poe, who included poems in "The Fall of the House of Usher" and "Ligeia" that are not only among his most memorable, but which are critical to the logic of the tales—has taken on a life of its own, especially when it was reprinted by itself in *Collected Poems* (1963). T. O. Mabbott, who charitably remarked that most of Lovecraft's poetry was "written 'with his left hand,'" quotes the magnificent line "Better under the table than under the ground" as an instance of what a fine poet Lovecraft might have been.[19] Indeed, it is difficult to resist something like this:

Anacreon had a red nose, so they say;
But what's a red nose if ye're happy and gay?
Gad split me! I'd rather be red whilst I'm here,
Than white as a lily—and dead half a year!
So Betty, my miss,
Come give me a kiss;
In hell there's no innkeeper's daughter like this!

There is good reason for regarding this poem as a separate entity, for it was written separately and perhaps years before the story itself. Indeed, its inclusion in the story could be considered something of an indulgence. The manuscript of the poem survives in the John Hay Library: it is part of a letter, one perhaps that was never actually sent (the fifth page is incomplete, bearing no closing). We do not know to whom the letter was addressed, as the first two pages are missing. I suspect that Lovecraft kept these pages for himself solely because he liked the drinking song he had written; perhaps he even then conceived some future use for it.

The relevant part of the letter begins: "As for 'Gaudeamus', the best I can say is, that its rather too Epicurean subject is as ancient as literature itself, and its treatment mediocre. I believe, without any egotism, that I could do better myself—witness the following: . . ." There follows the drinking song, entitled "Gaudeamus." The reference in the letter is evidently to a poem entitled "Gaudeamus" written by a Miss Renning or Ronning (the handwriting is difficult to read), presumably in the amateur press. I cannot date this letter from any internal references, but the handwriting is very youthful; it could date to as early as 1914.

Will Murray makes an interesting case that the song may have been inspired by a similar song contained in Thomas Morton's *New English Canaan or New Canaan* (1637);[20] but this is only one of many such songs Lovecraft may have been familiar with, and his letter suggests that he was attempting to imitate a Georgian (not a Jacobean) drinking song. Accordingly, a perhaps more likelier source (if one is to be sought) may be a song included in Sheridan's *School for Scandal* (1777), which we know Lovecraft to have read (he owned an 1874 edition of Sheridan's *Works*):

Here's to the maiden of bashful fifteen;
Here's to the widow of fifty;
Here's to the flaunting extravagant quean,
And here's to the housewife that's thrifty.
Chorus. Let the toast pass,—
Drink to the lass,
I'll warrant she'll prove an excuse for a glass.[21]

William Fulwiler is, however, undoubtedly correct in pointing out some other literary influences on "The Tomb."[22] The use of the name Hyde is a clear tip of the hat to Stevenson's *Strange Case of Dr Jekyll and Mr Hyde,* suggesting that both works involve a double. The theme of psychic possession—used again and again by Lovecraft—is in this instance very likely derived from Poe's "Ligeia," in which a man's dead wife insidiously possesses the spirit of his new wife to such a degree that the latter actually takes on the physical appearance of the former.

In spite of any borrowings, "The Tomb" is an admirable piece of work for a twenty-seven-year-old who had not written a line of fiction in nine years. Lovecraft himself retained a fondness for it, a significant fact in itself given his later repudiations of much his early work. Its brooding atmosphere, its mingling of horror and pathos, the subtlety of its supernatural manifestations, the psychological probing of the narrator, and the hilarious drinking song that does not quite shatter the atmosphere of the story make "The Tomb" a surprising success.

"Dagon" is also a commendable tale, although it is different in almost every way from its predecessor. Here we are also dealing with an individual whose hold on sanity does not appear firm: he is about to kill himself after writing his account because he has no more money for the morphine that prevents him from thinking of what he has experienced. A supercargo on a vessel during the Great War, this unnamed first-person narrator is captured by a German sea-raider but manages to escape five days later in a boat. As he drifts in the sea, encountering no land or other ship, he lapses into despair as to whether he will ever be rescued. One night he falls asleep, and awakes to find himself half-sucked in "a slimy expanse of hellish black mire which extended about me in monotonous undulations as far as I could see"; evidently there had been an upheaval of some subterranean land mass while he slept. In a few days the mud dries, permitting the narrator to walk along its vast expanse. He aims for a hummock far in the distance, and when finally attaining it finds himself looking down into "an immeasurable pit or canyon." Climbing down the side of the canyon, he notices a "vast and singular object" in the distance: it is a gigantic monolith "whose massive bulk had known the workmanship and perhaps the worship of living and thinking creatures."

Stunned by the awareness that such a civilisation existed unknown to human science, the narrator explores the monolith, finding repellent marine bas-reliefs and inscriptions on it. The figures depicted on it are highly anomalous: "Grotesque beyond the imagination of a Poe or a Bulwer, they were damnably human in general outline despite webbed hands and feet, shockingly wide and flabby lips, glassy, bulging eyes, and other features less pleasant to recall." But a still greater shock is coming to the narrator, for now a living creature emerges from the waves: "Vast, Polyphemus-like, and loathsome, it darted like a stupendous monster of nightmares to the monolith, about which it flung its gigantic scaly arms, the while it bowed its hideous head and gave vent to certain measured sounds." The narrator concludes: "I think I went mad then."

Fleeing, he somehow finds himself in a San Francisco hospital, having been rescued by an American ship. But his life is shattered; he cannot forget what he has seen, and morphine is only a temporary palliative. He is concluding his narrative when he suddenly cries out: "God, *that hand!* The window! The window!"

In spite of the rough similarity of the opening—a clearly deranged (or, at the very least, disturbed) individual telling his story after the fact—there is much less psychological analysis of the narrator of "Dagon" than there is of Jervas Dudley of "The Tomb." This is because it is essential to establish the fundamental rationality of the narrator prior to his encounter with the monster, for it not only inspires our confidence in the veracity of his account but also suggests that some genuinely horrific event (not merely a dream or hallucination) has led him to drugs and contemplated suicide. "Dagon" is the first of many tales in which knowledge *in itself* can cause mental disturbance. As the narrator remarks poignantly at the end:

> I cannot think of the deep sea without shuddering at the nameless things that may at this very moment be crawling and floundering on its slimy bed, worshipping their ancient stone idols and carving their own detestable likenesses on submarine obelisks of water-soaked granite. I dream of a day when they may rise above the billows to drag down in their reeking talons the remnants of puny, war-exhausted mankind—of a day when the land shall sink, and the dark ocean floor shall ascend amidst universal pandemonium.

True, there is potential danger from attacks by this alien race, but it is the simple knowledge of the race's existence that has unhinged the narrator. One should not, of course, hastily conclude that Lovecraft was somehow hostile to knowledge itself—a ridiculous assumption for one who so ardently pursued the life of the mind himself. Instead, it is the weakness of our psychological state that is at issue: "All rationalism tends to minimise the value and importance of life, and to decrease the sum total of human happiness. In many cases the truth may cause suicidal or nearly suicidal depression."[23] Lest one think that Lovecraft is placing too much value on the power of truth to affect the emotions, it should be noted that the above remark was made in the context of a discussion on religion, and he went on to maintain that the truth, as he saw it (i.e., the absence of a God governing the cosmos), could well cause irreparable harm to those who could not accept such a fact. Evidence suggests that he is correct on this point.

In "Dagon" the truth that so affects the narrator is the suddenly revealed existence, not merely of a single hideous monstrosity, but of an entire alien civilisation that had once dwelt literally on the underside of the world. As Matthew H. Onderdonk long ago remarked, the true horror of the tale is "the terrible and acknowledged antiquity of the earth and man's tenuous sinecure thereon."[24] Onderdonk is right to see this is the central theme in all Lovecraft's work, and it would achieve deeper and more exhaustive expression in a dozen or more of his later tales.

Some features of the plot are worth examining. Our credulity is strained at the outset by two implausible occurrences: first, the ease with which the narrator escapes from the Germans (he tries to explain it by remarking that at that time "the ocean forces of the Hun had not completely sunk to their later degradation; so that . . . we . . . were treated with all the fairness and consideration due us as naval prisoners"); and secondly, the fact that the oceanic upheaval occurs while the narrator is asleep and fails to awaken him. But these are minor points. One critical issue is the very end of the tale: what, if anything, does the narrator see? Has the monster who made obeisances at the monolith come to pursue him? The idea that such a monster could walk down the streets of San Francisco and somehow know where the narrator is must surely be regarded as utterly preposterous; and yet, some readers evidently believe that the narrator's vision is genuine. But we are surely to understand that the narrator is hallucinating here. Passages from two letters may lend support to this view. In August 1917, a month after writing the story, he wrote: "Both ['The Tomb' and 'Dagon'] are analyses of strange monomania, involving hallucinations of the most hideous sort."[25] The only hallucination in "Dagon" is the concluding vision of the monster outside the window. (The "hallucinations" in "The Tomb" presumably refer to the narrator's seeming participation in events in the eighteenth century while possessed by his ancestor.) In 1930 Lovecraft wrote: "In 'Dagon' I shewed a horror that *may appear,* but that has not yet made any effort to do so."[26] Surely he would not have made this remark if he wished us to understand that the monster actually emerged from his slimy bed.

I am not wholly clear what the connexion with the Philistine fish-god Dagon is meant to be. Lovecraft cites the god by name toward the end of the story, but we are left to draw our own conclusions. Later Dagon appears as a figure in Lovecraft's pseudomythology, but whether he is to be literally identified with the Philistine god is certainly open to doubt.

"Dagon" is remarkable merely for its contrast in tone, theme, and setting from "The Tomb." Lovecraft, the eighteenth-century fossil, has found inspiration in the great cataclysm—World War I—going on across the sea, and it is perhaps no accident that the story was written only a month or two after American forces actually entered the conflict. If the general stylistic influence of Poe is still evident, then we are nevertheless facing a substantially updated Poe, in a story whose *density* of idiom is by no means to be equated with *archaism* of idiom. Indeed, the mention of the Piltdown man—"discovered" as recently as 1912—foreshadows what would become a hallmark of Lovecraft's fiction: its scientific contemporaneousness. We will find that he would on occasion revise a story at the last moment in order to be as up to date on the scientific veracity of his tale as he could be. Ultimately, this sort of realism became a central component in Lovecraft's theory of the weird, and also led to his effecting a union between the supernatural tale and the nascent field of science fiction. "Dagon" itself could be considered proto-science-fiction in that the phenomena of the tale do not so much *defy* as *expand* our conceptions of reality.

On the whole, "Dagon" is a substantial bit of work. It broaches a number of themes that Lovecraft would develop in later tales, and its tense, forward-driving narration glosses over implausibilities and leads to a hypnotic and cataclysmic conclusion. A poignant moment occurs when the narrator flees after seeing the monster: "I believe I sang a great deal, and laughed oddly when I was unable to sing." Rarely has Lovecraft so concisely captured the unnerving effects of a cataclysmic revelation. "Dagon" was also a tale for which Lovecraft long retained a fondness; in this case, too, his approval was justified.

Lovecraft notes that "Dagon" was at least in part inspired by a dream. John Ravenor Bullen, writing in the Transatlantic Circulator about the story, noted: "We are told that [the narrator] crawled into the stranded boat (which lay grounded some distance away). Could he, half-sucked into mire, crawl to his boat?" Lovecraft responded: ". . . the hero-victim *is* half-sucked into the mire, yet he *does* crawl! He pulls himself along in the detestable ooze, tenaciously though it cling to him. I know, for I dreamed that whole hideous crawl, and can yet feel the ooze sucking me down!" ("The Defence Reopens!," 1921). Lovecraft does not make clear how much of the plot of "Dagon" was already in the dream.

As is, however, fitting for a tale set in the contemporary world, there may also be contemporary literary influences on the story. William Fulwiler[27] is probably correct in sensing the general influence of Irvin S. Cobb's "Fishhead"—a tale of a loathsome fishlike human being who haunts an isolated lake, and a tale that Lovecraft praised in a letter to the editor when it appeared in the *Argosy* on January 11, 1913—although that story's influence on a later work by Lovecraft is still more evident. Fulwiler also points to some other works appearing in the *All-Story*—Edgar Rice Burroughs's *At the Earth's Core* and *Pellucidar;* Victor Rousseau's *The Sea Demons*—that involve underground realms or anthropomorphic amphibians; but I am less certain of the direct influence of these tales on Lovecraft's.

"The Tomb" was accepted by W. Paul Cook for the *Vagrant* as early as the middle of June 1917; Lovecraft thought it would appear around December, but it did not.[28] He then thought it might appear in Cook's *Monadnock Monthly*[29] around 1919 or 1920, but it did not appear there either. The story was only published in the *Vagrant* for March 1922. "Dagon" had been accepted by the amateur journal, the *Phoenician* (edited by James Mather Mosely),[30] but did not appear there. It was published, as we have seen, in the *Vagrant* for November 1919.

Around 1923 Lovecraft showed "Dagon" to Clark Ashton Smith, who in turn passed it on to his friend and mentor George Sterling. Sterling, while liking the tale, thought the ending needed pepping up a bit, so recommended that the monolith topple over and kill the monster. This piece of advice, Lovecraft wrote in a letter, "makes me feel that poets should stick to their sonneteering . . ."[31]

Both "The Tomb" and "Dagon" are, as we shall see, the nuclei of other and still better tales by Lovecraft: the former is the ultimate origin of *The Case of Charles Dexter Ward* (1927), and the latter was writ large in "The Call of Cthulhu" (1926) and "The Shadow over Innsmouth" (1931). This is a phenomenon we shall find repeatedly in his fictional work. A case could be made that Lovecraft conceived—or, more precisely, executed—only a relatively small number of different plots or scenarios and spent much of his career reworking and refining them. Even if this is the case, we ought to be grateful that in the end he did refine the plots so that many of them achieved transcendent levels of expression.

A third work of fiction presumably written in 1917 has frequently been overlooked. "A Reminiscence of Dr. Samuel Johnson" appeared in the *United Amateur* for September 1917 under the pseudonym "Humphry Littlewit, Esq."—one of the few instances in which Lovecraft published a story under a pseudonym. Even if, as is likely, it was written not long before publication, it could still conceivably have been written even before "The Tomb" and "Dagon"; the *United Amateur* was, however, often late, appearing a month or two after its cover date. In any event, this work has no doubt been ignored simply because it is so singular; and yet, it ranks as one of Lovecraft's finest comic stories.

"A Reminiscence of Dr. Samuel Johnson" is not, of course, a weird tale, unless one interprets its premise—that the narrator is entering his 228th year, having been born on August 20, 1690—very literally. Lovecraft/Littlewit goes on to provide some familiar and not-so-familiar "reminiscences" of the Great Cham of Letters and of his literary circle—Boswell, Goldsmith, Gibbon, and others—all written in the most flawless re-creation of eighteenth-century English that I have ever read. Most of the information is clearly derived from Boswell's *Life* and from Johnson's own works. Lovecraft owned an impressive array of the latter, including the *Idler* and *Rambler,* the *Lives of the Poets, Rasselas, A Journey to the Western Islands of Scotland,* and a 12th (1802) edition of the *Dictionary.*

The piece is a delight from beginning to end. Clearly Lovecraft was having fun with what had by now become an endless refrain amongst amateurs that he was two centuries out of date. Lovecraft boldly plays upon this notion:

> Tho' many of my readers have at times observ'd and remark'd a Sort of antique Flow in my Stile of Writing, it hath pleased me to pass amongst the Members of this Generation as a young Man, giving out the Fiction that I was born in 1890, in *America.* I am now, however, resolv'd to unburthen myself of a secret which I have hitherto kept thro' Dread of Incredulity; and to impart to the Publick a true Knowledge of my long years, in order to gratifie their taste for authentick Information of an Age with whose famous Personages I was on familiar Terms.

Littlewit is the author of a periodical paper, the *Londoner,* like Johnson's *Rambler, Idler,* and *Adventurer,* and—like Lovecraft—he has a reputation for revising the poetry of others. When Boswell, "a little the worse for Wine," attempts to lampoon Littlewit with a squib, the latter chides Boswell that "he shou'd not try to pasquinade the Source of his Poesy." This leads to one of the most delightful touches in the whole piece, one that only those familiar with the *Life of Johnson* would understand. Johnson shows Littlewit a wretched little poem written by a servant on the marriage of the Duke of Leeds:

When the Duke of *Leeds* shall marry'd be
To a fine young Lady of high Quality
How happy will that Gentlewoman be
In his Grace of *Leeds'* good Company.

This poem actually appears in the *Life of Johnson* as an instance of how Johnson "retained in his memory very slight and trivial, as well as important things."[32] What does not appear is Littlewit's revision of the poem:

When Gallant LEEDS auspiciously shall wed
The virtuous Fair, of antient Lineage bred,
How must the Maid rejoice with conscious Pride
To win so great an Husband to her Side!

This, of course, is Lovecraft's own emendation of the eighteenth-century doggerel. It is competent, but Johnson is right to note: "Sir, you have straightened out the Feet, but you have put neither Wit nor Poetry into the Lines."

"A Reminiscence of Dr. Samuel Johnson" is endlessly refreshing, and only the later stories "Sweet Ermengarde" and "Ibid" can match it for deft comic touches. It certainly dynamites the myth that Lovecraft had no sense of humour or took himself too seriously, and its perfect Georgianism makes one wonder whether he wasn't correct after all in stating that "I am probably the only living person to whom the ancient 18th century idiom is actually a prose and poetic mother-tongue."[33] And it may not be so clearly separable from Lovecraft's other fiction as one might imagine: does it not play, as "The Tomb" does, on Lovecraft's quite sincere longing to drift insensibly back into the eighteenth century? And does it not too embody what Lovecraft, in "Notes on Writing Weird Fiction," held to be the dominant theme in all his weird work—"conflict with time"?

It would be nearly a year before Lovecraft would write another tale—a fact that suggests that fiction-writing was still very far from the forefront of his mind. The result was "Polaris," a very short tale whose mere existence has given rise to some interesting speculation. In this story an unnamed narrator appears to have a dream in which he is initially a disembodied spirit contemplating some seemingly mythical realm, the land of Lomar, whose principal city Olathoë is threatened with attack from the Inutos, "squat, hellish, yellow fiends." In a subsequent "dream" the narrator learns that he has a body, and is one of the Lomarians. He is "feeble and given to strange faintings when subjected to stress and hardships," so is denied a place in the actual army of defenders; but he is given the important task of manning the watch-tower of Thapnen, since "my eyes were the keenest of the city." Unfortunately, at the critical moment Polaris, the Pole Star, winks down at him and casts a spell so that he falls asleep; he strives to wake up, and finds that when he does so he is in a room through whose window he sees "the horrible swaying trees of a dream-swamp" (i.e., his "waking" life). He convinces himself that "I am still dreaming," and vainly tries to wake up, but is unable to do so.

There is much poignancy in this tale, which appears to describe a man who has confused the "real" and the dream worlds; but in fact the story is not a dream-fantasy at all but rather—like "The Tomb"—a case of psychic possession by a distant ancestor. This is the meaning of the poem inserted in the tale, which the narrator fancies the Pole Star speaks to him:

Slumber, watcher, till the spheres
Six and twenty thousand years
Have revolv'd, and I return
To the spot where now I burn.

This appears to be what the ancients called the "great year"—the period it would take for the constellations to resume their positions after an entire circuit of the heavens—although in antiquity the figure was thought to be about 15,000 years. In other words, the man's spirit has gone back twenty-six thousand years and identified with the spirit of his ancestor. This means that Lomar is postulated not as a dream-realm but as a truly existing land in the prehistory of the earth; moreover, it is situated somewhere in the Arctic, since the narrative suggests that modern-day Eskimos are the descendants of the Inutos. (The coined term "Inutos" is clearly meant to allude to *Inuit,* the native term for what Westerners call Eskimos. That term is the plural of *Inuk.*) This point is of significance only because many of Lovecraft's fantasies have been taken as dream-stories, when in fact only "Celephaïs" (1920) and *The Dream-Quest of Unknown Kadath* (1926–27) can be so regarded—and even these with significant qualifications.

What makes "Polaris" remarkable, however, is its apparently uncanny echo of the work of Lord Dunsany, whom Lovecraft would not read for more than a year. Lovecraft himself commented on the resemblance in 1927:

> "Polaris" is rather interesting in that I wrote it in 1918, *before* I had ever read a word of Lord Dunsany's. Some find it hard to believe this, but I can give not only assurance but absolute proof that it is so. It is simply a case of similar types of vi-

> sion facing the unknown, and harbouring similar stores of mythic and historical lore. Hence the parallelism in atmosphere, artificial nomenclature, treatment of the dream theme, etc.[34]

I do not wish entirely to downplay this parallelism—which really is remarkable—but it may be possible to adduce other factors that led to the apparent anomaly. In the first place, purely from the point of view of style, both Dunsany and Lovecraft were clearly influenced by Poe, although Lovecraft the more obviously; but Dunsany admits in his autobiography that he too came under Poe's spell at an early age: "One day at Cheam I was introduced to Poe's Tales, from the school library, and I read them all; and the haunted desolation and weird gloom of the misty mid-region of Weir remained for many years something that seemed to me more eerie than anything earth had . . ."[35] Whereas Lovecraft was influenced principally by Poe's tales of pure horror—"Ligeia," "The Fall of the House of Usher," "The Black Cat"—Dunsany may have found more inspiration in Poe's fantasies and prose-poems ("Silence—a Fable"; "Shadow—a Parable"; "The Masque of the Red Death"), which may have worked in tandem with his reading of the King James Bible to produce that sonorous, bejewelled manner associated with his early work. Lovecraft himself remarks in "Supernatural Horror in Literature" that these latter stories by Poe "employ[ed] that archaic and Orientalised style with jewelled phrase, quasi-Biblical repetition, and recurrent burthen" and that they had left their mark upon such "later writers [as] Oscar Wilde and Lord Dunsany." But clearly Lovecraft also found Poe's prose-poems affecting, and traces of their influence can be found in his own work.

What has gone relatively unnoticed is the fact that the immediate inspiration for "Polaris" is not a literary work by Poe or anyone else but a philosophical discussion in which Lovecraft was engaged with Maurice W. Moe. In a letter to Moe of May 1918 Lovecraft describes at length a dream he had just had, a dream that is manifestly the nucleus for "Polaris":

> Several nights ago I had a strange dream of a strange city—a city of many palaces and gilded domes, lying in a hollow betwixt ranges of grey, horrible hills. . . . I was, as I said, aware of this city visually. I was in it and around it. But certainly I had no corporeal existence. . . . I recall a lively curiosity at the scene, and a tormenting struggle to recall its identity; for I felt that I had once known it well, and that if I could remember, I should be carried back to a very remote period—many thousand years, when something vaguely horrible had happened. Once I was almost on the verge of realisation, and was frantic with fear at the prospect, though I did not know what it was that I should recall. But here I awaked . . . I have related this in detail because it impressed me very vividly.[36]

It is likely that the actual story was written shortly afterwards. Many features of the story match the account of the dream: the unbodied state of the narrator ("At first content to view the scene as an all-observant uncorporeal presence . . ."), the connexion with the distant past, the fear of some nameless realisation ("Vainly did I struggle with my drowsiness, seeking to connect these strange words with some lore of the skies which I had learnt from the Pnakotic manuscripts").

Much of the letter to Moe is a polemic on religion. What Lovecraft is keen on establishing is the "distinction between dream life and real life, between appearances and actualities." Moe was maintaining that belief in religion is useful for social and moral order regardless of the question of its truth or falsity. Lovecraft, after relating his dream, replies: ". . . according to your pragmatism that dream was as real as my presence at this table, pen in hand! If the truth or falsity of our beliefs and impressions be immaterial, then I am, or was, actually and indisputably an unbodied spirit hovering over a very singular, very silent, and very ancient city somewhere between grey, dead hills." This *reductio ad absurdum* is reflected a little impishly in the story:

> . . . I now desired to define my relation to [the scene], and to speak my mind amongst the grave men who conversed each day in the public squares. I said to myself, "This is no dream, for by what means can I prove the greater reality of that other life in the house of stone and brick south of the sinister swamp and the cemetery and the low hillock, where the Pole Star peers into my north window each night?"

The fact that the narrator at the end seems permanently confused between the real and the waking world (actually his present life and his past incarnation) may be a final tweaking of Moe's nose on the need to maintain such distinctions in real life.

"Polaris" is a quiet little triumph of prose-poetry, its incantatory rhythm and delicate pathos sustaining it in spite of its brevity. Critics have carped on a possible plot defect—why would the narrator, given to spells of fainting, be appointed the sole sentry in the watch-tower in spite of his keen eyes?—but only hard-headed literalists would see this as a significant flaw. The tale was first published in the one and only issue of Alfred Galpin's amateur journal, the *Philosopher* (December 1920).

The one other work of fiction that can definitively—or perhaps not so definitively—be dated to 1918 is one that we do not have. In a letter to Rheinhart Kleiner of June 27, 1918, Lovecraft speaks of his manuscript magazine, *Hesperia:*

> My *Hesperia* will be critical & educational in object, though I am "sugar-coating" the first number by "printing" a conclusion of the serial *The Mystery of Murdon Grange*. . . . It is outwardly done on the patchwork plan as before—each chapter bears one of my different *aliases*—Ward Phillips—Ames Dorrance Rowley—L. Theobald, &c. It was rather a good diversion to write it. Really, I think I could have been a passable dime novelist if I had been trained in that noble calling![37]

A mention of what appears to be a second issue of *Hesperia* occurs in a letter to Long in 1921: "I will send . . . two papers containing collaborated work which you have not seen before. *Hesperia* is a manuscript magazine which I circulate in Great Britain."[38] This second remark in some ways clarifies, and in other ways confuses, the first. All we know is that *Hesperia* was, in the parlance of amateur journalism, a "manuscript magazine"—a magazine typed on the typewriter[39] and sent on a definite round of circulation—distributed among amateur journalists in the United Kingdom. Arthur Harris, the Welshman who printed Lovecraft's *The Crime of Crimes,* was clearly on the circulation list, for an issue of *Interesting Items* contains the only known mention of *Hesperia* by someone other than Lovecraft: "MS. magazines have appeared again. . . . The second received was 'Hesperia' edited by H. P. Lovecraft of America, a noteworthy production, well-typewritten. 'The Green Meadow' is a fascinating story and the poems and editorial make up an excellent issue."[40] This at least tells us that "The Green Meadow" (a collaborative tale written by Lovecraft and Winifred Virginia Jackson) was among the contents of what was probably a second issue, distributed in 1921. Of the first issue, distributed in 1918, Lovecraft remarks to Harris: "Its leading feature will be an able reply by Mr [Ernest Lionel] McKeag to the sociological article by Mr. Temple."[41] This shows that *Hesperia* included material by writers other than Lovecraft.

Matters have been confused still further by the recent discovery of one segment of "The Mystery of Murdon Grange"—but it is not by Lovecraft. The Christmas 1917 issue of *Spindrift,* edited by Ernest Lionel McKeag of Newcastle-upon-Tyne, England, contains a segment of what appears to be a round-robin story entitled "The Mystery of Murdon Grange," signed "B[enjamin] Winskill," a British amateur of the period. Moreover, Lovecraft himself, in the unsigned "Department of Public Criticism" columns of January, March, and May 1918, discusses the work, noting that the first instalment (in an unspecified issue) was written by Joseph Parks, the second (published in the December 1917 issue) by Beryl Mappin, the third by Winskill (the one in the Christmas 1917 issue), and the fourth (in the January 1918) issue by McKeag. All this leads one to think that Lovecraft did in fact write only the "conclusion" to the story, probably published in the summer or fall of 1918. But if this conclusion appeared in *Spindrift,* why does Lovecraft say it will appear in *Hesperia,* along with other segments written under his own pseudonym? Is it possible that he did not like the way the story was evolving under its actual authors, and that he tried to do better? The matter still remains a considerable mystery.

Another item that may date to 1918 is a genuine collaboration, "The Green Meadow." This story, written with Winifred Virginia Jackson, was not published until it appeared in the long-delayed final issue (Spring 1927) of the *Vagrant;* but Lovecraft, in speaking of this story and another collaboration with Jackson, "The

Crawling Chaos," says in a letter that the dream by Jackson that inspired the latter tale "occurred in the early part of 1919" and that the "Green Meadow" dream was "of earlier date,"[42] so that the dream itself may date to 1918, even if the actual writing of the story took place a little later. Indeed, Lovecraft's confession that he did not complete the story until a few months after his mother "broke down"[43] (i.e., her hospitalisation in March 1919) suggests that the full narrative was not finished until May or June 1919. Lovecraft goes on to note that Jackson's dream "was exceptionally singular in that I had one exactly like it myself—save that mine did not extend so far. It was only when I had related my dream that Miss J. related the similar and more fully developed one. The opening paragraph of 'The Green Meadow' was written for my own dream, but after hearing the other, I incorporated it into the tale which I developed therefrom."[44] Elsewhere Lovecraft says that Jackson supplied "a *map*" of the scene of "The Green Meadow," and that he added the "quasi-realistic . . . introduction from my own imagination."[45]

"The Green Meadow" is, quite frankly, a pretty sorry excuse for a story, its meandering vagueness robbing it of any cumulative power. The story was published as "Translated by Elizabeth Neville Berkeley and Lewis Theobald, Jun.," the respective pseudonyms of the collaborators. The ponderous introduction added by Lovecraft states that the document presented in the body of the text was found in a notebook embedded in a meteorite that landed in the sea near the coast of Maine. This notebook was made of some unearthly substance and the text was *"Greek of the purest classical quality."* The idea, evidently (as Lovecraft explains in a letter), is that this is the "narrative of an ancient Greek philosopher who had escaped from the earth and landed on some other planet",[46] although there are simply not enough clues in the text to arrive at such a conclusion.

The narrative itself tells of a person who finds himself (or, conceivably, herself) on a peninsula near a rushing stream, not knowing who he is and how he got there. The peninsula breaks off its land mass and floats down the river, which is gradually wearing away the soil of the newly created island. The narrator sees in the distance a green meadow, "which affected me oddly," whatever that means. His island is approaching the green meadow, and gradually he hears a weird singing on it; but as he approaches close enough to see "the *source* of the chanting," he suddenly experiences a cataclysmic revelation: "therein was revealed the hideous solution of all which had puzzled me." But after a few coy hints the text becomes illegible, since it was conveniently announced at the beginning that during the examination of the notebook "several pages, mostly at the conclusion of the narrative, were blurred to the point of utter effacement before being read . . ."

I am not at all clear what Lovecraft and Jackson were intending with this story. It seems as if they were merely trying to capture the impressions engendered by their curiously similar dreams, but they could not be bothered to make an actual *story* out of them, so that all we have here is a nebulous sketch or a study in mood. The prose (all Lovecraft's, surely, since he announces that "in prose technique she fails, hence can utilise *story* ideas only in collaboration with some technician"[47]) is actually rather good—smooth, hypnotic, and just on this side of being purple—but the story goes nowhere, and fails to be clear at exactly the moments it needs to be. To choose only one example, the narrator at one point looks behind him and sees "weird and terrible things": "in the sky dark vaporous forms hovered fantastically . . ." This won't do; no reader can visualise what those forms could be from such a description.

Lovecraft did learn better in early 1919, when he wrote "Beyond the Wall of Sleep." This is the story of Joe Slater, a denizen of the Catskill Mountains who in the year 1900 has been interred in a mental institution because of the horrible murder of another man. Slater seems clearly mad, filled with strange cosmic visions which his "debased patois" is unable to articulate coherently. The narrator, an interne at the asylum, takes a special interest in Slater because he feels that there is something "beyond my comprehension" in Slater's wild dreams and fancies. He contrives a "cosmic 'radio'" by which he hopes to be able to establish mental communication with Slater. After many fruitless attempts the sought-for communication finally occurs, prefaced by weird music and visions of spectacular beauty: Slater's body has in fact been occupied all his life by an extraterrestrial entity which for some reason has a burning desire for revenge against the star Algol (the Daemon-Star). With the impending death of Slater, the entity will now be free to exact the vengeance it has always desired. Sure enough, on February 22, 1901, come reports of a celebrated nova near Algol.

There are some powerful conceptions in this story, but on the whole it is marred by stilted prose, confusion in critical points of plot and conception, and a vicious class-consciousness. The first puzzle we have to examine is why Lovecraft chose the setting he did. He at this time had no first-hand knowledge of the Catskill Mountains; indeed, he never would do so, although in later years he would explore the colonial areas of New Paltz and Hurley considerably south of the Catskills. He probably first heard about the area from the aged amateur poet Jonathan E. Hoag (1831–1927), who had come to Lovecraft's notice around 1916 and for whom, beginning in 1918, Lovecraft wrote annual birthday tributes. Hoag lived in Troy, New York, and Lovecraft's birthday poems appeared simultaneously in various amateur papers and in Hoag's hometown newspaper, the *Troy Times.* But Lovecraft himself supplies the source of the story when he notes that it was "written spontaneously after reading an account of some Catskill Mountain degenerates in a *N.Y. Tribune* article on the New York State Constabulary."[48] The article in question is "How Our State Police Have Spurred Their Way to Fame" by F. F. Van de Water, published in the *New York Tribune* for April 27, 1919. This extensive feature article actually mentions a backwoods family named Slater or Slahter

(Lovecraft reflects the variant spelling by noting: "His name, as given on the records, was Joe Slater, or Slaader").

But the real reason, perhaps, that Lovecraft chose this area is that it allowed him to express a snobbishness based simultaneously upon class, region, and intellect. Slater's wild imaginings are regarded as so anomalous to this backwoodsman that they require a supernatural explanation. Lovecraft paints a harsh picture of the locale and its inhabitants:

> [Slater's] appearance was one of the typical denizen of the Catskill Mountain region; one of those strange, repellent scions of a primitive colonial peasant stock whose isolation for nearly three centuries in the hilly fastnesses of a little-travelled countryside has caused them to sink to a kind of barbaric degeneracy, rather than advance with their more fortunately placed brethren of the thickly settled districts. Among these odd folk, who correspond exactly to the decadent element of "white trash" in the South, law and morals are non-existent; and their general mental status is probably below that of any other section of the native American people.

For all Lovecraft's pretensions to a quasi-rural upbringing, the above is the scorn of a city man for crude and ignorant countryfolk. Slater is, for Lovecraft, scarcely human: when he dies he displays "repulsively rotten fangs" like some wild animal.

Then there is the problem of the extraterrestrial entity occupying Slater. Lovecraft never provides any rationale for *why* this entity finds itself trapped in Slater's body to begin with. The message delivered to the narrator by this entity merely states that "He has been my torment and diurnal prison for forty-two of your terrestrial years" and that it has been prevented from exacting the revenge it seeks "by bodily encumbrances." But why this should be so is never explained, and Lovecraft does not seem to feel that it requires explanation.

Lovecraft concludes the story with a sober citation from Garrett P. Serviss: "On February 22, 1901, a marvellous new star was discovered by Dr. Anderson, of Edinburgh, *not very far from Algol.* No star had been visible at that point before. Within twenty-four hours the stranger had become so bright that it outshone Capella. In a week or two it had visibly faded, and in the course of a few months it was hardly discernible with the naked eye." This is taken verbatim from Serviss's *Astronomy with the Naked Eye,*[49] which Lovecraft owned in his library; and it of course accounts for why the tale is set in 1900–01. This nova really was a remarkable event in modern astronomy, as the most significant previous novas had been sighted as far back as 1054 and 1572.[50] The discovery just predates Lovecraft's boyhood interest in astronomy, but no doubt it was still being much discussed in the first decade of the twentieth century. But commentators have pointed out that, since Algol is many light-years away from the earth, the light from the nova originated well before 1901.

The tale does have a few virtues, even if they merely anticipate some features of Lovecraft's later tales. Still more than "Dagon," this is Lovecraft's first authentically "cosmic" story, using the entire universe as a backdrop for what appears to be merely a tale of a sordid crime. The "brother of light" who communicates with the narrator states at the end: "'We shall meet again—perhaps in the shining mists of Orion's Sword, perhaps on a bleak plateau in prehistoric Asia. Perhaps in unremembered dreams tonight; perhaps in some other form an aeon hence, when the solar system shall have been swept away.'" That concluding future perfect, already rare in English prose, adds a archaic stateliness strangely in keeping with the cosmicism of the conception.

The dream motif connects the tale to both "The Tomb" and "Polaris"; for what we have here again are not dreams as such but visions of some other realm of entity. Hence the narrator's rumination at the outset: "I have frequently wondered if the majority of mankind ever pause to reflect upon the occasionally titanic significance of dreams, and of the obscure world to which they belong." While most dreams are "no more than faint and fantastic reflections of our waking experiences," there are some "whose immundane and ethereal character permits of no ordinary interpretation"; perhaps in these cases we are "sojourning in another and uncorporeal life of far different nature from the life we know." And the narrator of "Polaris" would agree with the narrator's conclusion that "Sometimes I believe this less material life is our truer life, and that our vain presence on the terraqueous globe is itself the secondary or merely virtual phenomenon."

"Beyond the Wall of Sleep" is Lovecraft's first quasi-science-fiction tale—"quasi" because the field of science fiction cannot be said to have been in existence at this time, and would not be for another decade or so. But the fact that the extraterrestrial entity in the tale cannot meaningfully be termed supernatural makes this story an important foreshadowing of those later works that abandon the supernatural altogether for what Matthew H. Onderdonk termed the "supernormal."[51]

The question of literary influence is worth some attention. Lovecraft notes[52] that Samuel Loveman introduced him to the work of Ambrose Bierce in 1919, and there is indeed a story in *Can Such Things Be?* (1893) entitled "Beyond the Wall"; but I think this is a coincidental similarity, for Bierce's tale is a conventional ghost story that bears no resemblance at all to Lovecraft's. Instead, I posit the influence of Jack London's *Before Adam* (1906), although I have no evidence that Lovecraft read this work. (Lovecraft did, however, have London's *Star Rover* in his library.) This novel is a fascinating account of hereditary memory, whereby a man from the modern age has dreams of the life of his remote ancestor in primitive times. At the very outset of the novel London's character remarks: "Nor . . . did any of my human kind ever break through the wall of my sleep."[53] Here the expression is used with exactly the same connotation as Lovecraft's. Later London's narrator declares:

> . . . the first law of dreaming . . . [is that] in one's dreams one sees only what he has seen in his waking life, or combinations of the things he has seen in his waking life. But all my dreams violated this law. In my dreams I never saw *anything* of which I had knowledge in my waking life. My dream life and my waking life were lives apart, with not one thing in common save myself.[54]

In effect, Lovecraft is presenting a mirror-image of *Before Adam:* whereas London's narrator is a modern (civilised) man who has visions of a primitive past, Joe Slater is in effect a primitive human being whose visions, as Lovecraft declares, are such as "only a superior or even exceptional brain could conceive."

"Beyond the Wall of Sleep" appeared in the amateur journal *Pine Cones* (edited by John Clinton Pryor) for October 1919. *Pine Cones* was a mimeographed magazine, and the physical appearance of the story—with its text typed out on a typewriter and its title crudely drawn by hand at the top—is not very aesthetically pleasing, but the story was printed surprisingly accurately. Lovecraft—as he would do for many of his early tales—revised it slightly for later appearances.

Lovecraft continued his fictional experimentation with "Memory" (*United Co-operative,* June 1919), a very slight prose-poem that betrays the influence of Poe's own experiments in prose-poetry. Once again there is uncertainty on the exact date of writing, but it was probably written not long before its first appearance. "Memory" features a Daemon of the Valley who holds a colloquy with "the Genie that haunts the moonbeams" about the previous inhabitants of the valley of Nis, through which the river Than flows. The Genie has forgotten these creatures, but the Daemon declares:

> "I am Memory, and am wise in lore of the past, but I too am old. These beings were like the waters of the river Than, not to be understood. Their deeds I recall not, for they were but of the moment. Their aspect I recall dimly, for it was like to that of the little apes in the trees. Their name I recall clearly, for it rhymed with that of the river. These beings of yesterday were called Man."

All this is a trifle obvious, and Lovecraft would later learn to express his cosmicism and his belief in the insignificance of human beings more indirectly. Poe's influence dominates this very short piece: there is a Demon in Poe's "Silence—a Fable"; "the valley Nis" is mentioned in Poe's "The Valley of Unrest" (whose original title was "The Valley Nis,"[55] although Lovecraft may not have been aware of the fact); and "The Conversation of Eiros and Charmion," which features a dialogue like that of Lovecraft's tale, speaks of the destruction of all earth life by means of a fire caused by a comet passing near the earth. Nevertheless, as Lance Arney points out, this is Lovecraft's first tale involving, not merely the *insignificance* of mankind, but its *extinction;*[56] and the fact that mankind has left so few traces of itself upon its extinction is as potent an expression of its insignificance as we are likely to find even in Lovecraft's later tales.

A tale that was never published in Lovecraft's lifetime is "The Transition of Juan Romero," dated on the manuscript September 16, 1919. It is the curious story of an incident occurring in 1894 at the Norton Mine (somewhere in the Southwest, one imagines, although Lovecraft is not specific as to the actual location). The narrator is an Englishman who because of nameless "calamities" has migrated from his native land (after spending many years in India) to work as a common labourer in America. At the Norton Mine he becomes friendly with a Mexican peon named Juan Romero, who exhibits a strange fascination for the Hindu ring he owns. One day it is decided to use dynamite to blast a cavity for further mining; but the result is the opening up of an immeasurable cavern that cannot be sounded. That night a storm gathers, but beyond the roar of the wind and rain there is another sound, which the frightened Romero can only deem *"el ritmo de la tierra*—THAT THROB DOWN IN THE GROUND!" The narrator also hears it—a huge rhythmical pounding in the newly opened abyss. Possessed by some fatality, they both descend down ladders into the cavern; Romero then dashes off ahead of the narrator, only to plunge into a further abyss, screaming hideously. The narrator cautiously peers over the edge, sees something—*"but God! I dare not tell you what I saw!"*—and flees back to the camp. That morning he and Romero are both found in their bunks, Romero dead. Other miners swear that neither of them left their cabin that night. The narrator later discovers that his Hindu ring is missing.

There are the elements of an interesting tale here, but the execution is confused and unsatisfying. Lovecraft would later claim that his later stories were marred by overexplanation; but, like "The Green Meadow" and a few later tales, "The Transition of Juan Romero" suffers from excessive vagueness. The narrator's coy refusal to tell what he saw in the abyss makes one think that Lovecraft himself is unsure of what the revelation could have been. In a late letter he advises Duane W. Rimel on a critical point in story-conception: "A sort of general clarification *in your own mind* (not necessarily to be revealed in toto to the reader) of what is supposed to happen, & why each thing happens as it does, would produce a certain added convincingness worth securing."[57] In "The Transition of Juan Romero" Lovecraft has apparently failed to follow this recommendation.

There is some suggestion that Romero is not in fact Mexican but is descended from the Aztecs, a suggestion enhanced by his crying out of the name *"Huitzilopotchli"* as he descends into the abyss. The narrator remarks of this word: "Later I definitely placed that word in the works of a great historian—and shuddered when the association came to me." Lovecraft explicitly footnotes Prescott's *Conquest of Mexico,* which contains the following passage on the Aztec god:

> At the head of all stood the terrible Huitzilopotchli, the Mexican Mars; although it is doing injustice to the heroic war-god of antiquity to identify him with this sanguinary monster. This was the patron deity of the nation. His fantastic im-

> age was loaded with costly ornaments. His temples were the most stately and august of the public edifices; and his altars reeked with the blood of human hecatombs in every city of the empire. Disastrous, indeed, must have been the influence of such a superstition on the character of the people.[58]

But again, the exact connexion is vague: is Lovecraft suggesting that the Aztec civilisation extended up into the American Southwest? And what is the relation of the Hindu ring? "Somehow I doubt if it was stolen by mortal hands," the narrator reflects, but it is difficult to know what to make of this.

The portrayal of Romero bears some resemblance to that of Joe Slater, but Lovecraft is thankfully less crudely class-conscious here. Although Romero is referred to as "one of a large herd of unkempt Mexicans" working at the mine, the narrator later remarks: "It was not the Castilian conquistador or the American pioneer, but the ancient and noble Aztec, whom imagination called to view when the silent peon would rise in the early morning and gaze in fascination at the sun as it crept above the eastern hills, meanwhile stretching out his arms to the orb as if in the performance of some rite whose nature he did not himself comprehend." This sounds like Joe Slater, possessed by some intelligence vastly greater than himself, but later the narrator cites Romero's "untutored but active mind," and at the end we feel a sympathy for Romero that Lovecraft emphatically denies us in Slater.

Lovecraft recognised that "The Transition of Juan Romero" was a false start, and he refused to allow it to be published, even in the amateur press. He disavowed it relatively early in life, and it fails to appear on most lists of his stories; he does not even seem to have shown it to anyone until 1932, when R. H. Barlow badgered him into sending him the manuscript so that he could prepare a typescript of it. The story was finally published in *Marginalia* (1944).

Steven J. Mariconda has pointed out[59] that the first five surviving weird tales of Lovecraft's "mature" period—"The Tomb," "Dagon," "Polaris," "The Green Meadow," and "Beyond the Wall of Sleep"—are all experiments in variety of tone, mood, and setting. If we include "Memory" and "The Transition of Juan Romero"—as different from these stories as they are from each other—then we have still greater diversity. When the two comic stories, "A Reminiscence of Dr. Samuel Johnson" and "Old Bugs," are thrown in, then the first nine tales of Lovecraft's maturity, written over a two-year period, are about as varied as they possibly can be. It is clear that he was testing his own literary powers to see what type of work he wanted to write and what methods would best convey what he wished to convey. The weird tales break down fairly evenly between supernatural realism ("The Tomb," "Dagon," "The Transition of Juan Romero") and fantasy ("Polaris," "The Green Meadow," "Memory"), with "Beyond the Wall of Sleep" initiating Lovecraft's experiments in proto-science-fiction. The thematic links between many of these stories—dream as providing access to other realms of entity; the overwhelming influence of the past upon the present; the insignificance of humanity in the universe and its eventual obliteration from this planet—adumbrate many of the central concerns of Lovecraft's later fiction. The dominant influence, at least from the point of view of style, is Poe, although only two tales—"The Tomb" and "Memory"—can be said to echo Poe both stylistically and conceptually. Lovecraft was already emerging slowly as a fiction-writer of originality and power.

But in the fall of 1919 Lovecraft fell under the influence of the Irish fantaisiste Lord Dunsany, and for at least two years would do little but write imitations of his new mentor. In many ways the Dunsany influence was positive, in that it suggested to Lovecraft new ways of conveying his cosmicism and in demonstrating new modes of expression, particularly delicate prose-poetry; but in some ways it was a retarding influence, temporarily derailing that quest for topographical and historical realism which would ultimately be the hallmark of his work. It would take Lovecraft years to assimilate the Dunsany influence, but when at last he did so—having in the meantime encountered such other writers as Arthur Machen and Algernon Blackwood—he was ready to initiate the most significant and characteristic phase of his writing.

In this period Lovecraft also learned to express weird conceptions in verse. Whereas up to 1917 his poetry had been wholly Georgian in character, Lovecraft now began to see that poetry could do more than merely recapture the atmosphere of the eighteenth century. The dominant influence on his early weird verse is, of course, Poe; for although Lovecraft owned and read the "Graveyard Poets" of the later eighteenth century—James Hervey's *Meditations and Contemplations* (1746–47), Edward Young's *Night-Thoughts* (1742–45), among others—they do not appear to have influenced him appreciably.

One spectacular anticipation of his weird verse is a 302-line poem written sometime in 1916,[60] "The Poe-et's Nightmare." As it stands, this work is something of a hodgepodge: it is introduced by 72 lines in heroic couplets; the body of the poem, in pentameter blank verse, bears the added title "Aletheia Phrikodes" ("The Frightful Truth"), with a delightful coined phrase in Latin (*Omnia risus et omnis pulvis et omnia nihil* = "All is laughter, all is dust, all is nothing"); this is then followed by a 38-line conclusion in heroic couplets. The general thrust of the poem is, in fact, a sort of tongue-in-cheek morality, suggested both by the subtitle of the poem itself ("A Fable") and its epigraph from Terence, *Luxus tumultus semper causa est* ("Disturbance is always caused by excess"). We are introduced to Lucullus Languish, who is at once a "student of the skies" and a "connoisseur of rarebits and mince pies"; in other words, he longs to write cosmic poetry, but is repeatedly distracted by his ravenous appetite. His name, as R. Boerem has pointed out,[61] is highly appropriate: Lucullus is a clear echo of the Roman general L. Licinius Lucullus, who gained notoriety as a gourmand; while Languish is a tip of the hat to Lydia Languish, the heroine in Sheridan's *The Rivals,* who, as Boerem notes, is like Lucullus Languish in being "a romantic of simple-minded display."

Although he is a "bard by choice," Lucullus is merely a "grocer's clerk" by actual trade. Then one day he stumbles upon a set of Poe; charmed by the "cheerful horrors there display'd," he turns his attention to the writing of horrific verse. In this, however, he has little success until one day he overindulges at a meal and experiences the wild nightmare related in the blank verse section. This comic introduction really is quite clever, directing genial but sharp barbs at the hungry poetaster. Here is the description of the meal that brought on the Poe-et's nightmare:

> Tho' it were too prosaic to relate
> Th' exact particulars of what he ate
> (Such long-drawn lists the hasty reader skips,
> Like Homer's well-known catalogue of ships),
> This much we swear: that as adjournment near'd,
> A monstrous lot of cake had disappear'd!

One of the best strokes is an exquisite parody of Shakespeare: ". . . or cast a warning spell / On those who dine not wisely, but too well."

With the 192 lines in blank verse the mood changes abruptly—perhaps a little too abruptly. Here Lucullus narrates in the first person how his soul drifts into space and encounters a cosmic spirit who promises to unveil to him the secrets of the universe. This scenario allows Lovecraft to express his cosmicism in its purest form:

> Alone in space, I view'd a feeble fleck
> Of silvern light, marking the narrow ken
> Which mortals call the boundless universe.
> On ev'ry side, each as a tiny star,
> Shone more creations, vaster than our own,
> And teeming with unnumber'd forms of life;
> Tho' we as life would recognise it not,
> Being bound to earthy thoughts of human mould.

And yet, the cosmic spirit tells Lucullus that "all the universes in my view / Form'd but an atom in infinity . . ." The fundamental message of this section—that the universe is boundless both in time and in space; that there may be other forms of intelligent life in the universe aside from ourselves, life that we would scarcely recognise as such—is exactly that found in his early letters. This vision leads Lucullus to the contemplation of our own planet:

> Then turn'd my musings to that speck of dust
> Whereon my form corporeal took its rise;

That speck, born but a second, which must die
In one brief second more; that fragile earth;
That crude experiment; that cosmic sport
Which holds our proud, aspiring race of mites
And mortal vermin; those presuming mites
Whom ignorance with empty pomp adorns,
And misinstructs in specious dignity . . .

Lucullus (and Lovecraft) gain contempt for humanity because of its "presumption" of cosmic importance in the universe. A letter of August 1916 exactly echoes these ideas:

> How arrogant of us, creatures of the moment, whose very species is but an experiment of the *Deus Naturae,* to arrogate to ourselves an immortal future and considerable status! . . . How do we know that that form of atomic and molecular motion called "life" is the highest of all forms? Perhaps the dominant creature—the most rational and God-like of all beings—is an invisible gas![62]

This section of "The Poe-et's Nightmare" embodies Lovecraft's early cosmic views as compactly as any work in his oeuvre. Lucullus, in any event, is horrified at this spectacle—truly it is to him a "frightful truth"—but the cosmic spirit now offers to unveil to him a still greater secret:

Yet changing now his mien, he bade me scan
The wid'ning rift that clave the walls of space;
He bade me search it for the ultimate;
He bade me find the Truth I sought so long;
He bade me brave th' unutterable Thing,
The final Truth of moving entity.

But the dream-Lucullus withdraws in fear, his spirit "shrieking in silence thro' the gibbering deeps."

At this point Lucullus wakes up, and the third-person heroic couplets resume. The narrator now ponderously relates the lesson Lucullus has learned: "He vows to all the Pantheon, high and low, / No more to feed on cake, or pie, or Poe." He is now glad to be a humble grocer's clerk; and the narrator warns other bad poets (who "bay the moon in numbers strange and new") to think before they write: "Reflect, ere ye the draught Pierian take, / What worthy clerks or plumbers ye might make . . ."

All this is clever too, but to my mind it has the effect of dynamiting the cosmicism of the previous section, rendering it retroactively parodic. Note especially these lines, where Lucullus "thanks his stars—or cosmoses—or such / That he survives the noxious nightmare's clutch." I think Lovecraft was trying to do too much here: he has produced both a piece of terrifying cosmicism and a satire against poetasters; but the two do not work well together. Lovecraft ultimately came to realise this. Toward the end of his life, when R. H. Barlow wished to include "The Poe-et's Nightmare" in a collection of Lovecraft's verse, he advised Barlow to omit the comic framework.[63]

It should be pointed out that "The Poe-et's Nightmare" is not influenced by Poe. For all his fondness for Poe, Lovecraft came to realise that his mentor fundamentally lacked the cosmic sense; relatively little of his poetry is, in any case, horrific or fantastic, and there is not even the remotest parallel in Poe for this extended use of blank verse. If there is any influence at all on that central section, it is Lucretius, as certain lines in Lovecraft's poem—". . . whirling ether bore in eddying streams / The hot, unfinish'd stuff of nascent worlds"—make clear. Although Lucretius, in his fervent exposition of the atomic theory and the making of the worlds (especially in Books I and II of the *De Rerum Natura*), finds only awe and not horror in the contemplation of infinite space, both poets see in the vastness of the cosmos a refutation of human self-importance. As we examine Lovecraft's philosophy, it will become evident that he gained both the fundamentals of materialism and a sense of the cosmic in part from the line of ancient atomists beginning with Leucippus and Democritus and continuing through Epicurus and Lucretius.

Another, less striking anticipation of Lovecraft's later attempts in weird verse is the recently discovered "The Unknown." Actually, it is not the poem but its attribution that has only now come to light; for it appeared in the *Conservative* for October 1916, but under the byline of Elizabeth Berkeley (pseudonym of Winifred Virginia Jackson). In a later letter Lovecraft explains that he allowed this poem (as well as "The Peace Advocate" in the *Tryout* for May 1917) to appear under Jackson's pseudonym "in an effort to mystify the [amateur] public by having widely dissimilar work from the same nominal hand";[64] and in a still later letter he clearly acknowledges the work as "another of my old attempts at weird verse."[65] This very short three-stanza poem, in an iambic metre Lovecraft had never used before and would never use again, is a purely imagistic vignette that speaks of a "seething sky," a "mottled moon," and "Wild clouds a-reel"; it concludes:

> Thro' rift is shot
>   The moon's wan grace—
> But *God! That blot*
>   *Upon its face!*

As an experiment in mood and metre it is interesting, but is too insubstantial to be of much account.

Later poems seek, like "The Poe-et's Nightmare," to unite a moral and a horrific message. There is in several poems a sense of the insignificance, even the vileness, of humanity even in the absence of a cosmic framework. Many poems unfortunately tend, however, toward stock images or contrived shudders. "The Rutted Road" (*Tryout,* January 1917) speaks of a man who, like Lucullus Languish, fears some revelation at the end of his traversing of a rutted road: "What lies ahead, my weary soul to greet? / *Why is it that I do not wish to know?*" But the preceding stanzas have been so contentless that one has not even the remotest sense of what such a revelation could be. Similarly, in "Astrophobos" (*United Amateur,* January 1918) the narrator hopes to find "Worlds of happiness unknown" in the heavens, but instead finds only horror and woe, for no reason anyone can tell. Even Lovecraft's most famous early weird poem, "Nemesis" (written in the "sinister small hours of the black morning after Hallowe'en" of 1917;[66] first published *Vagrant,* June 1918), is open to the charge of vagueness and empty horrific imagery. Lovecraft supplies the purported scenario of the poem: "It presents the conception, tenable to the orthodox mind, that nightmares are the punishments meted out to the soul for sins committed in previous incarnations—perhaps millions of years ago!"[67] Tenable or not, this framework seems only to provide Lovecraft an excuse for poetic cosmicism:

I have whirl'd with the earth at the dawning,
    When the sky was a vaporous flame,
I have heard the dark universe yawning,
    Where the black planets roll without aim;
Where they roll in their horror unheeded, without knowledge or lustre or name.

This is quite effective, and Lovecraft is justified in using some of these lines as the epigraph to his late tale "The Haunter of the Dark" (1935); but what, ultimately, is their import? Like many of Lovecraft's poems, "Nemesis" is open to Winfield Townley Scott's brutal charge: "To scare is a slim purpose in poetry."[68]

Fortunately, some poems go beyond this shudder-coining. "The Eidolon" (*Tryout,* October 1918) may be superficially derived in part from Poe (Lovecraft speaks of a quest to find "the Eidolon call'd *Life,*" while Poe in "Dream-Land" makes note of "an Eidolon, named Night"[69]), but beyond this, and the use of the octosyllabic metre, the resemblances to Poe are not strong. Here the narrator, "at a nameless hour of night," fancies he looks upon a beauteous landscape:

Fair beyond words the mountain stood,
Its base encircled by a wood;
Adown its side a brooklet bright
Ran dancing in the spectral light.
Each city that adorn'd the crest
Seem'd anxious to outvie the rest,
For carven columns, domes, and fanes
Gleam'd rich and lovely o'er the plains.

But the daylight shows a grimmer scene:

> The East is hideous with the flare
> Of blood-hued light—a garish glare—
> While ghastly grey the mountain stands,
> The terror of the neighb'ring lands.

Lovecraft is careful to indicate that the horror is more than a spook or a haunted wood:

> Aloft the light of knowledge crawls,
> Staining the crumbling city walls
> Thro' which in troops ungainly squirm
> The foetid lizard and the worm.

Repelled by the sight, the narrator asks to see "the living glory—Man!" But an even more loathsome sight greets his eyes:

> Now on the streets the houses spew
> A loathsome pestilence, a crew
> Of things I cannot, dare not name,
> So vile their form, so black their shame.

In its way "The Eidolon" is as nihilistic as "The Poe-et's Nightmare," although lacking its cosmic scope. What is more interesting is the notion—which we have already seen in "Dagon"—that knowledge (here symbolised by the light of day) is in itself a source of horror and tragedy. This same conception is found in another fine poem, "Revelation" (*Tryout,* March 1919). The narrator, "in a vale of light and laughter," decides to scan "the naked skies of Jove"; but the result is that he emerges "ever wiser, ever sadder" from a realisation of his lowly place in the cosmic scheme of things. Seeking to return to earth, he now finds that the blight of revelation has poisoned it also:

> But my downward glance, returning,
>   Shrank in fright from what it spy'd;
> Slopes in hideous torment burning,
>   Terror in the brooklet's ride;
> For the dell, of shade denuded
>   By my desecrating hand,
> 'Neath the bare sky blaz'd and brooded
>   As a lost, accursed land.

Many later stories will harp on this theme: the inability to derive any pleasure from existence once the horrors of the cosmos are known.

Other weird poems of this period are less substantial but pleasant enough to read: a trilogy of poems entitled "A Cycle of Verse" ("Oceanus," "Clouds," and "Mother Earth"; *Tryout,* July 1919); "The House" (*Philosopher,* December 1920; written July 16, 1919[70]) and "The City" (*Vagrant,* October 1919), which adapt the metre of "Nemesis"—itself derived, of course, from Swinburne's "Hertha." "The House" is based upon the same house at 135 Benefit Street that later inspired "The Shunned House" (1924).

One long weird poem that may be worth a little consideration is "Psychopompos: A Tale in Rhyme." This 312-line poem was begun in the fall of 1917 but not completed until May or June of 1918.[71] Unlike the bulk of Lovecraft's weird verse written up to this time, the apparent influence on this poem—the second-longest single poem Lovecraft ever wrote, just shorter than "Old Christmas" and just longer than "The Poe-et's Nightmare"—is not Poe but the ballads of Sir Walter Scott, although I have not found any single work in Scott exactly analogous to "Psychompos." In this poem an aged grandam, Mère Allard, tells the story of Sieur and Dame De Blois, who occupy a shunned castle in the Auvergne region of France. They have developed a bad reputation because of whispered rumours about them: that they do not worship the god of the Christians; that the Dame has an evil eye and a serpentine gait. One Candlemas, the bailiff's son Jean falls ill and dies; it is then recalled that Dame De Blois had passed by the other day and spotted the child ("Nor did they like the smile which seem'd to trace / New lines of evil on her proud, dark face"). That night, when Jean's grieving parents are holding a vigil over their dead son, a huge snake suddenly appears and makes for the corpse; but the bailiff's wife springs to action—"With ready axe the serpent's head she cleaves," and it crawls away with a mortal wound.

Later people notice a change in Sieur De Blois's bearing. He hears the gossip about the incident with the bailiff's wife and the snake, and "low'ring rode away, / Nor was he seen again for many a day." That summer the Dame is found in some shrubbery, her head cleaved with an axe. The body is brought to the castle of Sieur De Blois, where it is received "with anger, more than with surprise." The next Candlemas arrives, and that evening the bailiff and his family are startled to notice that their home is surrounded by a pack of anomalously intelligent wolves. The leader of the wolfpack bursts through the window and attacks the bailiff's wife, but her husband strikes the creature down with the same axe used on the hideous serpent. The wolf falls dead, but the rest of the pack begin to close in around the house as a furious storm rises. But at the sight of the shining cross on the chimney each wolf "Drops, fades, and vanishes in empty air!"

The listener, wearied of the confused story of Mère Allard, thinks that two stories have been intertwined into one—the tale of the De Blois's, and the tale of the wolfpack. But he receives little clarification from the grandam, who concludes:

"For Sieur De Blois . . . / Was lost to sight for evermore."

Few readers will be so dense as the listener of this "tale in rhyme"; they will have quickly realised that the snake killed by the bailiff's wife was Dame De Blois and that the leader of the wolfpack was Sieur De Blois. In effect, they were werewolves or shapeshifters. This work is, in fact, the only instance of Lovecraft's use of this conventional myth (at least, in its orthodox form); and the general mediaeval setting of the poem makes "Psychopompos" a sort of versified Gothic tale. I am not clear what the significance of the title is: psychopomps (from the Greek *psychopompos,* "conveyer of the dead" [i.e., to the underworld]) are used in some later tales, but werewolves have never been regarded as psychopomps. Interestingly, Lovecraft himself seems to have classified the work among his prose tales, as it is found on several lists of his short stories.

I have pointed to the general influence of Scott on this poem; but a more immediate influence can also be adduced. Lovecraft prefaces the body of the poem (written in heroic couplets) with two striking quatrains:

> I am He who howls in the night;
> I am He who moans in the snow;
> I am He who hath never seen light;
> I am He who mounts from below.
>
> My car is the car of Death;
> My wings are the wings of dread;
> My breath is the north wind's breath;
> My prey are the cold and the dead.

This is manifestly an echo of the first stanza of a poem, "Insomnia," by Winifred Virginia Jordan (later Jackson), published by Lovecraft in his *Conservative* for October 1916:

> The Thing, am I, that rides the Night,
> That clips the wings of Sleep;
> The Thing, am I, in sunshine bright
> That goads, with hag-mind, deep;
> The Thing, am I, with forked knife
> That prods the weary brain,
> And snarls when Pleasure strives for life
> Within my haunts of Pain.

It is possible that Lovecraft revised this poem for Jackson, but she was herself an accomplished poet and probably did not require much help from Lovecraft. Another small point can be noted: the name De Blois is derived from a set of tombstones bearing this name in the churchyard of St John's Episcopal Church in Providence, a favourite haunt of Lovecraft's.

Regardless of its literary influences and the intentional obviousness of its plot, "Psychopompos" is a triumph, full of deft and subtle touches. The narrative opens as if in sympathy with the reclusiveness of the De Bloises: it is natural that evil legends would accrue against people who (like Lovecraft) were not conventionally religious and kept to themselves:

> So liv'd the pair, like many another two
> That shun the crowd, and shrink from public view.
> They scorn'd the doubts by ev'ry peasant shewn,
> And ask'd but one thing—to be let alone!

The use of the cross as the ultimate defence against the supernatural wolves—curious for an unbeliever—is merely a bow to weird tradition.

Lovecraft is surprisingly effective in depicting the grief of the parents of little Jean:

> Around the corpse the holy candles burn'd,
> The mourners sigh'd, the parents dumbly yearn'd.
> Then one by one each sought his humble bed,
> And left the lonely mother with her dead.

And sympathy is later extended even to Sieur De Blois as he contemplates the body of his wife, "By some assassin's stroke most foully slain."

"Psychopompos" appeared in Cook's *Vagrant* for October 1919. We have seen that Cook was not at all receptive to Lovecraft's Georgian poetry; but he clearly appreciated both his weird tales and his weird poems, and a good many of the latter were published in the *Vagrant,* including "Psychopompos" and "The Poe-et's Nightmare" (July 1918). I have not found much comment in the amateur papers on his weird verse, but it and the satiric poetry are easily the two most consistently meritorious branches of his poetic work.

Weird fiction and poetry was, as I have suggested, still a relatively minor concern in Lovecraft's life at this period; amateur politics, political events, relations with his mother, and his gradual emergence from the hermitry of his post-high-school years dominated his interests, and it is to these subjects that I shall now turn.

9. Feverish and Incessant Scribbling (1917–1919 [II])

Meanwhile political events were not failing to attract Lovecraft's attention. Even if he could not himself serve in the Great War, he could at least closely follow the course of that conflict—especially America's belated entry into it. Lovecraft predictably wrote a number of poems commemorating the United States' joining of her "mother" England to battle Germany—"Iterum Conjunctae" (*Tryout,* May 1917), "An American to the British Flag" (*Little Budget,* December 1917), "The Link" (*Tryout,* July 1918)—or more generally urging on the British soldiers: "Britannia Victura" (*Inspiration,* April 1917), "Ad Britannos, 1918" (*Tryout,* April 1918). A number of these poems were reprinted in the professional *National Enquirer.* None of them amount to anything.

A few political poems of this period address slightly more interesting issues. "To Greece, 1917" (*Vagrant,* November 1917) is a fiery broadside urging the Greeks to take action against the invading Germans. At the outset of the war Greece was very divided on its course of action, and Lovecraft upbraids King Constantine I for his pledge of neutrality ("Shame on thee, Constantinos! Reign no more, / Thou second Hippias of the Attic shore!"). Naturally, Lovecraft lauds Eleutherios Venizelos, the Greek premier since 1909, who had sided with the Allies and in 1916 had established a separate government, forcing Constantine to flee the country:

> Say not your plains of heroes are bereft,
> Nor cry that Clisthenes no heir hath left;
> False is the tongue that such a slander gives
> To Grecian soil, while VENIZELOS lives!

If nothing else, it contains one memorable line, as it records how the Greeks at Thermopylae "Snatch'd infant Europe from a Persian grave." This poem must have been written before June 1917, when the Greeks actually entered the war on the Allied side.

"On a Battlefield in Picardy" (*National Enquirer,* May 30, 1918) is a poignant Pindaric ode about the devastation of France:

> Here all is dead.
> The charnel plain a spectral legion knows,
> That cannot find repose,
> And blank, grey vistas endless stretch ahead,
> Mud-carpeted,

And stain'd with red,
Where Valour's sons for Freedom bled.
And in the scorching sky
The carrion ravens fly,
Scanning the treeless waste that rots around,
Where trenches yawn, and craters pit the ground.
And in the night the horn'd Astarte gleams,
And sheds her evil beams.

This and several other poems show what a fine (or, at least, respectable) poet Lovecraft could have been had he not been so slavishly addicted to the heroic couplet in his youth. Less successful is "To the Nurses of the Red Cross" (written in 1917[1] but apparently not published in Lovecraft's lifetime), a maudlin poem about the "heav'n-descended train" who "ease the anguish and . . . purge the pain" of soldiers on the battlefield.

Lovecraft's most reprinted poem is "The Volunteer," which first appeared in the *Providence Evening News* for February 1, 1918, and was then reprinted in the *National Enquirer* (February 7, 1918), *Tryout* (April 1918), the *Appleton* [Wis.] *Post* (surely at the instigation of Maurice W. Moe), the *St. Petersburg* [Fla.] *Evening Independent* (perhaps through John Russell?), and *Trench and Camp,* the military paper at San Antonio, Texas. The dates of the latter three appearances have not been ascertained. The poem was a reply to "Only a Volunteer" by Sergeant Hayes P. Miller, 17th Aero-Squadron, U.S.A., which appeared in the *National Enquirer* for January 17, 1918, and also in the *Providence Evening News.* Neither poem is exactly a stellar piece of work: Miller laments bitterly that his treatment as a volunteer is far inferior to that of the drafted men (". . . the honor goes to the drafted man, / And the work to the volunteer!"), forcing Lovecraft to counter that the volunteer is the true patriot and will be so recognised by the people:

We honour the ranks of the conscripts,
For we know they are average men—
The plumber and clerk snatched up from their work
To be thrown in the dragon's den;
They are bearing their fate rather nobly,
Who is perfect enough to sneer?
But the laurels of fame and the patriot's name
Go first to the volunteer!

This is worth comparing to a curious poem entitled "The Conscript," written probably in 1918 but apparently not published at the time. Here we are taken into the mind of an ordinary conscript ("I am a peaceful working man— / I am not wise or strong . . .") who has no idea why he has been "told . . . I must write my name / Upon a scroll of death":

> I hate no man, and yet they say
> That I must fight and kill;
> That I must suffer day by day
> To please a master's will.

These are highly uncharacteristic remarks for Lovecraft to make—if, that is, the poem is not intended somehow parodically or cynically. It is, indeed, a little difficult to know what the drift of the poem is, or what the significance of the final stanza can be:

> Yet hark—some fibre is o'erwrought—
> A giddying wine I quaff—
> Things seem so odd, I can do naught
> But laugh, and laugh, and laugh!

Does this mean that the conscript has suddenly gained a sense of his role in the great war machine? I am not at all clear as to the occasion or purpose of this poem.

By December 1917 Lovecraft noted that "My questionnaire arrived yesterday, and I discussed it with the head physician of the local draft board." At the advice of this individual—who was both a family friend and also a remote relative—Lovecraft, although he himself wished to place himself in Class I, put himself down in Class V, Division G—"totally and permanently unfit."[2] Lovecraft observed poignantly that "It is not flattering to be reminded of my utter uselessness twice within the space of six months," but realised that the doctor was correct in noting that "my lack of physical endurance would make me a hindrance rather than a help in any work requiring schedule and discipline."

In terms of the actual progress of the war, Lovecraft here remarked: "As to the general situation, it seems very discouraging just now. It may take a second war to adjust things properly." This comment—seemingly but, surely, unwittingly prophetic—was made at the lowest point of the war for the Allies: the Germans were making considerable headway and seemed on the brink of winning the war before the new American forces could be mobilised. It is therefore possible that Lovecraft was actually conceiving the possibility of a victory for the Germans, so that the "second war" would be one required to restore national borders to the pre-1914 state. Curiously enough, I cannot find any remark by Lovecraft on the actual end of the war; but this may only be because letters of the 1918–19 period have probably been lost or destroyed and the surviving ones have not on the whole been made available to me.

Lovecraft's ponderous essay, "The League" (*Conservative,* July 1919), on the League of Nations, shows that he was paying considerable attention to the peace conference at Versailles. The essay was published only two months after the covenant of the League was unanimously adopted on April 28, 1919. "The League" is nothing more than a broadside on the inevitability of war and the uselessness of treaties to prevent it. Opening pompously with a grandiose pseudo-philosophical rumination like that used in some of his stories ("Endless is the credulity of the human mind"), Lovecraft goes on to say: "Having just passed through a period of indescribable devastation caused by the rapacity and treachery of an unwisely trusted nation which caught civilisation unarmed and unawares, the world purposes once more to adopt a policy of sweet trustfulness, and to place its faith again in those imposing 'scraps of paper' known as treaties or covenants . . ." Lovecraft's objections to the League focus on three issues: first, he does not see that it can genuinely do much to prevent war from occurring, since any nation that wants something badly enough will fight for it regardless of the consequences; second, the League's goal of universal disarmament is dangerous unless there is some means of verifying that countries are not secretly hoarding arms; and third, if a serious conflict did arise, the League would quickly "be undermined by a score of clandestine inner leagues" based upon prior allegiance of the countries involved.

These objections are a mixture of hard-headed common sense and right-wing paranoia. The principal means by which the League would have "prevented" war by a single determined country would be the imposition of economic sanctions. Lovecraft no doubt gained tremendous satisfaction that the United States in early 1920 refused to ratify American entry into the League, the brainchild of the hated President Wilson; but what Lovecraft did not know is that the withdrawal of what was already the world's leading economic power effectively nullified the threat of economic sanctions, since the United States would always be theoretically capable of ignoring them against a country it supported. The point about disarmament is valid enough, and indeed the League's World Disarmament Conference, which met periodically during the later 1920s, essentially fell apart after being unable to resolve the question of Hitler's demand for rearmament in the early 1930s. The point about "clandestine inner leagues" does not seem borne out by the history of the League. In fact, the League of Nations worked quite well in resolving minor disputes in the 1920s, and the United States began half-officially participating in League business by the end of the decade. Lovecraft's alternate recommendation—that the major powers (United States, Great Britain, France, and Italy) form a "simple and practical alliance" to prevent Germany or some other belligerent from starting another war sounds good on paper, even though he could not predict that in three years the rise of Mussolini would cause Italy to go in a very different direction from the other Allied powers. Lovecraft always liked to think of himself as a tough, unsentimental political realist; and the man who would say in 1923 that "The one sound power in the world is the power of a hairy muscular right arm"[3] was not likely to look kindly on an organisation he considered soft-headed and leftist.

One comment in "The League" is very interesting: "It is to be a very nice and attractive League, we are told; brimful of safeguards against ordinary war, even though somewhat deficient in safeguards against Bolshevism." This signifies Lovecraft's predictable involvement in the "Red Scare" of the postwar period. I cannot find any remark contemporary with the October Revolution, but it was only in the immediate postwar period that the tendencies of Russian socialism became evident. In another essay in the July 1919 *Conservative,* "Bolshevism," Lovecraft worries about the "alarming tendency observable in this age . . . a growing disregard for the established forces of law and order." Some of this disregard is caused by the "noxious example of the almost sub-human Russian rabble," but other factors are closer to home:

> . . . long-haired anarchists are preaching a social upheaval which means nothing more or less than a reversion to savagery or mediaeval barbarism. Even in this traditionally orderly nation the number of Bolsheviki, both open and veiled, is considerable enough to require remedial measures. The repeated and unreasonable strikes of important workers, seemingly with the object of indiscriminate extortion rather than rational wage increase, constitute a menace which should be checked.

All one can say about something like this is that Lovecraft changed his tune considerably—indeed, antipodally—in a decade. It is unlikely that he himself had any personal knowledge of any "Bolsheviki," either open or veiled; and as someone not in the workforce, he could of course have no conception of the appalling working conditions prevailing in many key industries at this period, and he is parroting many right-wing commentators in accepting the fantasy that labour unrest was largely led by foreign socialists. Once again, Lovecraft as an armchair political analyst proves himself to be naive, prejudiced, and fundamentally ignorant of the actual state of affairs in the nation.

The remark about a "reversion to savagery" suggests the basic tenet of Lovecraft's entire political philosophy at this juncture, one that was perhaps maintained throughout his life even if expressed slightly less hyperbolically. Lovecraft's statement in 1929—"All that I care about is *the civilisation*—the state of development and organisation which is capable of gratifying the complex mental-emotional-aesthetic needs of highly evolved and acutely sensitive men"[4]—could serve as the core of his entire political thought. It may be true that his idea of a "civilisation" was a state of society that would make things comfortable for people like him; but most philosophy and politics tend to be self-serving, so that Lovecraft is not unique on this point. His prime concern was to prevent a collapse of civilisation, a concern that became very keen in the period directly following the world war, especially given his low view of humanity.

The fact is, as Lovecraft states in "At the Root" (*United Amateur,* July 1918), we have not advanced very far from primitivism at all: "We must recognise the essential underlying savagery in the animal called man, and return to older and sounder principles of national life and defence. We must realise that man's nature will remain the same so long as he remains man; that civilisation is but a slight coverlet beneath which the dominant beast sleeps lightly and ever ready to awake." Many things—liquor; war; Bolshevism—could bring about a collapse, and society must be constituted in such a way as to prevent a collapse from occurring. For Lovecraft, at this period (and, really, for his entire life, even during and after his conversion to moderate socialism), the answer was aristocracy. I shall examine this branch of his thought later.

Right now we can tie in Lovecraft's racism into the picture, since he manifestly regarded the influx of foreigners—who, to his mind, could not maintain the cultural standards he valued—as a threat to the dominant Anglo-Saxon civilisation of New England and the United States as a whole. The essay "Americanism" (*United Amateur,* July 1919) embodies this conception. For Lovecraft, Americanism is nothing more than "expanded Anglo-Saxondom": "It is the spirit of England, transplanted to a soil of vast extent and diversity, and nourished for a time under pioneer conditions calculated to increase its democratic aspects without impairing its fundamental virtues. . . . It is the expression of the world's highest race under the most favourable social, political, and geographical conditions." None of this is, as we have already seen, especially new or unusual for someone in Lovecraft's socioeconomic position. Nor, indeed, is the complete rejection of the "melting-pot" idea:

> Most dangerous and fallacious of the several misconceptions of Americanism is that of the so-called "melting-pot" of races and traditions. It is true that this country has received a vast influx of non-English immigrants who come hither to enjoy without hardship the liberties which our British ancestors carved out in toil and bloodshed. It is also true that such of them as belong to the Teutonic and Celtic races are capable of assimilation to our English types and of becoming valuable acquisitions to the population. But from this it does not follow that a mixture of really alien blood or ideas has accomplished or can accomplish anything but harm. . . . Immigration cannot, perhaps, be cut off altogether, but it should be understood that aliens who choose America as their residence must accept the prevailing language and culture as their own; and neither try to modify our institutions, nor to keep alive their own in our midst.

I repeat that this statement—offensive as it may be to many—was not in any way unusual amongst Yankees of Lovecraft's class. Let us bypass the flagrant untruth that immigrants have somehow come here merely to enjoy the "liberties" carved out by those sturdy Saxons: again Lovecraft's complete ignorance of the hardships willingly endured by immigrants to establish themselves in this country has betrayed him into clownish error. The critical term here is "assimilation"—the idea that foreign culture-streams should shed their own cultural heritage and adopt that of the prevailing (Anglo-Saxon) civilisation. Current thinking on this idea rejects the "melting-pot" idea as violently as Lovecraft did, although from a different direction. What Israel Zangwill envisioned in his play, *The Melting-Pot* (1909), was the fusing of cultures among the divergent culture-streams of America to produce a new civilisation unlike that of any of the separate cultures of Europe or Asia or Africa. Many of us now, evidently, wish to see ethnic or culture-groups retain their own folkways to produce a new metaphor—a "rainbow"; but it is by no means clear that the severe fragmentation of the American people along ethnic lines has produced much aside increased racial tensions and a fundamental lack of unity of purpose. In Lovecraft's time it was *expected* that immigrants would "assimilate"; as one modern historian has noted: "The predominant expectation [in the early twentieth century] has been that the newcomer, no matter what his place of origin, would conform to Anglo-Saxon patterns of behavior."[5] Lovecraft, although on the far right in his views on World War I and on the League of Nations, was a centrist in the matter of immigrant assimilation.

I have no doubt that Lovecraft approved of the three important immigration restriction laws of the period: those of 1917 (which introduced a literacy test), of 1921 (which limited immigration from Europe, Australia, the Near East, and Africa to 3% of each foreign nation's population then residing in the U.S.), and, most significantly, of 1924, reducing the quota to 2%, but taking as its basis the census of 1890, which had the added effect of radically reducing immigration from eastern and southern Europe, since immigrants from those countries were an insignificant number in 1890. Lovecraft does not mention any of these immigration laws, but his general silence on the matter of foreign incursions in the 1920s (except during his New York period) suggests that he felt this matter had been, at least for the time being, satisfactorily dealt with. Politics during the relatively tranquil and Republican-governed 1920s becomes for Lovecraft less a matter of immediate crises than an opportunity for theoretical speculation. It was during this time that he evolved his notions of aristocracy and "civilisation," ideas that would undergo significant modification with the onset of the Depression but retain their fundamental outlines, leading to the evolution of the distinctive notion of "fascistic socialism."

The late teens saw Lovecraft emerge as a towering figure in the tiny world of amateur journalism. Having been elected President for the 1917–18 term, he seemed in a good position to carry out his programme for a UAPA that would both promote pure literature and serve as a tool for education. Under the capable official editorship of Verna McGeoch (pronounced Ma-GOO), who held the office for two consecutive terms (1917–19), the *United Amateur* really did flower into a substantial literary organ. But signs of trouble were already in the air. As early as January 1917, when Lovecraft published the article "Amateur Standards" in the *Conservative,* he was having to fend off attacks on the literary orientation of the UAPA. The piece opens resoundingly: "Amateur journalism has always been a battle-ground betwixt those who, cognisant of its better possibilities, wish to improve their literary skill; and those who, viewing it merely as a field of amusement to which they can obtain easy access, wish to indulge in mock-politics, pseudo-feuds, and cheap social frivolities." This is Lovecraft's old distinction of literati and politicians. He goes on to note that "there has arisen in opposition to the progressive policies of [the current administration] a reactionary movement of such blatant vulgarity and puerile crudeness, that the *Conservative* feels impelled to protest at the display of impotent malice and infantile bitterness shewn by some of the treacherous anti-administration elements." This refers, of course, to the administration of 1916–17, of which Paul J. Campbell was president. One phase of the attack cut Lovecraft to the quick: "One of these peace-disturbers has wailed against the improvement of the *The United Amateur,* declaring . . . that it has become a mere purveyor of 'literary twaddle' . . ." This is exactly the sort of "improvement" he was aiming to bring about, and his July 1917 *United Amateur* may have been a veiled response to such an accusation. I believe Lovecraft's object of attack is William J. Dowdell and other members of what Lovecraft fancied to be a clique in the area of Cleveland, Ohio.

But for the time being Lovecraft was in a position to carry forward his own agenda. An amendment creating a third and fourth vice-president passed at the 1917 convention, and these officers were to be responsible for recruiting at the college and high-school levels, respectively. Lovecraft appointed Mary Henrietta Lehr as the third vice-president and, by November 1917, Alfred Galpin as the fourth vice-president.[6] Recruitment at these institutions would, in Lovecraft's view, markedly improve the overall literacy of the membership, counteracting the generally undereducated "boy printers" of the NAPA tradition and the tyros, young and old, who saw in amateurdom a place for the publication of ill-formed writings not publishable elsewhere.

Verna McGeoch originated a plan for a regular column in the *United Amateur* called "The Reading Table," which would offer elementary histories of the great literatures of the world and guides to the "great books" of the Western world.[7] The plan took a little while to get under way, but in the September 1918 issue McGeoch herself published an article on "Greek Literature." Lovecraft followed with "The Literature of Rome" in November 1918. This is a competent enough piece that allows Lovecraft to rhapsodise about the greatness of the Romans, to whom he always felt closer than to the Greeks. He confesses this bias openly:

> In considering Rome and her artistic history, we are conscious of a subjectivity impossible in the case of Greece or any other ancient nation. Whilst the Hel-

> lenes, with their strange beauty-worship and defective moral ideals, are to be admired and pitied at once, as luminous but remote phantoms; the Romans, with their greater practical sense, ancient virtue, and love of law and order, seem like our own people.

The "defective moral ideals" refers, apparently to Greek homosexuality. Lovecraft evidently went on a little too long in this piece, as parts of it were relegated to the back of the issue in small type without attribution; this section of the article was not reprinted until its appearance in the second volume of *Collected Essays* (2004).

A later piece, "Literary Composition" (*United Amateur,* January 1920), although not part of "The Reading Table," continues Lovecraft's effort to educate amateurs in basic literary craft. It is an elementary, sometimes simple-minded, survey of grammar, syntax, and the rudiments of prose fiction. This bias toward fiction is itself interesting—as are the frequent citations of Poe, Bierce, and Lord Dunsany as models of style and narration—in pointing to Lovecraft's shift away from essays and poetry; he promises later articles on these latter subjects, but they were never written. Some features of the article reveal Lovecraft's antiquated grammatical and syntactical preferences, as when he objects to the use of "barbarous compound nouns" such as *viewpoint* or *upkeep,* which had already become relatively common in standard English; but he is dead right on the misuse of *like* for *as* or *as if,* even though this distinction is now virtually a lost cause thanks to the ignorance of the supposedly literate general public. He highlights this misuse with a piquant example: "I strive to write like Pope wrote."

Another idea Lovecraft put forward to encourage amateur activity was the issuing of cooperative papers—papers in which a number of individuals would pool their resources, both financial and literary. He announced in his "President's Message" of March 1918 that he was heading such an operation, and announced the rates: "$1.50 will pay for one page, 7 × 10, and each contributor is at liberty to take as many pages as he desires at that rate." But the next "President's Message" (May 1918) declared that "Responses to the proposal for a co-operative paper have been slow in coming in," so clearly the project did not take off as Lovecraft wished.

But no one could accuse Lovecraft of not trying to teach by example. He himself participated in such a journal, the *United Co-operative,* which published three issues: December 1918, June 1919, and April 1921. Lovecraft had contributions in each issue: "The Simple Spelling Mania" (3 pages) and the poem "Ambition" (½ page) in December 1918; "The Case for Classicism" (3 pages), the poem "John Oldham: A Defence" (½ page), and the prose-poem "Memory" (½ page) in June 1919; the collaborative story "The Crawling Chaos" (with Winifred Virginia Jackson; 6 pages) and "Lucubrations Lovecraftian" (8 pages) in April 1921. Jackson was also one of the cooperative editors.

Lovecraft also served on the editorial board of a paper, the *Bonnet,* which was the organ of the United Women's Press Club of Massachusetts. Winifred Virginia Jackson was official editor. I know of only one issue to appear (June 1919), containing an unsigned editorial undoubtedly by Lovecraft, "Trimmings," and an unsigned poem, "Helene Hoffman Cole: 1893–1919: The Club's Tribute," also clearly by him. I have already mentioned that Lovecraft was Assistant Editor of the *Credential* (April 1920). Earlier he had served as Assistant Editor for at least one issue (June 1915) of the *Badger* (edited by George S. Schilling) and for the Tribute Number (April 1917) of the *Inspiration* (edited by Edna von der Heide).

When Lovecraft's term as President expired in the summer of 1918, he was appointed to his old job of Chairman of the Department of Public Criticism by the new president, Rheinhart Kleiner. For the 1919–20 term Lovecraft held no office, although he was no doubt gratified to have won the Story, Essay, and Editorial laureateships for the year (for "The White Ship," "Americanism," and "The Pseudo-United," respectively). In the summer of 1920, however, he was elected Official Editor, serving for four of the next five years. He was now in still greater control of the editorial content of the *United Amateur,* and he made the most of it, opening its pages to literary matter by many of his colleagues old and new. Moreover, he wrote editorials for nearly every issue and was also in charge of writing "News Notes" recounting comings and goings of various amateurs, including himself.

The rumblings of discontent from some members became more emphatic around this time. In July 1919, in recommending Anne Tillery Renshaw for official editor (she in fact won the office), Lovecraft was forced to battle the "turbulent Cleveland element," waging a direct attack on William J. Dowdell—who was running against Renshaw—and his paper, the *Cleveland Sun:*

> Mr. Dowdell is clever, and could go far in literature if he chose; but up to now he has shewn no inclination to succeed except on a very low cultural plane—the plane of commercial "yellow" newspaper journalism. His artistic birth has not yet taken place. It is probably no exaggeration to say that the *Bearcat* and *Sun,* as now conducted, are fair specimens of the grade of official organ which Mr. Dowdell would give us—when he might condescend to give us any. Need more be said? Forewarned is forearmed! ("For Official Editor—Anne Tillery Renshaw," *Conservative,* July 1919)

By November 1920, now himself official editor, he was having to respond to this accusation:

> For several years our foes have reproached us for excessive centralisation of authority; asserting that the control of our society is anything from oligarchical to monarchial, and pointing to the large amount of influence wielded by a very few leaders. Denials on our part, prompted by the conspicuous absence of any dictatorial ambitions in the minds of our executives, have been largely nullified by the fact

> that while power has not been autocratically usurped and arbitrarily exercised, the burden of administrative work has certainly been thrust by common consent on a small number of reluctant though loyal shoulders. ("Editorial," *United Amateur,* November 1920)

At this point it is difficult to gauge the accuracy of Lovecraft's remarks. It is true that for the period 1917–22 a relatively small number of people held office in the UAPA, many of them doing so repeatedly: Winifred V. Jackson was Second Vice-President for 1917–20; Verna McGeoch was Official Editor for 1917–19; W. Paul Cook was Official Publisher for 1917–20 and E. E. Ericson for 1920–22; Alfred Galpin was Chairman of the Department of Public Criticism for 1919–22; and, as I have noted, Lovecraft was Official Editor for 1920–22. It seems as if a certain apathy had set in among UAPA members whereby they were content to have these individuals continue holding office year in and year out. Individual papers were declining, and Lovecraft's own *Conservative,* because of his other official involvements, only appeared annually in 1918 and 1919, and then ceased altogether until 1923.

But there is also a case to be made that Lovecraft himself, if not his colleagues, was beginning to conduct himself in a sort of fascistic way. Perhaps irritated at the slowness of the progress in literary development on the part of most members, he increasingly called for improvement by main force. We have already seen his demands for editors to band together to eliminate simple spelling ("Department of Public Criticism," *United Amateur,* May 1917) and his pleas for a Department of Instruction that would correct the contributions of the cruder members. Now, in a lecture entitled "Amateur Journalism: Its Possible Needs and Betterment" (probably delivered at an amateur convention in Boston on September 5, 1920),[8] he proposed establishing "some centralised authority capable of exerting a kindly, reliable, and more or less invisible guidance in matters aesthetic and artistic." This is how the plan would work:

> Certain qualified members must undertake the entirely new burden of offering help to both writers and publishers. They must approach crude authors whose work shews promise, and crude publishers whose papers appear to possess the spark of aspiration; offering a revision and censorship which shall ensure the publication of the articles or journals in question, free from all the main errors in taste and technique.

Lovecraft attempted to anticipate the objections of "any idealistic and ultra-conscientious person" who might object to the plan's "possible oligarchical tendencies" by pointing to the fact that all great periods in literature—Periclean Athens, Augustan Rome, eighteenth-century England—were led by "dominant coteries." It is evident that Lovecraft had simply reached the limit of his patience with sporting pages, bad poetry, and unhelpful official criticism. It is needless to say that the plan was never adopted.

If criticism of Lovecraft had come from people like Dowdell, he might have been able to fend it off; but instead, it now came from more responsible elements. Lovecraft must have been taken aback when the October 1921 *Woodbee* contained an attack upon him by Leo Fritter, a longtime UAPA member whom Lovecraft himself had supported for president in 1915. Fritter had cited a "wide-spreading dissatisfaction" with Lovecraft's editorial policy in the *United Amateur* and went on to accuse Lovecraft of trying to force the members into a mould he had arbitrarily cast according to his own ideas. Lovecraft countered that he himself had received "numerous and enthusiastic assurances of an opposite nature," and repeated once more his ideal for the UAPA:

> What justifies the separate existence and support of the United is its higher aesthetic and intellectual cast; its demand for the unqualified best as a goal—which demand, by the way, must not be construed as discriminating against even the crudest beginner who honestly cherishes that goal. . . . We must envisage a genuine scale of values, and possess a model of genuine excellence toward which to strive. ("Editorial," *United Amateur,* September 1921)

When Lovecraft concluded that "The question is one which should ultimately be decided at the polls," he spoke better than he knew, as we shall see presently.

This period, however, saw Lovecraft evolving socially from an extreme misfit to one who, while by no means gregarious, could take his place in the society of congenial individuals. This transformation, as successive waves of friends—most of them amateurs—came to visit him or as he actually ventured forth on brief excursions, is heart-warming to see.

Two visits by amateurs occurring in 1917 are instructive by their very contrast. In mid-September 1917 W. Paul Cook, who had only recently become acquainted with Lovecraft, paid him a call in Providence. Cook tells the story piquantly:

> The first time I met Howard I came very near not meeting him. . . . I was bound from New York to Boston, and broke my trip in Providence purposely to see Lovecraft. I was traveling by train, which enabled me to announce in advance the time of my arrival and with a variation of only a few minutes. Arriving at the address on Angell street which later was to be the best known street address in amateur journalism, I was met at the door by Howard's mother and aunt. Howard had been up all night studying and writing, had just now gone to bed, and must under no circumstances be disturbed. If I would go to the Crown hotel, register, get a room and wait, they would telephone when, and if, Howard woke up. This was one of the occasions in my life when I have blessed the gods for giving me a sense of humor, however perverted. It was essential that I be in Boston early that evening, which allowed me about three hours in Providence, but there was a train leaving in half an hour which I could catch if I kept moving. I had a life-like pic-

> ture of myself hanging around Providence until His Majesty was ready to receive me! In later years Mrs. Clark and I laughed more than once in recalling the incident. I was part way to the sidewalk and the door was almost latched when Howard appeared in dressing gown and slippers. Wasn't that W. Paul Cook and didn't they understand that he was to see me immediately on my arrival? I was almost forcibly ushered by the guardians of the gate and into Howard's study.[9]

Cook's account of the three hours spent with Lovecraft—they mostly talked amateur journalism, naturally enough—is unremarkable save in one detail I shall consider later. Let us now hear Lovecraft's account of the meeting, recorded in a letter to Rheinhart Kleiner:

> Just a week ago I enjoyed the honour of a personal call from Mr. W. Paul Cook . . . I was rather surprised at his appearance, for he is rather more rustic & carelessly groomed than I had expected of a man of his celebrity to be. In fact, his antique derby hat, unpressed garments, frayed cravat, yellowish collar, ill-brushed hair, & none too immaculate hands made me think of my old friend Sam Johnson . . . But Cook's conversation makes up for whatever outward deficiencies he may possess.[10]

Before examining these accounts, we should consider the details of Rheinhart Kleiner's meeting with Lovecraft, which also occurred sometime in 1917—presumably after Cook's visit, since Lovecraft says in the above letter that he had previously met only William B. Stoddard and Edward H. Cole (in 1914), but does not mention having met Kleiner himself. Kleiner tells the story as follows: "I was greeted at the door of 598 Angell Street by his mother, who was a woman just a little below medium height, with graying hair, and eyes which seemed to be the chief point of resemblance between herself and her son. She was very cordial and even vivacious, and in another moment had ushered me into Lovecraft's room."[11] Why the very different responses by his mother to Cook and Kleiner? I believe that the overriding factor is social snobbery. Cook's unkempt appearance could not have sat well with either Susie or Lillian, and they were manifestly going to make it as difficult as possible for Cook to pass through their door. Lovecraft confesses in a candid moment that "Of amateurdom in general her [Susie's] opinion was not high, for she had a certain aesthetic hypersensitiveness which made its crudenesses very obvious and very annoying to her."[12] Elsewhere he goes on to admit that Lillian also did not care for amateurdom—"an institution whose extreme democracy and occasional heterogeneity have at times made it necessary for me to apologise for it."[13] If these were the reasons why Lillian did not like amateurdom, then it is clear that social considerations weighed heavily in her mind: "democracy and occasional heterogeneity" can scarcely stand for anything but the fact that people of all classes and educational backgrounds were involved in the amateur movement.

Kleiner, a polished and debonair Brooklynite, was cordially received because his social standing was, in Susie's eyes, at least equal to Lovecraft's. Kleiner's account continues:

> Just before broaching the subject of an outdoor stroll, I absentmindedly took my pipe out of my pocket. I don't know why, but I suddenly felt that pipe-smoking in that house might not be quite the thing, and put it back into my pocket. At that very moment his mother appeared in the doorway again and espied the pipe sliding back into my pocket. To my surprise, she gave an exclamation of pleasure and wished that I could persuade Howard to smoke a pipe, as it would be "so soothing" for him. This may have been New England courtesy to cover a guest's embarrassment, but I knew that I never made the slightest attempt to convert Lovecraft to pipe-smoking!

Lovecraft's hostility to smoking nearly equalled his disapprobation of drinking. Kleiner is not entirely accurate in saying that he never attempted to convert Lovecraft to pipe-smoking, for the general matter of smoking crops up several times in their correspondence. Lovecraft admits to Kleiner that "though I smoked when about twelve years old—just to seem like a grown man—I left off as soon as I acquired long trousers"; going on to say, "I cannot see yet what anyone finds attractive about the habit of imitating a smokestack!"[14] But the most interesting part of the above account is again social: Kleiner instinctively sensed that smoking in the house would be a *faux pas,* and perhaps Susie, acknowledging Kleiner's tact, tried to cover up his "embarrassment" with a suggestion that she must have known her son would have scorned.

These accounts are among the most illuminating as to Lovecraft's life—and his relations with his mother—in this period. Both Cook and Kleiner are united on the extreme solicitude exercised by Susie and Lillian over Lovecraft. Cook notes: "Every few minutes Howard's mother or his aunt, or both, peeped into the room to see if he had fainted or shown signs of strain . . ." Kleiner tells a more remarkable story: "I noticed that at every hour or so his mother appeared in the doorway with a glass of milk, and Lovecraft forthwith drank it." It is this constant babying of Lovecraft by Susie and Lillian that no doubt helped to foster in Lovecraft's own mind a sense of his "invalidism."

Kleiner suggested that they go out for a stroll, and Lovecraft took him to see the colonial antiquities of Providence—a tour he invariably gave to all his out-of-town guests, for he never tired of showing off the wondrous remains of the eighteenth century in his native city. But Lovecraft's unfamiliarity with normal social conduct is made evident when Kleiner states:

> On our way back to his home, and while we were still downtown, I suggested stopping in at a cafeteria for a cup of coffee. He agreed, but took milk himself, and watched me dispose of coffee and cake, or possibly pie, with some curiosity. It oc-

curred to me later that this visit to a public eating-house—a most unpretentious one—might have been a distinct departure from his own usual habits.

This is very likely to be the case: not only because of the family's dwindling finances, but because of Lovecraft's continuing hermitry in spite of his ever-growing correspondence, a trip to a restaurant was at this time not likely to have been a common occurrence.

That correspondence, however, did lead at this time to Lovecraft's contact with two individuals, each remarkable in their own way, who would become lifelong friends—Samuel Loveman and Alfred Galpin. Loveman (1887–1976)—a friend or correspondent of three of the most distinctive writers in American literature (Ambrose Bierce, Hart Crane, and H. P. Lovecraft) and also well acquainted with George Sterling and Clark Ashton Smith—appears to be merely a sort of hanger-on to the great. But he was himself an accomplished poet—a greater poet than any in the Lovecraft circle except, perhaps, Clark Ashton Smith, and vastly superior to Lovecraft himself. His infrequently issued amateur journal, the *Saturnian,* contained his own exquisite, neo-Grecian, *fin-de-siècle* poems as well as translations from Baudelaire and Heine; and he scattered his poetry in other amateur or little magazines with bewildering insouciance, caring so little about its preservation that in the 1920s Lovecraft would compel Loveman to recite his poems so that Lovecraft could get them down on paper, something Loveman had not bothered to do. His greatest work is a long poem, *The Hermaphrodite* (written perhaps in the late teens and published in 1926 by W. Paul Cook), a gorgeous evocation of the spirit of classical Greece:

> I murmured: "For three thousand years
> Is that tale done, yet bitter tears
> Come to me now—to clasp and close
> The delicate ecstasy of those
> That vanished by no fault of mine.
> Radiant, remote, these friends of thine,
> So long ago! Another says
> That in Pieria many days
> The vintage through an autumn mist
> Shone purple amid amethyst,
> While in their vines one eve of gold
> The tortured god walked as of old,
> Bacchus, no doubt."[15]

It was to Loveman that Bierce wrote one of his last letters before vanishing into Mexico in late 1913: "This is only to say goodbye. I am going away to South America in a few weeks, and have not the faintest notion when I shall return."[16]

Lovecraft states that he came in direct contact with Loveman in 1917.[17] Loveman was at this time stationed at an army base, Camp Gordon, in Georgia, where he was in Company H of the 4th Infantry, Replacement Regiment. According to the UAPA membership lists, he remained there until the middle of 1919, when he returned to his native Cleveland. In the early to mid-1910s, however, he must have been in California, where his friendships with Smith and Sterling were established. (Bierce, although a longtime San Franciscan, was mostly in Washington, D.C., at the time of his correspondence with Loveman [1908–13].) By November 1917 Lovecraft was already announcing that "Loveman has become reinstated in the United through me."[18] Loveman, although heavily involved in the amateur movement from about 1905 to 1910, had been out of organised amateurdom for some years, and he attests that Lovecraft's first letter was essentially a query as to whether Loveman was in fact still in the land of the living:

> The gist of the letter was this: the writer had long been an ardent admirer of my poetry, and its appearance had, from time to time, excited his admiration to such a degree that he had made bold to institute inquiries as to my whereabouts. He had, he asserted, practically given up any hope of finding me, when a clue to my location was indicated. Hence, his letter of inquiry: was I alive or dead?[19]

Loveman, finding the antique diction of the letter (which he here parodies) both charming and faintly ridiculous, duly relieved Lovecraft's doubts on this score.

Lovecraft proceeds in his letter: "Jew or not, I am rather proud to be his sponsor for the second advent to the Association." Robert H. Waugh[20] has pointed to the deliciously doubtful grammar of this remark—who is the Jew, Loveman or Lovecraft?—and it would be pleasant to think that Loveman had some eventual effect in relieving Lovecraft of his prejudice; but in fact Loveman was, in Lovecraft's mind, what all Jews and other non-Anglo-Saxons should be: a totally assimilated American who had renounced his cultural ties to Judaism. Whether this is in fact the case or not is another matter—I do not know enough about Loveman's own religious or cultural views to pass any judgment—but clearly Lovecraft thought it to be the case. In addition, the neoclassicism of Loveman's poetry and his general air of languid sophistication could only appeal to Lovecraft. For several years their association was largely conducted on paper, but in 1922 they met in Cleveland and then, in 1924–26, they became close friends in New York.

Alfred Galpin (1901–1983) is an entirely different case. This brilliant individual—as gifted in pure intellect as Loveman was in aesthetic sensitivity—would eventually become a philosopher, composer, and teacher of French, although his rapid alterations in intellectual aspirations may have prevented him from distinguishing himself in any one of them. Galpin first came to Lovecraft's attention in late 1917, when he was appointed to the new position of 4th Vice-President, in charge of recruiting high-school students into amateurdom. This appointment was very likely suggested by Maurice W. Moe, since Galpin was at that time already emerging as a star pupil in the Appleton (Wis.) High School and specifically in Moe's Appleton High School Press Club. By January 1918, the date of the first surviving letter by Lovecraft to Galpin, the two were already cordial correspondents.

Galpin's most profound effect upon Lovecraft may have been philosophical, for as early as August 1918 Lovecraft was announcing that Galpin's "system of philosophy . . . comes nearest to my own beliefs of any system I have ever known,"[21] and in 1921:

> he is intellectually *exactly like me* save in degree. In degree he is immensely my superior—he is what I should like to be but have not brains enough to be. Our minds are cast in precisely the same mould, save that his is finer. He alone can grasp the direction of my thoughts and amplify them. And so we go down the dark ways of knowledge; the poor plodding old man, and ahead of him the alert little link-boy holding the light and pointing out the path. . . .[22]

This obviously was meant half in jest, although Lovecraft clearly believed there was more than a grain of truth to it; and perhaps Galpin did indeed help to give shape to Lovecraft's still nebulous philosophical conceptions, encouraging this "old man" of thirty-one to hone his mechanistic materialism. But it is not that that I wish to study here; rather, Galpin had a more immediate effect upon Lovecraft's literary work, and it involved the production of some delightfully playful poetry.

Lovecraft of course wrote some more or less conventional tributes to Galpin, especially on his birthday ("To the Eighth of November," *Tryout,* November 1919; "To Alfred Galpin, Esq.," *Tryout,* December 1920; "To a Youth," *Tryout,* February 1921). "To the Eighth of November" was published a year late, as it commemorates Galpin's seventeenth birthday (November 8, 1918). About this time a student named Margaret Abraham joined the Appleton High School Press Club; curiously, she was exactly one year younger than Galpin, so in 1919 Lovecraft commemorated both their birthdays in "Birthday Lines to Margfred Galbraham," a poem that was apparently not published in Lovecraft's lifetime.

Whether Galpin had amorous inclinations toward Margaret Abraham is unclear; he certainly seems to have had such inclinations toward other girls in his high school, and Lovecraft had great fun with the whole subject. Galpin, in his memoir of Lovecraft, made brief note of "the petty incidents of a sophomore's (or junior's) life, including a number of 'crushes' in which he [Lovecraft] took an expressive interest—expressive to the point of commemorating them in verse."[23] Galpin refrains from elaborating on the matter, but an examination of Lovecraft's poetry of the period, as well as his letters to Galpin for 1918, will allow us to do so.

The poems we have to deal with are "Damon and Delia, a Pastoral" (*Tryout,* August 1918), "To Delia, Avoiding Damon" (*Tryout,* September 1918), "Damon—a Monody" (*United Amateur,* May 1919), and perhaps "Hylas and

Myrrha" (*Tryout,* May 1919) and "Myrrha and Strephon" (*Tryout,* July 1919), if these latter two are in fact about Galpin. Damon in these poems is clearly Galpin; the name is derived from the shepherd who is featured in the eighth eclogue of Virgil (a Damon also figures as a character in the first of Pope's *Pastorals*). Is Delia a real person? She certainly seems so, although her name too is taken from Graeco-Roman pastoral: she is a minor character in Virgil's third eclogue. In referring to some tongue-in-cheek love poems included in a letter to Galpin dated August 21, 1918, Lovecraft concluded: "They ought to melt even the beautiful perverse Delia!"[24] This is probably the same as the "Hibernian Chloë"[25] mentioned in a previous letter. If this girl was Irish, can we identify her? The membership list of the UAPA, printed in the *United Amateur* for November 1918, lists five girls of the proper age (the "b" category—16–21 years old) in Appleton: Gertrude L. Merkel, Muriel P. Kelly, Matilda E. Harriman, Ruth C. Schumacher, and Helen Mills. Perhaps Muriel P. Kelly is the Delia in question. A later reference by Lovecraft to "Delia-Margarita"[26] makes one think that perhaps Margaret Abraham herself is Delia. Of course, the girl need not have been in the UAPA at all. She was apparently scorning Galpin's overtures, and most of Lovecraft's poems play with this scenario. "To Delia, Avoiding Damon" opens with a prefatory note: "The old Bard *Tityrus* addresseth a Beautiful Perverse Nymph on behalf of his young Amorous Friend *Damon,* ending with a Threat of Satire if the Maid prove not kind to the youth." Then he rebukes Delia in no uncertain terms:

> Senseless creature! thus to scorn
> One to wit and glory born;
> Future times with proud acclaim
> Shall revere thy Damon's name:
> If thou prove not his, thy lot
> Bleak shall be—thy name forgot!

Well, Lovecraft's prediction has certainly come true. All this is amusing enough, although several hundred lines of this sort of thing can become a little wearying.

In May 1918 another girl came to Galpin's attention, one to whom Lovecraft refers as "the beauteous Miltonico-Shakespearian fellow-prodigy"[27] at the Appleton High School. This girl seems to have been of French extraction, as Lovecraft later calls her Mlle Shakespeare. I cannot identify this person, as no one with a French-sounding name appears on the UAPA membership list for Appleton; perhaps she never joined the association. In August Lovecraft wrote to her, singing Galpin's praises:

> In my Galpinian interpolations, I took care to avoid any appearance of fulsomeness, but merely stated casually that Mr. Galpin is indeed a very remarkable young man, who despite his few years has come to be one of the leading workers in our

> cause, *& who has a great future before him.* Note this last item. By predicting a great future, I imply, of course, that anyone who *shares* that future will be fortunate indeed! . . . All hail to Theobald the Matchmaker!![28]

Lovecraft spoke a little too soon, for Galpin did not marry for another several years—although, by coincidence, he did in fact marry a Frenchwoman.

By October Galpin has apparently been lured back to Delia, and a new girl—called by Lovecraft "the wingèd Eleanora"[29]—has taken second place, with Mlle Shakespeare dropping to third. This is probably Eleanor Evans Wing, who shows up in the UAPA membership list for Appleton in November 1919; her classification is "a," meaning that she is under sixteen. Lovecraft urges Galpin to pay more attention to the latter two than to Delia, who appears only to have good looks but does not have a keen mind like the others and is also shrewish and quarrelsome.

All this is great entertainment, and some of the best of Lovecraft's parodic love poetry is found in letters to Galpin. The letter for May 27, 1918, contains "A Pastoral Tragedy of Appleton, Wisconsin." Galpin had himself evidently attracted the attention of some other girl—apparently not very good looking—and Lovecraft urges Galpin to cultivate her affections so as to prick Delia's jealousy: "Such is the approved method of fiction." In the poem he depicts this scenario, with the result that the blighted Hecatissa—the ugly girl whom Strephon uses only to make Chloë jealous—hurls herself "with desperate intent / Into the swift Fox River!" But there is an anomalous P.S.:

> The river-god her face espy'd,
> And felt a sudden pain—
> Declin'd to claim her as his bride,
> And cast her back again!

The letter of August 21, 1918, contains a handful of parodies of love poems designed for "a lady's album," playing off an actual poem for such an album written by Rheinhart Kleiner. Lovecraft affixes hilarious pseudonyms to the poems—Kleinhart Reiner, Anacreon Microcephalos, and (my favourite) A. Saphead. Here is Saphead's poem:

> Were the blue of the sea and the blue of the skies
> Half as sweet and as pure as the blue of your eyes;
> Were the scent of the fields, and the flow'r-laden air
> Half as potent and rich as your dear golden hair
> { nut-brown
> raven
> silver
> crimson }

Then the world were an Heaven, and mine were the bliss
To write verses forever as freely as this!

Lovecraft adds: "Note the adaptability of the above gem to all varieties of maidens. True, there is no alternative for *blue* eyes—but in poesy all eyes are blue." Lovecraft gives Galpin permission to "use any or all of these specimens if occasion arises . . ."

Lovecraft's final word on Galpin's schoolboy crushes occurs in the delightful two-act play in pentameter blank verse entitled *Alfredo: A Tragedy,* the manuscript of which declares it to be "By Beaumont and Fletcher" and which is dated September 14, 1918. This date makes it clear that two of the chief characters—Rinarto, King of Castile and Aragon, and Alfredo, the Prince Regent—are meant to be Kleiner and Galpin, since Kleiner was president of the UAPA and Galpin was 1st vice-president during the 1918–19 term. Other obviously recognisable characters are Mauricio (= Maurice W. Moe), a Cardinal, Teobaldo (= Lovecraft), the prime minister, and three principal female characters: Margarita (= Delia = Margaret Abraham?), Hypatia (= Mlle Shakespeare), and Hecatissa (= the unattractive girl who had a crush on Galpin).

Those who have read Lovecraft's earlier poems on Damon and Delia will find little new here in terms of plot. Alfredo burns for Margarita, but she scorns him. Teobaldo advises him to pretend to be attracted to Hecatissa in order to arouse Margarita's jealousy, but Alfredo discounts the idea. Meanwhile Teobaldo perceives that Alfredo is close friends with Hypatia, who combines beauty and a love of books; Teobaldo urges him to forget Margarita and make Hypatia his wife. Alfredo takes the advice, but in the process excites the ire of both Margarita and Hecatissa. At the nuptials a play written by Teobaldo is to be acted as a preface to the marriage ceremony; but Hecatissa, who is from the East, has devised a fatal poison which both Alfredo and Hypatia unwittingly drink in the course of the play. At this point characters begin killing one another in revenge until scarcely anyone is left alive.

Alfredo was not published until 1966, and clearly Lovecraft wrote it as a jeu d'esprit. But there are some fine touches, especially the now customary deprecation of his own dour bookishness (Hypatia refers to "that ancient prattler Teobaldo, / Whose very face casts gloom on youthful bliss"). Lovecraft really does capture the flavour of Elizabethan tragedy—or perhaps tragicomedy—with songs and other interruptions of the predominant pentameter metre; and—as in "The Poe-et's Nightmare"—the blank verse permits a liberal use of enjambement:

ALF. Fair nymphs,
I greet you all! No lovelier train e'er danc'd
O'er velvet turf, and 'mid the vernal flow'rs,
Since Cytheraea, fresh from Paphos, led
Her melting followers o'er Arcadian meads!

The portrayals of characters aside from Alfredo and Teobaldo are not especially distinctive—at least, there seems little in the character of Rinarto to make us recall Kleiner. Mauricio is virtually the only character left alive at the end of the play, and Lovecraft cannot help poking fun at Moe's religiosity by having Mauricio trudge off the stage counting his beads.

I don't know that we need read a great deal into all these mock-love poems about Galpin: certainly Lovecraft's beloved Georgians had made a specialty of it, and *The Rape of the Lock* is only the best-known example. But I think there is something to be said for the view that by consistently deflating the emotion of love in these and other poems Lovecraft was thereby shielding himself from falling under its influence. The probability that he would so fall was, at the moment, comparatively small, but Lovecraft was not about to take any chances. During his involvement with the Providence Amateur Press Club in 1914–16 a few of the members decided to play a rather malicious joke on him by having one of the female members call him up and ask him to take her out on a date. Lovecraft stated soberly, "I'll have to ask my mother," and of course nothing came of the matter.[30] In a letter to Galpin Lovecraft notes in passing that "so far as I know, no feminine freak ever took the trouble to note or recognise my colossal and transcendent intellect."[31] Whether this was exactly true or not is something I shall take up later.

Galpin did have one further effect on Lovecraft's literary work—he was the inspiration for the curious piece called "Old Bugs." This too is a charming little frivolity, even though it treats a subject Lovecraft customarily regarded with great seriousness: liquor. Galpin had become interested in getting one quick taste of alcohol before Prohibition took effect in July 1919, so he purchased a bottle of whiskey and a bottle of port wine and drank them (in their entirety?) in the woods behind the Appleton golf course. He managed to drag himself back home without attracting notice, but when he recounted the event in a letter to Lovecraft, "Old Bugs" was the response.

This tale is set in the year 1950 and speaks of a derelict, Old Bugs, who haunts Sheehan's Pool Room in Chicago. Although a drunkard, he exhibits traces of refinement and intelligence; and no one can figure out why he carries an old picture of a lovely and elegant woman on his person at all times. One day a young man named Alfred Trever enters the place in order to "see life as it really is." Trever is the son of Karl Trever, an attorney, and a woman who writes poetry under the name Eleanor Wing (recall Eleanor Evans Wing in the Appleton High School Press Club). Eleanor had once been married to a man named Alfred Galpin, a brilliant scholar but one imbued with "evil habits, dating from a first drink taken years before in woodland seclusion." These habits cause the termination of the marriage; Galpin gains fleeting fame for his writing but eventually drops out of sight. Meanwhile Old Bugs, listening to Alfred Trever tell of his background, suddenly leaps up and dashes the uplifted glass from Trever's lips, shattering a number of bottles in the process. (At this point "Numbers of men, or things which had been men, dropped to the floor and began lapping at the puddles of spilled liquor . . .") Old Bugs dies of overexertion, but Trever is sufficiently repulsed at the whole turn of events that his curiosity for liquor is permanently quenched. Naturally, when the picture of the woman found on Old Bugs is passed around, Trever realises that it is of his own mother.

The story is not nearly as ponderous as it sounds, even though no reader can have failed to predict the outcome after the first few paragraphs. Lovecraft does manage to poke fun at himself (through Old Bugs) in the course of his heavy-handed moralising: "Old Bugs, obtaining a firmer hold on his mop, began to wield it like the javelin of a Macedonian hoplite, and soon cleared a considerable space around himself, meanwhile shouting various disconnected bits of quotation, among which was prominently repeated, '. . . the sons of Belial, blown with insolence and wine.'" And his attempt at lower-class slang isn't bad: "'Well, here's yer stuff,' announced Sheehan jovially as a tray of bottles and glasses was wheeled into the room. 'Good old rye, an' as fiery as ya kin find anyw'eres in Chi'.'" Galpin notes that at the end of the story Lovecraft has added: "*Now* will you be good?!"

Although Lovecraft suggested that his closeness to Galpin stemmed largely from the similarity of their philosophical views, Galpin also had a taste for weird fiction. This taste did not persist very long, and Galpin noted in his memoir that in high school "I was in a passing phase of fondness for Poe and the weird." But that phase allowed the production of at least two interesting experiments by Galpin in weird writing, the poem "Selenaio-Phantasma" (*Conservative,* July 1918) and the story "Marsh-Mad: A Nightmare" (*Philosopher,* December 1920), written under Galpin's pseudonym Consul Hasting. "Selenaio-Phantasma" is a rather able pastiche of Lovecraft's "Nemesis":

When, in midst of this immundane dreaming
Come effulgent the first rays of light,
Bringing back my rapt soul with their beaming,
Lending splendour to all within sight;
And I wake to the sunrise at dawning, fit close to the dusk's mad delight.

"Marsh-Mad" is just what its title declares: a nightmare about being lost in a weird, quasi-sentient swamp. It is an effective piece of atmosphere, although it doesn't amount to much as a story and is more adjective-choked than Lovecraft's work ever was. It was written in August 1918, and Lovecraft claimed to find great merit in the piece: he addressed his letter to Galpin of August 29, 1918 to "Edgar A. Poe, Esq.," deeming the tale "fully up to your usual standard, though in some respects surpassed by your former story 'The Fall of the House of Usher.'"

* * *

Although the amateur world was still the focal point of Lovecraft's world, he was slowly—probably through his mother's urging—making tentative forays at professional employment. His scorn of commercial writing prevented him from submitting his work to paying magazines, and the small number of his poems that were reprinted in the *National Magazine* all saw prior publication in amateur journals, and moreover were presumably not sent in by Lovecraft but were selected by the editors of the magazine itself from an examination of amateur papers. But if Lovecraft was not at the moment inclined to make money by writing, in what way could he earn an income? Whipple Phillips's inheritance, some of it already squandered by bad investments, was slowly but inexorably diminishing; even Lovecraft probably saw that he could not indulge himself as a gentleman-author forever.

The first sign we have that Lovecraft was actually attempting to earn an income occurs in a letter to John T. Dunn in October 1916. In explaining why he is unable to participate as thoroughly in amateur affairs as he would like, Lovecraft stated: "Many of my present duties are outside the association, in connection with the Symphony Literary Service, which is now handling a goodly amount of verse."[32] There was no mention of this service in previous letters to Dunn, so one imagines that Lovecraft's participation in it commenced about this time. This was a revisory or ghostwriting service featuring Lovecraft, Anne Tillery Renshaw (who edited the amateur journal the *Symphony*), and Mrs J. G. Smith, a colleague of Renshaw's (although not in the UAPA), both of whom lived at this time in Coffeeville, Mississippi. Three years later, in "For Official Editor—Anne Tillery Renshaw" (*Conservative,* July 1919), Lovecraft noted that Renshaw was now an instructor at Pennsylvania State College; he did not mention any revisory service, but perhaps that is because it was irrelevant to her amateur activity or because it had already ceased to exist.

If all this is a reasonable conjecture, then it means that Lovecraft had already commenced what would become his only true remunerative occupation: revising and ghostwriting. He never managed to turn this occupation into anything like a regular source of income, as he generally took on jobs only from colleagues and placed advertisements for his services very sporadically and, apparently, with little result. In many senses it was exactly the wrong job for him in terms of his creative work: first, it was too similar in nature to his fiction writing, so that it frequently left him too physically and mentally drained to attempt work of his own; and second, the very low rates he charged, and the unusual amount of effort he would put into some jobs, netted him far less money than a comparable amount of work in some other profession.

Nevertheless, it is clear that this work grew directly out of his amateur activity, specifically his work as Chairman of the Department of Public Criticism, his editing of the *Conservative,* and his assistance in issuing the paper of "credentials" in 1916 (which, as we have seen, may never have appeared): "I am now struggling with reams of crude MSS. for the forthcoming paper of credentials; in fact, I have before me the entire contents of both MSS. Bureaus for revision. It is a monstrous task, and I fear I shall delay the appearance of the paper with my tardiness in completing work."[33] This is exactly the sort of thing he would later do for pay. As for editing the *Conservative,* the frequency with which Lovecraft remarks how some item or other by a contributor had *not* been revised shows how routinely he did revise the contributions he received: in the "Department of Public Criticism" for July 1917 he noted that Ira A. Cole's poem "In Vita Elysium" was printed "practically without revision." No doubt he touched up most of the contributions to the two issues of the *Providence Amateur* and also to the *United Amateur* during his editorship. This work very likely would now be classified as copy editing, and it is a pity that Lovecraft could not have secured an actual position in this capacity with a publisher. He attempted to do so during his New York period, but in vain.

The reference to the Symphony Literary Service in October 1916 is anomalous in that there appears to be no mention of it in any subsequent correspondence that I have seen, although in a later letter to Dunn he made note of "the increasing amount of professional work I am doing for writers outside the Association."[34] There is then little on this subject until early 1920, when Lovecraft noted that "I have just emerged from a veritable 'killer' [i.e., a headache], contracted by working half the forenoon and all the afternoon on Bush junk."[35] This, of course, refers to Lovecraft's most pestiferous revision client, the Rev. David Van Bush (1882–1959), a preacher, itinerant lecturer, pop psychologist, and would-be poet who would be the bane of Lovecraft's existence for several years. In the "News Notes" section of the *United Amateur* for May 1922 Lovecraft described him as follows:

> Dr. David V. Bush, introduced to the United in 1916 by Andrew Francis Lockhart, is rejoining this year and observing the progress lately achieved. Dr. Bush is now a psychological lecturer, speaking in the largest cities of the country and drawing record-breaking crowds wherever he goes. He is the author of several published volumes of verse and prose, the latter mainly psychological in nature, and has been rewarded by phenomenally extensive sales.

This is clearly a "puff," but it tells us several things of importance. First, it is obvious that Lovecraft came into contact with Bush through his amateur connexions. A letter by Bush (February 28, 1917) to the Symphony Literary Service requests information on "the costs for Mr. Lovecraft's revising of 38 pages of poetry."[36] As the bulk of Lovecraft's work for Bush occurred at a slightly later date, I shall discuss him in greater detail later.

One further enigmatic reference to possible remunerative work occurs in the *In Defence of Dagon* essays of 1921. Lovecraft remarked that one of his "verses on

America and England," when published in the professional *National Magazine* of Boston, "brought me an offer (albeit an impracticable one) from the book-publishing house of Sherman, French, & Co." I know neither what the poem might have been (probably "Ode for July Fourth, 1917," the only poem by Lovecraft in the *National Magazine* that might be thought to be about America and England) nor what sort of "offer" might have been involved. Was Lovecraft asked to write a book of patriotic propaganda? Actually, it is likely that Sherman, French & Co. was offering to publish a book of Lovecraft's poetry—at his expense. This is no doubt why he found the suggestion "impracticable," and he must have turned it down.

In August 1919 Lovecraft and Maurice W. Moe claimed to have teamed up in a "new professional literary partnership": hack writing. In a letter to Kleiner, Lovecraft outlines the plan:

> Mo has long been urging me to try professionalism, but I have been reluctant on account of my variation from the tastes of the period. Now, however, Mo has proposed a plan for collaboration in which his modern personality will be merged with my antique one. I am to write the material—mainly fiction—because I am the more fertile in plots; whilst he is to revise to suit the market, since he is the more familiar with contemporary conditions. He will do all the business part, also; since I detest commercialism. Then, IF he is able to "land" anything with a remunerative magazine, we shall "go halves" on the spoils of victory.
>
> The pseudonym under which we shall offer our composite wares for sale, is a compound of our own full names: *Horace Philter Mocraft.*[37]

All this sounds very amusing, and no doubt Lovecraft regarded it as a lark; but it came to nothing, and probably he and Moe never really made any attempt to put the plan into practice. In later years he would scorn the idea of writing for a specific market, and one of the pillars of his aesthetic theory became the need for "self-expression" without any thought of an audience. Collaboration, too, proved very difficult for Lovecraft, as he and his coauthors could never mesh their ideas into a satisfactory amalgam. It is one of Lovecraft's great virtues that he never buckled down to hackwork even in the face of ever-increasing poverty; as he wrote poignantly in 1924, "Writing after all is the essence of whatever is left in my life, and if the ability or opportunity for that goes, I have no further reason for—or mind to endure—the joke of existence."[38]

What of Lovecraft and his family at this time? We have seen that aunt Lillian, upon the death of her husband Franklin Chase Clark in 1915, lived in various rented quarters in the city. W. Paul Cook's account of his visit in 1917 makes it clear that she spent considerable time with her sister and nephew. Aunt Annie, upon her separation from Edward F. Gamwell (probably in 1915 or 1916) and the death of her son Phillips at the end of 1916, returned from Cambridge and probably lived with her brother Edwin in Providence. The death of Edwin E. Phillips on November 14, 1918, passes entirely unnoticed in the surviving correspondence by Lovecraft that I have seen; letters from this period are admittedly few, but the silence is nonetheless significant. I have no doubt that Lovecraft attended Edwin's funeral in Swan Point Cemetery as a matter of duty, but he was clearly on less intimate terms with Edwin than he was with any of Whipple Phillips's other surviving offspring.

Meanwhile Lovecraft himself, as he had been doing since 1904, continued to live alone with his mother at 598 Angell Street. The nature of their relations for much of the period 1904–19 is a mystery. We have seen that both Susie and Lillian disapproved of amateur journalism in general and Lovecraft's ardent enthusiasm for it in particular. Susie's son may have quickly become a giant in this tiny field, but that was not helping in any way to retard the family's inexorable decline into shabby gentility. His sporadic efforts to earn an income by revision, and his whimsical thoughts of turning into a hack writer, give the impression that he was not very serious about supporting himself; but we shall see that Susie was very concerned about this matter. Lovecraft may have come out of his hermitry of 1908–13 to some degree, but his singular lack of interest in women did not bode well for the eventual continuance of the Lovecraft family in America.

All in all, relations between Lovecraft and Susie could not have been very wholesome. Lovecraft was still doing almost no travelling outside the city, and the lack of a regular office job must have kept him at home nearly all day, week after week. And yet, Clara Hess, their neighbour of twenty-five years, remarks disturbingly: "In looking back, I cannot ever remember to have seen Mrs. Lovecraft and her son together. I never heard one speak to the other. It probably just happened that way, but it does seem rather strange . . ."[39]

Then, in May 1917, came Lovecraft's attempt at enlistment in the R.I.N.G. and, later, in the regular army. We have seen how Susie put a stop to the first of these efforts by pulling strings; but Lovecraft's remark to Kleiner that she was "almost prostrated with the news"[40] speaks eloquently of the mental perturbation she must have felt at the prospect (relatively remote, admittedly, since it is unlikely that Lovecraft would actually have been sent overseas) of losing her only son to the war. Lovecraft goes on in this letter to say: "My mother has threatened to go to any lengths, legal or otherwise, if I do not reveal all the ills which unfit me for the army." And if he is sincere in declaring that "If I had realised to the full how much she would suffer through my enlistment, I should have been less eager to attempt it," then it reveals a staggering failure of communication and empathy between mother and son. Susie must have been aware of Lovecraft's militarism and his eagerness to see the United States enter the war on England's side; but she must genuinely have been caught off guard at this attempt at enlistment—which, let us recall, came before President Wilson's announcement of the resumption of the draft. Susie was forced to acquiesce in Lovecraft's registering for the draft, since Lovecraft was legally obliged to do so; but it was by then a foregone conclusion that he would have been deemed suitable only for clerical work, and in the end he was rejected even for that.

Kenneth W. Faig, Jr, is surely correct in noting that "Susie's sharp decline . . . seems to have begun at about the time of her brother's death"[41] in November 1918. Edwin was the closest surviving male member of Susie's generation: of two cousins (both sons of Whipple Phillips's brother James Wheaton Phillips), Jeremiah W. Phillips had died in 1902, while Walter H. Phillips (1854–1924) was still alive, but his whereabouts at this time are not well known and in any event he does not seem to have had much contact with Susie or her sisters.[42] This means that Susie, Lillian, and Annie were all wholly reliant on Whipple Phillips's and (in the case of Lillian) Franklin C. Clark's estates for their income. (Since Annie never formally divorced her husband, Edward F. Gamwell, it is not clear whether she received any financial support from him; I think it unlikely.) Lovecraft was the only possible wage-earner in the family, and he was clearly not doing much to support himself, let alone his mother and aunts.

The result, for Susie, was perhaps inevitable. In the winter of 1918–19 she finally cracked under the strain of financial worries. On January 18, 1919, Lovecraft wrote to Kleiner: "My mother, feeling no better here, has gone on a visit to my elder aunt for purposes of complete rest; leaving my younger aunt as autocrat of this dwelling."[43] It is not entirely clear where Lillian was residing at this time: the 1917 city directory gives her address as 144 Dodge Street (in the West Side, several miles away from 598 Angell Street), but she disappears from the city directories thereafter; the 1920 federal census lists her as residing with a Mrs C. H. Babbit at 135 Benefit Street on the East Side,[44] but here she was serving as a companion to Mrs Babbit and it is not likely that Susie was staying there in early 1919. On March 13, Susie, "showing no signs of recovery,"[45] was admitted to Butler Hospital, where her husband had died more than twenty years before and where she herself would remain until her death two years later.[46]

Lovecraft noted in his January letter to Kleiner that "such infirmity & absence on her part is so *unprecedented*," but one wonders whether this was really the case. Once again Clara Hess provides some very disturbing testimony:

> I remember that Mrs. Lovecraft spoke to me about weird and fantastic creatures that rushed out from behind buildings and from corners at dark, and that she shivered and looked about apprehensively as she told her story.
>
> The last time I saw Mrs. Lovecraft we were both going "down street" on the Butler Avenue car. She was excited and apparently did not know where she was. She attracted the attention of everyone. I was greatly embarrassed, as I was the object of all her attention.[47]

I believe that these incidents occurred just before Susie's breakdown. But Clara Hess already noted, when finally visiting at 598 Angell Street after Susie's frequent urgings, that "She was considered then to be getting rather odd"; this may have occurred as early as 1908, since it was the time when Susie referred to Lovecraft as being "hideous." Again, if Lovecraft was oblivious to Susie's gradual decline, he must have had very little close or meaningful contact with his mother.

And yet, Lovecraft himself was profoundly shaken by Susie's nervous collapse. In the January letter to Kleiner he wrote:

> . . . you above all others can imagine the effect of maternal illness & absence. I cannot eat, nor can I stay up long at a time. Pen-writing or typewriting nearly drives me insane. My nervous system seems to find its vent in feverish & incessant scribbling with a pencil. . . . She writes optimistic letters each day, & I try to make my replies equally optimistic; though I do not find it possible to "cheer up", eat, & go out, as she encourages me to do.

One of the things he was "scribbling" was a poem, "Despair," which he included in his February 19, 1919, letter to Kleiner. It is one of his most powerful weird poems, even if its general atmosphere, and even some of its specific language, are clearly influenced by Poe's late poem "For Annie." "Once," the narrator writes, "I think I half remember . . . Liv'd there such a thing as bliss," but now there is only the "Deadly drowsiness of Dis"; what will be the end?

> Thus the living, lone and sobbing,
> In the throes of anguish throbbing,
> With the loathsome Furies robbing
> Night and noon of peace and rest.
> But beyond the groans and grating
> Of abhorrent Life, is waiting
> Sweet Oblivion, culminating
> All the years of fruitless quest.

Rarely has Lovecraft's "cosmic pessimism" achieved such concentrated expression as this.

It is obvious that Lovecraft felt very close to his mother, however much he may have failed to understand her or she to understand him. I have no warrant for saying that his response to her illness is pathological; rather, I see it as part of a pattern whereby any serious alteration in his familial environment leads to extreme nervous disturbance. The death of his grandmother in 1896 leads to dreams of "night-gaunts"; the death of his father in 1898 brings on some sort of "near-breakdown"; the death of Whipple Phillips and the loss of his birthplace in 1904 cause Lovecraft seriously to consider suicide. Even less tragic events result in severe traumas: school attendance in 1898–99 and violin lessons produce another "near-breakdown"; yet another breakdown causes or is caused by his inability to complete high school and leads to a several-year period of vegetation and hermitry.

The state of Lovecraft's own health during this entire period is somewhat of a mystery, since we have only his own testimony on the matter. He obviously had no physical ailments: his R.I.N.G. examination, however cursory, was clear on that score. To Arthur Harris, Lovecraft made the remarkable assertion in 1915: "I can remain out of bed but three or four hours each day, and those three or four hours are generally burdened with an array of amateur work far beyond my capabilities."[48] His letters to John Dunn and Alfred Galpin of the period 1915–18 are full of references to his pseudo-invalidism:

> I was offered the official editorship [of the UAPA in June 1916], but was forced to decline on account of ill health.[49]

> . . . it is rather difficult for me to determine how I can best help [in the war effort]; for my feeble health makes me very unreliable where steady work is concerned.[50]

> I am only about half alive—a large part of my strength is consumed in sitting up or walking. My nervous system is a shattered wreck, and I am absolutely bored & listless save when I come upon something which peculiarly interests me. However—so many things *do* interest me, & interest me intensely, . . . that I have never actually desired to die . . .[51]

That last remark is, strictly speaking, untrue, if we believe that his thoughts of suicide in 1904 were seriously conceived; there may also be a certain amount of posturing here, as Lovecraft appears to have become wryly (if perhaps unconsciously) fond of appearing to the world as a feeble invalid or valetudinarian. But on the whole these statements unwittingly reveal that many of Lovecraft's ailments were purely psychological—perhaps fostered, as I have noted before, by his mother's and his aunts' oversolicitousness—and that whenever he became engrossed in some intellectual subject, his "ill health" would be sloughed off and he would pursue studies as vigorously as anyone. It is perhaps not too early to bring in the testimony of a relatively impartial witness, George Julian Houtain, who met Lovecraft in Boston in 1920:

> Lovecraft honestly believes he is not strong—that he has an inherited nervousness and fatigue wished upon him. One would never suspect in his massive form and well constructed body that there could be any ailment. To look at him one would think seriously before 'squaring off.' . . .
>
> Many of us are Lovecrafts, in the peculiar sense, that we have lots of things wished upon us—and are ignorant how to throw them off. We react always to the suggestion—shall I call it curse?—placed upon us. It was never intended in the great scheme of things that such a magnificent physique should succumb to any mental dictation that commanded it to be subject to nervous ills and fatigue—nor

> that that wonderful mentality should weakly and childishly listen to that—WHICH ISN'T.[52]

Lovecraft responded to this in a letter to Frank Belknap Long:

> If Houtain knew how constant are my struggles against the devastating headaches, dizzy spells, and spells of poor concentrating power which hedge me in on all sides, and how feverishly I try to utilise every available moment for work, he would be less confident in classifying my ills as imaginary. I do not arbitrarily pronounce myself in invalid *because* of a nervous heredity. The condition itself is only too apparent—the hereditary part is only one explanatory factor.[53]

Lovecraft's account must be given its due, but in the event it appears that Houtain was more on the mark, and eventually Lovecraft realised it:

> Lovecraft did not express surprise at my pronouncements. In fact he was receptive to them. I came to the conclusion that he was willing to overcome this and would but he isn't allowed to do so, because others in his immediate household won't permit him to forget this hereditary nervousness. As it is Lovecraft is a mental and physical giant, not because of, but in spite of these conditions. I venture the prediction that were he to lose all thoughts of this handed down idea, get out in the world, and rub elbows with the maddening crowd, that he would stand out as a National figure in Belles-Lettres; that his name would top the list in the annals of the literature of the day and I will go so far as to say it would become a house-hold name throughout the breadth and length of this land.

Even now that final pronouncement is a bit of an exaggeration, but it is more accurate than Houtain—or Lovecraft—could ever have imagined. How Lovecraft finally emerged—intellectually, creatively, and personally—from the claustrophobic influence of 598 Angell Street to become the writer, thinker, and human being we know will be the subject of the subsequent chapters of this book.

Samuel Loveman

Rheinhart Kleiner and Lovecraft
in front of 598 Angell Street

Lovecraft and William J. Dowdell
in Boston

Lovecraft and Sonia Greene
in Boston

Alan H. Teague

Clark Ashton Smith
showing one of his sculptures

Donovan K. Loucks

The Lovecrafts' apartment
at 259 Parkside Avenue, Brooklyn

Donovan K. Loucks

The John Mawney House at 135 Benefit Street, Providence
(featured in "The Shunned House")

10. Cynical Materialist (1919–1921 [II])

The immediate effects of Susie's absence from the household at 598 Angell Street were mixed: at times Lovecraft seemed incapable of doing anything because of "nerve strain";[1] at other times he found himself possessed of unwonted energy: "I wrote an entire March critical report [i.e., the "Department of Public Criticism" for March 1919] one evening recently, & I am this morning able to write letters after having been up all night."[2] A month after Susie came to Butler, Lovecraft reported that she was "slightly improved in general physical condition, but not so far as nerves are concerned";[3] two months later it seems that "My mother's health remains so stationary that I fear present arrangements must be considered as semi-permanent."[4] In a sense, this turn of events—especially in light of Lovecraft's repeated assurances, which he himself no doubt received from Susie's doctors, that she was in no physical danger—may have been a relief, for it definitively moved Susie out of the picture as far as Lovecraft's daily life was concerned.

What exactly was the matter with Susie is now difficult to say, since her Butler Hospital records were among those destroyed in a fire several decades ago. Winfield Townley Scott, however, consulted them when they were still in existence, and he paraphrases them as follows:

> She suffered periods of mental and physical exhaustion. She wept frequently under emotional strains. In common lingo, she was a woman who had gone to pieces. When interviewed, she stressed her economic worries, and she spoke . . . of all she had done for "a poet of the highest order"; that is, of course, her son. The psychiatrist's record takes note of an Oedipus complex, a "psycho-sexual contact" with the son, but observes that the effects of such a complex are usually more important on the son than on the mother, and does not pursue the point.
>
> It was presumed that Mrs. Lovecraft was suffering from an "insufficiency complex." This had been brought about by the increasingly perilous state of her finances, complicated by the fact that neither she nor her son was a wage earner. However she adored him, there may have been a subconscious criticism of Howard, so brilliant in promise but so economically useless. Or perhaps not; perhaps she would not have changed him any more than she could have changed herself, and so, distraught and helpless, she at last collapsed.[5]

I imagine the second paragraph is Scott's, not Susie's doctor's, interpretation of the medical evidence. The most seemingly spectacular item is the curious mention of a "psycho-sexual contact"; but it is surely inconceivable that any actual abuse could have occurred between two individuals who so obviously shared the rigid Victorian sexual mores of the time. There seems every reason to regard Susie's collapse as primarily brought on by financial worries: there was, let us recall, only $7500 for the two of them from Whipple's estate, and in addition there was a tiny sum in mortgage payments (usually $37.08 twice a year, in February and August[6]) from a quarry in Providence, the Providence Crushed Stone and Sand Co., managed by a tenant, Mariano de Magistris. Given that Lovecraft at the age of twenty-eight was still showing no ability at—nor even much inclination toward—economic self-sufficiency, Susie's distress was entirely understandable.

Scott adds one further note of interest: "[Lovecraft] used to visit his mother at the hospital, but he never entered the buildings: always she met him on the grounds, usually at 'the grotto,' and they would stroll together through the Butler woods above the river. To other patients she spoke constantly and pridefully of her son, but they never saw him. And in her final illness, when she was confined to her bed, he apparently did not visit her." I do not know that much need be made of this: there are many who are disinclined to enter hospitals—especially someone who had suffered so many youthful ailments as Lovecraft—and the grounds at Butler are to this day exquisitely maintained and very pleasant for strolling. It may not even be very surprising that Lovecraft did not see her during her final illness; for it was not believed to be life-threatening until almost the very end.

In the meantime Lovecraft restricted himself to visiting Susie on the grounds and to writing leters and occasional birthday and Christmas poems to her. Even if he himself was never seen by other patients, perhaps Susie showed these brief and insignificant ditties as proof that her son was a "poet of the highest order." The first birthday tribute, "Oct. 17, 1919," is a slight eight-line poem that concludes with the wish "that future birthdays bright / May this excel, as noon excels the night!" No Christmas poem for this year survives, but probably Lovecraft did write one. For her next birthday Lovecraft wrote "To S. S. L.—October 17, 1920," which evidently accompanied a box of chocolates, which are designed to "shew that life, howe'er its course unfold, / Amidst the gall some sweetness yet can hold." "S. S. L.: Christmas 1920" was written to accompany some further unspecified "trivial tokens of a festive day." Oddly enough, the only two surviving letters by Lovecraft to Susie date to February and March of 1921; there were probably others, now lost.

It was perhaps inevitable that Susie's absence from 598 produced at least the possibility of a certain liberation on Lovecraft's part, if only in terms of his physical activities. By now a giant in the world of amateur journalism, he was increasingly in demand at various local and national amateur conventions. It was some time before Lovecraft actually ventured forth; but when he did so, it betokened the definitive end of his period of "eccentric reclusiveness." In October 1919 (as I shall relate in detail in the next chapter) he accompanied several amateurs to Boston to hear his new literary idol, Lord Dunsany. On the evening of June 21, 1920, Edward F.

Daas—the man who had introduced Lovecraft to amateur journalism six years before, and was currently First Vice-President of the UAPA—came to Providence. Lovecraft met him at Union Station at 9 P.M. and took him back to 598 for conversation till midnight. The next day he met Daas downtown and showed him various points of interest. Daas caught the 2:20 train to Boston to meet with the members of the Hub Club (a NAPA group).[7] That summer and fall Lovecraft himself made three separate trips to the Boston area for amateur gatherings.

The first meeting took place at 20 Webster Street in the suburb of Allston. This house—occupied jointly by Winifred Jackson, Laurie A. Sawyer, and Edith Miniter—no longer exists, as the entire block has been razed; but at the time it was a central meeting-place for the Hub Club. The members had decided that, since most of them could not attend the national NAPA convention in Cleveland, they would hold their own gathering—one that appeared to go on for nearly two weeks. Lovecraft arrived on Monday, July 4, in the company of Rheinhart Kleiner, who—along with others of a New York delegation of amateurs including E. Dorothy McLaughlin and George Julian Houtain—had come to Providence the day before. On this occasion Lovecraft spent the night under a roof other than his own for the first time since 1901.[8] His sleeping-place was the home of Alice Hamlet at 109 Greenbriar Street in Dorchester. But, lest we look askance at Lovecraft's spending the night alone in a young lady's home, let us be reassured: a convention report in the *Epgephi* for September 1920 discreetly informs us that "he said he'd just got to have a 'quiet room to himself'" and that he and Hamlet were properly chaperoned by Michael Oscar White and a Mrs Thompson.[9] The Dorchester party returned to 20 Webster Street the next day to resume festivities, and Lovecraft caught a train home in the early evening. He commemorated the event with a whimsical piece in *Epgephi,* "The Conquest of the Hub Club," in which he declared that the club had been "captured" by such stalwart UAPA members as himself and Winifred V. Jordan.

Edith Miniter (1869–1934) was perhaps the most noted literary figure at the gathering. In 1916 she had published a realistic novel, *Our Natupski Neighbors,* to good reviews, and her short stories had been widely published in professional magazines. But in spite of her professional success, she was devoted to the amateur cause; she had entered amateurdom as early as 1883 and remained a lifelong member. Her loyalty, however, extended to the NAPA and not the UAPA: she was NAPA's Official Editor for part of the 1895–96 term and its President in 1909–10. Among her amateur journals were *Aftermath,* generally issued after conventions and giving lively convention reports, *The Varied Year,* and *True Blue.* She also issued at least one issue of a journal entitled the *Muffin Man* in April 1921, which contained her exquisite parody of Lovecraft, "Falco Ossifracus: By Mr. Goodguile." It is, perhaps, the first such work of its kind and deserves some attention in its own right.

This little squib is a clear take-off of "The Statement of Randolph Carter." It opens: "Any form of inquisition into the meaning of this will be fruitless. Favour me, an' you will, with eternal confinement in a gaol, and everything that I now relate will be repeated with perfect candour." Along the way Miniter manages to get in effective jabs at Lovecraft's heavily laid-on atmosphere of grue ("A few skulls and crossbones lay in the foreground, while coffinplates, shreds of shrouds, and mattocks which I instinctively knew appertained to gravediggers, scattered around loosely, completed the remarkable scene"), his occasionally *recherché* diction ("'I am really sorry to have to ask you to absquatulate'"), and even his habit of Latinising his friends's names ("the name was originally John Smith, but it is always my will that my friends bear a name of my choosing and as cumbersome a one as possible"). I am sure Lovecraft took the whole thing in good humour: in his 1934 memoir of Miniter he notes her "highly amusing parody . . . though it was not of a nature to arouse hostility."[10]

Miniter had invited Lovecraft to attend the Hub Club picnic on August 7. Lovecraft accepted, although he did so largely in the hope of meeting his ex-nemesis James F. Morton; Morton, however, was called away to New Hampshire. This gathering consisted largely of old-time amateurs who had been active before the turn of the century. At one point, as the group was wandering through the Middlesex Fells Reservation, Miniter fashioned a chaplet of bays for Lovecraft and insisted that he wear them at a banquet that evening in honour of his triple laureateship. Lovecraft caught a late train from South Station, reached Providence at 1.30 A.M., came home half an hour later, and "slept like a mummy until the following noon."[11]

Lovecraft's third Boston trip began on September 5. He arrived at noon at 20 Webster Street and unexpectedly encountered Morton, whom he had not realised would be at the gathering: "Never have I met so thoroughly erudite a conversationalist before, and I was quite surprised by the geniality and friendliness which overlay his unusual attainments. I could but regret the limited opportunities which I have of meeting him, for Morton is one who commands my most unreserved liking."[12] Clearly, the rancour surrounding Isaacson's *In a Minor Key*—which led to Lovecraft's unpublished poem "The Isaacsonio-Mortoniad"—had died away. Lovecraft would later have plenty of opportunities to meet Morton during his two-year stay in New York. In the afternoon Lovecraft delivered his lecture, "Amateur Journalism: Its Possible Needs and Betterment," which he reports "was received with admirable courtesy."[13] Again he caught a late train back to Providence.

Some months earlier, at the very beginning of 1920, Lovecraft met an individual who would play a very large role in his life: Frank Belknap Long, Jr (1901–

1994). At this time Long, a lifelong New Yorker, was not quite nineteen,[14] and would enter New York University that fall to study journalism, transferring two years later to Columbia. His family was quite well-to-do—his father was a prominent New York dentist—and resided in comfortable quarters on the Upper West Side of Manhattan, at 823 West End Avenue (the building does not now survive). Long had developed an interest in the weird by reading the Oz books, Verne, and Wells in youth, and he exercised his talents both in prose and in poetry. He discovered amateurdom when he won a prize for the *Boy's World* and received an invitation to join the UAPA; he seems to have done so around the end of 1919.[15] In an unsigned article, "The Work of Frank Belknap Long, Jr." (*United Amateur,* May 1924) Lovecraft declares that Long's first published work in amateurdom—"Dr. Whitlock's Price" (*United Amateur,* March 1920)—was "a frankly boyish and elementary story"; it is, in fact, a wildly flamboyant and rather ridiculous mad scientist tale. His next work of fiction—"The Eye above the Mantel" (*United Amateur,* March 1921)—is, however, a very different proposition.

The story is also a trifle sophomoric, but still very striking in its way. In a rhythmic and incantatory prose that occasionally recalls Dunsany, but with an atmosphere of clutching horror that is clearly Poe-esque, "The Eye above the Mantel" professes to tell of the end of the human race and the "supermen" who will succeed it. It is scarcely to be wondered that Lovecraft would be attracted to it, since he had already indirectly dealt with this theme in "Memory." Lovecraft also published, in the May 1922 *United Amateur,* Long's "At the Home of Poe," a brief prose-poem about the Poe cottage in Fordham. And in his own *Conservative* for July 1923 he published Long's "Felis: A Prose Poem." an exquisite story inspired by his pet cat. How could the ailurophile Lovecraft have resisted this passage?

> Some day I shall drown in a sea of cats. I shall go down, smothered by their embraces, feeling their warm breath upon my face, gazing into their large eyes, hearing in my ears their soft purring. I shall sink lazily down through oceans of fur, between myriads of claws, clutching innumerable tails, and I shall surrender my wretched soul to the selfish and insatiate god of felines.

It is not difficult to see why Lovecraft took to Long, and why he saw in him a sort of pendant to his other young disciple, Alfred Galpin. Long may not have had Galpin's incandescent brilliance as a philosopher, but he was an aesthete, fictionist, and poet; and it was exactly at this time that Lovecraft's own creative focus was shifting from arid antiquarian poetry and essays to weird fiction. Indeed, in a letter to Kleiner in which he notes getting in touch with Long, Lovecraft remarks: "Naturally my changed literary province tends to group around me a new set of proteges and clients—the budding story writers."[16] Long's early Poe-esque work, by no means markedly inferior to Lovecraft's, no doubt helped convince the latter that the new direction in which he was heading was a potentially fruitful one.

Long, of course, was not at all temperamentally or intellectually similar to Lovecraft. His aesthetic foci were the Italian Renaissance and nineteenth-century French literature. As befits a fiery youth, he tended to go through phases of passionate rapture—for avant-garde literary sophistication, for mediaeval Catholicism (although he himself was an agnostic and perhaps an atheist), and, some years later, Bolshevism. Lovecraft looked upon these sudden shifts of interest with a certain cynical amusement, but he could not remain unaffected by them; if nothing else, they inspired voluminous argumentative letters that helped to clarify his own aesthetic, philosophical, and political views. Indeed, it is very likely that Long helped to initiate a significant shift in Lovecraft's own aesthetic.

For now, however, the bond that linked the two men was weird fiction, and Long would be the privileged first reader of many of Lovecraft's stories in manuscript. They could know that they would remain the closest of friends for the next seventeen years.

Toward the end of 1919 Lovecraft and Kleiner began a desultory discussion of women, love, and sex. Kleiner, apparently, had always been susceptible to the temptations of the fair, and Lovecraft looked upon his varied involvements with a mixture of mild surprise, amusement, and perhaps a certain lofty contempt. At one point he remarks:

> Of course, I am unfamiliar with amatory phenomena save through cursory reading. I always assumed that one waited till he encountered some nymph who seemed radically different to him from the rest of her sex, and without whom he felt he could no longer exist. Then, I fancied, he commenced to lay siege to her heart in businesslike fashion, not desisting till either he won her for life, or was blighted by rejection.[17]

On the matter of sex, Lovecraft was equally resolute: "Eroticism belongs to a lower order of instincts, and is an animal rather than nobly human quality. . . . The primal savage or ape merely looks about his native forest to find a mate; the exalted Aryan should lift his eyes to the worlds of space and consider his relation to infinity!!" One suspects that that double exclamation mark, plus the generally bombastic tone of the entire passage, are indicative of a certain self-parody. But Lovecraft goes on:

> About romance and affection I never have felt the slightest interest; whereas the sky, with its tale of eternities past and to come, and its gorgeous panoply of whirling universes, has always held me enthralled. And in truth, is this not the natural attitude of an analytical mind? What is a beauteous nymph? Carbon, hydrogen, nitrogen, a dash or two of phosphorus and other elements—all to decay soon. But what is *the cosmos?* What is the secret of time, space, and the things that lie beyond time and space?[18]

Well, that seems to settle that. But is it really the case that Lovecraft was "unfamiliar with amatory phenomena"? that he had "never felt the slightest interest" in romance? There is perhaps some small reason for doubt on the matter; and it centres upon an individual who has been mentioned sporadically during the last several chapters—Winifred Virginia Jackson (1876–1959).

According to research done by George T. Wetzel and R. Alain Everts, Jackson had married Horace Jordan, an African American, around 1915; at that time she resided at 57 Morton Street in Newton Centre, Massachusetts, a suburb of Boston. Wetzel and Everts believe that she divorced in early 1919,[19] although she continues to be listed in the UAPA membership list under her married name until September 1921. By January 1920 she is living, along with two other female amateurs, at 20 Webster Street in Allston.

Jackson had joined the UAPA in October 1915,[20] and Lovecraft must have got in touch with her, at least by correspondence, very shortly thereafter, for the January 1916 issue of the *Conservative* contains two poems by her (signed Winifred Virginia Jordan), "Song of the North Wind" and "Galileo and Swammerdam." Three of her poems—"April," "In Morven's Mead," and "The Night Wind Bared My Heart"—appeared in the *Conservative* for April 1916. Two more, "Insomnia" and "The Pool," were published in the October 1916 issue; and I have noted already that Lovecraft's poem "The Unknown" appeared in this issue under Jackson's pseudonym, "Elizabeth Berkeley," a situation that was repeated in May 1917 when "The Peace Advocate" appeared under the same pseudonym in the *Tryout*.

Jackson and Lovecraft certainly do seem to have done a considerable amount of amateur work together. She herself issued only a single issue of the amateur journal *Eurus* (February 1918), which contained Lovecraft's poem on Jonathan E. Hoag's eighty-seventh birthday; as President of the United Women's Press Club of Massachusetts, she helped to publish one issue of the *Bonnet* (June 1919). She and Lovecraft, along with several others, edited and published three issues of the *United Co-operative* (1918–21), and she was associate editor of the *Silver Clarion* at a time when Lovecraft was giving a certain amount of attention to that journal. Jackson was Second Vice-President of the UAPA for three consecutive years (1917–20), when Lovecraft was President (1917–18) and Chairman of the Department of Public Criticism (1918–19).

Then, of course, there are the two stories co-written by Jackson and Lovecraft. One, "The Green Meadow" (1918/19), has already been discussed. The other, "The Crawling Chaos" (1920/21), was similarly based on a dream by Jackson and is similarly insubstantial; it was published in the *United Co-operative* for April 1921. All this suggests that a considerable amount of correspondence must have passed between the two, but only five letters by Lovecraft for the period 1920–21 survive, and these only in transcripts made by R. H. Barlow; there are, to my knowledge, no surviving letters by Jackson to Lovecraft.

None of this would suggest that Lovecraft and Jackson were anything but occasionally close working colleagues were it not for some remarks made by Wilametta Keffer, an amateur of a somewhat later period, to George T. Wetzel in the 1950s. According to Wetzel, Keffer told him that (and here Wetzel is paraphrasing a letter by Keffer) "everybody in Amateur Journalism thought Lovecraft would marry Winifred Jordan"; Keffer herself stated to Wetzel, "A long time member of NAPA who knew and met both HPL and Winifred Virginia told me of the 'romance.'"[21]

It is difficult to know what to make of this. Lovecraft must have met Jackson in person no later than the summer of 1920, since she was then residing at 20 Webster Street in Allston, where Lovecraft stopped on at least two occasions; but strangely enough, he does not mention her in any of his various accounts of his trips there. He did write an effusive article, "Winifred Virginia Jackson: A 'Different' Poetess," in the *United Amateur* for March 1921; and he spent Christmas Day of 1920 writing a quaint poem upon receiving a photograph of her—presumably her Christmas gift to him. "On Receiving a Portraiture of Mrs. Berkeley, ye Poetess" is rather charming, and naturally lauds both her beauty and her poetical skill:

> Tho' outward form the fair indeed would place
> Within the ranks of Venus' comely race,
> Yon shapely head so great an art contains
> That *Pallas'* self must own inferior strains.

Jackson really was a very attractive woman, and the fact that she was fourteen years older than Lovecraft need not preclude a romance between the two. But one other fact must now be adduced: although by this time divorced, Jackson (according to Wetzel and Everts) was carrying on an affair with the noted black poet and critic William Stanley Braithwaite (1878–1962), and she would remain his mistress for many years.[22] Did Lovecraft know this? I find it impossible to believe, given his extraordinarily strict views on the need to maintain an absolute "colour line" prohibiting any sort of sexual union between blacks and whites; if he had known, he would have dropped Jackson immediately even as a colleague. He might not even have known that Horace Jordan was black. Lovecraft of course did know of Braithwaite, who by this time was already the most prominent black critic in the country; he would correspond with him briefly in 1930. As literary editor of the influential *Boston Transcript* and as editor of the annual *Anthology of Magazine Verse* (1913–29), Braithwaite occupied a formidable position in American poetry at this time. Lovecraft casually mentions that Jackson's verse had appeared in the *Boston Transcript*,[23] and her verse was also reprinted in a number of the Braithwaite anthologies; it would be uncharitable to think that they did so merely because she was Braithwaite's mistress, for much of her poetry is rather good—better as a whole than Lovecraft's early verse. Lovecraft was no doubt appreciative of what he in his 1921 article called her "poems of potent terror and dark suggestion"; and I see no reason to believe that he had much of a hand in writing or revising them, although he does mention revising a poem for Jackson in 1916.[24] Her poem "April" (*Conservative,* April 1916) has a delicacy Lovecraft could not hope to duplicate:

Winter's sway
Pass'd away
'Neath a blue sky's leaven;
In its place
Out of space
Dropp'd a golden heaven!

There are two further bits of evidence that seem to clinch the matter of a romance between Lovecraft and Jackson. A photograph was taken at some point by Lovecraft (probably in 1921) of Jackson at the seaside; and Lovecraft's wife Sonia Greene told R. Alain Everts in 1967 that "I stole HPL away from Winifred Jackson."[25] How this happened will be the subject of a later chapter; but this romance, if it could really be called that, appears to have been very languidly pursued on both sides. There is no evidence that Jackson ever came to Providence to visit Lovecraft, as Sonia frequently did even though she lived much farther away (Brooklyn), and after Sonia "stole" him we hear little of Winifred either from Lovecraft or in the amateur press generally. She published only two books of verse, *Backroads: Maine Narratives, with Lyrics* (1927) and *Selected Poems* (with Major Ralph Temple Jackson) (1944).

One also does not know what, if anything, to make of some of the other amateur women who were associated with Lovecraft at this time. It is understandable that he would go to Boston to hear Lord Dunsany in the company of Alice Hamlet, since she was the one who introduced him to the Irish master; and we hear very little of her after that point. Lovecraft visited Myrta Alice Little a few times in New Hampshire during 1921, and one long and rambling letter to her survives. Then there is the enigma of Anna Helen Crofts, the only other woman with whom Lovecraft collaborated (as opposed to doing unsigned revision work), in the curious fantasy "Poetry and the Gods" (*United Amateur,* September 1920). I shall investigate each of these relationships further in their proper place, but I doubt if anything romantic was involved, at least on Lovecraft's side. It is not unlikely that a man of Lovecraft's great accomplishment in the tiny amateur world might have been the object of affection on the part of female amateurs, but aside from the Jackson matter we have not even the remotest evidence of any such thing.

Meanwhile Lovecraft was not done travelling. Two more trips to Boston were made in the early months of 1921, both again for amateur conventions. On February 22 the Boston Conference of Amateur Journalists was held at Quincy House. In the afternoon session, beginning at 2 P.M., Lovecraft delivered a paper, written the previous day,[26] on a prescribed subject, "What Amateurdom and I Have Done for Each Other." I have earlier noted the benefits Lovecraft claims (rightly) to have derived from amateur journalism: the broadening of his perspective by encountering other minds, and the chance to offer his writings to an appreciative public. Lovecraft is also perspicacious, if predictably modest, on what he has done for the amateur cause: he initiated a searching but constructive brand of criticism through the official public and private criticism bureaux; he issued his own paper, the *Conservative,* from 1915 to 1919, even if "circumstances have since forced me to suspend its publication" (he would fleetingly resume it in 1923); he contributed voluminously to other papers; and he performed "my share of administrative drudgery both official and unofficial." It is, on the whole, an eloquent statement, full of keen self-awareness. Lovecraft writes to his mother: "My own remarks were received with a surprising amount of applause, which naturally gratified me immensely."[27]

Lovecraft, still largely a United man, found himself greatly outnumbered by Nationalites at the conference; so he kept closely in the company of Winifred Jackson and Mrs S. Lilian McMullen (Lilian Middleton) as a "compact minority of purely United enthusiasts."[28] His skill in conversational repartee—which would reach its height at gatherings of the Kalem Club in New York in 1924–26—was beginning to emerge. When Laurie A. Sawyer, a devoted Nationalite, pointed out that her association was older and larger, Lovecraft produced a biological analogy: just as the dinosaur was older and larger than man, so was it also slower and duller!

After the banquet Lovecraft was to give a set speech on the designated subject, "The Best Poet." He reports not reading it verbatim from the manuscript but instead making a number of extemporaneous asides which "evoked fairly thunderous applause."[29] Lovecraft does not specify the content of this speech, but it may possibly be the essay published in the March 1921 *United Amateur* as "Winifred Virginia Jackson: A 'Different' Poetess." This is, however, only a conjecture.

Afterward Lovecraft engaged in various discussion—mostly with W. Paul Cook and George Julian Houtain—but declined an invitation to sing, even though he had apparently done so at the September 1920 gathering.[30] So Lovecraft's days as a plaintive tenor were not wholly over! He caught a late train home, but because of an accident to a previous train did not reach 598 Angell Street until 3.30 A.M.

A month later Lovecraft returned to Boston for a St Patrick's Day gathering of amateurs on March 10.[31] This took place at 20 Webster Street. Members were seated in a circle in the parlour, and literary contributions were recited in sequence. Lovecraft on this occasion read the story "The Moon-Bog," written expressly for the occasion; it received abundant applause, but did not win the prize. In the general discussion that followed, Lovecraft got into a philosophical discussion with a new recruit, Dr Joseph Homer (listed in the UAPA membership lists as living in Roxbury); this was not an argumentative debate, since Lovecraft and Homer saw things pretty much eye to eye, but it "drew about us rather a large circle of wide-eyed listeners; two or three of whom may have understood some of the words we used."[32]

Lovecraft was the only out-of-town guest at the gathering, and was to stay overnight; so that the discussion proceeded far into the night. He stayed up till 1.30 A.M. talking with Winifred Jackson and Edith Miniter, then retired to a guest room. The next day (Friday the 11th) was spent largely in varied discussions and in Lovecraft's playing with the household cat, named Tat; ordinarily a shy creature, it deigned to be picked up by Lovecraft and sat purring in his lap. Lovecraft again caught a late train, but this time there were no mishaps and he returned home by 1.30 A.M.

Lovecraft was planning yet another trip in early June, this time to New Hampshire to visit Myrta Alice Little in Hampstead, near Westville (just over the Massachusetts border, a few miles north of Haverhill). I am not sure how Lovecraft got in touch with Miss Little; she had been a member since at least September 1920, and she may have been a friend of Charles W. ("Tryout") Smith of Haverhill, whom Lovecraft had known at least by correspondence since 1917. Lovecraft reports that Little was a former college professor who was now attempting to be a professional writer.[33] In spite of the length of the proposed trip, he wished to stay only one night, since he had felt very tired on the second days of his two overnight stops in Boston (July 1920 and March 1921). He planned therefore to visit Little on June 8, stay overnight, and then move on to Boston to attend a Hub Club meeting in Boston on the 9th. This would have been only the fourth state he had set foot in—Rhode Island and Massachusetts in 1890, Connecticut in 1903 (a visit about which we know nothing), and now New Hampshire. But Lovecraft's one surviving letter to Little, written on May 17, 1921,[34] was written only a week before the most traumatic event of his entire life up to this point: the death of his mother on May 24. How this happened, and how Lovecraft dealt with it, I shall examine in a later chapter.

In "A Confession of Unfaith" Lovecraft suggests that the immediate postwar period led to the solidification of his philosophical thought: "The Peace Conference, Friedrich Nietzsche, Samuel Butler (the modern), H. L. Mencken, and other influences have perfected my cynicism; a quality which grows more intense as the advent of middle life removes the blind prejudice whereby youth clings to the vapid 'all's right with the world' hallucination from sheer force of desire to have it so." These "influences" are certainly a heterogeneous lot, and they seem primarily influential in Lovecraft's ethical, political, and social philosophy. What he does not state here are what appear to be the two central influences on his metaphysical thought of the time—Ernst Haeckel's *The Riddle of the Universe* (1899; English translation 1900) and Hugh Elliot's *Modern Science and Materialism* (1919). This is by no means to say that these two volumes alone shaped Lovecraft's metaphysics, which in many important particulars can be traced back to the Presocratics, Epicurus, and nineteenth-century science; but these volumes, read apparently in 1918–19, helped to give direction to his views for several years to come, until new influences would compel him to modify his outlook significantly.

It cannot be said that Lovecraft chose especially eminent figures as the immediate sources for his metaphysics. Ernst Haeckel (1834–1919) was, indeed, a highly noted biologist, zoologist, and anthropologist, and with Thomas Henry Huxley was one of the leading proponents of Darwin's theory of evolution. Lovecraft also read his *The Evolution of Man* (1903; a translation of *Anthropogenie,* 1874). *The Riddle of the Universe* (a translation of *Die Welträthsel*) is the summation of nineteenth-century thought on biology and physics, but the biological section is much sounder than the physical section, which was significantly vitiated only half a decade later by the Einstein theory. Haeckel is, perhaps justifiably, no longer held in much esteem as a pure philosopher. The English writer Hugh Elliot (1881–1930) was never held in much esteem as a philosopher, since he was merely a populariser of the subject and not a pioneer in any capacity; he wrote a few other books, including *Modern Science and the Illusions of Professor Bergson* (1912) and *Herbert Spencer* (1917). I cannot find any evidence that Lovecraft read any other work of his except *Modern Science and Materialism,* but this book encapsulated the doctrine of pure materialism ably enough to give him a clear foundation for his metaphysics.

Elliot lays down three main principles of mechanistic materialism:

> 1. The uniformity of law.
>
> 2. The denial of teleology.
>
> 3. The denial of any form of existence other than those envisaged by physics and chemistry, that is to say, other existences that have some kind of palpable material characteristics and qualities.[35]

Lovecraft espoused all these tenets to the end of his life, feeling that even the revolutionary findings of relativity and quantum theory did not upset them in essence. Let us consider each of these principles in greater detail.

1) The uniformity of law means that the sequence of cause and effect is constant throughout the universe, from the smallest sub-atomic particle to the largest quasar or nebula. This is the "mechanistic" part of mechanistic materialism—the

universe is a mechanism that runs by fixed laws of Nature. It is not necessary for us to know all these laws—indeed, according to most materialists it is not even possible for us to do so—but it is theoretically conceivable. But what Elliot and many other nineteenth-century materialists ignored—or, more likely, were careful to brush under the rug—is that the uniformity of law is not a datum of physics but (as Hume was the first to suggest) an inference from all the accumulated data of physics. Before the introduction of quantum theory, there never had been discovered any genuine violations of causality, as physics, chemistry, and biology were explaining with ever-increasing thoroughness the purely mechanical activity of all entity. Even after quantum theory it is possible to "save causality" after a fashion.

2) The denial of teleology generally refers to the denial that the cosmos *as a whole* is progressing in some direction, especially—as in religious metaphysics—under the direction of a deity. The more restricted notion that the human race is evolving toward some (presumably better) state of existence is not a purely metaphysical conception, even in its religious guise, for ethical and political considerations can enter into it; but as propounded by most religious or quasi-religious thinkers, the notion refers to the divine guidance of mankind to a more exalted spiritual state.

3) Elliot's formulation of this principle is a little unfortunate, since it is exactly the assertion of religionists and spiritualists that there are "other existences" which do *not* have "palpable material characteristics"—i.e., soul or spirit. Nevertheless, denial of spirit—or any non-material entity—is really the cardinal tenet and defining quality of materialism. It is conceivable to reject the first two of Elliot's principles (most modern physicists would, at least in theory, reject the first, and several eighteenth-century *philosophes* denied the second, in that they asserted the ultimate perfectibility of the human race) and still remain a materialist; but the third cannot be so rejected.

Mechanistic materialism as a philosophy, of course, goes back to the Presocratics, specifically Leucippus and Democritus, the co-founders of atomism and very strong proponents of determinism. Epicurus followed Democritus in metaphysics but rejected him in ethics, at least insofar as he espoused free will, something that a rigid adherence to the "uniformity of law" principle renders theoretically impossible. The Roman poet Lucretius did no more than versify Epicurus' philosophy, although he did so with breathtaking panache, and in so doing helped to introduce Epicurean principles to the Roman world and, ultimately, to the Renaissance.

Lovecraft displays considerable familiarity with all these ancient thinkers, but I am still unclear how he gained this information. Leucippus, Democritus, and Epicurus exist only in fragments. The remains of the first two were collected in Hermann Diels's landmark compilation, *Die Fragmente der Vorsokratiker* (1903), but Lovecraft's Greek was never good enough to enable him to pore through this work; Epicurus' fragments were not definitively collected until Cyril Bailey's edition of 1926, long after Lovecraft was citing him as an influence. Perhaps he read (in translation) Diogenes Laertius' *Lives of the Philosophers,* which offer sound enough accounts of these philosophers' views, although they tend to be chatty, biographical, and at times unreliable. Lovecraft certainly read Lucretius in Latin: he owned Jacob Bernays's Teubner edition of 1879, and in 1927 he actually recited a line of Lucretius in a dream. Even handbooks on ancient philosophy were not common in Lovecraft's day, but one has to assume that he read some such at a relatively early stage—perhaps during his hermitry of 1908–13. He owned Fénélon's *Lives of the Ancient Philosophers* in an 1824 English translation, and this is as good a source as any.

Among modern thinkers materialism made considerable headway in the seventeenth (Hobbes), eighteenth (Helvétius, La Mettrie, d'Holbach), and nineteenth centuries, in part through the rediscovery of the ancient materialists and much more importantly through increasing advances in science. It is, however, a myth that Lovecraft was in any significant way influenced by eighteenth-century philosophy. Although he was very much influenced by the (English) literature of the period, he shows little familiarity with the great thinkers of the age, not even with the *philosophes* whom he would have found congenial. He tends to rattle off names such as "La Mettrie, Diderot, Helvetius, Hume, & dozens of others . . . in the supremely rational 18th century,"[36] but with little suggestion that he has genuinely absorbed these philosophers.

In fact, Lovecraft's chief philosophical influences are all from the nineteenth century—Darwin, Huxley, Haeckel, and others who by their pioneering work in biology, chemistry, and physics systematically brought more and more phenomena under the realm of the known and the natural. There is nothing to criticise in all this—Lovecraft, as a creative artist, had no need to be an encyclopaedia on the history of philosophy, and his philosophical mentors were, on the whole, about as sound as one could want for the type of outlook he came to evolve.

Let us return to Elliot's three principles and see where Lovecraft stands in relation to them. The first—the uniformity of law—had by Lovecraft's day become such an axiom of science that he accepted it as a matter of course; indeed, it was because he so firmly accepted it—and made it the foundation not merely of his metaphysics but of certain features of his ethics and even aesthetics—that he had so much difficulty coming to terms with quantum theory. Nevertheless, he did accept Elliot's notion that human beings can never know all the "laws" of Nature because of the inescapable limitations of our senses. Elliot writes provocatively:

> Let us first ask why it is that all past efforts to solve ultimate riddles have failed, and why it is that they must continue to fail. It is, in the first place, due to the fact that all knowledge is based on sense-impressions, and cannot, therefore, go beyond what the senses can perceive. Men have five or six different senses only, and

> these are all founded on the one original sense of touch. . . . Now, supposing that we happened to have a thousand senses instead of five, it is clear that our conceptions of the Universe would be extremely different from what it now is. We cannot assume that the Universe has only five qualities because we have only five senses. We must assume, on the contrary, that the number of its qualities may be infinite, and that the more senses we had, the more we should discover about it. (2–3)

I shall return to this staggering conception later; it is one that Lovecraft clearly found very stirring to his imagination, and it led Elliot himself to write with unwonted cynicism, "Our achievements are like the scratchings of a field-mouse on the side of a mountain" (27). Lovecraft, in any case, echoes Elliot when he states in the *In Defence of Dagon* essays of 1921: "Beyond a certain limit knowledge may be impossible to acquire with man's present sensory and intellectual equipment." This seems to leave open the possibility of some future development of humanity's sensory and intellectual equipment, but Lovecraft probably did not intend such an implication; in any case, epistemology was the weakest area of his philosophical thought, simply because he did not pay much attention to it or felt it needed much attention.

It is on Elliot's second principle—the denial of teleology—that Lovecraft felt most passionate. His cosmicism, engendered by his astronomical studies, had relegated the entire history of the human race to an inessential nanosecond in the realm of infinite space and time; and any suggestion—whether in metaphysics or in ethics—that humanity might conceivably have some *cosmic* (as opposed to local) importance caused him to unleash all his rhetorical weapons with a vengeance. One of the theories he toyed with in his battle against teleology was Nietzsche's eternal recurrence—the idea that, given the infinity of space, time, and matter, all entities and events in the universe are bound to recur an infinite number of times. Nietzsche, like Lovecraft, used this argument against religious conceptions of the universe as divinely created for the human race. As early as 1918—perhaps even before he had read Nietzsche—Lovecraft wrote: "I am inclined to think that all entity evolves in cycles—that sooner or later everything occurs practically all over again."[37] In *In Defence of Dagon* he is a little more cautious:

> As to the origin of a supposed deity—if one *always existed* and *always will exist,* how can he be developing creation from one definite state to another? Nothing but a *cycle* is in any case conceivable—a cycle or an infinite rearrangement, if that be a tenable thought. Nietzsche saw this when he spoke of the *ewigen Wiederkunft.* In absolute eternity there is neither starting-point nor destination.

Gradually, however, Lovecraft was forced to give up the notion of eternal recurrence and replace it with the more scientifically plausible notion of entropy—the eventual degradation of all the energy of the cosmos to a state of mere radiant heat. Here he follows Elliot over Haeckel, who had denied entropy because he was so wedded to the conception of the eternity of the cosmos that he could not envision a time when all matter might be obliterated. Elliot counters:

> If transformations of matter and energy are entirely reversible, taking place with equal facility in any direction, then the Universe might be regarded as a permanent existence, in more or less its present form. . . . [But] transformations do *not* take place equally readily in all directions; they tend very unmistakably towards what may be called a degradation of matter and energy. The Universe is running down; and, theoretically at least, a time may be imagined when it will have run down altogether, becoming still and "lifeless." (61)

As early as 1915 Lovecraft postulated a similar conception in one of his astronomy articles: "A vast, sepulchral universe of unbroken midnight gloom and perpetual arctic frigidity, through which will roll dark, cold suns with their hordes of dead, frozen planets, on which will lie the dust of those unhappy mortals who will have perished as their dominant stars faded from their skies. Such is the depressing picture of a future too remote for calculation" ("Clusters and Nebulae," Part II, *Asheville Gazette-News,* 6 April 1915). This is in fact not entropy, since there would be no suns or planets at all; but the idea is analogous. We shall see it recur after a fashion in some of his stories, where he imagines the eventual cooling of the sun and the extinction of all life on this planet and throughout the solar system. It is not entirely certain that Lovecraft actually embraced entropy, for he too was very wedded to the notion of the eternity and infinity of the universe—he required these conceptions as the means to deflate human self-importance—and this is why he regarded Einstein's notion of curved space with a certain unease.

Another way in which Lovecraft differed from Haeckel is in the latter's wild extension of a very sound principle—Darwin's theory of evolution—to cosmic proportions. Like Lovecraft, Haeckel found in Darwin a great weapon against terrestrial teleology:

> Darwin was the first to point out that the "struggle for life" is the unconscious regulator which controls the reciprocal action of heredity and adaptation in the gradual transformation of species; it is the great "selective divinity" which, by a purely "natural choice," without preconceived design, creates new forms, just as selective man creates new types by an 'artificial choice" with a definite design. That gave us the solution of the great philosophical problem: "How can purposive contrivances be produced by purely mechanical processes without design?" . . . Thus have we got rid of the transcendental "design" of the teleological philosophy of the schools, which was the greatest obstacle to the growth of a rational and monistic conception of nature.[38]

The refutation of the religious "argument from design"—the notion that the entities of the world are so well adapted to their environments that they must have been produced by a deity—far antedates Voltaire's *Candide;* the Epicureans very powerfully pointed to the imperfections of the world in opposition to this conception. But the scientific proof had to wait till Darwin. But Haeckel then extravagantly assumes that the principle of evolution is somehow inherent in the cosmos at large: "It is true that there were philosophers who spoke of the evolution of things a thousand years ago; but the recognition that such a law dominates the entire universe, and that the world is nothing else than an eternal "evolution of substance," is a fruit of the nineteenth century" (4). Lovecraft, amusingly enough, refutes this argument soundly when, in *In Defence of Dagon,* he attacks a Mr Wickenden who was putting forth a somewhat analogous religious argument:

> [Wickenden] sees a process of evolution in operation at one particular cosmic moment in one particular point in space; and at once assumes gratuitously that *all the cosmos* is evolving steadily *in one direction* toward a fixed goal. Moreover, he *feels* that it all must amount to something—he calls it a thing of "heroism and splendour"! So when it is shewn that life on our world will (relatively) soon be extinct through the cooling of the sun; that space is full of such worlds which have died; that human life and the solar system itself are the merest *novelties* in an eternal cosmos; and that all indications point to a gradual breaking down of both matter and energy which will eventually nullify the results of evolution in any particular corner of space; when these things are shewn Mr. Wickenden recoils, and . . . cries out that it's all nonsense—it just *can't* be so!! But what of the actual probability, apart from man's futile wishes? If we cannot prove that the universe means *nothing,* how can we prove that it means *anything*—what right have we to invent a notion of purpose in the utter absence of evidence?

Elliot's third principle—denial of spirit—was scarcely less thoroughly espoused by Lovecraft. It is here that Elliot, Haeckel, and Lovecraft (and for that matter Nietzsche) are all in accord. At one point in *The Riddle of the Universe* (204–5) Haeckel posits a six-stage argument to demolish the notion of an immaterial soul, using physiological, histological, experimental, pathological, ontogenic, and phylogenetic arguments. Lovecraft follows Haeckel's argument closely in *In Defence of Dagon:*

> One might ask, to the confounding of those who aver that men have "souls" whilst beasts have not, . . . just how the evolving organism began to acquire "spirit" after it crossed the boundary betwixt advanced ape and primitive human? It is rather hard to believe in "soul" when one has not a jot of evidence for its existence; when all the psychic life of man is demonstrated to be precisely analogous to that of other animals—presumably "soulless". But all this is too childish. When we investigate both ontogeny and phylogeny we find that man had both individually and racially evolved from the unicellular condition. . . . This development occurs both prenatally and post-natally in the individual, and can be followed with much exactitude. In the species, we can follow it hardly less exactly by means of comparative anatomy and biology.

It is clear that Lovecraft is heavily reliant on the theory of evolution in this argument. I am not certain whether Lovecraft actually read Darwin: his books are not found in Lovecraft's library (but then, neither are Elliot's, Haeckel's, or Nietzsche's), and although Lovecraft does mention *The Origin of Species* and *The Descent of Man* in the *In Defence of Dagon* essays, I cannot sense any genuine familiarity with these works. In all likelihood, he absorbed evolution chiefly from Thomas Henry Huxley and Haeckel.

It is somewhat interesting to note that both Elliot and Haeckel share, to some degree, Lovecraft's sense of cosmic insignificance. Haeckel branded as "anthropism" the mistaken idea that the human race had some sort of cosmic importance: "I designate by this term 'that powerful and world-wide group of erroneous opinions which opposes the human organism to the whole of the rest of nature, and represents it to be the preordained end of the organic creation, an entity essentially distinct from it, a godlike being'" (11; Haeckel is quoting an earlier work of his own). Elliot is no less explicit:

> Just as the savage supposes the whole Universe to be specially created for the benefit of himself or his tribe; just as the more civilised man supposes the Universe to be specially subservient to the human race; so in the most recondite problems of philosophy our arguments tend to be vitiated by infusion of the subjective element, in such a way that we read into external nature the human interests and egocentric habits which belong to our own minds. (167)

This passage is remarkable in that Lovecraft provided an anticipation of it in 1916: "Our philosophy is all childishly *subjective*—we imagine that the welfare of our race is the paramount consideration, when as a matter of fact the very existence of the race may be an obstacle to the predestined course of the aggregated universes of infinity!"[39] It is no wonder that Elliot's book was so stimulating for him: it may have seemed to Lovecraft that he had written it himself.

Lovecraft sees this "anthropism" working in most religious conceptions of the universe, and he devastates it in an argument on the subject with Maurice W. Moe in 1918:

> What am I? What is the nature of the energy about me, and how does it affect me? So far I have seen nothing which could possibly give me the notion that cosmic force is the manifestation of a mind and will like my own infinitely magnified; a potent and purposeful consciousness which deals individually and directly with the miserable denizens of a wretched little flyspeck on the back door of a microscopic universe, and which singles this putrid excrescence out as the one spot whereto to send an onlie-begotten Son, whose mission is to redeem these accursed flyspeck-inhabiting lice which we call human beings—bah!! Pardon the "bah!" I feel several "bahs!", but out of courtesy I say only one. But it is all so very childish. I cannot help taking exception to a philosophy which would force this rubbish down my throat.[40]

In all honesty, there is not much actual *reasoning* in this passage, and Lovecraft was aware of it; and of course he intentionally prejudices his account by all manner of pejorative designations ("miserable denizens," "putrid excrescence," etc.). If any argument can be derived from this, it is the argument from probability. And yet, Lovecraft knew that there was no other way to prove a negative proposition (i.e., the proposition that God does not exist). It is worth quoting a much later letter here, since its basic philosophic thrust is the same:

> I certainly can't see any sensible position to assume aside from that of *complete scepticism tempered by a leaning toward that which existing evidence makes most probable.* All I say is that I think it is *damned unlikely* that anything like a central cosmic will, a spirit world, or an eternal survival of personality exist. They are the most preposterous and unjustified of all the guesses which can be made about the universe, and I am not enough of a hair-splitter to pretend that I don't regard them as arrant and negligible moonshine. In theory I am an *agnostic,* but pending the appearance of rational evidence I must be classed, practically and provisionally, as an *atheist.* The chances of theism's truth being to my mind so microscopically small, I would be a pedant and a hypocrite to call myself anything else.[41]

One of the greatest weapons Lovecraft found in his battle against religious metaphysics (and, for that matter, ethics) was anthropology. The anthropological thought of the later nineteenth century had, in Lovecraft's mind, so convincingly accounted for the natural *origin* of religious belief that no further explanation was required for its tenacious hold on human beings. He writes in the *In Defence of Dagon* essays: "This matter of the explanation of 'spiritual' feelings is really the most important of all materialistic arguments; since the explanations are not only overwhelmingly forcible, but so adequate as to shew that man could not possibly have developed without acquiring just such false impressions." This conception is elaborated at length in the essay "Idealism and Materialism—A Reflection," which was published in an issue of the *National Amateur* dated July 1919. This may not mean, however, that the essay was written at this time or earlier; for this issue (printed by W. Paul Cook) was held up for some two years, and seems to have come out shortly after the NAPA election in the summer of 1921.[42] In any event, Lovecraft's essay is a sort of updated "natural history of religion":

> Since to the untutored mind the conception of impersonal action is impossible, every natural phenomenon was invested with purpose and personality. If lightning struck the earth, it was wilfully hurled by an unseen being in the sky. If a river flowed toward the sea, it was because some unseen being wilfully propelled it. And since men understood no sources of action but themselves, these unseen creatures of imagination were endowed with human forms, despite their more than human powers. So rose the awesome race of anthropomorphic gods, destined to exert so long a sway over their creators.

This notion—that primitive human beings were, to put it crudely, merely bad philosophers who misapprehended the true nature of phenomena—was evolved by a number of important anthropologists of the later nineteenth century. I would like to believe that Lovecraft read Edward Burnett Tylor's *Primitive Culture* (1871), a landmark work in its field that is still of value, but can find no evidence that he ever did so. Tylor is cited as one of the anthropological authorities cited by Henry Wentworth Akeley in "The Whisperer in Darkness" (1930), and for some data in his stories Lovecraft pillaged several of Tylor's entries in the 9th edition of the *Encyclopaedia Britannica,* which he owned; but that is all. We are on more certain ground if we contend that Lovecraft's anthropology of religion comes from John Fiske's *Myths and Myth-Makers* (1872) and Sir James George Frazer's *The Golden Bough* (1890f.), which he clearly did read (although Frazer perhaps not this early). Fiske's book was in his library. Like Haeckel, John Fiske (1842–1901) has suffered somewhat of a decline in esteem, but in his day he was highly noted as an anthropologist, philosopher, and (in his later years) historian. Lovecraft also owned his *American Political Ideals Viewed from the Standpoint of Universal History* (1885) and *The Beginnings of New England; or, The Puritan Theocracy in Its Relation to Civil and Religious Liberty* (1889).

Here is Fiske on the subject of the origin of religion:

> The same mighty power of imagination which now, restrained and guided by scientific principles, leads us to discoveries and inventions, must have wildly run riot in mythologic fictions whereby to explain the phenomena of nature. Knowing nothing whatever of physical forces, of the blind steadiness with which a given effect invariably follows its cause, the men of primeval antiquity could interpret the actions of nature only after the analogy of their own actions. The only force they knew was the force of which they were directly conscious,—the force of will. Accordingly, they imagined all the outward world to be endowed with volition, and to be directed by it. They personified everything,—sky, clouds, thunder, sun, moon, ocean, earthquake, whirlwind.[43]

Fiske goes on to state that dreams and the fear of death led to the ideas of an immaterial soul that survives the body, and Lovecraft follows him in many essays and letters. And once religion became established in early civilised communities, it was perpetuated by the systematic brainwashing of the young into conventional religious belief. (There is relatively little in Lovecraft of Nietzsche's idea that religion is perpetuated by cynical clerics who wish to maintain their power and standing in their communities.) Curiously, in spite of Lovecraft's awareness of the pervasiveness of religious belief, in his early years he occasionally expressed sanguine beliefs about its downfall:

> The progress of science will eventually, I believe . . . put an end to spiritualism amongst the educated and even the half-educated. . . . A mere knowledge of the

> approximate dimensions of the visible universe is enough to destroy forever the notion of a personal godhead.[44]
>
> Dr. Sigmund Freud of Vienna, whose system of psycho-analysis I have begun to investigate, will probably prove the end of idealistic thought.[45]

This is one of the many occasions where Lovecraft places an exaggerated emphasis on the power of the rational mind to shape beliefs and to govern actions; and in a somewhat different way the notion enters into his fiction as well. Somewhat later Lovecraft came to a different and more seasoned view of religious belief:

> My contention is that religion is still useful amongst the herd—that it helps their orderly conduct as nothing else could, and that it gives them an emotional satisfaction they could not get elsewhere. I don't say that it does either of these things as well as it used to do, but I do say that I believe nothing else could do them so well even now. The crude human animal is ineradicably superstitious, and there is every biological and historical reason why he should be. An irreligious barbarian is a scientific impossibility. Rationalistic conceptions of the universe involve a type of mental victory over hereditary emotion quite impossible to the undeveloped and uneducated intellect. Agnosticism and atheism mean nothing to a peasant or workman. Mystic and teleological personification of natural forces is in his bone and blood—he cannot envisage the cosmos (i.e., the earth, the only cosmos he grasps) apart form them. Take away his Christian god and saints, and he will worship something else.[46]

Taking the cynicism of this passage into account, Lovecraft certainly seems to be pretty much on target here; what he would say about the recrudescence of very ignorant fundamentalist belief in the last three decades it is difficult to imagine. And yet, Lovecraft was perhaps not so wrong in thinking that a cleavage between the agnostic intelligentsia and the religious "herd" was occurring in his day and would continue to occur as science continued to advance. One historian, James Turner, has traced the rise of agnosticism in America after the Civil War to the weakening of three central arguments for religious belief: 1) Scripture (whose claim to be the "word of God" was thrown in doubt by the "higher criticism" of the middle nineteenth century, which found disturbing inconsistencies throughout the Old and New Testaments); 2) the argument from design (demolished by Darwin); and 3) the "hearts" of human beings (explained by psychology and anthropology).[47] Lovecraft, in the *In Defence of Dagon* essays, sympathetically if somewhat condescendingly discusses an anonymous article, "Whither?," published in the *Atlantic Monthly* for March 1915, which lamented the decline of religious belief:

> There is no real argument of importance in the harangue of the anonymous author, but the atmosphere of sorrow at the passing of the old illusions makes the whole complaint an absorbing human document. Certainly, there is much in the

> modern advance of knowledge which must of necessity shock and bewilder the mind accustomed to uncritical tradition. That the old illusions cheered and stimulated the average person to a more or less considerable degree cannot be denied—the dream-world of our grandsires was undoubtedly a sort of artificial paradise for mediocrity. . . . A phase of primitive allegory has retreated into the past, and we must make the best of what we cannot help. If we tried to believe now we should feel the sham, and despise ourselves for it—we simply know better, like the small boy deprived of "Santa Claus".

I want at last to return to those curious statements made in "A Confession of Unfaith," wherein Lovecraft attests to his "cynical materialism" and his "pessimistic cosmic views," for they will provide a transition to a study of Lovecraft's early ethics. Why cynical? why pessimistic? What is there in materialism or cosmicism that could lead to such an ethical stance? Well, as a matter of pure logic, nothing: materialism and cosmicism, as metaphysical principles, have *no* direct ethical corollaries, and it therefore becomes our task to ascertain how and why Lovecraft felt that they did. Let us consider some statements of the 1919–20 period:

> There is a real restfulness in the scientific conviction that nothing matters very much; that the only legitimate aim of humanity is to minimise acute suffering for the majority, and to derive whatever satisfaction is derivable from the exercise of the mind in the pursuit of truth.[48]

> The secret of true contentment . . . lies in the achievement of a *cosmical* point of view.[49]

Once again it must be emphasised that neither of these ethical precepts is a direct corollary of cosmicism; they are, rather, varying *psychological* responses to Lovecraft's awareness of the cosmic insignificance of humanity in a boundless universe. In effect, they are somewhat bizarre conjoinings of Epicureanism and Schopenhauerianism. Just prior to the utterance of the second statement above, Lovecraft has written: "To enjoy tranquillity, and to promote tranquillity in others, is the most enduring of delights. Such was the doctrine of Epicurus, the leading ethical philosopher of the world." But Lovecraft surrounds this utterance with the following:

> One should come to realise that all life is merely a comedy of vain desire, wherein those who strive are the clowns, and those who calmly and dispassionately watch are the fortunate ones who can laugh at the acts of the strivers. The utter emptiness of all the recognised goals of human endeavour is to the detached spectator deliciously apparent—the tomb yawns and grins so ironically! . . . If one's interest in life wanes, let him turn to the succour of others in a like plight, and some grounds for interest will be observed to return.

This is remarkably similar to a passage in Arthur Schopenhauer's *Studies in Pessimism,* virtually the only volume of Schopenhauer's that Lovecraft appears to have read: "The best consolation in misfortune or affliction of any kind will be the thought of other people who are in a still worse plight than yourself; and this is a form of consolation open to every one. But what an awful fate this means for mankind as a whole!"[50]

A later passage in this same letter of Lovecraft's is one of his most poignant early ethical remarks, and here he explicitly ties Epicureanism, Schopenhauerianism, and cosmicism into a neat (if not logically defensible) whole:

> About the time I joined the United I was none too fond of existence. I was 23 years of age, and realised that my infirmities would withhold me from success in the world at large. Feeling like a cipher, I felt I might as well be erased. But later I realised that even success is empty. Failure though I be, I shall reach a level with the greatest—and the smallest—in the damp earth or on the final pyre. And I saw that in the interim trivialities are not to be despised. Success is a relative thing—and the victory of a boy at marbles is equal to the victory of an Octavius at Actium when measured by the scale of cosmic infinity. So I turned to observe other mediocre and handicapped persons about me, and found pleasure in increasing the happiness of those who could be helped by such encouraging words or critical services as I am capable of furnishing. That I have been able to cheer here and there an aged man, an infirm old lady, a dull youth, or a person deprived by circumstances of education, affords to me a sense of being not altogether useless, which almost forms a substitute for the real success I shall never know. What matter if none hear of my labours, or if those labours touch only the afflicted and mediocre? Surely it is well that the happiness of the unfortunate be made as great as possible; and he who is kind, helpful, and patient with his fellow-sufferers, adds as truly to the world's combined fund of tranquillity as he who, with greater endowments, promotes the birth of empires, or advances the knowledge of civilisation and mankind.

Touching as this is, I wonder how it is to be reconciled with statements made in 1921 ("I expect nothing of man, and disown the race. . . . It is better to laugh at man from outside the universe, than to weep for him within"[51]) or 1923 ("Honestly, my hatred of the human animal mounts by leaps and bounds the more I see of the damned vermin, and the more I see exemplified the workings of their spiteful, shabby, and sadistic psychological processes"[52]). But perhaps there is no real contradiction: Lovecraft, without being a genuine pessimist or misanthrope, was never blind to the follies and contemptibilities of humanity. But the long quotation above may help us to understand why Lovecraft initially derived pessimism from cosmicism. His various comments to the contrary notwithstanding, I suspect he did suffer a sort of disillusion when he contemplated the myriad worlds of infinite space; the first reaction may well have been one of exhilaration, but perhaps not much later there came to him the sensation of the utter futility of all human effort in light of the vastness of the cosmos and the inconsequentiality of mankind in it. At a still later stage Lovecraft turned this pessimism to his advantage, and it became a bulwark against the little tragedies of his own existence—his failure to graduate from high school and enter college; his failure to secure a job; his dissatisfaction with the progress of his writing—since these things could be regarded as cosmically unimportant, however large they loomed in his own circumstances. Lovecraft largely abandoned Schopenhauerian pessimism over the next decade or so, evolving instead his notion of "indifferentism"; but this should be treated at a later stage.

I have adduced the influence of Nietzsche on a number of occasions, but it is again not entirely certain which of his works Lovecraft read. As early as 1916, in the "Department of Public Criticism" for June 1916, he makes passing reference to Nietzsche as the "German iconoclast"; but "A Confession of Unfaith" makes clear that Lovecraft read Nietzsche only after the war. The first mention I have found in Lovecraft occurs in September 1919: "With Nietzsche, I have been forced to confess that mankind as a whole has no goal or purpose whatever, but is a mere superfluous speck in the unfathomable vortices of infinity and eternity."[53] So far as I know, Nietzsche never makes this exact utterance anywhere, and it may be Lovecraft's not entirely sound inference from a variety of Nietzsche's works. In a letter of 1921 he makes a pun on Kant's name (cant), which Nietzsche had made (in English) in *Twilight of the Idols* (Poe had also made it in "How to Write a Blackwood Article"). In this same letter Lovecraft continues:

> Lest you fancy that I am making an idol of Nietzsche as others do of Kant, let me state clearly that I do not swallow him whole. His ethical system is a joke—or a poet's dream, which amounts to the same thing. It is in his method, and his account of the basic origin and actual relation of existing ideas and standards, which make him the master figure of the modern age and founder of unvarnished sincerity in philosophical thought.[54]

This is a trifle vague, and I do not know what Lovecraft's comment on Nietzsche's ethical system is meant to suggest. But the second sentence is clearly a reference to several of Nietzsche's works, chiefly *On the Genealogy of Morals,* which strove to find the natural (as opposed to divine or objective) origin of the notions of justice, democracy, and equality in primitive social customs. Lovecraft echoes these ideas in a single sentence of the *In Defence of Dagon* essays ("Then out of the principle of barter comes the illusion of 'justice'") and in his later philosophical thought as well. But Nietzsche's influence on Lovecraft, at least in the short term, seemed chiefly to be manifested in the realm of social and political theory, and I shall examine this elsewhere.

The whole issue of how Lovecraft could offer moral precepts at all, even to himself, in light of his confirmed determinism and denial of free will did not trouble him much, as it has rarely troubled other determinists from Democritus on down. Lovecraft was indeed a determinist, and a very acute one, as he discusses the idea with Rheinhart Kleiner in 1921:

> Determinism—which you call Destiny—rules inexorably; though not exactly in the personal way you seem to fancy. We have no specific destiny against which we can fight—for the fighting would be as much a part of the destiny as the final end. The real fact is simply that every event in the cosmos is caused by the action of antecedent and circumjacent forces, so that whatever we do is unconsciously the inevitable product of Nature rather than of our own volition. If an act correspond with our wish, it is Nature that made the wish, and ensured its fulfilment.[55]

But Lovecraft was aware of the possible conflict between determinism and conventional ethics, as a much later essay, "Some Causes of Self-Immolation" (1931), establishes:

> It was of course recognised by determinists that behind any proximate base must lie the general flux of the universe, be it simple or complex; that is, that in the last analysis each human act can be no less than the inevitable result of every antecedent and circumambient condition in an eternal cosmos. This recognition, however, did not prevent such thinkers from continuing to seek for the more proximate base or bases, and to speculate upon the immediate strings by which human puppets are moved.

Perhaps Lovecraft is trying to have his cake and eat it too, here; but what he wishes to establish is simply that "free will" (in the conventional sense of conscious moral decisions for or against a given course of action) is in most, perhaps all, cases a myth because of those "antecedent and circumambient" conditions that cause a given ethical situation to occur and that cause each individual to make a decision in one way or another.

Curiously enough, Lovecraft once did believe in free will. In "A Confession of Unfaith" he records that among the benefits he derived from philosophical discussion with his fellow amateurs was that "I ceased my literal adherence to Epicurus and Lucretius, and reluctantly dismissed free-will in favour of determinism." This does not tell us *why* Lovecraft relinquished free will, and a letter of 1921 helps only marginally: "As to free-will—like the Epicureans, whose school I followed, I used to believe in it. Now, however, I am forced to admit that there is no room for it. It is fundamentally opposed to all those laws of causality which every phenomenon of Nature confirms and verifies."[56] If this tells us anything, it is that—Lovecraft's remark notwithstanding—he did not yield on free will through discussion with amateurs (unless it was with the Nietzschean Alfred Galpin) but through his absorption of the great trilogy of Nietzsche, Haeckel, and Elliot, who all unite on the issue. Incidentally, when Lovecraft refers to his former "literal" adherence to Epicurean free will, I can hardly believe that he is referring to the bizarre contrivance by which Epicurus (and Lucretius) tried to save free will. Epicurus first unwisely deviated from Democritus by asserting that atoms primordially did not fly in all directions but all fell downward in space; this itself is bad enough, but then—solely in order to salvage free will—he postulated a random "swerve" of atoms that ultimately led to the creation of material objects, and which also in some fashion guaranteed free will. The notion was much ridiculed in antiquity, in spite of what we can now see as a wholly fortuitous similarity to quantum theory. I cannot imagine Lovecraft accepting the swerve: what he terms his "literal adherence" to Epicurus must be merely his provisional acceptance of the principle of free will and not the specifically Epicurean reasoning behind it.

I have referred frequently to the so-called *In Defence of Dagon* essays. This title was devised by R. H. Barlow for a series of three pieces, "The Defence Reopens!" (January 1921), "The Defence Remains Open!" (April 1921), and "Final Words" (September 1921), which Lovecraft sent through the Transatlantic Circulator; it was perhaps the first time when he was compelled to defend his entire metaphysical, ethical, and aesthetic philosophy, and these essays are among his most scintillating and rhetorically effective philosophical writing, far outshining the wooden and pedantic "Idealism and Materialism." Lovecraft's involvement in this group has been much misunderstood, and a detailed examination of it may be in order.

The Transatlantic Circulator has sometimes been taken to be an amateur journal of some kind, but in fact it was a loose organisation of amateur journalists in England and the United States who exchanged stories and poems in manuscript and criticised them. How long the organisation was in existence before Lovecraft's entrance into it in July 1920 is unknown, but it is certainly not correct, as some have believed, that Lovecraft himself organised the group. Indeed, there is nothing to suggest either this nor that the organisation collapsed after Lovecraft's exit from it in September 1921, for new members were entering it at precisely the time Lovecraft was withdrawing.

Also in doubt is the matter of who introduced Lovecraft to the Circulator. The choice would perhaps fall on John Ravenor Bullen, a Canadian amateur and a central figure in the organisation. Bullen is the only one of the known members of the Circulator with whom Lovecraft continued an acquaintance in later life; but did he know Bullen as early as 1920? There is no especial reason to doubt it. Bullen shows up in the UAPA membership list for the first time in July 1920, and it is quite likely that he got in touch with Lovecraft—who had just been elected Official Editor of the UAPA—then or slightly later. Lovecraft published a poem of Bullen's in the July 1923 issue of the *Conservative,* but this issue may have been prepared much earlier; and in 1927 Lovecraft edited and wrote the preface to Bullen's posthumous collection of poems, *White Fire.*

The preserved letters of comment from other members of the Transatlantic Circulator allow us to know precisely the number and dates of the pieces by Lovecraft sent through the organisation. Lovecraft made his debut with "The White

Ship," sent in July 1920; this was followed by two works, "Dagon" and "Old Christmas," sent in November 1920; then followed "The Tree," "Nemesis," and "Psychopompos" in January 1921; "The Nameless City," "To Mistress Sophia Simple, Queen of the Cinema," "On Religion," and "Quinsnicket Park" were submitted in June 1921; and "The Doom That Came to Sarnath," in September 1921, heralded Lovecraft's exit from the group. There must, however, have been at least one original essay, now evidently not extant, sent through the Circulator, as in "The Defence Reopens!" Lovecraft refers to "the Wickenden objections to my philosophical views"; this was presumably sent in November 1920. Indeed, the autograph manuscripts of the three surviving essays may be rough drafts that Lovecraft typed up for distribution through the Circulator. No letters or essays from Wickenden himself survive, so that we have no idea of his identity or location; but letters by several other members, mostly commenting on Lovecraft's stories and poems, are extant, and a number of these are quite acute. Lovecraft revised the final couplet of "Psychopompos" and the poem included in "Polaris" based on criticisms made in the Circulator.

Wickenden was Lovecraft's chief philosophical opponent, and he does not appear to have been a very astute one, for he allows Lovecraft many opportunities to demolish his obviously false and poorly conceived theistic views. If Lovecraft is occasionally a little hard on Wickenden, he never indulges in mere abuse and actually ends up taking Wickenden's views more seriously than they deserve. At one point he makes one of his noblest utterances, as he attempts to free Wickenden from the immortality myth:

> No change of faith can dull the colours and magic of spring, or dampen the native exuberance of perfect health; and the consolations of taste and intellect are infinite. It is easy to remove the mind from harping on the lost illusion of immortality. The disciplined mind fears nothing and craves no sugar-plum at the day's end, but is content to accept life and serve society as best it may. Personally I should not care for immortality in the least. There is nothing better than oblivion, since in oblivion there is no wish unfulfilled. We had it before we were born, yet did not complain. Shall we then whine because we know it will return? It is Elysium enough for me, at any rate.

There is every reason to believe that Lovecraft actually practised the above precept in the subsequent course of his life.

Philosophy was only one of Lovecraft's many concerns in this period. Perhaps more significantly for his future career, he simultaneously began—or attempted to begin—separating himself from amateur activity and turning determinedly to fiction-writing. We can at last study the influence of Lord Dunsany on his fiction, as well as the many other tales of supernatural horror that laid the groundwork for his later, more substantial fiction.

11. Dunsanian Studies (1919–1921 [II])

Edward John Moreton Drax Plunkett (1878–1957) became the eighteenth Lord Dunsany (pronounced Dun-SAY-ny) upon the death of his father in 1899. He could trace his lineage to the twelfth century, but few members of this Anglo-Norman line had shown much aptitude for literature. Dunsany himself did not do so in his early years, spent alternately in various homes in England and in Dunsany Castle in County Meath. He had gone to Eton and Sandhurst, had served in the Boer War, and appeared on his way to occupying an undistinguished place among the Anglo-Irish aristocracy as sportsman, hunter, and socialite. He married Beatrice Villiers, daughter of the Earl of Jersey, in 1904, the year he ran unsuccessfully for Parliament in England on the conservative ticket.

Dunsany had published a mediocre poem, "Rhymes from a Suburb," in the *Pall Mall Gazette* for September 1897 but otherwise gave little indication that he had any literary aspirations. But in 1904 he sat down and wrote *The Gods of Pegāna.* Having no literary reputation, he was forced to pay for its publication with Elkin Mathews of London. Never again, however, would Dunsany have to resort to vanity publishing.

The Gods of Pegāna opens thunderously:

> Before there stood gods upon Olympus, or even Allah was Allah, had wrought and rested Mānā-Yood-Sushāī.
>
> There are in Pegāna—Mung and Sish and Kib, and the maker of all small gods, who is Mānā-Yood-Sushāī. Moreover, we have a faith in Roon and Slid.
>
> And it has been said of old that all things that have been were wrought by the small gods, excepting only Mānā-Yood-Sushāī, who made the gods amd hath thereafter rested.
>
> And none may pray to Mānā-Yood-Sushāī but only to the gods whom he hath made.[1]

This rhythmic prose and cosmic subject-matter, both self-consciously derived from the King James Bible—and, as Dunsany admits in his charming autobiography, *Patches of Sunlight* (1938), from recollections of Greek mythology in school[2]—introduced something unique to literature. The last decades of the nineteenth century had seen such things as the jewelled fairy tales of Oscar Wilde and the prose and verse epics of William Morris; but this was very different. Here was an entire theogony whose principal motivation was not the expression of religious fervour (Dunsany was in all likelihood an atheist) but an instantiation of Oscar Wilde's imperishable dictum: "The artist is the creator of beautiful things."[3] While there are a number of provocative philosophical undercurrents in *The Gods of Pegāna,* as in Dunsany's work as a whole, its main function is merely the evocation of beauty—beauty of language, beauty of conception, beauty of image. Readers and critics alike responded to this rarefied creation of exotic loveliness, with its seamless mixture of naiveté and sophistication, archaism and modernity, sly humour and brooding horror, chilling remoteness and quiet pathos. Generally favourable reviews began to appear—including one by the poet Edward Thomas—and Dunsany's career was launched.

By the time Lovecraft discovered him, Dunsany had published much of the fiction and drama that would gain him fame, even adulation, on both sides of the Atlantic: *Time and the Gods* (1906); *The Sword of Welleran* (1908); *A Dreamer's Tales* (1910); *The Book of Wonder* (1912); *Five Plays* (1914); *Fifty-one Tales* (1915); *The Last Book of Wonder* (1916); *Plays of Gods and Men* (1917). *Tales of Three Hemispheres* would appear at the very end of 1919, marking the definite end of this phase of his work. By this time, however, Dunsany had achieved idolatrous fame in America, thanks in part to the editions of his work published by John W. Luce & Co. in Boston. In 1916 he became the only playwright to have five plays simultaneously produced in New York, as each of the *Five Plays* appeared in a different "little" theatre. His work was appearing in the most sophisticated and highbrow magazines—*Vanity Fair,* the *Smart Set, Harper's,* and (a little later) the *Golden Book.* By 1919 Dunsany would probably have been considered one of the ten greatest living writers in the English-speaking world. Shaw Desmond's article on him in the November 1923 *Bookman,* "Dunsany, Yeats and Shaw: Trinity of Magic," places him ahead of two now canonical figures.

It is difficult to specify in brief compass the principal characteristics of even this early work of Dunsany's, to say nothing of the novels, tales, and plays he wrote during the remaining four decades of his career; but Dunsany himself provides a few clues as to the basic import of all his work in *Patches of Sunlight,* as he recounts how at an early age he saw a hare in a garden: "If ever I have written of Pan, out in the evening, as though I had really seen him, it is mostly a memory of that hare. If I thought that I was a gifted individual whose inspirations came sheer from outside earth and transcended common things, I should not write this book; but I believe that the wildest flights of the fancies of any of us have their homes with Mother Earth . . .[4] Lovecraft would have been taken aback by this utterance, since it was precisely the apparent *remoteness* of Dunsany's realm—a realm of pure fantasy with no connexion with the human world—that initially captivated him; and, strangely enough, Lovecraft came to express dissatisfaction at what he thought was the "dilution" of this otherworldliness in Dunsany's later work, when in fact his own creative writing of the 1920s and 1930s was on a largely similar path to Dunsany's in its greater topographical realism and evocation of the natural world.

But many readers can be excused for seeing the early Dunsany in this light, since the pure exoticism and lack of any significant reference to the "real" world in his early volumes appeared to signal it as virtually the creation of some non-human imagination. The realm of Pegāna (which is featured in *The Gods of Pegāna* and *Time and the Gods,* and in those volumes only) is wholly distinct from the "real" world; the first sentence of *The Gods of Pegāna* seems to refer to the *temporal* priority of Dunsany's God Mānā-Yood-Sushāī to the Graeco-Roman or Islamic gods, but beyond this citation there is no allusion to the "real" world at all. Dunsany himself, in his autobiography, remarks that his early tales were written "as though I were an inhabitant of an entirely different planet,"[5] something Lovecraft no doubt found very captivating, given his own cosmicism; but Dunsany could not keep this up for long, and already by *The Sword of Welleran* the real world has entered, as it would continue increasingly to do in his later writing. Indeed, it could be said that the uneasy mingling of the real and the unreal in *The Sword of Welleran* and *A Dreamer's Tales* produces some of the most distinctive work in Dunsany's entire canon.

It should, however, not be thought that Dunsany's early work is uniform either in import or in quality. By the time *A Dreamer's Tales* was published, he seems to have reached a certain exhaustion of imagination. Most of the tales in *The Book of Wonder* were written around pictures drawn by Sidney H. Sime, who had illustrated most of Dunsany's earlier volumes; and these tales show a regrettable tendency toward self-parody and ponderously owlish humour. The result is a sort of snickering sarcasm and cheap satire sadly out of keeping with the high seriousness of his early work. Lovecraft, in a late letter, put his finger directly on the problem:

> As he gained in age and sophistication, he lost in freshness and simplicity. He was ashamed to be uncritically naive, and began to step aside from his tales and visibly smile at them even as they unfolded. Instead of remaining what the true fantaisiste must be—a child in a child's world of dream—he became anxious to shew that he was really an adult good-naturedly pretending to be a child in a child's world. This hardening-up began to shew, I think, in *The Book of Wonder* . . .[6]

Lovecraft is exactly right on the result but not, I think, on the cause: it was not, certainly, that Dunsany was "uncritically naive" in his early work, for that work clearly displays his sophisticated awareness of the symbolic function of fantasy for the conveying of philosophical conceptions; it is simply that now Dunsany no longer wished to preserve the *illusion* of naiveté as he had done in the *Gods of Pegāna* period. *The Last Book of Wonder,* some of which was written during the early stages of the war, is a little more in line with his earlier manner, but *Tales of Three Hemispheres* is easily his weakest collection, containing many ephemeral and insignificant items. It was just as well that, after a few years, Dunsany found a new direction with his early novels.

An examination of Dunsany's early tales and plays reveals many thematic and philosophical similarities with Lovecraft: cosmicism (largely restricted to *The Gods of Pegāna*); the exaltation of Nature; hostility to industrialism; the power of dream to transform the mundane world into a realm of gorgeously exotic beauty; the awesome role of Time in human and divine affairs; and, of course, the evocative use of language. It is scarcely to be wondered at that Lovecraft felt for a time that Dunsany had said all he had wished to say in a given literary and philosophical direction.

Lovecraft could hardly have been unaware of Dunsany's reputation. He admits to knowing of him well before he read him in 1919, but he had passed him off as a writer of whimsical, benign fantasy of the J. M. Barrie sort. The first work he read was not Dunsany's own first volume, *The Gods of Pegāna,* but *A Dreamer's Tales,* which may well be his best single short story collection in its diversity of contents and its several powerful tales of horror ("Poor Old Bill," "The Unhappy Body," "Bethmoora"). Lovecraft admits: "The book had been recommended to me by one whose judgment I did not highly esteem . . ."[7] This person was Alice M. Hamlet, an amateur journalist residing in Dorchester, Massachusetts, and probably a member of Winifred Virginia Jackson's informal coterie of writers. Some months later Lovecraft acknowledged Hamlet in a poem, "With a Copy of Wilde's Fairy Tales" (July 1920):

> Madam, in whom benignant gods have join'd
> The gifts of fancy, melody, and mind;
> Whose kindly guidance first enrich'd my sight
> With great DUNSANY'S Heliconian light . . .

Lovecraft's present of Wilde's fairy tales was a small recompense for the realms of wonder Hamlet had opened up in introducing him to Dunsany, for Lovecraft would repeatedly say, even late in life, that Dunsany "has certainly influenced me more than any other living writer."[8] The first paragraph of *A Dreamer's Tales* "arrested me as with an electrick shock, & I had not read two pages before I became a Dunsany devotee for life."[9]

Hamlet had given Lovecraft *A Dreamer's Tales* in anticipation of Dunsany's lecture at the Copley Plaza in Boston on October 20, 1919, part of his extensive American tour. Lovecraft read the book about a month or so before the visit, for he later remarks that he first encountered Dunsany in September.[10] In a letter of November 9 to Rheinhart Kleiner describing the lecture he states that "a party consisting of Miss H[amlet], her aunt, young Lee, and L. Theobald set out for the great event."[11] I do not know who young Lee is. There must have been others whom Lovecraft met in Boston prior to the lecture; in particular, at some point he met Kleiner, and with him wrote a series of light-hearted poems that I have grouped together under the title "On Collaboration" (derived from one poem so titled). One of these, written to Verna McGeoch, runs as follows:

Madam, behold with startled eyes
A source of wonder and surprise;
Your humble serfs are two of many
Who will this night hear Ld DUNSANY!

"Wonder" presumably prefers to Dunsany's *Book of Wonder.* But Kleiner clearly could not have accompanied Lovecraft and the others to the lecture, else Lovecraft would not have had to write to him about it in his letter. In any case, the group secured seats in the very front row, "not ten feet" from Dunsany; it was the closest Lovecraft would ever come to meeting one of his literary idols, since he was too diffident to meet or correspond with Machen, Blackwood, or M. R. James. Lovecraft describes Dunsany aptly: "He is of Galpinian build—6 ft. 2 in. in height, and very slender. His face is fair and pleasing, though marred by a slight moustache. In manner he is boyish and a trifle awkward; and his smile is winning and infectious. His hair is light brown. His voice is mellow and cultivated, and very clearly British. He pronounces *were* as *wair,* etc." After an account of his literary principles Dunsany read his magnificent short play, *The Queen's Enemies* (in *Plays of Gods and Men*), then an exquisite parody of himself, "Why the Milkman Shudders When He Perceives the Dawn" (in *The Last Book of Wonder*). After the lecture "Dunsany was encircled by autograph-seekers. Egged on by her aunt, Miss Hamlet almost mustered up courage enough to ask for an autograph, but weakened at the last moment. . . . For mine own part, I did not need a signature; for I detest fawning upon the great." Dunsany's own account of this lecture scarcely occupies more than a few sentences in his second autobiography, *While the Sirens Slept:* "At Boston in a big hall called the Copley Plaza the chair was taken for me by Mr. Baker, lecturer on the drama at Harvard . . . There Mr. Ellery Sedgewick, editor of the *Atlantic Monthly,* entertained us in what, as I said there was one word that I would not use here again, I may call the American way."[12] Clearly he was entirely unaware that the lanky, lantern-jawed gentleman in the front row would become his greatest disciple and a significant force in the preservation of his own work.

Alice Hamlet, however, could not give up the idea of an autograph by Dunsany, so she wrote him a personal letter, enclosing as a present an original letter by Abraham Lincoln. Dunsany acknowledged this gift with customary graciousness ("It is a stately letter, and above all, it is full of human kindness; and I doubt if any of us by any means can achieve anything better than that").[13] Perhaps it was this that led Dunsany to agree to act as Laureate Judge of Poetry of the UAPA for the 1919–20 term. In this function Dunsany probably read some of Lovecraft's poetry published during that period, but in his letter to UAPA President Mary Faye

Durr announcing his decision he makes no reference to any work by Lovecraft; instead, he grants top honours to a poem by Arthur Goodenough, second place to one by John Milton Samples, and third place to one by S. Lilian McMullen, also mentioning work by Rheinhart Kleiner and Winifred Jackson.[14]

Another gift to Dunsany by Hamlet was the *Tryout* for November 1919, which contained one of two poems written on Dunsany by Lovecraft. "To Edward John Moreton Drax Plunkett, 18th Baron Dunsany" (*Tryout,* November 1919) must have been written very shortly after Lovecraft's attendance of the lecture; it is a dreadful, wooden poem that starkly reveals the drawbacks of using the Georgian style for subjects manifestly unsuited to it:

> As when the sun above a dusky wold
> Springs into sight, and turns the gloom to gold,
> Lights with his magic beams the dew-deck'd bow'rs,
> And wakes to life the gay responsive flow'rs;
> So now o'er realms where dark'ning dulness lies,
> In solar state see shining *Plunkett* rise!

And so on for another sixty lines. Dunsany, however, remarked charitably in a letter published in the *Tryout* that the tribute was "magnificent" and that "I am most grateful to the author of that poem for his warm and generous enthusiasm, crystallised in verse."[15]

And yet, a few months later Lovecraft wrote a much better tribute in three simple stanzas of quatrains, "On Reading Lord Dunsany's *Book of Wonder*" (*Silver Clarion,* March 1920). Here is the last stanza:

> The lonely room no more is there—
>   For to the sight in pomp appear
> Temples and cities pois'd in air,
>   And blazing glories—sphere on sphere.

Dunsany apparently never read this poem.

Lovecraft very quickly acquired and read most or all of Dunsany's published books: *The Gods of Pegāna* (given to him by his mother[16]); two Modern Library editions, one containing *A Dreamer's Tales* and *The Sword of Welleran* (1917), the other containing *The Book of Wonder* and *Time and the Gods* (1918); *Five Plays; Fifty-one Tales; The Last Book of Wonder; Plays of Gods and Men; Tales of Three Hemispheres;* and *Unhappy Far-Off Things* (1919), Dunsany's pensive reflections on the end of the war. Lovecraft's edition of *Five Plays* dates to 1923, but he had probably read the contents earlier. He never seems to have acquired the non-fantastic *Tales of War* (1918), although he probably read it. For the rest of his life Lovecraft continued to acquire (or, at least, read) almost all of Dunsany's new books as they came out, in spite of his dwindling enthusiasm for Dunsany's later work.

It is easy to see why a figure like Dunsany would have had an immediate appeal for Lovecraft: his yearning for the unmechanised past, his purely aesthetic creation of a gorgeously evocative ersatz mythology, and his "crystalline singing prose" (as Lovecraft would memorably characterise it in "Supernatural Horror in Literature") made Lovecraft think that he had found a spiritual twin in the Irish fantaisiste. As late as 1923 he was still maintaining that "Dunsany *is myself*. . . His cosmic realm is the realm in which I live; his distant, emotionless vistas of the beauty of moonlight on quaint and ancient roofs are the vistas I know and cherish."[17] And one must also conjecture that Dunsany's position as an independently wealthy nobleman who wrote what he chose and paid no heed to popular expectations exercised a powerful fascination for Lovecraft: here was an "amateur" writer who had achieved tremendous popular and critical success; here was a case where the aristocracy of blood and the aristocracy of intellect were conjoined.

It is, of course, the prose style of those early works that is so fatally alluring, and it is this, more than the philosophy or themes in Dunsany's work, that Lovecraft first attempted to mimic. There is much truth in C. L. Moore's comment: "No one can imitate Dunsany, and probably everyone who's ever read him has tried."[18] Lovecraft's first consciously Dunsanian story is "The White Ship," which was probably written in October 1919. In early December he remarked to Kleiner: "As you infer, 'The White Ship' is in part influenced by my new Dunsanian studies."[19] The phrase "in part" is interesting, and in fact quite accurate: although it strives to imitate Dunsany's prose-poetic style, it is also in large part a philosophical allegory that reflects Lovecraft's, not Dunsany's, world view.

"The White Ship" tells of Basil Elton, "keeper of the North Point light," who one day "walk[s] out over the waters . . . on a bridge of moonbeams" to a White Ship that has come from the South, captained by an aged bearded man. They sail to various fantastic realms: the Land of Zar, "where dwell all the dreams and thoughts of beauty that come to men once and then are forgotten"; the Land of Thalarion, "the City of a Thousand Wonders, wherein reside all those mysteries that man has striven in vain to fathom"; Xura, "the Land of Pleasures Unattained"; and finally Sona-Nyl, in which "there is neither time nor space, neither suffering nor death." Although Elton spends "many aeons" there in evident contentment, he gradually finds himself yearning for the realm of Cathuria, the Land of Hope, beyond the basalt pillars of the West, which he believes to be an even more wondrous realm than Sona-Nyl. The captain warns him against pursuing Cathuria, but Elton is adamant and compels the captain to launch his ship once more. But they discover that beyond the basalt pillars of the West is only a "monstrous cataract, wherein the oceans of the world drop down to abysmal nothingness." As their ship is destroyed,

Elton finds himself on the platform of his lighthouse. The White Ship comes to him no more.

The surface plot of "The White Ship" is clearly derived from Dunsany's "Idle Days on the Yann" (in *A Dreamer's Tales*). The resemblance is, however, quite superficial, for Dunsany's delightful tale tells only of a dream-voyage by a man who boards a ship, the *Bird of the River,* and encounters one magical land after another; there is no significant philosophical content in these realms, and their principal function is merely an evocation of fantastic beauty. (Dunsany wrote the story in anticipation of a boat trip down the Nile.) Lovecraft's tale is meant to be interpreted allegorically or symbolically, and as such enunciates several central tenets of his philosophical thought.

The fundamental message of "The White Ship" is the folly of abandoning the Epicurean goal of *ataraxia,* tranquillity (interpreted as the absence of pain). Sona-Nyl is such a state, and by forsaking it Basil Elton brings upon his head a justified doom—not death, but sadness and discontent. The non-existence of Cathuria is anticipated by the land of Thalarion: this realm embodies all those "mysteries that man has striven in vain to fathom," and therein "walk only daemons and mad things that are no longer men"; such mysteries are not meant to be penetrated, and the hope of penetrating them (Cathuria is the Land of Hope) is both vain and foolish. Elton compounds his folly by egotism: as he approaches the basalt pillars of the West, he fancies that "there came the notes of singer and lutanist; sweeter than the sweetest songs of Sona-Nyl, and sounding mine own praises."

It is worth pointing out that "The White Ship" is not a dream-fantasy. Both Dunsany's early tales and Lovecraft's Dunsanian imitations are carelessly referred to as dream-stories, but only a few by either author can be so designated. "Idle Days on the Yann" is one of them: the narrator tells his ship-captain that he comes "from Ireland, which is of Europe," feeling that this laborious circumlocution is necessary on the chance that the crew have not heard of such a place; but it is of no use: "the captain and all the sailors laughed, for they said, 'There is no such place in all the land of dreams.'"[20] But in most of Dunsany's stories, there is no clear distinction between dream and reality: the fantasy realm of Pegāna *is* the "real" world, for there is no other. We will also find that this is the case in most of Lovecraft's tales; if anything, Lovecraft follows up dim suggestions in Dunsany that these fantastic realms have a *temporal* priority to the "real" world—i.e., that they existed in the distant past of the known world. "Polaris" already makes this clear. In "The White Ship" we do not know where the North Point lighthouse is, but the implication is that it exists in the real world; and yet, the realms visited by the White Ship are so patently symbolic that no suggestion of their actual existence is made, or is even required by the logic of the tale.

"The White Ship" was first published in the *United Amateur* for November

1919. Alfred Galpin, chairman of the Department of Public Criticism, gave a warm reception to the story, commending Lovecraft's turn to fiction-writing in general ("his natural trend is leading him toward more and more appropriate paths") and the story in particular ("The lover of dream literature will find all he might long for in the carefully sustained poetry of language, the simple narration, and the profound inner harmonies of 'The White Ship'"). Galpin concludes: "If this fickle devotion to other gods will subserve ultimately to the finding of Mr. Lovecaft's own original voice, it will sustain a purpose which will mean something to wider fields than amateur journalism."[21]

I wish to study "The Street" (*Wolverine,* December 1920) here for two reasons, even though it is probably the single worst tale Lovecraft ever wrote. Firstly, it was written late in 1919, sometime after "The White Ship";[22] and secondly, it is just possible that the tale was inspired at least indirectly by some of Dunsany's own war parables, particularly those in *Tales of War.* The story is only marginally weird, and it in fact proves to be is a transparent and crude story of racism. It opens laboriously and ponderously: "There be those who say that things and places have souls, and there be those who say they have not; I dare not say, myself, but I will tell of The Street."

It is clear that this Street is in New England; for the "men of strength and honour" who built it were "good, valiant men of our blood who had come from the Blessed Isles across the sea." These were "grave men in conical hats" who had "bonneted wives and sober children" and enough "courage and goodness" to "subdue the forest and till the fields." Two wars came; after the first, there were no more Indians, and after the second "they furled the Old Flag and put up a new Banner of Stripes and Stars." After this, however, things become ominous; for there are "strange puffings and shrieks" from the river, and "the air was not quite so pure as before"; but, reassuringly, "the spirit of the place had not changed." But now come "days of evil," a time when "many who had known The Street of old knew it no more; and many knew it, who had not known it before." The houses fall into decay, the trees are all gone, and "cheap, ugly new buildings" go up. Another war comes, but by this time "only fear and hatred and ignorance" brood over the Street because of all the "swarthy and sinister" people who now dwell in it. There are now such unheard-of places as Petrovitch's Bakery, the Rifkin School of Modern Economics, and the Liberty Café.

There develops a rumour that the houses "contained the leaders of a vast band of terrorists," who on a designated day are to initiate an "orgy of slaughter for the extermination of America and of all the fine old traditions which The Street had loved"; this revolution is to occur, picturesquely, on the fourth of July. But a miracle occurs: "For without warning, in one of the small hours beyond midnight, all the ravages of the years and the storms and the worms came to a tremendous climax; and after the crash there was nothing left standing in The Street save two ancient chimneys and part of a stout brick wall. Nor did anything that had been alive come alive from the ruins." I guess this proves that streets have souls after all.

Lovecraft supplies the genesis of the story in a letter:

> The Boston police mutiny of last year is what prompted that attempt—the magnitude and significance of such an act appalled me. Last fall it was grimly impressive to see Boston without bluecoats, and to watch the musket-bearing State Guardsmen patrolling the streets as though military occupation were in force. They went in pairs, determined-looking and khaki-clad, as if symbols of the strife that lies ahead in civilisation's struggle with the monster of unrest and bolshevism.[23]

The Boston police had gone on strike on September 8, 1919, and remained on strike well into October. No doubt it was a very disturbing event, but at this time unionisation and strikes were almost the only option available to the working class for better wages and better working conditions.

I have gone into this wild, paranoid, racist fantasy in such excruciating detail to show how spectacularly awful Lovecraft can be when riding one of his hobby-horses, in particular his stereotyped lament on the decline of New England at the hands of foreigners. "The Street" is nothing more than a prose version of such early poems as "New-England Fallen" and "On a New-England Village Seen by Moonlight": there is the same naive glorification of the past, the same attribution of all evils to "strangers" (who seem to have ousted those hardy Anglo-Saxons with surprising ease), and, remarkably, even a gliding over of the devastating economic and social effects of the industrial revolution. Although in late 1920 he expressed a wish to see the tale published professionally,[24] he apparently did not make any such attempt, and eventually he included it among his disavowed tales; but the fact that he allowed it to be published twice in the amateur press (first in the *Wolverine* and then, just over a year later, in the *National Amateur* for January 1922), under his own name, suggests that, at least at the time of its writing (however much before its first publication that may have been), Lovecraft was fully prepared to acknowledge this tale and its sentiments as his own.

Things are very different with "The Doom That Came to Sarnath," the next of Lovecraft's Dunsanian imitations, written on December 3, 1919. This tale is less philosophically interesting than "The White Ship," but it too is rather more than a mere pastiche. The narrator tells the story of the land of Mnar, where "ten thousand years ago" stood the stone city of Ib near a vast still lake. Ib was inhabited by "beings not pleasing to behold": they were "in hue as green as the lake and the mists that rise above it . . . they had bulging eyes, pouting, flabby lips, and curious ears, and were without voice." Many aeons later new folk came to Mnar and founded the city of Sarnath; these were the first human beings of the region, "dark shepherd folk with their fleecy flocks." They loathed the creatures of Ib and destroyed both the town and the inhabitants, preserving only the "sea-green stone idol chiselled in the likeness of Bokrug, the water-lizard." After this Sarnath flourished greatly, becoming the "wonder of the world and the pride of all mankind." Every year was a festival commemorating the destruction of Ib, and the thousandth year of this festival was to be of exceptional lavishness. But during the feasting and celebrating Sarnath is overrun by "a horde of indescribable green voiceless things with bulging eyes, pouting, flabby lips, and curious ears." Sarnath is destroyed.

In this rather elementary tale of vengeance the borrowings from Dunsany are all in externals. Lovecraft thought he had come by the name Sarnath independently, but maintained that he later found it in a story by Dunsany; this is not, however, the case. He may have been thinking of Sardathrion, the city mentioned repeatedly in the title story of Dunsany's *Time and the Gods*. Sarnath is also a real city in India, but Lovecraft was probably not aware of the fact. The green idol Bokrug is reminiscent of the green jade gods of Dunsany's magnificent play *The Gods of the Mountain* (in *Five Plays*). Mention of a throne "wrought of one piece of ivory, though no man lives who knows whence so vast a piece could have come" is an echo of a celebrated passage in "Idle Days on the Yann" (noted by Lovecraft in "Supernatural Horror in Literature") of an ivory gate "carved out of one solid piece!"[25] The style of "The Doom That Came to Sarnath" is also only superficially Dunsanian, and in fact reveals the degree to which Lovecraft (like many others) failed to understand the true sources of Dunsany's effectiveness as a prose-poet. The descriptions of Sarnath allow Lovecraft to unleash a lush, bejewelled style that is actually not Dunsanian in essence: "Many were the pillars of the palaces, all of tinted marble, and carven into designs of surpassing beauty. And in most of the palaces the floors were mosaics of beryl and lapis-lazuli and sardonyx and carbuncle and other choice materials, so disposed that the beholder might fancy himself walking over beds of the rarest flowers." It never seems to have occurred to Lovecraft that Dunsany achieved his most striking effects not through dense passages like this—which are more reminiscent of Wilde's fairy tales—but through a staggeringly bold use of metaphor. Consider that quixotic quest by King Karnith Zo and his army to lay siege to Time:

> But as the feet of the foremost touched the edge of the hill Time hurled five years against them, and the years passed over their heads and the army still came on, an army of older men. But the slope seemed steeper to the King and to every man in his army, and they breathed more heavily. And Time summoned up more years, and one by one he hurled them at Karnith Zo and at all his men. And the knees of the army stiffened, and the beards grew and turned grey . . .[26]

This is the sort of thing Lovecraft almost never managed in his Dunsanian imitations.

But "The Doom That Came to Sarnath" has other virtues. Simple as the moral here is, it can readily be seen that Lovecraft is portraying the doom of Sarnath as well deserved on account of its citizens' race prejudice against the inhabitants of Ib ("with their marvelling was mixed hate, for they thought it not meet that beings of such aspect should walk about the world of men at dusk") and their greed (Sarnath was founded "at a spot where precious metals were found in the earth"). Sarnath furthermore becomes increasingly artificial in its design, aping the natural world but in fact repudiating it. Each house in Sarnath has a "crystal lakelet," parodying the actual "vast still lake" where Sarnath had consigned the ruins of Ib. The gardens of Sarnath defy the seasons: "In summer the gardens were cooled with fresh odorous breezes skilfully wafted by fans, and in winter they were heated with concealed fires, so that in those gardens it was always spring." All this is presented in superficial terms of praise (or, at least, wonder), but in truth it is Sarnath's excessive wealth, its irrational hatred of Ib, and its corrupt religion, founded upon hate (for the priests of Sarnath "often performed the very ancient and very secret rite in detestation of Bokrug"), that bring about its doom.

Lovecraft also makes it abundantly clear that the setting of the tale is the primitive real world, not an imaginary realm or dream-world. Ib was founded "when the world was young," but we know little of its inhabitants because man "knows but little of the very ancient living things." At the very end we learn that "adventurous young men of yellow hair and blue eyes, who are no kin to the men of Mnar" enter the region, suggesting a racial succession of some kind. Most of Lovecraft's Dunsanian tales will follow this pattern.

"The Doom That Came to Sarnath" first appeared in the Scottish amateur journal the *Scot* (edited by Gavin T. McColl) for June 1920. McColl, living in Dundee, was the only Scottish member of the UAPA at this time. Several years earlier Lovecraft had written to McColl praising his journal (a portion of his letter had been published in the *Scot* for March 1916), and no doubt he wished to do all he could to foster transatlantic amateur activity.

"The Terrible Old Man" (written on January 28, 1920) is not generally considered a Dunsanian story, and indeed it is not in the sense of being a tale set in an imaginary or ancient realm. We are here very clearly situated in contemporary New England, but the tale nevertheless is likely derived from some of Dunsany's work. It opens ponderously:

> It was the design of Angelo Ricci and Joe Czanek and Manuel Silva to call on the Terrible Old Man. This old man dwells all alone in a very ancient house on Water Street near the sea, and is reputed to be both exceedingly rich and exceedingly feeble; which forms a situation very attractive to men of the profession of Messrs. Ricci, Czanek, and Silva, for that profession was nothing less dignified than robbery.

The Terrible Old Man dwells in Kingsport, a city somewhere in New England. In the "far-off days of his unremembered youth" he was a sea-captain, and seems to have a vast collection of ancient Spanish gold and silver pieces. He has now become very eccentric, appearing to spend hours speaking to an array of bottles from which a small piece of lead is suspended from a string. On the night of the planned robbery Ricci and Silva enter the Terrible Old Man's house while Czanek waits outside. Screams are heard from the house, but there is no sign of the two robbers; and Czanek wonders whether his colleagues were forced to kill the old man and make a laborious search through his house for the treasure. But then the Terrible Old Man appears at the doorway, "leaning quietly on his knotted cane and smiling hideously." Later three unidentifiable bodies are found washed in by the tide.

The heavy-handed sarcasm with which "The Terrible Old Man" is told recalls many of the tales in *The Book of Wonder*, which similarly deal with owlish gravity of attempted robberies which usually end badly for the perpetrators. Consider the opening of "The Probable Adventure of the Three Literary Men": "When the nomads came to El Lola they had no more songs, and the question of stealing the golden box arose in all its magnitude. On the one hand, many had sought the golden box, the receptacle (as the Aethiopians know) of poems of fabulous value; and their doom is still the common talk of Arabia."[27] Although this tale is still set in an imaginary realm, Dunsany had already allowed the real world to enter into his work as early as "The Highwayman" and "The Kith of the Elf-Folk" (in *The Sword of Welleran*). In "The Terrible Old Man" it is not clear where exactly the imaginary city of Kingsport is; it was only later, in "The Festival" (1923), that it was situated in Massachusetts and identified with the town of Marblehead. Here it is stated only that the three robbers in question "were not of Kingsport blood; they were of that new and heterogeneous alien stock which lies outside the charmed circle of New-England life and traditions."

This comment itself brings to the fore the issue of racism in this story. The remark is certainly double-edged—it can be considered as much a satire on New England Yankee social exclusiveness as an attack on foreigners—but the racist overtones cannot be ignored. Ricci, Czanek, and Silva each represent one of the three leading ethnic minorities in Providence—Italian, Polish, and Portuguese. It can scarcely be doubted that Lovecraft derived some measure of satisfaction from the dispatching of these three criminals.

Is the tale actually supernatural? There is certainly reason to think so. The Terrible Old Man may appear feeble, but he is clearly endowed with vast strength to be able to subdue two presumably young and vigorous thieves. Whence did he derive it? This is never made clear, but the suggestion is that the Terrible Old Man is not merely superhuman in strength but also preternaturally aged: the fact that he possesses only very old Spanish money implies that he may actually be hundreds of years old—especially since "no one can remember when he was young." And then there are those bottles with the pendulums: the Terrible Old Man has given them names such as Jack, Scar-Face, and Long Tom; and when he talks to them, "the little lead pendulum within makes certain definite vibrations as if in answer." What else can these things be but the souls of his old shipmates, whom he (or some other force) has trapped in the bottles?

"The Terrible Old Man" is the shortest of Lovecraft's horror tales (exclusive of his prose-poems), and—in spite of one critic's attempt to read it in mythic and psychoanalytical terms[28]—really does not amount to much. It first appeared in C. W. Smith's *Tryout* for July 1921.

The next of Lovecraft's "Dunsanian" tales is "The Tree," written sometime in the first half of 1920: in chronologies of Lovecraft's stories it is customarily listed after "The Terrible Old Man" (January 28) and before "The Cats of Ulthar" (June 14). The story concerns a contest proposed by the "Tyrant of Syracuse" between the two great sculptors, Kalos and Musides, to carve a statue of Tyché for the Tyrant's city. The two artists are the closest of friends, but their lives are very different: whereas Musides "revelled by night amidst the urban gaieties of Tegea," Kalos remains home in quiet contemplation. The two begin working on their respective statues; but Kalos gradually takes ill, and in spite of Musides' constant nursing eventually dies. Musides wins the contest by default, but both he and his lovely statue are weirdly destroyed when a strange olive tree growing out of Kalos' tomb suddenly falls upon Musides' residence.

The clear implication of the tale is that Musides, for all his supposed devotion to his friend, has poisoned Kalos and suffers supernatural revenge. Lovecraft says as much when discussing the story with the Transatlantic Circulator the following year:

> Regarding "The Tree"—Mr. Brown finds the climax insufficient, but I doubt if a tale of that type could possess a more obvious denouement. The climactic effect sought, is merely an emphasis—amounting to the first direct intimation—of the fact that there is something hidden behind the simple events of the tale; that the growing suspicion of Musides' crime and recognition of Kalos' posthumous vengeance is well founded. It is to proclaim what has hitherto been doubtful—to shew that the things of Nature see behind human hypocrisy and perceive the baseness at the heart of outward virtue. All the world deems Musides a model of fraternal piety and devotion although in truth he poisoned Kalos when he saw his laurels in peril. Did not the Tegeans build to Musides a temple? But against all these illusions the trees whisper—the wise trees sacred to the gods—and reveal the truth to the midnight searcher as they chaunt knowingly over and over again *"Oida! Oida!"* This, then, is all the climax so nebulous a legend can possess. ("The Defence Remains Open!")

Lovecraft is, aware that this sort of supernatural justice is not even metaphorically true to life:

> About the plot of "The Tree"—it was the result of some rather cynical reflection on the possible real motives which may underlie even the most splendid appearing acts of mankind. With this nucleus I developed a tale based on the Greek idea of divine justice and retribution, (a very pretty though sadly mythical idea!) with the added Oriental notion of the soul of a man passing into something else.[29]

The story's relative lack of vital connexion to Dunsany's work can be gauged by the fact that the basic plot was evolved more than a year before Lovecraft ever read Dunsany. In an August 1918 letter to Alfred Galpin, Lovecraft outlined the plot of "The Tree," saying that it had already by that time been "long conceived but never elaborated into literary form";[30] he postponed writing the story because he evidently felt that Galpin's own tale "Marsh-Mad" had pre-empted him by utilising the "living tree" idea. The plot as recorded here is identical in all essential features to the story as we have it, save that at the end "the tree was found uprooted—as if the roots had voluntarily relinquished their hold upon the ground—and beneath the massive trunk lay the body of the faithful mourner—crushed to death, & with an expression of the most unutterable fear upon his countenance."

What was not included in this plot synopsis was the setting of the tale in ancient Greece; but even this feature is not likely to have been derived from Dunsany, save perhaps indirectly in the sense that many of Dunsany's early works have a vaguely Grecian or archaic air to them. Dunsany actually used the ancient world as a setting not in any tales but in two plays: *Alexander* (a play about Alexander the Great written in 1912, but not published until *Alexander and Three Small Plays* [1925], hence not read by Lovecraft until after he had written "The Tree") and *The Queen's Enemies* (published separately in 1916 and included the next year in *Plays of Gods and Men*), a delightful and celebrated play about Queen Nitokris of Egypt and the hideous (but not supernatural) vengeance she carries out upon her enemies. This was, let us recall, one of the works Dunsany read during his Boston appearance.

Wherever he derived the Grecian setting and atmosphere, Lovecraft pulls it off ably; his lifelong study of ancient history paid dividends in this satisfying and elegantly written little story. The names of the artists—Kalos ("handsome" or "fair") and Musides ("son of the Muse(s)")—are both apt, although they are not actual Greek names. Tyché means "chance" (or sometimes "fate"), and actual cults of Tyché were established in Greece sometime after 371 B.C.E. This helps to date the tale fairly precisely: there were tyrants of Syracuse (in Sicily) from c. 485 to c. 467 and again from c. 406 to 344, but the cult of Tyché clearly establishes the latter period as the temporal setting for the story. One other detail helps to establish an even more precise date: mention of a tomb for Kalos "more lovely than the tomb of Mausolus" refers to the tomb built for Mausolus, the satrap of Caria, in 353, so that "The Tree" must take place in the period 353–344, when Dionysius II was Tyrant of Syracuse.[31]

"The Tree" was first published, pitiably misprinted, in the *Tryout* for October 1921. Lovecraft later came to despise the story, maintaining that it, along with several other tales, "might—if typed on good stock—make excellent shelf-paper but little else."[32] The tale may be a trifle obvious, but it is an effective display of Lovecraft's skill in handling an historical setting.

"The Cats of Ulthar" (June 15, 1920), conversely, always remained one of Lovecraft's favourites, probably because cats are the central focus of the tale. This tale owes more to Dunsany than many of his other "Dunsanian" fantasies. The narrator proposes to explain how the town of Ulthar passed its "remarkable law" that no man may kill a cat. There was once a very evil couple who hated cats and who brutally murdered any that strayed on their property. One day a caravan of "dark wanderers" comes to Ulthar, among which is the little boy Menes, owner of a tiny black kitten. When the kitten disappears, the heartbroken boy, learning of the propensities of the cat-hating couple, "prayed in a tongue no villager could understand." That night all the cats in the town vanish, and when they return in the morning they refuse for two entire days to touch any food or drink. Later it is noticed that the couple has not been seen for days; when at last the villagers enter their house, they find two clean-picked skeletons.

Here too some of the borrowings from Dunsany may be only superficial: the name of the boy Menes may be derived from King Argimēnēs of the play, *King Argimēnēs and the Unknown Warrior* (in *Five Plays*); the "dark wanderers" seem an echo of the "Wanderers . . . a weird, dark tribe" mentioned toward the end of "Idle Days on the Yann."[33] But the entire scenario—once again a consciously elementary tale of vengeance—is likely inspired by the many similar tales in *The Book of Wonder.*

One wonders whether Lovecraft was thinking of himself when he wrote, with unexpected poignancy, of the orphan Menes, "when one is very young, one can find great relief in the lively antics of a black kitten." Is this a remembrance of Nigger-Man and all that that lone pet meant to Lovecraft? He had outlined the plot of the story to Kleiner as early as May 21,[34] but it would be another three weeks before he actually set it down. It first appeared in the *Tryout* for November 1920.

It would be some months before Lovecraft produced another Dunsanian tale, but it would be both one of his best and most significant in terms of his later work. "Celephaïs" (the dieresis over the *i* is frequently omitted) was written in early November 1920,[35] although it did not appear in print until Sonia Greene published it in her *Rainbow* for May 1922. Kuranes (who has a different name in waking life) escapes the prosy world of London by dream and drugs. In this state he comes upon the city of Celephaïs, in the Valley of Ooth-Nargai. It is a city of which he had dreamed as a child, and there "his spirit had dwelt all the eternity of an hour one summer afternoon very long ago, when he had slipt away from his nurse and let the warm sea-breeze lull him to sleep as he watched the clouds from the cliff near the village." It is a realm of pure beauty:

> When he entered the city, past the bronze gates and over the onyx pavements, the merchants and camel-drivers greeted him as if he had never been away; and it was the same at the turquoise temple of Nath-Horthath, where the orchid-wreathed priests told him that there is no time in Ooth-Nargai, but only perpetual youth. Then Kuranes walked through the Street of Pillars to the seaward wall, where gathered the traders and sailors, and strange men from the regions where the sea meets the sky.

But Kuranes awakes in his London garret and finds that he can return to Celephaïs no more. He dreams of other wondrous lands, but his sought-for city continues to elude him. He increases his intake of drugs, runs out of money, and is turned out of his flat. Then, as he wanders aimlessly through the streets, he comes upon a cortege of knights who "rode majestically through the downs of Surrey," seeming to gallop back in time as they do so. They leap off a precipice and drift softly down to Celephaïs, and Kuranes knows that he will be its king forever. Meanwhile, in the waking world, the tide at Innsmouth washes up the corpse of a tramp, while a "notably fat and offensive millionaire brewer" purchases Kuranes' ancestral mansion and "enjoys the purchased atmosphere of extinct nobility."

Lovecraft indicates that the story was ultimately based upon an entry in his commonplace book (for which see below) reading simply: "Dream of flying over city." Note that this is a pure *image*, and that none of the philosophical or aesthetic conceptions actually imbedded in the story are at all suggested by it. We will come upon this phenomenon repeatedly: tales are triggered by some innocuous, fragmentary image that comes to occupy a very small place—or indeed no place—in the finished tale. Another entry in the commonplace book was perhaps also an inspiration: "Man journeys into the past—or imaginative realm—leaving bodily shell behind."

But if we are to find the inspiration for "Celephaïs," we shall not have to look far; for the tale is embarrassingly similar in conception to Dunsany's "The Coronation of Mr. Thomas Shap" (in *The Book of Wonder*). There a small businessman imagines himself the King of Larkar, and as he continues to dwell obsessively on (and in) this imaginary realm his work in the real world suffers, until finally he is placed in the madhouse of Hanwell. Other, less significant details also derive from Dunsany: the oft-repeated phrase "where the sea meets the sky" echoes "where sky meets ocean" from "When the Gods Slept"[36] (in *Time and the Gods*) and analogous phrases in other tales. Even the small detail whereby Kuranes floats down "past dark, shapeless, undreamed dreams, faintly glowing spheres that may have been partly dreamed dreams" is clearly derived from the opening pages of *The Gods of Pegāna,* where all the gods and the separate worlds are seen to be merely the dreams of Mānā-Yood-Sushāī. And yet, it is also possible that this image of horses drifting dreamily over a cliff is an echo of a fantastic-seeming but very realistic story by Ambrose Bierce, "A Horseman in the Sky" (in *Tales of Soldiers and Civilians*), where a man seems to see such a sight after he has shot the rider—who proves to be his own father.

Nevertheless, "Celephaïs" enunciates issues of great importance to Lovecraft. It is difficult to resist an autobiographical interpretation of Kuranes at he appears at the outset:

> . . . he was the last of his family, and alone among the indifferent millions of London . . . His money and lands were gone, and he did not care for the ways of people about him, but preferred to dream and write of his dreams. What he wrote was laughed at by those to whom he shewed it, so that after a time he kept his writings to himself . . . Kuranes was not modern, and did not think like others who wrote. Whilst they strove to strip from life its embroidered robes of myth, and to shew in naked ugliness the foul thing that is reality, Kuranes sought for beauty alone.

This is a trifle maudlin and self-pitying, but we are clearly meant to empathise with Kuranes' psychological dissociation from his environment. That final sentence, perfectly encapsulating Lovecraft's aesthetic at this stage of his career, is worth studying in detail later. But "Celephaïs" seeks to do more than merely create beauty; the thrust of the story is nothing less than an escape from the "groans and grating / Of abhorrent life" (as he put it in "Despair") into a realm of pure imagination—one which, nevertheless, is derived from "the nebulous memories of childhood tales and dreams." The man who in January 1920 wrote "Adulthood is hell"[37] had found in Lord Dunsany a model for the glorious re-creation of those memories of youth for which he would yearn his entire life.

"Celephaïs" is a gorgeously evocative prose-poem that ranks close to the pinnacle of Lovecraft's Dunsanian tales. But it will gain added importance for the contrast it provides to a much later work superficially (and only superficially) in the Dunsanian vein, *The Dream-Quest of Unknown Kadath.* This novel, written after Lovecraft's New York experience, exhibits a marked, almost antipodal, alteration in Lovecraft's aesthetic of beauty, and when Kuranes reappears in it he and his imagined realm will take on a very different cast.

"The Quest of Iranon" (February 28, 1921) may be the most beautiful of all Lovecraft's Dunsanian fantasies, although in later years he savagely condemned it as mawkish. A comment made shortly after the tale was written may be more on target: "I am picking up a new style lately—running to pathos as well as horror. The best thing I have yet done is 'The Quest of Iranon', whose English Loveman calls the most musical and flowing I have yet written, and whose sad plot made one prominent poet actually weep—not at the crudity of the story, but at the sadness."[38] The note about the "new style" presumably refers to "Celephaïs," the only other tale of this period that could be said to mix horror and pathos. "The Quest of

Iranon" is really all pathos. A youthful singer named Iranon comes to the granite city of Teloth, saying that he is seeking his far-off home of Aira, where he was a prince. The men of Teloth, who have no beauty in their lives, do not look kindly on Iranon, and force him to work with a cobbler. He meets a boy named Romnod, who similarly yearns for "the warm groves and the distant lands of beauty and song." Romnod thinks that nearby Oonai, the city of lutes and dancing, might be Iranon's Aira. Iranon doubts it, but goes there with Romnod. It is indeed not Aira, but the two of them find welcome there for a time. Iranon wins praises for his singing and lyre-playing, and Romnod learns the coarser pleasures of wine. Years pass; Iranon seems to grow no older, as he continues to hope one day to find Aira. Romnod eventually dies of drink, and Iranon leaves the town and continues his quest. He comes to "the squalid cot of an antique shepherd" and asks him about Aira. The shepherd looks at Iranon curiously and says:

> "O stranger, I have indeed heard the name of Aira, and the other names thou hast spoken, but they come to me from afar down the waste of long years. I heard them in my youth from the lips of a playmate, a beggar's boy given to strange dreams, who would weave long tales about the moon and the flowers and the west wind. We used to laugh at him, for we knew him from his birth though he thought himself a King's son."

At twilight an old, old man is seen walking calmly into the quicksand. "That night something of youth and beauty died in the elder world."

There is perhaps a certain sentimentality in this story—as well as the suggestion of social snobbery, since Iranon cannot bear the revelation that he is not a prince but only a beggar's boy—but the fundamental message of the shattering of hope is etched with great poignancy and delicacy. In a sense, "The Quest of Iranon" is a mirror-image of "Celephaïs": whereas Kuranes dies in the real world only to escape into the world of his childhood imaginings, Iranon dies because he is unable to preserve the illusion of the reality of those imaginings.

In the city of Teloth Lovecraft has devised a pungent satire of Christianity, specifically of the Protestant work ethic. When Iranon asks why he must work as a cobbler, the archon tells him: "All in Teloth must toil, . . . for that is the law." Iranon responds: "Wherefore do ye toil; is it not that ye may live and be happy? And if ye toil only that ye may toil more, when shall happiness find you?" To this the archon states: "'The words thou speakest are blasphemy, for the gods of Teloth have said that toil is good. Our gods have promised us a haven of light beyond death, where there shall be rest without end, and crystal coldness amidst which none shall vex his mind with thought or his eyes with beauty. . . . All here must serve, and song is folly.'"

Aside from its musical language, "The Quest of Iranon" bears no influence of any specific work by Dunsany, and may be the most original of Lovecraft's Dunsanian imitations. It was a long time appearing in print. Lovecraft wished to use it in his own *Conservative* (whose last issue had appeared in July 1919), but the next issue did not appear until March 1923, and Lovecraft had by then evidently decided against using it there. It languished in manuscript until finally published in the *Galleon* for July–August 1935.

Lovecraft's final explicitly Dunsanian story is "The Other Gods" (August 14, 1921). The "gods of earth" have forsaken their beloved mountain Ngranek and have betaken themselves to "unknown Kadath in the cold waste where no man treads"; they have done this ever since a human being from Ulthar, Barzai the Wise, attempted to scale Mt. Ngranek and catch a glimpse of them. Barzai was much learned in the "seven cryptical books of Hsan" and the "Pnakotic Manuscripts of distant and frozen Lomar," and knew so much of the gods that he wished to see them dancing on Mt. Ngranek. He undertakes this bold journey with his friend, Atal the priest. For days they climb the rugged mountain, and as they approach the cloud-hung summit Barzai thinks he hears the gods; he redoubles his efforts, leaving Atal far behind. He cries out:

> "The mists are very thin, and the moon casts shadows on the slope; the voices of earth's gods are high and wild, and they fear the coming of Barzai the Wise, who is greater than they. . . . The moon's light flickers, as earth's gods dance against it; I shall see the dancing forms of the gods that leap and howl in the moonlight. . . . The light is dimmer and the gods are afraid. . . ."

But his eagerness turns to horror. He thinks he actually sees the gods of earth, but instead they are "'The *other* gods! The *other* gods! The gods of the outer hells that guard the feeble gods of earth!'" Barzai is swept up ("'Merciful gods of earth, *I am falling into the sky!*'") and is never seen again.

"The Other Gods" is a textbook example of hubris, and not an especially interesting one. Dunsany had already treated the matter several times in his own work; in "The Revolt of the Home Gods" (in *The Gods of Pegāna*) the humble home gods Eimes, Zanes, and Segastrion declare: "We now play the game of the gods and slay men for our pleasure, and we be greater than the gods of Pegāna."[39] But, even though they be gods, they suffer a dismal fate at the hands of the gods of Pegāna.

"The Other Gods" is a little more interesting in that it establishes explicit links with other of Lovecraft's Dunsanian tales. The mention of the Pnakotic Manuscripts ties the story to the pre-Dunsanian "Polaris"; the mention of Ulthar connects with "The Cats of Ulthar," as does the character Atal, who had already appeared in that story as an innkeeper's son. This sort of thing had in fact been happening all along in these tales: "The Quest of Iranon" made passing mention of Lomar ("Polaris") and to Thraa, Ilarnek, and Kadatheron (cited in "The Doom That Came to Sarnath"). The only tales exempt from this type of interconnexion are "The White Ship" (clearly an allegory), "The Tree" (set in ancient Greece), and "Celephaïs," where the distinction between the real world of Surrey and the realm of Celephaïs (a product of Kuranes' imagination) is at the heart of the story.

What this seems to suggest is that the Dunsanian tales (now including "Polaris") occupy a single imagined realm; but it should be pointed out that this realm is systematically and consistently presented as being situated not in a "dream-world" (there are no dream-stories among these works except, in a special way, "Polaris" and "Celephaïs") but in the distant past of the earth. I have already pointed out that the reference in "Polaris" to "Six and twenty thousand years" dates that story to 24,000 B.C. Other Dunsanian tales follow this pattern: Ib (in "The Doom That Came to Sarnath") stood "when the world was young"; "The Other Gods," by mentioning Lomar and Ulthar, incorporates the latter (and by extension the entire story "The Cats of Ulthar") into the earth's prehistory; and "The Quest of Iranon," by mentioning Lomar in conjunction with the cities named in "The Doom That Came to Sarnath," does the same (recall also the final sentence of "The Quest of Iranon": "That night something of youth and beauty died in the *elder world*").

Some of this interconnectedness may have been inspired by Dunsany's example, although even in these early tales Lovecraft carries it to far greater lengths than Dunsany ever did. *The Gods of Pegāna* and *Time and the Gods* are generally set in the realm of Pegāna, but no other of Dunsany's works are. "Idle Days on the Yann" has two sequels, "The Shop in Go-by Street" and "The Avenger of Perdóndaris"; "The Hashish Man" is a lame sequel to "Bethmoora"; but this is all the cross-referencing that exists in Dunsany's work.

Lovecraft's non-Dunsanian stories, from as early as "The Nameless City" (1921), similarly refer to sites and artifacts from the Dunsanian stories, and in such a way as to suggest their existence in the distant past. This whole schema, however, becomes confused and even paradoxical when Lovecraft writes *The Dream-Quest of Unknown Kadath,* whose very title proclaims it to be a dream-fantasy.

For now it is of interest to realise the degree to which Lovecraft's stories are already becoming intertextually related, a phenomenon that would continue with his later stories. It is, to be sure, unusual for an author to be so self-referential, and there is certainly no doubt about the thematic or philosophical unity of all Lovecraft's work, from fiction to essays to poetry to letters; but it does not strike me as helpful to regard all his tales as interconnected on the level of plot—which they manifestly are not—or even in their glancing and frequently insignificant borrowings of names, entities, and characters. Nevertheless, it is a singular phenomenon that will require further analysis.

What, then, did Lovecraft learn from Dunsany? The answer may not be immediately evident, since it took several years for the Dunsany influence to be assimilated, and some of the most interesting and important aspects of the influence are manifested in tales that bear no superficial resemblance to Dunsany. For now, however, one lesson can be summed up in Lovecraft's somewhat simple-minded characterisation in "Supernatural Horror in Literature": "Beauty rather than terror is the keynote of Dunsany's work." Whereas, with the exceptions of "Polaris" and such non-weird ventures as "A Reminiscence of Dr. Samuel Johnson," Lovecraft's experiments in fiction up to 1919 had been entirely within the realm of supernatural horror, he was now able to diversify his fictional palette with tales of languorous beauty, delicacy, and pathos. To be sure, horror is present as well; but the fantastic settings of the tales, even given the assumption that they are occurring in the earth's prehistory, causes the horror to seem more remote, less immediately threatening.

In this sense a remark made as early as March 1920 may stand as Lovecraft's most perceptive account of Dunsany's influence on him: "The flight of imagination, and the delineation of pastoral or natural beauty, can be accomplished as well in prose as in verse—often better. It is this lesson which the inimitable Dunsany hath taught me."[40] This comment was made in a discussion of Lovecraft's verse writing; and it is no accident that his verse output declined dramatically after 1920. There had been a dichotomy between Lovecraft's fictional and poetic output ever since he had resumed the writing of stories: how could tales of supernatural horror have any relation to the empty but superficially "pretty" Georgianism of his verse? With the decline of verse writing, that dichotomy disappears—or, at least, narrows—as the quest for pure beauty now finds expression in tales. Is it any wonder, then, that as early as January 1920 Lovecraft is noting that, "since all habits must be broken gradually, I am breaking the poesy habit that way"?[41]

More to the point, Lovecraft learned from Dunsany how to enunciate his philosophical, aesthetic, and moral conceptions by means of fiction, beyond the simple cosmicism of "Dagon" or "Beyond the Wall of Sleep." The relation of dream and reality—dimly probed in "Polaris"—is treated exhaustively and poignantly in "Celephaïs"; the loss of hope is etched pensively in "The White Ship" and "The Quest of Iranon"; the perfidy of false friendship is the focus of "The Tree." Lovecraft found *Time and the Gods* "richly philosophical,"[42] and the whole of Dunsany's early—and later—work offers simple, affecting parables on fundamental human issues. Lovecraft would in later years express his philosophy in increasingly complex ways as his fiction itself gained in breadth, scope, and richness.

At the outset it was one particular phase of Dunsany's philosophy—cosmicism—that most attracted Lovecraft. He would maintain hyperbolically in "Supernatural Horror in Literature" that Dunsany's "point of view is the most truly cosmic of any held in the literature of any period," although later he would modify this opinion considerably. What is somewhat strange, therefore, is that Lovecraft's own imitations are—with the sole exception of "The Other Gods"—not at all cosmic in scope, and rarely involve that interplay of "gods and men" which is so striking a characteristic of Dunsany's early work. Perhaps Lovecraft felt that this *Gods of Pegāna* style or subject-matter was simply not to be duplicated (in this he was probably right); but what we will discover is that this cosmicism becomes exhibited in Lovecraft's real-world stories, where the metaphysical and aesthetic implications are very different.

For it will become evident that Dunsany's influence extends far beyond Lovecraft's "Dunsanian" fantasies. We will find many instances of influence in small and large particulars in later tales; and Lovecraft's remarkable claim that it was Dunsany's imagined pantheon in *The Gods of Pegāna* that led him to create his own pseudomythology will have to be given consideration at the proper time. In a later chapter I shall also wish to consider Dunsany's role in what proved to be a significant shift in Lovecraft's aesthetic stance over the next several years.

In spite of his own assertions to the contrary, Lovecraft's "Dunsanian" fantasies are far more than mechanical pastiches of a revered master: they reveal considerable originality of conception while being only superficially derived from Dunsany. It is true that Lovecraft might never have written these tales had he not had Dunsany's example at hand; but he was, at this early stage, an author searching for things of his own to say, and in Dunsany's style and manner he merely found suggestive ways to say them. Interestingly, Dunsany himself came to this conclusion: when Lovecraft's work was posthumously published in book form, Dunsany came upon it and confessed that he had "an odd interest in Lovecraft's work because in the few tales of his I have read I found that he was writing in my style, entirely originally & without in any way borrowing from me, & yet with my style & largely my material."[43] Lovecraft would have been grateful for the acknowledgement.

For the time being, however, Dunsany, more than Poe, was Lovecraft's "God of Fiction." He would write an interesting, but not notably perceptive, lecture, "Lord Dunsany and His Work," in late 1922; as early as May 1920, when "Literary Composition" was published in the *United Amateur,* he would single out Dunsany and Bierce as models of short story technique; and in 1921 he would complain that "Dunsany has met with nothing but coldness or lukewarm praise" ("The Defence Reopens!"). Lovecraft would, in fact, be indirectly responsible for the revival of Dunsany's work in the 1970s: his paean to Dunsany in "Supernatural Horror in Literature" caused August Derleth to take note of his work and to sign up the Irish writer for an early Arkham House title (*The Fourth Book of Jorkens,* 1948), which in turn led to efforts by Arthur C. Clarke, Ursula K. Le Guin, and Lin Carter to resurrect Dunsany's early work. Dunsany is still vastly underappreciated, and both the Irish and the fantasy communities appear either uninterested in or intimidated by him; but the richness and substance of his entire work, early and late, would seem to single him out for study and appreciation. A Dunsany renaissance has yet to occur, and one can only hope that it may one day do so, even if on Lovecraft's coattails.[44]

12. A Stranger in This Century (1919–1921 [III])

During this period Lovecraft of course did not cease to write tales of supernatural horror, and a number of these display his increasing grasp of short story technique; some of them are also rather good in their own right. One of the most interesting of these, at least in terms of its genesis, is "The Statement of Randolph Carter." It is well known that this story is—or was claimed by Lovecraft to be—an almost literal transcript of a dream Lovecraft had, probably in early December 1919, in which he and Samuel Loveman make a fateful trip to an ancient cemetery and Loveman suffers some horrible but mysterious fate after he descends alone into a crypt. The story purports to be a kind of affidavit given to the police by Randolph Carter (Lovecraft) concerning the disappearance of Harley Warren (Loveman).

We have three separate phenomena to deal with here: 1) the dream itself; 2) a letter to the Gallomo (the correspondence cycle, analogous to the Kleicomolo, between Alfred Galpin, Lovecraft, and Maurice W. Moe) of December 11, 1919, in which Lovecraft recounts the dream;[1] and 3) the finished tale, written later in December. Only the last two, of course, are recoverable. This point is important because it is already evident in the letter that Lovecraft has begun to fashion the dream creatively so that it results in an effective and suspenseful narrative, with its powerful climactic last line ("YOU FOOL, LOVEMAN IS DEAD!" in the letter; *"YOU FOOL, WARREN IS DEAD!"* in the story). To what degree, then, the letter diverges from the dream it is now impossible to say; and all we can do is to study the suggestive similarities and differences between the letter and the story.

One of the most obvious changes, as noted above, is that of the names of the characters: H. P. Lovecraft and Samuel Loveman become Randolph Carter and Harley Warren. This change, however, must be taken in conjunction with another possible, but not certain, change—a change of setting. Both the letter and the story are remarkably vague in the actual location of the events of the narrative. In the letter Lovecraft suggests, but does not explicitly declare, that the dream occurred in some old New England cemetery: writing to two Midwesterners, Lovecraft states, "I suppose no Wisconsinite can picture such a thing—but we have them in New-England; horrible old places where the slate stones are graven with odd letters and grotesque designs such as a skull and crossbones." Later in the letter he remarks that "my tale 'The Tomb' . . . was inspired by one of these places"; "The Tomb" clearly is set in New England, but nothing in the letter clearly commits the dream to this setting.

In "The Statement of Randolph Carter" mention is made of the "Gainsville [*sic*] pike" and "Big Cypress Swamp"; these are the only topographical sites mentioned in the story. It is here that the names of the characters gain some importance, for I have now been convinced by the arguments of James Turner[2] that the tale takes place in Florida: Lovecraft seems to have misspelled the name of the well-known city of Gainesville, and cypress swamps are certainly more common in the South than in New England. If we may draw upon evidence of later stories, we can note that in "The Silver Key" (1926) Harley Warren is referred to as "a man in the South," while in "Through the Gates of the Silver Key" (1932–33) he is called a "South Carolina mystic." Recall that Loveman had for part of the war been stationed at Camp Gordon, Georgia, so perhaps he described certain features of the local terrain to Lovecraft in letters.

The name Randolph Carter, however, offers ambiguous evidence. There certainly were Carters in New England, and Lovecraft was from an early age familiar with John Carter, founder of Providence's first newspaper in 1762. Lovecraft at this time probably already knew (as he declares in a letter of 1929) that John Carter himself came from the celebrated Virginia Carters; he goes on to add here that "This transposition of a Virginia line to New England always affected my fancy strongly—hence my frequently recurrent fictional character 'Randolph Carter.'"[3] This might lead one to believe that "The Statement of Randolph Carter" is set in New England: it is undeniable that all the other Randolph Carter tales ("The Unnamable" [1923], "The Silver Key" [1926], *The Dream-Quest of Unknown Kadath* [1926–27], "Through the Gates of the Silver Key") are set entirely or in part in New England. In these later tales, of course, Carter becomes a resident of Boston. But Lovecraft is ordinarily quite explicit in declaring the New England locality of his tales—even "The Tomb," the most nebulously situated of these, contains references to "New England dialect," "Boston gentry," and the like—and the absence of any such references in "The Statement of Randolph Carter" is telling. Of course, Lovecraft clearly wished to retain some atmosphere of the dream—Carter's testimony is full of gaps and lapses of memory, as if he himself were in a dream—so that clear topographical specification may have been undesirable.

There are, of course, many details—and even points of language—common to the letter and the story. The dream itself, Lovecraft declares, had been inspired by a lengthy discussion of weird fiction, as Loveman had been recommending many books and authors (Bierce among them?) not familiar to Lovecraft. The correspondence between Loveman and Lovecraft for this period has, unfortunately, not come to light, so that we have no way of gauging the tenor of this discussion. In any event, Lovecraft in the letter declares complete ignorance of the *purpose* of the cemetery visit: "We were, for some terrible yet unknown reason, in a very strange and very ancient cemetery . . . He [Loveman] seemed to know exactly what he was about to do, and I also had an idea—though I cannot now remember what it was!" The letter does declare that in the dream Loveman had acquired some secret knowledge from "some rare old books," adding parenthetically: "Loveman, you may know, has a vast library of rare first editions and other treasures precious to the bibliophile's heart." Harley Warren is similarly endowed (Carter speaks of "his vast collection of strange, rare books on forbidden subjects"), but in the story Lovecraft feels it necessary to provide at least some motivation for the graveyard trek: "I remember how I shuddered at his facial expression on the night before the awful happening, when he talked so incessantly of his theory, *why certain corpses never decay, but rest firm and fat in their tombs for a thousand years.*"

Carter declares that this knowledge had been gained from a "fiend-inspired book which . . . he carried in his pocket out of the world." Many have believed this book to be the *Necronomicon,* Lovecraft's celebrated mythical book of forbidden lore, but it is very unlikely that this is the book in question. Carter declares that he had read every book in Warren's library in the languages known to him; this must mean that Carter is at least versed in the common languages (Latin, Greek, French, German, English), and he even mentions that some books were in Arabic. But of the "fiend-inspired book" Carter declares that it was "written in characters whose like I never saw elsewhere," which suggests that the book was *not* in Arabic or any other common language; later Carter states that the book came from India. Since, according to Lovecraft's later testimony, the *Necronomicon* exists only in Arabic, Greek, Latin, and English, Warren's book cannot be that volume.

The degree to which Lovecraft drew upon the letter (which he probably recalled from memory) for the story is very evident by comparison of a passage in the two documents relating to the first sight of the cemetery:

> Such was the scene of my dream—a hideous hollow whose surface was covered with a coarse, repulsive sort of long grass, above which peeped the shocking stones and markers of decaying slate. In a hillside were several old tombs whose facades were in the last stages of decrepitude. I had an odd idea that no living thing had trodden that ground for many centuries till Loveman and I arrived.

> The place was an ancient cemetery; so ancient that I trembled at the manifold signs of immemorial years. It was in a deep, damp hollow, overgrown with rank grass, moss, and curious creeping weeds, and filled with a vague stench which my idle fancy associated absurdly with rotting stone. On every hand were the signs of neglect and decrepitude, and I seemed haunted by the notion that Warren and I were the first living creatures to invade a lethal silence of centuries.

The letter is already a little overheated; the story is more so. This sort of parallelism can be found throughout the two works, right down to the incessant repetition of "waning crescent moon." In both letter and story Loveman/Warren and Lovecraft/Carter pause at one particularly ancient sepulchre, lying flat on the ground;

Loveman/Warren is unable to pry open the top of the sepulchre by his own spade, so Lovecraft/Carter lends him assistance with his own. An aperture is uncovered, revealing a long flight of steps descending downward, and a miasmal stench wafting from the cavity causes the two momentarily to pause (Lovecraft's dreams clearly brought every sense organ into play). At this point Loveman/Warren compels Lovecraft/Carter to remain on the surface while the former descends the crypt alone; in both letter and story the justification given is the fragile state of Lovecraft/Carter's nerves. Although the latter protests, Loveman/Warren is adamant, threatening to cancel the entire enterprise if Lovecraft/Carter proves obdurate. The letter notes that Loveman threatened to bring in one "Dr. Burke" to replace Lovecraft; this detail is omitted from the story. The letter also adds one telling remark made by Loveman that Lovecraft quietly omitted from the story: "'At any rate, this is no place for anybody who can't pass an army physical examination.'" Two and a half years after the fact, Lovecraft's humiliating experience with the R.I.N.G. and the U.S. Army still rankled in his subconscious. But the two protagonists will stay in touch by means of a sort of telephone cable device; as letter and story identically have Loveman/Warren declare, "you see I've enough wire here to reach to the centre of the earth and back!" This is, admittedly, a trifle implausible, but by this time the atmosphere of the story has eliminated such concerns.

As Loveman/Warren descends into the crypt, he begins speaking to Lovecraft/Carter in tones of amazement at what he is seeing. In the story Warren's exclamations are much elaborated, going on for several italicised paragraphs; but in both letter and story Loveman/Warren soon finds his wonder turning to horror as he encounters some nameless entity which causes him to plead frantically to his companion on the ground above, with chilling colloquialism, *"Beat it!"* This single expression—repeated frequently in both letter and story—is one of the first instances of Lovecraft's sloughing off his customarily stately diction for the purpose of augmenting the horror of the situation; it is far more telling than Joe Slater's crude descriptions of his extraterrestrial possession in "Beyond the Wall of Sleep," since these are still expressed generally in the language of the sober narrator. In a very short time Lovecraft would evolve his use of a backwoods New England patois that could evoke the loathsomeness of a scenario far more powerfully than the most adjective-choked purple prose; and this—along with his concomitant adaptation of the prose-poetry of Dunsany—went far in replacing the stiff Johnsonianism of his early work with a much more fluid and wide-ranging prose style.

The rest of "The Statement of Randolph Carter" is very similar in diction to the letter. Of course, the actual entity that makes the final utterance—in English—is left unexplained: throughout the story Carter merely refers to it melodramatically as "the *thing*." The repeated use of this term is itself moderately interesting, in that it suggests a clearly material entity—as opposed to a ghost or spirit—and thereby indirectly confirms Lovecraft's materialism. There will be those who find the complete silence as to the actual nature of the entity disappointing and even a sort of cop-out; but in the dream Lovecraft clearly had no idea what the entity was, and his similar inconclusiveness in the story is another attempt to preserve for himself the nightmarish qualities of his dream.

"The Statement of Randolph Carter" remained a favourite of Lovecraft's throughout his life, perhaps more because it captured a singularly distinctive and memorable dream than because it was a wholly successful weird tale. It first appeared in W. Paul Cook's *Vagrant* for May 1920.

Very shortly after writing "The Statement of Randolph Carter," Lovecraft initiated a project that would again signal a clear shift in his aesthetic focus from poetry and essays to fiction. It must have been around the very beginning of 1920 that he began his commonplace book; he describes its content and purpose in a brief preface to it written in 1934: "This book consists of ideas, images, & quotations hastily jotted down for possible future use in weird fiction. Very few are actually developed plots—for the most part they are merely suggestions or random impressions designed to set the memory or imagination working. Their sources are various—dreams, things read, casual incidents, idle conceptions, & so on." To this assessment there is little to add except masses of detail. David E. Schultz, whose annotated edition of the commonplace book is one of the landmarks of Lovecraft scholarship, has shown how virtually every one of the 222 entries in this book played a role in the shaping of Lovecraft's subsequent fictional output, and even some of his weird poetry. While the sources for some entries are still obscure, enough of them have been elucidated to confirm Lovecraft's statement as to their variegated nature: very few books, dreams, and personal events failed to leave their mark on Lovecraft's imagination.

There has been some debate as to when Lovecraft began keeping his commonplace book. The first reference to it appears to occur in a letter to the Gallomo written some months after the letter in which Lovecraft recorded the dream that inspired "The Statement of Randolph Carter." August Derleth printed this letter (apparently dating to April 1920) in *Dreams and Fancies* (1962), but not all of it; in an editorial note he remarks: "In this very long rambling letter . . . Lovecraft makes an intriguing reference to 'mere dreams' which he says, he has 'recorded for future fictional development in my commonplace book.'"[4] There are other references to the commonplace book in letters to Kleiner dated January 23 and February 10, 1920. The first letter declares: "I have lately . . . been collecting ideas and images for subsequent use in fiction. For the first time in my life, I am keeping a 'commonplace-book'—if that term can be applied to a repository of gruesome and fantastick thoughts."[5] Since Lovecraft's previous letter to Kleiner is dated December 27, 1919, one presumes that the commonplace book was begun somewhere between this date and January 23, 1920. The February 10 letter quotes several actual entries from the commonplace book, none of them later than entry 21.

I have emphasised the likelihood of a very late 1919 or very early 1920 date for the commencement of the commonplace book because Lovecraft himself suggests a date of 1919. This is the date he has written between entries 24 and 25 in the commonplace book itself; but this and other dates were written around 1934 at the urging of R. H. Barlow, who was preparing a transcript of the item. In spite of some remarkable instances of memory of remote events (especially from his childhood), Lovecraft's memory was by no means infallible, and all the dates he has supplied in the commonplace book must be regarded as tentative and in some cases plainly erroneous. Entries 150 and 151 unquestionably date to 1928, but Lovecraft has dated them to 1926. Entry 6 explicitly derives from Dunsany's "Idle Days on the Yann"; but it is my belief that this entry was jotted down not when Lovecraft *first* read that story in *A Dreamer's Tales* in September 1919, but when he *reread* the story in its appearance in *Tales of Three Hemispheres,* probably in early 1920. That volume was published in November 1919 by John W. Luce & Co.,[6] and Lovecraft does not seem to have read it any earlier than the beginning of the next year. Entry 24 derives from Dunsany's "A Shop in Go-by Street," one of the sequels to "Idle Days on the Yann" in *Tales of Three Hemispheres.* The likelihood is that Lovecraft, having come up with the idea of a commonplace book, wrote many entries in a rush in the first few weeks, then wrote only a handful of entries a year for the remainder of his life.

In any event, the commonplace book would prove to be a mine of images and impressions upon which Lovecraft would draw for his subsequent fictional work. More significantly, it clearly calls attention to the fact that fiction is now to be his dominant mode of creative expression: we have no commonplace book entries for essays and very few for poetry, and the rapid waning of these two later bodies of his work becomes evident from this point onward.

Lovecraft certainly seemed to be flexing his fictional muscles in 1920. By March he reported that "I am at present full of various ideas, including a hideous novel to be entitled 'The Club of the Seven Dreamers.'"[7] There is no other mention of this work in any other letters I have ever seen, and I suspect that the novel was never even begun. Lovecraft was simply not at the stage where he could undertake a novel-length work. Even though we know absolutely nothing about the work, it is possible to make some conjectures regarding it. Perhaps, indeed, it was not intended to be a genuine novel but rather a series of short stories with different narrators—these being the "seven dreamers" of the title. If so, then the conception would be somewhat similar to Poe's plans for a volume entitled *Tales of the Folio Club;* in his preface to this volume (first printed in James A. Harrison's collected edition of Poe [1902]) Poe declares that "The number of the club is limited to eleven."[8] One may perhaps also suspect the influence of John Osborne Austin's *More Seven Club Tales* (1900), a volume about strange happenings in Rhode Island which Lovecraft had in his library. This slim book contains seven stories, each narrated by a different individual, mostly figures from seventeenth-century Rhode Island. Only a few of the tales are genuinely weird, and even these are rather innocuous ghost stories; but Lovecraft may have found the format suggestive.

At this moment, however, Dunsany was still in the ascendant. Even if we include "The Terrible Old Man," it would be a half year or more before Lovecraft would write a non-Dunsanian tale of supernatural horror. "The Temple" was written sometime after "The Cats of Ulthar" (June 15, 1920) but before "Celephaïs" (early November), since it is so situated in Lovecraft's chronologies of his fiction. My guess is that it was written sometime in late summer. At nearly 6000 words it is the longest story Lovecraft had written up to this point, and amidst some painful flaws it reveals several points of interest.

A German submarine commanded by a Prussian nobleman, Karl Heinrich, Graf von Altberg-Ehrenstein, sinks a British freighter; later a dead seaman from the freighter is found clinging to the railing of the submarine, and in his pocket is found a "very odd bit of ivory carved to represent a youth's head crowned with laurel." The German crew sleep poorly, have bad dreams, and some think that dead bodies are drifting past the portholes. Some crewmen actually go mad, claiming that a curse has fallen upon them; Altberg-Ehrenstein executes them to restore discipline.

Some days later an explosion in the engine room cripples the submarine, and still later a general mutiny breaks out, with some sailors further damaging the ship; the commander again executes the culprits. Finally only two men, Altberg-Ehreinstein and Lieutenant Klenze, are left alive. The ship sinks lower and lower toward the bottom of the ocean. Klenze then goes mad, shouting: "*He* is calling! *He* is calling! I hear him! We must go!" He voluntarily leaves the ship and plunges into the ocean. As the ship finally reaches the ocean floor, the commander sees a remarkable sight:

> What I saw was an extended and elaborate array of ruined edifices; all of magnificent though unclassified architecture, and in various stages of preservation. Most appeared to be of marble, gleaming whitely in the rays of the searchlight, and the general plan was of a large city at the bottom of a narrow valley, with numerous isolated temples and villas on the steep slopes above.

"Confronted at last with the Atlantis I had formerly deemed largely a myth," Altberg-Ehrenstein notices one especially large temple carved out of the solid rock; later he sees that a head sculpted on it is exactly like the figurine taken from the dead British sailor. The commander, finishing his written account of his adventure on August 20, 1917 (Lovecraft's twenty-seventh birthday), prepares to explore the temple after he sees an anomalous phosphorescence emerging from far within the temple. "So I will carefully don my diving suit and walk boldly up the steps into that primal shrine; that silent secret of unfathomed waters and uncounted years."

Like "Dagon," "The Temple" is aggressively contemporary in its World War I setting; this might have been considered a virtue were it not for the extraordinarily crude and clumsy satire directed against the German commander, who in his first-person account makes himself ridiculous by referring constantly to "our victorious German exploits," "our great German nation," "my own German will," and the like. Why Lovecraft, nearly two years after the war was over, felt the need to carry out this sort of vicious satire is difficult to imagine, especially since the commander actually proves to be quite admirable for his courage and his undaunted facing of the unknown: "Though I knew that death was near, my curiosity was consuming . . ."—a sentiment we will find in many later tales.

Another serious flaw in the story is that it contains *too much supernaturalism.* There are too many anomalous phenomena, and they cannot be unified into a coherent pattern: why does the dead British sailor appear to swim away after his hands are pried off the railing? why do a school of dolphins follow the ship to the bottom of the sea and not come up for air? and what do these matters have to do with the undersea city and the temple? Lovecraft seems to have thrown these elements in to increase the general weirdness of the scenario, but their unaccountability dilutes the force of the central weird phenomenon.

But that central phenomenon—not so much the supposed existence of Atlantis (in which Lovecraft did not believe) as the existence of an entire human civilisation unknown to history—is what redeems "The Temple": it will become a dominant motif in many of Lovecraft's later tales, in which both human and extraterrestrial civilisations are found to have existed long before the emergence of known human civilisations, rendering our own physical and cultural supremacy tentative and perhaps transitory. One detail is of consuming interest: the commander notes that the pictorial and architectural art of the undersea city is "of the most phenomenal perfection, largely Hellenic in idea, yet strangely individual. It imparts an impression of terrible antiquity, as though it were the remotest rather than the immediate ancestor of Greek art." The suggestion is that this civilisation was in fact the ancestor of all Western art, and that our own culture represents a sad decline from the "phenomenal perfection" of this race. That phosphorescence at the end seems to suggest that that race is perhaps not as extinct as the ruined state of the city implies, but Lovecraft in a letter remarks curiously that "the flame that the Graf von Altberg-Ehrenstein beheld was a witch-fire lit by spirits many millennia old";[9] how any reader could ever make this deduction in the utter absence of any textual evidence escapes me.

Lovecraft seemed to retain a fondness for "The Temple," but it never appeared in an amateur journal and was first published only in *Weird Tales* for September 1925. Perhaps its length made amateur publication difficult, since space was always at a premium.

Another tale of which Lovecraft was justifiably proud is "Facts concerning the Late Arthur Jermyn and His Family," written some time after "The Temple," probably no later than autumn. This compact story—notable for its taut, restrained language in contrast to the flamboyance of some of his other early tales—tells of why Sir Arthur Jermyn doused himself in oil and set himself aflame one night. He had come from a venerable but eccentric family. In the eighteenth century Sir Wade Jermyn "was one of the earliest explorers of the Congo region," but was placed in a madhouse after speaking wildly of "a prehistoric white Congolese civilisation." He had brought back from the Congo a wife—reportedly the daughter of a Portuguese trader—who was never seen. The offspring of the union were very peculiar both in physiognomy and mentality. In the middle of the nineteenth century a Sir Robert Jermyn killed off nearly his entire family as well as a fellow African explorer who had brought back strange tales (and perhaps other things) from the area of Sir Wade's explorations.

Arthur Jermyn seeks to redeem the family name by continuing Sir Wade's researches and perhaps vindicating him. Pursuing reports of a white ape who became a goddess in the prehistoric African civilisation, he comes upon the remains of the site in 1912 but finds little confirmation of the story of the white ape. This confirmation is supplied by a Belgian explorer who ships the object to Jermyn House. The hideous rotting thing is found to be wearing a locket containing the Jermyn coat of arms; and what remains of its face bears an uncanny resemblance to that of Arthur Jermyn. When he sees this object, Jermyn douses himself in oil and sets himself aflame.

This seemingly straightforward story—Sir Wade had married the ape-goddess, whose offspring bore the physical and mental stigmata of the unnatural union—is actually rather more complicated than it seems. Consider the resounding opening utterance, one of the most celebrated passages in Lovecraft's fiction:

> Life is a hideous thing, and from the background behind what we know of it peer daemoniacal hints of truth which make it sometimes a thousandfold more hideous. Science, already oppressive with its shocking revelations, will perhaps be the ultimate exterminator of our human species—if separate species we be—for its reserve of unguessed horrors could never be borne by mortal brains if loosed upon the world.

The critical phrase here is the clause "if separate species we be": this *generalised* statement concerning the possibility that human beings may not be entirely "human" is not logically deducible from a *single* case of miscegenation. But let us return to that "prehistoric *white* Congolese civilisation" and a later description of it: "the living things that might haunt such a place [were] creatures half of the jungle and half of the impiously aged city—fabulous creatures which even a Pliny might describe with scepticism; things that might have sprung up after the great apes had overrun the dying city with the walls and the pillars, the vaults and the weird carvings." This, really, is the crux of the story, for what Lovecraft is suggesting is that the inhabitants of this city are not only the "missing link" between ape and human but also *the ultimate source for all white civilisation.* For someone of Lovecraft's well-known racialist bent, such a thing would be a horror surpassing any isolated case of miscegenation. Of course, the "white ape" whom Sir Wade marries is not a member of the original white civilisation (which is long extinct), but a product of the mingling of apes with the descendants of this civilisation. How else could the ape be "white"?

The overall implication of "Arthur Jermyn" is that all white civilisation is derived from this primal race in Africa, a race that has corrupted itself by intermingling with apes. This is the only explanation for the narrator's opening statement, "If we knew what we are, we should do as Sir Arthur Jermyn did [i.e., commit suicide]": we may not have a white ape in our immediate ancestry, but we are all the products of an ultimate miscegenation. More broadly, Lovecraft is suggesting that the distinction between apes and human beings is a highly tenuous one—not merely in the case of the Jermyns, but of us all. Recall "At the Root" (1918): "We must recognise the essential underlying savagery in the animal called man . . . civilisation is but a slight coverlet beneath which the dominant beast sleeps lightly and ever ready to awake."

Lovecraft made two suggestive remarks on the sources and genesis of this tale. First, he wrote to Arthur Harris: "The only tale of mine to be published in sections is 'Arthur Jermyn', & this was written with that form in mind."[10] What this means is that the tale was written expressly for the *Wolverine* (edited by Horace L. Lawson), where the tale appeared serially in the issues for March and June 1921. The two sections fall neatly into an account of the history of the Jermyn line and the narrative of Arthur Jermyn himself. Lovecraft's second comment is still more suggestive:

> [The] origin [of "Arthur Jermyn"] is rather curious—and far removed from the atmosphere it suggests. Somebody had been harassing me into reading some work of the iconoclastic moderns—these young chaps why pry behind exteriors and unveil nasty hidden motives and secret stigmata—and I had nearly fallen asleep over the tame backstairs gossip of Anderson's *Winesburg, Ohio.* The sainted Sherwood, as you know, laid bare the dark area which many whited village lives concealed, and it occurred to me that I, in my weirder medium, could probably devise some secret behind a man's ancestry which would make the worst of Anderson's disclosures sound like the annual report of a Sabbath school. Hence Arthur Jermyn.[11]

As I shall discuss later, it was just at this time when Lovecraft (perhaps in part through the influence of Frank Belknap Long) was attempting to bring himself literarily up to date by investigating the modernists. If the above is to be taken at its face value, it suggests Lovecraft's dawning realisation that weird fiction could be a mode of social criticism as probing in its way as the grimmest literary realism. "Arthur Jermyn," of course, represents only a minor foray of this sort, but a much later tale of which it is a source—"The Shadow over Innsmouth"—is a very different proposition.

"Facts concerning the Late Arthur Jermyn and His Family" was, as I have mentioned, first published as a serial in the *Wolverine* for March and June 1921. This is the only appearance until the recent corrected edition in which the full, correct title as recorded on the surviving typescript was printed. It got a favourable notice in "The Vivisector" for November 1921, written (as I shall demonstrate later) by Alfred Galpin:

> "Facts Concerning the Late Arthur Jermyn and His Family", by Mr. Lovecraft, shows another phase of that writer's gloomy but powerful genius. It is perfect in execution, restrained in manner, complete, and marked by Mr. Lovecraft's uniquely effective handling of introductory and concluding portions. The legend is not so powerful as many of Mr. Lovecraft's dreamings have been, but it is unquestionably original and does not derive from Poe, Dunsany, or any other of Mr. Lovecraft's favorites and predecessors. Its affiliations are rather closer with Ambrose Bierce, and I personally should place it beside much of Bierce's best work without fearing for the fame of the United's representative.[12]

The comparison to Bierce seems to me a trifle strained, and may apply only in the relative plainness of the style and the brooding pessimism of the opening. Whether it is "unquestionably original" is another matter. I have not found any direct influence, but one wonders whether a novel that was serialised in the *Cavalier* (a Munsey magazine) in April 1912—*The Ape at the Helm* by Patrick Gallagher, which Sam Moskowitz describes as dealing with "a ship that loses its first mate and finds the captain taking aboard a half-man, half-ape from an island"[13]—is a source for the story. Since Lovecraft declares that "I read every number of *The Cavalier*,"[14] he must have read Gallagher's novel; I myself, however, have not done so, so can only note the very general similarity of conception between it and Lovecraft's story.

We now come to "Poetry and the Gods," published in the *United Amateur* for September 1920 as by "Anna Helen Crofts and Henry Paget-Lowe." Aside from the two stories written with Winifred Virginia Jackson, this is Lovecraft's only signed collaboration with a woman writer. Some have believed Anna Helen Crofts to be a pseudonym (perhaps for Jackson), but she appears under her own name in the UAPA membership lists, residing at 343 West Main Street in North Adams, Massachusetts, in the far northwestern corner of the state. I have no idea how Lovecraft came in touch with her or why he chose to collaborate on this tale; he never mentions it or his coauthor in any correspondence I have ever seen.

"Poetry and the Gods" tells the somewhat mawkish story of Marcia, a young woman who, though "outwardly a typical product of modern civilisation," feels strangely out of tune with her time. She picks up a magazine and reads a piece of free verse, finding it so evocative that she lapses into a languid dream in which Hermes comes to her and wafts her to Parnassus where Zeus is holding court. She is shown six individuals sitting before the Corycian cave; they are Homer, Dante, Shakespeare, Milton, Goethe, and Keats. "These were those messengers whom the Gods had sent to tell men that Pan had passed not away, but only slept; for it is in poetry that Gods speak to men." Zeus tells Marcia that she will meet a man who is "our latest-born messenger," a man whose poetry will somehow bring order to the chaos of the modern age. Sure enough, she later meets this person, "the young poet of poets at whose feet sits all the world," and he thrills her with his poetry.

This is surely one of the most peculiar items in Lovecraft's fictional corpus, not only for its utterly unknown genesis but for its anomalous theme. At whose urging was this story written? The fact that Crofts's name is placed before Lovecraft's does not mean much, as Lovecraft would have considered it gentlemanly to have taken second billing; much of the language clearly is Lovecraft's, and it is difficult to imagine what Crofts's contribution can have been. The prose verges on Dunsanianism, especially Hermes' long speech to Marcia; but in reality this bit sounds like a conventional translation of the period from Greek or Latin literature. It is facile to say that the idea of using a female protagonist must have come from Crofts, but perhaps not so facile to think that the description of her attire ("in a low-cut evening dress of black") is not likely to have been arrived at by a man so seemingly unworldly as Lovecraft.

Then there is the long bit of free verse in the story. Is this Crofts's addition? I have found only one other contribution by Crofts in the amateur press, but it is a one-page story, "Life" (*United Amateur,* March 1921), and not a poem; she could, however, have published poetry in other journals. Lovecraft, of course, cannot help poking fun at the specimen: "It was only a bit of *vers libre,* that pitiful compromise of the poet who overleaps prose yet falls short of the divine melody of numbers . . ."; but the passage goes on to say: "but it had in it all the unstudied music of a bard who lives and feels, and who gropes ecstatically for unveiled beauty. Devoid of regularity, it yet had the wild harmony of winged, spontaneous words; a harmony missing from the formal, convention-bound verse she had known." The poetic fragment—rather effective in its imagistic way—is certainly not meant parodically, and is presumably supposed to be by that "poet of poets" whom Marcia meets later. The encounters with Homer and the rest are a trifle embarrassing, as each soberly spouts some familiar chestnut which Marcia appreciates even though she does not know Greek, German, or Italian and hence cannot understand three of the six bards. On the whole, "Poetry and the Gods" is simply a curiosity, and will become of interest only if more information on its writing and its collaborator emerges.

A more representative story is "From Beyond," written on November 16, 1920, as noted on the autograph manuscript. Like so many of Lovecraft's early tales, it is severely flawed but full of significance for its adumbration of themes that are developed to much better advantage in later works. This is the histrionic story of Crawford Tillinghast, a scientist who has devised a machine that will "break down the barriers" erected by our five senses that limit our perception of phenomena. He shows to his friend, the narrator, "a pale, outré colour or blend of colours" that he maintains is ultraviolet, ordinarily invisible to the human eye. As he continues his experiment, the narrator begins to perceive all sorts of amorphous, jellylike objects drifting through what he previously thoguht was empty air; he even sees them "brushing past me and occasionally *walking or drifting through my supposedly solid body.*" Later, as the experiment becomes increasingly peculiar and as Tillinghast begins shouting madly about the creatures he controls through his machine, the narrator suddenly fires a shot from a pistol, destroying the machine. Tillinghast is found dead of apoplexy.

This tale remained unpublished until its appearance in the *Fantasy Fan* for June 1934; at this time or earlier, Lovecraft made several changes that are not recorded on the surviving autograph manuscript. In the first place, the scientist's name has been changed from Henry Annesley. Perhaps Lovecraft thought this a little too colourless; Crawford Tillinghast is a combination of two celebrated old families in the history of Providence (as Lovecraft notes in *The Case of Charles Dexter Ward:* ". . . the great brigs of the Browns, Crawfords, and Tillinghasts") and befits a tale set, however nominally, in Providence: Tillinghast resides in an "ancient, lonely house set back from Benevolent Street," on College Hill near Brown University. There may in fact be a subtle historical in-joke here, since in the late eighteenth century property on Benevolent Street was owned, on one side of the street, by Joseph Crawford, and, on the other, by a J. Tillinghast.[15] Another curious addition is the narrator's account of why he has a revolver, something "I always carried after dark since the night I was held up in East Providence." To my knowledge, Lovecraft was never himself held up in East Providence or anywhere else; but perhaps this phrase was added after his frequent visits to the weird writer C. M. Eddy and his wife in East Providence, then and now a rather seedy community.

The true significance of the tale, however, is its spectacular idea of expanding the range of sense-perception to make visible what we otherwise think of as empty space. As one studies the wording of the story, it becomes clear that it is little more than a sort of extrapolation of some conceptions in Hugh Elliot's *Modern Science and Materialism.* Elliot's book not merely helped to firm up Lovecraft's early metaphysics, but also triggered his imagination. Each of the following three entries in his commonplace book have fairly precise analogues in Elliot's work:

> 34 Moving away from earth more swiftly than light—past gradually unfolded—horrible revelation.
>
> 35 Special beings with special senses from remote universes. Advent of an external universe to view.
>
> 36 Disintegration of all matter to electrons and finally empty space assured, just as devolution of energy to radiant heat is known. Case of *acceleration*—man passes into space.

The first entry relates to the old conception (now rendered false by relativity) that it is possible to travel faster than the speed of light and that in doing so one would go backward in time. The third entry is merely an echo of the notion of entropy. For our present concerns, it is the second entry that is of greatest relevance, since it echoes the passage I have already quoted from Elliot in which he expresses the bold conjecture of how the universe might appear to us if we had a thousand senses. Compare this with Tillinghast's utterance near the beginning of "From Beyond":

> "What do we know," he had said, "of the world and the universe about us? Our means of receiving impressions are absurdly few, and our notions of surrounding objects infinitely narrow. We see things only as we are constructed to see them, and can gain no idea of their absolute nature. With five feeble senses we pretend to comprehend the boundlessly complex cosmos, yet other beings with a wider, stronger, or different range of senses might not only see very differently the things we see, but might see and study whole worlds of matter, energy, and life which lie close at hand yet can never be detected with the senses we have. . . ."

When Tillinghast shows the narrator the anomalous colour, he asks him, "Do you know what that is? . . . *That is ultra-violet*." This is a direct echo of a passage in Elliot in which he mentions, "Not only are our senses few, but they are extremely limited in range," and he goes on specifically to cite the case of ultraviolet rays as one of the many phenomena we cannot see.

But the clearest borrowing from Elliot relates to the central weird phenomenon of the tale—the fact that every particle of space is populated by a mass of loathsome creatures that can flow through our own bodies. This is really nothing more than a horrific presentation of the common fact that most material objects consist largely of empty space. Elliot writes about this notion at length:

> Let us now . . . see what matter would look like if magnified to, say, a thousand million diameters, so that the contents of a small thimble appeared to become the size of the earth. Even under this great magnification, the individual electrons would still be too small to be seen by the naked eye. . . . The first circumstance that

> strikes us is that nearly the whole structure of matter consists of the empty spaces between electrons. . . . It ceases, therefore, to be remarkable that X-rays can penetrate matter and come out on the other side.

"From Beyond" is, however, a very poorly written and conceived tale. Its use of the already hackneyed motif of the mad scientist (which entered weird fiction no later than *Frankenstein*) is crude to the point of caricature: "It is not pleasant to see a stout man suddenly grown thin, and it is even worse when the baggy skin becomes yellowed or greyed, the eyes sunken, circled, and uncannily glowing, the forehead veined and corrugated, and the hands tremulous and twitching." Tillinghast's speeches become comically grotesque in their self-important bombast; toward the end he makes the inexplicable assertion: "I have harnessed the shadows that stride from world to world to sow death and madness. . . . Space belongs to me, do you hear?" I am not even clear on some points of plot in the story. Some of Tillinghast's servants have died inexplicably; did the monsters evoked by the machine kill them, or Tillinghast himself dispose of them? The story offers contradictory clues on the matter.

But "From Beyond" is important for its adumbration of such issues as the expansion of sense-perception (we will see that several of Lovecraft's later extraterrestrials possess more senses than human beings), the strange "colour or blend of colours" (perhaps the ultimate nucleus of "The Colour out of Space"), and the attempt to visualise what a supra-sensory world might be like. For these reasons, "From Beyond" must be regarded as an important formative tale in Lovecraft's corpus—a tale that, like "Polaris" in a somewhat different way, shows him employing explicitly philosophical conceptions for the purpose of horror fiction.[16]

The two stories, "Nyarlathotep" (a prose-poem) and "The Crawling Chaos" (written in collaboration with Winifred Virginia Jackson), must be considered together for a reason I shall discuss presently. "Nyarlathotep" was published in the issue of the *United Amateur* dated November 1920; but since the magazine was at this time habitually late, sometimes by two or three months, it is difficult to know exactly when the prose-poem was written. Lovecraft first discusses it in a letter to Rheinhart Kleiner dated December 14, 1920,[17] but it is unclear whether Lovecraft has sent the tale in manuscript to Kleiner or whether Kleiner has read the story in the presumably delayed *United Amateur.* The former seems somewhat more likely, since Lovecraft wrote the letter to accompany several recent stories he was then sending to Kleiner.

"Nyarlathotep" is of interest both intrinsically and for its genesis. Like "The Statement of Randolph Carter," it is the direct product of a dream; but more to the point, the first paragraph was written *"before I fully awaked,"* as Lovecraft wrote to Kleiner. By "first paragraph" Lovecraft cannot be referring to the brief, fragmentary opening ("Nyarlathotep . . . the crawling chaos . . . I am the last . . . I will tell the audient void. . . .") but the lengthy paragraph that follows; otherwise, his remark that he changed only three words of it would not be particularly noteworthy. In any case, the dream again involved Samuel Loveman, who writes Lovecraft the following note: "Don't fail to see Nyarlathotep if he comes to Providence. He is horrible—horrible beyond anything you can imagine—but wonderful. He haunts one for hours afterward. I am still shuddering at what he showed." Lovecraft notes that the peculiar name Nyarlathotep came to him in this dream, but one can conjecture at least a partial influence in the name of Dunsany's minor god Mynarthitep (mentioned fleetingly in "The Sorrow of Search," in *Time and the Gods*) or of the prophet Alhireth-Hotep (mentioned in *The Gods of Pegāna*). Of course, *-hotep* is an Egyptian root, and Nyarlathotep is in fact said in the prose-poem to have come "out of Egypt . . . he was of the old native blood and looked like a Pharaoh." In the dream Nyarlathotep is supposed to be a sort of "itinerant showman or lecturer who held forth in publick halls and aroused widespread fear and discussion with his exhibitions"—exhibitions that included "a horrible—possibly prophetic—cinema reel" and, later, "some extraordinary experiments with scientific and electrical apparatus." Lovecraft decides to go hear Nyarlathotep, and the story follows the dream pretty closely up to the conclusion: Nyarlathotep's lecture seems to inspire a sort of collective madness, and people march mechanically in various mindless formations, never to be heard of again.

"Nyarlathotep" is, plainly, an allegory on the downfall of civilisation—the first of many such ruminations in the length and breadth of Lovecraft's fiction and his philosophical thought. In the tale we find ourselves in a "season of political and social upheaval" in which people "whispered warnings and prophecies which no one dared consciously repeat." And what does the narrator see "shadowed on a screen" during Nyarlathotep's cinema presentation? "And I saw the world battling against blackness; against the waves of destruction from ultimate space; whirling, churning; struggling around the dimming, cooling sun." Civilisation's downfall heralds the decline of the whole planet with the extinction of the sun. Later the world seems to be falling apart:

> Once we looked at the pavement and found the blocks loose and displaced by grass, with scarce a line of rusted metal to shew where the tramways had run. And again we saw a tram-car, lone, windowless, dilapidated, and almost on its side. When we gazed around the horizon, we could not find the third tower by the river, and noticed that the silhouette of the second tower was ragged at the top.

The entire prose-poem is one of Lovecraft's most powerful vignettes, and shows how deeply imbued was his mingled terror of and fascination with the decline of the West. The fact that Nyarlathotep "had risen up out of the blackness of twenty-seven centuries" places him at the end of the fourth dynasty of the Old Kingdom, either in the reign of Khufu (Cheops) in 2590–68 B.C.E. or in that of Khafre (Chephren) in 2559–35 B.C.E. Khafre, of course, is the builder of the Sphinx, and perhaps Lovecraft was wishing to draw indirectly upon the eternal mystery of this cryptic monument.[18]

Can there be a real source for Nyarlathotep? Will Murray[19] has made the provocative conjecture that this "itinerant showman" was based upon Nicola Tesla (1856–1943), the eccentric scientist and inventor who created a sensation at the turn of the century for his strange electrical experiments. Lovecraft mentions Tesla at least once in his correspondence—most tellingly in a letter in which he is free-associating about the events he recalls in the year 1900: "Nikola Tesla reports signals from Mars."[20] Physically, of course, Tesla looked nothing like Nyarlathotep: one biographer describes him as a "weird, storklike figure on the lecture platform in his white tie and tails" and "nearly seven feet tall" because of the cork soles he wore to protect himself during his electrical demonstrations.[21] Nevertheless, there are enough suggestive similarities between Tesla's and Nyarlathotep's lecture performances—and the shock and disturbance they inspired—to make a connexion likely, even if, because of the dream-inspiration of "Nyarlathotep," such a connexion can only be regarded as subconscious.

Nyarlathotep, of course, recurs throughout Lovecraft's later fiction and becomes one of the chief "gods" in his invented pantheon. But he appears in such widely divergent forms that it may not be possible to establish a single or coherent symbolism for him; to say merely, as some critics have done, that he is a "shapeshifter" (something Lovecraft never genuinely suggests) is only to admit that even his physical form is not consistent from story to story, much less his thematic significance. But whatever the ultimate "meaning" of Nyarlathotep, he rarely made a more dramatic appearance than in the brief tale laconically bearing his name.

"The Crawling Chaos," as will now be evident, must be considered in conjunction with "Nyarlathotep" only because the title is clearly derived from the previously cited opening of the prose-poem, although Nyarlathotep himself makes no appearance in the story. Lovecraft admits in a letter: "I took the title C. C. from my Nyarlathotep sketch . . . because I liked the sound of it."[22] I do not know how helpful this is in dating the collaboration; it cannot, at least, have been written before the prose-poem, hence probably does not date any earlier than December 1920. It was published in the *United Co-operative* for April 1921 as by "Elizabeth Berkeley and Lewis Theobald, Jun." Lovecraft appears to allude to the genesis of the story in a letter of May 1920, in which he notes the previous collaboration with Jackson, "The Green Meadow": "I will enclose—subject to return—an account of a Jacksonian dream which occurred in the early part of 1919, and which I am some time going to weave into a horror story . . ."[23] It is, of course, not entirely certain whether this dream was the nucleus of "The Crawling Chaos"; but since there are no other story collaborations with Jackson, the conjecture seems likely.

In certain external features of the plot "The Crawling Chaos" is surprisingly reminiscent of "The Green Meadow"; but it is, on the whole, a somewhat more interesting tale than its predecessor, although still quite insubstantial. The narrator tells of his one experience with opium, when a doctor unwittingly gave him an overdose to ease his pain. After experiencing a sensation of falling, "curiously dissociated from the idea of gravity or direction," he finds himself in a "strange and beautiful room lighted by many windows." A sense of fear comes over him, and he realises that it is inspired by a monotonous pounding that seems to be coming from below the house in which he finds himself. Looking out a window, he sees that the pounding is caused by titanic waves that are rapidly washing away the piece of land on which the house stands, transforming the land into an ever-narrowing peninsula. Fleeing through the back door of the house, the narrator finds himself walking along a sandy path and rests under a palm tree. Suddenly a child of radiant beauty drops from the branches of the tree, and presently two other individuals—"a god and goddess they must have been"—appear. They waft the narrator into the air and are joined by a singing chorus of other heavenly individuals who wish to lead the narrator to the wondrous land of Teloe. But the pounding of the sea disrupts this throng, and in imagery very reminiscent of "Nyarlathotep" ("Down through the aether I saw the accursed earth turning, ever turning, with angry and tempestuous seas gnawing at wild desolate shores and dashing foam against the tottering towers of deserted cities"), the narrator appears to witness the destruction of the world.

"The Crawling Chaos" is redeemed only by its apocalyptic conclusion; for up to this point it has merely been a confused, verbose, histrionic dream-phantasy without focus or direction. Various points in the account carry the implication that the narrator is not actually dreaming or hallucinating but envisioning the far future of the world—a point made very clumsily by his conceiving of Rudyard Kipling as an "ancient" author. But the final passage is impressive on its own as a set piece, and is the sole connexion with the prose-poem that inspired the story's title. It is manifest that the entire tale was written by Lovecraft; as with "The Green Meadow," Jackson's only contribution must have been the dream whose imagery probably laid the foundations for the opening segments.

Once again Alfred Galpin reviewed the story favourably: ". . . I recall the attention of amateurs to the most important story recently published, 'The Crawling Chaos,' pseudonymously written by Winifred Virginia Jackson and H. P. Lovecraft. The narrative power, vivid imagination and poetic merit of this story are such as to elevate it above certain minor but aggravating faults of organisation and composition."[24] But not everyone was so enthusiastic. Lovecraft, in the "News Notes" for the January 1922 *United Amateur,* takes a certain glee in reporting the hostile reaction of one amateur: ". . . during a denunciation of Lovecraftian stories [he] remarked, 'We can hardly go them. That Crawling Chaos is the limit. His attempts at Poe-esque tales will hand him—'" I do not know who this person is; Lovecraft merely identifies him, archly, as a "prominent politician with a distaste for the 'wild, weird tales' of H. P. Lovecraft."

Another tale written late in 1920—"The Picture in the House," written on December 12—is a very different proposition, and can rank as one of Lovecraft's pioneering stories of his early period. Its opening is very celebrated:

> Searchers after horror haunt strange, far places. For them are the catacombs of Ptolemais, and the carven mausolea of the nightmare countries. They climb to the moonlit towers of ruined Rhine castles, and falter down black cobwebbed steps beneath the scattered stones of forgotten cities in Asia. The haunted wood and the desolate mountain are their shrines, and they linger around the sinister monoliths on uninhabited islands. But the true epicure in the terrible, to whom a new thrill of unutterable ghastliness is the chief end and justification of existence, esteems most of all the ancient, lonely farmhouses of backwoods New England; for there the dark elements of strength, solitude, grotesqueness, and ignorance combine to form the perfection of the hideous.

Resounding as this is, it is generally overlooked that the narrator of the tale is no "epicure in the terrible" but merely an individual "in quest of certain genealogical data" who, travelling on bicycle, finds himself forced to take shelter at a decrepit farmhouse in the "Miskatonic Valley." When his knocks fail to summon an occupant, he believes it to be uninhabited and enters; but shortly the occupant, who had been asleep upstairs, makes an appearance.

> In the doorway stood a person of such singular appearance that I should have exclaimed aloud but for the restraints of good breeding. Old, white-bearded, and ragged, my host possessed a countenance and physique which inspired equal wonder and respect. His height could not have been less than six feet, and despite a general air of age and poverty he was stout and powerful in proportion. His face, almost hidden by a long beard which grew high on the cheeks, seemed abnormally ruddy and less wrinkled than one might expect; while over a high forehead fell a shock of white hair little thinned by the years. His eyes, though a trifle bloodshot, seemed inexplicably keen and burning. But for his horrible unkemptness the man would have been as distinguished as he was impressive.

The old man, seemingly a harmless backwoods farmer speaking in "an extreme form of Yankee dialect I had thought long extinct" ("'Ketched in the rain, be ye?'"), notes that his visitor had been examining a very old book on a bookcase, Pigafetta's *Regnum Congo,* "printed in Frankfort in 1598." This book continually turns, as if from frequent consultation, to plate XII, depicting "in gruesome detail a butcher's shop of the cannibal Anziques." The old man avers that he obtained the book from a sailor from Salem years ago, and as he continues babbling on in his increasingly loathsome patois he begins to make vile confessions of the effects of that plate: "'Killin' sheep was kinder more fun—but d'ye know, 'twan't quite *satis-fyin'.* Queer haow a *cravin'* gits a holt on ye— As ye love the Almighty, young man, don't tell nobody, but I swar ter Gawd thet picter begun ta make me *hungry fer victuals I couldn't raise nor buy—'"* At that point a drop of liquid falls from the ceiling directly upon the plate. The narrator thinks it is rain, but "rain is not red." "I did not shriek or move, but merely shut my eyes." But a thunderbolt destroys the house and its tenant, although somehow the narrator survives.

There are so many points of interest in this compact, 3000-word story that it is difficult to know where to begin. This tale is celebrated for its introduction of the second, and perhaps most famous, city in Lovecraft's mythical New England—Arkham. Here it is clearly implied that the city is in the Miskatonic Valley, since the narrator "found myself upon an apparently abandoned road which I had chosen as the shortest cut to Arkham." It is not entirely clear where the mythical Miskatonic Valley itself is, but there is no compelling reason to assume (as Will Murray did in a provocative series of articles whose conclusions were substantially refuted by Robert D. Marten) that Arkham was not at this time a fictional analogue of the coastal town Salem, as Lovecraft frequently declared in later years. Murray's conjecture that the name Arkham was founded on the central Massachusetts town of Oakham also seems implausible—no less implausible than Marten's conjecture that the source of the name was an archaic Rhode Island town, Arkwright.[25] Until further evidence emerges, we shall have to remain in the dark as to the precise origin of the name Arkham.

More significant is the fact that "The Picture in the House" is the first of Lovecraft's tales not merely to utilise an authentic New England setting but to draw upon what Lovecraft himself clearly felt to be the weird heritage of New England history, specifically the history of Massachusetts. As a Rhode Islander (but one who spent his very early years in Massachusetts and would probably have become a resident of the state had his father not taken ill), Lovecraft could look upon the "Puritan theocracy" of Massachusetts with suitably abstract horror and even a certain condescension; in the story he somewhat flamboyantly paints the lurking hideousness of the repressed colonial tradition:

> In such houses have dwelt generations of strange people, whose like the world has never seen. Seized with a gloomy and fanatical belief which exiled them from their kind, their ancestors sought the wilderness for freedom. There the scions of a conquering race indeed flourished free from the restrictions of their fellows, but cowered in an appalling slavery to the dismal phantasms of their own minds. Divorced from the enlightenment of civilisation, the strength of these Puritans turned into singular channels; and in their isolation, morbid self-repression, and struggle for life with relentless Nature, there came to them dark furtive traits from the prehistoric depths of their cold Northern heritage. By necessity practical and by philosophy stern, these folk were not beautiful in their sins. Erring as all mortals must, they were forced by their rigid code to seek concealment above all else; so that they came to use less and less taste in what they concealed.

These sentiments, expressed perhaps less hyperbolically, would remain with Lovecraft throughout his life. It becomes clear from this passage that the principal cause, in the atheist Lovecraft's mind, of the Puritans' ills was their religion. In discussing "The Picture in the House" with Robert E. Howard in 1930, he remarks: "Bunch together a group of people deliberately chosen for strong religious feelings, and you have a practical guarantee of dark morbidities expressed in crime, perversion, and insanity."[26] In a much earlier discussion of Puritans with Frank Belknap Long, in 1923, Lovecraft says (again a trifle hyperbolically and pretentiously): "Verily, the Puritans were the only really effective diabolists and decadents the world has known; because they hated life and scorned the platitude that it is worth living."[27]

Regardless of the validity of Lovecraft's interpretation of early New England, this gesture of imbuing horror in seventeenth-century Puritan Massachusetts was of vital significance to his entire aesthetic of horror. Maurice Lévy remarks correctly that the American fantastic tradition up to Lovecraft's time "lacks unity and depth"; he goes on to contrast European and American weird writing:

> To create an adequate atmosphere for a fantastic tale, we must have old houses and medieval castles that materialize in space the hallucinatory presence of the past, the houses we can find *authentically* only on the old continent. We need an old, legendary foundation, a national heritage of obscure beliefs and antiquated superstitions. We need millennia of history, the progressive accumulation in the racial memory of prodigious facts and innumerable crimes, so that the necessary sublimations and schematizations can take place. Above all, we need a history that has become myth, so that the fantastic tale can be born through the irruption of myth into history.[28]

Lévy maintains that Lovecraft created a sort of ersatz historical tradition by drawing upon the colonial past—the only "ancient" historical period (aside from the Indians) that this country can acknowledge. We may not have millennia of history, but even two or three hundred years—in a land that was changing rapidly even in Lovecraft's day, to say nothing of our own—is sufficient for those "sublimations and schematizations" to take place. Lovecraft did not know it yet, but he had found the locus of horror on his doorstep. At the moment, he was regarding the colonial past as a "pure other"—something of which he, the eighteenth-century Rhode Island rationalist, had no part; it was only after his New York period that he would come to internalise it, recognise it as his own, and treat the land, its people, and its history with both sympathy and horror.

Returning specifically to "The Picture in the House," it is not merely the case that, as Colin Wilson remarks, the tale presents "a nearly convincing sketch of sadism."[29] It is true that the old man is a sadist of sorts, or at least an individual who is psychologically very disturbed; but the tale is not simply a *conte cruel* but actually supernatural in its implication that the old man has lived far beyond his normal span by resorting to cannibalism. He himself states, "'They say meat makes blood an' flesh, an' gives ye new life, so I wondered ef 'twudn't make a man live longer an' longer ef 'twas *more the same*—'" That sailor from Salem who gave the old man the *Regnum Congo* is someone whose name the narrator recognises only from the Revolutionary period.

The *Regnum Congo* by Filippo Pigafetta (1533–1604) is of some interest in revealing an embarrassing lapse on Lovecraft's part. The book was, to be sure, printed in Frankfort in 1598; but its first edition was not in Latin, as that edition was, but in Italian (*Relatione del reame di Congo et della cironvicine contrade,* Rome, 1591); it was subsequently translated into English (1597) and German (1597) prior to its Latin translation; and it was in the German (as well as the Latin) translation that the plates by the brothers De Bry were introduced. Lovecraft appears not to have known any of this because he derived his information on the book entirely from Thomas Henry Huxley's essay "On the History of the Man-like Apes," in *Man's Place in Nature and Other Anthropological Essays* (1894). Lovecraft must have read this book prior to 1915, for it was from another essay in it—"On the Methods and Results of Ethnology"—that he derived the term "Xanthochroi" mentioned in "The Crime of the Century" (*Conservative,* April 1915). What is more, Lovecraft never consulted the De Bry plates themselves but only some rather inaccurate engravings of them printed in an appendix to Huxley's essay. As a result, Lovecraft makes errors in describing the plates; for example, the old man thinks the natives drawn in them are anomalously white-looking, when in fact this is merely the result of a poor rendering of the plates by Huxley's illustrator. All this is only of interest because it reveals Lovecraft on occasion to have used exactly that "second-hand erudition"[30] for which he later chided Poe.[31]

Finally, what are we to make of the *deus ex machina* conclusion? Lovecraft has been roundly abused for it, but the convenient stroke of lightning seems clearly derived from Poe's "The Fall of the House of Usher," where a bolt of lightning causes the "once barely-discernible fissure" in the house to crack open so that the entire house collapses. This may or may not be much of an excuse, but Lovecraft at least has an impressive precedent for what is really a relatively insignificant aspect of a tale that otherwise offers tremendous richness of theme and conception.

The use of the backwoods New England dialect by the old man calls for some comment. The fact that the narrator believes it to have been "long extinct" is another clue that the old man must be hundreds of years old. But where, in fact, did Lovecraft derive this peculiar dialect, which he will use at considerable length in some later stories, notably "The Dunwich Horror" (1928) and "The Shadow over Innsmouth" (1931)? Lovecraft admits in 1929 that the dialect did not exist in the New England of his day:

> As for Yankee farmers—oddly enough, I haven't noticed that the majority talk any differently from myself; so that I've never regarded them as a separate class to whom one must use a special dialect. If I were to say, "Mornin', Zeke, haow ye be?" to anybody along the road during my numerous summer walks, I fancy I'd receive an icy stare in return—or perhaps a puzzled inquiry as to what theatrical troupe I had wandered out of![32]

We will, however, see that in the summer of 1928 he found some reason to modify this judgment. But if this dialect was not (or was no longer) in existence, where did Lovecraft come by it? Jason C. Eckhardt has, with much plausibility, suggested a literary source: James Russell Lowell's *Biglow Papers* (1848–62).[33] Lovecraft owned Lowell's poems and was clearly familiar with much of his work; he notes reading the *Biglow Papers* as early as August 1916.[34] In the introduction to the first series of *Biglow Papers* Lowell specifically addresses the issue of the "Yankee dialect" found in the poems, claiming that many of the dialectical variants derive from the usage of the earliest colonists. He presents a dialectical rendition of a celebrated passage:

> Neow is the winta uv eour discontent
> Med glorious summa by this sun o' Yock,
> An' all the cleouds thet leowered upon eour heouse
> In the deep buzzum o' the oshin buried . . .

These are not exactly the *same* dialectical variants found in Lovecraft, but they are close enough to make one suspect that he has chosen to make his own variations from them. Eckhardt goes on to note astutely that Lovecraft's awareness that this dialect was already regarded by Lowell as archaic further augments the sense of the preternatural age of the old man in "The Picture in the House."

"The Picture in the House" appeared, with "Idealism and Materialism—a Reflection," in the "July 1919" *National Amateur,* which I have already noted was actually issued only in the summer of 1921. It remains one of Lovecraft's most reprinted stories. Later reprints derive from a revised version in which Lovecraft made some interesting changes. In particular, he subtilised his description of the old man. At the conclusion of his initial portrayal Lovecraft had added, in the *National Amateur* text: "On a beard which might have been patriarchal were unsightly stains, some of them disgustingly suggestive of blood." This would have been a catastrophic telegraphing of the final "punch," and Lovecraft wisely omitted it for subsequent appearances.

It may be worth covering some of the other stories that presumably date to 1920 before turning to those written in the early part of 1921. One of the most interesting items—interesting precisely because we do not have it—is "Life and Death." This is supposedly one of Lovecraft's few "lost" stories, and it has haunted generations of Lovecraftians by its very absence. The pieces of the puzzle are widely scattered, and we must begin with entry 27 in the commonplace book:

> *Life & Death*
>
> Death—its desolation & horror—bleak spaces—sea-bottom—dead cities. But Life—the greater horror! Vast unheard-of reptiles & leviathans—hideous beasts of prehistoric jungle—rank slimy vegetation—evil instincts of primal man—Life is more horrible than death.

This entry is in a group of entries dated to 1919; but, as I have already indicated, the dates Lovecraft affixed to his commonplace book years after jotting the entries down are highly unreliable, and I have my doubts whether any part of the commonplace book dates to even late 1919.

The query we must face is whether the story was written at all; there are, of course, dozens of entries in the commonplace book that were not used, although few are of such detail and length. Aside from the very next entry (for "The Cats of Ulthar"), this is the only one that has a title affixed to it; but the entry for "The Cats of Ulthar" has been indicated as "used," whereas there is no such indication for "Life and Death." Was this story, then, actually written and published in an amateur journal?

The first piece of evidence that suggests that it was comes from the first Lovecraft bibliography, compiled by Francis T. Laney and William H. Evans and published in 1943. In the listing of stories there is the citation: "LIFE AND DEATH. (c. 1920) (D) Unpublished?" (D indicates a disavowed story.) The bibliography was compiled with the assistance of many of Lovecraft's later associates, in particular R. H. Barlow, who may have been told of "Life and Death" in person by Lovecraft (it is not mentioned in the correspondence to Barlow). Barlow wrote to August Derleth in 1944: "As for the sort [of] pieces you ask about, I can be of no help . . . THE STREET I saw once, I think and LIFE AND DEATH."[35]

The most important piece of evidence, however, comes from George T. Wetzel, whose bibliography of 1955 was a landmark of Lovecraft scholarship. In an essay, "The Research of a Biblio" (1955), in which he told of his bibliographic work, Wetzel wrote:

> While in Philadelphia [in 1946] I showed some of my initial compilation to Oswald Train . . . The Lovecraft story "Life and Death" was found by me at this time, but the amateur paper and date were on one page of my biblio which vanished while I was visiting at Train's home. I attempted to re-locate this item on a later trip, but I feel I've not back-tracked enough. Suffice it to say that it exists in those files and may one day be uncovered by some one more blessed with funds for research expenses than myself.[36]

Wetzel's sanguine prediction has proved vain. His initial research on amateur appearances of Lovecraft was done at the Fossil Collection of Amateur Journalism, at that time in the Franklin Institute in Philadelphia. Later it was transferred to the Fales Library of New York University, where I consulted it in 1978; but by then the collection had been vandalised by someone who had cut out many Lovecraft appearances with a razor blade. I have looked through nearly every major repository of amateur journals in this country but have failed to turn up this item.

It is, I suppose, futile to speculate on the content of "Life and Death," but my feeling is that there really is no such work, and that researchers have confused it with an actual prose-poem that may date to this time, "Ex Oblivione." This work was published in the *United Amateur* for March 1921 under the "Ward Phillips" pseudonym, one of the few instances in which a story appeared under a pseudonym. This unusually bitter and cheerless fantasy ("When the last days were upon me, and the ugly trifles of existence began to drive me to madness like the small drops of water that torturers let fall ceaselessly upon one spot of their victim's body, I loved the irradiate refuge of sleep") tells of a man who seeks various exotic worlds in dream as an antidote to the grinding prosiness of daily life; later, when "the days of waking became less and less bearable from their greyness and sameness," he begins to take drugs to augment his nightly visions. In the "dream-city of Zakarion" he comes upon a papyrus containing the thoughts of the dream-sages who once dwelt there, he reads of a "high wall pierced by a little bronze gate" which may or may not be the entrance to untold wonders. Realising that "no new horror can be more terrible than the daily torture of the commonplace," the narrator takes more and more drugs in an effort to find this gate. Finally he seems to come upon it—the door is ajar.

> But as the gate swung wider and the sorcery of drug and dream pushed me through, I knew that all sights and glories were at an end; for in that new realm was neither land nor sea, but only the white void of unpeopled and illimitable space. So, happier than I had ever dared hoped to be, I dissolved again into that native infinity of crystal oblivion from which the daemon Life had called me for one brief and desolate hour.

As can be seen, this is a precise instantiation of the "Life is more horrible than death" trope that "Life and Death" is supposed to have embodied. It is true that the prose-poem does not include much of the imagery found in the corresponding commonplace book entry (there is nothing about "vast unheard-of reptiles & leviathans" and so forth), but we have seen that many elements of an entry that inspired a tale do not actually make it into the finished story. "Ex Oblivione" also constitutes a parable on that poignant utterance in *In Defence of Dagon* (spoken there, however, with an awareness of the bountiful pleasures of life): "There is nothing better than oblivion, since in oblivion there is no wish unfulfilled." In its union of a powerful philosophical message with rhythmic, musical, yet relatively restrained diction it may be intrinsically the best of Lovecraft's four surviving prose-poems, although "Nyarlathotep" is perhaps a more central work in Lovecraft's *oeuvre.*

Then there is the oddity called "Sweet Ermengarde; or, The Heart of a Country Girl" (by "Percy Simple"). This is the only work of fiction by Lovecraft which we cannot date at all precisely. The manuscript of the story is written on stationery from the Edwin E. Phillips Refrigeration Company, which was a going concern around 1910 or so, but since the story alludes to the passage of the 18th Amendment it must clearly date to 1919 or later. Since Phillips (Lovecraft's uncle) died on November 14, 1918, perhaps the stationery came into Lovecraft's possession shortly thereafter; but it is by no means certain that Lovecraft wrote the story at that time. From the handwriting the tale could date to as late as 1922 or 1923. The pseudonym may be a clue: Lovecraft's one surviving letter to Myrta Alice Little (May 17, 1921) includes a brief parody of a Sunday-school story entitled "George's Sacrifice: By Percy Vacuum, age 8." "Sweet Ermengarde," too, is very clearly a parody, this time on the Horatio Alger stories (which Lovecraft, conceivably, may have read in dime-novel form at the turn of the century). The tale makes me think of a curious P.S. to Lovecraft's letter in the *Argosy* for March 1914: "I have a design of writing a novel for the entertainment of those readers who complain that they cannot secure enough of Fred Jackson's work. It is to be entitled: 'The Primal Passion, or The Heart of 'Rastus Washington.'" It is, in fact, possible that Jackson is a subsidiary (or even primary) target for attack here. Jackson's "The First Law" has exactly the sort of implausibility of plot and sentimentality of action that is so hilariously lampooned in "Sweet Ermengarde." This story is, in short, a little masterpiece of comic deflation. In basic plot and even in tone and texture it oddly anticipates Nathanael West's *A Cool Million* (1936).

Ermengarde Stubbs is the "beauteous blonde daughter" of Hiram Stubbs, a "poor but honest farmer-bootlegger of Hogton, Vt." She admits to being sixteen years old, and "branded as mendacious all reports to the effect that she was thirty." She is pursued by two lovers who wish to marry her: 'Squire Hardman, who is "very rich and elderly" and, moreover, has a mortgage on Ermengarde's home; and Jack Manly, a childhood friend who is too bashful to declare his love, but who unfortunately has no money. Jack, however, manages to find the gumption to propose, and Ermengarde accepts with alacrity. Hardman observes this and in fury demands Ermengarde's hand from her father lest he foreclose on the mortgage (he has, incidentally, found that the Stubbses' land has gold buried in it). Jack, learning of the matter, vows to go to the city and make his fortune and save the farm.

Hardman, however, takes no chances and has two disreputable accomplices kidnap Ermengarde and hole her up in a hovel under the charge of Mother Maria, "a hideous old hag." But as Hardman ponders the matter, he wonders why he is even bothering with the girl, when all he really wants is the farm and its buried gold. He lets Ermengarde go and continues to threaten to foreclose. Meanwhile a band of hunters strays on to the Stubbses' property and one of them, Algernon Reginald Jones, finds the gold; not revealing it to his companions or to the Stubbses, Algernon feigns snakebite and goes to the farm, where he instantly falls in love with Ermengarde and wins her over with his sophisticated city ways. She elopes with Algernon a week later, but on the train to the city a piece of paper falls out of Algernon's pocket; picking it up, she finds to her horror that it is a love letter from another woman. She pushes Algernon out the window.

Unfortunately, Ermengarde fails to take Algernon's wallet, so she has no money when she reaches the city. She spends a week on park benches and in breadlines; she tries to look up Jack Manly, but can't find him. One day she finds a purse; finding that it has not much money in it, she decides to return it to its owner, a Mrs Van Itty. This aristocrat, amazed at the honesty of the "forlorn waif," takes Ermengarde under her wing. Later Mrs Van Itty hires a new chauffeur, and Ermengarde is startled to find that it is Algernon! "He had survived—this much was almost immediately evident." It turns out that he had married the woman who wrote the love letter, but that she had deserted him and run off with the milkman. Humbled, Algernon asks Ermengarde's forgiveness.

Ermengarde, now ensconced as a replacement for the daughter Mrs Van Itty lost many years ago, returns to the old farmstead and is about to buy off the mortgage from Hardman when Jack suddenly returns, bringing a wife, "the fair Bridget Goldstein," in tow. All this time Mrs Van Itty, sitting in the car, eyes Ermengarde's mother Hannah and finally shrieks: "You—you—Hannah Smith—I know you now! Twenty-eight years ago you were my baby Maude's nurse and stole her from the cradle!!" Then she realises that Ermengarde is in fact her long-lost daughter. But Ermengarde is now doing some pondering: "How could she get away with the sixteen-year-old stuff if she had been stolen twenty-eight years ago?" She, knowing of the gold on the Stubbses' farm, repudiates Mrs Van Itty and compels 'Squire Hardman's to foreclose on the mortgage and marry her lest she prosecute him for last year's kidnapping. "And the poor dub did."

The mere narration of this spectacularly convoluted and ridiculous plot (all told in 3000 words) clearly reveals the absurdity of the dime-novel sentimental romance being parodied here. Some of Lovecraft's humour is a bit sophomoric ("She was about 5 ft 5.33... in tall, weighed 115.47 lbs. on her father's copy scales—also off them—and was adjudged most lovely by all the village swains who admired her father's farm and liked his liquid crops"), but on the other hand much of it is rather good. The portrayal of the stereotyped 'Squire Hardman is delightful—at one point he indulges "in his favourite pastime of gnashing his teeth and swishing his riding-crop." When Jack proposes to Ermengarde, she cries, "Jack—my angel—at last—I mean, this is so unexpected and quite unprecedented!" The conclusion of this tender love-scene can only be quoted:

> "Ermengarde, me love!"
> "Jack—my precious!"
> "My darling!"
> "My own!"
> "My Gawd!"

When Jack vows to the Stubbses that "You shall have the old home still," the narrator is forced to add in brackets: "[adverb, not noun—although Jack was by no means out of sympathy with Stubbs' kind of farm produce]."

It is a shame that Lovecraft never made an effort to prepare this outrageous little squib for publication, but perhaps he considered it a *jeu d'esprit* whose purpose had been served by the mere writing of it. With "A Reminiscence of Dr. Samuel Johnson" and "Ibid," "Sweet Ermengarde" forms a trilogy of Lovecraft's comic gems.

"The Nameless City" appears to be the first story of 1921, written in mid- to late January; in a letter to Frank Belknap Long of January 26, 1921, he reports it as "just finished and typed."[37] This tale, for which Lovecraft always retained an inexplicable fondness, is really one of the worst of his purely weird efforts—a fact Lovecraft should have suspected from its repeated rejections in professional markets over the years. After its predictable appearance in the amateur press (*Wolverine,* November 1921) it was finally published in the semi-professional fanzine *Fanciful Tales* for Fall 1936, a few months before Lovecraft's death. Like many of his early works, it is more important for what it suggests and foretells than for what it actually contains.

A somewhat overexcited archaeologist seeks to explore the nameless city, which lies "remote in the desert of Araby." It was of this place that Abdul Alhazred "the mad poet" dreamed the night before he wrote his "unexplainable couplet":

> That is not dead which can eternal lie,
> And in strange aeons even death may die.

The narrator burrows into the sand-choked apertures that lead into some of the larger structures of the city. He is disturbed by the odd proportions of a temple into which he crawls, for the ceiling is very low to the ground and the man can scarcely kneel upright in it. He descends an immense staircase that leads down into the bowels of the earth, where he finds a large but still very low-built hall with odd cases lining the walls and frescoes covering the walls and ceiling. The creatures in the cases are very peculiar:

> They were of the reptile kind, with body lines suggesting sometimes the crocodile, sometimes the seal, but more often nothing of which either the naturalist or the palaeontologist ever heard. In size they approximated a small man, and their fore legs bore delicate and evidently flexible feet curiously like human hands and fingers. But strangest of all were their heads, which presented a contour violating all known biological principles. To nothing can such things be well compared—in one flash I thought of comparisons as varied as the cat, the bulldog, the mythic Satyr, and the human being.

In spite of the fact that it is these anomalous entities who are portrayed in the frescoes, the narrator manages to convince himself that they are mere totem-animals for the human builders of the nameless city and that the historical tableaux depicted in the frescoes are metaphors for the actual (human) history of the place. But this comforting illusion is shattered when the narrator perceives a gust of cold wind emerging from the end of the hallway, where a great bronze gate lies open and from which a strange phosphorescence is emerging, and then sees in the luminous abyss the entities themselves rushing in a stream before him. Somehow he manages to escape and tell his story.

The absurdities and implausibilities in this tale, along with its wildly overheated prose, give it a very low place in the Lovecraft canon. Where, for example, did the creatures who built the nameless city come from? There are no indications that they came from another planet; but if they are simply early denizens of the earth, how did they come to possess their physical shape? Their curiously *composite* nature seems to rule out any evolutionary pattern known to earth's creatures. How do they continue to exist in the depths of the earth? The narrator must also be very foolish not to realise at once that the entities were the ones who built the city. Lovecraft does not seem to have thought out the details of this story at all carefully.

Lovecraft admitted that it was largely inspired by a dream, which in turn was triggered by a suggestive phrase in Dunsany's *Book of Wonder,* "the unreverberate blackness of the abyss" (the last line of "The Probable Adventure of the Three Literary Men"). Lovecraft goes on to say that he began the story twice but was dissatisfied, and only "hit the right atmosphere the third time."[38] A slightly more concrete source, perhaps, is the entry on "Arabia" in the 9th edition of the *Encyclopaedia Britannica,* which Lovecraft owned. He copied down part of this entry in his commonplace book (entry 47), especially the part about "Irem, the City of Pillars . . . supposed to have been erected by Shedad, the latest despot of Ad, in the regions of Hudramut, and which yet, after the annihilation of its tenants, remains entire, so Arabs say, invisible to ordinary eyes, but occasionally, and at rare intervals, revealed to some heaven-favoured traveller." Lovecraft mentions Irem casually in his tale, suggesting that the nameless city was even older than this antediluvian place. The Irem connexion presumably accounts for the citation of the "unexplainable couplet" ("That is not dead which can eternal lie, / And with strange aeons even death may die") attributed to Abdul Alhazred, who here makes his first appearance in Lovecraft. A later entry in the commonplace book (59) is clearly an account of the dream that inspired the story: "Man in strange subterranean chamber—seeks to force door of bronze—overwhelmed by influx of waters."

The remarkable thing about "The Nameless City" is that Lovecraft took its basic scenario—a scientist investigating a millennia-abandoned city and deciphering historical bas-reliefs on the walls—and made it not only plausible but immensely powerful in a tale written exactly ten years later, *At the Mountains of Madness.* In that short novel we even find the same sort of desperate rationalising as the protagonists seek to convince themselves that the entities (extraterrestrials this time) depicted on the bas-reliefs are not the actual builders of the city but are somehow meant as symbols for human beings; but this feature too is handled more cogently and with greater psychological acuity.

"The Moon-Bog," as we have seen, was written to order for a St Patrick's Day gathering of amateurs in Boston, and it betrays its thinness of inspiration by being a very conventional supernatural revenge story. Denys Barry, who comes from America to reclaim an ancestral estate in Kilderry, Ireland, decides to empty the bog on his hand: "For all his love of Ireland, America had not left him untouched, and he hated the beautiful wasted space where peat might be cut and land opened up." The peasants refuse to help him in this work for fear of disturbing the spirits of the bog; but Barry calls in outside workers and the project continues apace, even though the workers confess suffering from strange and troublesome dreams. One night the narrator, Barry's friend, awakes and hears a piping in the distance: "wild, weird airs that made me think of some dance of fauns on distant Maenalus" (a curious nod to "The Tree"). Then he sees the labourers dancing as if under some form of hypnosis, along with "strange airy beings in white, half indeterminate in nature, but suggesting pale wistful naiads from the haunted fountains of the bog." But the next morning the workers seem to remember nothing of the night's events. The next night things reach a climax: the piping is heard again, and the narrator again sees the "white-clad bog-wraiths" drifting toward the deeper waters of the bog, followed by the mesmerised labourers. Then a shaft of moonlight appears, and "upward along that pallid path my fevered fancy pictured a thin shadow slowly writhing; a vague contorted shadow struggling as if drawn by unseen daemons." It is Denys Barry, who is spirited off and never seen again.

The elementary nature of the moral in "The Moon-Bog"—the spirits of Nature avenging or warding off desecration by human beings—renders the story unusually trite and commonplace, even though some of the language is evocative and relatively subdued. Strangely enough, twelve years after Lovecraft wrote this story, Lord Dunsany would write a novel based very largely on the same conception—

The Curse of the Wise Woman (1933)—but with infinitely greater richness of texture and complexity of theme. It need hardly be said that Dunsany could not possibly have been influenced by Lovecraft's harmless little story, whose only appearance prior to his death was in *Weird Tales* for June 1926.

The last story I wish to consider here is "The Outsider." This tale has been seen as prototypical of Lovecraft's work, and in some ways even emblematic of his entire life and thought; but I think there are reasons to doubt such assertions. As one of Lovecraft's most reprinted stories, its plot is very well known. A strange individual who has spent his entire life virtually alone except for some aged person who seems to take care of him decides to forsake the ancient castle in which he finds himself and seek the light by climbing the tallest tower of the edifice. With great effort he manages to ascend the tower and experiences "the purest ecstasy I have ever known: for shining tranquilly through an ornate grating of iron . . . was the radiant full moon, which I had never before seen save in dreams and in vague visions I dared not call memories."

But horror follows this spectacle, for he now observes that he is not at some lofty height but has merely reached *"the solid ground."* Stunned by this revelation, he walks dazedly through a wooded park where a "venerable ivied castle" stands. This castle is "maddeningly familiar, yet full of perplexing strangeness to me"; but he detects the sights and sounds of joyous revelry within. He steps through a window of the castle to join the merry band, but at that instant "there occurred one of the most terrifying demonstrations I had ever conceived": the partygoers flee madly from some hideous sight, and the protagonist appears to be alone with the monster who has seemingly driven the crowd away in frenzy. He thinks he sees this creature "beyond the golden-arched doorway leading to another and somewhat similar room," and finally does catch a clear glimpse of it:

> I cannot even hint what it was like, for it was a compound of all that is unclean, uncanny, unwelcome, abnormal, and detestable. It was the ghoulish shade of decay, antiquity, and desolation; the putrid, dripping eidolon of unwholesome revelation; the awful baring of that which the merciful earth should always hide. God knows it was not of this world—or no longer of this world—yet to my horror I saw in its eaten-away and bone-revealing outlines a leering, abhorrent travesty on the human shape; and in its mouldy, disintegrating apparel an unspeakable quality that chilled me even more.

He seeks to escape the monster, but inadvertently falls forward instead of retreating; and at that instant he touches *"the rotting outstretched paw of the monster beneath the golden arch."* It is only then that he realises that that arch contains *"a cold and unyielding surface of polished glass."*

On the level of plot, "The Outsider" makes little sense. What exactly is the nature of the "castle" in which the Outsider dwells? If it is truly underground, how is it that the creature spends time in the "endless forest" surrounding it? Taking these and other implausibilities—if the story is to be held to rigid standards of realism—into account, and noting the epigraph from Keats's *Eve of St Agnes* ("That night the Baron dreamt of many a woe; / And all his warrior-guests . . . / Were long be-nightmared"), William Fulwiler has suggested that "The Outsider" is merely the account of a dream.[39] There is something to be said for this, and this explanation would certainly account for the seemingly "irrational" elements in the tale; but the story does offer some further complexities of plot. From the various remarks by the Outsider regarding his puzzlement at the present shape of the ivied castle he enters (as well as a path "where only occasional ruins bespoke the ancient presence of a forgotten road"), it becomes evident that the Outsider is some long-dead ancestor of the current occupants of the castle. His emergence in the topmost tower of his underground castle places him in a room containing "vast shelves of marble, bearing odious oblong boxes of disturbing size": clearly the mausoleum of the castle on the surface. Of course, even if the Outsider is some centuried ancestor, there is no explanation for how he has managed to survive—or rise from the dead—after all this time.

The conclusion of the story—in which the Outsider touches the mirror and realises that the monster is himself—can scarcely be a surprise to any reader, even though Lovecraft deftly puts off the actual stating of the revelation and allows the Outsider to tell of his actions following it: he suffers a merciful lapse of memory, finds himself unable to return to his underground castle, and now "ride[s] with the mocking and friendly ghouls on the night-wind, and play[s] by day amongst the catacombs of Nephren-Ka in the sealed and unknown valley of Hadoth by the Nile." But that climactic image of touching the glass has correctly been seen to be representative of a significant number of Lovecraft's fictional works. Donald R. Burleson writes:

> The rotting finger that touches the glass sets ringing a vibration that will endure, will continue to resonate in varying pitches and intensities, throughout the whole experience of Lovecraft's fiction. . . . The grand theme of the soul-shattering consequences of self-knowledge is the one defining notion into which Lovecraft's other themes feed in confluence, rivers running to a common sea.[40]

Many commentators have attempted to speculate on a literary influence for this image. Colin Wilson[41] has suggested both Poe's classic story of a double, "William Wilson," and also Wilde's fairy tale "The Birthday of the Infanta," in which a twelve-year-old princess is initially described as "the most graceful of all and the most tastefully attired" but proves to be "a monster, the most grotesque monster he had ever beheld. Not properly shaped as all other people were, but hunchbacked, and crooked-limbed, with huge lolling head and a mane of black hair."[42] George T. Wetzel[43] has put forth Hawthorne's curious sketch, "Fragments from the Journal of a Solitary Man," in which a man has the following revelation in a dream: "'I passed not one step farther, but threw my eyes on a looking-glass which stood deep within the nearest shop. At first glimpse of my own figure I awoke, with a horrible sensation of self-terror and self-loathing. No wonder that the affrighted city fled! I had been promenading Broadway in my shroud!'" Then, of course, there is a celebrated passage in *Frankenstein:*

> "I had admired the perfect forms of my cottagers—their grace, beauty, and delicate complexions; but how was I terrified when I viewed myself in a transparent pool! At first I started back, unable to believe that it was indeed I who was reflected in the mirror; and when I became fully convinced that I was in reality the monster that I am, I was filled with the bitterest sensations of despondence and moritification."[44]

This influence seems more likely in view of the fact that the earlier scene, where the Outsider disturbs the party by stepping through the window, may also have been derived from *Frankenstein:* "'One of the best of [the cottages] I entered, but I had hardly placed my foot within the door before the children shrieked, and one of the women fainted.'"[45] A less distinguished predecessor is a story in the *All-Story Weekly* for September 2, 1916, "The Man in the Mirror" by Lillian B. Hunt, in which again the protagonist only learns of his own hideousness by looking in a mirror.

Preeminently, however, the story is a homage to Poe. August Derleth frequently bestowed upon "The Outsider" the dubious honour of claiming that it would pass as a lost tale of Poe's if presented as such; but Lovecraft's own later judgment, expressed in a 1931 letter to J. Vernon Shea, seems more accurate:

> Others . . . agree with you in liking "The Outsider", but I can't say that I share this opinion. To my mind this tale—written a decade ago—is too glibly *mechanical* in its climactic effect, & almost comic in the bombastic pomposity of its language. As I re-read it, I can hardly understand how I could have let myself be tangled up in such baroque & windy rhetoric as recently as ten years ago. It represents my literal though unconscious imitation of Poe at its very height.[46]

Lovecraft perhaps spoke better than he knew, for the opening of the tale is a startlingly close pastiche of the first four paragraphs of Poe's "Berenice"; and yet, Lovecraft probably is correct in speaking of the Poe influence as unconscious at this stage.

In 1934 Lovecraft provided an interesting sidelight into the composition of the story. As recollected by R. H. Barlow, Lovecraft stated: "'The Outsider' [is] a series of climaxes—originally intended to cease with the graveyard episode; then he wondered what would happen if people would see the ghoul; and so included the second climax; finally he decided to have the Thing see itself!"[47] There are those who think Lovecraft had too many "climaxes" here; among them is W. Paul Cook:

> When I first saw *The Outsider* it was in the typed manuscript, and at the bottom of a page were the words: "My fingers touched the rotting outstretched paw

> of the monster beneath the golden arch." There was the revelation; there was the story; and I thought that was the end of the story. I was struck with admiration at the artistic restraint of the work, and started a note of praise to Lovecraft when, lifting the sheet, I found there was more of it. Restraint disappeared and the author enjoyed himself throwing words around. All the rest was just verbiage, words, padding, anti-climax. I wrote him then that the story should have ended there. And I still think so.[48]

This somewhat jaundiced account perhaps has some merit as a criticism of the lack of a genuine "surprise" ending in the story; but, Cook's comments notwithstanding, if the story really had ended where Cook wished it to, there would have remained unacceptable ambiguity as to the actual revelation. Cook, however, frequently expressed dissatisfaction with Lovecraft's later stories, much preferring his early, nebulous, purely supernatural short narratives.

"The Outsider" will always remain a popular favourite, and indeed it is not entirely undeserving of its celebrity: its rhetoric, if a little overdone, is effective in its flamboyant, Asianic way; the climax, while predictable, is structurally clever in being placed at the very last line of the tale; and the figure of the Outsider is distinctive (although here again the influence of *Frankenstein* may perhaps be evident) in that it inspires both horror and pathos. The tale was not published in an amateur journal: it was scheduled to appear in the first (and, as it proved, only) issue of Cook's *Recluse,*[49] but Lovecraft persuaded Cook to release it and allow it to be published in *Weird Tales* for April 1926, where it created a sensation.

It is, however, now time to examine the question of the story's autobiographical character. The opening sentence reads: "Unhappy is he to whom the memories of childhood bring only fear and sadness." One of the Outsider's final remarks—"I know always that I am an outsider; a stranger in this century and among those who are still men"—has been taken as prototypical of Lovecraft's entire life, the life of an "eccentric recluse" who wished himself intellectually, aesthetically, and spiritually in the rational haven of the eighteenth century. I think we have already learnt enough about Lovecraft to know that such an interpretation greatly overstates the case: without denying his emphatic and sincere fondness, and even to some degree nostalgia, for the eighteenth century, he was also very much a part of his time, and was an "outsider" only in the sense that most writers and intellectuals find a gulf between themselves and the commonality of citizens. Lovecraft's childhood was by no means unhappy, and he frequently looked back upon it as idyllic, carefree, and full of pleasurable intellectual stimulation and the close friendship of at least a small band of peers.

Is, then, "The Outsider" a symbol for Lovecraft's own self-image, particularly the image of one who always thought himself ugly and whose mother told at least one individual about her son's "hideous" face? I find this interpretation rather superficial, and it would have the effect of rendering the story maudlin and self-pitying. The plausibility of this view would perhaps be augmented if the exact date of writing of "The Outsider" could be ascertained—especially if it could be established that it was written on or around the time of Susie's death on May 24, 1921. But Lovecraft never discusses the story in any letters of 1921–22 that I have seen, never supplies an exact date of writing for the tale on the relatively few later instances where he talks about it, and in his various lists of stories it usually appears sandwiched between "The Moon-Bog" (March) and "The Other Gods" (August 14). I think it is more profitable not to read too much autobiographical significance in "The Outsider": its large number of apparent literary influences seem to make it more an experiment in pastiche than some deeply felt expression of psychological wounds.

It is difficult to characterise the non-Dunsanian stories of this period. Lovecraft was still experimenting in different tones, styles, moods, and themes in an effort to find out what might work the best. Once again we should note the relative absence of "cosmic" stories in this period, in spite of Lovecraft's manifest declaration (in the *In Defence of Dagon* essays) of his scorn for the "humanocentric" pose. Only the prose-poem "Nylarlathotep" can be considered genuinely cosmic. Still, other themes that would be greatly elaborated in later tales find their origins here: miscegenation ("Arthur Jermyn"); alien civilisations dwelling unknown in obscure corners of the world ("The Temple," "The Nameless City"); the horror latent in old New England ("The Picture in the House"); the transcending of the limitations of sense-perception ("From Beyond").

Perhaps the fact that so many of these tales were inspired by dreams is the most important thing about them. Lovecraft's letters of 1920 are full of accounts of incredibly bizarre dreams, some of which served as the nuclei for tales written years later. It would be a facile and inexpert psychoanalysis to maintain that Lovecraft's worries over Susie's health were the principal cause of these disturbances in his subconscious; as a matter of fact, it appears that Susie's health had, after a fashion, stabilised and that there was no suspicion of any impending collapse until only a few days before her death. Suffice it to say that the dozen or more stories Lovecraft wrote in 1920—more than he wrote in any other year of his life—point to a definitive shift in his aesthetic horizons. Lovecraft still did not know it yet, but he had come upon his life-work.

13. The High Tide of My Life (1921–1922)

Sarah Susan Phillips Lovecraft died on May 24, 1921, at Butler Hospital, where she had been confined since March 13, 1919. Her death, however, was not a result of her nervous breakdown but rather of a gall bladder operation from which she did not recover. Winfield Townley Scott, who had access to Susie's now destroyed medical records, tells the story laconically: "She underwent a gall-bladder operation which was thought to be successful. Five days later her nurse noted that the patient expressed a wish to die because 'I will only live to suffer.' She died the next day . . ."[1] Her death certificate gives the cause of death as "cholecystitis cholangitis," or inflammation of the gall bladder and the bile ducts.

Lovecraft's reaction was pretty much what one might expect:

> I am answering letters promptly these last few days, because I lack the will and energy to do anything heavier. The death of my mother on May 24 gave me an extreme nervous shock, and I find concentration and continuous endeavour quite impossible. I am, of course, supremely unemotional; and do not weep or indulge in any of the lugubrious demonstrations of the vulgar—but the psychological effect of so vast and unexpected a disaster is none the less considerable, and I cannot sleep much, or labour with any particular spirit or success.[2]

Later on in this letter, written nine days after the event, Lovecraft adds disturbingly:

> For two years she had wished for little else [than death]—just as I myself wish for oblivion. Like me, she was an agnostic with no belief in immortality . . . For my part, I do not think I shall wait for a natural death; since there is no longer any particular reason why I should exist. During my mother's life-time I was aware that voluntary euthanasia on my part would cause her distress, but it is now possible for me to regulate the term of my existence with the assurance that my end would cause no one more than a passing annoyance . . .

Evidently his aunts did not figure much in this equation. But it was a passing phase, and three days later he was urging Frank Long: "The only real tranquillity—the true Epicurean ataraxia,—comes from the assumption of the objective, external point of view whereby we stand off as spectators and watch ourselves without caring much; a triumph of mind over feeling."[3]

What, in the end, are we to make of Lovecraft's relations with his mother? He writes after her death: "My mother was, in all probability, the only person who thoroughly understood me, with the possible exception of Alfred Galpin."[4] There is too little evidence to judge whether this was truly the case, but it is of some interest that Lovecraft *thought* it to be so. Susie Lovecraft has not fared well at the hands of Lovecraft's biographers, and her flaws are readily discernible: she was overly possessive, clearly neurotic, failed (as Lovecraft himself and the rest of his family did) to foresee the need for training her son in some sort of remunerative occupation, and psychologically damaged Lovecraft at least to the point of declaring him physically hideous and perhaps in other ways that are now irrecoverable. It is telling that in one of the two surviving letters to her—February 24, 1921, telling of his trip to Boston—Lovecraft cannot help remarking on his appearance: "The new suit, worn for the first time, was a work of art, and made me appear as nearly respectable as my face permits—and even the face was almost at its best."

But the verdict on Susie should not be entirely negative. Kenneth W. Faig, Jr correctly remarks: "Lovecraft's finely honed aesthetic sensibilities and seasoned artistic judgment undoubtedly owed something to the early influence of his mother. . . . The wonderful home which Susie and her young son shared with her parents and sisters at 454 Angell Street during the 1890s must have been truly a delight . . ."[5] Her indulging Lovecraft in many of his early whims—the *Arabian Nights,* chemistry, astronomy—may seem excessive, but it allowed Lovecraft fully to develop these intellectual and aesthetic interests, and so to lay the groundwork for both the intellect and the creativity he displayed in later years.

The critical issue is whether Lovecraft knew and acknowledged—at least to himself—the ways in which his mother affected him, both positively and adversely. In letters both early and late he speaks of her with nothing but praise and respect. In many letters of the 1930s, when recalling his early years, he makes statements such as: "My health improved vastly and rapidly, though without any ascertainable cause, about 1920–21";[6] which gives—or appears to give—little hint that Susie's death might actually have been a liberating factor of some kind. But was Lovecraft really so lacking in self-awareness on this issue? I have already cited Sonia's noting that Lovecraft once admitted to her that Susie's influence upon him had been "devastating." Another very interesting piece of evidence comes not from a letter or an essay, or from a memoir by a friend, but from a story.

"The Thing on the Doorstep" (1933) tells the tale of Edward Derby, who was an only child and "had organic weaknesses which startled his doting parents and caused them to keep him closely chained to their side. He was never allowed out without his nurse, and seldom had a chance to play unconstrainedly with other children." Is Lovecraft recollecting that summer vacation in Dudley, Massachusetts, in 1892, when Susie told Ella Sweeney to stoop when walking with Howard so as not to pull his arm out of its socket?

Lovecraft continues in the story: "Edward's mother died when he was thirty-four, and for months he was incapacitated by some odd psychological malady. His father took him to Europe, however, and he managed to pull out of his trouble without visible effects. Afterward he seemed to feel a sort of grotesque exhilaration, as if of partial escape from some unseen bondage." That last sentence is all the evidence we need: it makes it abundantly clear that Lovecraft knew (by 1933, at any rate) that Susie's death had in a sense made the rest of his own life possible. It is telling that, in his litany of "near-breakdowns" beginning in 1898, he lists no breakdown of 1921.

In the short term Lovecraft did the most sensible thing he could have done—continue the normal course of his existence. He may not, like Derby, have travelled to Europe, but there was always New Hampshire. He had naturally thought of cancelling Myrta Alice Little's invitation to visit her in Westville on June 8–9, but his aunts—Lillian Clark had by now moved into 598 Angell Street to accompany her sister Annie Emeline Phillips Gamwell, who had already been there since March 1919—urged him to go, and he did so. On the morning of the 9th both Little and Lovecraft went to visit Tryout Smith in Haverhill, Massachusetts, and Lovecraft found himself captivated by the old man (he was sixty-nine) with a young boy's heart. His *Tryout* was one of the most pathetically misprinted journals in the history of amateur journalism, but it emerged almost like clockwork month after month for thirty-four years (300 issues were produced from 1914 to 1948). Smith, adhering in old age to the "boy printer" ideal of the NAPA, set the type himself in a shed behind his house at 408 Groveland Street. Lovecraft pays unaffected tribute to him:

> . . . I like him immeasurably, for he is the most unspoiled, simple, contented, artless, and altogether delightful small boy of his age that I have ever beheld. He never grew up, but lives on without any of the dull complexities of adulthood—active, busy with his little press, stamp album, cat, and woodland excursions—in short, a perfect old Damoetas whom Theocritus would have loved to delineate.[7]

Lovecraft wrote up the trip charmingly in "The Haverhill Convention" (*Tryout,* July 1921). He had already penned a whimsical poem to Smith, "Tryout's Lament for the Vanished Spider" (*Tryout,* January 1920), and when Smith's cat died on November 15, 1921, he produced a touching elegy, "Sir Thomas Tryout" (*Tryout,* December 1921):

> There's many an eye that fills tonight,
> And many a pensive strain
> That sounds for him who stole from sight
> In the November rain.

Lovecraft returned to New Hampshire in August. On the 25th he visited Tryout Smith in Haverhill; on the 26th he visited the museum of the Haverhill Historical Society with Myrta Alice Little and her mother, who were acquainted with the director and so were allowed into the museum even though it was not open to the public on that day; he returned home the next day.[8]

Need we make anything of these two visits to Little in quick succession? She seems virtually to drop out of the picture after this date, except for one further visit Lovecraft paid her in the summer of 1922. Even if, as I doubt, there was some romantic—or even the nascent nucleus of a romantic—involvement here, it was clearly terminated, perhaps for reasons that will soon become apparent.

August was, indeed, a travelling month for Lovecraft. On the 8th Harold Bateman Munroe summoned Lovecraft out of the bath at 9.30 A.M. to revisit their Great Meadow Country Clubhouse in Rehoboth. Munroe, now a businessman as well as a deputy sheriff, had some calls to make in nearby Taunton, and wanted to spend the rest of the day reminiscing with his boyhood pal about their long-lost youth. (An unnamed woman accompanied them on this trip, but Lovecraft remarks that she was properly quiet and unobtrusive.) For Lovecraft, ever ready to return in spirit to his idyllic youth, the moment was full of emotion, especially since the clubhouse was found to be nearly intact in spite of its fifteen-year-long abandonment:

> There had been no decay, nor even vandalism. Tables stood about as of yore, pictures we knew still adorned the walls with unbroken glass. Not an inch of tar paper was ripped off, & in the cement hearth we found still embedded the small pebbles we stamped in when it was new & wet—pebbles arranged to form the initials G.M.C.C. Nothing was lacking—save the fire, the ambition, the ebulliency of youth in ourselves; & that can never be replaced. Thus two stolid middle-aged men caught for a moment a vision of the aureate & iridescent past—caught it, & sighed for days that are no more.[9]

Twelve days before his thirty-first birthday Lovecraft is declaring himself "middle-aged." But for an afternoon he could revel in the past. There was even a plan (suggested by Harold) to revive the G.M.C.C., and holding monthly meetings with Ronald Upham and Stuart Coleman, who were still in Providence. But Lovecraft correctly declared a week and a half later that "H B M has no doubt forgotten all about it now. He does not miss youth as I do." It was probably just as well: the worst thing that could have happened to Lovecraft, so soon after his mother's death, was a return to childhood and its irresponsibility: he needed to move on and engage himself in the world.

On August 17 Lovecraft made another trip to Boston to meet amateurs. An increasing tension between the UAPA and the NAPA created some awkwardness. Lovecraft was forced to meet his UAPA group on Wednesday the 17th rather than take in the Hub Club meeting (consisting mostly of Nationalites) on the next day. In addition, Alice Hamlet wanted Lovecraft to visit her in Dorchester, since she hated the Nationalites so much that she did not even wish to risk meeting any of them at the scheduled UAPA meeting. But Lovecraft missed the 11.00 A.M. train to Boston, and had to catch the 12.25 instead; he arrived in Dorchester at 1.44, but by this time Hamlet and her party had already left to visit an invalid friend in a nursing home in Quincy. "As a matter of prosaic fact, my loss of this trip caused me no very profound grief; but the Dorcastrians seemed amazingly disappointed. . . . Miss H. appeared to view the exploded schedule as little short of calamitous."[10] One gets the impression that Alice Hamlet was more fond of Lovecraft than he was of her.

Moving on to Boston, Lovecraft went to the Curry School of Expression on Huntington Avenue near Copley Square, where he met for the first time Anne Tillery Renshaw, a longtime amateur whom he had supported for various official posts almost from the time he entered amateurdom. She had come from Washington, D.C., where she was head of the English department at Research University. Lovecraft pays her a mixed tribute: "In aspect stout & homely, she is in conversation pleasant, cultivated, & intelligent; with all the force of mind & speech becoming a philosopher, poet, & professor of English, drama, & public speaking." Lovecraft and Renshaw argued philosophy most of the afternoon. In the evening the main gathering occurred at Lilian McMullen's home at 53 Morton Street in Newton Centre, where Winifred Jackson, Edith Miniter, and others congregated; but Lovecraft was diverted all evening by a grey kitten brought by one of the amateurs. Once again he refused to sing, although both McMullen and Renshaw gave renditions. At one point Renshaw made a suggestion that Lovecraft write a textbook on English—an irony given that Renshaw herself would write a wretched textbook on speech which Lovecraft would revise at the end of his life. As usual, Lovecraft caught a late train and returned home at 1.20 A.M.

Meanwhile events in the amateur world were heating up. Lovecraft had easily been elected Official Editor for the 1920–21 and 1921–22 terms, and his "literary" faction was in both political and editorial control of the association: Alfred Galpin was President in 1920–21 (serving, anomalously, also as Chairman of the Department of Public Criticism), and Ida C. Haughton of Columbus, Ohio, was President in 1921–22; other associates of Lovecraft such as Paul J. Campbell, Frank Belknap Long, and Alice Hamlet all held official positions. All this puts the lie to the statement Lovecraft had made as early as August 1919: "But I am gradually getting through with amateur journalism. What I have done for it has brought me only slights and insults, except from an intensely appreciated few to whom I shall ever be fervently grateful. I shall always cling to the Kleicomolo and Gallomo circle, and shall always be glad to help any writer who wishes me to do so; but with the organisation I am done."[11] But the picture was by no means rosy. Lovecraft had considerable disagreements with President Haughton, and years later he claimed that she "ran the very gamut of abuse & positive insult—culminating even in an aspersion on my stewardship of the United funds!"[12] (This latter point refers to Lovecraft's running of the Official Organ Fund, a record of dues or donations by members for the publishing of the *United Amateur.*) It does not appear as if this dispute got into print, at least from Haughton's side; but Lovecraft did indeed respond by writing "Medusa: A Portrait" in late 1921. This is the most vicious and unrestrained of his poetic satires, and in it he mercilessly flays Haughton for her large bulk and her supposed foulness of temper:

> Soak'd in her noxious venom, puff'd with gall,
> Like some fat toad see dull MEDUSA sprawl;
> Foul with her spleen, repugnant to the sight,
> She crudely whines amidst eternal night.

When the poem was published in the *Tryout* for December 1921, it lacked the prefatory letter to Haughton (found in the typescript); even so, I suspect that the object of attack was evident to most of the amateur public.

There was trouble on other fronts also. I have already told how such individuals as William J. Dowdell and Leo Fritter had expressed resentment against what they believed to be Lovecraft's high-handed running of the *United Amateur,* filling it with material by his own colleagues. In the *Woodbee* for January 1922 Fritter continued his attacks, writing: "The Official Organ is the medium of all the members, and as such should become a clearing-house for all shades of literary endeavor within the Association."[13] Lovecraft spat back in his "Editorial" in the January 1922 *United Amateur:*

> Our constitution does not define the functions of *The United Amateur* beyond making imperative the publication of certain official documents. The rest is left to an unwritten combination of tradition and editorial judgment. Any editor, once elected, is absolutely in control of the magazine aside from the essential official matter; his only external obligation being a tacit recognition of the prevailing objects of the Association.

He fended off complaints of high-handedness by declaring that the standards he was attempting to maintain were those established when the UAPA split into two factions in 1912—what he now uncharitably called "the departure of the chronically political element." He continued: "Prior to that time the Official Organ was mainly a bulletin of reports; not, as the present agitators would imply, a repository for indiscriminate amateur writings. The standard developed since then is the creation of no one person, but a logical outgrowth of the rising calibre of a vital and progressive society." To seal the matter, Lovecraft declared that "this office has received *not so much as one complaint* as to policy" save from two "politicians," and that "throughout the present editor's service *not more than three manuscripts have been rejected.*" Those italics betray Lovecraft's impatience and irritation even more than the general tone of the editorial does.

But in this case Lovecraft was not to prevail. In the UAPA election in July 1922, the "literature" side lost out to its opponents. Howard R. Conover was President; Edward T. Mazurewicz was First Vice-President; Stella V. Kellerman was Second Vice-President; Edward Delbert Jones was Chairman of the Department of Public Criticism. None of these individuals was a close associate of Lovecraft. He himself lost to Fritter for Official Editor by a vote of 44–29. It was, no doubt, a staggering blow, and may have gone a long way in showing Lovecraft that this phase of his amateur career was coming to an end.

But the battle over the content of the *United Amateur* was not over. Anthony F. Moitoret—who had been both Official Editor (1919–20) and President (1920–21) of the NAPA—greeted the first issue of Fritter's *United Amateur* as follows:

> Official Editor Fritter makes an auspicious beginning with his first number of "The United Amateur," happily issued and mailed in the month for which it is dated. In his conception of an official organ that is just what the name implies—a compilation of current official business communications and notes which it is the right of every member to scan—the September "United Amateur" returns to the practice of former days before the Association's paper became the dumping ground for a hodge-podge of alleged literary material that could not possibly find publication elsewhere.[14]

That last stinger was clearly a jab at Lovecraft (as was the bit about the timeliness of Fritter's issue, as issues under Lovecraft's editorship were indeed perennially late); but since he was not on the official board and since his own *Conservative* was in abeyance, Lovecraft did not reply. He had regarded Moitoret with apprehension for some years. As early as 1916 he had noted that Moitoret "is working against the best literary interests of the association";[15] and in 1919, in the midst of an election controversy, Lovecraft reports that Moitoret "expresses his determination to 'kill off' the 'highbrow' element if he can."[16]

But if Lovecraft did not respond, his colleagues did so. Horace L. Lawson, editor of the *Wolverine,* wrote hotly: "Mr. Moitoret resorted to absolute falsehood in his rancor against the previous administration when he termed Mr. Lovecraft's excellent volume a 'dumping ground for a hodge-podge of alleged literary material that could not possibly find publication elsewhere.' The utter absurdity of this charge must be apparent even to Mr. Lovecraft's bitterest enemies."[17] Paul J. Campbell wrote with unwonted sarcasm just prior to the 1922 election:

> In order to save the association from the High-Brows every member must have access to the Official Organ on equal terms without literary restrictions. The raw recruit and the hungry yearner after space must be "encouraged" by having their grammatical errors conspicuously displayed on the front page. No longer will they

> submit to the insult of being told to improve their style or seek original ideas! Down with the tyrrany [*sic*] of literary standards![18]

But Lovecraft had the last laugh. The new official board did manage to produce six issues of the *United Amateur,* but at the convention in late July 1923 Lovecraft's literary party was almost entirely voted back into office; incredibly enough, Sonia H. Greene was elected President even though she had not knowingly placed herself on the ballot.[19] This whole turn of events appeared to rile Fritter, Moitoret, and their colleagues, and they acted in an obstructionist manner toward the new official board; the Secretary-Treasurer, Alma B. Sanger, withheld funds and failed to answer letters,[20] so that no *United Amateur* could be printed until May 1924. Sometime in the fall of 1923 Sonia issued a mimeographed flyer, "To the Members of the United,"[21] pleading with the members to pull together by resuming activity, renewing memberships, and in general making some effort to rescue the UAPA from its moribund condition.

In his "Editorial" in the May 1924 *United Amateur* Lovecraft responded to the entire situation with surprising bitterness:

> Once more the United, well-nigh asphyxiated by the tender ministrations of those who sought to shield it from the rude winds of literature, commences the long and arduous climb "back to normalcy". One is tempted to dilate upon the theme of "I-told-you-so", and draw various salutary morals from the utter disintegration following the revolt against high standards; but in sober fact such gloating de luxe would be supremely futile. The situation teaches its own lesson, and we are not yet far enough out of the woods to indulge in leisurely exultation. The future is in our own hands, and the downfall of the anti-literati will avail us nothing unless we are ready to rebuild on the ruins of the edifice they demolished in 1922.

The UAPA was not, indeed, out of the woods; in fact, it was in its terminal decline. Realising the apathy that was overtaking the entire membership in the absence of regularly issued *United Amateurs,* Lovecraft in the editorial endorses, with reservations and modifications, the plan of James F. Morton (who had joined the UAPA for the first time in thirty-five years of amateurdom, serving as the Chairman of the Department of Public Criticism) for a partial consolidation of the three amateur associations (UAPA, UAPA of A, and NAPA): the UAPA of A would cover the western portions of the country, since it was still largely based in Seattle; the NAPA would represent "amateurdom's historical tradition and diverse activities social and political"; and the UAPA would continue in its advocacy of pure literature. It was a pipe dream, and one senses that Lovecraft knew it. No convention was held in 1924, and evidently the official board for that year was reelected by a mail vote; but that administration produced only one more issue (July 1925)—an issue remarkable for its complete dominance by members of Lovecraft's literary circle (Frank Belknap Long, Samuel Loveman, Clark Ashton Smith, and of course

Lovecraft himself). This ended Lovecraft's official involvement with the UAPA. Although he strove valiantly to establish the next official board (Edgar J. Davis as President, Victor E. Bacon as Official Editor), it never really took off and, after one or two skimpy issues of the *United Amateur,* it died sometime in 1926.

Although Lovecraft had not served as Chairman of the Department of Public Criticism since 1919, he continued to offer his views on the state of current amateur prose and verse. One of the most curious venues he chose for this enterprise was a column entitled "The Vivisector," published under the pseudonym (or, more properly, house name) Zoilus in Horace L. Lawson's *Wolverine.* The authorship of the five "Vivisector" pieces (which appeared in the *Wolverine* for March 1921, June 1921, November 1921, March 1922, and Spring 1923) has long been a matter of doubt, but correspondence between Lovecraft and Lawson clarifies the matter. All the articles could certainly not have been written by the same hand, since the November 1921 piece states, "My 'Zoilian' colleague shows fine common-sense in the March number . . ." Who, then, were the authors of these articles?

That Lovecraft wrote at least some of them is confirmed by an undated letter (perhaps early 1921) from Lawson to Lovecraft: "As for your 'Zoilus' article, it reads about like a review of *The Cleveland Sun.*"[22] This seems to refer to the March 1921 article. In a letter dated March 20, 1921, Lawson writes: "May I have the next instalment of 'The Visisector' soon? I must start preparation for the May number immediately." The issue, of course, actually came out in June, and Lawson's letter clinches Lovecraft's authorship of the first two pieces. The third article—clearly not by Lovecraft—is, as mentioned earlier, a lengthy analysis of Lovecraft's own "Facts concerning the Late Arthur Jermyn and His Family." Lawson writes to Lovecraft in an undated letter (c. Autumn 1921):

> I think that a vivisection of the "Wolverine" might interest its readers, but I fear that you would not do justice to your own work in it. How would it do to do the larger part of the work yourself, and let Galpin or Kleiner or someone else criticize your own stories? That would help to justify my statement in regard to the department in the June "W". However, this is merely a suggestion. You are the editor of the department, and so may do as you see fit in the matter.

This establishes that Lovecraft was a sort of informal "editor" of "The Vivisector" and had control of what material was published in the column. A later letter by Lawson to Lovecraft (September 19, 1921) clarifies the authorship of the November 1921 article:

> I enclose Galpin's review of *The Wolverine,* written at your request. He suggests in an accompanying letter, that it be changed to suit. It could never be run as it is, for we do not wish to have it in the form of a letter written by request; in several places it mentions you as the author of the previous criticisms; and we should keep

it anonymous, don't you think? If you will be kind enough to make this over to your taste, and return it, I'll try to get to work on the issue.

As it happens, Lovecraft does not seem to have revised the article greatly; it begins: "An invitation to criticise the last two issues of *The Wolverine* gives one an excellent opportunity for evil-doing. . . ." Mentions of Lovecraft's authorship of the previous "Vivisector" columns have, however, been eliminated. This letter raises the question of who decided that the column should be anonymous, and why. Was it Lawson's idea? Perhaps Lovecraft's views on amateur affairs were by this time so well known that anything appearing under his name might be subject to violent rebuttal or dismissal by those who disagreed with him.

For the authorship of the last two articles no external evidence is available, but internal evidence points to Lovecraft. The article for March 1922 discusses the work of Lovecraft's fellow amateur poet Lilian Middleton and seems to be largely an extract or abridgement of an essay written on January 14, 1922 (unpublished during his lifetime), entitled "The Poetry of Lilian Middleton." The final article studies the poetry of Lovecraft's close friend Rheinhart Kleiner.

The house name Zoilus—taken from the fourth-century B.C.E. Greek critic who gained notoriety for severely criticising the Homeric poems—is not very apt, since the articles are not notably censorious; most of them are quite lavish in their praise of amateur work. The first discusses several amateur papers, heaping especial praise on, of all things, George Julian Houtain's *Zenith* for January 1921, which contains Houtain's writeup of the amateur gathering at 20 Webster Street in July of the previous year; the second article lauds the one and only issue of Galpin's *Philosopher* (December 1920). The contents of the remaining articles have already been noted. No one would want to read great significance into the "Zoilus" pieces, but they can be seen as the ultimate distillation of all the plodding work that Lovecraft did as Chairman of the Department of Public Criticism.

I have already noted the lengthy tirade entitled "Lucubrations Lovecraftian," published in the *United Co-operative* for April 1921. Its laborious and surprisingly bitter defence of the role of public criticism in amateurdom seems to be anomalously late, given that Lovecraft himself had ceased to be Chairman of the Department of Public Criticism in July 1919; but he still cherished enough hope for this department (now manned successively by his own colleagues, Alfred Galpin and James F. Morton) that he did not wish attacks upon it to go unanswered. The political content of this article will be discussed later. The only remarkable thing about this piece, aside from its sharpness of tone, is how Lovecraft bibliographers could have overlooked it in spite of a title that transparently betrays its authorship.

Lovecraft was by no means aloof from the affairs of the NAPA. It is somewhat ironic that the only two national conventions he ever attended, in 1921 and 1930, were those of the NAPA, not the UAPA. The NAPA convention of 1921 was held on July 2–4 in Boston. Oddly enough, I have been unable to find any discussions of the event in Lovecraft's correspondence—perhaps because, in spite of his devotion to the UAPA, he and most of his colleagues were also members of the NAPA and attended the convention, so that there would be no need to rehash it afterwards in letters—but two documents are of some interest. The first is an apparently unpublished essay, "The Convention Banquet," giving an account of the NAPA banquet held at the Hotel Brunswick in Boston on July 4 at 8 P.M. Lovecraft tells of speeches given by James F. Morton, William J. Dowdell, Edward H. Cole, and—to culminate events—a tribute to W. Paul Cook, who in spite of his long and fruitful amateur career was attending his first actual convention and was given a silver loving-cup for his services to the cause. After Cook gave a brief and halting speech, the audience—rather in the manner of a crowd at a sporting event or a campaign rally—began chanting, "What's the matter with Cook? He's all right! Who's all right? W. Paul Cook!" A number of other speeches—by George Julian Houtain, Laurie A. Sawyer, Edith Miniter, and others—followed.

In this account Lovecraft passes very briefly over a speech he himself gave at the banquet, one that apparently directly followed the opening remarks by Toastmaster Willard O. Wylie. The speech survives under the title: "Within the Gates: By 'One Sent by Providence.'" Next to some of his humorous short stories, it is one of the wittiest of Lovecraft's prose performances. The title alludes to the fact of his unbending devotion to the UAPA—or, as he puts it in the speech, "the presence of a strictly United man in the midst of the National's Babylonish revelry"—and he goes on to cite a line about another gate "which appears in the celebrated epic of my fellow-poet Dante"—"All hope abandon, ye who enter here." The speech is full of genial barbs directed at Houtain, Edith Miniter, and other amateurs, and concludes by apologising for the "long and sonorous intellectual silence" of the speech (it is less than 1000 words).

Clever as "Within the Gates" is, it is of importance merely for its existence: six weeks after his mother's death, Lovecraft is resolutely making efforts to resume the course of his life, to the point of attending his first national amateur convention and being able to exchange harmless banter with amateur associates. In "The Convention Banquet" Lovecraft modestly fails to give any indication of how his speech was received, but I have no doubt it went over very well.

One of the individuals who must have been in the audience was Sonia Haft Greene (1883–1972).[23] Sonia had been introduced to amateur journalism by James F. Morton; in an autobiography written in 1967 she claims to have known him since 1917.[24] She was one of a contingent of NAPA members from the New York area (among them Morton, Rheinhart Kleiner, and others) to go to the convention, and Kleiner later testified that he introduced her to Lovecraft at the event.[25] Very shortly thereafter Sonia became an ardent supporter of the amateur cause, not only joining the UAPA but contributing the unheard-of sum of $50.00 to the Official Organ Fund. In the "News Notes" for the September 1921 *United Amateur* Lovecraft acknowledges this contribution as an "example of amateur devotion and enthusiasm which should be heeded by all members as an inspiration to renewed activity." In private letters he is less restrained:

> *Some* liberality! Upon sending in her United application, and merely after having read a few stray papers and old official organs, Mme. Greene unsolicitedly and unexpectedly came across with a pledge of FIFTY (count 'em—50!) refulgent rubles—HALF A HUNDRED scintillant simoleons—for the Official Organ Fund. Ten of 'em cash down. Oh, boy! Is that the ideal amateur spirit? We'll notify the cosmos!![26]

It is a pity that we know so relatively little about the woman whom Lovecraft would marry less than three years later. She was born Sonia Haft Shafirkin on March 16, 1883, in Ichnya (near Kiev) in the Ukraine. Her father, Simyon Shafirkin, apparently died when she was a child. Her mother, Racille Haft, left Sonia with her brother in Liverpool—where Sonia received her first schooling—and herself came to America, where she married Solomon H——— in 1892. Sonia joined her mother later that year. She married Samuel Seckendorff in 1899—she was not quite sixteen, her husband twenty-six. A son, born in 1900, died after three months, and a daughter, Florence, was born on March 19, 1902. Seckendorff, a Russian, later adopted the name Greene from a friend in Boston, John Greene.[27] In her memoir of Lovecraft, Sonia tells very little about this marriage; but Alfred Galpin provides an interesting sidelight:

> Her first marriage in Russia [*sic*] had been most unhappy, to a man of brutal character, and quarrels became bitter. "Let me tell you, Alfred, things have happened to me that never, *never* happened before to *any living creature on earth!"* In one of their quarrels—the last?—"I walked to the window," which looked down several stories of the street, "and I said, 'Georgi Fedorovitch, *if you take one step forward, I shall hurl myself from this window!'"*[28]

I do not know what the name "Georgi Federovitch" is supposed to signify; perhaps this was a misrecollection on Galpin's part. Samuel Greene himself died in 1916, apparently by his own hand.

Sonia had taken some extension courses at Columbia University and had secured what she called "a highly paid executive position with a fashionable women's wear establishment in Fifth Avenue,"[29] with a salary of $10,000 a year—probably at least five to ten times as much as Lovecraft ever made in any given year of his entire career. This establishment is Ferle Heller's, which had two shops, one at 36 West 57th Street and the other at 9 East 46th Street; Sonia, whose specialty was hats, apparently worked at the former shop, since in her late autobiography she states that the establishment was "a few doors west of Fifth Avenue."[30] She resided at 259 Parkside Avenue in the then fashionable Flatbush section of Brooklyn.

Lovecraft supplies an effusive biographical account of her in the "News Notes" for the September 1921 *United Amateur,* an account surely derived from Sonia but with the lavish praise added by Lovecraft:

> Mrs. Greene is a Russian by birth, and descended from an illustrious line of artists and educators. Coming at an early age to the United States, she acquired a remarkable degree of erudition mainly through her own initiative; being now a master of several languages and deeply read in all the literatures and philosophies of modern Europe. Probably no more thorough student of Continental literature has ever held membership in amateurdom . . .

Kleiner describes her physically as "a very attractive woman of Junoesque proportions"; Galpin, while using exactly the same classical adjective, paints a more piquant portrait:

> When she dropped in on my reserved and bookish student life at Madison [in 1921 or 1922], I felt like an English sparrow transfixed by a cobra. Junoesque and commanding, with superb dark eyes and hair, she was too regal to be a Dostoievski character and seemed rather a heroine from some of the most martial pages of *War and Peace.* Proclaiming the glory of the free and enlightened human personality, she declared herself a person unique in depth and intensity of passion and urge me to Write, to Do, to Create.

Sonia was taken with Lovecraft from the start. Kleiner notes that "On our return to Brooklyn, she sought out all those who were friends of Lovecraft—myself among them—and spent most of the time talking about him." Sonia bluntly confesses that, when first meeting Lovecraft, "I admired his personality but frankly, at first, not his person"—a clear reference to Lovecraft's very plain looks (tall, gaunt frame, lantern jaw, possible problems with facial hair and skin) and perhaps also his stiff, formal conduct and (particularly annoying to one in the fashion industry) the archaic cut of his clothes.

But a correspondence promptly ensued. Lovecraft heard from Sonia as early as mid- to late July of 1921, by which time she had already read some of Lovecraft's stories that had appeared in the amateur press. Lovecraft professed to be taken with her, at least as an intellect: "Mrs. G. has an acute, receptive, and well-stored mind; but has yet to learn that impersonal point of view which weighs evidence irrespective of its palatability. She forms a welcome addition to the United's philosophical arena . . ."[31]

Up to this point, there does not seem any immediate attraction between the two except that of two intelligent and congenial minds. What of the fact, however, that (according to testimony cited earlier) Lovecraft and Winifred Virginia Jackson were considered to be having some sort of romance at this time? Lovecraft does not mention Jackson in his admittedly few discussions of the NAPA convention of 1921; and yet, it would have been remarkable (even given that she was a loyal UAPA member) for her not to have been there. The last of Lovecraft's surviving letters to Jackson was written on June 7, 1921, two weeks after his mother's death, and contains the following interesting notes:

> It may indeed be said with justice that you have lost a friend in my mother, for although you never heard directly from her, she may be reckoned among the earliest and most enthusiastic admirers of your work. . . . In case it would interest you to know my mother's appearance during these latter days, I enclose a snap-shot—inadequate enough, I regret to say—which I took a year ago last autumn. Her appearance was as handsome as mine is homely, and her youthful pictures would form close rivals to your own in a contest for aesthetic supremacy.[32]

Kenneth W. Faig, Jr wryly remarks: "What Miss Jackson thought of a man who sent her a snapshot of his mother along with praises of her own beauty, history has not recorded . . ."[33] This letter is, however, still very formal, and I have trouble envisioning any real intimacy between the two. Perhaps, indeed, it was Susie who had been encouraging such a liaison (if that is what it was)—she would surely have approved of Winifred far more than she would have approved of Sonia had she lived to meet her. But we hear nothing of Winifred after this date.

It was Sonia who took things into her own hands. She visited Lovecraft in Providence on September 4–5, staying at the Crown Hotel. This is rather remarkable in itself—note that Winifred never seems to have made an effort to visit Lovecraft in his native city—and Sonia must have taken at least Monday the 5th off from work to make the trip. Lovecraft, as had already become customary with his out-of-town visitors, showed her the antiquarian treasures of Providence, took her back to 598, and introduced her to Aunt Lillian ("Both seemed delighted with each other, and my aunt has ever since been eloquent in her praise of Mme. G."[34]), and then Sonia invited both Lovecraft and Lillian to dinner at the Crown; but as the latter had already had a noon meal, Lillian declined and Lovecraft had only coffee and ice cream. Perhaps neither of them wished to give the impression of taking advantage of Sonia's generosity, since she manifestly wished to pick up the cheque for the meal. More antiquarian exploration followed, including the "cloistral hush" of the Brown University campus. The next day Sonia did manage to get Lovecraft and his aunt to come to the Crown for a noon meal, and presumably left on the long train ride back to New York (about five hours) shortly thereafter. Lovecraft sang her praises: "Mme. G. is certainly a person of the most admirable qualities, whose generous and kindly cast of mind is by no means feigned, and whose intelligence and devotion to art merit the sincerest appreciation. The volatility incidental to a Continental and non-Aryan heritage should not blind the analytical observer to the solid work and genuine cultivation which underlie it."[35]

Prior to her departure Sonia strongly urged Lovecraft to participate in (as he termed it in this letter) a "convention of freaks and exotics" in New York, including Samuel Loveman and Alfred Galpin from Cleveland, Lovecraft from Providence, and such New Yorkers as Frank Belknap Long, Rheinhart Kleiner, and James F. Morton. Lovecraft was tempted by the prospect, but was doubtful whether the thing could come off.

In the meantime Sonia contributed to the amateur cause in other than monetary ways. In October 1921 the first of two issues of her *Rainbow* appeared; both would be forums for the poetic, fictional, essayistic, and polemical outpourings of Lovecraft and his inner circle of amateur colleagues. This first issue contains Galpin's substantial essay, "Nietzsche as a Practical Prophet," Lovecraft's "Nietzscheism and Realism," poems by Rheinhart Kleiner, Samuel Loveman, James F. Morton, and Sonia herself, and an editorial by Sonia, "Amateurdom and the Editor." Of her two poems, "Ode to Florence" is a rather sappy little ditty on her daughter; the other, "Mors Omnibus Communis (Written in a Hospital)," is of slightly greater interest. Lovecraft admitted to revising this poem for Sonia,[36] and it indeed features several characteristics of Lovecraft's own verse (including archaic elisions, absent from "Ode to Florence") and even some sentiments that seem much more his than hers:

> And as the dying groan and scream
> Beneath the futile knife,
> They pray their gods to end the dream;
> The noxious dream call'd life.

As for Lovecraft's own "Nietzscheism and Realism" (the first word unfortunately misprinted as "Nietscheism"), an editor's note announces: "This article is taken from correspondence not originally meant for publication." Lovecraft himself declared that the extracts were made from two letters to Sonia.[37] This compendium of philosophical *bon mots* comprises, sadly enough, almost the sole remnant (aside from a handful of postcards and one other item to be discussed later) of what must have been an extensive and exceptionally fascinating correspondence—one which we would, from a biographical perspective, wish to have perhaps more than any other of Lovecraft's. But Sonia is clear on its fate: "I had a trunkful of his letters which he had written me throughout the years but before leaving New York for California [around 1935] I took them to a field and set a match to them."[38] No doubt Sonia, after all she had been through, was within her rights to do this, but all students of Lovecraft must groan when reading this terse utterance.

The first issue of the *Rainbow* was not only impressive in substance but exquisitely typeset and printed; it must have cost Sonia a significant sum. Kleiner hypothesises that it cost "a couple of hundred dollars."[39] It featured photographs of Alfred Galpin, Rheinhart Kleiner, Lovecraft (a rather wooden one, and one that appears already to show him becoming somewhat stout), and a very attractive one of Sonia wearing a fetching hat—of her own design, presumably. Lovecraft again praises the issue in the "News Notes" of the September 1921 *United Amateur:* "Beyond a doubt, the leading amateur publication of the season is Mrs. Sonia H. Greene's resplendent October *Rainbow.*"

Being a professional amateur was perfectly suited to Lovecraft's aristocratic temperament, but as time went on and the family inheritance increasingly dwindled, some thought must be paid to making money. He was surely aware of the principal reason for his mother's nervous collapse—her worries about the financial future of herself and her son. Perhaps it was this that finally led him to make some effort at earning an income. I have already noted his doing some revisory work around 1916 for some amateur writers, and his casual, flippant, and probably never realised plans to collaborate with Maurice W. Moe on hack fiction under the pseudonym Horace Philter Mocraft. Then David Van Bush appeared on the scene.

As noted earlier, Bush joined the UAPA in 1916. Lovecraft first mentions him, to my knowledge, in the summer of 1918. In speaking of helping a Mrs Arnold, an elderly woman friend of Alfred Galpin's, with some of her poetry, Lovecraft remarks: ". . . if she has any large amount of work to be prepared for outside publication, I shall be pleased to handle it as I handle Rev. David V. Bush's. It will not be such hard work, since Mrs. A. could not possibly perpetuate such utter & unqualified asininity as Rev. D. V. B."[40] At this point it may be worth giving as complete a list of Bush's published books as is currently known, arranged chronologically:

Peace Poems and Sausages. [Webster, SD: Reporter & Farmer Print, 1915.]
"Pike's Peak or Bust"; or, The Possibilities of the Will. [Webster, SD: The Reporter & Farmer, 1916.]
Soul Poems and Love Lyrics. St Louis: David Van Bush, [1916].
What to Eat. St Louis: David Van Bush, [192-; rev. 1924].
Grit and Gumption. [St Louis: David Van Bush, 1921.]
Inspirational Poems. St Louis: Hicks Almanac & Publishing Co., [1921].
Will Power and Success. [St Louis: Hicks Almanac & Publishing Co., 1921.]
Applied Psychology and Scientific Living. [St Louis: David Van Bush, 1922; rev. 1923.]
The Law of Vibration and Its Use. [St Louis: David Van Bush, 1922.]
Poems of Mastery and Love Verse. [St Louis: David Van Bush, 1922.]

The Power of Visualization: How to Make Your Dreams Come True. [St Louis: David Van Bush, 1922.]

Practical Psychology and Sex Life. Chicago: David Van Bush, [1922].

Affirmations and How to Use Them. Washington, DC: David Van Bush, [1923].

Character Analysis: How to Read People at Sight. With W. Waugh. [St Louis: David Van Bush, 1923; rev. 1925.]

Kinks in the Mind: How to Analyze Yourself and Others for Health. Chicago: David Van Bush, [1923].

The Universality of the Master Mind. Chicago, [1923].

What Is God? Dayton, OH: Otterbein Press, 1923.

Your Mind Power. Chicago: David Van Bush, [1923].

How to Put the Subconscious Mind to Work. Chicago: David Van Bush, 1924.

Psychology of Healing. Chicago: David Van Bush, [1924].

Psychology of Sex: How to Make Love and Marry. Chicago, [1924].

Spunk. Chicago: David Van Bush, [1924].

Concentration Made Effective and Easy. Chicago: David Van Bush, [1925].

The Influence of Suggestion: Auto-Suggestion. St Louis: David Van Bush, [1925?].

How to Hold "the Silence." Chicago: David Van Bush, [1925].

Relaxation Made Easy. Chicago: David Van Bush, [1925].

(Editor) *Practical Helps for Health, Poise, Power: Being Selected Articles from* Mind Power Plus. Chicago: David Van Bush, [1928].

The New Law, Radiation: How to Fulfill Your Desires. Chicago: David Van Bush, [1929].

If You Want to Be Rich. Mehoopany, PA, 1954.

Several things become evident from this list: first, most of Bush's works were self-published; second, Bush initially attempted to write poetry, but later switched to a sort of inspirational pop psychology that, at least from the number of books published, was relatively successful; third, most of his publications are in the 1922–25 period. It is a dreary possibility that Lovecraft revised the bulk of these books, both prose and verse; on a flyer for *Applied Psychology and Scientific Living* (1922), Lovecraft has written: "I did 2 or 3 chapters in this. His regular staff did the rest."[41] Since, however, he did not encounter Bush before 1917, it is mercifully unlikely that he revised the first three of Bush's books; of that first title Lovecraft notes, in discussing "Lord" Timothy Dexter's book, *A Pickle for the Knowing Ones,* "In 1796, stung by the ridicule of the publick, Dexter publish'd what was probably America's queerest book—Bush's *Peace Poems & Sausages* not excepted."[42]

The fact of the matter is that Bush became quite popular as a writer and lecturer on popular psychology. Lovecraft did not begin working in earnest for Bush until around 1920, and it is no accident that Bush's titles begin appearing at a rapid rate thereafter. Lovecraft regarded Bush with a mixture of irritation and lofty condescension. In speaking of headaches, he writes: "I have just emerged from a veritable 'killer', contracted by working half the forenoon and all the afternoon on Bush junk."[43] Lovecraft met him in the summer of 1922, when Bush was lecturing in Cambridge, Massachusetts, and paints a vivid portrait of him:

> David V. Bush is a short, plump fellow of about forty-five, with a bland face, bald head, and very fair taste in attire. He is actually an immensely good sort—kindly, affable, winning, and smiling. Probably he has to be in order to induce people to let him live after they have read his verse. His keynote is a hearty good-fellowship, and I almost think he is rather sincere about it. His "success-in-life" stuff is no joke so far as finance is concerned; for with his present "psychological" mountebank outfit, his Theobaldised books of doggerel, and his newly-founded magazine, *Mind Power Plus,* he actually shovels in the coin at a very gratifying rate. Otherwise he'd never have a suite at the Copley-Plaza.[44]

The letter goes on at some length, touching on Bush's rural upbringing, his wife, his odd jobs (trick cyclist in a circus, "ham" actor, clergyman), and his "new gospel of dynamic psychology" ("which has all the virtues of 'New Thought' plus a saving vagueness which prevents its absurdity from being exposed before the credulous public amongst whom his missionary labours lie"). The above passage implies that Lovecraft only revised Bush's poetry volumes; but I suspect he must have had a hand with the psychology manuals as well. Sonia Davis suggests as much in her memoir:

> One man in particular . . . became a public lecturer on many scientific subjects of which he knew very little. When he wanted a quotation from the Bible or any other source, he would mention a word or two, not knowing what he really wanted, and H. P. would supply the necessary information. I listened to this man when he "lectured" on psychology in Los Angeles, to a large crowd, mostly women who were seeking healing for lost causes . . .[45]

Lovecraft, in his classified ad in the *New York Times* in 1924 (for which see Chapter 15), states that he "has for seven years handled all the *prose and verse* [my emphasis] of a leading American public speaker and editor," which can only be a reference to Bush. What is more, some of the psychology manuals contain bits of poetry, which Lovecraft no doubt revised. This poetry really is screamingly awful, and even Lovecraft could do little with it:

Grit Your Teeth

Are you bound down on every side,
With sorrow underneath?
Don't quail or stop—you'll land on top—
But you must grit your teeth!

You can do much in life, young man,
Though starting far beneath.
On top you'll rise, 'neath adverse skies,
If you but grit your teeth!

Are you the under dog today?
Dare not your sword to sheath,
But firmly stand—on top you'll land—
If you will grit your teeth!

Ay, set your jaw though gods and Fate
Their darkest ills bequeath;
You're bound to win if you but grin
And bravely grit your teeth![46]

This poem even employs that internal rhyme which we have seen in Lovecraft's own verse from as early as "The Poem of Ulysses."

The mention of *Mind Power Plus* is of some interest. The magazine is not listed in the *National Union Catalogue* or the *Union List of Serials,* and does not seem to be housed in any library in the world. Recently the issue of October 1923 was offered for sale, and it contains a wide array of articles, not merely on psychological subjects (e.g., "Psycho-Analysis: How It Is Done"), but a surprising number of pieces on religious or spiritualistic topics ("The Universal Consciousness of Christ," "Do the Spirits of the Dead Return?"), along with recommendations for a healthy diet and a concluding section of "laughs." It is not clear how typical this issue is. Otherwise, all we have is, among Lovecraft's papers, a one-sheet clipping from it containing a signed article by Lovecraft, "East and West Harvard Conservatism." This piece of frank promotion for Bush's New England lecture campaign is surely one of the most degrading things Lovecraft was ever forced to write—for no doubt Bush commissioned it and paid him for it. The article seeks to explain why the lecture tour was not quite as thunderously successful in New England as in other regions of the country, and Lovecraft trots out any number of hackneyed saws about the New England temperament (it "is uniquely non-receptive because of its extreme unemotionalism . . . Spontaneous impulses have for so long been regarded as reprehensible weaknesses"); but he nonetheless concludes that "Dr.

Bush . . . leaves behind him a gratifying number of new friends and active supporters." It is impossible to tell from the clipping which issue of *Mind Power Plus* this article appeared in, but it probably dates to the summer or fall of 1922; the remarkable thing is that Lovecraft felt it worth the bother of saving. He also admitted revising at least one issue of the magazine in 1923, adding charitably that the material (by various hands, evidently) is "not as technically bad as DVB's own drool."[47]

But Lovecraft could scarcely scorn David Van Bush: he was a regular customer, and he paid promptly and well. In 1917 Lovecraft was charging a rate of $1.00 for sixty lines of verse;[48] by 1920 Bush had agreed to pay $1.00 for forty-eight lines;[49] and by September 1922 Bush was paying $1.00 for every eight lines of verse revised.[50] This really is a pretty remarkable rate, given that the best Lovecraft could do with his own professionally published poetry was to get 25¢ per line for verse in *Weird Tales.* Lovecraft goes on to note: "I told him that only at this high price could I guarantee my own personal service—he doesn't like Morton's work so well, and asked me to do as much as possible myself." What this clearly means is that Lovecraft and Morton have teamed up to do revisory work. How formal was such an arrangement? It is difficult to tell, but consider the following ad that appeared in the amateur journal *L'Alouette* (edited by Charles A. A. Parker) in September 1924:

> THE CRAFTON SERVICE BUREAU offers the expert assistance of a group of highly trained and experienced specialists in the revision and typing of manuscripts of all kinds, prose or verse, at reasonable rates.
>
> THE BUREAU is also equipped with unusual facilities for all forms of research, having international affiliations of great importance. Its agents are in a position to prepare special articles on any topic at reasonable notice. It has a corps of able translators, and can offer the best of service in this department, covering all of the important classical and modern languages, including the international language Esperanto. It is also ready to prepare and supervise courses of home study or reading in any field, and to furnish expert confidential advice with reference to personal problems.
>
> APPLICATIONS and INQUIRIES may be addressed to either of the heads of THE BUREAU:
>
> Howard P. Lovecraft,
> 598 ANGELL STREET, PROVIDENCE, R.I.
> James F. Morton, Jr.,
> 211 WEST 138TH STREET, NEW YORK, N.Y.

Well, Lovecraft (or Morton) has certainly caught the spirit of advertising! I have no idea how much business this wildly exaggerated ad—suggesting that Lovecraft and Morton were "heads" of a non-existent bureau of editors, revisors, translators, and solvers of "personal problems"—brought in; Bush seemed to remain Lovecraft's chief revision client until well into the 1920s. It is likely that many of the "services" noted above were provided by Morton: it was he who was a former vice president of the Esperanto Association of North America, he who probably knew the modern languages better than Lovecraft, he who may have had better "international affiliations" than Lovecraft (unless this refers merely to amateur colleagues in Great Britain and the British Commonwealth). Even those "personal problems" were probably under Morton's jurisdiction, since among his published works was at least one collaborative treatise on sex morality. It is, in any case, difficult to imagine Lovecraft at this stage dealing with anyone's personal problems but his own.

There were other, possibly flippant or wistfully considered job prospects. At the beginning of 1920 Lovecraft became involved in correcting arithmetic papers for the Hughesdale Grammar School. Hughesdale is a village in the township of Johnston, now at the western edge of the Providence metropolitan area, and the school board had urgent need of a substitute mathematics teacher; as a result of family connexions, the job was offered to one of Lovecraft's aunts (probably Lillian), and Lovecraft himself was brought in to assist in the task. He did not actually go to the school, but merely corrected papers as they were brought back by his aunt.[51]

This job was of very short duration; but perhaps as a result of the experience, in early 1920 Lovecraft mused about the following:

> I have been wondering lately if I could ever manage, under the pressure of poverty, to accept a position in an *evening* school. A day school, of course, would be out of the question—for I can rarely keep up that long for two successive days. If fairly frequent absences could be pardoned, I might manage to keep up with the evening hours—but fancy my trying to hold in check a roomful of incipient gangsters! It seems as though every avenue of remunerative activity is closed to a total nervous wreck![52]

This is one of the most pathetic passages in Lovecraft's early letters. How he could have imagined that any night school would hire a high-school dropout who might be subject to "fairly frequent absences" is beyond fathoming. One wonders whether the remark about "incipient gangsters" is a recollection of the Providence Amateur Press Club, made up of seemingly quite normal, if lower-class, night-school students from North Providence.

In the midst of all this activity, both amateur and professional, Lovecraft finally embarked upon a career of professional fiction publication; inevitably, the opportunity was afforded him by amateur connexions. Around September 1921 George Julian Houtain (who had married the amateur writer E. Dorothy MacLaughlin) conceived the idea of launching a peppy and slightly off-colour humour magazine named *Home Brew.* As contributors he called upon his various amateur colleagues and managed to secure pieces from James F. Morton, Rheinhart Kleiner, and others for early issues. For some strange reason he wished Lovecraft to write a serial horror story, even though such a thing would seemingly clash with the general humorous tone of the magazine. He offered Lovecraft the princely sum of $5.00 per 2000-word instalment (¼¢ a word). "You can't make them too morbid," Lovecraft reports Houtain telling him.[53] The first issue of the magazine duly appeared in February 1922, selling for 25¢ and with a subtitle—"A Thirst Quencher for Lovers of Personal Liberty"—that was clearly a code for a certain element of sexual daring in both literary content and artwork. It was edited by "Missus and Mister George Julian Houtain." A blurb on the cover—"Do Dead Come to Life?"—refers to Lovecraft's serial, which he titled "Herbert West—Reanimator" but which Houtain ran under the title "Grewsome Tales" ("grewsome" was a legitimate variant of "gruesome" at this time). A later issue proclaims on the cover that the author of "Grewsome Tales" is "Better Than Edgar Allen [*sic*] Poe"!

Lovecraft takes a certain masochistic pleasure in complaining at being reduced to the level of a Grub Street hack. Over and over for the next several months he emits whines like the following:

> In this enforced, laboured, and artificial sort of composition there is nothing of art or natural gracefulness; for of necessity there must be a superfluity of strainings and repetitions in order to make each history compleat. My sole inducement is the monetary reward, which is a guinea per tale . . .[54]

> Now this is manifestly inartistic. To write to order, to drag one figure through a series of artificial episodes, involves the violation of all that spontaneity and singleness of impression which should characterise short story work. It reduces the unhappy author from art to the commonplace level of mechanical and unimaginative hack-work. Nevertheless, when one needs the money one is not scrupulous—so I have accepted the job![55]

One gets the impression that Lovecraft actually got a kick out of this literary slumming.

In spite of the fact that the six episodes of "Herbert West—Reanimator" were clearly written over a long period—the first two were finished by early October;[56] the fourth was written in early March;[57] the sixth was finished no later than mid-June, and perhaps earlier[58]—the tale does maintain unity of a sort, and Lovecraft seems to have conceived it as a single entity from the beginning: in the final episode all the imperfectly resurrected corpses raised by Herbert West come back to despatch him hideously. In other ways the story builds up a certain cumulative power and suspense, and it is by no means Lovecraft's poorest fictional work. The structural weaknesses necessitated by the serial format are obvious and unavoidable: the need to recapitulate the plot of the foregoing episodes at the beginning of each new one, and the need for a horrific climax at the end of each episode. But, in fact, one wonders whether the plot summaries were in fact necessary: why did Lovecraft not have Houtain supply synopses as headnotes to each successive story? There are in fact headnotes to each segment, but they are wholly fatuous puffs or teasers written by Houtain to spur reader interest. Lovecraft appears to have learnt better in his second *Home Brew* serial, "The Lurking Fear," where he must have instructed Houtain to provide just such synopses to free him from the burden of doing so.

"Herbert West—Reanimator" is narrated in the first person by an unnamed friend and colleague of Dr Herbert West; both he and West attended the Miskatonic University Medical School in Arkham and later went on to experience various adventures as practising physicians. It was in medical school that West derived his peculiar theories about the possibility of reanimating the dead:

> His views . . . hinged on the essentially mechanistic nature of life; and concerned means for operating the organic machinery of mankind by calculated chemical action after the failure of natural processes. . . . Holding with Haeckel that all life is a chemical and physical process, and that the so-called "soul" is a myth, my friend believed that artificial reanimation of the dead can depend only on the condition of the tissues; and that unless actual decomposition has set in, a corpse fully equipped with organs may with suitable measures be set going again in the peculiar fashion known as life.

It is unlikely that even the most astute readers of *Home Brew* expected a mention of Ernst Haeckel in a story of this kind. The amusing thing, of course, is that the above actually expresses Lovecraft's own philosophical view, as noted in *In Defence of Dagon* and elsewhere; what is still more amusing is that the narrator later admits that he still "held vague instinctive remnants of the primitive faith of my forefathers." Clearly Lovecraft is having a little fun both at his own philosophy and at the naive beliefs of the average citizen as to the existence of the soul.

The six episodes show West producing more and more hideous instances of reanimation. In the first, West injects a serum in a corpse, but it seems to produce no results; the two doctors bury the corpse in the potter's field, only to learn later that it came to life after all. In the second, West impishly decides to resurrect Dr Allan Halsey, who as head of the medical school had vigorously opposed West's experiments and had died in the typhoid epidemic that raged through Arkham. The creature is caught and locked up in Sefton Asylum. In the third, West and the narrator have set up practice in the small Massachusetts town of Bolton, and attempt to resurrect the body of a black man—an amateur boxer named Buck Robinson, "The Harlem Smoke"—but seem to find that the serum "prepared from experience with white specimens only" will not work on black corpses; later they learn otherwise. In the fourth episode the narrator, returning from a vacation with his parents in Illinois, finds West in a state of unusual excitement. He has designed an embalming fluid that will preserve a corpse in a state of freshness indefinitely, and claims that a travelling salesman who had come to visit West had died unexpectedly and would therefore serve as a perfect specimen because of the freshness of the corpse. When it is reanimated, the narrator finds that West's account of the matter is perhaps not wholly accurate. The fifth episode takes us to the horrors of the Great War, where West and the narrator have enlisted in a Canadian regiment in 1915. West now seeks to put into practice still more eccentric views on the reanimation of the dead, and does so in a loathsome manner. The sixth episode finds the two doctors in Boston after the war, and it ends with the various reanimated bodies returning to tear West to pieces and bear off the fragments of his corpse through ancient underground tunnels leading to a cemetery.

No one would deem "Herbert West—Reanimator" a masterpiece of subtlety, but it is rather engaging in its lurid way. It is also my belief that the story, while not *starting out* as a parody, *became* one as time went on. In other words, Lovecraft initially attempted to write a more or less serious, if quite "grewsome," supernatural tale but, as he perceived the increasing absurdity of the enterprise, abandoned the attempt and turned the story into what it in fact was all along, a self-parody. The philosophical subtext of the story may bear out this interpretation. We have already seen that Lovecraft initially endows West with his own mechanistic views, so that the reanimation of the dead becomes merely an extrapolation upon them. But consider West's later theories during his World War I experience:

> Two biological points he was exceedingly anxious to settle—first, whether any amount of consciousness and rational action be possible without the brain, proceeding from the spinal cord and various nerve-centres; and second, whether any kind of ethereal, intangible relation distinct from the material cells may exist to link the surgically separated parts of what has previously been a single living organism.

That second point is so manifestly a contradiction of materialism that it can only be intended parodically—or, rather, as an excuse for a particularly grisly tableau in which a severed head placed in a vat cries out when West reanimates the trunk. If this were not enough to indicate parody at this stage of the story, consider this passage in the same segment (the fifth): "The scene I cannot describe—I should faint if I tried it, for there is madness in a room full of classified charnel things, with blood and lesser human debris almost ankle-deep on the slimy floor, and with hideous reptilian abnormalities sprouting, bubbling, and baking over a winking bluish-green spectre of dim flame in a far corner of black shadows." I have to believe this is intended more to provoke a smirk than a shudder.

The question of influence might be worth studying briefly. It has been taken for granted that the obvious influence upon the story is *Frankenstein;* but I wonder whether this is the case. The method of West's reanimation of the dead (whole bodies that have died only recently) is very different from that of Victor Frankenstein (the assembling of a huge composite body from disparate parts of bodies), and only the most general influence can perhaps be detected. The core of the story is so elementary a weird conception that no literary source need be postulated.

"Herbert West—Reanimator" does have some importance in Lovecraft's evolving imaginary New England topography. It is the first story where Miskatonic University is mentioned, although of course the word *Miskatonic* had already appeared in "The Picture in the House." Five of the six segments are set in New England, even if there is not much in the way of realistic landscape description in any of them. The mention of Bolton is interesting: it is a real town in east-central Massachusetts; but it was not at the time a "factory town" as Lovecraft describes it, but merely a tiny agricultural community. Lovecraft has a few topographical in-jokes along the way as well. In the first segment the two doctors find the "deserted Chapman farmhouse beyond Meadow Hill" a suitable place for their experiments; later it burns to the ground when their first experiment goes awry. Recall this passage from a letter to Rheinhart Kleiner of February 1920:

> But *the* event of the season was the burning of the large Chapman house last Wednesday night—the yellow house across two lawns to the north of #598 Angell. . . . There, in full view, was the most impressive sight I ever beheld. Where that evening had stood the unoccupied Chapman house, recently sold and undergoing repairs, was now a titanic pillar of roaring, living flame amidst the deserted night—reaching into the illimitable heavens and lighting the country for miles around.[59]

No one but Lovecraft—and perhaps Kleiner—would ever have gotten this joke.

I do not know whether much need be made of the apparent racism in the third episode. Buck Robinson is described as "a loathsome, gorilla-like thing, with abnormally long arms which I could not help calling fore legs, and a face that conjured up thoughts of unspeakable Congo secrets and tom-tom poundings under an eerie moon." The latter part of the sentence is so extravagant that I again suspect parody. And, interestingly, far from confirming the doctors' belief that the serum prepared for white patients would not work on a black corpse, the resurrection of Buck Robinson actually establishes the reverse.

It has frequently been believed—based upon Lovecraft's remark in June 1922 that "the pay was a myth after the second cheque"[60]—that Lovecraft was never fully paid for the serial; but a letter to Samuel Loveman in November 1922 reports that Houtain has "paid up his past debts" and even advanced Lovecraft $10 for the first two segments of "The Lurking Fear."[61]

Lovecraft managed to write two other stories while working desultorily on "Herbert West—Reanimator," and they are very different propositions altogether. "The Music of Erich Zann" appears to have been written in late 1921, probably December, since in Lovecraft's chronologies of his fiction it is always listed as the last story of the year; a letter of early February 1922 states: "'Erich Zann' I wrote only recently."[62] The first of its many appearances was in the *National Amateur* for March 1922.

"The Music of Erich Zann" justifiably remained one of Lovecraft's own favourite stories, for it reveals a restraint in its supernatural manifestations (bordering, for one of the few times in his entire work, on obscurity), a pathos in its depiction of its protagonist, and a general polish in its language that Lovecraft rarely achieved in later years.

The first-person narrator, again nameless, has "examined maps of the city with the greatest of care," but he cannot find the Rue d'Auseil, where he once dwelt as an "impoverished student of metaphysics" and heard the music of Erich Zann. Zann is a mute viol-player who played in a cheap theatre orchestra and dwelt in the garret apartment of a boarding-house run by "the paralytic Blandot"; the narrator, occupying a room on the fifth floor, occasionally hears Zann playing wild tunes featuring harmonies that seem to have no relation to any known style of music. One night he meets Zann in the hallway and asks to listen in while he plays; Zann accedes, but plays only ordinary music, although it is nevertheless affecting and apparently of his own composition. When the narrator asks Zann to play some of his weirder numbers, and even begins to whistle one of them, Zann reacts with horror and covers the narrator's mouth with his hand. When the narrator then seeks to look out the curtained window of the apartment, Zann furiously tugs at his coat and prevents him from doing so. Later Zann has the narrator move to a lower floor so that he does not hear the music anymore.

One night, as the narrator comes to Zann's door, he hears "the shrieking viol swell into a chaotic babel of sound" and later hears an "awful, inarticulate cry which only the mute can utter, and which rises only in moments of the most terrible fear or anguish." Demanding entry, he is let in by a harried Zann, who manages to calm himself and writes a scribbled note saying that he will prepare "a full account in German of all the marvels and terrors which beset him." An hour passes while Zann writes; then a strange sound seems to come from the curtained window: ". . . it was not a horrible sound, but rather an exquisitely low and infinitely distant musical note . . ." Zann immediately stops writing, picks up his viol, and commences to play with daemoniac fury: "He was trying to make a noise; to ward something off or drown something out . . ." The glass of the window breaks, blowing out the candle and plunging the room into darkness; a sudden gust of wind catches up the manuscript and bears it out the window. As the narrator attempts to save it, he gains his first and last look out that lofty window: "Yet when I looked from that highest of all gable windows, looked while the candles sputtered and the insane viol howled with the night-wind, I saw no city outspread below, and no friendly lights gleaming from remembered streets, but only the blackness of space illimitable; unimagined space alive with motion and music, and having no semblance to anything on earth." The narrator runs into Zann in an effort to flee, encountering the mad player still playing mechanically even though he seems to be dead. Rushing out of the building, he finds the outside world seemingly normal: "And I recall that there was no wind, and that the moon was out, and that all the lights of the city twinkled." And he has, from that time, been unable to find the Rue d'Auseil.

Lovecraft in later years was aware that "The Music of Erich Zann" had a sort of negative value: it lacked the flaws—notably overexplicitness and overwriting—that marred some of his other works, both before and after. He somewhat mechanically declared that it was his second-favourite of his own stories, next to "The Colour out of Space," but he admitted late in life that this was "because it isn't as bad as most of the rest. I like it for what it *hasn't* more than for what it *has*."[63] The reference, of course, is to the very nebulous nature of the horror involved. What, exactly, is Zann trying to "ward off"? Why does the narrator see empty space "alive with motion and music," and what is this supposed to signify? There are those who find this sort of restraint effective because it leaves so much to the imagination; and there are those who find it ineffective because it leaves *too much* to the imagination, and there is a suspicion that the author himself did not have a fully conceived understanding of what the central weird phenomenon of the story is actually meant to be. I fear I am in the latter camp. Lovecraft was, I think, regrettably correct in later years in believing that pulp fiction had insidiously and unwittingly corrupted his style by making his stories a little too histrionic and overexplanatory; but in "The Music of Erich Zann" I cannot help feeling that he has erred in the opposite direction.

Robert M. Price, in a provocative close reading of the story, finds tantalising hints that Zann is a kind of otherworldly figure who by the end of the tale has spiritually returned to the black abysses where he always belonged. Why, argues Price, would Zann's German be "execrable" even though he is presumably a native German? Why is Zann twice described as "satyr-like," and why does the narrator seem to see "shadowy satyrs and Bacchanals dancing and whirling insanely" at the end? Price's subtle analysis deserves much consideration, although it must inevitably leave some elements of the story unexplained.[64]

It should be pointed out that the instrument Zann is playing is a viol—the archaic stringed instrument played between the legs and shaped like a cello—not a violin. This may seem a little grotesque—even more so as Zann is supposed to be playing this instrument in a "cheap theatre orchestra"; but Lovecraft confirms the matter when in a letter he refers to Zann as a "'cellist."[65]

The setting of the story is worth considering. Is it, in fact, Paris? It has always been assumed to be so, but Lovecraft never states so explicitly, and the Rue d'Auseil is the only place name mentioned in the story. One curious piece of evidence—if it can be called that—comes from the French critic Jacques Bergier, who claimed to have corresponded with Lovecraft late in the latter's life and specifically asked Lovecraft how and when he had ever seen Paris in order to derive the convincing atmosphere of the tale, to which Lovecraft is said to have replied, "In a dream, with Poe."[66] But there is, quite frankly, reason to doubt whether Bergier corresponded with Lovecraft at all, and the entire story may be apocryphal. In any case, Lovecraft declares shortly after writing the story, "It is not, as a whole, a dream, though I have dreamt of steep streets like the Rue d'Auseil."[67] The word *Auseil* does not exist in French (nor does *Zann* exist in German), but it has plausibly been suggested that the place name is meant to convey *au seuil* ("at the threshold")—i.e., that Zann's room (and his music) is at the threshold between the real and the unreal. Lovecraft had only a smattering of French, but he could have come up with an elementary coinage of this sort.

The other story of this period is "Hypnos," probably written in March 1922.[68] It is a curious but quite substantial tale that has not received the attention it deserves, perhaps because Lovecraft himself in later years came to dislike it. A recently discovered typescript of the tale bears the dedication "To S. L.," although it is not clear that Samuel Loveman was in any way instrumental in its conception or writing. Probably the dedication refers to the references to Greek antiquity, which Loveman included in much of his own verse. A relatively early entry in the commonplace book (23) provides the plot-germ for the story: "The man who would not sleep—dares not sleep—takes drugs to keep himself awake. Finally falls asleep—& *something* happens—"

"Hypnos" tells the tale of a sculptor who encounters another man at a railway station. This person had fallen unconscious, and the narrator, struck with the man's appearance ("the face [was] . . . oval and actually *beautiful* . . . I said to myself, with all the ardour of a sculptor, that this man was a faun's statue out of antique Hellas"), takes it upon himself to rescue the man, who becomes the sculptor's only friend. The two engage in "studies" of some nameless sort, studies "of that vaster and more appalling universe of dim entity and consciousness which lies deeper than matter, time, and space, and whose existence we suspect only in certain forms of sleep—those rare dreams beyond dreams which never come to common men, and but once or twice in the lifetime of imaginative men." The sensations experienced by the two in these "dreams" are almost inexpressible, but the narrator's teacher is always "vastly in advance" in the exploration of these realms of quasi-entity. But at some point the teacher encounters some awesome horror that causes him to shriek into wakefulness. Previously they had augmented their dream-visions with drugs; now they take drugs in a desperate effort to keep awake. They reverse their previous reclusiveness (they had dwelt in an "old manor-house in hoary Kent") and seek as many "assemblies of the young and the gay" as they can. But it all goes for naught: one night the teacher cannot stay awake for all the efforts of his sculptor friend; something nameless happens, and all that is left of the teacher is an exquisitely sculpted bust of "a godlike head of such marble as only old Hellas could yield", with the word HYPNOS in Greek letters at the base. People maintain that the narrator never had a friend, but that "art, philosophy, and insanity had filled all my tragic life."

It would seem as if the interpretation of this story would rest on whether the narrator's friend actually existed or not; but this point may not affect the analysis appreciably. What we have here, ultimately, is, as with "The Other Gods," a case of hubris, but on a much subtler level. At one point the narrator states: "I will hint—only hint—that he had designs which involved the rulership of the visible universe and more; designs whereby the earth and the stars would move at his command, and the destinies of all living things be his." This sounds somewhat extravagant, but in the context of the story it is powerful and effective, even though (and perhaps this is a point in its favour) not much evidence is offered as to how the person could have effected this rulership of the universe. If the person really existed, then he is merely endowed with overweening pride and his doom—at the hands of the Greek god of sleep, Hypnos—is entirely merited. On a psychological interpretation, this "friend" becomes merely an aspect of the narrator's own personality; note how, after the above statement, he adds harriedly, "I affirm—I swear—that I had no share in these extreme aspirations"—a textbook instance of the conscious mind sloughing off responsibility for its subconscious fantasies.

In the end, "Hypnos" is a subtilisation of a theme already broached in several earlier tales, notably "Beyond the Wall of Sleep"—the notion that certain "dreams" provide access to other realms of entity beyond that of the five senses or waking world. There are, indeed, several points of similarity between "Hypnos" and "Beyond the Wall of Sleep": aside from the above passage on the nature of dreams, there is the narrator's sensations of "occasionally *tearing* through certain well-marked and typical obstacles," similar to Joe Slater's desire (or that of the astral body possessing him) to "soar through abysses of emptiness, *burning* every obstacle that stood in his way"; and just as Slater has some connexion with the star Algol, the narrator of "Hypnos" finds that his friend is weirdly attracted to the constellation Corona Borealis. "Hypnos," therefore, already begins that tendency which we will find over and over again in Lovecraft—the tendency to rewrite certain scenarios in order to produce the most effective treatment of the core idea.

The fact that the narrator of "Hypnos" is a sculptor is of some importance. A paper by Steven J. Mariconda provides a brilliant analysis of the story and its relation to Lovecraft's developing aesthetic theory.[69] I shall treat that theory at length in a later chapter, but here it is worth noting that the theme of expanding sense-perception—already broached in several tales, notably "From Beyond"—becomes a crucial element in Lovecraft's conception of the aesthetic process. In a 1929 letter he declares that the function of each work of art is to provide a distinctive vision of the world, in such a way that this vision becomes comprehensible to others:

> I'd say that good art means the ability of any one man to pin down in some permanent and intelligible medium a sort of idea of what he sees in Nature that nobody else sees. In other words, to make the other fellow grasp, through skilled selective care in interpretative reproduction or symbolism, some inkling of what only the artist himself could possibly see in the actual objective scene itself.

The result is that, by appreciating many different works of art each with their own distinctive vision, *"We see and feel more in Nature"* and accordingly attain a "faint approximation of an approach to *the mystic substance of absolute reality itself*. . ."[70] In "Hypnos" Lovecraft has rendered the conception horrific: the artist narrator and his friend (who, while not being an artist himself, is of such transcendent beauty that he is himself a work of art) now blasphemously seek to transfer this *aesthetic* conception into the realm of the real world—to attempt some actual (not aesthetic) mastery of the "visible universe and more . . ."

"Hypnos" appeared, without its dedication to Loveman, in the *National Amateur* for May 1923. It might be thought to be one of Lovecraft's few non-Dunsanian fantasies: while nominally set in England, so much of the action of the tale occurs either in the protagonists' minds or in the realms of supra-reality to which they gain access that the result is quite otherworldly. Although perhaps slightly overwritten, it deserves neither the contempt Lovecraft heaped upon it in later years nor the casual dismissal it has received at the hands of later critics.

Shortly after writing "Hypnos" Lovecraft began a series of peregrinations that would not end until October. First on the agenda was Lovecraft's first trip out of New England—his New York jaunt of April 6–12. The trip was, of course, arranged by Sonia. She had visited Cleveland on business sometime in late 1921 or early 1922, and there met both Samuel Loveman and Alfred Galpin, who had temporarily settled there after finishing his work at Lawrence College. Still taken with the idea of convening a group of Lovecraft's best friends in New York, Sonia persuaded Loveman to come to the metropolis to look for work. Loveman arrived on April 1 but had little success in job-hunting, although in later years he would secure good work with various antiquarian book dealers. As a way of keeping Loveman in the city—and, coincidentally, of uprooting Lovecraft from his hermitry—Sonia telephoned Lovecraft and urged him to come down to meet his longtime correspondent. Loveman, Morton, and Kleiner added their encouragement, and Lovecraft's new protégé Frank Long was also likely to be on hand. These massed invitations did the trick, and Lovecraft caught the 10.06 train from Providence on the 6th.

Five hours later he saw the "Cyclopean outlines of New-York"[71] for the first time. Lovecraft's lengthiest account of his six-day journey, in a letter to Maurice W. Moe of May 18, 1922, is (at least as published in *Selected Letters*) a trifle difficult to follow on a day-to-day basis, but there was clearly an endless round of discussion along with museum visiting, sightseeing (they ascended to the top of the Woolworth Building, then the tallest structure in the city), bookstore-hunting, and all the other things that most tourists of a bookish sort do when they hit the big city. Sonia magnanimously turned over her own apartment at 259 Parkside Avenue in Brooklyn to Loveman and Lovecraft, herself sleeping in a neighbour's apartment. She reports in her memoir at being "amazed at myself" for her "boldness"[72] in inviting two men to be guests in her flat. She also notes that she took Lovecraft for the first time to an Italian restaurant, where he fell in love with spaghetti and meatballs but refused to drink wine.

Certainly the high point for Lovecraft was meeting two of his closest friends, Loveman and Long. Loveman read his works-in-progress, *The Hermaphrodite* and *The Sphinx* (a prose drama), which Lovecraft pronounced (correctly) to be masterpieces. As for Long, he is

> an exquisite boy of twenty who hardly looks fifteen. He is dark and slight, with a bushy wealth of almost black hair and a delicate, beautiful face still a stranger to the gillette. I think he likes the tiny collection of lip-hairs—about six on one side and five on the other—which may with assiduous care some day help to enhance his genuine resemblance to his chief idol—Edgar Allan Poe. . . . A scholar; a fantaisiste; a prose-poet; a sincere and intelligent disciple of Poe, Baudelaire, and the French decadents.[73]

Lovecraft—whose objection to moustaches and beards was unrelenting—would tease Long about his "moustachelet" for years. It really never did seem to get much bigger.

Lovecraft of course met often with Sonia, and even once met her "flapper offspring" Florence—a "pert, spoiled, and ultra-independent infant rather more hard-boiled of visage than her benignant mater." Sonia cooked several meals for the gang at her place, which even the ascetic Lovecraft admitted to enjoying. One of the most provocative passages in her memoir relates to an event toward the end of Lovecraft's stay:

> Soon S. L. returned to Cleveland and H. P. remained. My neighbor who so kindly made room for me had a beautiful Persian cat which she brought to my apartment. As soon as H. P. saw that cat he made "love" to it. He seemed to have a language that the feline brother understood, for it curled right up in his lap and purred contentedly.
>
> Half in earnest, half in jest I remarked, "What a lot of perfectly good affection to waste on a mere cat, when some woman might highly appreciate it!" His retort was, "How can any woman love a face like mine?" My counter-retort was, "A mother can and some who are not mothers would not have to try very hard." We all laughed while Felis was enjoying some more stroking.[74]

At this point one hardly need belabour Lovecraft's inferiority complex about his appearance, a simultaneous result of his mother's influence (which makes Sonia's remark about mothers a trifle unfortunate) and an actual problem with ingrown facial hairs. But Sonia's intentions were already becoming clear, although she herself may not yet have been wholly aware of them. I doubt if anyone—even Winifred Jackson—had ever said anything like the above to Lovecraft before.

Lovecraft naturally rhapsodised about the spectacular New York skyline, which he saw from a fine vantage point on Manhattan Bridge. But when he examined some parts of the city at somewhat closer range, his views were quite different. Consider this description of the lower East Side:

> My gawd—what a filthy dump! I thought Providence had slums, and antique Bostonium as well; but damn me if I ever saw anything like the sprawling sty-atmosphere of N.Y.'s lower East Side. We walked—at my suggestion—in the middle of the street, for contact with the heterogeneous sidewalk denizens, spilled out of their bulging brick kennels as if by a spawning beyond the capacity of the places, was not by any means to be sought. At times, though, we struck peculiarly deserted areas—these swine have instinctive swarming movements, no doubt, which no ordinary biologist can fathom. Gawd knows what they are . . . a bastard mess of stewing mongrel flesh without intellect, repellent to eye, nose, and imagination—would to heaven a kindly gust of cyanogen could asphyxiate the whole gigantic abortion, end the misery, and clean out the place.[75]

The racism of this passage is only what one would have expected of Lovecraft; in effect, he was finally waking up to the realities of the world. The walls of his sheltered and sequestered life were tumbling brick by brick, and an initial reaction of fear and loathing was predictable.

By Tuesday, April 11, Lovecraft was already quite tired, and upon returning home on the 12th he found himself utterly exhausted; there was also a mass of letters, parcels, and papers awaiting him. He gradually pulled himself together and by early May was already expressing the opinion that "now I must meet that delectable little imp Galpin, and life would be complete!"[76] But Cleveland seemed such an enormous distance away that a trip there seemed a pipe dream. Instead, after six weeks Lovecraft undertook a further round of travelling a little closer to home.

In late May he visited Myrta Alice Little again in New Hampshire. After several days in Westville, Myrta dropped him off at Dover (the "farthest north I ever was in my life!"[77]) as she and her mother continued up to their summer camp at Lake Winnepesaukee. Lovecraft found this car trip "the crowning event of the journey":

> . . . a trip back through Time, extending 75 to 200 years, and plunging me into the heart of an ancient New-England which I had mourned as dead and buried. Words cannot convey the charms of the winding, hilly road; the placid pastoral panoramas at every turn; the magic glimpses of cool centuried farmhouses amidst

> old gardens and under venerable and gigantic trees. . . . The villages were enchanting—opium-dreams of delicate foliage and old white houses. Portsmouth is a city of the Georgian age—there is a glorious atavism to be derived from a ride through its shady residence streets . . .[78]

It is not too early to remark here a feature that we will find again and again on Lovecraft's journeys—the *keenness of perception* that allows him to absorb to the full the topographical, historical, and social features of regions that many of us might heedlessly pass over. Lovecraft was exceptionally alive to whatever milieu he found himself in, and this accounts both for raptures like the above and for the violence of his reaction to places like Chinatown, which defied all his norms of beauty, repose, and historic rootedness.

In early or mid-June was the Cambridge trip to hear David Van Bush lecture. Coming back to Boston, he stopped off at a house jointly occupied by Edith Miniter and Charles A. A. Parker, spent the night at the Hotel Brunswick (where the NAPA convention had been held the year before), and "'did' the art museum and all the old grave-yards."[79]

Later that month Sonia, striking while the iron was hot, found a way to spend time in New England and do much visiting with Lovecraft. She was representing her firm at Magnolia, Massachusetts, which Lovecraft describes as "an ultra-fashionable watering-place on the coast near Gloucester, an hour's ride northeast from Boston."[80] She came down to Providence on Sunday, June 16, meeting both aunts and becoming so carried away that she tried to persuade Annie to move permanently to New York and share her apartment. Although this idea was naturally rejected, Lovecraft added tellingly: ". . . strange to say, my aunt [Annie] likes her immensely despite a racial and social chasm which she doesn't often bridge." It is a plausible conjecture that Annie's friends were ordinarily neither Jewish nor independent businesswomen.

Sonia persuaded Lovecraft to spend several days with her in Gloucester and Magnolia in late June and early July. The cliffs of Magnolia really are a delight—a place where "pearl-grey mists surge out of the sky to mix with the sea."[81] Lovecraft went up around June 26 and stayed until July 5, stopping at the same house (whether a private residence or a boarding-house is unclear) in Magnolia where Sonia was staying and taking meals at a boarding-house in the main village square. Sonia tells what happened one evening when they were strolling along the esplanade:

> . . . the full moon reflecting its light in the water, a peculiar and unusual noise heard at a distance as of a loud snorting and grunting, the shimmering light forming a moon-path on the water, the round tops of the submerged piles in the water exposed a rope connecting them like a huge spider's guy-line, gave the vivid imagination full play for an interesting weird tale. "Oh, Howard," I exclaimed, "here you have the setting for a real strange and mysterious story." Said he, "Go ahead, and write it." "Oh, no, I couldn't do it justice," I answered. "Try it. Tell me what the

> scene pictures to your imagination." And as we walked along we neared the edge of the water. Here I described my interpretation of the scene and the noises. His encouragement was so enthusiastic and sincere that when we parted for the night, I sat up and wrote the general outline which he later revised and edited.[82]

The result was "The Horror at Martin's Beach," which appeared in *Weird Tales* for November 1923 (under Sonia's name only) as "The Invisible Monster." It is, I fear, not much of a story. Chronologically, this is the first weird story that Lovecraft could be said to have revised instead of collaborated on, although the distinction here is perhaps not very significant: it only affects his refusal to affix his name on the piece as an actual collaborator (as gentlemanly a gesture as his taking second billing for the collaborations with Winifred Jackson and Anna Helen Crofts); he certainly accepted no pay for his revisory work, as he would for later tales revised or ghostwritten for clients.

"The Horror at Martin's Beach" is the wild and improbable story of an enormous sea creature ("fifty feet in length, of roughly cylindrical shape, and about ten feet in diameter") killed by the crew of a fishing smack at Martin's Beach—an unspecified and imaginary locale, but presumably near Gloucester, which is mentioned several times by name. The creature is proved by scientists to be a mere infant, hatched only a few days previously, and probably originating from the deep sea; the day after it is placed on a wooden frame for exhibition, it and the vessel that caught it disappear without a trace. Some days later a terrified cry for help emerges from the sea, and the lifeguards throw out a life-preserver to assist the stricken individual; but the life-preserver, attached to a long rope, appears to have been grasped by some nameless entity that pulls it out to sea, and when the lifeguards and other individuals attempt to reel it in, they not only find themselves unable to do so, but find that they cannot release their hands from the rope. They are inexorably dragged to their deaths in the sea.

The idea is that the parent of the huge infant creature has not only grasped the life-preserver but has also hypnotised the rescuers so that their wills no longer function (this is why a scholarly article, "Are Hypnotic Powers Confined to Recognized Humanity?" by a Prof. Alton, is cited early in the text). This does not seem a very compelling kernel for even a 3000-word short story, so Lovecraft (and it is surely he) is forced to pep up the narrative with his now typical verbal flamboyance: "I recall thinking of those heads, and the bulging eyes they must contain; eyes that might well reflect all the fright, panic, and delirium of a malignant universe—all the sorrow, sin, and misery, blasted hopes and unfulfilled desires, fear, loathing and anguish of the ages since time's beginning; eyes alight with all the soul-racking pain of eternally blazing infernos." A passage like this fails because it is *inappropriate to the circumstances:* there has been an insufficient build-up for it, and it comes off sounding forced and bathetic.

Another story that may have been written at this time is "Four O'Clock." In a letter to Winfield Townley Scott, Sonia declared that Lovecraft only suggested changes in the prose of the tale,[83] hence I concluded that it does not belong in the Lovecraft corpus and did not include it in the revised version of *The Horror in the Museum and Other Revisions* (1989). Judging, however, from her later memoir, it does not appear as if Sonia was a very skilled, polished, or even coherent writer, so that Lovecraft probably did contribute something to this story, which is even slighter than its predecessor. Here we find some individual (whether a man or a woman is never made clear) whose mortal enemy died at four o'clock in the morning and who now fears that some nameless fate will now overtake him at that same hour. He sees some cloud of vapour outside his window gradually form itself into the shape of a clock with hands pointing to four, and later sees other nebulous objects take the same shape. The vapour turns to flame and takes the form of the enemy's face, and the narrator realises that "the end is near."

As a study of monomania—it is never clarified whether the visions seen by the narrator are real or imagined—this story is intermittently effective, but it too is spoiled by overwriting. And it certainly seems as if some of the prose is Lovecraft's, since it features so many of the mannerisms—piled-up adjectives, frequent italicisation of key words, even characteristic punctuational usages—typical of his fiction at this time. But it is not a work we would be much the poorer without. The story was not published in Lovecraft's lifetime, appearing only in *Something about Cats and Other Pieces* (1949). There is, apparently, a third and as yet unpublished weird tale by Sonia; whether Lovecraft had any involvement in it is not known.[84]

Sonia adds a startling note about what transpired the day after "The Horror at Martin's Beach" was conceived:

> His continued enthusiasm the next day was so genuine and sincere that in appreciation I surprised and shocked him right then and there by kissing him. He was so flustered that he blushed, then he turned pale. When I chaffed him about it he said he had not been kissed since he was a very small child and that he was never kissed by any woman, not even by his mother or aunts, since he grew to manhood, and that he would probably never be kissed again. (But I fooled him.)[85]

This really is pretty remarkable. First, if Lovecraft's statement here is true, it certainly makes his "romance" with Winifred Jackson an exceptionally platonic one. Second, the matter of his not being kissed even by his aunts or mother since he was a young man makes us wonder about the degree of reserve in this old New England family. Lovecraft's affection for his aunts—and theirs for him—is unquestioned; but such an unusual lack of physical intimacy is anomalous even for the time and for their social milieu. No wonder Lovecraft was so slow to respond to a woman who so openly expressed affection for him. His emotions had clearly been stunted in this direction.

This week-long trip with Sonia was, as far as I can tell, the first time Lovecraft had spent any considerable amount of time alone in the company of a woman with whom he was not related. There is no evidence that Lovecraft made any such excursions with Winifred Jackson. Sonia was keen on pursuing matters and managed to get up to Rhode Island again on Sunday, July 16, when she and Lovecraft went to Newport and wrote a joint postcard to Lillian (the predictable "wish you were here" stuff).[86]

Ten days later, on Wednesday, July 26, we find Lovecraft writing again from Sonia's apartment in Brooklyn: somehow she had managed to persuade him to undertake the long trip to Cleveland to see Galpin and Loveman. He spent only three days in a stopover in New York (clearly staying in Sonia's apartment, while she again presumably stayed with the neighbour), for on Saturday, July 29, at 6.30 P.M., he boarded the Lake Shore Limited at Grand Central Station for the long train ride to Cleveland. The midwestern scenery did not impress him: "It is quite unlike—and inferior to—New England, having vast level stretches, sparser vegetation and foliage, and different types of architecture. (Flatter roofs, etc.) The villages are insufferably dismal—like 'Main St.' They have no ancient features, and totally lack the mellow charm and scenery which make New-England villages so delightful."[87] The reference to Sinclair Lewis's novel of 1920 does not mean that Lovecraft had actually read it, since it was both a critical and popular success and was no doubt on everybody's tongue; *Babbitt* (1922) would come out later that summer and would add several words to the English language—Babbitesque, Babbitry—that Lovecraft, in his Decadent *épater le bourgeois* phase, would find very useful.

The train ride took sixteen hours, and Lovecraft arrived in Cleveland at 10.30 A.M. on the 30th. He was greeted at the station by Galpin, who, Lovecraft recognised immediately. Their initial exchange of greetings was not a very distinguished one for these two Nietzschean philosophers:

"So this is my Son Alfredus!"

"It sure is!"

But after that a steady stream of conversation flowed. Lovecraft stayed until August 15, mostly at Galpin's residence at 9231 Birchdale Avenue (the building is now no longer standing). Their habits were roughly in accord with Lovecraft's own behaviour-patterns at home: "We rise at noon, eat twice a day, and retire after midnight . . ." Lovecraft takes pride in telling Lillian how boyish and unconventional he has become: he has given up wearing his vest and has bought a belt (probably because of the hot weather); he has bought *soft* collars for the first time; and he is going about *hatless* like Galpin except on formal occasions. "Can you picture me vestless, hatless, soft-collared, and belted, ambling about with a boy of twenty, as if I were no older?" But Lovecraft is careful to reassure Lillian that no social *faux pas* is being committed: "One can be free and easy in a provincial city—when I hit

New York again I shall resume the solemn manner and sedate vestments befitting my advanced years . . ."

An interesting note on the state of Lovecraft's physical and psychological health is recorded in a later letter to Lillian:

As for the kind of time I am having—it is simply great! I have just the incentive I need to keep me active & free from melancholy, & I look so well that I doubt if any Providence person would know me by sight! I have no headaches or depressed spells—in short, I am for the time being really alive & in good health & spirits. The companionship of youth & artistic taste is what keeps one going![88]

And Lovecraft would later wonder why, around the age of thirty, his health suddenly began to improve! Freedom from his mother's (and, to a lesser degree, his aunts') stifling control, travel to different parts of the country, and the company of congenial friends who regarded him with fondness, respect, and admiration will do wonders for a cloistered recluse who never travelled more than a hundred miles away from home up to the age of thirty-one.

Naturally, they met Samuel Loveman (staying at the Lonore Apartments around the corner) frequently, and it was through Loveman that Lovecraft met several other distinguished littérateurs—George Kirk (1898–1962), the bookseller who had just published Loveman's edition of Ambrose Bierce's *Twenty-one Letters* (1922), and, most notably, the young Hart Crane (1899–1932) and his circle of literary and artistic friends. Lovecraft reports attending a meeting of "all the members of Loveman's literary circle": "It gave me a novel sensation to be 'lionised' so much beyond my deserts by men as able as the painter Summers [*sic*], Loveman, Galpin, &c. I met some new figures—Crane the poet, Lazar [*sic*], an ambitious young literary student now in the army, & a delightful young fellow named Carroll Lawrence, who writes weird stories & wants to see all of mine."[89] I shall have more to say about both Kirk and Crane later, since Lovecraft would meet them again during his New York period; for now we can note this brief meeting with William Sommer, the watercolourist and draughtsman, William Lescaze, later to become an internationally known architect, Edward Lazare (whom Lovecraft would meet again in New York, and who in later years would become distinguished as a longtime editor of *American Book-Prices Current*), and others of Crane's circle. Crane had just begun to publish his poetry in magazines, although his first volume, *White Buildings,* would not appear until 1926. Lovecraft must, however, have read Crane's "Pastorale" (in the *Dial* for October 1921), for he wrote a parody of it entitled "Plaster-All." While an amusing take-off of what Lovecraft believed to be the formless free verse of the modernists, the poem is really a sort of impressionistic—dare one say imagistic?—account of his Cleveland trip:

Here it was,
That in the light of an interpreter,

Soon I met and succeeded
In surrounding myself
With a few of the Intelligentsia
That Cleveland affords,
Loveman, Sommer, Lescaze, Hatfield, Guenther. . . .
But Loveman
Left the fold early—pity, yes!

The mention of the minor composer Gordon Hatfield is interesting, since by all accounts this is the first openly homosexual person Lovecraft ever met. His response—as recorded about a year and a half later—is predictable: "To be sure, I recall him! Dear, dear! how he used to sit cross-legged on the floor at Eglin's, little white sailor's cap tucked gracefully under one arm, sport shirt open at the neck, gazing soulfully up at Samuelus and discoursing of arts and harmonies of life! I'm afraid he thought me a very crude, stupid, commonplace, masculine sort of person . . ."[90] He says elsewhere: "I didn't know whether to kiss it or kill it!"[91] Interestingly, he remarks that Hatfield and Crane were mortal enemies. Evidently Lovecraft either did not know that Crane was gay (as was Loveman) or never held it against him—probably the former.

Another person with whom Lovecraft came into contact at this time, although only by correspondence, was Clark Ashton Smith. Loveman and Smith were longtime correspondents, and the former showed Lovecraft Smith's paintings and sketches, while Galpin and Kirk, respectively, presented Lovecraft with copies of Smith's early collections of poetry, *The Star-Treader and Other Poems* (1912) and *Odes and Sonnets* (1918). So taken was Lovecraft with both the pictorial and literary material that he forthwith wrote Smith a fan letter toward the end of his Cleveland stay:

> I trust you will pardon the liberty taken by an absolute stranger in writing you, for I cannot refrain from expressing the appreciation aroused in me by your drawings & poetry, as shown me by my friend, Mr. Samuel Loveman, whom I am now visiting in Cleveland. Your book, containing matter only chronologically classifiable as juvenilia, impresses me as a work of the most distinguished genius . . .[92]

This almost effusively flattering letter initiated a fifteen-year correspondence that would end only with Lovecraft's death.

Clark Ashton Smith (1893–1961) has suffered an anomalous fate precisely because his work is so distinctive and unclassifiable. His two early collections of poetry—followed by several more, including *Ebony and Crystal* (1922), *Sandalwood* (1925), and *The Dark Chateau* (1951), and culminating with the enormous but much-delayed *Selected Poems* (1971)—were in a *fin de siècle* vein somewhat in the manner of Swinburne or George Sterling, but very distinctively Smith's own.

Indeed, upon the publication of that first volume, at the age of nineteen, Smith—a native of California who was born in Long Valley and lived most of his life in Auburn—was hailed by local reviewers as a new Keats or Shelley. These accolades were perhaps not far from the truth. Consider the opening of "The Star-Treader":

> A voice cried to me in a dawn of dreams,
> Saying, "Make haste: the webs of death and birth
> Are brushed away, and all the threads of earth
> Wear to the breaking; spaceward gleams
> Thine ancient pathway of the suns,
> Whose flame is part of thee;
> And the deep gulfs abide coevally
> Whose darkness runs
> Through all thy spirit's mystery. . . ."

To my mind, this and other of Smith's early poems are quite superior to the "cosmic" poetry of George Sterling (1869–1926), although Smith has clearly learnt from Sterling's two long poems, *The Testimony of the Suns* (1903) and *A Wine of Wizardry* (1907). The problem for Smith—or, rather, for his recognition as a significant poet—is that the tradition of weird or fantastic poetry is not very deep or substantial; moreover, modern enthusiasts (and critics) of weird literature seem uncomfortable with poetry, so that the tremendous body of Smith's verse has been ignored by exactly those readers who might be expected to champion it and keep it alive. And although Smith wrote some free verse, much of his work is written both in formal metres and in a very elevated, metaphor-laden diction in utter contrast to the flat, conversational, and (to my thinking) entirely prosaic work of the "poets" who, following the dreary example of William Carlos Williams and Ezra Pound, are currently fashionable. Is it any wonder that Smith's poetry, after its initial praise on the West Coast, fell on deaf ears and remains one of the lost jewels of twentieth-century literature?[93]

Smith did not help his cause by churning out reams of fantasy and science fiction tales in the late '20s and early '30s, some of it inspired by Lovecraft, or at least written under Lovecraft's encouragement. This body of work retains a following, although it is something of an acquired taste, but to me it is much inferior to his verse; I shall have more to say of it later. If Smith did any good work in prose, it is in the prose-poem, some of which Lovecraft read and admired in *Ebony and Crystal.* This work is toweringly impressive, and it could be maintained quite plausibly that Smith is the best prose-poet in English; but this form is too recondite to inspire much of a following or much critical attention.

As for Smith's art work, I find it quite amateurish and crude, and have no idea why Lovecraft so rhapsodised over it. Smith was a self-taught artist, and it shows; this work is, to be sure, reminiscent of primitive art, and occasionally some startlingly weird effects are produced, but much of it—in pen and ink, crayon, and oil—is imaginatively powerful but technically very backward. His small sculptures and figurines are somewhat more interesting. Lovecraft, however, never ceased to admire Smith as another Blake who could both write great work and illustrate it.

Smith did in fact come into contact with George Sterling prior to the publication of his first volume, and their voluminous joint correspondence—full of Sterling's careful dissections of Smith's early work—is highly revealing;[94] but even Sterling's star is falling, and it is an open question whether the forthcoming three-volume edition of his collected poems and verse plays will reverse his descent into obscurity.[95] Smith was at this time living in Auburn with his aged and steadily declining parents. He affected a certain debonair, decadent air: he was fond of wine and women (although he would not marry until he was past sixty), and heaped towering scorn upon the ignorant suburbanites who failed to acknowledge his genius. In the early 1920s he had a column in the *Auburn Journal* that he filled with barbed aphorisms, but these are not very distinguished. His lack of financial success as a writer and his difficult home life left him in poverty for most of his career: his cottage outside of Auburn had no running water, and there were times when he was compelled to work at fruit-picking and other menial jobs. But literature remained his chief object of devotion until at least the mid-1930s. Two years before meeting Lovecraft he wrote his longest and greatest poem, *The Hashish-Eater; or, The Apocalypse of Evil* (included in *Ebony and Crystal*). It is by no means remarkable that Lovecraft would be transported by this nearly 600-line riot of cosmic imagery:

> Bow down: I am the emperor of dreams;
> I crown me with the million-colored sun
> Of secret worlds incredible, and take
> Their trailing skies for vestment when I soar,
> Throned on the mounting zenith, and illume
> The spaceward-flown horizon infinite.

As Lovecraft remarked: "The magnificence of *The Hashish-Eater* is beyond description . . ."[96] He would, in his small way, help to promote Smith by reviewing *Ebony and Crystal* in *L'Alouette* for January 1924—the only formal book review Lovecraft ever wrote.

For the time being, however, it was the benefits and delights of travel that were in the forefront of Lovecraft's mind. Leaving for New York on August 15, he spent at least two months as Sonia's guest in Brooklyn, making an unheard-of total of nearly three solid months away from 598 Angell Street. This long trip was made possible by the unstinting generosity of Lovecraft's friends: just as Loveman, Galpin, and Kirk insisted on picking up many of his expenses (especially meals) in

Cleveland, so did Long (or, more precisely, his parents) frequently have Lovecraft over for lunch or dinner, and no doubt Sonia made or paid for many meals as well. I do not believe there was any condescension in this: Lovecraft's friends surely knew of his lean purse, but their hospitality was both a product of their own kindness and their genuine fondness for Lovecraft and their desire to have him stay as long as possible. We shall find this becoming a repeated pattern in all Lovecraft's peregrinations for the rest of his life.

How did the aunts take this extended departure of their only nephew? As early as August 9, in Cleveland, Lovecraft writes to Lillian, rather touchingly: "I am sorry you miss me—though much flattered that you should do so!" In September Sonia and Lovecraft attempted to persuade one or both of the aunts to come and join them in New York; the staid Lillian declined, but Annie—who in her younger days was very much the socialite—accepted. On September 24 Sonia and Lovecraft wrote a joint letter to her; Sonia's bit is typically saccharine ("Gee! I'm so glad you can come! . . . My Dear, I do hope you can stay a long time!"), and Lovecraft's segment states that he has by now become such an expert guide to New York City that he can lead her anywhere.

Lovecraft's travels in the area were indeed becoming extensive. Among the sites taken in on this jaunt were the very recently opened George Grey Barnard Cloisters on the northern tip of Manhattan, a spectacular mediaeval French chapel brought piecemeal from Europe and reassembled stone by stone; the Van Cortlandt mansion (1748) and the Dyckman Cottage (1783); the lavish expanse of Prospect Park in Brooklyn (no doubt seen on his earlier trip also, since it is near 259 Parkside); the great second-hand bookshops on Fourth Avenue (on the lower East Side) and East 59th Street, which Long, although a native of the city, had incredibly never explored (they are now all gone); James Ferdinand Morton's apartment in Harlem (Lovecraft's first experience with the area that, for the past decade, had been steadily becoming a black enclave); the Jumel mansion (1765) on Washington Heights, containing relics of George Washington; Greenwich Village (whose bohemians did not impress him); the Bronx Zoo; the very fine New York Historical Society museum; the sleepy villages on Staten Island; Fraunces' Tavern (built as a residence in 1719, opened as a tavern in 1762), on the southern tip of Manhattan; and many other places. Lovecraft's accounts of these journeys, in long letters to his aunts, are a delight to read.

Relatively few new acquaintances were made on this trip, Lovecraft staying pretty much with Long, Morton, Kleiner, and Sonia (who was free only on weekends). In late September Lovecraft was introduced to the young amateur Paul Livingston Keil, who accompanied Lovecraft, Morton, and Long to the Poe cottage in Fordham and took a celebrated photograph of them at that site. Years later Keil wrote a brief memoir of the excursion.[97]

Another interesting colleague encountered at this time was Everett McNeil, a writer of boys' stories whom Lovecraft would meet frequently during his New York period. He was then living in one of the worst areas of the city, Hell's Kitchen on the far west side of Manhattan in the 40s. Lovecraft, ever fascinated by urban and social decay, writes of the region vividly:

> Hell's Kitchen is the last remnant of the ancient slums—& by ancient I mean slums in which the denizens are not sly, cringing foreigners; but "tough" and energetic members of the superior Nordic stock—Irish, German, & American. The slinking Dago or Jew of the lower East Side is a strange, furtive animal . . . he uses poison instead of fists, automatic revolvers instead of bricks & blackjacks. But west of Broadway the old toughs have made their last stand. . . . Squalor is extreme, but not so odorous as in the foreign districts. Churches flourish—for all the natives are devout & violent Roman Catholics. It was odd to see slums in which the denizens are Nordic—with shapely faces, & often light hair & blue eyes.[98]

Lovecraft evidently failed to conclude from this that it was not "inferior" blood but socioeconomic disparity that produced these "Nordic" slums.

On the evening of September 16th Lovecraft and Kleiner explored the exquisite Dutch Reformed Church (1796) on Flatbush Avenue in Brooklyn, quite near to Sonia's apartment. This magnificent structure contains a sinister old churchyard at its rear, full of crumbling slabs in Dutch. What did Lovecraft do? "From one of the crumbling gravestones—dated 1747—I chipped a small piece to carry away. It lies before me as I write—& ought to suggest some sort of a horror-story. I must some night place it beneath my pillow as I sleep . . . who can say what *thing* might not come out of the centuried earth to exact vengeance for his desecrated tomb?"[99] True enough, the incident led directly to the writing of "The Hound," probably in October after he returned home.[100] This story involves the escapades of the narrator and his friend St John (based very loosely on Kleiner, whom Lovecraft referred to in correspondence as Randolph St John, as if he were a relative of Henry St John, Viscount Bolingbroke) in that "hideous extremity of human outrage, the abhorred practice of grave-robbing." These two "neurotic virtuosi," who are "wearied with the commonplaces of a prosaic world," can find in this loathsome activity the only respite from their "devastating ennui." They are true aesthetes in morbidity:

> The predatory excursions on which we collected our unmentionable treasures were always artistically memorable events. We were no vulgar ghouls, but worked only under certain conditions of mood, landscape, environment, weather, season, and moonlight. These pastimes were to us the most exquisite form of aesthetic expression, and we gave their details a fastidious technical care. An inappropriate hour, a jarring lighting effect, or a clumsy manipulation of the damp sod, would almost totally destroy for us that ecstatic titillation which followed the exhumation of some ominous, grinning secret of the earth.

One day they seek the grave of an especially redoubtable individual in Holland—"one buried for five centuries, who had himself been a ghoul in his time and had stolen a potent thing from a mighty sepulchre." When they unearth this grave, they find "much—amazingly much" left of the object despite the lapse of half a millennium. They find an amulet depicting the "oddly conventionalised figure of a crouching winged hound, or sphinx with a semi-canine face," and realise that they must bear this prize off for the unholy museum of charnel things they keep in their home in England.

Upon their return, strange things begin to happen. Their home seems besieged with a nameless whirring or flapping, and over the moors they hear the "faint, distant baying" as of a gigantic hound. One night, as St John is walking home alone from the station, he is torn to ribbons by some "frightful carnivorous thing." As he lies dying, he manages to utter, "The amulet—that damned thing—" The narrator realises that he must return the amulet to the Holland grave, but one night in Rotterdam thieves rob him of the thing. Later the city is shocked by a "red death" in a "squalid thieves' den," The narrator, driven by some fatality, returns to the churchyard and digs up the old grave. As he uncovers it, he finds "the bony thing my friend and I had robbed; not clean and placid as we had seen it then, but covered with caked blood and shreds of alien flesh and hair, and leering sentiently at me with phosphorescent sockets and sharp ensanguined fangs yawning twistedly in mockery of my inevitable doom." The narrator, after telling his tale, proposes to "seek with my revolver the oblivion which is my only refuge from the unnamed and unnamable."

"The Hound" has been roundly abused for being wildly overwritten; but it has somehow managed to escape most critics' attention that the story is an obvious self-parody. Lovecraft has rarely been given credit for being master, not slave, of his prose style: we have already seen how earlier stories—"Beyond the Wall of Sleep," "Facts concerning the Late Arthur Jermyn and His Family," "The Music of Erich Zann"—show an admirable restraint in diction and imagery, and it becomes transparently obvious that Lovecraft has chosen the overheated prose and histrionic incidents of "The Hound" deliberately. Parody becomes increasingly evident from the obvious literary allusions (St John's "that damned thing" echoing the celebrated tale by Ambrose Bierce; the "red death" and the indefinite manner of dating ["On the night of September 24, 19—"], meant as playful nods to Poe; the baying of the hound clearly meant to recall Doyle's *The Hound of the Baskervilles;* and, as Steven J. Mariconda has demonstrated,[101] many tips of the hat to Joris-Karl Huysmans, particularly *A Rebours*) and also from such grotesque utterances as "Bizarre manifestations were now too frequent to count." And yet, the story is undeniably successful as an experiment in sheer flamboyance and excess, so long as one keeps in mind that Lovecraft was clearly aiming for such an effect and was doing so at least partially with tongue in cheek.

Some autobiographical touches in the story are worth commenting upon. While St John is clearly meant to be Kleiner, the connexion rests only in the name, as there is not much description of his character. I wonder whether the museum of tomb-loot collected by the two protagonists is a playful reference to Samuel Loveman's quite impressive collection of *objets d'art* (not taken from tombs, one must hasten to add): Lovecraft first saw this collection in September and was tremendously impressed by it. The original typescript of the story includes a reference to a very recent colleague: "A locked portfolio, bound in tanned human skin, held the unknown and unnamable drawings of Clark Ashton Smith." Lovecraft revised this passage (on the advice of C. M. Eddy, Jr[102]) before submitting it to *Weird Tales,* where the tale was published in the issue for February 1924. Another piquant autobiographical connexion relates to one of the most striking images in the tale. As the narrator is attempting to rebury the amulet, he encounters a "queer interruption": "a lean vulture darted down out of the cold sky and pecked frantically at the grave-earth until I killed him with a blow of my spade." Consider a letter to Maurice W. Moe in which he tells of his pilfering of the gravestone fragment: "A flock of birds descended from the sky and pecked queerly at the ancient turf, as if seeking some strange kind of nourishment in that hoary and sepulchral place."[103]

In terms of Lovecraft's developing pseudomythology, "The Hound" gains importance as the first explicit mention of the *Necronomicon* and as the first time that that work is clearly attributed to Abdul Alhazred. The passage is a curious one: "Alien it [the amulet] indeed was to all art and literature which sane and balanced readers know, but we recognised it as the thing hinted of in the forbidden *Necronomicon* of the mad Arab Abdul Alhazred; the ghastly soul-symbol of the corpse-eating cult of inaccessible Leng, in Central Asia." As with Nyarlathotep, the word "Necronomicon" came to Lovecraft in a dream; and when he, whose Greek was at best rudimentary, later attempted a derivation of the term (*nekros,* corpse; *nomos,* law; *eikon,* picture = "An Image [or Picture] of the Law of the Dead"[104]), the result was wildly inaccurate. In fact, by the rules of Greek etymology the derivation is: *nekros,* corpse; *nemo,* to consider or classify; *-ikon,* neuter adjectival suffix = "A Consideration [or Classification] of the Dead." In interpreting the term, however, one must at least take note of Lovecraft's mistaken derivation. In order to account for a Greek title to a work by an Arab, Lovecraft later claimed that the *Necronomicon* was the Greek translation of a work in Arabic entitled *Al Azif*—a term he cribbed from Samuel Henley's notes to William Beckford's *Vathek* (1786), where *azif,* referring to the buzzing of insects, is defined as "a nocturnal sound . . . believed to be the howling of demons."

Vathek—which Lovecraft first read in late July 1921[105]—is of some interest in itself, as this spectacular work of exotic fantasy—in which a decadent caliph is forced for his sins to descend to Eblis, the Islamic underworld, and face nameless tortures—seems to have fired Lovecraft's imagination at this time and later. The frequent mentions of ghouls in *Vathek* may have had some influence on "The Hound"; Henley notes: "Goul or *ghul,* in Arabic, signifies any terrifying object which deprives people of the use of their senses; hence it became the appellative of that species of monster which was supposed to haunt forests, cemeteries, and other lonely places, and believed not only to tear in pieces the living, but to dig up and devour the dead." Lovecraft was taken with this piquant idea and used ghouls—rubbery, doglike creatures for the most part—in many later tales. *Vathek* also clearly influenced another work written a little earlier—a proposed novel entitled "Azathoth," which Lovecraft describes in June 1922 as a "weird Vathek-like novel."[106] What Lovecraft perhaps means by this is that "Azathoth" is an attempt both to capture *Vathek's* air of dreamlike fantasy and to imitate its continuous flow of narrative and absence of chapter divisions. He had been thinking of writing "a weird Eastern tale in the 18th century manner; a tale perhaps too long for publication in amateurdom"[107] as early as October 1921, only a few months after reading *Vathek* and very shortly after borrowing *The Episodes of Vathek* (long stories narrated by various characters in *Vathek* but not published until 1912); but unlike Lovecraft's previous novel idea, *The Club of the Seven Dreamers,* which was probably never even begun, "Azathoth" was actually started, although only to the extent of about 500 words. Its opening is ponderous:

> When age fell upon the world, and wonder went out of the minds of men; when grey cities reared to smoky skies tall towers grim and ugly, in whose shadow none might dream of the sun or of spring's flowering meads; when learning stripped earth of her mantle of beauty, and poets sang no more save of twisted phantoms seen with bleared and inward-looking eyes; when these things had come to pass, and childish hopes had gone away forever, there was a man who travelled out of life on a quest into the spaces whither the world's dreams had fled.

Lovecraft quotes the entire extant text of "Azathoth" in a letter to Long, adding:

> The rest—for which this introduction prepares the reader, will be material of the *Arabian Nights* type. I shall defer to no modern critical canon, but shall frankly slip back through the centuries and become a myth-maker with that childish sincerity which no one but the earlier Dunsany has tried to achieve nowadays. I shall go out of the world when I write, with a mind centred not in literary usage, but in the dreams I dreamed when I was six years old or less—the dreams which followed my first knowledge of *Sinbad,* of *Agib,* of *Baba-Abdallah,* and of *Sidi-Nonman.*[108]

This may or may not suggest that "Azathoth" was to be a non-supernatural adventure story (such as Clark Ashton Smith wrote voluminously in his youth), but probably the work would at least have had some dreamlike elements. "Azathoth" gains its importance only in light of Lovecraft's developing aesthetics and in terms of some stories written several years later, so I will take it up again farther on.

Lovecraft did not do much other writing during his New York stay—he was too busy gallivanting about town and was also occasionally burdened by Bush work, which was tedious but at least brought prompt and welcome cheques that permitted him to extend his sojourn. One little spoof produced probably in late August was the poem "To Zara," which Lovecraft attempted to pass off to Galpin as a lost poem by Edgar Allan Poe. Although Galpin did not swallow the Poe authorship—he believed the poem to be copied from some standard poet, perhaps the obscure Arthur O'Shaughnessy—he nevertheless praised the poem highly. When, in September, he was let in on the joke, Galpin's enthusiasm waned. Lovecraft certainly had a laugh here, since Galpin was ordinarily very censorious of Lovecraft's poetry. The spasm is nothing to write home about: it attempts to imitate Poe's many variations on the "death of a beautiful woman" trope:

> Pale, lovely ghost—so young, so fair,
> To flutter in sepulchral air—
> To flutter where the taper dies
> Amidst a mourner's choking sighs!

Lovecraft finally returned home in mid-October, presumably writing "The Hound" shortly after he got back. Meanwhile Houtain was already asking him for another serial, this time to run in four parts. Lovecraft dawdled on the task through mid-November, but—perhaps because Houtain finally paid up for "Herbert West—Reanimator" and advanced him half the payment for the new story—finally got down to work and wrote "The Lurking Fear" later in the month.[109] Since this story was written in a far more condensed period of time than "Herbert West—Reanimator," it presents a somewhat greater impression of unity than its predecessor, in spite of the need to provide a shocking conclusion at the end of each segment.

No one is likely to regard "The Lurking Fear" as one of Lovecraft's masterworks, even among his early tales; and yet, it is not as contemptible a tale as many critics have deemed it, and once again it contains many foreshadowings of techniques and devices used to better advantage in later works. In spite of a hackneyed melodramatic opening ("There was thunder in the air on the night I went to the deserted mansion atop Tempest Mountain to find the lurking fear") the tale moves briskly in its account of the narrator's search for the unknown entity that had wreaked havoc amongst the squatters of the Catskills near the Martense mansion. The narrator is convinced that the haunted mansion must be the seat or locus of the horror, and he takes two colleagues, George Bennett and William Tobey, with him to the place one night. They all sleep in the same bed in one room of the mansion, having provided exits either through the door of the room or the window. Although one of the three is to stay awake while the others rest, some strange drowsiness affects all three. The narrator wakes and finds to his horror that both Bennett and Tobey—sleeping on either side of him—have been snatched away by the thing. But why was he spared?

The second episode finds the narrator coming upon another associate, Arthur Munroe, to assist him in his endeavours. They know that the lurking fear customarily roams abroad during thunderstorms, and during one such storm they stop in a hamlet to wait it out. Munroe, who has been looking out the window, seems anomalously fascinated by something outside and does not respond to a summons. When the narrator shakes his shoulder, he finds that "Arthur Munroe was dead. And on what remained of his chewed and gouged head there was no longer a face."

In the third episode the narrator realises that he must explore the history of the mansion to come to terms with its lurking horror. The mansion had been built in 1670 by Gerrit Martense, a wealthy Dutchman who hated the English; his descendants similarly shunned the people around them and and took to intermarrying with the "numerous menial class about the estate." One descendant, Jan Martense, seeks to escape this unhealthy reclusiveness and is killed for his pains. The episode ends with a cataclysmic sight of a "nameless thing" in a subterranean tunnel he stumbles upon as he digs in Jan Martense's grave.

In the final episode the truth is finally learned: there is not one monster but a whole legion of them. The entire mountain is honeycombed with underground passageways housing loathsome creatures, half apes and half moles: they are the "ultimate product of mammalian degeneration; the frightful outcome of isolated spawning, multiplication, and cannibal nutrition above and below the ground; the embodiment of all the snarling chaos and grinning fear that lurk behind life." In other words, they are the degenerate descendants of the house of Martense.

The theme of hereditary degeneration will be a significant one in Lovecraft's less openly "cosmic" tales; we have already seen it in "Arthur Jermyn," and we will see it again in "The Rats in the Walls" and "The Shadow over Innsmouth." Here the evils of inbreeding are exposed at their ghastliest. It would be easy to make an armchair Freudian analysis of this theme—involving such things as Lovecraft's general coolness toward sex, the frequency with which members of his own ancestry married their cousins, perhaps even his possible awareness of the cause of his father's death—but I think a racialist interpretation is perhaps more plausible. Perhaps the two work in tandem. But I do not think this theme can be explained away by appeal to the facts of biography: it is expressed with great power in several of Lovecraft's stories, and its social implications go well beyond the circumstances of his own life.

There are, of course, some autobiographical touches, although they are rather on the trivial side. Arthur Munroe's name is clearly borrowed from the Munroe brothers, while Jan Martense was probably taken from the Jan Martense Schenck house (1656) in Flatbush, the oldest existing house in New York City. Lovecraft did not see this house during either of his 1922 New York visits, and may not in fact have learnt of it until after writing "The Lurking Fear": he speaks of the house in a letter to Maurice W. Moe of July 31, 1923, but only visited it in 1928.[110] There is, however, a Martense Street very near 259 Parkside, so perhaps this is the origin of the name.

"The Lurking Fear" is more of a detective story than most of his other works, and Lovecraft ably conceals the true state of affairs until at least the third episode. It is only at the conclusion that we learn of the fatal error in reasoning—the belief in only a single monster as the cause of the horror—that led to the deaths of Bennett and Tobey: each were snatched away by different creatures coming from either direction.

The third episode is perhaps the most significant in terms of Lovecraft's later work: this historical investigation will be much elaborated in future tales, and reflects the sentiment Lovecraft expressed in a letter of 1929: "The past is *real*—it is *all there is.*"[111] The narrator of "The Lurking Fear" makes a strangely poignant utterance in justifying his investigation of the past: "History, indeed, was all I had after everything else ended in mocking Satanism." That the heavy hand of the past weighs upon the present and future; that historical study (and, by extension, all scientific enquiry) can somehow help us to come to terms with our fate; that there are facets of the past that are perhaps best left unexplored, but that nevertheless must be explored if we are to understand our place in the world—all these things are perhaps only suggested in "The Lurking Fear," but they will be treated much more exhaustively in the great tales of his final decade.

But we read "The Lurking Fear" not for its element of mystery or its historical or philosophical ruminations, but, quite simply, for its flagrantly overblown prose—a prose that so exquisitely treads the thin line between seriousness and parody, between humour and horror, that we scarcely know how to react to it. Throughout the tales of this period Lovecraft is fond of including, toward the end, an hysterical series of stream-of-consciousness ramblings that somehow epitomise the entire work; and he has never done it better than here:

> Shrieking, slithering, torrential shadows of red viscous madness chasing one another through endless, ensanguined corridors of purple fulgorous sky . . . formless phantasms and kaleidoscopic mutations of a ghoulish, remembered scene; forests of monstrous overnourished oaks with serpent roots twisting and sucking unnamable juices from an earth verminous with millions of cannibal devils; mound-like tentacles groping from underground nuclei of polypous perversion . . . insane lightning over malignant ivied walls and daemon arcades choking with fungous vegetation . . .

Later the narrator piquantly "destroy[s] certain overnourished trees whose very existence seemed an insult to sanity."

Presumably at Lovecraft's request, Clark Ashton Smith was commissioned to illustrate the serial, supplying two illustrations per instalment. They are very curious line drawings. Lovecraft later complained (to others, not to Smith) that Smith had not followed his text very well in the illustrations.[112] Still later Frank Long, probably thinking of these illustrations, pointed out that Smith's artwork contained systematically sexual implications; Lovecraft pooh-poohed the idea,[113] but Smith was clearly having a not-so-private laugh, for many of the trees and vegetation in the illustrations are obviously in the shape of penises, testicles, and vaginas. Lovecraft quite literally could not conceive of such a thing, and I am convinced this joke never dawned upon him.

"The Lurking Fear" appeared in *Home Brew* from January to April 1923. I have not found any evidence that Lovecraft received the $10 he was owed for the last two instalments, but there is also no evidence that he did not. The last issue announces that the magazine will change its name to *High Life;* Lovecraft later reports that after this change of name the magazine folded in 1924.[114] He was no doubt glad to see the end of the "vile rag."[115]

Although it was late in the year and Lovecraft's sensitivity to cold would not allow him to venture abroad very much, his travels for 1922 were not quite over. In mid-December he visited Boston to participate in a Hub Club meeting with Edith Miniter and others. Afterward he decided to do some solitary antiquarian exploration of some of the towns on the North Shore, specifically Salem. This was either on Sunday the 17th or Monday the 18th.[116] Salem was certainly a delight—it was Lovecraft's first true experience of the seventeenth century, and he canvassed the Witch House (1642), the House of the Seven Gables, and other celebrated sites—but while there he learnt from natives that there was another town a little farther up the coast called Marblehead that was even quainter. Taking a bus there, Lovecraft was "borne into the most marvellous region I had ever dream'd of, and furnished with the most powerful single aesthetick impression I have receiv'd in years."[117]

Marblehead was—and, on the whole, today remains—one of the most charming little backwaters in Massachusetts, full of well-restored colonial houses, crooked and narrow streets, and a spectral hilltop burying-ground from which one can derive a magnificent panoramic view of the city and the nearby harbour. In the old part of town the antiquity is strangely *complete,* and very little of the modern intrudes there. It was this that so captivated Lovecraft:

> Immemorial pinnacle of fabulous antiquity! As evening came I look'd down at the quiet village where the lights came out one by one; at the calm contemplative chimney-pots and antique gables silhouetted against the west; at the glimmering small-paned windows; at the silent and unillumined fort frowning formidably over the snug harbour where it hath frown'd since 1742, when 'twas put up for defence against

> the French King's frigates. Shades of the past! How compleatly, O Mater Novanglia, am I moulded of thy venerable flesh and as one with thy century'd soul![118]

More than seven years later Lovecraft was still attesting to the poignancy of this vision:

> God! Shall I ever forget my first stupefying glimpse of MARBLEHEAD'S huddled and archaick roofs under the snow in the delirious sunset glory of four p.m., Dec. 17, 1922!!! I did not know until an hour before that I should ever behold such a place as Marblehead, and I did not know *until that moment itself* the full extent of the wonder I was to behold. I account that instant—about 4:05 to 4:10 p.m., Dec. 17, 1922—the most powerful single emotional climax experienced during my nearly forty years of existence. In a flash all the past of New England—all the past of Old England—all the past of Anglo-Saxondom and the Western World—swept over me and identified me with the stupendous totality of all things in such a way as it never did before and never will again. That was the high tide of my life.[119]

The most powerful emotional climax he had ever experienced—the high tide of his life: these statements were uttered after his marriage had begun and ended, after his two hellish years in New York and his ecstatic return to Providence, but before his sight of Charleston and Quebec in 1930, which in their way perhaps matched his Marblehead glimpse of 1922. What exactly was it about Marblehead that so struck him? Lovecraft clarifies it himself: with his tremendous imaginative faculty—and with the visible tokens of the present almost totally banished for at least a short interval—Lovecraft felt himself united with his entire cultural and racial past. The past is real—it is all there is; and for a few moments on a winter afternoon in Marblehead the past really was all there was.

It would take Lovecraft nearly a year—and several more trips to Marblehead—to internalise his impressions and transmute them into fiction; but when he did so, in "The Festival" (1923), he would be well on his way to revivifying Mater Novanglia in some of the most topographically and historically rooted weird fiction ever written. He had begun haltingly to head in this direction, with "The Picture in the House"; but New England was still relatively undiscovered territory to him, and it would take many more excursions for him to imbibe the essence of the area—not merely its antiquities and its history, but its people and their intimate and centuried relations with the soil—and render it fit for fictional use. And it would also take those two years away from New England to make him realise how much he really was moulded of its flesh, so that he could express both the terror and the wonder of this ancient land.

14. For My Own Amusement (1923–1924)

Amateur activities still loomed large, in spite of the eviction of Lovecraft's "literary" party in the 1922–23 term. Sonia's second issue of the *Rainbow* appeared in May 1922, and as before it was filled with contributions by Lovecraft and his associates. Among them were such things as a long rumination on amateur journalism ("Certain Ideals") by Edith Miniter, poems by Lilian Middleton and Samuel Loveman ("A Letter to G—— K——," i.e., George Kirk), James F. Morton's disquisition "Misconceptions of Art," the first appearance of Lovecraft's "Celephaïs," and several pieces by Sonia. In the lead article ("Amateurdom and the Editor") she defends the editorial policy of the *United Amateur* against the attacks of Leo Fritter and others, although oddly enough she never mentions Lovecraft in the long piece. This may be a sign that Lovecraft co-wrote it, as indeed internal evidence suggests. "Commercialism—The Curse of Art" is an echo of Lovecraft's own views on the deleterious effects of writing for pay. As before, many photographs of the authors graced the issue, although there is none of Lovecraft this time.

Another piece, "Heins versus Houtain," although bearing Sonia's byline, also seems clearly co-written with Lovecraft, as it contains some of his characteristic mannerisms of style and some of his pet ideas in regard to the proper running of amateurdom. The article is a harsh censure of a feud in the NAPA between the young John Milton Heins and E. Dorothy Houtain; it takes no sides on the feud but criticises its mere existence, saying that its descent into vicious name-calling casts the whole of amateurdom in a bad light. It proposes establishing a "special committee or tribunal" to deal with such disputes and, if necessary, to eject repeat offenders from the world of amateur journalism. This seems very much Lovecraft's idea, echoing as it does his notion (expressed in "Amateur Journalism: Its Possible Needs and Betterment") of setting up an informal academy to correct and even censor inferior writing.

At just the time when Lovecraft's activity in the UAPA seemed on the wane, his involvement with the NAPA took on a sudden and wholly unforeseen turn: it was nothing less than his appointment as interim President to replace William J. Dowdell, who was forced to resign. It is not clear what led to Dowdell's decision: a scholar of amateur journalism has curtly referred merely to "changes in his business life,"[1] but one wonders whether a remark Lovecraft let slip a few years later—that Dowdell "ran off with a chorus girl in 1922"[2]—has anything to do with the matter. In any case, the appointment was made by the three Executive Judges—Mrs E. Dorothy Houtain, Mrs Annie Cross Ellis, and A. V. Fingulin—who acted as adjudicators of constitutional amendments and had other supervisory functions, but who rarely involved themselves in the day-to-day operation of the association. The UAPA had a set of three Directors who appear to have served an analogous function.

Kleiner describes the remarkable turn of events vividly:

> The occasion of his capitulation, in the home of Mr. and Mrs. George Julian Houtain, on Bedford Avenue, Brooklyn, was a memorable one. It is true that he had begun to waver in his first resolution not to accept, but a final plea from Mrs. Houtain—a plea most irresistibly offered—completely shattered his last defences. The amateur world rocked with the sensation when Lovecraft's name was announced as that of the new president.[3]

It has been thought that this event occurred in September 1922, during Lovecraft's extended New York trip; but in fact the "capitulation" took place on November 30, as Lovecraft stated much later.[4] On that date he also wrote a letter to the Executive Judges (probably in their presence) accepting the position; the letter was published in the *National Amateur* for November [1922]–January 1923. One curious remark occurs so early as a letter to Lillian Clark for August 31: "I had not intended to be active in amateurdom this year; but such are recent developments, that I may shortly make a political move well fitted to startle the entire fraternity and jolt my ungrateful colleagues in the *United*—of this more later." But a footnote to this sentence reads: "Later—I probably shan't make the move after all!"[5] This may or may not refer to some preliminary broaching of the idea of the presidency. In "The President's Annual Report" (*National Amateur,* September 1923) Lovecraft for some reason dates the beginning of his appointment to November 20.

In any event, Lovecraft's first objective was to form an official board. Several other elected officials had resigned shortly after Dowdell; these included Wesley H. Porter (Secretary) and Elgie A. Andrione (Second Vice-President). They were replaced, respectively, by Juliette Harris and Mary F. Kennedy. Samuel Loveman, whom Dowdell had appointed Chairman of the Bureau of Critics (the NAPA's department of public criticism), had initially chosen Lovecraft as a colleague; but upon his ascension to the presidency Lovecraft resigned this post, turning it over instead to Edward H. Cole. (Loveman's chairmanship had, incidentally, inspired a clever poem by Lovecraft, "To Saml: Loveman, Gent., with a Fellow-Martyr's Heartfelt Sympathy.") Harry E. Martin—whom Lovecraft had met briefly but cordially in Cleveland earlier that year—remained as Official Editor and did solid work.

Lovecraft made the first of five official reports (four "President's Messages" and a "President's Annual Report") for the *National Amateur* dated November [1922]–January 1923. There had been no *National Amateur* since September 1922; the July 1922 issue had been typeset but not issued, and it emerged only later that winter. Lovecraft's report, written on January 11, 1923, is an eloquent plea for the resumption of activity in light of the confusion involving the official board and the general apathy apparently overtaking all amateurdom; Lovecraft himself promised to issue another number or two of his *Conservative* and came through on the promise. He also announced a cooperative journal, the *National Co-operative*, which he planned to issue along the lines of the old *United Co-operative*, but I find no evidence that such a paper actually appeared. Most incredible of all, given his chronic poverty, Lovecraft himself contributed $10 (the equivalent of a week's rent in his New York period) to the official organ fund. Approaching the completion of his ninth year of amateur activity, Lovecraft found himself still drawn to the cause.

The actual content of the five issues of the *National Amateur* published under Lovecraft's presidency does not wholly reflect his predilections, since of course Harry E. Martin had editorial control of the official organ; but Lovecraft worked closely with Martin on the selection of contents, naturally recommending the work of his old and new colleagues. And, of course, the presidency gave him a bully pulpit from which to express his own views of the proper course and direction of amateur activity. Just as he had done with the UAPA, he stressed abstract literary expression as the loftiest desideratum of the amateur; but he was forced to be a little circumspect in so doing, since the NAPA had long emphasised the typographical, social, and political side of amateurdom and Lovecraft was clearly loath to create ill-will by attempting any sort of violent break with tradition. His first "President's Message" is a monument to tact on this matter. Recognising that the NAPA had been initially founded for the purpose of "laying principal stress upon the mechanical exercise of typography and the wit-sharpening regimen of political manoeuvring," he claims that "social changes of the period"—in particular, the decreasing proportion of youthful members who could practice the "small boy ideal" of amateur printing—have rendered these goals obsolete. "Much more effective and desirable, as I view it, is the later conception developed by experience and exemplified in the golden age of the eighties and nineties, whereby literary advancement and liberal culture through mutual aid were recognised as paramount." Lovecraft could speak with authority on these "Halcyon days" of amateurdom, since three years earlier C. W. Smith had lent him the leading journals of that period from which Lovecraft had written *Looking Backward*, serialised in the *Tryout* from February to July 1920 and shortly thereafter issued by Smith as a booklet—one of the earliest and rarest of Lovecraft's separate publications.

Lovecraft's second "President's Message" was written on March 7, 1923, and published in the March *National Amateur*. In it he reports progress on various fronts. The official board was now filled, while Dowdell himself returned to act as Secretary of Publicity, using his own funds for the office. In January Lovecraft had written a letter and had it mimeographed by J. Bernard Lynch[6] (it has not yet come to light, nor is it likely to do so), in which he asked for further contributions to the official organ fund, and he reported gradual but sufficient responses to it. Individual papers were starting to appear, including Horace L. Lawson's *Wolverine* and Paul J. Campbell's *Liberal* (whose February 1922 issue had included Lovecraft's seminal autobiographical essay, "A Confession of Unfaith").

Lovecraft's final two "President's Messages" (May and July 1923) do not say much of consequence, but "The President's Annual Report" for September 1923 (written on July 1) is a substantial document in which Lovecraft both expressed relief at his "official emancipation" and regret that he was unable to attend the upcoming convention in Cleveland. He scattered praise liberally to his fellow-members of the official board (especially Official Editor Martin), noted that forty-six papers were issued during his term as President, regretted the relative lack of new recruits, and once again encouraged abstract "self-expression" as the highest goal for the amateur. His concluding statement is eloquent, and shows that he has thoroughly enjoyed his official duties—perhaps because his being called upon to rescue a flagging organisation bolstered his self-esteem:

> The official year is over, and the present board will not be sorry to lay down its responsibilities. To the effective coöperation of my colleagues I owe whatever level short of failure my executive striving may have reached, and for that coöperation I wish to thank them as we retire. I have encountered no intentional obstacles and have found so much encouragement at every turn that I am forced to look outside the National in order to maintain my cosmic attitude of perfect cynicism. I believe that the coming year holds brilliant developments, and hope that the newly elected board may receive as undivided a support and as active a background as the members can give it. I for one shall not be half-hearted in my endeavours.

That last sentence was no doubt sincere, but it proved to be wish-fulfilment; for Lovecraft did not in fact do much more work for the NAPA in the short term. As early as February, Edward H. Cole was urging Lovecraft to run for President for the 1923–24 term; Lovecraft blanched at the idea (for he profoundly disliked the tedious administrative burdens that went with the office), and he discovered shortly thereafter that Hazel Pratt Adams was keen on running and was being supported vigorously by James F. Morton.[7] As a result, he felt that his own candidacy would cause a schism among his own colleagues. (Adams in fact won the presidency.) His reelection as Official Editor of the UAPA in July 1923 compelled him in any event to turn his attention back to his original amateur organisation. It would be a decade before he would resume ties with the NAPA.

Lovecraft's presidency did not by any means signify the end of his own individual amateur work. His *Conservative* was revived for two final issues in March and July 1923. These issues had been planned long in advance; one of the "News Notes" in the July 1921 *United Amateur* declares: "A revival of *The Conservative* is to be expected in the near future, at least two numbers being likely to appear during the official year. The first will contain a notable group of poems likely to win the approval of the discriminating." I do not know the causes for the long delay; perhaps there was a shortage of funds in the family coffers (especially given that Lillian, now head of the household, did not look at all kindly on amateur journalism). Lovecraft's travels of April and August–September 1922 further depleted the exchequer, as Lovecraft confessed in letters to Samuel Loveman, who was urging him to visit Cleveland again for the NAPA convention in July (where, as president, Lovecraft would preside):

> De re Clevelandica—I wish to hell I could be more certain about the cash question! It looks like a damn gloomy season, for nerves & household illness have reduced my Bushic capacity to a minimum, & I gotta helluva lotta expenses ahead. . . . So as I say, when I think of finance, my naturally long face tends to acquire an exaggeration of its original proportions! But still—if I can get me noives together enough to punish a record pile of Bush junk, there's no telling what I can do by July . . . provided my conservative aunt doesn't make too big a kick against my barbaric extravagance.[8]

Among the expenses Lovecraft speaks of here is the printing of the *Conservative* and the purchase of a new suit. In this letter he avers that "nothing respectable comes for less than XXX shiners nowadays," but the suit ended up costing $42, which made his aunts "dead set against any wholesale expenditures at this melancholy season of monetary sterility."[9] Unfortunately, the suit was stolen two years later in Brooklyn.

The two issues of the *Conservative*—printed by Charles A. A. Parker of Boston, editor of *L'Alouette*—were, however, well worth of cost of printing. They feature many of Lovecraft's closest colleagues, including Loveman, Morton, Galpin, and Long. Issue number twelve (March 1923) is only eight pages, but contains Loveman's poignant poem, "Thomas Holley Chivers" (the friend of Poe), Long's "An Amateur Humorist" (on which more later), and editorial comments by Lovecraft. The thirteenth number, however (July 1923), is, at twenty-eight pages, the longest *Conservative* ever issued, although this is in some senses misleading, for the page dimensions of both these final issues are far smaller than those of earlier issues. In any event, this last issue leads off boldly with Loveman's exquisite ode "To Satan" (dedicated to Lovecraft), followed by "Felis: A Prose Poem" by Long (a tribute to his cat), an essay and a prose-poem by Galpin (under the pseudonyms A. T. Madison and Anatol Kleinst), a long poem in Scots dialect by Morton, poems by Lilian Middleton and John Ravenor Bullen, and more editorial matter by Lovecraft. It was a triumphant conclusion to his amateur periodical.

But even if Bush work was not providing much income, there were other venues for Lovecraft's revisory talents, even in the amateur community. One of the most notable was nothing less than Lovecraft's first appearance in hardcover, in a volume entitled *The Poetical Works of Jonathan E. Hoag*. Hoag, it will be remembered, was the ancient poet (born 1831) in Troy, New York, for whom Lovecraft had been writing annual birthday odes since 1918. Now he wished to see a bound book of his verse and enlisted Lovecraft to gather, revise, and publish his work. Lovecraft in turn called upon Loveman and Morton to aid him. By November 1922 he had received some of the poems as revised by Loveman; he instructed Hoag to pay Loveman $5.00 for 120 lines (or $1.00 for 20 lines, considerably less than the $1.00 for 8 lines that Lovecraft was getting from Bush). The book's publication was being funded by Allen C. Balch, a wealthy entrepreneur who was apparently a friend of Hoag. This point is worth emphasising, since it has long been believed that Lovecraft himself helped to subsidise the book, a highly unlikely prospect given the leanness of his purse. Morton also helped with the revision and was evidently responsible for overseeing the reading of the final page proofs: Lovecraft expresses irritation at Morton's failure to correct some last-minute errors.[10] Lovecraft had an unbound copy by late April, and presumably the finished book emerged shortly thereafter. In the end he waived "all monetary remuneration for my share of the editing"[11] in exchange for twenty copies of the book!

The Poetical Works of Jonathan E. Hoag contains an introduction by Lovecraft in which he bends over backwards to find something good to say about Hoag's mediocre and conventional poetry. Probably what attracted him to Hoag in the first place was that sense of defying time which was at the core of Lovecraft's own sense of the weird:

> Penned in this age of chaos and change, fever and flourish, by a man born when Andrew Jackson was President, when Poe was an unknown youth with his second thin volume of verses in the press, when Coleridge, Moore, Crabbe, Southey, and Wordsworth were living bards, and when the memory of Byron, Shelley, Blake, and Keats was still recent; the present collection of poems is probably unique in its defiance of time and whim.

Even here Lovecraft is exaggerating a bit, since Hoag began writing poetry only at about the age of eighty-five, or around 1915. Still, Lovecraft finds charitable things to say about Hoag's "odes to Nature's primal forces," which "sometimes reach impressive depths, as where in speaking of the Grand Canyon of the Colorado he refers to black caverns where 'Vast nameless satyrs dance with noiseless feet.'" The volume also contains the first six of Lovecraft's birthday odes (1918–23); he would write four more, followed by an elegy in the autumn of 1927, when Hoag died at the age of ninety-six.

Two poems in the volume are of some interest—"Death" and "To the American Flag." They are of interest not because of any intrinsic merit in them—they are as conventional as the rest of Hoag's verse—but because they have been attributed to Lovecraft. After Lovecraft's death Rheinhart Kleiner supplied Hyman Bradofsky with a set of six poems for the memorial issue (Summer 1937) of the *Californian;* these included four poems undoubtedly by Lovecraft ("Sunset," "Phaeton," "August," and "Providence") along with the two Hoag poems; August Derleth subsequently included both in *Collected Poems* (1963). "Death" had already appeared, as by Hoag, in the amateur press (*Silver Clarion,* November 1918); there was probably an amateur periodical appearance for "To the American Flag," but I have not found it. I asked Bradofsky why Kleiner had come to the opinion that these works were by Lovecraft, and Bradofsky said he did not know. It is possible that Lovecraft revised them rather more extensively than he did the remainder of Hoag's poems; certainly "Death" has sentiments that might be thought Lovecraftian:

> What goal of growth could Life possess,
> If stretch'd out into emptiness,
> With bleak unbounded range?
>
> What bard with grace could ever sing
> The cloying charm of endless Spring,
> Or praise eternal day?

"To the American Flag" is no better or worse than Lovecraft's own forgettable patriotic verse. In a 1925 letter Lovecraft speaks of virtually ghostwriting a poem for Hoag, "Alone" (I have found no published appearance for this work, but Lovecraft transcribed the entire poem in his letter),[12] so it is conceivable that these poems really are Lovecraft's; but the matter will have to await further confirmation.

Meanwhile there was much more travel in the offing—in particular the wonders of Salem, Marblehead, and other Massachusetts sites, some of which he had discovered late in 1922. Lovecraft visited the Salem-Marblehead area at least three times early in 1923—in early February,[13] in March, and again in April. Of the first trip we do not know much; of the second, occurring on March 10–11, Lovecraft took in a meeting of the Hub Club in Boston, stayed overnight with Edward H. Cole, and returned home. It was on this occasion that he met Albert A. Sandusky, who had printed the earliest issues of the *Conservative.* Sandusky indulged in the rampant use of contemporary slang, and his "wise-cracks"[14] charmed Lovecraft, who shortly thereafter wrote an engaging poem about the Hub Club dinner—"The Feast (Hub Journalist Club, March 10, 1923)"—with a ponderous dedicatory letter to "Wisecrack Sandusky, B.I., M.B.O. (Bachelor of Intelligence, Massachusetts Brotherhood of Owls)," in which he dynamited both his own adherence to archaism and Sandusky's very different orientation: "I, Sir, am an old-fashion'd man still partial to the language of Dr. Johnson's aera; you are a creator of that lively speech which will be classical a century hence." In the poem itself Lovecraft, aside from exhibiting Sandusky's lively speech ("'Nobody home there, bo—no use to knock on ye! / But bozo, can that line of low-grade Socony!'"), cannot resist making a gorgeous pun on Cole's name: "A radiant Cole supplies th' enlightening spark . . ."

We know more about Lovecraft's third trip. He first went to Boston on Thursday, April 12, for his now customary attendance of a Hub Club meeting; he spent the night at the residence jointly occupied by Charles A. A. Parker and Edith Miniter at 30 Waite Street in Malden (a suburb of Boston), being regaled by a tiny six-week-old kitten named Victory who crawled all over him and finally went to sleep on the back of his neck. The next day he proceeded to Salem, then continued on to Danvers—the town, once called Salem-Village, founded in 1636 by some members of the original settlement of 1626, and where the 1692 witch trials had taken place. Spotting an ancient brick residence—the Samuel Fowler house (1809)—that was open as a museum, Lovecraft got off the trolley, went up to the house, and knocked on the door. Let him tell the rest:

> My summons was answer'd simultaneously by two of the most pitiful and decrepit-looking persons imaginable—hideous old women more sinister than the witches of 1692, and certainly not under eighty. . . . The "ell" in which they dwelt was in a state of indescribable squalor; with heaps of rags, books, cooking utensils, and the like on every hand. One meagre wood stove fail'd altogether to heat the barren room against the cold of that sharp afternoon.

Lovecraft goes on to tell how one of the women spoke to him—"in a hoarse rattling voice that dimly suggested death," but expressing "a courtly and aristocratick welcome in language an accents beyond question bespeaking the gentlest birth and proudest cultivation!" Lovecraft explored the place thoroughly, finding it well preserved—it had been purchased from the women by the Society for the Preservation of New England Antiquities, which was allowing them to reside in the place until their deaths—but in the end it was the occupants, not the house, that most struck him: "Yes—it was the old, old New-England story of family decay and aristocratick pauperism . . ."[15] One wonders whether Lovecraft—who had already written about a roughly analogous phenomenon in "The Picture in the House" (1920)—reflected on the parallel between the Fowlers and his own line. The Phillipses were never aristocrats in the proper sense, but their decline was no less precipitous than that of these decrepit crones.

Lovecraft then proceeded out into the countryside, seeking the farmhouse built by Townsend Bishop in 1636—the place occupied by Rebekah Nurse in 1692 when she was accused of witchcraft by the slave woman Tituba and, at the age of seventy, hanged on Gallows Hill. He found both the farmhouse and Rebekah Nurse's grave some distance away. Unlike the Fowler place, the farmhouse was of a cramped seventeenth-century design with low rooms and massive wooden beams; it made him think of the fundamental difference between his beloved Augustan age and the period immediately preceding it: "to my imagination the 17th century is as full of macabre mystery, repression, & ghoulish adumbrations as the 18th is full of taste, gayety, grace, & beauty."[16] He was allowed by the caretaker of the farmhouse to climb all the way up into the attic:

> Thick dust covered everything, & unnatural shapes loomed on every hand as the evening twilight oozed through the little bleared panes of the ancient windows. I saw something hanging from the wormy ridge-pole—something that swayed as if in unison with the vesper breeze outside, though that breeze had no access to this funereal & forgotten place—shadows . . . shadows . . . shadows . . .[17]

Returning that evening to the Parker-Miniter abode, Lovecraft set out the next day (Saturday the 14th) for Merrimac, where his young amateur friend Edgar J. Davis (age fifteen) lived. (Davis would become president of the UAPA during its death-throes in 1925–26.) The two of them visited graveyards in nearby Amesbury (where Whittier lived), and the next day they headed for Newburyport. This coastal town has now been made into a yuppie resort, but in 1923 it was a quiet little backwater that preserved its antiquities in almost as complete a state as Marblehead. So little life did the town have that Lovecraft and Davis rode the trolley car all the way through it without realising that they had passed through the centre of town, which was their destination. Returning on foot to the central square, Lovecraft and Davis revelled in the atmosphere of the past of a once-thriving colonial seaport. They returned to the Davis residence that evening, and on Monday the 16th Lovecraft began the leisurely trip home, passing through Boston and reaching 598 around midnight.

In early June Lovecraft was planning a trip with Edward H. Cole to Concord and Lexington—"those harbours of Yankee sedition"[18]—but I am not certain whether this visit actually occurred. Later that month he went again to Marblehead. Entering one of the mansions open to visitors, he learned from the occupants that he had on his previous visits not even seen the best (i.e., the oldest and best-preserved) parts of the town, and he promptly took steps to remedy the oversight. Once more he took a late train back to Providence, returning at 2 A.M.

Another visit to Boston and a Hub Club meeting followed on July 3–4. This may have been a sort of informal regional NAPA convention for all those amateurs who could not attend the official gathering in Cleveland. On the second day the amateurs took in the Fourth of July celebrations at Boston Common, but when it was time to sing the "Star-Spangled Banner," Lovecraft sang the "correct" words—the drinking-song "To Anacreon in Heaven," the tune upon which Francis Scott Key based his ditty.

Sonia paid Lovecraft a call in Providence on July 15–17. This is the first we hear of the two meeting since Lovecraft's visit to New York the preceding September (although he could have seen Sonia when he returned to the metropolis in November for discussions anent the NAPA presidency), but Sonia makes clear that in the two years preceding their marriage in March 1924 they engaged in "almost daily correspondence—H. P. writing me about everything he did and everywhere he went, introducing names of friends and his evaluation of them, sometimes filling 30, 40 and even 50 pages of finely written script."[19] What a shame that Sonia felt the need to burn all these letters! The visit in July was a joint business-pleasure trip on her part: on Monday the 16th Lovecraft showed Sonia the customary antiquities of Providence; then, on Tuesday the 17th, the two of them went to the coastal town of Narragansett Pier, in the southern part of the state overlooking the ocean, passing through Apponaug, East Greenwich, and Kingston along the way. On the return trip Sonia continued on to Boston while Lovecraft went home.

On August 10 occurred no less momentous an event than Lovecraft's first personal visit with his longtime friend Maurice W. Moe, who was making a tour of the East. Lovecraft met him at the Providence YMCA that morning, showing him all the local sites before boarding a bus to Boston, where they would meet Cole, Sandusky, and Moe's wife and two children, Robert (age eleven) and Donald (age nine). The next day Lovecraft performed his customary tour-guide act, as Cole relates in a memoir:

> I recall vividly the Saturday afternoon . . . when Lovecraft, Maurice Moe, Albert Sandusky, and I went to Old Marblehead to visit the numerous Colonial houses and other places of interest with which Howard was thoroughly familiar. He was so insistent that our friend from the West should not miss a single relic or point of view over lovely town and harbor that he walked us relentlessly for miles, impelled solely by his inexhaustible enthusiasm until our bodies rebelled and, against his protests, we dragged ourselves to the train. Lovecraft was still buoyant.[20]

Lovecraft himself tells the story still more piquantly: "I walked my associates so far that they rebelled—all lining up on a stone wall & refusing to budge an inch more except in a return direction!"[21] So much for the sickly recluse of a decade before! It is clear that Lovecraft functioned largely on nervous energy: he frequently admitted that he had no *intrinsic* interest in walking or other forms of exercise, but would undertake them only for some other purpose—in this case, the absorption of antiquity and, perhaps, the force-feeding of antiquity upon Moe, since just before his visit Moe had confessed that ancient things did not much attract him. This caused Lovecraft to unearth a withering contrast between the East and the West:

> For mine own Part, I do not see how any Man of acute Sensibilities can dwell in a new Town where there is nothing mellow & traditionally Beautiful. The West, Sir, is abominably crude & garish; because it rose up too quickly to possess any slow natural Growth, & because its Rise was in an Aera when nothing beautiful was created. Moreover, even its recent Adornments are of a blowsy mechanical kind, design'd at wholesale by some weary Hack who hath made plans for countless other Places, & who never expects to live in Sight of his Work. . . . Your Western

> towns, Sir, are as alike as Peas; so that any two of 'em cou'd be exchang'd without their Inhabitants being Sensible of the Fact.[22]

All this, of course, was based upon Lovecraft's one trip to Cleveland; but I think his point—when satiric exaggeration is taken into account—is still sound; at least, he felt it to be so for himself.

On Monday the 13th Lovecraft reluctantly bade Moe adieu as he put him on the New York bus. He did not know that another thirteen years would pass before he would meet him again; and in later years he expressed chagrin at the mental picture Moe must have carried of him, since at the time Lovecraft was rather portly. Clearly he was being well fed at home—perhaps for the last time. His later economies in diet—both during his New York period and during his last ten years in Providence—are painful to note.

On Tuesday the 14th Lovecraft went on a solitary tour of Portsmouth, New Hampshire, yet another colonial haven he had never seen; he was entirely captivated, for, unlike Marblehead and Newburyport, Portsmouth was a thriving and flourishing city that had nonetheless managed to keep its antiquities intact. Lovecraft found himself "merg'd for the first time in *the living whirl of the real eighteenth century*": "For Portsmouth is the one city which hath kept its own life and people as well as its houses and streets. There are scarce any inhabitants but the old families, and scarce any industries but the old ship-building and the navy yard which hath been there since 1800."[23] Much as Lovecraft found architectural antiquity charming, what most affected him *social continuity from the past.* Physical structures were not enough; it was when those structures were still used for their original purposes that he was most enthralled, perhaps again because it represented for him the sense of time-defiance that was so central to his imagination. Inevitably, there is a tinge of racism here: he makes particular note of the "pure ENGLISH faces" he sees in Portsmouth, and when he notes that "the Colonial age still liv'd untainted" there, one can scarcely resist the suggestion that that final word meant nothing more than the absence of foreigners.

Travels were by no means over, for in September James F. Morton stopped by for several days. Naturally, Lovecraft took him to Marblehead, remarking in a postcard on September 15: ". . . this time I have a sage companion whom I can't fatigue!"[24] Evidently his being dragged away from the place during Moe's visit still rankled. We do not know much else about Morton's visit, but on Wednesday the 19th the two of them made an expedition to Chepachet, a sleepy little village in the northwestern part of Rhode Island. From there they took the Putnam Pike (now Route 44) in an attempt to reach Durfee Hill, but Morton took a wrong turn and they went astray. They went instead to the nearby town of Pascoag, which Lovecraft found delightful: "The scene is magical—it is the early, half-forgotten, beautiful simple America that Poe and Hawthorne knew—a village with narrow winding streets and Colonial facades, and a sleepy square where merchants sit in their doorways."[25] They returned by train to Providence and went to the ancient wharves where Morton was to catch a boat to take him back to New York. After Morton left, Lovecraft went home and slept for twenty-one hours continuously; later rests of eleven, thirteen, and twelve hours show how much the exertion of the Chepachet expedition, and perhaps of Morton's trip generally, had told upon him. This would be a recurring pattern in Lovecraft's travels—intense activity for several days, followed by collapse. But to someone who, largely for monetary reasons, needed to squeeze as much as he could out of a trip, it was a price well worth paying.

Although he was scarcely aware of it at the time, the summer of 1923 brought a radical change in Lovecraft's literary career—perhaps as radical as his discovery of amateur journalism nine years previously. Whether the change was all for the good is a matter we shall have to consider at a later stage. In March of 1923 the first issue of *Weird Tales* appeared, and a month or two later Lovecraft was urged—initially by Everett McNeil[26] and Morton,[27] but probably by Clark Ashton Smith and others as well—to submit to it.

Weird Tales was the brainchild of Jacob Clark Henneberger, who with J. M. Lansinger founded Rural Publications, Inc., in 1922 to publish a variety of popular magazines. Henneberger had already achieved great success with the magazine *College Humor,* and he now envisioned founding a line of varied periodicals in the detective and horror field. In spite of the fairly significant amount of space given to weird and science fiction in the Munsey magazines (especially *Argosy, All-Story,* and *Cavalier*), there had never before been a magazine solely devoted to the weird. Henneberger had received assurances from such established writers as Hamlin Garland and Ben Hecht that they would be willing to contribute stories of the "unconventional" which they could not land in the "slicks" or other magazines, but they failed to come through when the magazine was actually launched.[28] As later events will show, Henneberger founded *Weird Tales* not out of some altruistic goal of fostering artistic weird literature but largely in order to make money by featuring big-name writers; and when this did not happen, he was quick to free himself of his creation. *Weird Tales* never made any significant amount of money, and on several occasions—especially during the depression—it came close to folding; but somehow it managed to hang on for thirty-one years and 279 issues, an unprecedented run for a pulp magazine.

Henneberger selected Edwin Baird (1886–1957) as editor, with assistance from Farnsworth Wright and Otis Adelbert Kline. Lovecraft no doubt read Baird's short novel "The Heart of Virginia Keep" in the *Argosy* for April 1915, although as it was not a weird tale he probably did not take much notice of it. Baird, indeed, did not appear to have any great sensitivity to the weird. The first several issues—which varied in dimensions from 6 × 9 to an ungainly "bedsheet" size (8½ × 11), all with very crude and amateurish covers—are a decidedly mixed bag: the March 1923 issue featured a striking novelette, "Ooze" by Anthony M. Rud, which Lovecraft enjoyed, but otherwise contained a rag-tag farrago of crude and outlandish stories largely written by beginning writers; subsequent issues are similar, every now and then containing some fairly distinguished work amidst a mass of rubbish. Few established writers, even from the pulp field, appeared in these early issues: Harold Ward, Vincent Starrett, Don Mark Lemon, and Francis Stevens (the latter two of whom had distinguished themselves in the Munseys) are the only recognisable names; and throughout its run *Weird Tales* was much more congenial to new writers than other pulps, a policy that had both advantages and drawbacks. In the May 1923 issue it began its long-running policy of reprinting weird "classics," in this case Bulwer-Lytton's "The Haunted and the Haunters"; as a result, some fairly rare weird fiction was indeed brought back into print, although valuable space was frequently occupied by very well-known and easily available works (the June 1923 issue contained Poe's "The Murders in the Rue Morgue," and years later the entirety of *Frankenstein* was serialised), and the magazine unconsciously lapsed into arrogance by reprinting "classic" tales from its own earlier issues.

Lovecraft, who may or may not have still been reading some of the Munseys at this time, no doubt read those early issues of *Weird Tales,* finding some of the tales quite powerful. Indeed, even if Morton and others had not advised him to submit to *Weird Tales,* he might eventually have done so on his own; for he was clearly making efforts—naive and clumsy as they may have been—to break into professional print on a somewhat higher grade than *Home Brew.* As early as late 1919, at the urging of one of his aunts, he submitted "The Tomb" to the *Black Cat;*[29] at some later date he submitted "Dagon" to *Black Mask.* Both stories were rejected.[30] This was perhaps not the wisest choice in either instance. Although Lovecraft read some of the early issues of *Black Cat* around the turn of the century, the magazine was not primarily devoted to weird fiction and published, proportionately, much less of it than the Munseys. As for *Black Mask,* it was initially founded as an all-purpose fiction magazine: its first issue (April 1920) featured the subtitle "An Illustrated Magazine of Detective, Mystery, Adventure, Romance, and Spiritualism." But it was just at this time that the earliest stories by Carroll John Daly and Dashiell Hammett were appearing in it, and under the editorship of Joseph T. Shaw, who took over in November 1926, *Black Mask* would by the end of the decade become the nurturing ground for the hard-boiled school of detective fiction. The occasional ghost story did appear, but such an excursion into archaic, Poe-esque horror as "The Tomb" was not likely to find a home there.

What is more, when Lovecraft did submit to *Weird Tales,* he sent five tales simultaneously—"Dagon," "Arthur Jermyn," "The Cats of Ulthar," "The

Hound," and "The Statement of Randolph Carter"—along with a cover letter that took pains to point out the rejection of "Dagon" by *Black Cat.* Baird replied to Lovecraft in a personal letter, saying that he would consider accepting these tales if they were typed double-spaced. Lovecraft, used to the relatively informal policies of the amateur journals and probably wanting to save paper, had typed them single spaced (these typescripts still survive in the John Hay Library). For one whose loathing of the typewriter would in later years reach epic proportions, the prospect of having to undergo such a labour for what he believed to be a not entirely certain assurance of acceptance was formidable; but he finally typed "Dagon," which was accepted, as were the other four.

It is one of the many anomalies of Lovecraft's involvement with *Weird Tales* that his first published work in the magazine was not a story but a letter. With a certain impishness, Baird printed the bulk of Lovecraft's cover letter accompanying his five tales; this letter appeared in the September 1923 issue, by which time his tales had been accepted. Baird's editorial preface to the letter (appearing in the letter column of the magazine, "The Eyrie") already calls Lovecraft a "master of the weird tale"; here are some extracts from the letter:

> My Dear Sir: Having a habit of writing weird, macabre, and fantastic stories for my own amusement, I have lately been simultaneously hounded by nearly a dozen well-meaning friends into deciding to submit a few of these Gothic horrors to your newly-founded periodical. . . .
>
> I have no idea that these things will be found suitable, for I pay no attention to the demands of commercial writing. My object is such pleasure as I can obtain from the creation of certain bizarre pictures, situations, or atmospheric effects; and the only reader I hold in mind is myself. . . .
>
> I like *Weird Tales* very much, though I have seen only the April number. Most of the stories, of course, are more or less commercial—or should I say conventional?—in technique, but they all have an enjoyable angle. . . .

No wonder Baird added at the end of this letter: "Despite the foregoing, or because of it, we are using some of Mr. Lovecraft's unusual stories . . ." One would like to think that the letter was in some senses a self-parody, but it does not appear to be. Highbrow and condescending as it may appear, it quite accurately reflects the aesthetic theory Lovecraft had by this time evolved. The mention of "half-a-dozen well-meaning friends" is interesting: a subsequent letter to Baird, published in the October 1923 issue, notes that "people in Massachusetts, New York, Ohio and California have been equally prompt in calling my attention" to the magazine. The New Yorker is surely Morton, just as the Californian is Smith; the Massachusetts friend is probably W. Paul Cook, and the Ohio friends might have been Alfred Galpin or Samuel Loveman.

This second letter (published in the same issue that contained "Dagon") is interesting in that it indicates that Lovecraft was also submitting his weird verse to the magazine. He quotes the opening stanza of "Nemesis" and says that he will one day send it to *Weird Tales* as a "filler"; Baird, in an editorial note, quotes the "prologue" to "Psychopompos" and declares that he may "some day" print it. The magazine had evidently begun with a "no-poetry" policy, and as early as May 1923 Lovecraft declared[31] that he had convinced Baird to overturn it: the July 1923 issue contained two poems by Clark Ashton Smith, and Lovecraft must have urged both Smith to submit them and Baird to accept them. "Nemesis" did in fact appear in the April 1924 issue, but "Psychopompos" was published only posthumously.

Lovecraft quickly became a fixture with *Weird Tales,* appearing in five of the six issues from October 1923 to April 1924 (there was no issue for December 1923). He might even be thought to have appeared in all six, if the publication of Sonia Greene's "The Horror at Martin's Beach" (retitled, to Lovecraft's chagrin, "The Invisible Monster") in the November 1923 issue can count as one of his appearances. The five tales he had initially submitted took their time appearing, and the last one, "The Cats of Ulthar," was not published until the February 1926 issue, long after several other tales submitted subsequently had already been printed.

Lovecraft no doubt found the money he received from the magazine a small but welcome relief from poverty. As he wrote in jest in October 1924: "O cheques, come to papa!"[32] *Weird Tales* paid upon publication, not (as the better grade of pulps and all the "slicks" did) on acceptance; and judging from the evidence of his early payments, he appears initially to have received much better than the standard 1¢ a word. Later this rate would decline, but Lovecraft would still receive *Weird Tales'* "highest" rate of 1½¢ a word.

Another event of the summer of 1923 that significantly affected Lovecraft's weird fiction was the discovery of the great Welsh writer Arthur Machen (1863–1947; pronounced MACK-en). As with his discoveries of Ambrose Bierce and Lord Dunsany in 1919, it is a wonder that he had not read him earlier, for Machen's greatest celebrity had been in the 1890s, and by 1923 he was already regarded (correctly, as it happens) as having done his best work long before. Machen had attained not merely fame but actual notoriety with such works as *The Great God Pan and The Inmost Light* (1894), *The Three Impostors* (1895), and *The House of Souls* (1906), which many believed to be the outpourings of a diseased mind; Machen soberly reprinted some of the bad reviews he had received in the volume *Precious Balms* (1924). In fact, Machen himself ascribed to the same Victorian sexual pruderies he seemingly flaunted; and the very covert intimations of aberrant sex in such tales as "The Great God Pan" and "The White People" were as horrifying to him as they were to his audience. Temperamentally Machen was not at all similar to Lovecraft: an unwavering Anglo-Catholic, violently hostile to science and materialism, seeking always for some mystical sense of "ecstasy" that might liberate him from what he fancied to be the prosiness of contemporary life, Machen would have found Lovecraft's mechanistic materialism and atheism repugnant in the extreme. They may have shared a general hostility to the modern age, but they were coming at it from very different directions. Lovecraft would sing Machen's praises in "Supernatural Horror in Literature," but in a letter of 1932 he offers a much more probing analysis:

> What Machen probably likes about perverted and forbidden things is their departure from and hostility to the commonplace. To him—whose imagination is not cosmic—they represent what Pegāna and the River Yann represent to Dunsany, whose imagination *is* cosmic. People whose minds are—like Machen's—steeped in the orthodox myths of religion, naturally find a poignant fascination in the conception of things which religion brands with outlawry and horror. Such people take the artificial and obsolete concept of "sin" seriously, and find it full of dark allurement. On the other hand, people like myself, with a realistic and scientific point of view, see no charm or mystery whatever in things banned by religious mythology. We recognise the primitiveness and meaninglessness of the religious attitude, and in consequence find no element of attractive defiance or significant escape in those things which happen to contravene it. The whole idea of "sin", with its overtones of unholy fascination, is in 1932 simply a curiosity of intellectual history. The filth and perversion which to Machen's obsoletely orthodox mind meant profound defiances of the universe's foundations, mean to us only a rather prosaic and unfortunate species of organic maladjustment—no more frightful, and no more interesting, than a headache, a fit of colic, or an ulcer on the big toe.[33]

And yet, because Machen so sincerely feels the sense of sin and transgression in those things that "religion brands with outlawry and horror," he manages to convey his sentiments to the reader in such a way that his work remains powerful and effective. Lovecraft himself came to regard "The White People" as perhaps second to Algernon Blackwood's "The Willows" as the greatest weird tale of all time; he may well be right.

Not all Machen's fiction—let alone the oceans of essays and journalism he wrote over his career—is to be considered horrific, and some of his most successful and artistically finished works are only on the borderline of the weird. The short novel *A Fragment of Life* (in *The House of Souls*) is an exquisite probing of the mysteries and wonders of ordinary life, portraying a stolid bourgeois couple in London who feel the call of their ancestry and return to their native Wales. As for *The Hill of Dreams* (1907), that agonising depiction of the anguish of artistic creation, Lovecraft waxed enthusiastic when he read it:

> And I have read *The Hill of Dreams!* Surely a masterpiece—though I hope it isn't quite as autobiographical as some reviewers claim. I'd hate to think of Ma-

> chen himself as that young neurotic with his sloppy sentimentalities, his couch of thorns, his urban eccentricities, and all that! But Pegāna, what an imagination! Cut out the emotional hysteria, and you have a marvellously appealing character—how vivid is that exquisite Roman day-dreaming! . . . even if the *spirit* is sadly un-Roman. Machen is a Titan—perhaps the greatest living author—and I must read everything of his.[34]

Lovecraft's reaction is typical: the novel is indeed very autobiographical, and it would be impossible to "cut out" all the "emotional hysteria" without disfiguring the work.

Lovecraft's reference to the "Roman day-dreaming" in the novel—that great fourth chapter where Lucian Taylor imagines himself back in Roman times with the Second Augustan Legion at Isca Silurum (Caerleon-on-Usk, where Machen himself grew up)—points to one of the bonds he immediately felt with Machen. In later life Lovecraft professed great fascination for Roman Britain—the one point where his Anglophilia and his love of Roman civilisation joined—and it is not surprising that Machen's own fascination helped to foster this interest.

Although Lovecraft dutifully read as much of Machen as he could—his quirky treatise on aesthetics, *Hieroglyphics: A Note upon Ecstasy in Literature* (1902), the curious mainstream novel *The Secret Glory* (1922), his three delightful autobiographies, *Far Off Things* (1922), *Things Near and Far* (1923), and *The London Adventure* (1924), even such minor works as *The Canning Wonder* (1926), a nonfiction account of a strange disappearance—it was the horror tales that remained closest to his heart. In particular, a whole series of works—including "The White People," "The Shining Pyramid," "Novel of the Black Seal" (a segment of the episodic novel *The Three Impostors*), and others—make use of the old legends of the "Little People," a supposedly pre-Aryan race of dwarfish devils who still live covertly in the secret places of the earth and occasionally steal human infants, leaving one of their own behind. Lovecraft would transform this topos into something even more sinister in some of his later tales.

Lovecraft's reference to Machen as the "greatest living author" was not a complete exaggeration, at least in terms of Machen's contemporary reputation. In 1923 Martin Secker issued a nine-volume collected edition of his work; the next year Knopf issued an exquisitely printed limited edition of his prose poems, *Ornaments in Jade;* the first edition of *The Hill of Dreams* was fetching enormous sums on the rare book market. Machen certainly was a distinctive figure, and the obscurity that has overtaken his work—partly because of the prejudice against weird fiction that continues to dominate the academic community, and partly because, like so many other writers, Machen wrote too much and in his later years babbled himself out into harmless verbosity—is quite undeserved. He, no less than Oscar Wilde or Walter Pater, helped to make the Yellow Nineties what they were; and although even his best work is marred by prolixity, formlessness, and even a certain self-indulgence, it remains a striking contribution to the literature of its time. On a much lesser scale than Lovecraft, Machen continues to attract a devoted band of followers who use the small press to keep his work alive after a fashion; he is one of those many authors who must suffer the indignity of periodic resurrection.

Lovecraft seems to have owed the discovery of Machen to Frank Long, as on one occasion he notes rereading "your Machen books."[35] I cannot detect any Machen influence on Lovecraft's tales prior to 1926, but the Welshman's work clearly filtered into Lovecraft's imagination and eventually emerged in a quite transformed but still perceptible manner in some of his best-known stories.

Lovecraft had, indeed, not written any stories since "The Lurking Fear" in November 1922; but then, in a matter of two or three months, he wrote three in quick succession—"The Rats in the Walls," "The Unnamable," and "The Festival." All three are of considerable interest, and the first is without question the greatest tale of Lovecraft's early period.

The plot of "The Rats in the Walls" is deceptively simple. A Virginian of British ancestry, a man named Delapore (his first name is never given), decides to spend his latter years in refurbishing and occupying his ancestral estate in southern England, Exham Priory, whose foundations go disturbingly far back in time, to a period even before the Roman conquest of the first century A.D. Delapore spares no expense in the restoration, and proudly moves into his estate on July 16, 1923. He has reverted to the ancestral spelling of his name, de la Poer, in spite of the fact that the family has a very unsavoury reputation with the local population—a reputation for murder, kidnapping, witchcraft, and other anomalies extending back to the first Baron Exham in 1261. Associated with the house or the family is the "dramatic epic of the rats—the lean, filthy, ravenous army which had swept all before it and devoured fowl, cats, dogs, hogs, sheep, and even two hapless human beings before its fury was spent."

All this seems merely conventional ghostly legendry, and de la Poer pays no attention to it. But shortly after his occupancy of Exham Priory, odd things begin to happen; in particular, he and his several cats seem to detect the scurrying of rats in the walls of the structure, even though such a thing is absurd in light of the centuries-long desertion of the place. The scurrying seems to be descending to the basement of the edifice, and one night de la Poer and his friend, Capt. Edward Norrys, spend a night there to see if they can elucidate the mystery. De la Poer wakes to hear the scurrying of the rats continuing "*still downward,* far underneath this deepest of sub-cellars," but Norrys hears nothing. They come upon a trap-door leading to a cavern beneath the basement, and decide to call in scientific specialists to investigate the matter. As they descend into the nighted crypt, they come upon an awesome and horrific sight—an enormous expanse of bones: "Like a foamy sea they stretched, some fallen apart, but others wholly or partly articulated as skeletons; these latter invariably in postures of daemoniac frenzy, either fighting off some menace or clutching some other forms with cannibal intent." When de la Poer finds that some bones have rings bearing his own coat of arms, he realises the truth—his family has been the leaders of an ancient cannibalistic witch-cult that had its origins in primitive times—and he experiences a spectacular evolutionary reversal: "Curse you, Thornton, I'll teach you to faint at what my family do! . . . 'Sblood, thou stinkard, I'll learn ye how to gust . . . wolde ye swynke me thilke wys? . . . *magna Mater! Magna Mater! . . . Atys . . . Dia ad aghaidh 's ad aodann . . . agus bas dunach ort! Dhonas 's dholas ort, agus leat-sa! . . . Ungl . . . ungl . . . rrrlh . . . chchch . . .*" He is found bending over the half-eaten form of Capt. Norrys.

It is difficult to convey the richness and cumulative horror of this story in any synopsis; next to *The Case of Charles Dexter Ward,* it is Lovecraft's greatest triumph in the old-time "Gothic" vein—although even here the stock Gothic features (the ancient castle with a secret chamber; the ghostly legendry that proves to be founded on fact) have been modernised and refined so as to be chillingly convincing. And the fundamental premise of the story—that a human being can suddenly reverse the course of evolution—could only have been written by one who had accepted the Darwinian theory.

"The Rats in the Walls" must have been written in late August or early September, for Lovecraft announced its completion in a letter of September 4.[36] It is notable for being both one of the most historically rich and one of the most contemporary stories he had written to date. The very first sentence ("On July 16, 1923, I moved into Exham Priory . . .") boldly places us in the modern world, unlike the Poe-esque nebulosity of "The Hound" ("On the night of September 24, 19—"), the 1896 setting of "The Picture in the House," or the unspecified chronology of "The Outsider," "The Nameless City," and others. This contemporaneousness will become a hallmark of Lovecraft's later work, creating an immediacy of effect that must have augmented the horror for his earliest readers. At the same time, this tale reaches farther back into the historic and prehistoric past than any other previous tale except "Dagon" and perhaps "The Temple": by an obvious but nonetheless effective symbolism, the narrator's descent into the successive layers of his cellar point to his descent into increasingly remote layers of history.

Lovecraft the Anglophile captures the English setting of the tale with notable felicity, although with some puzzling errors. The town nearest to Exham Priory is given as Anchester, but there is no such town in England. Lovecraft must have been thinking either of Ancaster in Lincolshire or (more likely) Alchester in the southern county of Oxfordshire. Perhaps this is a deliberate alteration; but then, what do we make of the statement that "Anchester had been the camp of the Third

Augustan Legion"? Neither Alchester nor Ancaster were the sites of legionary fortresses in Roman Britain; what is more, the Third Augustan Legion was never in England at all, and it was the Second Augustan Legion that was stationed at Isca Silurum (Caerleon-on-Usk) in what is now Wales. This is a strange error for Lovecraft to have made, and he repeats it in the fragment "The Descendant" (1927?). Even if this is a deliberate change, it is too clearly at variance with the known facts to be plausible.

Certain surface features of the tale—and perhaps one essential kernel of the plot—were taken from other works. As Steven J. Mariconda has pointed out,[37] Lovecraft's account of the "epic of the rats" appears to be derived from a chapter in S. Baring-Gould's *Curious Myths of the Middle Ages* (1869), of which Lovecraft speaks highly in "Supernatural Horror in Literature" and which he had probably read by this time. The Gaelic portions of de la Poer's concluding cries were lifted directly from Fiona Macleod's "The Sin-Eater," which Lovecraft read in Joseph Lewis French's anthology, *Best Psychic Stories* (1920).

More significantly, the very idea of atavism or reversion to type seems to have been derived from a story by Irvin S. Cobb, "The Unbroken Chain," published in *Cosmopolitan* for September 1923 (the issue, as is still customary with many magazines, was probably on the stands at least a month before its cover date) and later collected in Cobb's collection *On an Island That Cost $24.00* (1926). Lovecraft admitted that Long gave him the magazine appearance of this story in 1923,[40] and he alluded to it without citing its title in "Supernatural Horror in Literature." This tale deals with a Frenchman who has a small proportion of negroid blood from a slave brought to America in 1819. When he is run down by a train, he cries out in an African language—*"Niama tumba!"*—the words that his black ancestor shouted when he was attacked by a rhinoceros in Africa. The whole story, aside from being vilely racist, telegraphs its punch long before the end; but the sudden atavistic cry may have fired Lovecraft's imagination. It is, I suppose, to Lovecraft's credit that he has eliminated any racist overtones in his version. In an early passage in Cobb's story, a character ruminates on the general conception:

> ". . . the fear that some day, somehow, somewhere, some word from him, some involuntary spasmodic act of his, some throw-back manifestation of motive or thought that's been hiding in his breed for generation after generation, will betray his secret and utterly undo him. Call it by what scientific jargon or popular term you please—hereditary instinct, reversion to type, transmitted impulse, dormant primitivism, elemental recurrence—still the haunting dread of it must be walking with him in every waking minute."[41]

But it has to be admitted that Lovecraft has vastly enriched and subtilised the idea.

"The Rats in the Walls" is, technically, the first story Lovecraft wrote as a professional writer, for by this time his first tales had been accepted, though not published, in *Weird Tales.* It is, of course, a very different thing to say that Lovecraft somehow consciously wrote this story with a professional market in mind: I find no evidence of this. It is true that he did not submit this tale to an amateur journal; it is also true that he submitted the tale first, not to *Weird Tales,* but to the *Argosy All-Story Weekly,* a Munsey magazine whose managing editor, Robert H. Davis, rejected it as being (in Lovecraft's words) "too horrible for the tender sensibilities of a delicately nurtured publick."[42] Davis was, of course, the longtime editor of the *All-Story* during its entire run as a separate magazine (1905–20); when it was merged with the *Argosy* in 1920, he was forced to yield to Matthew White, Jr., who had edited the *Argosy* since 1886.[43] Davis left the Munsey organisation and founded his own literary agency, but it did not do well; around 1922 he returned to Munsey as managing editor under White. The *Argosy All-Story* may or may not have paid better than *Weird Tales* (it paid A. Merritt only 1¢ a word for *The Metal Monster* in 1920), but it clearly had a wider circulation and greater prestige; but when "The Rats in the Walls" was rejected, Lovecraft immediately sent it to Baird, who accepted it and ran it in the March 1924 issue. All this does not mean, however, that Lovecraft was suddenly becoming (as he later derisively termed it) a "pulp-hound" who sought acceptance in the pulps as a vindication of his self-worth.

In a late letter Lovecraft stated a little curiously that "The Rats in the Walls" was "suggested by a very commonplace incident—the cracking of wall-paper late at night, and the chain of imaginings resulting from it."[44] This is curious because this specific image does not in fact occur in the story. Lovecraft has recorded the kernel of the idea in his commonplace book: "Wall paper cracks off in sinister shape—man dies of fright" (entry 107). And yet, an earlier entry (79) is also suggestive: "Horrible secret in crypt of ancient castle—discovered by dweller." (This latter entry was probably inspired by Bram Stoker's final novel, *The Lair of the White Worm* [1911], which Lovecraft read around this time.[45]) The story may then be a fusion of images and conceptions that had been percolating in his mind for years.

"The Rats in the Walls," the longest of Lovecraft's tales by far to date (aside from the episodic "Herbert West—Reanimator" and "The Lurking Fear"), is similarly the broadest in scope and the most meticulously written. It is, in one sense, the pinnacle of his work in the Gothic/Poe-esque vein (it is, in effect, his "Fall of the House of Usher"), but in another sense it is very much a work of his own in its adumbration of such central themes as the influence of the past upon the present, the fragility of human reason, the baleful call of ancestry, and the ever-present threat of a reversion to primitive barbarism. It represents an exponential leap in quality from his past work, and he would produce nothing so good until "The Call of Cthulhu" in 1926.

"The Unnamable" and "The Festival," Lovecraft's two other original stories of 1923, return to New England in their different ways. The former is slight, but could be thought of as a sort of veiled justification for the type of weird tale Lovecraft was evolving; much of it reads like a treatise on aesthetics. It has gone relatively unnoticed that "The Unnamable" is the second story to involve Randolph Carter, even though he is referred to only once as "Carter." Still more unnoticed is the fact that this Carter is very different in temperament from that of "The Statement of Randolph Carter," as the Carters in the three later tales involving him will be as well; so that the blithe assumption that Carter is simply a stand-in for Lovecraft must be severely qualified or, at any rate, be examined with care.

The tale takes place in an "old burying ground" in Arkham, where Carter and his friend Joel Manton (clearly based upon Maurice W. Moe) are discussing the horror tales that Carter has written. Through Manton, Lovecraft satirises the stolid bourgeois objections to the weird—as contrary to probability; as not based on "realism"; as extravagant and unrelated to life—that he himself no doubt received on many occasions in the amateur press; he did so in the Transatlantic Circulator of 1921, leading to the first coherent enunciation of his theory of the weird in the *In Defence of Dagon* papers. The narrator paraphrases Manton's views: "It was his view that only our normal, objective experiences possess any aesthetic significance, and that it is the province of the artist not so much to rouse strong emotion by action, ecstasy, and astonishment, as to maintain a placid interest and appreciation by accurate, detailed transcripts of every-day affairs." This, and the rest of the passage, testify to Lovecraft's absorption of Decadent aesthetics and his revulsion from Victorian standards of mundane realism. The mention of "ecstasy" may reflect his reading, around this time, of Machen's *Hieroglyphics: A Note upon Ecstasy in Literature* (1902), which Lovecraft, although not accepting it in its entirety, found stimulating in its championing of literature that frees itself from the commonplace. Manton's objection to supernaturalism in literature, in spite of the fact that he "believ[es] in the supernatural much more fully than I," is a snide reference to Moe's theism: anyone who believes in an omnipotent God and in the resurrection of Jesus Christ from the dead can scarcely object to the depiction of the supernatural in fiction! The rest of the story—in which Manton scoffs at the very idea of something being termed "unnamable" but later encounters just such an entity in the burying ground—does not require much comment.

Aside from its interesting aesthetic reflexions, "The Unnamable" fosters that sense of the lurking horror of New England history and topography which we have already seen in "The Picture in the House," and which would become a dominant topos in Lovecraft's later work. The tale is set in Arkham, but the actual inspiration for the setting—a "dilapidated seventeenth-century tomb" and, nearby, a "giant willow in the centre of the cemetery, whose trunk has nearly engulfed an ancient, illegible slab"—is the Charter Street Burying Ground in Salem, where just such a tree-engulfed slab can be found. Later in the story Lovecraft records various "old-wives' superstitions," some of which are taken from Cotton Mather's *Magnalia Christi Americana* (1702), of which he owned an ancestral first edition. As in "The Picture in the House," Lovecraft's attempt to find horror in the seventeenth century is manifest: ". . . no wonder sensitive students shudder at the Puritan age in Massachusetts. So little is known of what went on beneath the surface—so little, yet such a ghastly festering as it bubbles up putrescently in occasional ghoulish glimpses."

One of those glimpses is presented in "The Festival" (written probably in October[46]), which for the sustained modulation of its prose can be considered a virtual 3000-word prose-poem. Although it is only in this tale that the mythical town of Kingsport (first cited in "The Terrible Old Man") is definitively identified with Marblehead, Lovecraft makes it clear that the seventeenth-century past is not in fact the true source of horror in the tale; in rhythmical, alliterative prose he suggests a horror of much older lineage: "It was the Yuletide, that men call Christmas though they know in their hearts it is older than Bethlehem and Babylon, older than Memphis and mankind." The Christian holiday is a mere veneer for a much older festival that reaches back to the agricultural rhythms of primitive man—the winter solstice, whose passing foretells the eventual reawakening of the earth in spring.

The narrator follows a course along the old town that can be traversed to this day. He passes by the old cemetery on the hill, where (in a literal borrowing from his letter of nearly a year previous) "black gravestones stuck ghoulishly through the snow like the decayed fingernails of a gigantic corpse," and makes his way to a house with an overhanging second story (a house clearly identifiable in the central square of Marblehead). There he encounters the past embodied in both furnishings and inhabitants:

> He beckoned me into a low, candle-lit room with massive exposed rafters and dark, stiff, sparse furniture of the seventeenth century. The past was vivid there, for not an attribute was missing. There was a cavernous fireplace and a spinning-wheel at which a bent old woman in loose wrapper and deep poke-bonnet sat back toward me, silently spinning despite the festive season.

For Lovecraft, the eighteenth-century rationalist, the seventeenth century in Massachusetts—dominated by the Puritans' rigid religion, bereft of the sprightliness of the Augustan wits, and culminating in the psychotic horror of the Salem witchcraft trials—represented an American "Dark Age" fully as horrifying as the early mediaeval period in Europe he so despised. Religion—seen by Lovecraft as the overwhelming of the intellect by emotion, childish wish-fulfilment, and millennia of pernicious brainwashing—proves to be the source of terror in "The Festival," whose culminating scene occurs in an old church in Marblehead (probably—as Donovan K. Loucks has ascertained—one of two churches no longer extant: the First Meeting House, built in 1648 on Old Burial Hill, or the Second Congregational Church, built in 1715 at 28 Mugford Street). But Lovecraft sees this Christian edifice as a mere façade for rituals of much older provenance; and when the band of townspeople descend robotically down a "trap-door of the vaults which yawned loathsomely open just before the pulpit," we can see both a relationship to "The Rats in the Walls" (where also a physical descent symbolises a descent into the archaic past) and an indication of the superficiality of Christianity's formalisation of primitive festivals from the depths of prehistory.

The conclusion of "The Festival"—marred by the luridness of grotesque winged creatures who carry off each of the celebrants on their backs—is not commensurate with its mesmeric opening and middle sections; but its evocation of the centuried past, in prose as fluid, restrained, and throbbingly vital as Lovecraft ever wrote, will always give this tale a high place among his lesser works.

It seems odd that Lovecraft required almost a year and at least four or five trips to Marblehead after his first visit of December 1922 to write the tale; but we will find that he frequently needed lengthy periods of reflection before topographical or other impressions settled sufficiently in his mind to emerge in the form of weird fiction. There is a literary (or scientific) influence as well. In 1933 Lovecraft stated in reference to the tale: "In intimating an alien race I had in mind the survival of some clan of pre-Aryan sorcerers who preserved primitive rites like those of the witch-cult—I had just been reading Miss Murray's *The Witch-Cult in Western Europe.*"[47] This landmark work of anthropology by Margaret A. Murray, published in 1921, made the claim (now regarded by modern scholars as highly dubious) that the witch-cult in both Europe and America had its origin in a pre-Aryan race that was driven underground but continued to lurk in the hidden corners of the earth. Lovecraft—having just read a very similar fictional exposition of the idea in Machen's stories of the "Little People"—was much taken with this conception and would allude to it in many subsequent references to the Salem witches in his tales; as late as 1930 he was presenting the theory seriously:

> Another and highly important factor in accounting for Massachusetts witch-belief and daemonology is the fact, now widely emphasised by anthropologists, that the traditional features of witch-practice and Sabbat-orgies *were by no means mythical. . . . Something actual was going on under the surface,* so that people really stumbled on *concrete experiences* from time to time which confirmed all they had ever heard of the witch species. . . . Miss Murray, the anthropologist, believes that the witch-cult actually established a "coven" (its only one in the New World) in the Salem region about 1690 . . . For my part—I doubt if a compact coven existed, but certainly think that people had come to Salem who had a direct personal knowledge of the cult, and who were perhaps initiated members of it. I think that some of the rites and formulae of the cult must have been talked about secretly among certain elements, and perhaps furtively practiced by the few degenerates involved. . . . Most of the people hanged were probably innocent, yet I do think

> there was a concrete, sordid background not present in any other New England witchcraft case.[48]

Lovecraft will not find many today who will agree with him on this point. I think that his enthusiastic response to Murray is one of those relatively few instances where his longing for some bizarre theory to be true convinced him that it actually was true. In this case the theory so perfectly meshed with some of his own *literary* tropes that he found it compelling in fact: he had conceived the notion of "alien" (i.e., non-human or not entirely human) races lurking on the underside of civilisation as early as "Dagon" and "The Temple," although the prime philosophical motivation had been the diminution of human self-importance and a refutation of the idea that we are the clear "rulers" of the planet; then he found it in an author (Machen) whose work he perhaps saw as a striking anticipation of his own; so that when a respected scholar actually propounded a theory that approximately echoed this trope, he naturally embraced it. Lovecraft makes the connexion explicit in a letter of 1924: "In this book the problem of witchcraft superstition is attacked from an entirely new angle—wherein the explanation of delusion and hysteria is discarded in favour of an hypothesis almost exactly like . . . the one used by Arthur Machen in fiction . . ."[49] It is also a fact that Murray's book was received as a significant work of anthropology, although many early reviewers disagreed with her conclusions; one critic, Robert Lynd (a literary man, not an anthropologist), wrote piquantly: "Miss Murray is to be congratulated on having produced a fascinating guide to the practices of witchcraft. Her book should be invaluable to romantic novelists."[50] Lovecraft cannot be blamed if her views were only later overturned or, at the very least, regarded as highly implausible.

Meanwhile Lovecraft had actually met a writer of weird fiction in his own hometown—Clifford Martin Eddy, Jr (1896–1967), who with his wife Muriel became fairly close to Lovecraft in the year or two preceding his marriage. The Eddys were at that time residents of East Providence, across the Seekonk River, and after an initial round of correspondence and a few telephone calls, Lovecraft walked three miles to visit them at their home on Second Street in August 1923.[51]

But how did Lovecraft come into contact with the Eddys at all? There is some doubt on the matter. Muriel Eddy wrote two significant memoirs of Lovecraft, one published in 1945, the other in 1961. The first memoir seems on the whole quite reliable; the second, written in a gushing and histrionic manner, makes many statements not found in the first, including the claim that Lovecraft's mother and Eddy's mother (Mrs Grace Eddy) had become friends by meeting at a women's suffrage meeting and that at this time (probably in 1918, although Muriel Eddy supplies no date) the two of them discovered their sons were both enthusiasts of the weird.[52] This is a remarkable assertion, and I am frankly sceptical of it. There is no other indication that Susie Lovecraft was interested in women's suffrage; although, given the paucity of information about her, especially her later years, I suppose it is at least conceivable. Muriel Eddy goes on to claim that there was extensive correspondence between Lovecraft and the Eddys until Susie was taken to the hospital in the spring of 1919; Lovecraft responded by sending them application blanks for the UAPA. The Eddys do not appear on any UAPA membership lists I have seen. Muriel then claims that the correspondence abruptly ceased, only to resume two years later, after Susie's death. Jim Dyer, Muriel Eddy's grandson, claims to have letters from Lovecraft dating to as early as 1918, but he has not made them public.

Lovecraft does not, to my knowledge, mention the Eddys in correspondence prior to October 1923, at which time he refers to Eddy as "the new Providence amateur."[53] He certainly gives no indication that he had once been in touch with the Eddys and was only now reestablishing contact. My feeling, then, is that the whole story about Susie Lovecraft and Grace Eddy—and about the Eddys' early association with Lovecraft—is a fabrication, made by Muriel so as to augment the sense of her and her husband's importance in Lovecraft's life. Muriel went on to write several more self-published pamphlets about her relations with Lovecraft, and it seems to me that she was attempting to capitalise on Lovecraft's growing renown. The "facts" that she tells about Susie Lovecraft in her 1961 memoir could all have been gleaned from others' writings—notably Winfield Townley Scott's "His Own Most Fantastic Creation" (1944). There is no mention at all of Susie or any involvement with her in Muriel's 1945 memoir. Accordingly, I see no reason to believe that Lovecraft was in any way familiar with the Eddys prior to the summer of 1923.

In any event, C. M. Eddy was already a professionally published author by this time. His first published story, "Sign of the Dragon," appeared in *Mystery Magazine* for September 1, 1919, and he had other mystery and horror stories in other early pulp magazines. Although he had clearly met Lovecraft through the amateur journalism movement, he was very anxious to become an established professional writer; Muriel Eddy reports that her husband had long been acquainted with Edwin Baird and that both she and Clifford urged Lovecraft to submit to *Weird Tales.* She also gives a piquant account of Lovecraft's reading them "The Rats in the Walls" one evening:

> He started to read this creepy yarn to us at midnight—and continued, placing special emphasis on certain words as he read, his facial expressions changing as he became so absorbed in what he was reading aloud that it seemed he was actually *living* the story, making it come alive. . . . I'll never forget that night! Many houses in Providence were gas-lighted at that time, and Lovecraft's face, as seen by the flickering rays of gaslight, while he read aloud his own ultra-fanciful creation, was

truly something "out of this world"—ever to be remembered. I shuddered myself to sleep that night!

In the meantime Eddy himself was working on stories for *Weird Tales.* Two of these—"Ashes" and "The Ghost-Eater"—had already been rejected, but Lovecraft "corrected"[54] them and Baird thereupon accepted them. "Ashes" (*Weird Tales,* March 1924) is perhaps the single worst tale among Lovecraft's "revisions," and no one would suspect his hand in it if he had not admitted it himself. This maudlin and conventional story about a mad scientist who has discovered a chemical compound that will reduce any substance to fine white ashes contains a nauseously fatuous romance element that must have made Lovecraft queasy: "The feel of her soft, yielding body held close to my own was the last straw. I cast prudence to the winds and crushed her tightly to my breast. Kiss after kiss I pressed upon her full red lips, until her eyes opened and I saw the lovelight reflected in them." Shades of Fred Jackson!

"The Ghost-Eater" (*Weird Tales,* April 1924) is a little better, although it is nothing but a stereotypical werewolf story. Lovecraft wrote to Muriel Eddy on October 20: "Here, at last, is the amended 'Ghost-Eater', whose appearance I trust Mr. Eddy will find satisfactory. I made two or three minor revisions in my own revised version, so that as it stands, it ought to be fairly acceptable to an editor."[55] Here again I cannot detect much actual Lovecraft prose, unless he was deliberately altering his style to make it harmonise with Eddy's more choppy, less prose-poetic idiom.

Lovecraft reported in late October that Eddy was working on another story, entitled "The Loved Dead";[56] Muriel Eddy refers to the original title as "The Beloved Dead." There was, as with its two predecessors, in all likelihood a draft written by Eddy for this tale; but the published version (*Weird Tales,* May–June–July 1924) certainly reads as if Lovecraft had written the entire thing. Here there is the sort of adjective-choked prose we have seen in "The Hound" and other tales of this period—references to a "foetid hollow," "poison-tongued gossips," an "exotic elixir," and other such things. The tale is, of course, about a necrophile, who works for one undertaking establishment after another so as to secure that intimacy with corpses he desires; some passages are remarkably explicit for their day: "One morning Mr. Gresham came much earlier than usual—came to find me stretched out upon a cold slab deep in ghoulish slumber, my arms wrapped about the stark, stiff, naked body of a foetid corpse! He roused me from my salacious dreams, his eyes filled with mingled detestation and pity." The final paragraph presents the same sort of perfervid free-association that concludes "The Hound," ending preposterously: "I—can—write—no—more. . . ." Muriel Eddy reports that Lovecraft, when visiting the Eddys on one occasion, was so "thoroughly delighted" with the tale as he had revised it that he read it to them aloud. What this suggests—as the tale itself does—is that "The Loved Dead" is a parody, both of itself and of this sort of lurid, sensationalist fiction. But, as we shall see, when it was published not everyone found it quite so amusing.

The final story revised for Eddy, "Deaf, Dumb, and Blind" (*Weird Tales,* April 1925), is a curious piece of work. It appears to have been revised by Lovecraft around February 1924, just prior to his move to New York. This tale about a deaf, dumb, and blind man who senses strange presences in his lonely cottage and records them in a manuscript or diary he is typing on the typewriter develops a curiously compelling power in spite of its stilted prose. Eddy reports: "He [Lovecraft] was unhappy with my handling of the note found in the typewriter at the very end of the protagonist's account of his eerie experiences, the final paragraph that seemed to have been typed by one of his persecutors. After several conferences over it, and an equal number of attempts on my part to do it justice, he finally agreed to rewrite the last paragraph."[57] This seems to suggest—although perhaps not by design—that Lovecraft revised only the last paragraph; in truth, the entire tale was probably revised, although again Eddy very likely had prepared a draft.

These four tales are among the earliest of Lovecraft's revisions of weird fiction, as opposed to collaborations (such as those with Winifred Jackson). The distinction between revisions and collaborations—in terms of Lovecraft's actual work on them—is perhaps not significant, for depending on the state of the original manuscript he would either merely touch it up or rewrite it wholesale. But there is some interest in ascertaining whether, and why, Lovecraft would affix his name to a work or not. In Eddy's case, the situation was close to the type of professional revision he would do later for Adolphe de Castro, Zealia Bishop, Hazel Heald, and others; but since the Eddys were friends of a sort, Lovecraft may have felt awkward actually charging them a fee for revisory work, so he seems to have worked out an agreement whereby they would type his manuscripts as recompense. Lovecraft declares explicitly that Eddy typed "The Hound" (that is, the double-spaced version that Baird wanted for *Weird Tales*) in exchange for the revised "Ghost-Eater."[58]

Eddy and Lovecraft did more than team up on writing projects. On November 4 the two of them returned to the Chepachet area where Lovecraft had taken Morton a month and a half before; this time the goal was not Durfee Hill but something called Dark Swamp, of which Eddy had heard "sinister whispers from the rusticks."[59] They encountered difficulty finding anyone who knew anything about the place or its precise location; even the town clerk, who had heard strange rumours of people entering the swamp but never coming out, did not know where it was. They looked up several other individuals, each of whom told them to consult some other person who would assuredly know where Dark Swamp was. Finally they found that the swamp was in the property of one Ernest Law, a farmer, but by this time it was too late to make the actual trip there; they vowed to return at some later date, but do not seem to have done so. Lovecraft and Eddy had covered an enormous amount of ground on this trip, and—although Lovecraft himself does not mention it in his two accounts of the adventure (in letters to Frank Belknap Long and Edwin Baird)—Muriel Eddy writes pungently: ". . . Mr. Eddy almost had to carry Lovecraft back from the rural excursion, at least a mile, to the trolley line, for, unaccustomed to such vigorous jaunts at that time, the writer of tales macabre soon became so exhausted he could hardly move one foot after the other." This does not quite seem to harmonise with other accounts of Lovecraft's tirelessness on foot; but perhaps in this case he did overexert himself. Lovecraft adds that on the trolley ride home Eddy, becoming inspired merely from the descriptions of Dark Swamp they had received from various natives, began a story called "Black Noon." This story remained unfinished up to the time of his death and appeared only posthumously in Eddy's collection *Exit into Eternity* (1973).

Lovecraft said to Baird in late 1923: "I find Eddy rather a delight—I wish I had known him before"[60] (another indication that his relationship with the Eddys was of relatively recent origin). Eddy was a somewhat crude and rough-hewn individual, far inferior to Lovecraft in intelligence and literary skill; and Lovecraft could not help regarding him with a sort of genial condescension, although this did not prevent him from doing him several good turns in later years. He clearly found it refreshing to find someone, even of Eddy's calibre, in Providence who shared his interest in weird fiction, but although he refers to him on one occasion as his "adopted son,"[61] Eddy never became as close a colleague as Long, Galpin, Loveman, and several others. Their friendship resumed upon Lovecraft's return to Providence in 1926, but we hear less and less of Eddy as the years pass.

In 1929 Lovecraft made the following evaluation of the progression of his aesthetic thought: "I can look back . . . at two distinct periods of opinion whose foundations I have successively come to distrust—a period before 1919 or so, when the weight of classic authority unduly influenced me, and another period from 1919 to about 1925, when I placed too high a value on the elements of revolt, florid colour, and emotional extravagance or intensity."[62] Simply put, these two phases (which would then be followed by a third and final phase combining the best features of both the previous two, and which might best be called "cosmic regionalism") are Classicism and Decadence. The classical phase I have treated already: Lovecraft's early absorption of the Augustan poets and essayists and the Graeco-Roman classics (either in the original or in translations deriving from the Augustan age), and his curious sense of psychic union with the eighteenth century, fostered a classicism that simultaneously condemned his poetry to antiquarian irrelevance and made him violently opposed to the radical aesthetic movements emerging in the early part of the century.

How, then, does an individual who professed himself, for the first thirty years of his life, more comfortable in the periwig and small-clothes of the eighteenth century suddenly adopt an attitude of "revolt, florid colour, and emotional extravagance or intensity"? How does someone who, in 1919, maintained that "The literary genius of Greece and Rome . . . may fairly be said to have completed the art and science of expression" ("The Case for Classicism") come to write, in 1923: "What is art but a matter of impressions, of pictures, emotions, and symmetrical sensations? It must have poignancy and beauty, but nothing else counts. It may or may not have coherence"?63 The shift may seem radical, but there are many points of contact between the older and the newer view; and in many ways the change of perspective occurring in Lovecraft's mind was a mirror of the change occurring in Anglo-American aesthetics in general. Much as he might have found the idea surprising or even repellent, Lovecraft was becoming contemporary; he was starting to live, intellectually, in the twentieth, not the eighteenth, century.

I do not wish to underestimate the extent and significance of the shift in Lovecraft's aesthetic; clearly he himself thought that something revolutionary was occurring. No longer was he concerned with antiquated notions of "metrical regularity" or the "allowable rhyme"; broader, deeper questions were now involved. Specifically, Lovecraft was attempting to come to terms with certain findings in the sciences that might have grave effects upon artistic creation, in particular the work of Sigmund Freud. One of Lovecraft's first references to Freud occurs only a week after his mother's death:

> Dr. Sigmund Freud of Vienna, whose system of psycho-analysis I have begun to investigate, will probably prove the end of idealistic thought. In details, I think he has his limitations; and I am inclined to accept the modifications of Adler, who in placing the ego above the eros makes a scientific return to the position which Nietzsche assumed for wholly philosophical reasons.[64]

All this is pretty nebulous, and it is not clear what work of Freud's (if any) Lovecraft had actually read; it is, in fact, more likely that he had read various accounts of it in books or magazines. A somewhat more revealing statement occurs in "The Defence Reopens!" (January 1921):

> Certainly, they [Freud's doctrines] reduce man's boasted nobility to a hollowness woeful to contemplate. . . . we are forced to admit that the Freudians have in most respects excelled their predecessors, and that while many of Freud's most important details may be erroneous—one should not be too hasty in substituting any single or simple instinct for the complex and dominant *Wille zur Macht* as the explanation of man's motive force—he has nevertheless opened up a new path in psychology, devising a system whose doctrines more nearly approximate the real workings of the mind than any heretofore entertained. We may not like to accept Freud, but I fear we shall have to do so.

Things now become a little clearer. Although Lovecraft rejects Freud's central notion of the libido as the principal motivating factor in human psychology—something he would have found difficult to comprehend, since his own libido seems to have been so sluggish—he nevertheless accepts the view that many of our beliefs and mental processes are the result, not of disinterested rationalism, but aggression (Nietzsche's will to power), ego-assertion, and in some cases pure irrationalism. Under the placid-seeming façade of civilised bourgeois life teem powerful emotional forces that social restraints are ill-equipped to control. The effect on art will necessarily be telling. Lovecraft expounds his view in "Lord Dunsany and His Work" (1922):

> Modern science has, in the end, proved an enemy to art and pleasure; for by revealing to us the whole sordid and prosaic basis of our thoughts, motives, and acts, it has stripped the world of glamour, wonder, and all those illusions of heroism, nobility, and sacrifice which used to sound so impressive when romantically treated. Indeed, it is not too much to say that psychological discovery, and chemical, physical, and physiological research, have largely destroyed the element of emotion among informed and sophisticated people by resolving it into its component parts—intellectual idea and animal impulse. The so-called "soul" with all its hectic and mawkish attributes of sentimentality, veneration, earnestness, devotion, and the like, has perished on analysis.

This is an intensely interesting utterance. In spite of Lovecraft's claim of intellectual independence from his time, it is clear that he had absorbed enough of the Victorian belief in "heroism, nobility, and sacrifice" to be shaken by the revelation, via Freud and Nietzsche, of their "sordid and prosaic basis." For the moment he adopted a sort of aesthetic Decadence that might allow these illusions to be preserved after a fashion precisely by recognising their artificiality. He continues in "Lord Dunsany and His Work":

> Art has been wrecked by a complete consciousness of the universe which shews that the world is to each man only a rubbish-heap limned by his individual perception. It will be saved, if at all, by the next and last step of disillusion; the realisation that complete consciousness and truth are themselves valueless, and that to acquire any genuine artistic titillation we must artificially invent limitations of consciousness and feign a pattern of life common to all mankind—most naturally the simple old pattern which ancient and groping tradition first gave us. When we see that the source of all joy and enthusiasm is wonder and ignorance, we shall be ready to play the old game of blindman's buff with the mocking atoms and electrons of a purposeless infinity.

We cannot regain that blissful ignorance of our triviality in the cosmic scheme of things and of the hollowness of our lofty ideals which allowed prior ages to create the illusion of significance in human affairs. What is the solution?

> It is then that we shall worship afresh the music and colour of divine language, and take an Epicurean delight in those combinations of ideas and fancies which we know to be artificial. Not that we can resume a serious attitude toward emotion—there is too much intellect abroad for that—but that we can revel in the Dresden-china Arcadia of an author who will play with the old ideas, atmospheres, types, situations, and lighting effects in a deft pictorial way; a way tinged with affectionate reminiscence as for fallen gods, yet never departing from a cosmic and gently satirical realisation of the true microscopic insignificance of the man-puppets and their petty relations to one another.

It is seriously to be doubted whether this is an accurate assessment of the foundations of Dunsany's art, but it was at this moment convenient to Lovecraft's purpose to maintain that it was; in any case, it is perfectly clear that he is speaking of himself and his own attempts to come to terms with the ethical and aesthetic implications (as he sees them) of modern science.

The interesting thing is that Lovecraft's new Decadent aesthetic fitted very well with a tendency he had long exhibited, and one that linked him significantly to the intelligentsia of his time: scorn of the nineteenth century. The little boy who had insensibly absorbed the prose and poetry of the Augustans and found only tedium in the great nineteenth-century authors (Dickens is despised for maudlin sentimentality, and Thackeray "induceth drowsiness"[65]) found himself entirely in sympathy with the repudiation of Victorianism that many of the poets and critics of the late nineteenth and early twentieth century were exhibiting. W. Jackson Bate, writing in 1970, speaks of

> the immense effort of the arts, including music, of the early and middle twentieth century to get the nineteenth century off their backs. So strenuous—at times single-minded—was the effort that, during the childhood and youth of those of us now middle-aged, many of us began to assume that the first requirement of the sophisticated poet, artist, or composer was to be as unlike his nineteenth-century predecessors as possible.[66]

Lovecraft, because of his early absorption in an anterior literary tradition, did not find this effort as difficult as many of his contemporaries; in fact, it might be said that his Decadent phase was really a means of retaining as much genuine classicism as he could in light of new scientific information.

Consider the issue of didacticism. Lovecraft had in fact never subscribed to classical notions of literature as a teacher or guide to behaviour; when he trumpeted classical ideals of "taste" and "elegance," he restricted their scope purely to matters of style and content (avoidance of slang and of "low" subject-matter), stripping them of their heavy moral overtones. In his early years, then, Lovecraft did not so much rebel against classical didacticism as simply ignore it. With his Decadent phase the rebellion became conscious; but, interestingly, Lovecraft chose to use Victorianism rather than Augustanism as his whipping-boy, probably because the actual morality preached by the latter was, as he came to realise, very much his own whereas the former was not. As he wrote in "In the Editor's Study" (*Conservative,* July 1923):

> It is time . . . definitely to challenge the sterile and exhausted Victorian ideal which blighted Anglo-Saxon culture for three quarters of a century and produced a milky "poetry" of shopworn sentimentalities and puffy platitudes; a dull-grey prose fiction of misplaced didacticism and insipid artificiality; an appallingly hideous system of formal manners, costume, and decoration; and worst of all, an artistically blasphemous architecture whose uninspired nondescriptness transcends tolerance, comprehension, and profanity alike.

Nothing is spared here—prose, poetry, architecture, social customs. Lovecraft was not always so harsh on the Victorians on this last point (in 1927 he would speak approvingly of the Victorians' "manners and conceptions of life as a fine art"[67]), but for his present purposes a uniform condemnation was much more rhetorically satisfying.

If there is any literary source for any of these views, it is Oscar Wilde. It is not likely that Wilde actually generated Lovecraft's views; rather, Lovecraft found Wilde a highly articulate spokesman for the sort of views he was nebulously coming to adopt. In "Final Words" (September 1921) he quotes the following sentences from Wilde's preface to *The Picture of Dorian Gray* (1891):

> No artist desires to prove anything. . . . No artist has ethical sympathies. An ethical sympathy in an artist is an unpardonable mannerism of style. No artist is ever morbid. The artist can express everything. All art is at once surface and symbol. . . . Those who read the symbol do so at their peril. . . . It is the spectator, and not life, that art really mirrors. . . . All art is quite useless.

Lovecraft found this especially helpful in his defence of the weird tale, as we shall see presently. In "The Defence Reopens!" he denies John Ravenor Bullen's claim that "The White Ship" was an allegory (or, rather, while not denying it, maintains that it was an "exception" in his work) by stating: "like Dunsany I protest that except in a few cases I have no thought of teaching." Lovecraft had gained this view of Dunsany from the appendix to Edward Hale Bierstadt's *Dunsany the Dramatist* (1917; rev. 1919), which printed several letters by Dunsany to various of his American supporters. One letter, to Emma Garrett Boyd, states bluntly: "Don't let them hunt for allegories. I may have written an allegory at some time, but if I have, it was a quite obvious one, and as a general rule, I have nothing to do with allegories."[68] Dunsany may have been a little disingenuous in this claim, for many of his tales—especially the prose-poems in *Fifty-one Tales* (1915)—are clear parables emphasising moral and aesthetic issues fundamental to his thought; but if this was what he wished to believe of his work, his disciple Lovecraft would willingly follow him.

There are two general caveats that should be borne in mind when studying

Lovecraft's Decadent stance: first, he clearly wished to believe that his position did not commit himself entirely, or at all, to the avant-garde; and second, he had no wish to follow the Decadents in the repudiation of Victorianism on the level of personal conduct. As to the first point, let me quote in full that statement from "In the Editor's Study" of July 1923 which I cited earlier:

> What is art but a matter of impressions, of pictures, emotions, and symmetrical sensations? It must have poignancy and beauty, but nothing else counts. It may or may not have coherence. If concerned with large externals or simple fancies, or produced in a simple age, it is likely to be of a clear and continuous pattern; but if concerned with individual reactions to life in a complex and analytical age, as most modern art is, it tends to break up into detached transcripts of hidden sensation and offer a loosely joined fabric which demands from the spectator a discriminating duplication of the artist's mood.

This statement—particularly the remark about "life in a complex and analytical age"—is remarkably similar to T. S. Eliot's celebrated definition and justification of Modernism, as expressed in "The Metaphysical Poets" (1921):

> We can only say that it appears likely that poets in our civilization, as it exists at present, must be *difficult.* Our civilization comprehends great variety and complexity, and this variety and complexity, playing upon a refined sensibility, must produce various and complex results. The poet must become more and more comprehensive, more allusive, more indirect, in order to force, to dislocate if necessary, language into his meaning.[69]

I do not think it is likely that Lovecraft was aware of this statement; if he had been, he would by no means have agreed with it. His own utterance seems to be as complete a repudiation of classicism—notably in the sense of clarity, unity, and "coherence"—as can be imagined. But Lovecraft pulls back at the last; perhaps aware that his amateur audience would be dumbfounded by the perception of the antiquated fossil Lovecraft becoming avant-garde, he hastily adds that he is "no convert to Dadaism," concluding:

> Nothing, on the contrary, seems more certain . . . than that the bulk of radical prose and verse represents merely the extravagant extreme of a tendency whose truly artistic application is vastly more limited. Traces of this tendency, whereby pictorial methods are used, and words and images employed without conventional connexions to excite sensations, may be found throughout literature; especially in Keats, William Blake, and the French symbolists. This broader conception of art does not outrage any eternal tradition, but honours all creations of the past or present which can shew genuine ecstatic fire and a glamour not tawdrily founded on utterly commonplace emotions.

Lovecraft is slowly carving out a place for himself between Victorian conventionality and Modernist radicalism: in this way he can continue to fulminate against such things as free verse, stream-of-consciousness, or the chaoticism of Eliot and Joyce as illegitimate extensions of his Decadent principles. Lovecraft seeks to unite his new views with what he saw as the best traditions of Western art in a provocative statement in "The Work of Frank Belknap Long, Jr.":

> Literary revolutions are not new. Elderly people who smirk complacently and predict the rapid subsidence of modernism forget utterly the Renaissance and even the romantic revival of the early nineteenth century. As in those times, the world has received a colossal influx of new ideas well calculated to remould all our impressions and recast all our utterances. We see the hollowness of things we believed before, and above all the disconnectedness of things we once thought indissolubly joined. It is the birth of a new aesthetic, grounded on the old but going beyond it, and demanding poignant, beautiful, and genuine sensation as the essence of artistic endeavour.

The fact that this utterance occurs in an essay on Long suggests that this young new colleague may have been instrumental in effecting this shift in Lovecraft's vision. Lovecraft himself describes Long as "a sincere and intelligent disciple of Poe, Baudelaire, and the French decadents."[70]

The second point in this entire issue—Decadence as a mode of conduct—is clarified in Lovecraft's discussion with Long in 1923–24 about the merits of Puritanism. This discussion occasionally becomes a little frivolous, and Lovecraft seems at times to be uttering hyperbole in a deliberate attempt to tease Long ("Verily, the Puritans were the only really effective diabolists and decadents the world has known"[71]). But he does manage to express quite sincere views on "Bohemians" and their wild lifestyle. The canonical utterance occurs in May 1923:

> Physical life and experience, with the narrowings of artistic vision they create in the majority, are the objects of my most profound contempt. It is for this reason that I despise Bohemians, who think it essential to art to lead wild lives. My loathing is not from the standpoint of Puritan morality, but from that of aesthetic independence—I revolt at the notion that physical life is of any value or significance.[72]

The extravagance of that last utterance—especially when it is followed by the sentence "To me the ideal artist is a gentleman who shows his contempt for life by continuing in the quiet ways of his ancestors, leaving his fancy free to explore refulgent and amazing spheres"—suggests that Lovecraft is not being entirely straightforward here, and that his objections to Bohemianism are not founded in aesthetics but in ethics and social conduct. This becomes evident in a later comment:

> An intellectual Puritan is a fool—almost as much of a fool as is an anti-Puritan—but a Puritan in the conduct of life is the only kind of man one may honestly re-

> spect. I have no respect or reverence whatever for any person who does not live abstemiously and purely—I can like him and tolerate him, and admit him to be a social equal as I do Clark Ashton Smith and Mortonius and Kleiner and others like that, but in my heart I feel him to be my inferior—nearer the abysmal amoeba and the Neanderthal man—and at times cannot veil a sort of condescension and sardonic contempt for him, no matter how much my aesthetick and intellectual superior he may be.[73]

Now we are getting to the root of the matter. Of course, the various code words in this utterance ("abstemiously," "purely") are a thin veil for restraint in sexual behaviour; the mentions of Smith and Kleiner—both of whom were openly fond of female companionship—are also telling. Lovecraft attempted to warn Long away from pornography or modern literature that explores sexual relations without Victorian inhibitions ("There is no more true sense and artistick discrimination in a modern coxcomb's praise of *Jurgen* or *Ulysses* . . . than there is in a small boy's praise of the dirty words which a bigger boy has dared to chalk up on the back wall of the stable"[74]), and copied over a poem he had written in 1921 to Kleiner, "The Pathetick History of Sir Wilful Wildrake," about a seventeenth-century rake who reforms late in life and becomes a loving husband and father. This poem is (along with a 1923 specimen, "Damon and Lycë," another squib on Alfred Galpin's love affairs) as close to sexual explicitness as Lovecraft ever got—

> 'Tis he that rails with righteous Zest
> At Modern Nymphs in Style undrest
> With shrinking Petticoats and naked Breast.

—but the message is quite the reverse of lasciviousness. Lovecraft had, therefore, sloughed off (or, in reality, never really adopted) the *aesthetics* of Victorianism but could not—or did not wish to—relinquish the sexual Puritanism he had no doubt gained at his mother's knee.

The middle ground that Lovecraft wished to occupy between a stale conventionalism and eccentric radicalism is evident in an amateur controversy of the early 1920s that linked him, Long, and Samuel Loveman with some of the old mossbacks of the amateur world. The source of the contretemps appears to have been a review of the first issue of Sonia Greene's *Rainbow* in the "Bureau of Critics" column in the *National Amateur* for March 1922. This review, although unsigned, is unquestionably by Lovecraft; and it goes on at great length praising Loveman's poem "A Triumph in Eternity" and Loveman's verse in general: "Samuel Loveman is the last of the Hellenes—a golden god of the elder world fallen among pygmies. Genius of the most poignant authenticity is his, opening in his mind a diamond-paned window which looks out clearly upon rarefied realms of dreams and scenes of immortal beauty seldom and dimly glimpsed by the modern age."

And so on. (I would remind readers who might be put off by this extravagant praise that Loveman really is a fine poet in a delicate *fin de siècle* sort of way.)

To this review one Michael Oscar White of Dorchester, Massachusetts—one of the members of the Hub Club, whom Lovecraft met on more than one occasion during his Boston visits of 1923—took issue in an article published in the *Oracle* (edited by Clyde G. Townsend) for December 1922. Writing on Loveman as the third instalment of a series on "Poets of Amateur Journalism," White—not knowing that Lovecraft was the author of the puff of Loveman in the *National Amateur*—criticised the review for praising a poet who was deliberately obscure, whose "insincere misanthropic" views tainted his work, and whose use of pagan gods was not only antiquated but possibly sacrilegious; remarking in particular of "A Triumph of Eternity," he wrote: "In anyone but an amateur poet with an amateur perception of things held sacred in a Christian country the whole piece would be considered blasphemous." White's article really is a piece of ham-fisted asininity, as he expects delicate poetry to follow the rules of prose syntax and logic. He concluded by saying that Loveman might win a following if he came down from Olympus and "adds his protest against the evils of the age."[75]

White's article was in turn attacked by Long in "An Amateur Humorist," in the March 1923 *Conservative,* and by Alfred Galpin in the August 1923 issue of the *Oracle.*[76] Both articles are extraordinarily vicious. Galpin, dripping with sarcasm, finally concludes: "It would seem as if Mr. White did not know what he was talking about." Long's response compares White to a court jester: "One characteristic of a jester is his utter lack of all sense of beauty. The divinest strain from the most enchanted lyre drives him to a gnashing of teeth and an insane stamping of feet. His appreciation of the arts is limited. He is in a small measure interested in 'thought' . . . And yet it is certain that all of the nuances and subtleties of thought escape him." And so on for four full pages. This article itself inspired a rebuttal by Edward H. Cole (in the "Bureau of Critics" column of the *National Amateur* for March 1923)—not so much a defence of White as a rebuke to Long for his sarcasm. Lovecraft remarked to Loveman that "Cole has a touch of New-England narrowness, but is not in any way a barbarian like that ass White. He really appreciates your poetry, & fully understands the absurd limitations of his dense fellow-townsman. What Cole disliked was the first half of Belknap's article, & that alone."[77] Nevertheless, Lovecraft no doubt took rich satisfaction in printing Loveman's superb ode "To Satan" on the cover of the July 1923 *Conservative* as a further tweaking of White's nose, although the bulk of this issue like its predecessor had been planned long before the controversy erupted.

Lovecraft himself made an actual response to White on at least two occasions: first, in a section of the "Bureau of Critics" column following Cole's piece (if this section, labelled "Contributed," is by Lovecraft, as I believe it is) and in "In the

Editor's Study" in the July 1923 *Conservative.* The former is studiously polite; the latter, which I have quoted on several occasions as typifying his condemnation of Victorian moral and aesthetic standards, is very much the opposite, and it is now evident that this new aesthetic stance was, at least superficially, being adopted as a stick with which to beat White over the head. There is no question of Lovecraft's sincerity in his views; but he found in them a convenient weapon against the naive moral criticism that White was putting forth. Lovecraft writes: "Certainly the position of Mr. White's circle is flawless if we are to accept art as an affair of the external intellect and commonplace, unanalysed emotions alone. *The Conservative* dissents only because he believes with most of the contemporary world that the actual foundations of art differ widely from those which the prim nineteenth century took for granted." So Lovecraft now welcomes the thought of being "contemporary"!

And yet, Lovecraft was by no means in the modernist camp. Several intensely interesting documents of this period bear this out with much emphasis. It is certainly odd that the two great landmarks of modernism—Joyce's *Ulysses* and Eliot's *The Waste Land*—appeared in the same year, 1922; but their fortuitously joint appearance compelled Lovecraft to address them in some fashion or other. He read *The Waste Land* in its first American appearance, in the *Dial* for November 1922 (it had appeared in England in Eliot's magazine, the *Criterion,* for October), and in fact preserved the issue; in May 1923 he urged Frank Long, who was planning to visit Lovecraft in Providence, to bring the book version (published by Boni & Liveright in late 1922, although dated 1923), since that contained Eliot's notes to the poem. He was particularly exercised over the final "Shantih. Shantih. Shantih," claiming that the "notes must tell or at least modernistically hint what it is."[78]

But well before this date, Lovecraft had written one or both of his responses to *The Waste Land.* The first is an editorial in the March 1923 *Conservative* headed "Rudis Indigestaque Moles" (taken from Ovid's *Metamorphoses:* "A rough and unfinished mass"). Beginning by lambasting the amateurs in general for their "complacent indifference . . . toward the present state of literature and general aesthetics," Lovecraft then turns to his argument that science has radically changed our attitude to the world, hence our attitude toward art. "The old heroics, pieties, and sentimentalities are dead amongst the sophisticated; and even some of our appreciations of natural beauty are threatened." *The Waste Land* is one result of this state of confusion and turbulence:

> We here behold a practically meaningless collection of phrases, learned allusions, quotations, slang, and scraps in general; offered to the public (whether or not as a hoax) as something justified by our modern mind with its recent comprehension of its own chaotic triviality and disorganisation. And we behold th[e] public, or a considerable part of it, receiving this hilarious melange as something vital and typical; as "a poem of profound significance," to quote its sponsors.

This is one of the most notorious pieces of evidence of Lovecraft's supposed insensitivity to modernism and to his innate aesthetic conservatism; but it is difficult to see what other reaction he could have made at this stage of his development. It should also be pointed out that many other reviewers—not merely stodgy Victorians like J. C. Squire but level-headed modernists like Conrad Aiken—also found the poem incomprehensible or at least ambiguous and incoherent, although some did not think it a bad poem on that account.[79] As for Lovecraft, he may by this time have given up his literal adherence to eighteenth-century forms—or, at least, his requirement that all other poets do so—but the outward form of *The Waste Land* with its free verse and its seemingly random progression so offended him that he saw in the poem an actual instance of the aesthetic fragmentation of modern civilisation that other reviewers felt it to be expressing. As Louis Untermeyer wrote in a review that reflects some of Lovecraft's own concerns about the work:

> As an echo of contemporary despair, as a picture of dissolution, of the breaking down of the very structures on which life has modelled itself, "The Waste Land" has a definite authenticity. But even the process of disintegration must be held within a pattern. This pattern is distorted and broken by Mr. Eliot's jumble of narratives, nursery-rhymes, criticism, jazz-rhythms, Dictionary of Favorite Phrases and a few lyrical moments.[80]

Eliot rejected this interpretation of the poem, but there were clearly many who read it as such.

I think too much has been made of the supposed similarities in philosophy and temperament of Eliot and Lovecraft: to be sure, they may both have been classicists (of a sort) and believed in continuity of culture; but Lovecraft rightly scorned Eliot's later royalism as a mere ostrich-act and heaped even more abuse on Eliot's belief in religion as a necessary foundation or bulwark of civilisation.

Lovecraft's immediate response to Eliot, and the modernists in general, was interesting:

> . . . I have a high respect for these moderns as *philosophers and intellectuals,* however much I may dismiss and disregard them *as poets.* T. S. Eliot himself is an acute *thinker*—but I do not believe he is an *artist.* An artist must always be a child . . . and live in dreams and wonder and moonlight. He must think of the lives and colours of things—of life itself—and never stop to pick the glittering fabric to pieces. Alas! Who ever caught and dissected the sunset gold without losing it?[81]

What this comment—and an analogous one in his *Conservative* editorial ("It is, for example, hardly possible that moonlight on a marble temple, or twilight in an old garden in spring, can ever be other than beautiful in our eyes")—indicates is Lovecraft's continued adherence to Poe's beauty/truth distinction (beauty is the province of art, truth is the province of science) as filtered through *fin de siècle* Decadence, notably Wilde's immortal first line from the preface to *The Picture of Dorian Gray:* "The artist is the creator of beautiful things." Lovecraft, indeed, never quite gave up on this belief, but he later refined it in such a way as still to convict the modernists of writing applied science, not literature.

But Lovecraft's other response to *The Waste Land*—the exquisite parody "Waste Paper: A Poem of Profound Insignificance"—merits much greater attention; for this is his best satiric poem. One wishes, therefore, that there was even the least bit of evidence as to when this poem was written and when it appeared in "the newspaper," as Lovecraft casually noted a decade later.[82] This is the only occasion, so far as is known, that Lovecraft even mentions his poem; searches have been made in at least some of the Providence papers of the period—*Evening Bulletin, Evening Tribune, Evening News*—with no results. One would very much like to know what if any reaction the poem—signed "Humphry Littlewit, Jun." on the manuscript—engendered among readers. It is, of course, unlikely that the printed version ever came to the attention of Eliot himself.

What Lovecraft very simply seeks to do in this work is to carry to a *reductio ad absurdum* his own claim in the *Conservative* editorial as to *The Waste Land* being a "practically meaningless collection of phrases, learned allusions, quotations, slang, and scraps in general." In many parts of this quite lengthy poem (135 lines) he has faithfully parodied the insularity of modern poetry—its ability to be understood only by a small coterie of readers who are aware of intimate facts about the poet—

> I used to sit on the stairs of the house where I was born
> After we left it but before it was sold
> And play on a zobo with two other boys.
> We called ourselves the Blackstone Military Band

There follow references to the popular songs of the turn of the century ("And the whippoorwill sings, Marguerite"), citations of his own earlier poetry ("Thro' the ghoul-guarded gateways of slumber"), quotations of other poets ("Achilles' wrath, to Greece the direful spring"—the first line of Pope's translation of the *Iliad*), various experiments in stream-of-consciousness or free-association, slang ("No, lady, you gotta change at Washington St. to the Everett train"), and on and on and on. The ending can only be quoted:

> Henry Fielding wrote *Tom Jones.*
> And cursed be he that moves my bones.
> Good night, good night, the stars are bright
> I saw the Leonard-Tendler fight
> Farewell, farewell, O go to hell.
> Nobody home
> In the shantih.

That delightful final pun "confirms the jerrybuilt quality of modern life and art," as Barton L. St Armand and John H. Stanley remark; and as for the poem as a whole, its "scraps of twentieth-century conversations, news bulletins, public announcements, newspaper headlines, and advertising jingles reflect the mundane tawdriness of the present as contrasted to the epic grandeur of the past."[83]

Lovecraft was, of course, by no means alone in being disturbed, even traumatised, by *The Waste Land* and its analogues; but he gradually came to terms with modernism, although by no means sympathising with it. He would simply pursue his own way—not lapsing back into stilted Victorianism but not throwing tradition entirely out the window as he believed the modernists were doing. His final answer to the issue can be found in a letter of 1927, when he cites Ben Hecht's *Erik Dorn* (a novel, published in 1921, whose mingling of Freudianism, Expressionism, and stream-of-consciousness with gritty realism and a fair amount of bawdiness was believed at the time to be a herald of the "new" literature) and *The Waste Land* as the high points of modernism and evaluates them and their congeners:

> The keynote of the modern doctrine is the dissociation of ideas and the resolving of our cerebral contents into its actual chaotic components, as distinguished from the conventional patterns visible on the outside. This is supposed to form a closer approach to reality, but I cannot see that it forms any sort of art at all. It may be good science—but art deals with beauty rather than fact, and must have the liberty to select and arrange according to traditional patterns which generations of belief and reverence have marked with the seal of empirical loveliness. Beyond or behind this seeming beauty lies only chaos and weariness . . .[84]

Here again the beauty/truth distinction is brought into play, along with the notion of art as a "selection" rather than as a literal transcript of phenomena. But the remark is full of paradoxes: if Lovecraft's much-vaunted science (especially the science of psychology) has so "greatly altered our view of the universe and the beliefs attendant upon that view" (as he says in his March 1923 *Conservative* editorial), how can the artist continue to "select and arrange according to traditional patterns"? Lovecraft is desperately attempting to maintain that certain forms of "empirical loveliness" (whatever that may be) continue to be valid no matter how much we know about the universe and about the workings of our own minds. He is really trying to have his cake and eat it too—he is trying to be modern scientifically, but conservative aesthetically. We shall see this as a problem in his later ethics as well. For the present, however, he could only regard Eliot and his colleagues with horror and contempt.

But what of Lovecraft's assertion, in "The Omnipresent Philistine" (*Oracle*, May 1924), that both *Ulysses* and James Branch Cabell's *Jurgen* are "significant contributions to contemporary art," especially given his earlier scorn of the sexual daring of these works in his letter to Long? In the first place, it should be noted that Lovecraft never actually read *Ulysses*—at least, not all of it. In a late letter he admitted: "I have not read *Ulysses,* because such extracts as I have seen convince me that it would hardly be worth the time & energy."[85] The reference to "extracts" may imply that Lovecraft saw some segments of the partial serialisation of Joyce's novel in the *Little Magazine* (March 1918–December 1920). But, more pertinently, the context of Lovecraft's remark in "The Omnipresent Philistine" must be examined with care. This article itself was part of yet another minor contretemps, this time between Lovecraft and Sonia Greene on one side and Paul Livingston Keil (the young man who had accompanied Lovecraft, Morton, and Long to the Poe cottage in 1922) on the other.

The source of this dispute was a brief unsigned piece in the May 1922 *Rainbow* entitled "Opinion." Although it is customary to regard unsigned articles in amateur journals as the work of the editor, my feeling is that Lovecraft at least contributed to this item, if not writing it entirely. It notes that several amateurs had remarked unfavourably on the philosophical views expressed in the first *Rainbow* (probably referring specifically to the Nietzschean sentiments of Lovecraft and Galpin), to which it responds that diversity of opinion is of value in expanding one's horizons and, moreover, that "philosophical opinion has nothing to do with aesthetic quality." Keil, in his journal *Pauke's Quill,* had attacked this view, declaring that a critic must always consider a writer's philosophical orientation when evaluating his or her work (a plausible view, although one that can lead to great mischief when used improperly) and going on to recommend a fairly broad censorship against "pornography" and other examples of literature that may present a "false" philosophical viewpoint. Sonia shot back with "Fact versus Opinion," in the *Oracle* for May 1924, maintaining that critics must consider only the manner, not the matter, of an artistic product (a debatable assertion, but one that might be effective against those who object to "unhealthy" philosophies of life embodied in literature) and saying that the distinction of what is true or false philosophically is not quite as easy as Keil seems to have believed. Lovecraft's response, in the same issue of the *Oracle,* went on in much the same way; and it is precisely because both *Ulysses* and *Jurgen* had been or were at that time the subject of such censorship (*Jurgen* had been seized by the New York Society for the Prevention of Vice in 1920, and the obscenity trial over it had ended in 1922 in an acquittal; *Ulysses* would remain banned in the United States until 1933) that Lovecraft felt the need to come to their defence. He took the standard, and sensible, liberal line against pornography:

> Not many of us, even in this age, have any marked leaning toward public pornography; so that we would generally welcome any agency calculated to banish offences against good taste. But when we come to reflect on the problem of enforcement, and perceive how absurdly any censorship places us in the hands of dogmatic and arbitrary officials with Puritan illusions and no true knowledge of life or

> literary values, we have to acknowledge that absolute liberty is the lesser evil. The literature of today, with its conscientious striving toward sincerity, must necessarily contain large amounts of matter repugnant to those who hold the hypocritical nineteenth-century view of the world. It need not be vulgarly presented, but it cannot be excluded if art is to express life.

Lovecraft's reserved approach to Modernism might perhaps be thought to have been vindicated by time. To what degree, really, does modernist prose continue to be the guiding light of contemporary writing? While Lovecraft would probably have had even less sympathy with certain aspects of postmodernism, conventional narrative made a quick recovery after World War II; very few writers use stream-of-consciousness much anymore. And as for poetry, it is not the chaoticism of Eliot that has dominated subsequent work but the slack, loose, colloquial, and utterly prosaic idiom of William Carlos Williams and his followers, to the point that one wonders whether there has been any genuine poetry written at all after the death of Frost, Auden, and Robert Lowell. The fact that contemporary poetry has dropped utterly out of the intellectual lives of even well-educated people may suggest that Lovecraft's warnings against too radical a departure from tradition may not have been entirely unsound.

Meanwhile Lovecraft had simultaneously been hammering out a theory of the weird tale that would, with some modifications, serve him his entire life. This theory is, like his aesthetics in general, an intimate outgrowth of his entire philosophical thought, especially his metaphysics and ethics. The central document here is the *In Defence of Dagon* essays. He begins by dividing fiction, in a somewhat unorthodox manner, into three divisions—romantic, realistic, and imaginative. The first "is for those who value action and emotion for their own sake; who are interested in striking events which conform to a preconceived artificial pattern." The second "is for those who are intellectual and analytical rather than poetical or emotional. . . . It has the virtue of being close to life, but has the disadvantage of sinking into the commonplace and the unpleasant at times." Lovecraft does not provide an explicit definition of imaginative fiction, but implies that it draws upon the best features of both the other two: like romanticism, imaginative fiction bases its appeal on emotions (the emotions of fear, wonder, and terror); from realism it derives the important principle of truth—not truth to fact, as in realism, but truth to human feeling. As a result, Lovecraft comes up with the startling deduction that "The imaginative writer devotes himself to art in its most essential sense."

The attack on what Lovecraft called "romanticism" is one he never relinquished. The term must not be understood here in any historical sense—Lovecraft had great respect and fondness for such Romantic poets as Shelley, Keats, and Coleridge—but purely theoretically, as embodying an approach not only to literature but to life generally:

> The *one* form of literary appeal which I consider *absolutely unsound, charlatanic, and valueless*—frivolous, insincere, irrelevant, and meaningless—is that mode of handling human events and values and motivations known as *romanticism.* Dumas, Scott, Stevenson—my gawd! Here is sheer puerility—the concoction of false glamours and enthusiasms and events out of an addled and distorted background which has no relation to anything in the genuine thoughts, feelings, and experiences of evolved and adult mankind.[86]

This remark, although made in 1930, makes clear that his enemy here is his whipping-boy of 1923, Victorianism. It was this approach—the instilling of "glamour" or significance into certain phases of human activity (notably love)—that Lovecraft believed to be most invalidated by the findings of modern science. And yet, his vehemence on this issue may stem from another cause as well: the possibility that his very different brand of weird fiction might conceivably be confused with (or be considered an aspect of) romanticism. Lovecraft knew that the weird tale had emerged in the course of the Romantic movement of the late eighteenth and early nineteenth centuries, so that, in the eyes of many, weird fiction itself was a phase of Romanticism and might be thought to have "no relation to anything in the genuine thoughts, feelings, and experiences of evolved and adult mankind."

Accordingly, Lovecraft always strove to associate weird fiction with realism, which he knew to be the dominant mode of contemporary expression. This realism extended not merely to technique—"a tale should be plausible—even a bizarre tale *except for the single element where supernaturalism is involved,*" he says in a letter of 1921[87]—but in terms of philosophical orientation. Of course, it cannot be realistic in terms of *events,* so it must be realistic in terms of *human emotions.* Lovecraft again contrasts romanticism (an "overcoloured representation of *what purports to be real life*") with fantasy: "But fantasy is something altogether different. Here we have an art based on the imaginative life of the human mind, *frankly recognised as such;* and in its way as natural and scientific—as truly related to natural (even if uncommon and delicate) psychological processes as the starkest of photographic realism."[88]

In defending himself, and his writing, from charges of "unwholesomeness" and immorality (charges still made today against weird fiction), Lovecraft stated that the weird, the fantastic, and even the horrible were as deserving of artistic treatment as the wholesome and the ordinary. No realm of human existence can be denied to the artist; everything depends upon the treatment, not the subject-matter. Lovecraft cited Wilde's pretty paradox (from "The Soul of Man under Socialism") that

> a healthy work of art is one the choice of whose subject is conditioned by the temperament of the artist, and comes directly out of it. . . . An unhealthy work of art, on the other hand, is a work . . . whose subject is deliberately chosen, not because

> the artist has any pleasure in it, but because he thinks that the public will pay him for it. In fact, the popular novel that the public calls healthy is always a thoroughly unhealthy production; and what the public calls an unhealthy novel is always a beautiful and healthy work of art.

In this way Lovecraft neatly justified his unusual subject-matter while simultaneously condemning the popular best-seller as a product of insincere hackwork. (He would use the same argument later for pulp fiction.) And yet, because Lovecraft realised that weird fiction was necessarily a cultivated taste, he was compelled to note repeatedly that he wrote only for the "sensitive"—the select few whose imaginations are sufficiently liberated from the minutiae of daily life to appreciate images, moods, and incidents that do not exist in the world as we know and experience it. Lovecraft stated in *In Defence of Dagon* that "There are probably seven persons, in all, who really like my work; and they are enough. I should write even if I were the only patient reader, for my aim is merely self-expression." This comes dangerously close to the sort of coterie-literature Lovecraft condemned in the modernists; although he would no doubt reply that the limited appeal or understanding of his work is based upon its unusual subject-matter, not its deliberate obscurity.

When asked by A. H. Brown, a Canadian member of the Transatlantic Circulator, why he didn't write more about "ordinary people," since this might increase the audience for his work, Lovecraft replied with towering scorn:

> I could not write about "ordinary people" because I am not in the least interested in them. Without interest there can be no art. Man's relations to man do not captivate my fancy. It is man's relation to the cosmos—to the unknown—which alone arouses in me the spark of creative imagination. The humanocentric pose is impossible to me, for I cannot acquire the primitive myopia which magnifies the earth and ignores the background.

This is Lovecraft's first *explicit* expression of the view he would later call "cosmicism." Cosmicism is at once a metaphysical position (an awareness of the vastness of the universe in both space and time), an ethical position (an awareness of the insignificance of human beings within the realm of the universe), and an aesthetic position (a literary expression of this insignificance, to be effected by the minimising of human character and the display of the titanic gulfs of space and time). The strange thing about it is that it was so late in being articulated, and also that it was so feebly exhibited in his weird fiction up to this time—indeed, really up to 1926. If Lovecraft is to be believed, cosmicism as a metaphysical and ethical position was initially inspired by his study of astronomy beginning in 1902 and was already established by his late teenage years. In terms of his fiction, "Dagon" (1917) and "Beyond the Wall of Sleep" (1919) only hint at cosmicism; and I have already noted that Lovecraft's fascination with Dunsany (of whom he extravagantly wrote in "Supernatural Horror in Literature": "His point of view is the most truly cosmic of any held in the literature of any period") did not seem to extend to the point of duplicating his cosmicism in his own "Dunsanian" tales.

One interesting development in Lovecraft's pure metaphysics occurred in May of 1923:

> I have no opinions—I believe in nothing . . . My cynicism and scepticism are increasing, and from an entirely new cause—the Einstein theory. The latest eclipse observations seem to place this system among the facts which cannot be dismissed, and assumedly it removes the last hold which reality or the universe can have on the independent mind. All is chance, accident, and ephemeral illusion—a fly may be greater than Arcturus, and Durfee Hill may surpass Mount Everest—assuming them to be removed from the present planet and differently environed in the continuum of space-time. There are no values in all infinity—the least idea that there are is the supreme mockery of all. All the cosmos is a jest, and fit to be treated only as a jest, and one thing is as true as another.[89]

The history of the acceptance of the theory of relativity would make an interesting study in itself. The theory was propounded by Einstein in 1905 but was the source of much scepticism on the part of philosophers and scientists; some merely ignored it, perhaps hoping it would go away. Lovecraft's mentor Hugh Elliot dismisses Einstein in a nervous footnote in *Modern Science and Materialism.* In early 1920 the matter was taken up by the Gallomo; Lovecraft's discussion (the only part that survives) begins:

> Next on the programme is the Einstein theory, which I must confess at the outset that I cannot discuss authoritatively. I have as yet seen no really coherent account, and many of the articles by professors in local papers admit freely imperfect comprehension on the part of the respective writers. Einstein himself says that only twelve living men can fully comprehend his theory.[90]

And so on for several more pages of windy and contentless verbiage. At least this indicates that Lovecraft was seeking to learn more about the matter, if only from the local paper.

The theory indeed remained largely deductive until the spring of 1923, when the results of observations of a total solar eclipse on September 21, 1922, were finally reported. The *New York Times* had a front-page article on April 12, 1923, entitled "Sun Eclipse Pictures Prove Einstein Theory" by W. W. Campbell, Director of the Lick Observatory, who declared: "The agreement [of the eclipse observations] with Einstein's prediction from the theory of relativity . . . is as close as the most ardent proponent of that theory could hope for."[91]

The curious thing about all this as far as Lovecraft is concerned is that Einstein is unquestionably alluded to in the story "Hypnos," written around March 1922. There the narrator states: "One man with Oriental eyes has said that all time and space are relative, and men have laughed. But even that man with Oriental eyes has done no more than suspect." I do not know if Lovecraft read any of the popular accounts of the Einstein theory that had emerged since 1905; but clearly the idea was beginning to gain currency, or at least to be talked about extensively. The mention here that Einstein "has done no more than suspect" clearly refers to the failure of definitive proof of the relativity theory to have emerged at this time; a year later that proof was manifestly at hand.

It is hardly worth remarking that Lovecraft's wild conclusions from Einstein, both metaphysical and ethical, are entirely unfounded; but his reaction is perhaps not atypical of that of many intellectuals—especially those who could not understand the precise details and ramifications of relativity—at the time. We will see that Lovecraft fairly quickly snapped out of his naive views about Einstein and, by no later than 1929, actually welcomed him as another means to bolster a modified materialism that still outlawed teleology, monotheism, spirituality, and other tenets he rightly believed to be outmoded in light of nineteenth-century science. In so doing he evolved a metaphysical and ethical system not at all dissimilar to that of his two later philosophical mentors, Bertrand Russell and George Santayana.

Some words about Lovecraft's political views might be in order. American entry into the world war had relieved him of the burden of fulminating against the "craven pacifism" of Woodrow Wilson, to the point that he could even poke fun at his own position in "Herbert West—Reanimator" (West "secretly sneered at my occasional martial enthusiasms and censures of supine neutrality"). In "A Confession of Unfaith" (1922) he states that "a German defeat was all I asked or hoped for." Later he made the cryptic comment that "The Peace Conference" and other forces "have perfected my cynicism": he did not elaborate upon this remark, and I do not know its precise import. I find no mentions in letters or essays that the harsh penalties imposed upon Germany by the Allies were unjust: Lovecraft later did indeed come to this opinion, although he came to regard it more as a tactical error than a matter of abstract ethics.

I have no doubt that Lovecraft voted for the Republican Warren G. Harding in the fall of 1920, if indeed he voted at all. I find no mention of Harding or of the repeated scandals that disgraced his administration, but Lovecraft did take note of Harding's sudden death of pneumonia on August 2, 1923. In "The Rats in the Walls," written probably a few weeks after this event, he interrupts the narrative oddly by remarking that "I felt poised on the brink of frightful revelations, a sensation symbolised by the air of mourning among the many Americans at the unexpected death of the President on the other side of the world." In a letter, remarking on a Harding stamp, he is a trifle more cynical: "Harding was a handsome bimbo—

I'm sure sorry he had the good luck to get clear of this beastly planet."[92] Of his successor Calvin Coolidge I find almost no mentions at all for the next five years.

What Lovecraft did instead in the relative political tranquillity of a Republican-dominated decade was to reflect more abstractly on the issues of government. "Nietzscheism and Realism," which we have already seen to be a compilation of letter excerpts to Sonia, contains a lot of cocksure aphorisms on the subject, largely derived from Nietzsche but with a sort of Schopenhauerian foundation. It does not begin auspiciously: "There is no such thing—and there never will be such a thing—as good and permanent government among the crawling, miserable vermin called human beings." Nevertheless, "Aristocracy and monarchy are the most efficient in developing the best qualities of mankind as expressed in achievements of taste and intellect . . ."

This view would, with much refinement, become the pillar of Lovecraft's later political theory. It is expressed here very compactly: "I believe in an aristocracy, because I deem it the only agency for the creation of those refinements which make life endurable for the human animal of high organisation." Lovecraft naturally assumed (correctly) that he was one of those animals of high organisation, and it was entirely logical for him, when speaking abstractly of the ideal government, to look for one that would suit his own requirements. What he seems to imagine is a society like that of Periclean Athens, Augustan Rome, or Augustan England, where the aristocracy both symbolised refinement and culture (if they did not always practise it) and provided enough patronage of artists to produce those "ornaments of life" that result in a rich and thriving civilisation. It is, certainly—at least in the abstract—an appealing system, but Lovecraft surely did not fancy that it could have much relevance to present-day concerns.

When he does address such concerns, it is in tones of magisterial condemnation. Democracy earns his wholesale scorn:

> Aristocracy alone is capable of creating thoughts and objects of value. Everyone, I fancy, will admit that such a state must precede democracy or ochlocracy in order to build the original culture. Fewer are willing to admit the cognate truth that democracies and ochlocracies merely subsist parasitically on the aristocracies they overthrow, gradually using up the aesthetic and intellectual resources which autocracy bequeathed them and which they never could have created for themselves.

And in a letter of February 1923: "democracy . . . is a false idol—a mere catchword and illusion of inferior classes, visionaries, and dying civilisations."[93] This is manifestly Nietzschean: "I have . . . characterised modern democracy . . . as the *decaying form* of the state."[94] I do not know that Lovecraft ever espoused democracy, but certainly his reading of Nietzsche just after the war seems to have given him the intellectual backbone to support his view.

The letter in which the above comment is imbedded occurs in a discussion of Mussolini and fascism. There should be scarcely any surprise that Lovecraft supported Mussolini's takeover of Italy (completed in late October 1922) and that he was attracted by the fascist ideology—or, at any rate, what he took it to be. I doubt that Lovecraft had any real understanding of the internal political forces that led to Mussolini's rise. Fascism was, at its base, opposed both to conventional liberalism and to socialism; its popularity grew rapidly after the end of the war when the socialists, winning a majority in 1919, could accomplish little to restore Italian society. Mussolini's takeover of the government was indeed supported, as Lovecraft would later remark, by a majority of the Italian populace; but each of the various groups supporting the dictatorship wished different benefits from it, and when after several years these benefits were not forthcoming, there was so much discontent that repressive measures had to be adopted.

For the time being, however, Lovecraft could revel in the fact that here was a "strong" ruler who scorned liberalism and could "get the sort of authoritative social and political control which alone produces things which make life worth living."[95] It cannot, certainly, be said that fascism produced any sort of artistic renaissance; but that was not of much concern to Lovecraft at the moment.

Lovecraft's political views were still very ill-considered, but at least he was beginning to think about broader issues than merely the reunification of England and America, the "crime" of Anglo-Saxons fighting each other in the Great War, and the evils of pacifism. It would be another five to seven years before he did any serious thinking about politics, economics, and society; but when he did so his thought showed a maturity born of actual experience in the world and deeper reflexion on the complex issues involved. In the short term, however, matters of a more personal nature were more pressing.

The end of 1923 saw still more small travels. On November 27 Lovecraft and his aunt Lillian went to the new private museum of George L. Shepley at 292 Benefit Street, where Annie Gamwell worked. (The museum is no longer in existence.) The next day he and C. M. Eddy visited various parts of Providence, especially south of the Great Bridge, that he had not seen before.[96] On December 27, Lovecraft gave Eddy and the visiting James F. Morton a tour of colonial Providence; it was on this occasion that the three of them went to the exquisite First Baptist Church (1775) on North Main Street and ascended to the organ loft, where Lovecraft attempted to play "Yes, We Have No Bananas" but was foiled, "since the machine is not a self-starter."[97]

In early February Lovecraft wrote a long letter to Edwin Baird of *Weird Tales,* expressing his irritation at the alteration of the titles of some of his stories, notably the retitling of "Arthur Jermyn" to "The White Ape" ("you may be sure that if I ever entitled a story 'The White Ape', *there would be no ape in it*'"[98]). In response to J. C. Henneberger's request for information on his life and beliefs, Lovecraft unearthed "A Confession of Unfaith" and copied much of it verbatim, prefaced by a somewhat smart-alecky biographical sketch. (Toward the end of his life, when the teenage Willis Conover somehow acquired this letter and wished to publish it, Lovecraft found the document so embarrassing that he threatened physical harm to Conover if he disseminated it.) *Weird Tales* was throwing a lot of work in his direction, in particular a rush ghostwriting job for Harry Houdini. Lovecraft also claimed to be working on a novel called "The House of the Worm," an idea that had apparently been percolating in his mind for a year or more, but about which we know nothing; it was probably never begun. But in the midst of all this literary activity we find an anomalous change of personal circumstances. On March 9, 1924, Lovecraft wrote a letter to his aunt Lillian from 259 Parkside Avenue, Brooklyn, New York. Was this another visit of longer or shorter duration, as the two New York trips of 1922 had been? Not exactly.

On March 3, at St Paul's Chapel at Broadway and Vesey Streets in lower Manhattan, H. P. Lovecraft had married Sonia Haft Greene.

15. BALL AND CHAIN (1924)

New York in 1924 was an extraordinary place. Far and away the largest city in the country, its five boroughs totalled (in 1926) 5,924,138 in population, of which Manhattan had 1,752,018 and Brooklyn (then and now the largest of the boroughs both in size and in population) had 2,308,631. A remarkable 1,700,000 were of Jewish origin, while the nearly 250,000 African Americans were already concentrating in Harlem (extending from 125th to 151st Streets on the west side and 96th Street northward on the east side of Manhattan) because of the severe prejudice that prevented their occupying many other areas of the city. The subway system, begun in 1904, was allowing easy access to many regions of the metropolis, and was supplemented by the extensive above-ground or elevated lines, now nearly all eliminated. Lovecraft, on some of his more remote jaunts around the area in search of antiquarian oases, nevertheless found it necessary to take the more expensive trolleys rather than the 5¢ subways or elevateds. The Hudson Tubes (now called the PATH trains) were constructed in 1908–10 to link Manhattan with the commuter terminals in Hoboken and Jersey City, New Jersey; ferry service was also common between the two states. The remoter areas of the region—say, Long Island or Westchester County to the north of the Bronx—were less easy of access, although the N.Y.N.H.&H. (New York, New Haven, and Hartford) railway lines brought in commuters from Connecticut to Grand Central Station. The mayor of the city was John F. Hylan, a Tammany politician; but he was ousted in 1925 and a "New Tammany" mayor, James J. Walker, was elected in 1926. The governor was the Democrat Alfred E. Smith (1923–28).

These facts and figures, of course, can convey only so much. Although neither the Empire State Building nor the Chrysler Building was as yet built, New York was already the city of skyscrapers, most of them at this time concentrated at the very southern tip of Manhattan, the Battery. (Skyscrapers cannot be built everywhere in Manhattan, since the schist foundation is not uniform; there are strict regulations governing the height and size of buildings in every portion of the island.) Lovecraft's first impression of the city in April 1922 is perhaps only a little more poeticised than that of most of those who come upon this almost unearthly sight:

> Out of the waters it rose at twilight; cold, proud, and beautiful; an Eastern city of wonder whose brothers the mountains are. It was not like any city of earth, for above purple mists rose towers, spires, and pyramids which one may only dream of in opiate lands beyond the Oxus; towers, spires and pyramids that no man could fashion, but that bloomed flower-like and delicate; the bridges up which fairies

> walk to the sky; the visions of giants that play with the clouds. Only Dunsany could fashion its equal, and he in dreams only.[1]

The reference to Dunsany is telling, for this passage, though no doubt sincere in its way, is a clear echo of Dunsany's "A City of Wonder" (in *Tales of Three Hemispheres,* 1919), a brief prose-poem in which he tells of his own first sight of New York ("One by one the windows shine from the precipices; some twinkle, some are dark; man's orderly schemes have gone, and we are amongst vast heights lit by inscrutable beacons"[2]).

Is it a surprise that Lovecraft the antiquarian found the skyline of New York stimulating? Hardly. He would later assert that the skyscraper was not a fundamentally modern form: "tall buildings hav[e] been common in mediaeval Italy, while Gothic towers approximate the same atmosphere. . . . A skyscraper (following Gothic lines or employing classical ornament) can be traditional, while a one-story building (abjuring traditional ornamentation & proportion) can be modernistic."[3] Lovecraft was well aware that historicist architecture—fostered in late nineteenth-century New York by such architects as Charles F. McKim, William Rutherford Mead, and Stanford White—had produced such landmarks as Pennsylvania Station (1903–10), modelled after the Baths of Caracalla, and other structures that satisfied his classical leanings.

It is difficult to convey in capsule form any impression of the vast metropolis, which then as now is as diverse as any place on the globe. The city's character can change in a single block, and the whole region defies neat generalisation. When we speak of Harlem or Hell's Kitchen or Greenwich Village, we are in danger of letting stereotypes take the place of realities. Lovecraft discovered the city gradually over two years of peregrinations, but his heart was in those surprisingly numerous pockets of antiquity (many now sadly obliterated) that still remained even in the heart of Manhattan. Some of the outer boroughs also preserved such pockets, and Lovecraft sought them out with the zeal of desperation. The Flatbush section of Brooklyn where he and Sonia settled was then on the outskirts of the borough, and was then (as it is not now) the residence of choice for the well-to-do in the area. It was not Providence, but neither was it a wholly inferior substitute.

There is no question that, at least for the first few months, the euphoria both of his marriage and of his residence in the nation's centre of publishing, finance, art, and general culture helped to ward off any doubts about the precipitancy of his departure from Providence. With a new wife, many friends, and even reasonably good job prospects Lovecraft had reason to believe that a promising new phase of his life was beginning.

In his 1975 memoir, Frank Belknap Long writes of first meeting Lovecraft in Sonia's apartment in April 1922. After a time, as he sat talking with the two of them, something began to dawn upon him:

> It was at this point that something which at first had been a mere suspicion began to lodge itself more firmly in my mind. During the brief talk by the window Howard had dwelt at some length on Sonia's meeting with his aunts and on two other occasions when they had spent considerable time together on New England terrain, with the Boston convention several weeks in the past.
>
> Could it be possible—
>
> It *was* possible, of course . . . his relationship with Sonia had taken on what could only be thought of as a just-short-of-engagement character. It still was only at the friendship stage perhaps, but with the distinct possibility that it might soon become something more.[4]

Long may perhaps be guilty of reading, in hindsight, more into this episode than is warranted; but he was probably not alone in sensing—at this time and on other occasions—that some sort of rapport was developing between Sonia and Lovecraft. And yet, the fact of their marriage seems to have produced, among their friends and associates, reactions ranging from surprise to shock to alarm. Rheinhart Kleiner writes: ". . . I do remember very well that it was while riding in a taxi with Mr. and Mrs. Houtain . . . that the news of the Lovecraft-Greene marriage was imparted to me. At once, I had a feeling of faintness at the pit of my stomach and became very pale. Houtain laughed uproariously at the effect of his announcement, but agreed that he felt as I did."[5] Even such recent friends as the Eddys were stunned: "The next news we had of Lovecraft was an engraved announcement of his marriage to Sonia Greene. It was a simple announcement, but it took us so completely by surprise that it was several hours before we thoroughly digested the news."[6] This engraved announcement, incidentally, was sent out shortly after the marriage; Lovecraft and Sonia spent $62 printing 200 copies of it.[7] It reads simply:

Howard Phillips Lovecraft
and
Sonia Haft Greene
announce their marriage
on
Monday the third of March
One thousand nine hundred and twenty-four.

Mr. and Mrs. Howard Phillips Lovecraft
At Home on and after March thirtieth, 1924
259 Parkside Avenue
Brooklyn, New York.

It is, indeed, telling that, on Lovecraft's last night in Providence, he visited the Eddys, saying he was leaving and offering them some furniture that he would not have use for, but never mentioning the marriage at this time.

This silence was duplicated by one of the most remarkable letters ever written by Lovecraft: the letter to his aunt Lillian announcing his marriage—*six days after the fact.* It is manifestly obvious that he simply boarded the 11.09 train on Sunday morning, March 2, married Sonia the next day, began settling in at 259 Parkside, and finally decided to spill the news to his elder aunt. Indeed, Lovecraft sent Lillian several postcards on March 4 and 5 from both New York and Philadelphia (where the couple honeymooned), but without any indication whatever of the true state of affairs. One such card, however, must have caused Lillian some wonderment, as Lovecraft speaks of a *"permanent literary position"* in New York that may fall in his lap.[8]

Some parts of the laborious preamble to the actual announcement in this letter are astounding:

> [A] more active life, to one of my temperament, demands many things which I could dispense with when drifting sleepily and inertly along, shunning a world which exhausted and disgusted me, and having no goal but a phial of cyanide when my money should give out. I had formerly meant to follow the latter course, and was fully prepared to seek oblivion whenever cash should fail or sheer ennui grow too much for me; when suddenly, nearly three years ago, our benevolent angel S. H. G. stepped into my circle of consciousness and began to combat that idea with the opposite one of effort and the enjoyment of life through the rewards which effort will bring.

Well, perhaps marriage and a move to the big city is better than suicide from poverty or boredom. But what about the critical issue of the pair's affection for each other?

> . . . meanwhile—egotistical as it sounds to relate it—it began to be apparent that I was not alone in finding psychological solitude more or less of a handicap. A detailed intellectual and aesthetic acquaintance since 1921, and a three-months visit in 1922 wherein congeniality was tested and found perfect in an infinity of ways, furnished abundant proof not only that S. H. G. is the most inspiriting and encouraging influence which could possibly be brought to bear on me, but that she herself had begun to find me more congenial than anyone else, and had come to depend to a great extent on my correspondence and conversation for mental contentment and artistic and philosophical enjoyment.

This is, certainly, one of the most glaring examples of Lovecraft's inability to speak of "love" or anything remotely connected to it. He does not say: "I love Sonia and Sonia loves me"; he says that he and she need each other for "mental contentment and artistic and philosophical enjoyment." Lovecraft's natural reserve in speaking of such matters to his aunt should certainly be taken into account; but we will also have to deal later with Sonia's own admission that Lovecraft never said the word "love" to *her.* In any event, he continues to explain why neither Lillian nor Annie were taken into the couple's confidence in the whole matter:

> At this point . . . you will no doubt ask why I did not mention this entire matter before. S. H. G. herself was anxious to do so, and if possible to have both you and A. E. P. G. present at the event about to be described. But here again appeared Old Theobald's hatred of sentimental spoofing, and of that agonisingly indecisive "talking over" which radical steps always prompt among mortals, yet which really exceeds the fullest necessary quota of sober and analytical appraisal and debate. . . . It hardly seemed to me that, in view of my well-known temperament, anyone could feel even slightly hurt by a decisive and dramatic gesture sweeping away the barnacles of timidity and of blindly reactionary holding-back.[9]

There can scarcely be any clearer indication of Lovecraft's fear—perhaps well founded—that his aunts would not approve of his marriage, although since he was thirty-three years old there was certainly nothing they could have done about it. The aunts' disapproval, as well as the possible reasons for it (was it because Sonia was not a New England Yankee? because she was a foreign-born businesswoman rather a member of the informal American aristocracy? because the marriage would mean Lovecraft's departure from home?), are all conjecture, for in the total absence of written documents by their hands, and even the lack of testimony by others on their attitude to Sonia, conjecture is all we have to go on. But that the aunts did in fact disapprove—or, at any rate, that Lovecraft thought they might—may become clearer as the course of the marriage unfolds.

What were Sonia's feelings on the whole matter? In speaking of the year or two prior to their marriage, she writes: "I well knew that he was not in a position to marry, yet his letters indicated his desire to leave his home town and settle in New York."[10] The first part of the statement presumably refers merely to financial capability; as for the second, although of course we do not have access to Lovecraft's letters to Sonia, I have to believe that this is somewhat of an exaggeration. The only indication of Lovecraft's wish to come to New York that I find in letters to other individuals is a mention to Clark Ashton Smith just five weeks before the marriage: "Like you, I don't know anyone who is at all congenial here; & I believe I shall migrate to New York in the end—perhaps when Loveman does."[11] My feeling is that this indicates Lovecraft had already resolved upon marriage by this time, and that he was simply disguising the fact from Smith; there is nothing particularly surprising about this, as Smith was a colleague of only a year and half's standing and one cannot expect someone like Lovecraft to reveal his personal life to him. His letter to Edwin Baird of February 3, exactly one month before the marriage, hints at the same thing (although for different reasons), when he notes that "finances will decree a final disintegration [i.e., of his Providence household] landing me in all probability in New York."[12] Financial considerations certainly were a factor in the marriage. It would, of course, be crass and quite unjust to Lovecraft to say that he married Sonia even in part because of her income; indeed, we may shortly discover that, in spite of her seeming prosperity, Sonia herself was not in very healthy financial shape herself at this juncture.

Sonia continues:

> We each meditated and remeditated upon the possibilities of a life together. Some of our friends suspected that we cared for one another, and upon friendly inquiry I admitted that I cared very much, that I took everything into consideration and decided that if he would have me I'd gladly be his wife. But nothing definitely had been said to any one. . . .
>
> During our few years of correspondence and the many business trips I took to New England I did not fail to mention many of the adverse circumstances that were likely to ensue, but that we would have to work out these problems between us, and if we really cared more for one another than for the problems that might stand in our way, there was no reason why our marriage should not be a success. He thoroughly agreed. . . .
>
> Before leaving Providence for N.Y. I requested him to tell his aunts that he was going to marry me but he said he preferred to surprise them. In the matter of securing the marriage license, buying the ring and other details incumbent upon a marriage, he seemed to be so jovial. He said one would think that he was being married for the nth time, he went about it in such a methodical way.[13]

This is all Sonia has to say on the matter. What she does not say is that she had written to Lillian a full month *before* the marriage, and in a manner that should clearly have tipped off to Lillian that something was afoot. In a letter dated February 9, 1924, Sonia writes:

> I have nothing in life to attract me to Life and if I can help the good and beautiful soul of Howard Lovecraft find itself financially as it has found itself spiritually, morally and mentally, my efforts shall not have been in vain. . . .
>
> Therefore little Lady, fear nothing. I am just as desirous of his success for his own sake as you are, and I am just as anxious, perhaps more so, that you should live to enjoy the fruits of his labor and the honors that will be heaped upon his beautiful and blessed name, as you may be.[14]

That "fear nothing" must have been in response to some letter by Lillian, perhaps asking Sonia bluntly what her "intentions" toward her nephew actually were.

Lovecraft's joviality during the ceremony is borne out by several amusing letters to his closest friends. To James Morton he writes, after another long and teasing preamble about the seeming strangeness of his residence at 259 Parkside:

> Yes, my boy, you got it the first time. Eager to put Colonial architecture to all of its possible uses, I hit the ties hither last week; and on Monday, March the Third, seized by the hair of the head the President of the United—S. H. G.—and

> dragged her to Saint Paul's Chapel, . . . where after considerable assorted genuflection, and with the aid of the honest curate, Father George Benson Cox, and of two less betitled ecclesiastical hangers-on, I succeeded in affixing to her series of patronymics the not unpretentious one of Lovecraft. Damned quaint of me, is it not? You never can tell what a guy like me is gonna do next![15]

The two ecclesiastical hangers-on were, according to the marriage licence, Joseph Gorman and Joseph G. Armstrong. To Frank Long he writes:

> The license stuff? Dead easy! We beat it to the Brooklyn borough hall, and got the papers with all the coolness and *savoir faire* of old campaigners . . . you ought to have seen your old Grandpa, Sonny! Brigham Young annexing his 27th, or King Solomon starting in on the second thousand, had nothing on the Old Gentleman for languid fluency and casual conversation![16]

It is as if Lovecraft is regarding the whole thing as a lark; and indeed, we will see increasing evidence that he was quite taken with the charm and novelty of being married but was simply not aware of the amount of effort it takes to make a marriage actually work. Lovecraft was, in all honesty, not emotionally mature enough for such an undertaking.

The testimony of two of Lovecraft's closest friends may be of some value here. Arthur S. Koki interviewed Samuel Loveman in 1959 and Frank Long in 1961, and he reports their views on the matter as follows: "Samuel Loveman thought Lovecraft had married Mrs. Greene out of a sense of obligation for the interest and encouragement she took in his work. Frank Belknap Long, Jr. said Lovecraft believed it befitted a proper gentleman to take a wife."[17] There is much to be said for both these opinions. The way in which Lovecraft soberly went through an Anglican ceremony at a colonial church indicates that his sense of aesthetics had overwhelmed his rationality; and his references in letters of the first few months of his marriage to "the wife" or "the missus" again suggest his being tickled at the state of being married without, perhaps, a realisation of what such a state actually meant either practically or emotionally.

It is worth pausing to ponder the sources for Lovecraft's attraction for Sonia. It seems facile to say that he was looking for a mother replacement; and yet, the emergence of Sonia into his life a mere six weeks after his mother's death is certainly a coincidence worth noting. Granted that the affection may initially have been more on Sonia's side than his—she came to Providence far more frequently than he came to New York—Lovecraft may nevertheless have felt the need to confide his thoughts and feelings to someone in a way that he does not seem to have done with his aunts. Those voluminous daily letters he wrote to Sonia would no doubt reveal much; one hopes that there is more intimacy and human feeling in them than the pompous declamations we find in "Nietzscheism and Realism." True, Lovecraft in his New York years wrote copiously to Aunt Lillian as well (less to Aunt Annie);

but these letters are largely chronicles of his daily activities, with only intermittent expressions of his moods, beliefs, and sensations.

Sonia was, of course, nothing like Susie Lovecraft: she was dynamic, emotionally open, contemporary, cosmopolitan, and perhaps a little domineering (this is the exact term Frank Belknap Long once used in describing Sonia to me), whereas Susie, although perhaps domineering in her own way, was subdued, emotionally reserved, even stunted, and a typical product of American Victorianism. But let us recall that at this moment Lovecraft was still in the full flower of his Decadent phase: his scorn of Victorianism and his toying with the intellectual and aesthetic avant-garde may have found a welcome echo in a woman who was very much an inhabitant of the twentieth century.

Their marriage occurred after what can only be called a long-distance romance—something that is, then and now, difficult to pull off. That Lovecraft fancied, on the basis of a three-month stay with Sonia in the summer of 1922, and in circumstances where he was really no more than a cordial friend, that they were fit for cohabitation strikes me as pitiably naive; what is more surprising is that Sonia herself, having already suffered through an unsuccessful marriage, managed to convince herself likewise.

Sonia has made one further admission that is of some interest. In a manuscript (clearly written after the dissolution of the marriage, as it is signed Sonia H. Davis) entitled "The Psychic Phenominon [*sic*] of Love" she has incorporated a part of one of Lovecraft's letters to her. In a note on the manuscript she has written: "It was Lovecraft's part of this letter that I believe made me fall in love with him; but he did not carry out his own dictum; time and place, and reversion of some of his thoughts and expressions did not bode for happiness."[18] Sonia submitted this manuscript to August Derleth for publication; he rejected it, but published Lovecraft's letter alone in the *Arkham Collector* as "Lovecraft on Love." It is a very strange document. Going on for about 1200 words in the most abstract and pedantic manner, Lovecraft thoroughly downplays the erotic aspect of love as a product of the fire of extreme youth, saying instead that "By forty or perhaps fifty a wholesome replacement process begins to operate, and love attains calm, cool depths based on tender association beside which the erotic infatuation of youth takes on a certain shade of cheapness and degradation. Mature tranquillised love produces an idyllic fidelity which is a testimonial to its sincerity, purity, and intensity."[19] And so on. There is actually not much substance in this letter, and some parts of it should have made Sonia a little nervous, as when he says that "True love thrives equally well in presence or in absence" or that each party "must not be too antipodal in their values, motive-forces, perspectives, and modes of expression and fulfilment" for compatibility. Nevertheless, Sonia did manage at least to get Lovecraft to talk about the subject; we shall have to examine at a later stage whether Lovecraft did or did not "carry out his own dictum" in actual practice.

But the months preceding and following the marriage were sufficiently hectic that neither had much time for reflexion. In the first place, Lovecraft had to finish the ghostwriting job for *Weird Tales.* The magazine was not doing well on the newsstands, and in an effort to bolster sales owner J. C. Henneberger enlisted the services of the escape artist Harry Houdini (born Erich Weiss, 1874–1926), then at the height of his popularity, to write a column and other items. "Ask Houdini" appeared in three issues beginning in March 1924, while two works of fiction—"The Spirit Fakers of Hermannstadt" (March, April, and May–June–July 1924) and "The Hoax of the Spirit Lover" (April 1924)—were also published. These latter two were ghostwritten by unknown hands, possibly Walter B. Gibson, the prolific pulp writer and editor (later to be known as the creator of The Shadow). (Some have conjectured C. M. Eddy, Jr, as the ghostwriter, but it does not appear as if Eddy was acquainted with Houdini at this time; Lovecraft himself notes in late September 1924 that he himself had given Eddy a letter of introduction to Houdini only a short time earlier.[20] Lovecraft believed that Farnsworth Wright ghostwrote the Houdini tales.[21]) Now Henneberger enlisted Lovecraft—who had to be regarded as one of the leading lights of the magazine in its first year—to write up a strange tale that Houdini was attempting to pass off as an actual occurrence. Lovecraft relates the account—involving Houdini's being kidnapped on a pleasure trip to Egypt, thrown bound and gagged down a deep aperture in Campbell's Tomb, and left to find his way out of the labyrinthine pyramid—in a letter to Long in mid-February, saying that the work would appear as "By Houdini and H. P. Lovecraft."[22] Shortly thereafter Lovecraft discovered that this account was entirely fictitious, so he persuaded Henneberger to let him have as much imaginative leeway as he could in writing up the story. By February 25 he had not yet begun to write the tale, even though it was due on March 1. Somehow he managed to finish it just shortly before he boarded the train to New York on March 2; but in his rush he left the typescript behind somewhere in Union Station in Providence. Harriedly he took out an advertisement that appeared the next day in the lost and found column of the *Providence Journal:*

> MANUSCRIPT—Lost, title of story, "Under the Pyramids," Sunday afternoon, in or about Union station. Finder please send to H. P. Lovecraft, 259 Parkside Ave., Brooklyn, N.Y.

Although the tale was published as "Imprisoned with the Pharaohs" in the first anniversary issue (May–June–July 1924) of *Weird Tales,* the ad verifies that "Under the Pyramids" was Lovecraft's original title for the work. It appeared, however, only as by Houdini; Lovecraft had written the story unexpectedly in the first person, causing Henneberger to feel awkward about affixing a collaborative byline on it.

Lovecraft's concern at the moment, however, was to get a newly typed version to Henneberger as quickly as possible. Fortunately, he had brought along the autograph manuscript, so the morning of the 3rd found him at the office of "The Reading Lamp" (on which more later) frantically retyping the long story; but he was only half done when it was time to go to St Paul's Chapel for the service.

Sonia had, incidentally, declared that a civil service would have been quite sufficient, but Lovecraft insisted on a church wedding. As she herself reports, it was his decision to have the service at this exquisite eighteenth-century relic—"where Washington and Lord Howe and many other great men had worshipped!"[23] St Paul's is an Episcopal church; and Lovecraft was quite aware that he was following in the tradition of his parents, who had married at St Paul's in Boston, also an Episcopal church.[24]

In any event, the couple was planning to go that evening to Philadelphia—whose colonial antiquities Lovecraft in November 1923 had expressed a wish to see[25]—for their honeymoon, but were too tired, so they presumably returned to 259 Parkside for the evening. There was also the matter of the Houdini manuscript remained to be dealt with. Sonia tells the tale this way:

> It was *not* "a public stenographer" who copied H. P.'s handwritten notes for the Houdini manuscript. It was I alone who was able to read these erased and crossed-out notes. I read them slowly to him while H. P. pounded them out on a borrowed typewriter, borrowed from the hotel in Philadelphia where we spent the first day and night copying that precious manuscript which had to meet the printer's deadline. When that manuscript was finished we were too tired and exhausted for honey-mooning or anything else.[26]

She is attempting to refute W. Paul Cook's claim that the story was typed by a public stenographer; but it was indeed typed *at* a public stenographer's office. Although the couple was staying at the Robert Morris Hotel, the only stenographer's office that was open in the evening was in the Hotel Vendig, and the two of them spent both their evenings in Philadelphia (March 4 and 5) there finishing the typing job.[27] The story was sent to *Weird Tales* immediately, and Lovecraft received payment of $100—the largest sum he had hitherto earned as a fiction writer—on March 21.[28] It was the only occasion on which he was paid by *Weird Tales* in advance of publication.

"Under the Pyramids" is quite an able piece of work, and it remains a much undervalued tale. It is true that some of the earlier parts read rather like a travelogue, or even an encyclopaedia:

> The pyramids stand on a high rock plateau, this group forming next to the northernmost of the series of regal and aristocratic cemeteries built in the neighbourhood of the extinct capital Memphis, which lay on the same side of the Nile, somewhat south of Gizeh, and which flourished between 3400 and 2000

> B.C. The greatest pyramid, which lies nearest the modern road, was built by King Cheops or Khufu about 2800 B.C., and stands more than 450 feet in perpendicular height.

Lovecraft had done considerable library work on Egyptian antiquities in preparation for writing the tale, and also had with him *The Tomb of Perneb* (1916), a volume issued by the Metropolitan Museum of Art; he had probably purchased it on one of his New York trips of 1922. Some of the imagery of the story probably also derives from Théophile Gautier's superb non-supernatural tale of Egyptian horror, "One of Cleopatra's Nights." Lovecraft owned Lafcadio Hearn's translation of *One of Cleopatra's Nights and Other Fantastic Romances* (1882).

In any case, the narrative nevertheless gains cumulative power as we see Houdini cast down some spectacularly deep chasm in the Temple of the Sphinx (Lovecraft had abandoned the idea of using Campbell's Tomb as the site of the central action of the story) and his laborious struggles not merely to escape from his bonds but to answer an "idle question" that had haunted him throughout his stay in Egypt: *"what huge and loathsome abnormality was the Sphinx originally carven to represent?"* This last bit is Lovecraft's addition, and it in fact becomes the focus of the entire tale. Houdini himself is, accordingly, removed from centre stage as an active participant in the narrative, becoming largely an observer of bizarre phenomena; and, in what can only be a tart spoof of one of the most physically robust individuals of his day, he faints on three different occasions during the entire escapade.

What Houdini encounters is an immense underground cavern—"Bases of columns whose middles were higher than human sight . . . mere bases of things that must each dwarf the Eiffel Tower to insignificance"—peopled with the most hideous entities imaginable. Houdini ponders the curiously morbid temperament of the ancient Egyptians ("All these people thought of was death and the dead"), in particular their notions of the spirit or *ka,* which can return to its body or other bodies after it had "wandered about the upper and lower worlds in a horrible way". There are "blood-congealing legends" of what "decadent priestcraft" fashioned on occasion—"*composite mummies* made by the artificial union of human trunks and limbs with the heads of animals in imitation of the elder gods." Considering all this, Houdini is dumbfounded to come upon *living embodiments* of such entities:

> I *would not* look at the marching things. That I desperately resolved as I heard their creaking joints and nitrous wheezing above the dead music and the dead tramping. It was merciful that they did not speak . . . but God! *their crazy torches began to cast shadows on the surface of those stupendous columns.* Heaven take it away! *Hippopotami should not have human hands and carry torches . . . men should not have the heads of crocodiles. . . .*

This is one of the most striking examples of a tendency we will see in much of Lovecraft's later fiction—the implication that myths and legends are imperfectly preserved memories of real, but loathsome, events or entities. But the crux of the tale is Houdini's discovery of the answer to that "idle question" he had asked himself earlier. The composite creatures appear to be laying down huge amounts of food as offerings to some strange entity that appears fleetingly out of an aperture in the underground cavern: "It was as large, perhaps, as a good-sized hippopotamus, but very curiously shaped. It seemed to have no neck, but five separate shaggy heads springing in a row from a roughly cylindrical trunk . . . Out of these heads darted curious rigid tentacles which seized ravenously on the *excessively great* quantities of unmentionable food placed before the aperture." What could this possibly be? "The five-headed monster that emerged . . . that five-headed monster as large as a hippopotamus . . . the five-headed monster—*and that of which it is the merest fore paw . . .*"

This is, perhaps, one of the relatively few instances where there is a genuine "surprise" ending in Lovecraft. On the whole, the tale is a rousing success, and it appropriately led off the huge May–June–July 1924 issue of *Weird Tales.* Lovecraft was, indeed, represented in three different contributions in this issue, the others being "Hypnos" and C. M. Eddy's "The Loved Dead."

One bizarre postscript to this entire affair concerns that last tale. A decade later Lovecraft, in discussing his relatively limited share of "real-life" experiences, noted in passing: "I have several times been in a police station . . . once to see the Chief of Police about the banning of a client's magazine from the stands . . ."[29] This can be nothing more than a reference to the fact that this issue of *Weird Tales* was banned on the grounds that "The Loved Dead" was about necrophilia (true enough, indeed) and apparently considered obscene. Lovecraft, oddly enough, does not discuss this matter in contemporary letters, and it is now hard to discover what actually happened. There are some indications, in Lovecraft's correspondence, that the magazine was banned only in the state of Indiana ("About poor Eddy's tale—it certainly did achieve fame of a sort! His name must have rung in tones of fiery denunciation all through the corridors & beneath the classic rotunda (if it has a rotunda) of the Indiana State Capitol!"[30]); but if so, I cannot see why Lovecraft would have gone to the Chief of Police in New York (it could hardly have been anywhere else) on the matter. To what degree the notoriety of the banning affected sales of *Weird Tales* is also in doubt: it can certainly not be said (as I myself have on occasion been careless enough to say) that this banning somehow "saved" the magazine by causing a run on the issue, especially since it would be four months before the next issue appeared. We may discover, however, that less fortunate consequences occurred—at least, as far as Lovecraft was concerned—in later years.

Meanwhile, Lovecraft was becoming very much involved with *Weird Tales*—perhaps more than he would have liked. In mid-March he reports that Henneberger "is making a radical change in the policy of *Weird Tales,* and that he has in mind a brand new magazine to cover the field of Poe-Machen shudders. This magazine, he says, will be 'right in my line', and he wants to know if I would consider moving to CHICAGO to edit it!"[31] There is a certain ambiguity in this utterance, but I believe the sense is not that Henneberger would start a "brand new magazine" but that *Weird Tales* itself would be made over into a "new" magazine featuring Poe-Machen shudders. Lovecraft had earlier noted that Baird had been ousted as editor and that Farnsworth Wright had been placed in his stead;[32] this was only a stop-gap measure (the May–June–July issue of *Weird Tales* appears to have been edited by Wright and Otis Adelbert Kline, although surely a large proportion of the contents consisted of material that had been previously accepted by Baird), and Lovecraft was indeed Henneberger's first choice for editor of *Weird Tales.*

Lovecraft has frequently been criticised for failing to take up this opportunity just at the time when, as a new husband, he needed a steady income; the thinking is that he should have overcome his purely aesthetic distaste of the modern architecture of Chicago and accepted the offer. But the matter is considerably more complicated than this scenario suggests. First, although Sonia was in favour of a move to Chicago "if [the offer] definitely materialises and is accompanied by the requisite guarantees,"[33] it would either have meant Sonia's search for uncertain job prospects in Chicago or the couple's having to live a thousand miles away from each other merely for the sake of employment. Second, Lovecraft knew that Henneberger was deeply in debt: he reports that Henneberger has "lost $51,000.00 on his two magazines"[34] (i.e., *Weird Tales* and *Detective Tales*), and there was no guarantee at all that either enterprise would continue in operation much longer; if Lovecraft had therefore left for Chicago, he might after a few months have been stranded there with no job and with little prospect of getting one. Lovecraft was, in my view, wise to decline the offer. In any case, even in the most ideal financial circumstances, he might not have made the best editor of a magazine like *Weird Tales.* His fastidious taste would have rejected much that was actually published in its pages: there was simply not enough artistically polished weird fiction—of the Machen-Dunsany-Blackwood grade—to fill what was really nothing more than a cheap pulp magazine paying a penny a word. It is a brutal fact that the overwhelming amount of material published in *Weird Tales* is, on the literary scale, complete rubbish, although this seems to matter little to those misguided souls who continue up to the present day to wax nostalgic about the magazine.

What actually happened to *Weird Tales* in this crisis was that Henneberger sold off his share of *Detective Tales* to the co-founder of Rural Publications, J. M. Lansinger (who retained Baird as editor of that magazine), appointed Farnsworth Wright as permanent editor of *Weird Tales* (he would retain that position until 1940), and then—as the only way to make up the $40,000 debt he had accrued—

come to an agreement with B. Cornelius, the printer of the magazine, as follows: "Cornelius became chief stockholder with an agreement that if the $40,000 owed him was ever repaid by profits from the magazine, Henneberger would be returned the stock."[35] A new company, the Popular Fiction Publishing Co., was formed to issue the magazine, with the stockholders being Cornelius, Farnsworth Wright, and William Sprenger (*Weird Tales'* business manager); after a several-month hiatus *Weird Tales* resumed publication with the November 1924 issue. Although Henneberger retained a minor interest in the new company, *Weird Tales* never made sufficient profits for him to buy it back; in any case, he seems to have lost interest in the venture after a few years and finally drifted entirely out of the picture.

Farnsworth Wright (1888–1940) deserves some mention, as Lovecraft would eventually develop a very curious relationship with him. He had been the magazine's first reader from the very beginning and had several undistinguished stories in early issues; Lovecraft dismissed him in February 1924 as a "mediocre Chicago author,"[36] and writing was indeed not where his strengths lay. He had served in World War I and afterward was music critic for the *Chicago Herald and Examiner,* continuing in this latter activity for a time even after he took over the editorship of *Weird Tales.* By early 1921 he had contracted Parkinson's disease, and the illness worsened throughout the rest of his life, so that by the end of the decade he could not sign his name. (One unexpected and rather despicable consequence of this is that letters with Wright's signature are highly prized collectors' items.)

It is difficult to gauge Wright's success as editor of *Weird Tales,* especially since very different yardsticks can be used to measure "success" in something of this kind. It is, certainly, something in his favour that he managed to keep the magazine going even during the worst years of the depression; but there can similarly be no denying that he published an appalling amount of trite, hackneyed, and simply bad fiction that would never have appeared elsewhere and, in an ideal world, should never have been published in the first place. Lovecraft felt that Wright was erratic, capricious, and even a little hypocritical, at least as regards his handling of Lovecraft's own work; and, in spite of those who have come to Wright's defence on this score, this view seems fairly plausible. Lovecraft may have had excessively high expectations of his success with Wright, so that rejections came with added bitterness. As early as March 1924 he wrote to Lillian about a letter Wright sent to Frank Long: "he mentioned my stories with extravagant praise—saying that I am the greatest short story writer since Poe, or something like that . . ."[37] In some senses Lovecraft's irritation with Wright stemmed from what he eventually realised was a somewhat naive view that aesthetically meritorious work should be rewarded commensurately. It would be years before he learned that writing for the pulps was simply a business, and that Wright looked upon the matter in that light. If most of

Weird Tales' readership wanted cheap, formula-ridden hackwork, Wright would make sure to give it to them.

In the short term, however, Lovecraft and Sonia had a household to set in order. The first thing to do was to persuade aunt Lillian (and perhaps Annie as well) to come to New York to live with them. This seems to have been an entirely sincere desire on the part of both Lovecraft and Sonia: the latter writes, on a joint postcard to Lillian, "Hope to see you in New York soon,"[38] while Lovecraft in his marriage-announcement letter states jovially, "Dost fancy the Old Gentleman would transfer the family seat without sending for his first-born daughter?" Lillian was at this time almost sixty-six years old and probably in declining health; Lovecraft says with a cheerfulness bordering on wish-fulfilment, "You will feel better and more active here," but it is clear that she herself had no desire to move—especially after her nephew failed to take her into his confidence regarding the most dramatic change in his personal circumstances—and she was even reluctant to visit the couple in New York, although she finally did come for more than a month late in the year.

In the meantime Lovecraft would need his papers and effects. He asked Lillian to send such things as his tin box full of unpublished manuscripts, his complete file of *Weird Tales* and *Home Brew,* his calendars (he had several), his Webster's Unabridged (also an older dictionary compiled by James Stormonth, which he preferred because it was British), his Gillette blades, and other items—including "my blue *jumbo cup,* whose capacious depths have dealt me out so much nourishment, and which has become so much a part of my essential background!"[39] Later much of his personal furniture was sent and somehow inserted into Sonia's four-room first-floor apartment at 259 Parkside.[40] This furniture did not arrive in its entirety until June 30,[41] but Kleiner reports seeing some of it as it arrived—"heaps of fine linen, quite a few pieces of heavy, old-fashioned silverware, and other items which had probably been stored away for years"—and also on how homelike the apartment looked. "Why, this looks as if you had lived here always." Lovecraft, beaming with pride, replied that a gentleman always made himself at home no matter where he happened to be.[42]

One occupant the couple would not have to worry about was Sonia's daughter. Florence Carol Greene appears to have had a falling out with her mother a few years previously: she had fallen in love with her half-uncle Sydney (only five years her elder), and Sonia, enraged, had adamantly refused to allow her to marry him. (Such a marriage would, in any event, have been prohibited by the tenets of the Orthodox Judaism.) This dispute led to a schism that, unfortunately, lasted for the duration of both women's lives. Florence left Sonia's apartment sometime after she came of age (March 19, 1923), although continuing to remain in New York.[43] There are reports that she herself did not care for Lovecraft and did not approve of her mother's marrying him.[44] Florence's later life is both distinguished and tragic: she married a newspaperman named John Weld in 1927 but divorced him in 1932; she herself went to Europe and became a reporter, attaining celebrity as the first reporter to cover the romance of the Prince of Wales (the future Edward VIII) and Mrs Wallis Simpson. Returning to America, she worked for newspapers in New York, later moving to Florida and becoming a film publicist. She died on March 31, 1979. But in all that time she refused to speak to her mother. And aside from a passing reference in her memoir, Sonia never speaks of her. Lovecraft too alludes to her only twice in all the correspondence I have seen.

In the meantime, however, Lovecraft had to think of work. This was, in fact, a somewhat pressing concern. Sonia had been making $10,000 per year at Ferle Heller's—a princely sum considering that the "minimum health and decency" wages for a family of four in the 1920s was $2000[45]—but had already lost this position, evidently, by February 1924. She wrote to Lillian: "Just at the moment I am down on my luck as it were but I know it can't last much longer. I simply must find a position, for I feel sure there is one waiting for me somewhere."[46] Nevertheless, she had savings in five figures,[47] so perhaps there was no immediate need to replenish the coffers.

It is true that Lovecraft had never held any regular salaried position, and it is also true that he seemed to have no especially regular revision client except David Van Bush; nevertheless, a likely prospect seemed in the offing in something called "The Reading Lamp." This was a magazine as well as a literary agency that would generate commissioned articles or books on behalf of its clients; it was run by one Gertrude E. Tucker. The one issue of the magazine that has come up for sale recently (no copy appears to exist in any library in the world) declares it to be "A Convenient Guide to the New Books including new editions of old favorites as issued by the Publishing Houses of Canada." The last part of that sentence relates to the fact that this issue—Volume 1, Number 1 (December 1923)—was published by the Ryerson Press, Toronto. Possibly there was also a corresponding edition of the magazine published in the United States, presumably from New York. In any case, it was Edwin Baird who had "recommended"[48] Lovecraft to Tucker in January 1924; Sonia, learning of this, took it upon herself to see Tucker and bring a sheaf of Lovecraft's manuscripts to her. On March 10 Lovecraft interviewed at the Reading Lamp office, with the following result:

> Miss T. thinks a book of my antiquarian & other essays would be quite practicable, & urges me to prepare at least three as samples at once. Also, she thinks she can get me a contract with a chain of magazines to write minor matter to order. And more—as soon as my MSS. arrive, she wants to see all of them, with a view

> to a weird book. . . . What Miss T. wants in the way of essays is quaint stuff with a flavour of the supernatural.[49]

All this sounds promising, and at one point Lovecraft even reports the possibility that The Reading Lamp might be able to secure him a regular position at a publishing house,[50] although this clearly did not happen. Later in the month he reported working on several chapters of a book on American superstitions; the idea evidently was that he would do three chapters and Tucker would then try to get a contract from a book publisher for the project. My feeling is that Lovecraft actually did write these chapters, although they have not come to light; but since on August 1 he made note of the "non-materialisation of sundry literary prospects,"[51] the obvious inference is that the Reading Lamp business came to nothing. He did, however, apparently write a review for the magazine—of J. Arthur Thomson's *What Is Man?* (London: Methuen, 1923; New York: G. P. Putnam's Sons, 1924), an anthropological work.[52] This item has not been located.

But, again, this was not in itself a disaster. Lovecraft always had Bush to rely on. He met him on May 25[53] and reported doing "Bush work" in July. Bush published at least eight books in 1924 and 1925 (all of them psychology manuals—he had evidently given up poetry), and no doubt Lovecraft derived at least a modest income from revising them. Checks from *Weird Tales* were no doubt trickling in also—for "The Hound" (February), "The Rats in the Walls" (March), "Arthur Jermyn" (April), and "Hypnos" (May–June–July) along with "Under the Pyramids," although I have no information on how much any of these stories aside from the Houdini job actually brought in.

The couple, indeed, felt so relatively prosperous that in May they purchased two home lots in Bryn Mawr Park, a development in Yonkers. The real estate company that negotiated the purchase, the Homeland Company of 28 North Broadway in Yonkers, has of course long ago ceased to exist. I cannot find much information on this matter and certainly do not know where in Yonkers this property actually was. A home lot would, of course, be much cheaper than a house, and in her autobiography Sonia declares that a home for Lovecraft, herself, and his two aunts was planned for the larger lot and that the other would be used for speculation.[54] Yonkers is the city immediately north of the Bronx in lower Westchester County, and within easy commuting distance of Manhattan by trolley or train. Since the turn of the century it had become a fashionable bedroom community for New Yorkers; but it was still an idyllic small town with plenty of greenery and a sort of New England feel to it, and might have been the ideal place for Lovecraft to have settled so long as he needed to remain in the New York area for purposes of employment.[55]

What is, of course, remarkable about this whole episode is that it exactly duplicates Lovecraft's parents' purchase of a home lot in Auburndale, Massachusetts, a few years after their marriage in 1889. Lovecraft knew of this matter, as he mentions it in an early letter to Kleiner;[56] was he consciously wishing to follow his parents' footsteps here, as he apparently did in going through an Anglican wedding service?

Although Lovecraft met with a Mr Bailey of the Homeland Company about "the type of house we would wish,"[57] on July 29 he wrote to the real estate firm that "Owing to financial difficulties of the most acute and unforeseen sort, I find myself unable at present to make the remittances now due on the property which I purchased last May at Bryn Mawr Park."[58] (Actually, Sonia states that she managed to retain control of the lots for some years by paying a rate of $100 per week.[59]) What was the nature of these difficulties?

We have already seen that Sonia either lost or gave up her very remunerative job at Ferle Heller's. Why? It appears that she attempted to start her own millinery business. This strikes me as an extremely risky undertaking. Even if she had simply lost her position at Ferle Heller's (as her letter to Lillian stating that she was "down on [her] luck" would seem to indicate), she might have been better off attempting to secure a position with an existing firm rather than striking out on her own—an undertaking that no doubt involved a considerable initial outlay of capital. In days when all men and women wore hats in public, the millinery business was an extraordinarily competitive one: the 1924–25 city directory for Manhattan and the Bronx lists a minimum of 1200 milliners. It is not surprising that Sonia would have gone into this profession: in both New York and Chicago, Russian Jewish immigrants specialised in the clothing trade.[60] My only thought as to Sonia's attempt to make it on her own is that, as a married woman, she did not wish to do the extensive amount of travelling that her position at Ferle Heller's evidently required her to do, and wished to open a shop of her own so as to remain in the city as much as possible. (I am not certain whether Sonia's shop was in Manhattan or Brooklyn; there is no city directory for Brooklyn at this time. The shop she attempted to establish in 1928 was certainly in Brooklyn.) But if this were the case, the ironic circumstance is that Sonia remained out of work for much of the rest of the year and was then forced to take a series of jobs in the Midwest, separating her from her husband far more than her Ferle Heller's position is likely to have done. She says nothing about this whole matter at all in her memoir; but Lovecraft, writing to Lillian on August 1, makes clear reference to "the somewhat disastrous collapse of S. H.'s *independent* [my emphasis] millinery venture," with the result that there is now "something of a shortage in the exchequer."[61]

The upshot of all this was that Lovecraft was forced to look much more vigorously for a job—any job—than before. Now, and only now, begins the futile and rather pathetic hunting through the classified ads every Sunday in the *New York Times* for any position that might conceivably be available; but Lovecraft came face to face with a realisation as true then as now: "Positions of every kind seem virtually unattainable to persons without experience . . ."[62] What he says is the job that "came nearest to materialisation" was a salesman's position with the Creditors' National Clearing House, located at 810 Broad Street in Newark, New Jersey. This was a bill collecting agency, and Lovecraft would be responsible, not for actually collecting bills, but for selling the agency's services among wholesalers and retailers in New York City. He appears to have been hired on a trial basis, and on Saturday, July 26, he attended a salesmen's meeting in Newark to learn the ropes after spending the better part of the previous week studying the literature given to him by the firm. On Monday the 28th he began the actual sales campaign with wholesalers, but did not generate a single sale; he tried again on Wednesday, canvassing retailers in Brooklyn, but with the same results. On Thursday Lovecraft was taken around by the head of the Newark branch, William J. Bristol, who quickly took him aside:

> my guide became very candid about the tone of the business, and admitted that a gentleman born and bred has very little chance for success in such lines of canvassing salesmanship . . . where one must either be miraculously magnetic and captivating, or else so boorish and callous that he can transcend every rule of tasteful conduct and push conversation on bored, hostile, and unwilling victims.

Bristol accepted Lovecraft's immediate resignation, without the usual one week's notice. And although Bristol, admiring Lovecraft's command of English, made vague proposals to go into business with him privately in the insurance business, this obviously came to nothing.

This whole episode—as well as a later one in which Lovecraft tried to secure a job in the lamp testing department of an electrical laboratory[63]—shows how difficult it was for Lovecraft to secure the job that most suited him, namely something in the writing or publishing business. There is no reason why, with his experience, he should not have been able to secure some such position; but he was unable to do so. Several of his friends have commented on a notorious letter of application that he sent out around this time (a draft of it is written on the back of his letter to the Homeland Company of July 29), the first paragraph of which reads as follows:

> If an unprovoked application for employment seems somewhat unusual in these days of system, agencies, & advertising, I trust that the circumstances surrounding this one may help to mitigate what would otherwise be obtrusive forwardness. The case is one wherein certain definitely marketable aptitudes must be put forward in an unconventional manner if they are to override the current fetish which demands commercial experience & causes prospective employers to dismiss unheard the application of any situation-seeker unable to boast of specific professional service in a given line.[64]

And so on for six more paragraphs, commenting pointedly that Lovecraft has, in the last two months, answered over a hundred advertisements without a single response (reminiscent of his noting to *Weird Tales* that "Dagon" and "The Tomb" had been previously rejected), and concluding with a feeble joke (Lovecraft is neither a round peg trying to fit a square hole nor a square peg trying to fit a round hole, but a trapezohedral peg).

To be sure, this may not have been the ideal letter, but standards of business writing were different seventy years ago. Nevertheless, Kleiner remarks of this letter, and others like it: "I think I am justified in saying that they were the sort of letters a temporarily straitened English gentleman might have written in an effort to make a profitable connection in the business world of the day before yesterday."[65] Frank Long is more blunt: "As specimens of employment-seeking correspondence, few letters could have been more incredibly off-target. But surprisingly enough, he received at least four sympathetic replies."[66] Long seems entirely unaware how the second half of his comment completely undercuts the first.

A paper among Lovecraft's effects appears to indicate the newspapers, magazines, and publishing houses to whom he sent this letter. Among the newspapers in New York are the *Herald Tribune,* the *Times,* the *Evening Post,* the *Sun,* the *World,* and the *Brooklyn Eagle.* (In another column, interestingly, are listed four papers in the Boston area—the *Transcript,* the *Herald,* the *Post,* and the *Christian Science Monitor.*) Magazines listed are the *Century, Harper's* (crossed out), *Munsey's,* and the *Atlantic* (in Boston). Publishers are Harper & Brothers, Charles Scribner's Sons, E. P. Dutton, G. P. Putnam's Sons, Doubleday, Page, George H. Doran, Albert & Charles Boni, Boni & Liveright, and Knopf. Lovecraft was certainly aiming high, and there is no reason why he shouldn't have. It is not clear that the letter of application was actually sent to all these places; some have check marks beside them, others do not. I do not know what the four responses alluded to by Long are.

Then, in the classified section of the *New York Times* for Sunday, August 10, appeared the following advertisement in the "Situations Wanted—Male" category:

> WRITER AND REVISER, free-lance, desires regular and permanent salared connection with any responsible enterprise requiring literary services; exceptionally thorough experience in preparing correct and fluent text on subjects assigned, and in meeting the most difficult, intricate and extensive problems of rewriting and constructive revision, prose or verse; would also consider situation dealing with such proofreading as demands rapid and discriminating perception, orthographical accuracy, stylistic fastidiousness and a keenly developed sense of the niceties of English usage; good typist; age 34, married; has for seven years handled all the prose and verse of a leading American public speaker and editor. Y 2292 Times Annex.[67]

This advertisement—taking many phrases from his application letter—is rather more open to criticism than the letter itself, for it is far longer than any other one in this section and really does go on at needless length when a more compact notice would have conveyed many of the same points far more cheaply. The expense was, indeed, quite considerable: the rate for ads in the "Situations Wanted" section was 40¢ per word, and this ad—99 words—cost a full $39.60. This would be the equivalent of a month's rent in the one-room apartment Lovecraft would occupy in 1925–26. I am amazed that Sonia let Lovecraft take out an ad of this length, for surely she paid for it with whatever savings she had at this time.

The ad generated at least one response, but not a very promising one. M. A. Katherman, Merchandising Counsellor, wrote to Lovecraft on August 11, saying: "If you will call at this office the writer will assist you to locate the position you are seeking."[68] In other words, Katherman himself was an agent of some sort (a head-hunter, in today's jargon) rather than someone who actually had a job to offer. Lovecraft makes no mention of this individual, nor of any other responses to his ad, in any correspondence I have seen.

Then, in September, an old friend reappeared on the scene—J. C. Henneberger. He may have visited Lovecraft in late March: Lovecraft states that he was planning to come then[69] (clearly to discuss the editorship of *Weird Tales*), but I cannot ascertain whether he actually did so. Nothing is heard of him until on September 18 we suddenly hear of the following:

> Am ceasing answering advts for a while, to give Henneberger a chance to prove his business sincerity. ¶ He has—or says he has—hired me for his new magazine at a salary beginning at $40.00 per wk & later going up (HE SAYS) to $100. I'll have to give him my undivided time, of course, but I'll lose nothing thereby, since the moment he stops paying I can stop working. First payment—a week from to-morrow. His plans sound more businesslike than ever before.[70]

Although Lovecraft met Henneberger in New York on September 7 and reported to his aunts that "he told me of the new lease of life achieved by Weird Tales, and of the fine job he had in store for me,"[71] it cannot have been the editorship of *Weird Tales* that Henneberger had in mind: Wright had surely been appointed by now (the first issue wholly under his editorship, dated November 1924, would appear in October). I think the two parts of Lovecraft's comment are meant to be taken separately; that is, that *Weird Tales* had achieved a new lease on life, thereby allowing Henneberger to create a new magazine for which Lovecraft would be editor. What was this magazine? *College Humor,* founded in 1922, was going strong and was not likely to need a new editor; but there was another magazine called the *Magazine of Fun* that Henneberger started about this time,[72] and, incredible as it seems, the editorship of this magazine or something like it is what Henneberger appears to have been offering. Lovecraft speaks of Henneberger telephoning him and "want[ing] me to turn out some samples of my adapting of jokes for his proposed magazine."[73] It was on the basis of these samples that Henneberger "hired" Lovecraft in mid-September.

But, of course, nothing came of the plans: either Henneberger did not have the resources for starting the magazine at this time (I can find no information on the *Magazine of Fun,* if this was indeed the magazine in question), or he decided that Lovecraft was not the appropriate editor. The former seems more likely, given that Henneberger did not have much cash at his disposal. The promised pay for Lovecraft's editorial work metamorphosed into a $60 credit at the Scribner Book Shop; and although Lovecraft tried to get this credit converted to cash, he was unable to do so and finally, on October 9, he took Long to the bookstore to purchase a sheaf of books—four by Lord Dunsany, seven by Arthur Machen, five on colonial architecture, two miscellaneous volumes, and one book for Long (*The Thing in the Woods* by Harper Williams, a recent horror novel) for his help in making the selection. Long treats the whole episode engagingly in his memoir,[74] but seems under the impression that the credit was a payment for stories in *Weird Tales,* when in fact it was for this editorial job that never materialised.

Lovecraft accordingly returned to answering the want ads, although by this time the strain was becoming pretty severe for someone who had no particular business sense and may perhaps have felt the whole activity somewhat beneath his dignity. He wrote to Lillian in late September: "That day [Sunday] was one of gloom and nerves—more advertisement answering, which has become such a psychological strain that I almost fall unconscious over it!"[75] Anyone who has been out of work for any length of time has perhaps felt this way.

Meanwhile Lovecraft's friends were trying to lend a hand. When Lovecraft completed "Under the Pyramids," Henneberger personally visited Houdini, who was then in Murfreesboro, Tennessee, to show it to him; Houdini was enthusiastic and in March wrote Lovecraft "a most cordial note."[76] Houdini maintained an apartment at 278 West 113th Street in Manhattan and urged Lovecraft to call. He may or may not have done so at the time, but he certainly got in touch with Houdini in September, when the latter offered to assist him in securing work. In a letter of September 28 he asked Lovecraft to telephone him at his private number in early October, "as I want to put you in touch with someone worth-while."[77] This person was one Brett Page, the head of a newspaper syndicate, whom Lovecraft met for an hour and a half at his office on Broadway and 58th Street on October 14; but he had no actual position to offer. In mid-November Samuel Loveman attempted to set up Lovecraft with the head of the cataloguing department of a bookshop on 59th Street, but this too proved fruitless.

Sonia was not, to be sure, unemployed during this entire period; no doubt she was also answering want ads, and in late September Lovecraft spoke of the "place where she has been the last few weeks"[78]—presumably a milliner's or a department store. But she felt that this position was insecure and was looking around for something better. But then things took a turn very much for the worse. On the evening of October 20 Sonia was stricken with "sudden gastric spasms . . . whilst resting in bed after a day of general ill-feeling."[79] Lovecraft took her in a taxicab to Brooklyn Hospital,[80] only a few blocks away. She would spend the next eleven days there, finally being released on the 31st.

There can hardly be any question but that Sonia's illness was in large part nervous or psychological in origin; Lovecraft himself acknowledged this later when referring to it as "a double breakdown, nervous and gastric."[81] Sonia herself must have been acutely worried over the many disasters, financial and otherwise, that had overtaken the couple, and had no doubt sensed Lovecraft's increasing discouragement at his failed job-hunting efforts and perhaps his belief that his entire life had taken a wrong turn. Lovecraft never makes any such statement in his letters of the period, but I have trouble believing that something of the sort was not going through his mind. Could there have been any actual quarrels? Neither party says so, and it is useless to conjecture.

Lovecraft was unusually solicitous to Sonia in the hospital: he visited her every day (this representing his first time he had actually set foot in a hospital, since he had never entered Butler when his mother was there), bringing her books, stationery, and an "Eversharp pencil," and—what must have been a great sacrifice in the name of married bliss—relearned the game of chess so that he could play it with Sonia. She beat him every time. (Lovecraft had a violent antipathy to games and sports of any kind, feeling them an utter waste of time. In speaking years later of puzzles, he remarked to Morton: "After I solve the problems—if I do—I don't know a cursed thing more about nature, history, and the universe than I did before."[82]) In turn he began learning to be more independent in the running of a household: he made coffee, a twenty-minute egg, and even spaghetti from Sonia's written instructions, and showed obvious pride in keeping the place well cleaned and dusted for her return. These remarks on cooking suggest that he had never made a meal for himself up to this time: he had either had his mother, his aunts, or Sonia to do it for him if he did not go to a restaurant.

Lovecraft states that one of Sonia's doctors, Dr Westbrook, actually recommended an operation for the removal of her gall bladder; but Lovecraft—consciously remembering that his mother had died of just such an operation—strongly urged Sonia to get a second opinion, and another doctor (an unnamed "woman graduate of the Sorbonne with a high Paris reputation"[83]) advised against surgery; it was either she or Dr Kingman, a nerve specialist, who then recommended six weeks' rest in the country before Sonia resumed work. Accordingly, she checked into a sort of private rest home in New Jersey on November 9. This was actually a farm run by a Mrs R. A. Craig and her two sons (her husband was a surveyor who did not spend much time at home) near Somerville, New Jersey, in the central part of the state. She would be given her own room and three meals a day for $12.50 a week.[84] Lovecraft was particularly taken with the place because it had at least seven cats. He stayed overnight at the farm on the 9th, then left the next morning to spend the rest of the week in Philadelphia examining colonial antiquities. Returning on the 15th, he was surprised to find that Sonia had come home the day before, one day early; evidently she had not found the place entirely to her liking: "the standard of immaculateness in housekeeping left something to be desired, whilst the company of the one other boarder—a nervous woman with alternating moroseness & loquacity—was not exactly inspiring."[85] She felt, however, good enough after only six days to resume job-hunting efforts.

Almost immediately after Sonia's return, a dramatic decision was made: Sonia would leave for a job in the Midwest while Lovecraft would relocate to a smaller apartment in the city. The couple planned to move out of 259 Parkside as early as the end of November, but as it happened the dispersal did not occur until the end of December. Lovecraft sent a telegram to Lillian (and perhaps to Annie also) to ask their assistance in the move, but later wrote that he and Sonia could manage everything by themselves. How all this came about is not entirely clear. All that Sonia says is the following:

> After we were married and I found it necessary to accept an exceedingly remunerative position out of town I suggested he have one of his friends live with him at our apartment, but his aunts thought it best that since I would be in town only a few days a time every three or four weeks when I'd come to town on a purchasing tour for my firm, it would be wiser to store most of *my* things and find a studio room large enough for Howard's book-cases and furniture that he brought with him from Providence.[86]

Sonia goes on to reveal considerable irritation and even anger that it was her furniture that was sold off and not Lovecraft's, since he clung to his "old (many of them dilapidated) pieces . . . with a morbid tenacity." Sonia's piano had already been sold for $350 in September,[87] although this was probably purely for the sake of money, since Lovecraft promptly cashed the cheque he had received for it and paid a $48 grocer's bill. Now more material was sold, including some of Sonia's books (for $20) and several items of furniture (whether Sonia's or Lovecraft's is not made clear; perhaps some from both). Unfortunately, an appraiser who looked at the latter said that his company would pay nothing for it, but Lovecraft thought that selling it to private individuals might net $25 or $30. Whether it did or not is unclear. He does reveal a certain "tenacity" in holding on to his Providence furnishings, whether it be morbid or not: "I *must* have the Dr. Clark table & chair, the cabinet, the typewriter table, the 454 library table, & several bookcases—to say nothing of some sort of bed or couch, & a bureau or chiffonier."[88]

Lovecraft's first choice for a place to settle was Elizabeth, New Jersey, which he had visited earlier in the year and found a delightful haven of colonial antiquity. It was not far from New York so far as a commute was concerned; presumably, as now, there was both rail and bus service, as well as a ferry. If this could not be managed, then Lovecraft would opt for Brooklyn Heights, where Loveman and Hart Crane lived. He continued to make a rather pitiable plea for Lillian to come down and set up housekeeping with him: "Best of all would be if . . . you & I could find some means of co-operative housekeeping here which might once more light the Phillips home-fires, albeit on distant sod."[89]

Lillian naturally did not accept this offer, but she did come down around December 1 to help in the transition. The month of December is a blank, since Lillian stayed the entire month and into early January, so naturally Lovecraft wrote no letters to her; no letters to others have come to light either. The one thing I am unclear on is exactly when or how Sonia secured her job in the Midwest. Lovecraft spoke in mid-November of her answering a want ad for a companion for an elderly lady[90]—which would be nothing more than a stopgap while she looked for a more permanent position in her field—and the next year, when recounting the year's events to Maurice Moe, he wrote: ". . . when, in December, she received a sudden offer of an important and highly salaried post in the largest department-store of Cincinnati she determined to try it for a while . . ."[91] Whether Lovecraft was wrong about the date of this offer, I cannot say: clearly the decision to leave 259 Parkside was made in mid-November, and I find it hard to imagine why such a move would be contemplated unless Sonia had already accepted the position in Cincinnati at this time.

It should be pointed out that this separation was not—at least outwardly—anything other than an economic move; there is no real indication that any dispute or emotional crisis had occurred. It is, to be sure, somewhat puzzling that Sonia, with her manifest qualifications in the millinery field, could not find suitable employment locally. When her own hat shop collapsed, her former employers, Ferle Heller, must have refused to take her back; and her gastric attack and subsequent stay in the rest home surely put an end to whatever job she had had in September. Still, these are the facts. Are we permitted to wonder whether Lovecraft was secretly pleased at this turn of events? Did he prefer a marriage by correspondence rather than one in person? It is time to backtrack and see what we can learn about the actual personal relations between Sonia and Lovecraft.

Sonia's dry remark that, after typing the Houdini manuscript, they were "too tired and exhausted for honey-mooning or anything else" is surely a tactful way of referring to the fact that she and Lovecraft did not have sex on their first night together.

The matter of Lovecraft's sexual conduct must inevitably be addressed, although the information we have on the subject is very sparse. We learn from R. Alain Everts, who interviewed Sonia on the matter, that:

1) he was a virgin at the time he married;

2) prior to his marriage he had read several books on sex;

3) he *never* initiated sexual relations, but would respond when Sonia did so.[92]

None of this, except 2), is a surprise. One wonders what books Lovecraft might have read (one hopes it was not David Van Bush's *Practical Psychology and Sex Life* [1922]!—quite possibly he may have read some of James F. Morton's writings on the subject). His Victorian upbringing—especially from a mother whose husband died under distasteful circumstances—clearly made him very inhibited as far as sex is concerned; but there is also every reason to believe that Lovecraft was simply one of those individuals who have a low sex drive, and for whom the subject is of relatively little interest. It is mere armchair psychoanalysis to say that he somehow sublimated his sex urges into writing or other activities.

Sonia herself has only two comments on the matter. "As a married man he was an adequately excellent lover, but refused to show his feelings in the presence of others. He shunned promiscuous association with women before his marriage."[93] I do not know what an "adequately excellent" lover is. The other remark is a trifle more embarrassing: "H. P. was inarticulate in expressions of love except to his mother and to his aunts, to whom he expressed himself quite vigorously; to all other[s] it was expressed by deep appreciation only. One way of expression of H. P.'s sentiment was to wrap his 'pinkey' finger around mine and say 'Umph!'"[94] Move over, Casanova! Sonia later admitted that Lovecraft did not like to discuss sex and became visibly upset even at the mention of the word "sex,"[95] although it is mentioned frequently—if disparagingly—in the "Lovecraft on Love" letter. The note about "appreciation" leads to one of the most celebrated passages in her memoir: "I believe he loved me as much as it was possible for a temperament like his to love. He'd never mention the word *love.* He would say instead 'My dear, you don't know how much I appreciate you.' I tried to understand him and was grateful for any crumbs from his lips that fell my way."[96] One of the very few times the word "love" is mentioned in the entire range of his correspondence occurs in a letter to Long written a month before his marriage: "One who so values love, shou'd realise that there are only two genuine kinds of it: matrimonial and parental."[97] This may well be another indication that Lovecraft and Sonia had decided to marry by this time; nevertheless, the word "love" does not seem otherwise to have crossed his lips, at least as far as Sonia was concerned. Again, none of this is entirely surprising given what we know about Lovecraft's upbringing. It is possible that that upbringing rendered him emotionally stunted, at least so far as sex and even personal relationships in general (especially with women) are concerned. In later years he would have a small number of women correspondents, but they would only be friends or associates whom he would address in an excessively formal and avuncular way. His letters to Helen Sully, Elizabeth Toldridge, C. L. Moore, and others are full of philosophical interest, but he never let his hair down to them the way he did to Long or Morton or Galpin.

If Sonia could not make Lovecraft perform sexually quite as much as she would like, she could change him in other ways. First there was his diet. Although he had put on considerable weight in the 1922–23 period, Sonia nevertheless remarks:

> When we were married he was tall and gaunt and "hungry-looking". I happen to like the apparently ascetic type but H. P. was too much even for my taste, so I used to cook a well-balanced meal every evening, make a substantial breakfast (he loved cheese soufflé!—rather an untimely dish for breakfast) and I'd leave a few (almost Dagwoodian) sandwiches for him, a piece of cake and some fruit for his lunch (he loved sweets), and I'd tell him to be sure to make some tea or coffee for himself.[98]

Elsewhere she says: "Living a normal life and eating the food I provided made him take on much extra weight, which was quite becoming to him."[99] She may have thought so, but Lovecraft didn't: he would later refer to himself as a "porpoise,"[100] and indeed he ballooned to nearly 200 pounds, which is certainly overweight for someone of his general build. It may be true that what he considered his ideal weight—140 pounds—is a trifle lean for a man of 5'11", but he came to hate the extra baggage he carried during this period. The amusing thing is that Sonia herself, according to George Kirk, was "continually bewail[ing] her avoirdupois"[101] at this time.

Both Sonia in her memoir and Lovecraft in his letters remark on the frequency with which, at least in the early months of their marriage, they would go out to restaurants. At a time when Sonia was making an enviable income (and when a reasonably good meal at a good restaurant could be had for a dollar or less), there is nothing to wonder at in this. Sonia gradually expanded Lovecraft's taste beyond the simple Anglo-Saxon fare to which he had no doubt been accustomed at 598 Angell Street. He became especially fond of Italian cuisine (which was at the time still regarded as "ethnic" food not meant for regular consumption by non-Italians), both in restaurants (especially the Milan at Eighth Avenue and 42nd Street) and as cooked by Sonia, with her special sauce; during his fifteen months alone in New York it would become his staple cuisine. Even with the impending breakup of their household, Sonia managed to cook a splendid Thanksgiving dinner for Lovecraft and his friends:

> And what a classick repast! Enchanted soup—apotheosised roast turkey with dressing of chestnuts & all the rare spices & savoury herbs that camel-caravans

> with tinkling bells bring secretly from forgotten orients of eternal spring across the deserts beyond the Oxus—cauliflower with cryptical creaming—cranberry sauce with the soul of Rhode Island bogs in it—salads that emperors have dreamed into reality—sweet potatoes with visions of pillar'd Virginia plantation-houses—gravy for which Apicius strove & Lucullus sigh'd in vain—plum pudding such as Irving never tasted at Bracebridge Hall—& to crown the feast, a gorgeous mince pie fairly articulate with memories of New-England fireplaces & cold-cellars. All the glory of earth sublimated in one transcendent repast—one divides one's life into periods of before & after having consumed—or even smelled or dream'd of—such a meal![102]

So Lovecraft was not always an ascetic—although no doubt some of this was meant as praise for Sonia's heroic efforts in preparing the meal, especially at such a trying time.

Another thing Sonia didn't like about Lovecraft, aside from his lean and hungry look, was his attire.

> I remember so well when I took him to a smart haberdashery how he protested at the newness of the coat and hat I persuaded him to accept and wear. He looked at himself in the mirror and protested, "But my dear, this is entirely too stylish for 'Grandpa Theobald'; it doesn't look like me. I look like some fashionable fop!" To which I replied, "Not all men who dress fashionably are necessarily fops."[103]

To someone in the fashion business, the conservative clothing customarily worn by Lovecraft must have been irritating indeed. Sonia adds with some tartness, "I really think he was glad that this coat and the new suit purchased that day were later stolen." Sure enough, when we read Lovecraft's catalogue of items stolen from him in the burglary of May 1925, we find "new Flatbush overcoat 1924." What still remained to him were overcoats dating to 1909, 1917 (both light), and 1918 (a winter coat); evidently the burglars felt these were not worth taking.

This simple incident may go far in suggesting what went wrong with the marriage. Although in later years Lovecraft charitably claimed that the marriage's failure was "98% financial,"[104] in reality both Sonia and Lovecraft had deceived themselves into thinking that they shared a "congeniality" (as Lovecraft stated in his marriage-announcement letter to Lillian) that went beyond intellectual and aesthetic matters and covered actual modes of behaviour and basic values. Granting that financial considerations were indeed of considerable—even paramount—importance, these differences in values would in any case have emerged in time and doomed the marriage sooner or later. In some senses it was better—at least for Lovecraft—that it occurred sooner than later.

But in those first few months the euphoria of being married, the excitement of the big city (and of fairly promising job prospects), the fortuitous arrival of Annie Gamwell at the end of March (she had been visiting a friend in Hohokus, New Jersey[105]), and of course his many friends in the area kept Lovecraft in a buoyant mood. Amateur work was still taking up some time: Sonia, as President, and Lovecraft, as Official Editor of the UAPA, managed to issue a *United Amateur* for May 1924, although it must have been a month or so late, as Sonia's "President's Message" is dated May 1. Here she announced that there would be no annual convention in late July—a consequence both of the obstructionism of the previous administration (the "anti-literati" group hostile to Lovecraft's faction) and of the general apathy overtaking the UAPA. The couple's financial and health problems later in the year forced them to place amateur affairs well to the rear of their priorities.

But social activity with amateurs still remained on the agenda. Sonia took Lovecraft frequently to the monthly meetings of the Blue Pencil Club (a NAPA group) in Brooklyn; Lovecraft did not much care for this group but would go to please his wife, and in 1925–26, when he was alone, he would skip meetings except when Sonia happened to be in town and made him go. There was some group called The Writers' Club whose meetings Lovecraft attended in March, although this does not seem to be an amateur organisation. When asked by Morton if he would attend a meeting in May, he writes: "It all depends on the ball-and-chain. If she feels equal to a wild night, we'll show up at The Writers. But if she doesn't, I'm afeard I'll have to be listed among those absent." However we are to take the "ball-and-chain" remark (one hopes it is meant in genial flippancy), Lovecraft adds rather touchingly: "She generally has to hit the hay early, and I have to get home in proportionate time, since she can't get to sleep till I do."[106] The couple did share a double bed, and no doubt Sonia had already become accustomed to having her husband beside her and felt uncomfortable when he was not there.

Lovecraft certainly found the support of his friends indispensable for maintaining emotional equilibrium during this entire period, when first the many changes in his social and professional life and, later, the successive disappointments and hardships threatened to disrupt his own mental stability. The most heartwarming portions of his letters to his aunts of 1924 are not those involving Sonia (she is mentioned with remarkable infrequency, either because Lovecraft was not spending much time with her or, more likely, because the aunts did not wish to hear about her) but those dealing with his surprisingly numerous outings with friends old and new. This was, of course, the heyday of the Kalem Club, although that term was not coined until early the next year.

Some of these men (and they were all men) we have met already—Kleiner (then a bookkeeper at the Fairbanks Scales Co. and living somewhere in Brooklyn), Morton (living in Harlem; I am not sure of his occupation at this time), and

Long (living at 823 West End Avenue in the upper West Side of Manhattan with his parents and studying journalism at New York University). Now others joined "the gang."

There was Arthur Leeds (1882–1952?), a sort of rolling stone who had been with a travelling circus as a boy and now, at the age of roughly forty, eked out a bare living as a columnist for *Writer's Digest* and occasional pulp writer for *Adventure* and other magazines; he had two stories in *Weird Tales.* He was perhaps the most indigent of this entire group of largely indigent aesthetes. At this time he was living at a hotel in West 49th Street in Hell's Kitchen. I do not know how he was introduced to Lovecraft, but he must have been a friend of one of the other members; in any case, he was rapidly incorporated into the circle. Lovecraft speaks warmly of Leeds, but after leaving New York he had little contact with him.

There was Everett McNeil (1862–1929), who like Morton earned an entry in *Who's Who in America,* on the strength of sixteen novels for boys published between 1903 and 1929, mostly for E. P. Dutton.[107] The majority of these were historical novels in which McNeil would sugarcoat the history with stirring tales of action on the part of explorers or adventurers battling Indians or colonising the American frontier. The most popular was perhaps *In Texas with Davy Crockett* (1908), which was reprinted as late as 1937. George Kirk describes him in a letter to his fiancée as "an oldster—lovely purely white hair, writes books for boys and does not need to write down to them, he is quite equal mentally."[108] Kirk did not mean that last remark at all derogatorily. Lovecraft—who had already met McNeil on one of his New York trips of 1922—felt the same way and cherished McNeil's naive simplicity, even though gradually McNeil fell out of favour with the rest of the gang for being tiresome and intellectually unstimulating. He was living, as in 1922, in Hell's Kitchen, not far from Leeds.

There was George Kirk himself (1898–1962), who had of course met Lovecraft in Cleveland in 1922 and arrived in New York in August (just before Samuel Loveman, who came in early September[109]) to pursue his bookseller's trade, settling at 50 West 106th Street in Manhattan. Although having lived in Akron and Cleveland for most of his life up to this time, he had spent the years 1920–22 in California, where he had become acquainted with Clark Ashton Smith. His one venture into publishing was *Twenty-one Letters of Ambrose Bierce* (1922), Loveman's edition of Bierce's letters to him. He had become engaged to Lucile Dvorak in late 1923 but did not wish to marry until he had established himself as a bookseller in New York; this took nearly three years, and in the interim he wrote letters to Lucile that rival Lovecraft's letters to his aunts in their detailed vignettes of "the gang." They are the only other contemporaneous documents of the sort that we have, and they are of enormous help in filling in gaps in Lovecraft's own letters and in rounding out the general picture of the group.

The Kalem Club existed in a very rudimentary—and nameless—form prior to Lovecraft's arrival in the city; Kleiner, McNeil, and perhaps Morton appear to have met occasionally at each other's homes. Long declares that "there were several small gatherings at which three or four of them were present,"[110] although he says he himself was not one of them. But clearly the group—whose chief bond was their correspondence and association with Lovecraft—fully solidified as a club only with Lovecraft's arrival.

Frank Long provides a piquant glimpse at Lovecraft's conduct at these meetings:

> Almost invariably . . . Howard did most of the talking, at least for the first ten or fifteen minutes. He would sink into an easy chair—he never seemed to feel at ease in a straight-backed chair on such occasions and I took care to keep an extremely comfortable one unoccupied until his arrival—and words would flow from him in a continuous stream.
>
> He never seemed to experience the slightest necessity to pause between words. There was no groping about for just the right term, no matter how recondite his conversation became. When the need for some metaphysical hair-splitting arose, it was easy to visualize scissors honed to a surgical sharpness snipping away in the recesses of his mind. . . .
>
> In general the conversation was lively and quite variegated. It was a brilliant enough assemblage, and the discussions ranged from current happenings of a political or sociological nature, to some recent book or play, or to five or six centuries of English and French literature, art, philosophy, and natural science.[111]

This may be as good a place as any to explore the question of Lovecraft's voice, since several of Lovecraft's New York colleagues have given us their impressions of it. I will later quote Hart Crane's reference to Sonia's "piping-voiced husband," and there seems general consensus that his voice was indeed somewhat high-pitched. Sonia has the most detailed discussion:

> His voice was clear and resonant when he read or lectured but became thin and high-pitched in general conversation, and somewhat falsetto in its ring, but when reciting favorite poems he managed to keep his voice on an even keel of deep resonance. Also his singing voice, while not strong, was very sweet. He would sing none of the modern songs, only the more favored ones of about a half century ago or more.[112]

Wilfred Blanch Talman offers a somewhat less flattering account:

> His voice had that flat and slightly nasal quality that is sometimes stereotyped as a New England characteristic. When he laughed aloud, a harsh cackle emerged that reversed the impression of his smile and to the uninitiated might be considered a ham actor's version of a hermit's laughter. Companions avoided any attempt

to achieve more than a smile in conversation with him, so unbecoming was the result.[113]

One wonders on what occasion Talman heard Lovecraft laugh, since in 1934 Lovecraft himself declared that he had laughed out loud only once in the previous twenty years.[114]

The Kalem Club began meeting weekly on Thursday nights, although they later shifted to Wednesdays because Long had a night class at NYU. It was after one such meeting that Lovecraft began the diligent if unsystematic discovery of the antiquities of the metropolitan area. On Thursday, August 21, there was a gang meeting at Kirk's place at 106th Street. The meeting broke up at 1.30 A.M. and the group started walking down Broadway, leaving successively at various subway or elevated stations on their respective ways home. Finally only Kirk and Lovecraft remained, and they continued walking all the way down Eighth Avenue through Chelsea into Greenwich Village, exploring all the colonial remnants (still existing) along Grove Court, Patchin and Milligan Places, Minetta Lane, and elsewhere. By this time it was "the sinister hours before dawn, when only cats, criminals, astronomers, and poetic antiquarians roam the waking world!"[115] But they continued walking, down the (now largely destroyed) "colonial expanse" of Varick and Charlton Streets to City Hall. They must have covered at least seven or eight miles on this entire trip. Finally they broke up around 8 A.M., Lovecraft returning home by 9. (So much for his coming home early so that he and Sonia could retire together. On a slightly earlier all-night excursion with Kleiner and Leeds, he returned home at 5 A.M., and, "having successfully dodged the traditional fusilade of conjugal flatirons and rolling-pins, I was with Hypnos, Lord of Slumbers."[116] One assumes Lovecraft is being whimsical and not literal here.)

Although the next night Lovecraft and Sonia went to see Eugene O'Neill's *All God's Chillun,* the subsequent weeks were largely taken up with activities with the gang, especially as Sonia severely sprained her ankle on August 26 and remained home for several days. On the 29th Lovecraft made a solitary exploration of the colonial antiquities of lower Manhattan, some of which—especially around Grove, Commerce, and Barrow Streets—still remain. On Sunday, September 1, he took the Staten Island ferry to that most remote and least populous of the city's boroughs, whose sleepy villages made him think of home: "St. George is a sort of Attleboro. Stapleton suggests East Greenwich."[117] One wonders whether these analogies were made solely for Lillian's sake. Later in the day he took another ferry to Perth Amboy, New Jersey, which he discovered quite surprisingly to contain an abundance of colonial houses and a general New England atmosphere. (It does not anymore.) A few days later he met Edward Lazare, one of Loveman's Cleveland friends whom he had met in 1922. Lovecraft felt that Lazare would become a "fitting accession to our select circle of The Boys,"[118] but he drops out of the picture shortly after this date. Loveman himself arrived on September 10; he had initially wished to reside at a rooming house at 110 Columbia Heights in Brooklyn, where Hart Crane (who had come to the city in March 1923) lived, but finally settled nearby at 78 Columbia Heights.

On September 12 Lovecraft made an interesting exploration of the lower East Side—interesting because of his reaction to the extensive colony of orthodox Jews there:

> Here exist assorted Jews in the absolutely unassimilated state, with their ancestral beards, skull-caps, and general costumes—which makes them very picturesque, and not nearly so offensive as the strident, pushing Jews who affect clean shaves and American dress. In this particular section, where Hebrew books are vended from pushcarts, and patriarchal rabbins totter in high hats and frock coats, there are far less offensive faces than in the general subways of the town—probably because most of the pushing commercial Jews are from another colony where the blood is less pure.[119]

Whatever the validity of that concluding observation, Lovecraft's general attitude is worth considering: his response is more charitable than one might have expected, and it seems to stem from his implicit approval of a group of people practising their "ancestral" modes of behaviour. The Orthodox Jews' scorn of the modern found an echo in Lovecraft's heart, overcoming his customary anger at the sight of "foreigners" not adopting "American" ways on American soil.

On Saturday the 13th was another long exploration of colonial sites in lower Manhattan with Loveman, Kirk, Kleiner, and Lazare, which did not break up until 4 A.M. Yet another lone excursion took place on the 15th, "to get the taste out of my mouth" after a bootless job-hunting session at a publishing house; Lovecraft again went to lower Manhattan, where at the confluence of Hudson, Watts, and Canal Streets he saw the early construction work on what would become the Holland Tunnel. On the 18th, after meeting with Henneberger, he went to three separate museums—Natural History, Metropolitan, and Brooklyn—dropping Lillian a postcard from each of them. That evening was a gang meeting at Long's, and Lovecraft wandered the streets with all the members, seeing each of them off at various subway stops; he and Leeds did not part until near dawn. It is as if Lovecraft were reluctant to go home. The next day he went to Loveman's apartment and met Crane,

> . . . a little ruddier, a little puffier, and slightly more moustached than when I saw him in Cleveland two years ago. Crane, whatever his limitations, is a thorough aesthete; and I had some enjoyable conversation with him. His room is in excellent taste, with a few paintings by William Sommer . . ., a choice collection of modern books, and some splendid small objets d'art of which a carven Buddha and an exquisitely carved Chinese ivory box are the high spots.[120]

He and Loveman went up to the roof, where they saw a spectacular vista of the Brooklyn Bridge:

> It was something mightier than the dreams of old-world legend—a constellation of infernal majesty—a poem in Babylonian fire! . . . Added to the weird lights are the weird sounds of the port, where the traffick of all the world comes to a focus. Fog-horns, ships' bells, the creak of distant windlasses . . . visions of far shores of Ind, where bright-plumed birds are roused to song by the incense of strange garden-girt pagodas, and gaudy-robed camel-drivers barter before sandalwood taverns with deep-voiced sailors having the sea's mystery in their eyes.

The poetry of New York had not quite worn off after seven months. Lovecraft interestingly reports that "Crane is writing a long poem on Brooklyn Bridge in a modern medium": this would, of course, be Crane's masterpiece, *The Bridge* (1930), on which he had begun work as early as February 1923.[121] It should be pointed out that Crane was rather less charitable to Lovecraft in his various letters than Lovecraft was to Crane. Writing on September 14 to his mother and grandmother, Crane notes Loveman's arrival in the city but says that he has not spent much time with him because he has been occupied with his many friends—"Miss Sonia Green [*sic*] and her piping-voiced husband, Howard Lovecraft, (the man who visited Sam in Cleveland one summer when Galpin was also there) kept Sam traipsing around the slums and wharf streets until four this morning looking for Colonial specimens of architecture, and until Sam tells me he groaned with fatigue and begged for the subway!"[122] The former "invalid" Lovecraft had already become famous for outwalking all his friends!

Kleiner, in a memoir, supplies a partial answer to a question that has perhaps occurred to nearly everyone reading of Lovecraft's long walks all around Manhattan at night, whether alone or with others: how is it that he escaped being the victim of a crime? Kleiner writes:

> In Greenwich Village, for whose eccentric habitants he had little use, he was fond of poking about in back alleys where his companions preferred not to go. In prohibition years, with murderous affrays among bootleggers and rum-runners likely to break out anywhere, this was a particularly dangerous business. Every other house in this neighborhood was open to suspicion as a speakeasy. I recall that at least once, while stumbling around old barrels and crates in some dark corner of this area, Lovecraft found a doorway suddenly illuminated and an excited foreigner, wearing the apron that was an almost infallible sign of a speakeasy bartender, enquiring hotly what he wanted. Loveman and Kirk went in after Lovecraft and got him safely out. None of us, surely, was under any illusion as to what might very well happen in such an obscure corner of the city.[123]

Lovecraft was certainly fearless—perhaps a little foolhardy—on these jaunts. He was, of course, at this time a fairly imposing physical specimen at nearly six feet and

200 pounds; but physical size means nothing when one is faced with a knife or gun, and many criminals are also not put off by a prospective victim's apparent lack of prosperity. Lovecraft was, in effect, simply lucky in not coming to harm on these peregrinations.

Annie Gamwell paid a visit beginning on September 21; over the next several days he showed her the same antiquarian treasures in Greenwich Village and elsewhere that he had just seen—it is obvious that he could not get enough of them. On the 24th he and Loveman went to the Poe Cottage in Fordham and then to the Van Cortlandt mansion (1748) in the Bronx. The next day Lovecraft took Annie to the Poe Cottage. On the 26th the two of them wrote Lillian a joint postcard from the Dyckman House (c. 1783), a small Dutch colonial farmhouse in the far northern reaches of Manhattan; Annie writes charmingly, if a little wistfully, "Would like to buy this house—it's so homey & nice."[124] (In a long letter he wrote to Lillian on the 29th and 30th Lovecraft speaks even more wistfully of buying back "the old place in Foster," i.e., the Stephen Place home where his mother was born.) Later that day the two of them visited the spectacular but unfinished Cathedral of St John the Divine on the upper West Side near Columbia University. Annie went home the next day. That evening was a Blue Pencil Club meeting, and the prescribed topic for literary contributions was "The Old Home Town." It was a theme close to Lovecraft's heart, and he produced the thirteen-stanza poem "Providence" for the occasion—virtually the first creative writing he had done since writing "Under the Pyramids" in February. It was published in the *Brooklynite* for November 1924 and, sometime in November, in the *Providence Evening Bulletin,* for which he received $5.00.[125]

Early October saw his first visit to Elizabeth, New Jersey (which Lovecraft persistently calls by its eighteenth-century name of Elizabethtown). An editorial in the *New York Times* had alerted him to the existence of colonial antiquities there, and on the 10th he went there by way of the Staten Island ferry and then another ferry to Elizabeth. He was entirely captivated. After arming himself with an array of guidebooks and historical matter from a stationery store, the public library, and the newspaper office (presumably the *Elizabeth Daily Journal*), he had only a chance to do a small amount of investigation on the edge of town before night fell and he had to return to Brooklyn. But he came back the next day, taking in the old Presbyterian Church, the First Church and its ancient churchyard, and along the Elizabeth River where the oldest houses stand. "But lud, ma'am—I cou'd rave all night about Elizabethtown!" he wrote to Lillian.[126] But, as with Portsmouth, New Hampshire, and other sites, it was not only the prevalence of antique structures that delighted him:

> There is no taint of New York & its nasty cosmopolitanism. All the people of substance are native Yankees, & though the factory sections teem with low Poles, they

are not frequently met on the main streets. Niggers are quite thick in the byways of the town . . . The whole atmosphere of the place is marvellously colonial. . . . Elizabethtown is a balm, a sedative, & a tonic to the old-fashion'd soul rackt with modernity.

Is it any wonder that, when little more than a month later he and Sonia had to think of breaking up their household, Lovecraft wished to settle at least temporarily here?

On October 12 Lovecraft had Loveman over for dinner (prepared by Sonia, of course), after which the two men returned to Columbia Heights, met Crane, and went for a walk with him in the evening along the shore. Crane seemed to take note of this meeting when he said in a letter that Sam "brought along that queer Lovecraft person with him, so we had no particularly intimate conversation."[127] Later Lovecraft and Loveman crossed over to lower Manhattan for more colonial exploration, staying there till midnight.

Lovecraft's Elizabeth visit proved to be the catalyst for his first story in eight months, "The Shunned House." Part of his description of the place reads as follows:

. . . on the northeast corner of Bridge St. & Elizabeth Ave. is a terrible old house—a hellish place where night-black deeds must have been done in the early seventeen-hundreds—with a blackish unpainted surface, unnaturally steep roof, & an outside flight of steps leading to the second story, suffocatingly embowered in a tangle of ivy so dense that one cannot but imagine it accursed or corpse-fed. It reminded me of the Babbitt house in Benefit St., which as you recall made me write those lines entitled "The House" in 1920.[128]

This house in Elizabeth, unfortunately, is no longer standing. The poem "The House" is a finely atmospheric piece published in Galpin's *Philosopher* for December 1920; its source—what Lovecraft here calls the Babbitt house—was the house at 135 Benefit Street in Providence, where Lillian had resided in 1919–20 as a companion for Mrs C. H. Babbit (so spelled in the 1920 U.S. census). That house had been built around 1763 and is a magnificent structure—with basement, two stories, and attic—built on the rising hill, with shuttered doors in the basement leading directly out into the sidewalk. It has been considerably restored since Lovecraft's day, but at that time it must have been a spectral place. Lovecraft spent the whole of the 16th through the 19th of October writing a draft of the story, making considerable "eliminations & rearrangements"[129] and doing more revision the next day after having read it to Frank Long. (It was in the evening of this day that Sonia was stricken with her gastric attack and had to be taken to the hospital.)

"The Shunned House" opens sententiously: "From even the greatest of horrors irony is seldom absent." The irony in question is the fact that Edgar Allan Poe, "the world's greatest master of the terrible and the bizarre," in his late (1848–49) courtship of the minor poet Sarah Helen Whitman, walked frequently along

Benefit Street in Providence past a house whose bizarrerie, had he known of it, far surpassed any of his own fictional horrors. This house, occupied by several generations of the Harris family, is never considered "haunted" by the local citizens but merely "unlucky": people simply seem to have an uncanny habit of dying there, or at least of being afflicted with anaemia or consumption. Neighbouring houses are free of any such taint. It had lain deserted—because of the impossibility of renting it—since the Civil War.

The first-person unnamed narrator had known of this house since boyhood, when some of his childhood friends would fearfully explore it, sometimes even boldly entering through the unlocked front door "in quest of shudders." As he grows older, he discovers that his uncle, Elihu Whipple, had done considerable research on the house and its tenants, and he finds his seemingly dry genealogical record full of sinister suggestion. He comes to suspect that some nameless object or entity is causing the deaths by somehow sucking the vitality out of the house's occupants; perhaps it has some connexion with a strange thing in the cellar, "a vague, shifting deposit of mould or nitre . . . [that] bore an uncanny resemblance to a doubled-up human figure."

After telling, at some length, the history of the house since 1763, the narrator finds himself puzzled on several fronts; in particular, he cannot account for why some of the occupants, just prior to their deaths, would cry out in a coarse and idiomatic form of French, a language they did not know. As he explores town records, he seems at last to have come upon the "French element." A sinister figure named Etienne Roulet had come from France to East Greenwich, Rhode Island, in 1686; he was a Huguenot and fled France after the revocation of the Edict of Nantes, moving to Providence ten years later in spite of much opposition from the town fathers. What particularly intrigues the narrator is his possible connexion with an even more dubious figure, Jacques Roulet of Caude, who in 1598 was accused of lycanthropy.

Finally the narrator and his uncle decide to "test—and if possible destroy—the horror of the house." They come one evening in 1919, armed with both a Crookes tube (a device invented by Sir William Crookes involving the emission of electrons between two electrodes) and a flame-thrower. The two men take turns resting; both experience hideous and disturbing dreams. When the narrator wakes up from his dream, he finds that some nameless entity has utterly engulfed his uncle:

> Out of the fungus-ridden earth steamed up a vaporous corpse-light, yellowed and diseased, which bubbled and lapped to a gigantic height in vague outlines half-human and half-monstrous, through which I could see the chimney and fireplace beyond. It was all eyes—wolfish and mocking—and the rugose insect-like head dissolved at the top to a thin stream of mist which curled putridly about and finally vanished up the chimney. . . . That object was my uncle—the venerable Elihu Whipple—who with blackening and decaying features leered and gibbered at me,

> and reached out dripping claws to rend me in the fury which this horror had brought.

Realising that his uncle is past help, he aims the Crookes tube at him. A further daemoniac sight appears to him: the object seems to liquefy and adopt various temporary forms ("He was at once a devil and a multitude, a charnel-house and a pageant"); then the features of the Harris line seem to mingle with his uncle's. The narrator flees, heading down College Hill to the modern downtown business district; when he returns, hours later, the nebulous entity is gone. Later that day he brings six carboys of sulphuric acid to the house, digs up the earth where the doubled-up anthropomorphic shape lies, and pours the acid down the hole—realising only then that the shape was merely the "titan *elbow*" of some huge and hideous monster.

What is, of course, remarkable about "The Shunned House" is the exquisite linkage of real and imagined history throughout the tale. Much of the history of the house is real, although it has at no time been unoccupied; indeed, the 1919 date was surely chosen because this was when Lillian was residing there. Other details are also authentic—the straightening out of Benefit Street after the removal of the graves of the oldest settlers to the North Burial Ground; the mentions of the great floods of 1815 (which in fact caused much destruction of houses along Benefit, South Main, and Water Streets, as the many surviving structures from the 1816–20 period attest); even the random mention of the fact that "As lately as 1892 an Exeter community exhumed a dead body and ceremoniously burnt its heart in order to prevent certain alleged visitations injurious to the public health and peace." This last point has been studied by Faye Ringel Hazel, who points out that several articles on this subject appeared in the *Providence Journal* in March 1892,[130] and goes on to examine the vampire legendry of Exeter (in Washington County, south of Providence) and the neighbouring area.

But on the other hand, there are sly insertions of fictitious events and connexions into the historical record. Elihu Whipple is said to be a descendant of Capt. Abraham Whipple, who led the burning of the *Gaspee* in 1772. The sequence of births and deaths of the Harris family is largely, but not wholly, fictitious.

The most interesting elaboration upon history in the story is the figure of Etienne Roulet. This figure is imaginary, but Jacques Roulet of Caude is quite real. Lovecraft's brief mention of him is taken almost verbatim from the account in John Fiske's *Myths and Myth-Makers* (1872), which we have already seen was a significant source of Lovecraft's early views on the anthropology of religion. Part of Fiske's account of Roulet is, however, a direct quotation from S. Baring-Gould's *A Book of Were-wolves* (1865); but Lovecraft had not read this book at this time (he would do so only a decade or so later[131]), so that his information on Jacques Roulet must have come from Fiske. It is, of course, a little peculiar that the presumed grandson of a reputed werewolf should become some sort of vampiric entity; aside from "Psychopompos" and perhaps "The Hound," this is the only occasion where Lovecraft treats either of these standard myths, and here he has altered it beyond recognition—or, rather, accounted for it with a novel way.

For the most interesting part of the story—in terms of Lovecraft's future development as a writer—is a strange passage in the middle as the narrator is attempting to come to grips with the exact nature of the malevolent entity:

> We were not . . . in any sense childishly superstitious, but scientific study and reflection had taught us that the known universe of three dimensions embraces the merest fraction of the whole cosmos of substance and energy. In this case an overwhelming preponderance of evidence from numerous authentic sources pointed to the tenacious existence of certain forces of great power and, so far as the human point of view is concerned, exceptional malignancy. To say that we actually believed in vampires or werewolves would be a carelessly inclusive statement. Rather must it be said that we were not prepared to deny the possibility of certain unfamiliar and unclassified modifications of vital force and attenuated matter; existing very infrequently in three-dimensional space because of its more intimate connexion with other spatial units, yet close enough to the boundary of our own to furnish us occasional manifestations which we, for lack of a proper vantage point, may never hope to understand. . . .
>
> Such a thing was surely not a physical or biochemical impossibility in the light of a newer science which includes the theories of relativity and intra-atomic action. . . .

This remarkable passage suddenly transforms "The Shunned House" into a sort of science-fiction story (or perhaps proto-science-fiction, since the genre cannot be said to have come into true existence at this time), in that it enunciates the crucial principle of a scientific rationale for a seemingly supernatural occurrence or event. A year and a half after Lovecraft had expressed bafflement and perturbation at the Einstein theory, he was making convenient use of it in fiction. The reference to "intra-atomic action" is some sort of bow to the quantum theory, although I have not found any discussions of it at this time in letters. Whether this scientific account is at all convincing or plausible is not quite to the point; it is the gesture that is important. That the entity is killed not by driving a stake through its heart but by sulphuric acid is telling. The "titan elbow" seems an adaptation of the ending of "Under the Pyramids," where what appeared to be a five-headed hippopotamus proves to be the paw of an immense monster.

The figure of Elihu Whipple is clearly modelled upon that of Lovecraft's own uncle, Franklin Chase Clark. Naturally there are some divergences: Whipple is a bachelor (in this way Lovecraft could dispense with any grieving widow when Whipple dies), and is considerably older than Dr Clark, as he had begun his medical practice in 1860, when Clark was only thirteen. In fact, Whipple is not described in any great detail, and the two occasions on which the narrator expresses sadness at his passing—"I am lonely without that gentle soul whose long years were filled only with honour, virtue, good taste, benevolence, and learning"; ". . . I shed the first of the many tears with which I have paid unaffected tribute to my beloved uncle's memory"—are still very reserved, although even this level of personal emotion is unusual for a Lovecraft story. There is no question that Lovecraft did indeed feel the loss of Dr Clark poignantly; it is simply that he has not here characterised Dr Whipple sufficiently so that a reader will feel analogously.

"The Shunned House" is a dense, richly textured story with convincing historical background and a fine sense of cumulative horror. The account of the lives and deaths of the Harris family in the second chapter may perhaps go on a little too long: Lovecraft hoped that it will create an atmosphere of the eerily sinister (the narrator remarks: "In this continuous record there seemed to me to brood a persistent evil beyond anything in Nature as I had known it"), but it is perhaps a little too dry and clinical for that effect to occur. But the hideous climax (with another genuine surprise ending) and the thought-provoking scientific rationale for the horror make this a noteworthy landmark in Lovecraft's early corpus.

That he chose to write a story about Providence at this juncture is hardly surprising. "The Shunned House" is, indeed, the first significant tale to be set in Providence and to evoke its history and topography; earlier, minor stories such as "From Beyond" nominally take place there but have nothing of this tale's specificity of setting. The poem "The House" also lacks this specificity, and one would never know that it was based on 135 Benefit Street had Lovecraft not said so. For all his initial euphoria at coming to New York, he had never left Providence; the trip to Elizabeth had merely acted as a sort of mnemonic trigger for a tale that brings his hometown to life.

Lovecraft read the story to the gang on November 16 and was heartened at the response: they all "waxed incredibly enthusiastick in affirming that it is the best thing I ever writ."[132] Loveman was particularly keen, and wanted Lovecraft to type it by Wednesday the 19th so that he could show it to a reader at Alfred A. Knopf. This did not happen, as Lovecraft did not finish typing the story until the 22nd, but Loveman continued throughout the next year to try to promote the story. We shall discover, indeed, that its experiences in print were not entirely happy.

More gang activity followed, especially during Sonia's hospital stay in late October. A schism had developed in the gang when McNeil took offence at Leeds's inability to pay back $8.00 he had borrowed from him; McNeil therefore refused to attend any meetings at which Leeds was present. This proved to be more unfortunate for McNeil than for anyone else, since the other members (except Lovecraft) found him a trifle old-fashioned and not a good conversationalist. The result was that separate "McNeil" and "Leeds" meetings of the gang had to be held, and many members did not even bother attending the McNeil sessions; but Lovecraft always did.

Lovecraft and Kirk were becoming close friends. "In beliefs," said Lovecraft, "he & I are exactly as one—for despite a stern Methodist upbringing he is an absolute cynick & sceptick, who realises most poignantly the fundamental purposelessness of the universe."[133] Kirk, for his part, writes to his future wife: "I *do* enjoy HPL's company. Girl, if you ever give me a more enjoyable time I shall hand you the skid-proof banana peel."[134] The two had another all-night walking session on October 24–25, talking philosophy into the wee hours, exploring the cryptlike basement of the American Radiator Company in the morning, and stopping off at various coffee shops or automats along the way. Lovecraft described the latter to Lillian: "a restaurant where the food is arranged on plates in glass-doored pigeon-holes along the walls. A nickel in the slot unlocks the door, & the plate of food is taken by the purchaser to one of the many tables in the great room."[135] A great place for people with meagre funds to stop for refreshment. Although it may seem that these establishments were the havens of derelicts and homeless people, they were in fact clean and well lit, and served a wide spectrum of the middle and lower classes of the city; and since none of the gang except Kleiner, Long (who would rarely go on these nightly jaunts), and perhaps Morton had much money, they were welcome resting-places. There are almost no automats in New York anymore; what few there are do not cost a nickel anymore.

On Monday, November 3, Lovecraft welcomed Edward Lloyd Sechrist (1873–1953), an amateur associate from Washington. Sechrist, a beekeeper by trade who had spent much time in the South Seas and central Africa, had apparently visited Lovecraft in Providence just prior to the latter's move to New York.[136] Naturally, Sechrist was shown the city's museums and colonial antiquities by the indefatigable Lovecraft. On the 4th the two of them went to the Anderson Galleries on Park Avenue and 59th Street to meet a friend of Sechrist's, John M. Price; Lovecraft had some dim hope that Price might be able to help him get a job at the gallery, but obviously nothing came of this.

If Lovecraft gives the impression, in his various accounts of evenings or all nights out with the boys, that he was not spending much time with Sonia, it is perhaps because he actually wasn't—at least by August or September. Some months earlier the picture was a little different, and we get a charming vignette of a few days in early July:

> The next day—the so-called glorious fourth of the Yankee rebels—S.H. and I devoted to open-air reading in Prospect Park. We have discovered a delightfully unfrequented rock overhanging a lake not far from our own door; and there we while away many an hour in the pages of chosen friends from our well-stocked

> shelves. . . . Saturday, the fifth, this reading programme was repeated; and on Sunday we spent most of the day answering the help wanted advertisements in the Sunday papers. Monday the seventh, we dedicated to pleasure and travel—that is, after one business interview—meeting at Trinity about noon, paying our respects to [Alexander] Hamilton's grave, visiting the fine Colonial town house of President James Monroe . . ., threading some Colonial alleys in Greenwich-Village, and finally taking the omnibus at Washington Square and riding all the way up to Fort George, where we descended the steep hill to Dyckman Street, took lunch in a humble restaurant . . . and proceeded to the ferry. Here embarking, we crossed the spacious Hudson to the foot of the Palisades; changing to an omnibus which climbed the precipitous slope by a zigzag road arrangement affording some magnificent views, and which finally turned inland through a forest road lined with fine estates and terminating at the quaint and sleepy village of Englewood, N.J. . . . After that we rode down to Fort Lee (opposite 125th St.) by trolley, crossed to the ferry, and rode all the way home by various changes of open surface car. It was a great day . . .[137]

A great day indeed, and a perfectly wholesome way for a husband and wife to spend it, even if both are unemployed. But this sort of activity seems to stop with the passage of time. Indeed, it is typical that, after depositing Sonia at her rest home in Somerville, New Jersey, on November 9, he proceeded the next day down to Philadelphia, whose colonial marvels he wished to examine in greater detail than he was able to on his honeymoon. He arrived on the evening of November 10 (having stayed overnight in Somerville) and checked into the YMCA. Not willing to wait till the next morning, he began a "nocturnal tour of the colonial past—in the older section toward the Delaware waterfront."[138] The "mile on mile of Georgian houses of every sort" made Greenwich Village's colonial section seem meagre by comparison.

On the 11th he raided the public library for guidebooks and historical matter, then set forth. St Peter's Church at Third and Pine particularly captivated him, especially since "there was the most friendly big yellow cat imaginable on a corner diagonally across the street."[139] Next he saw the Market House, the Maritime Exchange, Independence Hall, Congress Hall, the Betsey Ross house (where he met a garrulous old antiquarian who gave him further tips), then, after a trolley car ride south, the Old Swedes' Church and churchyard. By this time it was evening, so he returned, had a bean and spaghetti dinner with a chocolate sundae for dessert, took his first shower-bath in twenty-five years (as opposed to his usual tub bath), and wrote postcards in his room. In his letter to Lillian he spoke of having no previous meal during this entire peregrination; this may be an oversight, but more likely he did not in fact have any meals. When antiquarian exploration was on the agenda, enthusiasm and sheer nervous energy took over.

On Wednesday the 12th there was more. First he examined both the exterior and interior of the superb Christ Church, one of the most magnificent Georgian churches in the country, then along the river to the Pennsylvania Historical Society with its rich collection of colonial memorabilia, then to William Penn's house in Fairmount Park. Again dusk set in, so he returned and had a dinner of beef pie, macaroni, apple pie, and coffee at an automat for 40¢. He noted at this point that he stocked up on "my breakfast supply of cheese and peanut butter sandwiches" (10¢).[140]

On Thursday the 13th he decided to do some exploration in more remote suburban areas. First was the peculiar Bartram house in the Kingsessing district in the southwestern part of the city, beyond the Schuylkill. This stone structure was built by the botanist John Bartram in 1731 with his own hands and is very eccentric and heterogeneous in design. Then Lovecraft proceeded to Chester, a separate community well to the southwest of the Philadelphia city limits on the Delaware River. Returning to Fairmount Park, he saw a number of fine colonial homes before stopping for dinner (beans, cinnamon bun, and coffee for 25¢). That evening he proceeded to the home of the amateur poet Washington Van Dusen in Germantown, a remote suburb to the northwest; he was evidently not asked to spend the night there, as he returned to the Y late in the evening.

On the 14th Lovecraft rose before dawn in order to "observe the gold & rose dawn from the hills beyond the Schuylkill."[141] He then went back to Germantown, exploring that colonial haven thoroughly before proceeding still farther west to the Wissahickon valley: "It is a deep, wooded gorge of prodigious scenic magnificence, at the bottom of which flows the narrow, limpid Wissahickon on its way to join the Schuylkill. Legend has woven many beautiful tales around this piny paradise with its precipitous walls . . ."[142] Regretfully he returned to Philadelphia where, at the Broad Street station, he caught the train back to New York.

Lovecraft was much taken with Philadelphia:

> None of the crude, foreign hostility & underbreeding of New York—none of the vulgar trade spirit & plebeian hustle. A city of real American background—an integral & continuous outgrowth of a definite & aristocratic past instead of an Asiatic hell's huddle of the world's cowed, broken, inartistic, & unfit. What a poise—what a mellowness—what a character in the preponderantly Nordic faces![143]

Now, perhaps, it could be said that the honeymoon with New York was over.

The rest of the month was tranquil. He and Sonia played more chess and went to see the museum of the New York Historical Society. James F. Morton took an examination for a job as curator of the Paterson (New Jersey) Museum, a job he would ultimately secure early the next year. On the 24th Lovecraft ate ravioli for the first time and read H. G. Wells's *The Time Machine* ("thoroughly entertaining in every detail"[144]). The next day he and Sonia went to the Bronx Zoo. The gang meeting on Wednesday the 26th was spoiled by Morton's urging the members to solve crossword puzzles, so that instead of scintillating conversation there were merely "grunts such as '23 vertical', '13 horizontal', 'word of 17 letters beginning with X & meaning cloudy in the attic', &c. &c. &c."[145] Crossword puzzles had only been introduced about a year or two before and must have been the Rubik's cubes of 1924. Nevertheless, after the meeting Lovecraft and Kirk went on another all-night walking tour, this time along East River Park, past the Gracie Mansion (now the residence of the mayor) and the Queensboro Bridge, across to the west side, down to Greenwich Village and finally, at 7 A.M., to their respective homes. Thursday, of course, was the lavish Thanksgiving banquet. On the 29th Loveman and Kirk were evidently to introduce Lovecraft to Allen Tate, then a reviewer for the *Nation;* but I cannot ascertain whether this meeting actually took place. Tate was also a great friend and supporter of Hart Crane.

Lillian herself arrived, as I have mentioned, on December 1 and stayed until January 10. Kirk wrote to his fiancée that Lovecraft talked with him one Saturday at his place from 10 P.M. till 8 A.M. Sunday; on the 20th the gang meeting lasted until 4.30 A.M.[146] But the breakup of the household was the prime activity. Lovecraft was still hankering to move to Elizabeth, but must later have decided that this was impracticable and resolved instead on Brooklyn Heights, specifically a one-room apartment (with two alcoves) for $40.00 a month at 169 Clinton Street. Sonia left for Cincinnati at 4 P.M. on the 31st, after which Lovecraft proceeded to Kirk's to see the old year out.

Lovecraft and Sonia cohabited for only ten continuous months; the occasions on which she returned to New York from the Midwest over the next year and a quarter amounted to a net total of about thirteen weeks. It is too early to pass judgment on Lovecraft as a husband; we must first examine what the next fifteen months would bring. He may or may not have been secretly pleased at Sonia's departure; but if he thought that 1924 was a year he would rather forget, he had no idea what 1925 would be like.

NOTES

Chapter 1: Unmixed English Ancestry

1. HPL to FBL, [November 1927] (*SL* 2.179).

2. *SL* 2.182 (note 1).

3. See Kenneth W. Faig, Jr., "Quae Amamus Tuemur: Ancestors in Lovecraft's Life and Fiction," in Faig's *The Unknown Lovecraft* (New York: Hippocampus Press, 2009), 20.

4. Ibid., 20–21.

5. HPL to RHB, [19 March 1934] (*SL* 4.392).

6. I am grateful to Suzanne Juta and to Oliver Watson, Curator of Ceramics and Glass at the Victoria and Albert Museum, for this information.

7. Longfellow, "The Luck of Edenhall," *The Poems of Longfellow* (New York: Illustrated Modern Library, 1944), 438–40.

8. See *Dictionary of National Biography* 6.1270–71.

9. HPL to AD, 5 June 1936 (*SL* 5.263).

10. HPL to MWM, 5 April 1931 (*SL* 3.360).

11. HPL to MWM, 1 January 1915 (*SL* 1.7).

12. Faig, "Quae Amamus Tuemur," 22.

13. See Kenneth W. Faig, Jr, *Moshassuck Review* (May Eve 1992): 29.

14. Kenneth W. Faig, Jr, *Moshassuck Review* (Halloween 1991): 14.

15. Ibid., 28.

16. Faig, "Quae Amamus Tuemur," 30.

17. *SL* 1.5 (note 11).

18. I am grateful to Kenneth W. Faig, Jr, and A. Langley Searles for this information. For further data on Lovecraft's paternal ancestry, see Docherty, Searles, and Faig, *Devonshire Ancestry of Howard Phillips Lovecraft* (Glenview, IL: Moshassuck Press, 2003).

19. *SL* 1.7 (note 11).

20. HPL to Edwin Baird, 3 February 1924 (*SL* 1.296).

21. *SL* 1.6 (note 11).

22. Obituary of Whipple V. Phillips, *Providence Journal* (31 March 1904).

23. *SL* 1.6 (note 11).

24. HPL spells his maternal grandmother's first name as "Rhoby," but Robie is given on the central shaft of the Phillips plot at Swan Point Cemetery in Providence.

25. HPL to Helen Sully, 26 July 1936 (ms., JHL).

26. Casey B. Tyler, *Historical Reminiscences, of Foster, Rhode Island,* first published c. 1884 in the *Pawtuxet Valley Gleaner* and in a revised form in the same newspaper in 1892–93; rpt. in *Early Historical Accounts of Foster, Rhode Island,* ed. Kenneth W. Faig, Jr (Glenview, IL: Moshassuck Press, 1993), 100–101.

27. In a letter to FBL, 26 October 1926 (*SL* 2.88) HPL states that Whipple Phillips's last two children were born in Greene, which would date Whipple's arrival to around 1864; but the 1860 U.S. census already lists the family at Greene.

28. Ibid.

29. Henry W. Rugg, *History of Freemasonry in Rhode Island* (Providence: E. L. Freeman & Son, 1895), 553. I am grateful to Kenneth W. Faig, Jr, for bringing this work to my attention.

30. Ibid., 554.

31. *SL* 3.363 (note 10).

32. *SL* 2.83 (note 27).

33. Tyler, in Faig, *Early Historical Accounts of Foster, Rhode Island,* 101. Faig reports that the typescript of this work at the Rhode Island Historical Society renders the name as Hugog, but the published version prints it as Hugag.

34. *Early Historical Accounts of Foster, Rhode Island,* 112.

35. *SL* 2.88 (note 27).

36. HPL dates the move to 1873 at *SL* 1.6 (note 11), but Whipple Phillips's obituary (note 22) unequivocally states that it occurred in 1874; moreover, Whipple does not appear in the Providence city directory until 1875, arguing for a settlement in 1874. For this information, and much else on Whipple Phillips, I am much indebted to the work of Kenneth W. Faig, Jr, most recently his *Some of the Descendants of Asaph Phillips and Esther Whipple of Foster, Rhode Island* (Glenview, IL: Moshassuck Press, 1993).

37. *Reports of the United States Commissioners to the Paris Universal Exposition 1878* (Washington, DC: Government Printing Office, 1880), 1.341.

38. HPL to RK, 16 November 1916 (*SL* 1.33).

39. HPL to F. Lee Baldwin, 13 January 1934 (*SL* 4.344).

40. See Kenneth W. Faig, Jr, "Whipple V. Phillips and the Owyhee Land and Irrigation Company" (*Owyhee Outpost*, May 1988); rpt. *The Unknown Lovecraft*, 50–55.

41. HPL to F. Lee Baldwin, 31 January 1934 (*SL* 4.350).

42. See note 39.

43. All three letters are at JHL. Mrs Ethel Phillips Morrish had in her possession another letter from Whipple Phillips to Lovecraft, but I am uncertain of its date or point of origin.

44. *SL* 4.351 (note 41).

45. Arthur S. Koki, "H. Lovecraft: An Introduction to His Life and Writings" (M.A. thesis: Columbia University, 1962), 3.

46. HPL to LDC, 17–18 November 1924 (ms., JHL).

47. H. Smith, "Growth of Public Education," in Edward Field, ed., *State of Rhode Island and Providence Plantations at the End of the Century: A History* (Boston: Mason Publishing Co., 1902), 2.368–69.

48. Kenneth W. Faig, Jr, *The Parents of Howard Phillips Lovecraft* (West Warwick, RI: Necronomicon Press, 1990), 23, 25.

49. *SL* 1.33 (note 38).

50. Faig, *Parents*, 40.

51. *SL* 1.6 (note 11).

52. *SL* 1.29 (note 38).

53. Faig, *Some of the Descendants*, 134.

54. *SL* 1.33–34 (note 38).

55. R. Alain Everts believes that she was educated at the Wheeler School in Providence.

56. Sarah Susan Lovecraft, *Commonplace Book* (ms., JHL).

57. Faig, *Parents*, 40.

58. Clara Hess in the *Providence Journal* (19 September 1948); quoted in Faig, *Parents*, 32.

59. Clara Hess in AD, "Lovecraft's Sensitivity" (1949); quoted in Faig, *Parents*, 33.

60. See Richard D. Squires, *Stern Fathers 'neath the Mould: The Lovecraft Family in Rochester* (1995).

61. *SL* 1.5 (note 11).

62. HPL to RK, 16 November 1916; *Letters to Reinhardt Kleiner* (New York: Hippocampus Press, 2005), 65 (this portion not printed in *SL*).

63. William G. McLoughlin, *Rhode Island: A Bicentennial History* (New York: W. W. Norton, 1978), 123.

64. Sonia H. Davis, *The Private Life of H. P. Lovecraft*, ed. S. T. Joshi (West Warwick, RI: 1985; rev. 1992), 7.

65. Koki, 4.

66. I am grateful to John H. Stanley of JHL, Brown University, for this information. The library is now the repository for the papers of the Providence branch of the Gorham Company, but it does not have the papers of the New York branch.

67. *SL* 1.296 (note 20).

Chapter 2: A Genuine Pagan

1. See McLoughlin, *Rhode Island: A Bicentennial History*, passim.

2. On this subject see now Charles Rappleye, *Sons of Providence: The Brown Brothers, the Slave Trade, and the American Revolution* (New York: Simon & Schuster, 2006).

3. HPL to Bernard Austin Dwyer, 3 March 1927 (*SL* 2.108).

4. Charles V. Chapin, "Epidemics and Medical Institutions," in Field, *State of Rhode Island and Providence Plantations at the End of the Century,* 2.57–58.

5. HPL to AEPG, 19 August 1921 (*SL* 1.147).

6. Chapin, in *Field, State of Rhode Island,* 2.66.

7. HPL to MWM, 1 January 1915 (*SL* 1.6).

8. HPL to RHB, [24 May 1935]; *O Fortunate Floridian: H. P. Lovecraft's Letters to R. H. Barlow* (Tampa: University of Tampa Press, 2007), 271.

9. HPL to LDC, 24 August 1925 (ms., JHL).

10. HPL to RK, 16 November 1916 (*SL* 1.31).

11. *SL* 1.6 (note 7).

12. HPL to Edwin Baird, 3 February 1924 (*SL* 1.296).

13. HPL to JVS, 19[–31?] July 1931 (*SL* 3.383).

14. HPL to JVS, 4 February 1934 (*SL* 4.354).

15. Cited in Faig, *Parents,* 8. There are no allusions to the Lovecrafts in the two-volume *Letters of Louise Imogen Guiney* (1926).

16. See Kenneth W. Faig, Jr, "The Friendship of Louise Imogen Guiney and Sarah Susan Phillips," in The *Unknown Lovecraft,* 70–86.

17. *SL* 2.107 (note 3).

18. "Medical Record of Winfield Scott Lovecraft," *LS* No. 24 (Spring 1991): 15.

19. *SL* 1.6 (note 7).

20. *SL* 1.33 (note 10).

21. *SL* 1.32 (note 10).

22. H. Smith, in Field, *State of Rhode Island,* 2.385.

23. Sister Mary Adorita, *Soul Ordained to Fail: (Louise Imogen Guiney: 1861–1920)* (New York: Pageant Press, 1962), 8.

24. Henry G. Fairbanks, *Louise Imogen Guiney: Laureate of the Lost* (Albany, NY: Magi Books, 1972), 2.

25. See Faig (note 16), 83.

26. *SL* 1.32 (note 10).

27. Cited in E. M. Tenison, *Louise Imogen Guiney: Her Life and Works 1861–1920* (London: Macmillan, 1923), 57–58.

28. Tenison, 29.

29. HPL to AD, [January 1930] (*SL* 2.100).

30. *SL* 1.33 (note 10).

31. HPL to RK, 16 November 1916; *Letters to Reinhardt Kleiner,* 66.

32. HPL to REH, 4 October 1930 (*SL* 3.184).

33. HPL to RK, 2 February 1916 (*SL* 1.20).

34. *SL* 1.296 (note 12).

35. HPL to Richard F. Searight, 4 November 1935; *Letters to Richard F. Searight* (West Warwick, RI: Necronomicon Press, 1992), 68–69.

36. *SL* 1.6 (note 7).

37. Cited in Koki, 10.

38. Quoted in Faig, *Parents,* 11.

39. Koki, 11.

40. M. Eileen McNamara, M.D., "Winfield Scott Lovecraft's Final Illness," *LS* No. 24 (Fall 1991): 14.

41. Quoted by Faig, *Parents,* 11.

42. Koki, 12.

43. Faig, Parents, 11, quoting Everts, "The Lovecraft Family in America," *Xenophile* 2, No. 6 (October 1975): 7.

44. Sonia H. Davis, "Memories of Lovecraft" (1969), in *Lovecraft Remembered,* ed. Peter Cannon (Sauk City, WI: Arkham House, 1998), 276. ["Gorham" has been erroneously rendered as "Gotham" here.]

45. Winfield Townley Scott, "His Own Most Fantastic Creation: Howard Phillips Lovecraft" (1944), in *Lovecraft Remembered,* 16. Sarah Susan Lovecraft's medical records no longer survive, but Scott consulted them around 1944.

46. I am grateful to John H. Stanley of JHL for this information.

47. *SL* 1.6 (note 7).

48. *SL* 1.33 (note 10).

49. HPL to JVS, 29 May 1933 (*SL* 4.191).

50. John McInnis, "'The Colour out of Space' as the History of H. Lovecraft's Immediate Family," in *H. P. Lovecraft Centennial Conference: Proceedings,* ed. S. T. Joshi (West Warwick, RI: Necronomicon Press, 1991), 37.

51. HPL to Alfred Galpin, 27 October 1932; *Letters to Alfred Galpin* (New York: Hippocampus Press, 2003), 164. This volume is not listed in my edition of Lovecraft's library, as it does not appear to have been present when his library was catalogued by Mary Spink shortly after Lovecraft's death.

52. HPL to JVS, 4 February 1934 (*SL* 4.370).

53. HPL to MWM, 5 April 1931 (*SL* 3.362).

54. *SL* 3.363 (note 53).

55. *SL* 1.34 (note 10).

56. Scott, 11.

57. Myra H. Blosser to Winfield Townley Scott, n.d. (ms., JHL).

58. *SL* 4.355 (note 52). The same anecdote is found in HPL to RK, 16 November 1916; *Letters to Reinhardt Kleiner,* 66 (this portion not in *SL*).

59. *SL* 3.362 (note 53).

60. *Providence Journal* (21 July 1898).

61. Faig, *Parents,* 7.

62. *SL* 3.366–67 (note 53).

63. *SL* 1.33 (note 7).

64. Ibid.

65. HPL to Marion F. Bonner, 4 May 1936 (*SL* 5.244).

66. HPL to RK, 21 May 1920 (*SL* 1.115).

67. HPL to FBL, 27 February 1931 (*SL* 3.317).

68. HPL to JVS, 8 November 1933 (ms.).

69. *SL* 1.33 (note 10).

70. HPL to Helen Sully, 24 November 1933 (ms., JHL).

71. HPL to RK, 7 March 1920 (*SL* 1.110).

72. See note 68.

73. Ibid.

74. *SL* 4.357 (note 52).

75. *SL* 1.34 (note 10).

76. HPL to REH, 16 January 1932 (*SL* 4.8).

77. HPL to REH, 16 January 1932; *A Means to Freedom: The Letters of H. P. Lovecraft and Robert E. Howard* (New York: Hippocampus Press, 2009), 1.265 (this portion not in *SL*).

78. See note 68.

79. *SL* 1.31 (note 10).

80. *SL* 1.34–35 (note 10).

81. HPL to Virgil Finlay, 24 October 1936 (*SL* 5.335).

82. *SL* 5.244 (note 65).

83. HPL to FBL, 26 October 1926 (*SL* 2.84).

84. HPL to AD, 9 September 1931 (*SL* 3.409).

85. *SL* 3.407–8 (note 84).

86. HPL to FBL, 8 January 1924 (*SL* 1.282).

87. Per *SL* 2.107 (note 3); at *SL* 1.7 (note 7) HPL dates his discovery of classical antiquity to the age of seven, but it will soon be evident that this must be an error.

88. Nathaniel Hawthorne, "Preface" to *A Wonder-Book, A Wonder-Book, Tanglewood Tales, and Grandfather's Chair* (Boston: Houghton Mifflin, 1883), 13.

89. Thomas Bulfinch, *Bulfinch's Mythology* (New York: Modern Library, n.d.), 15.

90. *SL* 1.7 (note 7).

91. HPL to Richard F. Searight, 26 January 1935; *Letters to Richard F. Searight,* 44.

92. *SL* 1.33 (note 10).

93. HPL to CAS, 13 December 1933 (*SL* 4.335).

94. HPL to REH, 30 January 1931 (*SL* 3.283).

95. *SL* 1.7 (note 7).

96. Coleridge, *Poems,* ed. Ernest Hartley Coleridge (London: Oxford University Press, 1912), 189.

97. *SL* 2.108 (note 3).

98. HPL to Richard F. Searight, 26 January 1935; *Letters to Richard F. Searight,* 44.

99. HPL to LDC, 4 October 1925 (ms., JHL).

199. *SL* 1.300 (note 12).

101. *Bulfinch's Mythology,* 7.

102. HPL to RK, 7 March 1920 (*SL* 1.110–11).

103. HPL to REH, 30 October 1931 (*SL* 3.431–32).

104. HPL to FBL, 27 February 1931 (*SL* 3.313). An earlier letter, however, dates this pseudonym to Lovecraft's fourteenth year (HPL to FBL, 26 January 1921 [AHT]).

105. *SL* 1.36 (note 10).

106. HPL to JVS, 25 September 1933 (ms.).

107. *SL* 1.37 (note 10).

108. HPL to JFM, March [?] 1937 (*SL* 5.432).

109. *SL* 2.109 (note 3).

Chapter 3: Black Woods & Unfathomed Caves

1. Frederick S. Frank, "The Gothic Romance: 1762–1820," in *Horror Literature,* ed. Marshall Tymn (New York: Bowker, 1981), 3–175.

2. William Hazlitt, "American Literature—Dr Channing," *Edinburgh Review* No. 99 (October 1829): 127–28.

3. G. R. Thompson, *Poe's Fiction: Romantic Irony in the Gothic Tales* (Madison: University of Wisconsin Press, 1973),.

4. "Preface" to *Tales of the Grotesque and Arabesque* (1840), in *Collected Works of Edgar Allan Poe,* ed. Thomas Ollive Mabbott (Cambridge, MA: Harvard University Press, 1978), 2.473.

5. *Collected Works of Edgar Allan Poe,* 3.853.

6. Maurice Lévy, *Lovecraft: A Study in the Fantastic,* tr. S. T. Joshi (Detroit: Wayne State University Press, 1988), 14.

7. HPL to Elizabeth Toldridge, 28 August 1933 (*SL* 4.239).

8. HPL to CAS, 24 June 1927 (*SL* 2.148).

9. *The Weird Tale* (Austin: University of Texas Press, 1990), 1f.

10. See note 4.

11. HPL to RHB, 25 June 1931; *O Fortunate Floridian,* 3.

12. HPL to JVS, 19–31 July 1931 (ms., JHL).

13. HPL to JVS, 4 February 1934 (*SL* 4.354).

14. Henry James, "Baudelaire" (1876), *French Poets and Novelists* (New York: Macmillan, 1878), 76.

15. HPL to Bernard Austin Dwyer, 3 March 1927 (*SL* 2.109).

16. HPL to RK, 16 November 1916 (*SL* 1.36).

17. Edmund Pearson, *Dime Novels* (Boston: Little, Brown, 1929), 4f.

18. See Pearson, passim; Quentin Reynolds, *The Fiction Factory* (New York: Random House, 1955), passim.

19. HPL to RHB, 25 March 1935; *O Fortunate Floridian,* 230.

20. In *The Dime Novel Detective,* ed. Gary Hoppenstand (Bowling Green, OH: Bowling Green University Popular Press, 1982), 7–34, is reprinted an entire Old King Brady novel, *The Haunted Churchyard; or, Old King Brady the Detective and the Mystery of the Iron Vault* (1890).

21. HPL to JVS, 19–30 July 1931 (ms., JHL).

22. L. Sprague de Camp, *Lovecraft: A Biography* (Garden City, NY: Doubleday, 1975), 33.

23. This version has now been published in *H. P. Lovecraft: The Fiction* (New York: Barnes & Noble, 2008).

24. HPL to Richard F. Searight, 13 October 1934; *Letters to Richard F. Searight,* 34.

25. HPL to Alfred Galpin, 29 August 1918 (*SL* 1.74).

26. *SL* 2.109 (note 15).

27. *SL* 1.37 (note 16).

28. Ibid.

29. W. Paul Cook, *In Memoriam: Howard Phillips Lovecraft* (1941); rpt. in *Lovecraft Remembered,* 112.

30. *SL* 4.355–56 (note 13).

31. HPL to MWM, 1 January 1915 (*SL* 1.8).

32. HPL to REH, 25–29 March 1933 (*SL* 4.172).

33. Transcript of HPL's transcript at Hope Street English and Classical High School, Providence, RI.

34. See *Lovecraft's Library* (1980 ed.), 39.

35. The manuscripts here are very confused, and some scholars now follow Lejay in reading *illa* (sc. *coepta*), but Lovecraft's text almost certainly read *illas* (sc. *formas*).

36. *John Dryden,* ed. Keith Walker (Oxford: Oxford University Press, 1987), 382.

37 HPL to RK, 23 January 1920 (*SL* 1.106).

38. HPL to AD, 4 March 1932 (*SL* 4.26).

39. HPL to MWM, 5 April 1931 (*SL* 3.368).

40. Faig, *Parents,* 23.

41. *SL* 1.32 (note 16).

42. HPL to Richard F. Searight, 5 March 1935; *Letters to Richard F. Searight,* 51.

43. JVS, "Did Lovecraft Suffer from Chorea?" *Outré* No. 5 (May 1977): 30–31.

44. *SL* 1.36 (note 16).

45 Winfield Townley Scott, "His Own Most Fantastic Creation: Howard Phillips Lovecraft" (1944), in *Lovecraft Remembered,* 12.

46. Myra H. Blosser to Winfield Townley Scott, n.d. (ms., JHL).

47. *SL* 3.367 (note 39).

48. HPL to the Gallomo, [April 1920] (*SL* 2.104).

49. Sonia H. Davis, *The Private Life of H. P. Lovecraft,* 8.

50. See frontispiece to *SL* 2.

51. *SL* 1.32 (note 16).

52. Frontispiece to *Something about Cats and Other Pieces* (1949).

53. RHB, *On Lovecraft and Life,* ed. S. T. Joshi (West Warwick, RI: Necronomicon Press, 1992), 18.

54. Ms., JHL.

55. *SL* 1.35 (note 16). HPL declared that the line is from "Cicero's oration [*sic*] against Catiline" (there are in fact four orations against Catiline), but it is actually from *Pro Mureno* 13.

56. *SL* 1.29–30 (note 16).

57. HPL to RHB, 10 April 1934; *O Fortunate Floridian,* 125.

58. See further my essay, "Further Notes on Lovecraft and Music," *Romantist* Nos. 4/5 (1980–81): 47–49.

59. HPL to Elizabeth Toldridge, 29 May 1929 (*SL* 2.348).

60. Faig, *Parents,* 26.

61. HPL to LDC, [18 May 1929] (postcard) (ms., JHL).

62. *SL* 1.7 (note 31).

63. *SL* 1.35 (note 16).

64. Interview of Ethel Phillips Morrish by Paul R. Michaud, August 1977.

65. HPL to JVS, 8 November 1933 (ms.).

66. HPL to MWM, 27–29 July 1929 (AHT).

67. HPL to JVS, 10 February 1935 (*SL* 5.104).

68. *SL* 1.36 (note 16).

69. Ibid.

70. *SL* 1.7 (note 31).

71. HPL to LDC, 11 November 1924 (ms., JHL).

72. HPL to JVS, 18 September 1931 (AHT).

73. HPL to JVS, 4 February 1934 (ms., JHL).

74. *SL* 1.37 (note 16); HPL to Richard F. Searight, 5 March 1935; *Letters to Richard F. Searight,* 47.

75. HPL to RK, 20 January 1916 (*SL* 1.19); *SL* 2.109 (note 15).

76. For this and other information on Antarctic exploration, see Walker Chapman, *The Loneliest Continent: The Story of Antarctic Discovery* (Greenwich, CT: New York Graphic Society, 1964).

77. See HPL to MWM, 18 September 1932 (*SL* 4.67) for titles; HPL to Marion F. Bonner, 26 April 1936 (*SL* 5.237) for dates. In this latter letter the title of the second treatise is given as "Ross's Explorations."

78. Chapman, 92.

79. Chapman, 98.

80. *Letters to Richard F. Searight,* 47.

81. C. L. Moore to HPL, 6 October 1936 (ms., JHL): "Thank you for the privilege of reading that early publication of the Royal Atlas Company, 'Wilks' Exploration' [*sic*] . . . I am returning 'Wilks' Exploration' with a sigh . . ." The Royal Atlas Company must have been yet another of Lovecraft's juvenile imprints.

82. *SL* 1.37 (note 16).

83. HPL to MWM, 27–29 July 1929 (AHT).

Chapter 4: What of Unknown Africa?

1. HPL to MWM, 1 January 1915 (*SL* 1.7).

2. HPL to LDC, 12 February 1926 (*SL* 2.39).

3. HPL to Richard F. Searight, 16 April 1936; *Letters to Richard F. Searight,* 55.

4. HPL to Alfred Galpin, 21 August 1918; *Letters to Alfred Galpin,* 27 (this portion not in *SL*).

5. HPL to RHB, 23 July 1936; *O Fortunate Floridian,* 356.

6. See, in general, Charles A. Whitney, *The Discovery of Our Galaxy* (New York: Knopf, 1971).

7. For an exhaustive discussion of Lovecraft's interest in and knowledge of astronomy, see T. R. Livesey, "Dispatches from the Providence Observatory: Astronomical Motifs and Sources in the Writings of H. Lovecraft," *Lovecraft Annual* 2 (2008): 3–87.

8. This, and all other juvenile publications cited in this chapter, are at JHL. A few of these items have been published in *Collected Essays,* but most remain unpublished.

9. I am grateful to Sam Moskowitz for information on the hectograph.

10. This essay was written in 1934.

11. HPL to RK, 16 November 1916 (*SL* 1.38).

12. HPL to LDC, 12 February 1926 (ms., JHL).

13. HPL to Duane W. Rimel, 29 March 1934 (*SL* 4.398).

14. *SL* 1.38 (note 11).

15. HPL to RK, 20 January 1916 (*SL* 1.19).

16. *SL* 1.39 (note 11).

17. HPL to MWM, 27–29 July 1929 (AHT).

18. HPL to JVS, 4 February 1934 (*SL* 4.353).

19. When HPL refers to the Munroes as his "next-door neighbours" (HPL to REH, 4 October 1930 [*SL* 3.184]), he is referring to the time after the spring of 1904, when he moved to 598 Angell Street and was in fact only a few houses away from the Munroes.

20. HPL to AD, 17 February 1931 (*SL* 3.290).

21. See *Rhode Island Journal of Astronomy* (7 May 1905).

22. HPL to AEPG, 19 August 1921 (*SL* 1.147).

23. HPL to the Gallomo, 31 August 1921 (*SL* 1.150). R. Alain Everts is responsible for the identification of Tanner's last name.

24. HPL to AEPG, 5 August [1928] (ms., JHL).

25. *SL* 3.184 (note 19).

26. *SL* 1.147 (note 22).

27. HPL to Helen Sully, 4 December 1935 (ms., JHL).

28. *SL* 1.38 (note 11).

29. HPL to RK, 16 November 1916; *Letters to Reinhardt Kleiner,* 73.

30. HPL to Alfred Galpin, 27 May 1918; *Letters to Alfred Galpin,* 19.

31. HPL to AD, 17 February 1931 (*SL* 3.289–90).

32. HPL to AD, 26 March 1927; *Essential Solitude: The Letters of H. P. Lovecraft and August Derleth* (New York: Hippocampus Press, 2008), 1.77. HPL probably refers to two tales appearing in *Collier's,* "The Singular Experience of Mr. John Scott Eccles" (a.k.a. "The Adventure of Wisteria Lodge") (15 August 1908) and "The Adventure of the Bruce-Partington Plans" (12 December 1908).

33. HPL to JVS, 25 September 1933 (ms., JHL).

34. HPL to RK, 2 February 1916 (*SL* 1.20).

35. HPL to the Gallomo, 1920 (*SL* 1.104–5).

36. Field, *State of Rhode Island and Providence Plantations,* 2.553.

37. Ibid., 2.556.

38. HPL to MWM, 18 September 1932 (*SL* 4.65).

39. *SL* 1.105 (note 35).

40. HPL to F. Lee Baldwin, 13 February 1934 (ms., JHL).

41. HPL to AD, 31 December 1930 (*SL* 3.246).

42. HPL to F. Lee Baldwin, 27 March 1934 (ms., JHL).

43. *SL* 1.29 (note 11).

44. *SL* 4.365 (note 18).

45. Stuart J. Coleman to Winfield Townley Scott, 30 December [1943] (ms., JHL).

46. Winfield Townley Scott, "His Own Most Fantastic Creation" (1944), in *Lovecraft Remembered,* 12.

47. Clara Hess in the *Providence Sunday Journal* (19 September 1948); quoted in Faig, *Parents,* 33.

48. *SL* 1.40 (note 11).

49. *SL* 4.357 (note 18).

50. HPL to Edwin Baird, 3 February 1924 (*SL* 1.298).

51. HPL to RK, 16 November 1916; *Letters to Reinhardt Kleiner,* (this portion not in *SL*).

52. HPL to LDC, 22–23 December 1925 (ms., JHL).

53. HPL to FBL, [November 1927] (*SL* 2.181).

54. HPL to MWM, 5 April 1931 (*SL* 3.367).

55. HPL to Harry O. Fischer, 10 January 1937; quoted in de Camp, 40.

56. Kenneth W. Faig, Jr, "Howard Phillips Lovecraft: The Early Years 1890–1914," *Nyctalops* 2, No. 1 (April 1973): 14n16, citing probate records.

57. *SL* 4.358–59 (note 18).

58. *SL* 3.369 (note 54).

60. *SL* 1.39 (note 11).

60. HPL to REH, 25–29 March 1933 (*SL* 4.172).

61. *SL* 1.30 (note 11).

62. *SL* 1.9 (note 1).

63. HPL to RHB, 24 May 1935 (*SL* 5.165).

64. HPL to JVS, 8 November 1933 (ms.).

65. *Rhode Island Journal of Astronomy* (30 July 1905).

66. HPL to Alfred Galpin, 29 August 1918; *Letters to Alfred Galpin,* 40 (this portion not in *SL*).

67. Surviving in AHT, Vol. XXXIII.

68. *SL* 1.105–6 (note 35).

69. HPL to MWM, 15 May 1918 (*SL* 1.60).

70. See note 64.

71. *SL* 1.146 (note 22).

72. Various Internet sources reveal the existence of one James M. Kay (d. 8 April 1904), who served in the West Virginia cavalry during the Civil War. This may be the person in question, as it seems to me that HPL's friend would have lived a bit longer than 1904.

73. *SL* 1.146 (note 22).

74. See note 64.

75. Harold W. Munro, "Lovecraft, My Childhood Friend" (1983), in *Lovecraft Remembered,* 70.

76. See *Rhode Island Journal of Astronomy* (April 1907); HPL to Samuel Loveman, [c. 5 January 1924]; *Letters to Samuel Loveman and Vincent Starrett* (West Warwick, RI: Necronomicon Press, 1994), 23.

77. HPL to LDC, 30 May 1931 (ms., JHL).

78. HPL to JVS, 14 August 1933 (ms.).

79. See Faig, *Some of the Descendants,* 135f. See also Faig's *Edward Francis Gamwell and His Family* (Glenview, IL: Kenneth W. Faig, Jr, 1991).

80. *SL* 1.34 (note 11).

81. *SL* 1.39 (note 11).

82. Faig, *Some of the Descendants,* 131. The fact that Clark studied at Harvard Medical School was discovered by Faig after the publi-

cation of his volume, and I am grateful to him for passing on this information.

83. Ibid.

84. HPL to Richard F. Searight, 31 May 1935; *Letters to Richard F. Searight,* 59.

85. *SL* 1.38 (note 11).

86. William Benjamin Smith, *The Color Line* (1905; rpt. New York: Greenwood Press, 1969), 185.

87. Smith, 192.

88. HPL to RK, 16 November 1916; *Letters to Reinhardt Kleiner,* 74–75 (this portion not in *SL*).

89. Thomas F. Gossett, *Race: The History of an Idea in America* (New York: Schocken Books, 1965), passim.

90. HPL to AEPG, 5 August [1931] (ms., JHL).

91. "In a Major Key," *Conservative* 1, No. 2 (July 1915): 9–11.

92. HPL to LDC, [2 May 1929] (postcard) (ms., JHL).

93. HPL to RK, 16 November 1916; *Letters to Reinhardt Kleiner,* 72 (this portion not in *SL*).

94. HPL to LDC, [15 July 1928] (postcard) (ms., JHL).

95. See note 64.

96. *SL* 4.360 (note 18).

97. *SL* 4.170 (note 60).

98. HPL to RHB, 10 April 1934; *O Fortunate Floridian,* 128.

99. HPL to MWM, [6 April 1935] (*SL* 5.140).

100. HPL to Robert Bloch, 1 June 1933; *Letters to Robert Bloch* (West Warwick, RI: Necronomicon Press, 1993), 15.

101. HPL to LDC, 14–19 November 1925 (ms., JHL).

102. Cited in *Uncollected Prose and Poetry* (West Warwick, RI: Necronomicon Press, 1978), 1.

103. Mathias Harpin, *The High Road to Zion* ([West Warwick, RI:] Harpin's American Heritage Foundation, 1976), 197.

104. *SL* 1.9 (note 1).

105. *SL* 1.40 (note 11).

106. AD, in an appendix to *H. P. L.: A Memoir* (New York: Ben Abramson, 1945), printed a brief item purportedly by Lovecraft entitled "Does Vulcan Exist?" (91–92), claiming that it dated to 1906 and that it was either a portion or the entirety of an astronomy column published in the *Providence Journal.* Lovecraft had, however, no astronomy column in the *Journal.* My feeling is that this is an unpublished manuscript that came into Derleth's hands and that he simply assumed it had been published in the *Journal,* probably the only Providence newspaper of which he was aware.

107. HPL to RK, 19 February 1916 (*SL* 1.22).

108. HPL to Richard F. Searight, 22 December 1934; *Letters to Richard F. Searight,* 37.

109. *SL* 5.141 (note 99).

110. HPL to Alfred Galpin, 21 August 1918 (*SL* 1.70).

111. HPL to RK, 7 March 1920 (*SL* 1.110–11).

112. HPL to the Kleicomolo, [April 1917] (*SL* 1.44).

113. *SL* 1.70 (note 110).

Chapter 5: Barbarian and Alien

1. HPL to MWM, 1 January 1915 (*SL* 1.9).

2. HPL to RK, 16 November 1916 (*SL* 1.40–41).

3. HPL to Bernard Austin Dwyer, 3 March 1927 (*SL* 2.110).

4. HPL to Helen Sully, 4 December 1935 (ms., JHL).

5. Will Murray, "An Interview with Harry Brobst," *LS* Nos. 22/23 (Fall 1990): 34.

6. Harold W. Munro, "Lovecraft, My Childhood Friend" (1983), in *Lovecraft Remembered,* 70–71.

7. HPL to REH, 25–29 March 1933 (*SL* 4.172).

8. R. Alain Everts, "Howard Phillips Lovecraft and Sex," *Nyctalops* 2, No. 2 (July 1974): 19.

9. HPL to RHB, 10 April 1934; *O Fortunate Floridian,* 125.

10. *SL* 1.9 (note 1).

11. *SL* 1.31 (note 2).

12. HPL to Alfred Galpin, 19 August 1918 (*SL* 1.75).

13. See Mark Owings and Irving Binkin, *A Catalog of Lovecraftiana* (Baltimore: Mirage Press, 1975), plate 20.

14. David H. Keller, "Lovecraft's Astronomical Notebook," *Lovecraft Collector* No. 3 (October 1949): 1–4.

15. Keller has transcribed "Providence Evening Journal," but this is evidently his error.

16. HPL to Jonquil Leiber, 29 November 1936 (*SL* 5.363).

17. Scott, "His Own Most Fantastic Creation" (1944), in *Lovecraft Remembered,* 15.

18. HPL to MWM, 5 April 1931 (*SL* 3.367).

19. Faig, *Parents,* 28.

20. Sonia H. Davis, "Memories of Lovecraft: I" (1969), in *Lovecraft Remembered,* 276.

21. Quoted in Faig, *Parents,* 32–33.

22. Munro, 69.

23. HPL to Duane W. Rimel, 13 April 1934 (ms., JHL).

24. HPL to Sarah Susan Lovecraft, 24 February 1921 (*SL* 1.123).

25. Davis, 276.

26. Quoted in Faig, *Parents,* 33.

27. Munro, 71.

28. HPL to FBL, 26 October 1926 (*SL* 2.85); HPL to RHB, 20 April 1935; *O Fortunate Floridian,* 241.

29. See the photograph published with Kenneth W. Faig, Jr, "Howard Phillips Lovecraft: The Early Years 1890–1914," *Nyctalops* 2, No. 1 (April 1973): 11.

30. HPL to RK, 4 December 1918 (*SL* 1.78).

31. HPL to RHB, 23 July 1936 (*SL* 5.282).

32. HPL to FBL, 8 February 1922 (AHT).

33. HPL to RHB, 11 December 1936; *O Fortunate Floridian,* 383.

34. HPL to RK, 9 November 1919 (*SL* 192).

35. HPL to LDC, [17 August 1929] (postcard) (ms., JHL).

36. HPL to F. Lee Baldwin, 27 March 1934 (ms., JHL).

37. See note 32.

38. HPL to LDC, 4–5 November 1924 (ms., JHL).

39. HPL to W. G. Bautz, 16 May 1935 (AHT).

40. HPL to AEPG, 19 August 1921 (*SL* 1145).

41. Faig, "Early Years," 6, citing city directories.

42. HPL to RK, 4 December 1918 (*SL* 1.77).

43. *SL* 1.41 (note 2).

44. Scott, 13.

45. Munro, 71.

46. Scott, 13.

47. HPL to Robert Bloch, 4 December 1935 (*SL* 5.208).

48. HPL to JVS, 19–31 July 1931 (*SL* 3.383).

49. HPL to Edwin Baird, 3 February 1924 (*SL* 1.298).

50. *SL* 2.110 (note 3).

51. Field, *State of Rhode Island,* 2.206.

52. "The Defence Remains Open!" (1921).

53. HPL to LDC, 23 September 1925; *Letters from New York* (San Francisco: Night Shade Books, 2005), 198.

54. HPL to RHB, 31 March 1932; *O Fortunate Floridian,* 28.

55. See, in general, Sam Moskowitz, *Under the Moons of Mars* (New York: Holt, Rinehart & Winston, 1970), passim.

56. *SL* 1.41 (note 2).

57. HPL to Richard F. Searight, 26 September 1935; *Letters to Richard F. Searight,* 64.

58. HPL to Richard F. Searight, 16 April 1935; *Letters to Richard F. Searight,* 54.

59. See note 54.

60. HPL to RHB, 14 April 1932; *O Fortunate Floridian,* 29.

61. HPL to JFM, 23 February 1936 (*SL* 5.227).

62. All letters by and about HPL in the *Argosy* and *All-Story* are collected in *H. P. Lovecraft in the Argosy* (West Warwick, RI: Necronomicon Press, 1994).

63. HPL to Zealia Bishop, 20 March 1929 (*SL* 2.325).

64. HPL to CAS, 3 December 1929 (*SL* 3.88).

65. See Will Murray, "Lovecraft and the Pulp Magazine Tradition," in *An Epicure in the Terrible,* ed. David E. Schultz and S. T. Joshi (Rutherford, NJ: Fairleigh Dickinson University Press, 1991), 103.

66. Cass was briefly considered to be a pseudonym of CAS, and a lengthy story by Cass that was to have appeared in the *Thrill Book* in 1919 (*As It Is Written* [1982]) has been published under Smith's name; but this theory has now been found to be false. See Will Murray, "As It Was *Not* Written; or, The Curious Conundrum of De Lysle Ferrée Cass," *Studies in Weird Fiction* No. 4 (Fall 1988): 3–12.

67. Fred Jackson, "The First Law," *Argosy* 72, No. 1 (April 1913): 35.

68. *SL* 1.41 (note 2).

69. *SL* 1.42 (note 2).

70. See Moskowitz, 293.

71. HPL to AD, 9 September 1931 (*SL* 3.407).

Chapter 6: A Renewed Will to Live

1. Truman J. Spencer, *The History of Amateur Journalism* (New York: The Fossils, 1957), 86.

2. *Looking Backward* (1920).

3. *United Amateur Press Association: Exponent of Amateur Journalism.*

4. HPL to JVS, 27 October 1932 (*SL* 4.97).

5. This was a speech given at the Boston Conference of Amateur Journalists on 21 February 1921.

6. See Spencer, 91–92.

7. HPL to RK, 8 November 1917; *Letters to Reinhardt Kleiner,* 120.

8. HPL to JFM, 6 August 1923 (*SL* 1.243).

9. "Amateur Journalism and the English Teacher," *English Journal* (high school edition) 4, No. 2 (February 1915): 113–14.

10. HPL to John T. Dunn, 10 June 1916; *Books at Brown* 39–39 (1991–92 [1995]): 179.

11. John Clinton Pryor, "Comment Pryoristic," *United Co-operative* 1, No. 1 (December 1918): 6–7; "Comment Pryoristic," *United Co-operative* 1, No. 3 (April 1921): 7; W. Paul Cook, "Official Criticism," *Vagrant* No. 11 (November 1919): 31–35.

12. See L. Sprague de Camp, "Young Man Lovecraft" (1975), in *Lovecraft Remembered,* 173.

13. HPL to Edward H. Cole, 23 November 1914 (ms., JHL).

14. See "Department of Public Criticism," *United Amateur,* December 1915: "The general tone of this individual publication [*Hit and Miss*] is Socialistic . . . Miss Baker's ideas on economics seem not unlike those of her fellow-amateurs, Messrs. Shufelt and Basinet . . ."

15. de Camp, "Young Man Lovecraft," in *Lovecraft Remembered,* 174.

16. HPL to John T. Dunn, 20 July 1915; *Books at Brown,* 171.

17. HPL to John T. Dunn, 15 August 1916; *Books at Brown,* 191 (and n. 2).

18. de Camp, "Young Man Lovecraft," in *Lovecraft Remembered,* 173–74.

19. HPL to RK, 28 March 1915; *Letters to Reinhardt Kleiner,* 15.

20. HPL to John T. Dunn, 25 October 1915; *Books at Brown,* 174–75.

21. See note 17.

22. HPL to John T. Dunn, 13 November 1916; *Books at Brown,* 204.

23. HPL to RK, 24 September 1917 (*SL* 1.50).

24. RK, "Howard Phillips Lovecraft," *Californian* 5, No. 1 (Summer 1937): 5.

25. HPL to John T. Dunn, 16 June 1916; *Books at Brown,* 179.

26. HPL to John T. Dunn, 28 June 1916; *Books at Brown,* 185.

27. See note 25.

28. See note 26.

29. See note 22.

30. *Year Book of the United Amateur Press Association of America* [Athol, MA: W. Paul Cook, 1914].

31. HPL to John T. Dunn, 16 May 1917; *Books at Brown,* 215.

32. HPL to John T. Dunn, 6 July 1917; *Books at Brown,* 217.

33. Ibid., 222.

34. See note 25.

35. HPL to RK, 16 November 1916 (*SL* 1.40).

36. HPL to Bernard Austin Dwyer, 3 March 1927 (*SL* 2.110).

37. HPL to Alfred Galpin, 27 May 1918; *Letters to Alfred Galpin,* 15.

38. See *Science versus Charlatanry: Essays on Astrology* by H. Lovecraft and J. F. Hartmann, ed. S. T. Joshi and Scott Connors (Madison, WI: Strange Co., 1979), xiv. The articles by both HPL and Hartmann are now in *Collected Essays,* volume 3.

39. HPL to MWM, 8 December 1914 (*SL* 1.4).

40. Ibid.

41. HPL to JFM, March [?] 1937 (*SL* 5.422).

Chapter 7: Metrical Mechanic

1. HPL to MWM, 8 December 1914 (*SL* 1.3–4).

2. HPL to RK, 4 April 1918 (*SL* 1.60).

3. HPL to Elizabeth Toldridge, 8 March 1929 (*SL* 2.314–15).

4. See HPL to RHB, [24 May 1935] (*SL* 5.168).

5. Untitled editorial note, *Conservative* (April 1915).

6. Gray and Collins, *Poetical Works* (Oxford: Clarendon Press, 1977), 34.

7. HPL to MWM, 5 April 1931 (*SL* 3.369–70).

8. HPL to RK, 14 September 1915 (*SL* 1.12).

9. HPL to RK, 5 June 1918; *Letters to Reinhardt Kleiner,* 143.

10. Cited in *In Defence of Dagon* (West Warwick, RI: Necronomicon Press, 1985), 6, 19.

11. *Plainsman* 1, No. 4 (December 1915): 2–3.

12. Winfield Townley Scott, "A Parenthesis on Lovecraft as Poet" (1945), in *H. P. Lovecraft: Four Decades of Criticism,* ed. S. T. Joshi (Athens: Ohio University Press, 1980), 214.

13. W. Paul Cook, "Howard Lovecraft's Fiction," *Vagrant* (November 1919); cited in Cook's *In Memoriam: Howard Phillips Lovecraft* (1941), in *Lovecraft Remembered,* 148.

14. The poem was included in a letter to John T. Dunn, 10 June 1916; *Books at Brown,* 180.

15. "Speaking of the ignorant rabble—James Lawrence Crowley hath just inundated me with some of his 'poetry' for revision. The task is repugnant, but I hate to disappoint the poor devil." HPL to MWM, [May 1920] (AHT).

16. RK, "A Note on Howard Lovecraft's Poetry," in *Lovecraft Remembered,* 401–2.

17. HPL to RK, 13 May 1921 (*SL* 1.132).

18. HPL to RK, 28 March 1915; *Letters to Reinhardt Kleiner,* 16.

19. Charles D. Isaacson, "Concerning the Conservative," *In a Minor Key* No. 2 [1915]: [10–11].

20. See note 1.

21. HPL to RK, 30 September 1915 (*SL* 1.14).

22. HPL to DW, [2 August 1927]; *Mysteries of Time and Spirit: The Letters of H. P. Lovecraft and Donald Wandrei* (San Francisco: Night Shade Books, 2002), 138.

23. DW to HPL, 12 August 1927; *Mysteries of Time and Spirit,* 149.

24. Steven J. Mariconda, "On Lovecraft's 'Amissa Minerva,'" *Etchings and Odysseys* No. 9 [1986]: 97–103.

25. HPL to the Kleicomolo, [October 1916]; *Letters to Reinhardt Kleiner,* 45–46.

26. HPL to RK, 23 August 1916 (*SL* 1.24).

27. RK, *Piper* (May 1915): 6.

28. HPL to RK, 28 March 1915 (*SL* 1.11).

29. See further my essay, "The Rationale of Lovecraft's Pseudonyms" (1992), in *Primal Sources: Essays on H. P. Lovecraft* (New York: Hippocampus Press, 2003), 81–89.

30. HPL to John T. Dunn, 28 June 1916; *Books at Brown,* 183.

31. Alan Seeger, *Poems* (New York: Scribner's, 1916), 162.

32. Thomas Henry Huxley, *Man's Place in Nature* (New York: D. Appleton & Co., 1894), 233.

33. See, in general, Thomas F. Gossett, *Race: The History of an Idea in America* (New York: Schocken Books, 1965), ch. 5.

34. de Camp, *Lovecraft: A Biography,* 95–99.

35. Gossett, 348.

36. HPL to RHB, 13 June 1936 (*SL* 5.266).

37. See Gossett, 353.

38. HPL to the Gallomo, 30 September 1919 (*SL* 1.89).

39. See note 19.

40. HPL to RK, 25 November 1915 (*SL* 1.17).

41. A complete list of Morton's pamphlets, as culled from the *National Union Catalogue of Pre-1956 Imprints* and the New York Public Library Catalogue, is as follows: *Anarchy* by Errico Malatesta (with *Is It All a Dream?* by Morton) (1900); *Better Than Socialism* (19—); *The Gospel of the Gutter* (19—); *The Philosophy of the Single Tax* (19—); *Do You Want Freedom of Speech?* (1902?); *The Rights of Periodicals* (1905?); *The Curse of Race Prejudice* (1906?); *Being on the Safe Side* (1910?); *The American Secular Union: Its Aims and Plans . . .* (191–); *Sex Morality, Past, Present and Future* (with William J. Robinson and others) (1912); *The Case of Billy Sunday* (with others) (1915); *Exempting the Churches* (1916); *Shall Church Property Be Taxed? A Debate* (with Lawson Purdy) (1921?). Morton also edited the short-lived periodical *Loyal Citizen Sovereignty* (Oct. 1922–June 1923). An extract from *The Curse of Race Prejudice* can now be found in *Lovecraft's New York Circle,* ed. Mara Kirk Hart and S. T. Joshi (New York: Hippocampus Press, 2006), p 210–15.

42. JFM, "'Conservatism' Gone Mad," *In a Minor Key* No. 2 [1915]: [15–16].

43. HPL to RK, 10 August 1915 (*SL* 1.12).

44. It is included in a letter to RK, 14 September 1915; *Letters to Reinhardt Kleiner,* 20.

45. It is dated to 1915 and listed as "unpublished" in HPL's list of his amateur poetry compiled in 1918 (*SL* 1.58).

46. HPL to John T. Dunn, 20 July 1915; *Books at Brown,* 169.

47. Edward Norman, *A History of Modern Ireland* (Harmondsworth, UK: Penguin, 1973), 155–56.

48. See McLoughlin, *Rhode Island: A Bicentennial History,* 141–42.

49. HPL to John T. Dunn, 10 June 1916; *Books at Brown,* 178.

50. HPL to John T. Dunn, 28 June 1916; *Books at Brown,* 182.

51. See note 49.

52. HPL to John T. Dunn, 14 October 1916; *Books at Brown,* 196.

53. *New York Times* (30 September 1916): 1.

54. HPL to John T. Dunn, 13 January 1917; *Books at Brown,* 210.

55. HPL to John T. Dunn, 6 July 1917; *Books at Brown,* 217.

56. HPL to Alfred Galpin, 29 August 1918; *Letters to Alfred Galpin,* 40.

57. See de Camp, "Young Man Lovecraft," in *Lovecraft Remembered,* 175.

58. HPL to John T. Dunn, 16 May 1917; *Books at Brown,* 214.

59. *SL* 1.12 (note 8).

60. HPL to RK, 23 May 1917 (*SL* 1.45–46).

61. HPL to RK, 27 August 1917 (*SL* 1.49).

62. Ibid.

63. See note 60.

64. HPL to MWM, 30 May 1917 (*SL* 1.47–48).

65. HPL to RK, 22 June 1917 (*SL* 1.48).

66. HPL to John T. Dunn, 6 July 1917; *Books at Brown,* 222.

67. HPL to RK, 16 November 1916 (*SL* 1.35).

68. See John Allen Krout, *The Origins of Prohibition* (New York: Knopf, 1925), 192–95.

69. *Rhode Island: A Guide to the Smallest State* (WPA) (Boston: Houghton Mifflin, 1937), 56.

70. Samuel Eliot Morison et al., *The Growth of the American Republic,* 7th ed. (New York: Oxford University Press, 1980), 2.285.

71. HPL to the Kleicomolo, [October 1916] (*SL* 1.26).

72. HPL to Zealia Bishop, 13 February 1928 (*SL* 2.229).

73. Ibid. (*SL* 2.230).

74. HPL to JVS, 10 November 1931 (*SL* 3.434).

75. HPL to MWM, 15 May 1918 (*SL* 1.64).

76. "We find it impossible to express with sufficient force our regret at the withdrawal of Mr. Daas from the United, and we can but hope that the retirement may prove merely temporary." "Department of Public Criticism," *United Amateur* (June 1916).

77. See HPL to Alfred Galpin, [October 1918]; *Letters to Alfred Galpin,* 23.

78. HPL to RK, 25 June 1920; *Letters to Reinhardt Kleiner,* 194.

79. Ibid.

80. *Tryout* 3, No. 4 (March 1917): [1–2].

81. HPL to John T. Dunn, 20 July 1915; *Books at Brown,* 170–71.

82. HPL to Edward H. Cole, 23 November and 14 December 1914 (mss., JHL).

83. HPL to RK, 21 September 1921 (*SL* 1.152). Cf. HPL to RK, 24 September 1917: "Cook makes only the third amateur with whom I have had a good talk; Stoddard and Edward H. Cole being the others" (*Letters to Reinhardt Kleiner,* 116). The order in which Stoddard and Cole are mentioned perhaps suggests that HPL saw Stoddard first.

84. "The Conservative and His Critics," *Conservative* (July 1915).

85. HPL to John T. Dunn, 4 July 1916; *Books at Brown,* 187–88.

86. HPL to FBL, 3 May 1922 (*SL* 1.170).

87. "The Kleicomolo," *United Amateur* 18, No. 4 (March 1919): 75–76.

88. Andrew F. Lockhart, "Little Journeys to the Homes of Prominent Amateurs," *United Amateur* 15, No. 2 (September 1915): 27–28, 34.

89. *SL* 3.370 (note 7).

90. HPL to RK, 16 November 1916 (*SL* 1.30).

91. HPL to LDC, 24–27 October 1925 (ms., JHL).

92. HPL to JFM, 24 June 1923 (*SL* 1.236).

93. Sean Dennis Cashman, *America in the Age of the Titans* (New York: New York University Press, 1988), 323–24.

94. HPL to JVS, 4 February 1934 (*SL* 4.355).

95. HPL to RK, 6 December 1915 (*SL* 1.18).

96. HPL to RK, 30 September 1915 (*SL* 1.14).

97. See note 95.

98. HPL to RK, 14 October 1917 (*SL* 1.51).

99. HPL to RK, 31 January 1917 (*SL* 1.42–43).

100. F. T., Review of *The Image Maker, New York Dramatic Mirror* (20 January 1917): 26.

101. HPL to John T. Dunn, 19 February 1917; *Books at Brown,* 212.

102. HPL to Sarah S. Lovecraft, 17 March 1921 (*SL* 1.127).

103. "Extracts from the Letters to G. W. Macauley" (1938), *LS* 1, No. 3 (Fall 1980): 14.

Chapter 8: Dreamers and Visionaries

1. For more on Cook, see Sean Donnelly, *W. Paul Cook: The Wandering Life of a Yankee Printer* (New York: Hippocampus Press, 2007).

2. HPL to RK, 24 September 1917 (*SL* 1.49–50).

3. HPL to Richard Ely Morse, 30 August [1932] (ms., JHL).

4. HPL to CAS, 11 January 1923 (*SL* 1.202).

5. *E'ch-Pi-El Speaks: An Autobiographical Sketch* (Saddle River, NJ: Gerry de la Ree, 1972), 9. This is a letter of July 1929 to an unidentified correspondent.

6. W. Paul Cook, "Howard Lovecraft's Fiction" (*Vagrant,* November 1919), cited in Cook's *In Memoriam: Howard Phillips Lovecraft* (1941), in *Lovecraft Remembered,* 147–48.

7. *Collected Works of Edgar Allan Poe,* ed. T. O. Mabbott (Cambridge, MA: Harvard University Press, 1978), 2.209.

8. HPL to Richard F. Searight, 4 November 1935; *Letters to Richard F. Searight,* 66.

9. HPL to CAS, 18 November 1930 (*SL* 3.219).

10. HPL to Elizabeth Toldridge, 8 March 1929 (*SL* 2.315). The printed text errs in reading "my 'Lovecraft' pieces?"

11. Edmund Wilson, "Tales of the Marvellous and the Ridiculous" (1945), in *H. P. Lovecraft: Four Decades of Criticism,* ed. S. T. Joshi (Athens: Ohio University Press, 1980), 48.

12. Poe, *Collected Works,* 2.579.

13. Henry Seidel Canby, Frederick Erastus Pierce, and W. H. Durham, *Facts, Thought, and Imagination: A Book on Writing* (New York: Macmillan, 1917), 56.

14. J. Berg Esenwein, *Writing the Short-Story: A Practical Handbook on the Rise, Structure, Writing, and Sale of the Modern Short-Story* (New York: Hinds, Noble & Eldredge, 1909; rev. ed. Springfield, MA: Home Correspondence School, 1928). I have not had access to the 1918 edition.

15. Ibid., 30.

16. I am grateful to Sam Moskowitz for some of this information.

17. HPL to the Gallomo, [April 1920]; *Letters to Alfred Galpin,* 81.

18. Poe, *Collected Works,* 2.209.

19. T. O. Mabbott, "H. Lovecraft: An Appreciation" (1944), in *H. P. Lovecraft: Four Decades of Criticism,* 43.

20. Will Murray, "A Probable Source for the Drinking Song from 'The Tomb,'" *LS* No. 15 (Fall 1987): 77–80.

21. Sheridan, *Plays* (London & New York: Dent/Dutton [Everyman's Library], 1906), 263. This suggestion was made to me by T. G. Cockcroft.

22. William Fulwiler, "'The Tomb' and 'Dagon': A Double Dissection," *CoC* No. 38 (Eastertide 1986): 8–14.

23. HPL to MWM, 15 May 1918 (*SL* 1.65).

24. "The Lord of R'lyeh" (1945), rpt. *LS* No. 7 (Fall 1982): 14.

25. HPL to RK, 27 August 1917; *Letters to Reinhardt Kleiner,* 114.

26. HPL to CAS, 7 November 1930 (*SL* 3.213).

27. See note 22.

28. HPL to RK, 17 July 1917; *Letters to Reinhardt Kleiner,* 112.

29. HPL to the Gallomo 11 December 1919 (*SL* 1.94).

30. See note 25.

31. HPL to Edwin Baird, c. June 1923; *Uncollected Letters* (West Warwick, RI: Necronomicon Press, 1986), 6.

32. Boswell, *Life of Johnson,* ed. R. W. Chapman, rev. J. D. Fleeman (Oxford: Oxford University Press, 1970), 1074.

33. HPL to AD, 9 September 1931 (*SL* 3.407).

34. HPL to Bernard Austin Dwyer, 26 March 1927 (*SL* 2.120).

35. Lord Dunsany, *Patches of Sunlight* (London: William Heinemann, 1938), 32.

36. HPL to MWM, 15 May 1918 (*SL* 1.62).

37. HPL to RK, 27 June 1918 (*SL* 1.68).

38. HPL to FBL, 4 June 1921 (*SL* 1.135–36).

39. "I am still struggling with the typing of *Hesperia.*" HPL to Alfred Galpin, 21 August 1918; *Letters to Alfred Galpin,* 33.

40. *Interesting Items* No. 511 (February 1921): [1–2].

41. HPL to Arthur Harris, 13 December 1918 (ms., JHL).

42. HPL to RK, 21 May 1920 (*SL* 1.116).

43. HPL to the Gallomo, [April 1920]; *Letters to Alfred Galpin,* 82.

44. See note 42.

45. *SL* 1.136 (note 38).

46. Ibid.

47. Ibid.

48. HPL to the Gallomo, [April 1920]; *Letters to Alfred Galpin,* 83.

49. Garrett Serviss, *Astronomy with the Naked Eye* (New York: Harper & Brothers, 1908), 152.

50. Charles A. Whitney, *The Discovery of Our Galaxy* (New York: Knopf, 1971), 21.

51. Matthew H. Onderdonk, "The Lord of R'lyeh" (1945), *LS* No. 7 (Fall 1982): 10.

52. HPL to Vincent Starrett, 10 January 1927 (*SL* 2.222).

53. Jack London, *Before Adam* (New York: Ace, n.d.), 3.

54. Ibid., 4–5.

55. See Poe, *Collected Works,* 1.191.

56. Lance Arney, "The Extinction of Mankind in the Prose Poem 'Memory,'" *LS* No. 21 (Spring 1990): 38–39.

57. HPL to Duane W. Rimel, 30 October 1934 (ms., JHL).

58. William H. Prescott, *History of the Conquest of Mexico and History of the Conquest of Peru* (New York: Modern Library, n.d.), 38.

59. Steven J. Mariconda, "Realism in Lovecraft's Early Work," *Ultimate Chaos* 2, No. 4 (December 1984): 1–11.

60. See HPL to RK, 4 April 1918 (*SL* 1.59).

61. R. Boerem, "A Lovecraftian Nightmare," in *H. P. Lovecraft: Four Decades of Criticism,* 218.

62. HPL to the Kleicomolo, 8 August 1916 (*SL* 1.24).

63. HPL to RHB, 13 June 1936; *O Fortunate Floridian,* 342.

64. HPL to the Gallomo, 12 September 1921; *Letters to Alfred Galpin,* 108.

65. HPL to CAS, 30 July 1923 (ms.).

66. HPL to RK, 8 November 1917 (*SL* 1.51).

67. Ibid.

68. Winfield Townley Scott, "A Parenthesis on Lovecraft as Poet" (1945), in *H. P. Lovecraft: Four Decades of Criticism,* 215.

69. Poe, *Collected Works,* 1.343.

70. HPL to RK, 16 July 1919 (*SL* 1.83).

71. HPL to the Gallomo, [April 1920]; *Letters to Alfred Galpin,* 82. HPL to RK, 5 June 1918; *Letters to Reinhardt Kleiner,* 143.

Chapter 9: Feverish and Incessant Scribbling

1. See HPL to RK, 4 April 1918 (*SL* 1.59).

2. HPL to RK, 23 December 1917 (*SL* 1.52).

3. HPL to JFM, 10 February 1923 (*SL* 1.209).

4. HPL to Woodburn Harris, 25 February–1 March 1929 (*SL* 2.290).

5. Samuel Eliot Morison et al., *The Growth of the American Republic,* 2.112.

6. "President's Message," *United Amateur* (September 1917; November 1917).

7. "President's Message," *United Amateur* (January 1918).

8. "This latest trip [to Boston] was in response to an invitation to deliver an address on amateurdom's future before the Hub Club Conference of Sept. 5th . . ." HPL to RK, 10 September 1920; *Letters to Reinhardt Kleiner,* 197.

9. Cook, *In Memoriam,* in *Lovecraft Remembered,* 110–11.

10. HPL to RK, 24 September 1917 (*SL* 1.49).

11. RK, "A Memoir of Lovecraft," in *Lovecraft Remembered,* 195.

12. HPL to Winifred Virginia Jackson, 7 June 1921 (*SL* 1.138).

13. HPL to RK, 21 September 1921 (*SL* 1.152–33).

14. HPL to RK, 9 November 1919 (*SL* 1.91).

15. Samuel Loveman, *The Hermaphrodite and Other Poems* (Caldwell, ID: Caxton Printers, 1936), 27. For as complete an edition of Loveman's poetry (including a selection of his other work) as we are likely to have, see *Out of the Immortal Night: Selected Works by Samuel Loveman* (New York: Hippocampus Press, 2004).

16. *Twenty one Letters of Ambrose Bierce,* ed. Samuel Loveman (1922; rpt. West Warwick, RI: Necronomicon Press, 1991), 19.

17. HPL to DW, 27 March 1927 (*SL* 2.121).

18. HPL to RK, 8 November 1917 (*SL* 1.51).

19. Samuel Loveman, "Howard Phillips Lovecraft," in *Lovecraft Remembered,* 204.

20. Robert H. Waugh, "Landscapes, Selves, and Others in Lovecraft," in *An Epicure in the Terrible,* 234.

21. HPL to Anne Tillery Renshaw, 24 August 1918 (*SL* 1.71).

22. HPL to RK, 23 April 1921 (*SL* 1.128).

23. Alfred Galpin, "Memories of a Friendship," in *Lovecraft Remembered,* 165.

24. HPL to Alfred Galpin, 21 August 1918; *Letters to Alfred Galpin,* 30.

25. HPL to Alfred Galpin, 27 May 1918; *Letters to Alfred Galpin,* 16.

26. HPL to Alfred Galpin, [October 1918]; *Letters to Alfred Galpin,* 51.

27. HPL to Alfred Galpin, 27 May 1918; *Letters to Alfred Galpin,* 23.

28. HPL to Alfred Galpin, 29 August 1918; *Letters to Alfred Galpin,* 37.

29. See note 26.

30. L. Sprague de Camp, "Young Man Lovecraft," in *Lovecraft Remembered,* 174.

31. See note 25.

32. HPL to John T. Dunn, 14 October 1916; *Books at Brown,* 198–99.

33. HPL to John T. Dunn, 10 June 1916; *Books at Brown,* 179.

34. HPL to John T. Dunn, 6 July 1917; *Books at Brown,* 222.

35. HPL to the Gallomo, [April 1920] (*SL* 1.103).

36. Ms., JHL.

37. HPL to RK, 12 August 1919 (*SL* 1.84–85).

38. HPL to LDC, 17 November 1924 (ms., JHL).

39. Clara Hess, letter to AD, 9 October 1948 (ms., JHL); quoted in Faig, *Parents,* 33.

40. HPL to RK, 23 May 1917 (*SL* 1.46).

41. Faig, *Parents,* 29.

42. See Faig, *Some of the Descendants,* 122–26.

43. HPL to RK, 18 January 1919 (*SL* 1.78).

44. Faig, *Some of the Descendants,* 131.

45. HPL to RK, 19 March 1919 (*SL* 1.80).

46. The date of admission is supplied by Winfield Townley Scott; see "His Own Most Fantastic Creation," in *Lovecraft Remembered,* 15.

47. See note 39.

48. HPL to Arthur Harris, 23 August 1915 (ms., JHL).

49. HPL to John T. Dunn, 10 June 1916; *Books at Brown,* 179.

50. See note 34.

51. HPL to Alfred Galpin, 27 May 1918 (*SL* 1.67).

52. George Julian Houtain, "Lovecraft" (*Zenith,* January 1921), in *Lovecraft Remembered,* 87.

53. HPL to FBL, 26 January 1921 (*SL* 1.122).

Chapter 10: Cynical Materialist

1. HPL to RK, 30 March 1919 (*SL* 1.81).

2. HPL to RK, 19 March 1919 (*SL* 1.81).

3. HPL to RK, 16 April 1919 (*SL* 1.82).

4. HPL to RK, 17 June 1919 (*SL* 1.82).

5. Winfield Townley Scott, "His Own Most Fantastic Creation," in *Lovecraft Remembered,* 16.

6. HPL to LDC, 13 August 1925 (ms., JHL); HPL to JFM, 19 May 1927 (*SL* 2.128).

7. HPL to RK, 25 June 1920; *Letters to Reinhardt Kleiner,* 194.

8. HPL to Edwin Baird, 3 February 1924 (*SL* 1.298).

9. *Epgephi* (September 1920): 6, 21.

10. "Falco Ossifracus" can be found in Miniter's *Dead Houses and Other Works,* ed. Kenneth W. Faig, Jr, and Sean Donnelly (New York: Hippocampus Press, 2008).

11. HPL to RK, 12 August 1920; *Letters to Reinhardt Kleiner,* 196.

12. HPL to RK, 10 September 1920; *Letters to Reinhardt Kleiner,* 197.

13. Ibid.

14. Long's date of birth has long been a source of debate: Lovecraft believed it to be 1902 (hence his writing a poem, "To Endymion," on his coming of age in 1923), and in later years Long himself stated that it was 1903; but a search by Peter Cannon in New York City birth records establishes conclusively that it was 1901. See Cannon, "FBL: When Was He Born and Why Was Lovecraft Wrong?" *Studies in Weird Fiction* No. 17 (Summer 1995): 33–34.

15. See Long's introduction to *The Early Long* (1975). He appears in the UAPA membership list no later than November 1919.

16. HPL to RK, 23 January 1920 (*SL* 1.107).

17. HPL to RK, 27 September 1919 (*SL* 1.88).

18. HPL to RK, 23 January 1920 (*SL* 1.106–7).

19. See George T. Wetzel and R. Alain Everts, *Winifred Virginia Jackson—Lovecraft's Lost Romance* [Madison, WI: R. Alain Everts, 1976].

20. HPL, "Winifred Virginia Jordan: Associate Editor," *Silver Clarion* (April 1919).

21. See note 19.

22. See note 19.

23. See note 20.

24. HPL to Sarah Susan Lovecraft, 17 March 1921 (ms., JHL). The poem in question was "The River of Life," which was printed as a wall card.

25. See note 19.

26. See headnote by Edwin Hadley Smith to "What Amateurdom and I Have Done for Each Other," *Boys' Herald* 46, No. 1 (August 1937): 6, who reports having secured the manuscript and noting that it is dated February 21.

27. HPL to Sarah Susan Lovecraft, 24 February 1921 (ms., JHL).

28. Ibid.

29. Ibid.

30. Ibid.

31. Cf. HPL to RK, 23 April 1921 (*SL* 1.128). The principal letter recording this trip—HPL to Sarah Susan Lovecraft, 17 March 1921—is misdated 24 March in *SL* 1.125 because Derleth thought that the gathering was actually on St Patrick's Day (March 17) and that therefore the mention of "My trip of a week ago" dated the letter to March 24.

32. Ibid.

33. HPL to RK, 12 June 1921 (*SL* 1.139).

34. Published in *LS* No. 26 (Spring 1992): 26–30.

35. Hugh Elliot, *Modern Science and Materialism* (London: Longmans, Green, 1919), 138–41. Hereafter cited in the text.

36. HPL to Elizabeth Toldridge, 24 April 1930 (*SL* 3.146).

37. HPL to RK, 23 February 1918 (*SL* 1.56–57).

38. Ernst Haeckel, *The Riddle of the Universe,* tr. Joseph McCabe (New York: Harper & Brothers, 1900), 263–64. Hereafter cited in the text.

39. HPL to the Kleicomolo, 8 August 1916 (*SL* 1.24).

40. HPL to MWM, 15 May 1918 (*SL* 1.63–64).

41. HPL to REH, 16 August 1932 (*SL* 4.57).

42. See Cook, *In Memoriam,* in *Lovecraft Remembered,* 148–49.

43. John Fiske, *Myths and Myth-Makers: Old Tales and Superstitions Interpreted by Comparative Mythology* (Boston: Houghton Mifflin, 1902), 23–24.

44. HPL to the Kleicomolo, April 1917 (*SL* 1.44).

45. HPL to Anne Tillery Renshaw, 1 June 1921 (*SL* 1.134).

46. HPL to Woodburn Harris, 25 February–1 March 1929 (*SL* 2.310).

47. James Turner, *Without God, Without Creed: The Origins of Unbelief in America* (Baltimore: Johns Hopkins University Press, 1985), 171–73.

48. HPL to RK, 14 September 1919 (*SL* 1.87).

49. HPL to RK, 7 March 1920 (*SL* 1.112).

50. Arthur Schopenhauer, *Studies in Pessimism,* in *Essays of Arthur Schopenhauer,* tr. T. Bailey Saunders (New York: Willey Book Co., [191–]), 2.

51. HPL to RK, 23 April 1921 (*SL* 1.130).

52. HPL to JFM, 1 March 1923 (*SL* 1.211).

53. HPL to RK, 14 September 1919 (*SL* 1.86).

54. HPL to Anne Tillery Renshaw, 1 June 1921 (*SL* 1.134).

55. HPL to RK, 13 May 1921 (*SL* 1.132).

56. HPL to FBL, 17 July 1921 (*SL* 1.142).

Chapter 11: Dunsanian Studies

1. *The Gods of Pegāna* (Boston: John W. Luce, n.d.), 1.

2. *Patches of Sunlight* (London: William Heinemann, 1938), 29–30.

3. Oscar Wilde, "Preface" to *The Picture of Dorian Gray* (1891).

4. *Patches of Sunlight,* 9.

5. Ibid., 135.

6. HPL to Fritz Leiber, 15 November 1936 (*SL* 5.354).

7. HPL to CAS, 14 April 1929 (*SL* 2.328).

8. HPL to Richard Ely Morse, 28 July 1932 (ms.).

9. See note 7.

10. HPL to CAS, 11 January 1923 (*SL* 1.203).

11. HPL to RK, 9 November 1919 (*SL* 1.91).

12. *While the Sirens Slept* (London: Jarrolds, 1944), 21.

13. Quoted by HPL in *SL* 1.93 (see note 11).

14. Lord Dunsany, Letter to Mary Faye Durr (10 July 1920), *United Amateur* 20, No. 2 (November 1920): 22–23.

15. *Tryout* 5, No. 12 (December 1919): 12.

16. HPL to the Gallomo, [April 1920]; *Letters to Alfred Galpin,* 83.

17. HPL to FBL, 3 June 1923 (*SL* 1.234).

18. C. L. Moore to HPL, 30 January 1936 (ms., JHL).

19. HPL to RK, 3 December 1919 (*SL* 1.93).

20. Lord Dunsany, *A Dreamer's Tales* (Boston: John W. Luce, n.d.), 60.

21. Alfred Galpin, "Department of Public Criticism," *United Amateur* 19, No. 4 (March 1920): 84.

22. Cf. the chronology of tales included in his letter to FBL, 8 November 1923 (AHT), where "The Street" is placed between "The White Ship" and "The Doom That Came to Sarnath."

23. HPL to FBL, 19 November 1920 (AHT).

24. "I echo your wish that 'The Street' might be professionally published and widely read . . ." Ibid.

25. *A Dreamer's Tales,* 78.

26. "In the Land of Time" (from *Time and the Gods*), *The Book of Wonder* (New York: Modern Library, 1918), 176.

27. *The Book of Wonder,* 16.

28. Carl Buchanan, "'The Terrible Old Man': A Myth of the Devouring Father," *LS* No. 29 (Fall 1993): 19–31.

29. HPL to FBL, 19 November 1920 (*SL* 1.121).

30. HPL to Alfred Galpin, 29 August 1918; *Letters to Alfred Galpin,* 35.

31. See further my article, "'The Tree' and Ancient History" (*Nyctalops,* April 1991), in *Primal Sources,* 162–66.

32. HPL to Wilfred B. Talman, 10 November 1936 (*SL* 5.348).

33. *A Dreamer's Tales,* 87.

34. HPL to RK, 21 May 1920 (*SL* 1.116–17).

35. HPL to FBL, 19 November 1920 (*SL* 1.121).

36. *The Book of Wonder,* 117.

37. HPL to the Gallomo, [April 1920] (*SL* 1.106).

38. HPL to RK, 23 April 1921 (*SL* 1.128).

39. *The Gods of Pegāna,* 35.

40. HPL to RK, 7 March 1920 (*SL* 1.110).

41. HPL to RK, 23 January 1920 (*SL* 1.107).

42. *SL* 1.93 (see note 11).

43. Lord Dunsany, Letter to AD (28 March 1952), quoted in *LS* No. 14 (Spring 1987): 38.

44. For an exhaustive treatment of Dunsany's writing, see my *Lord Dunsany: Master of the Anglo-Irish Imagination* (Westport, CT: Greenwood Press, 1995). I did manage to prepare a selection of Dunsany's stories for Penguin Classics (*In the Land of Time and Other Fantasy Tales,* 2004), and I have also prepared editions of *The Complete Jorkens Stories* (San Francisco: Night Shade Books, 2005–05; 3 vols.) and of Dunsany's final, previously unpublished novel, *The Pleasures of a Futuroscope* (New York: Hippocampus Press, 2003), but it still does not seem feasible to say that a genuine Dunsany renaissance is under way.

Chapter 12: A Stranger in This Century

1. HPL to the Gallomo, 11 December 1919 (*SL* 1.94–97).

2. Turner related this theory to me as we were preparing the corrected edition of *At the Mountains of Madness and Other Novels* (Arkham House, 1985).

3. HPL to Elizabeth Toldridge, 10 June 1929 (*SL* 2.353).

4. *Dreams and Fancies* (Sauk City, WI: Arkham House, 1962), 46; see David E. Schultz, ed., *Commonplace Book* (West Warwick, RI: Necronomicon Press, 1987), 1.viii.

5. HPL to RK, 23 January 1920 (*SL* 1.106).

6. See S. T. Joshi and Darrell Schweitzer, *Lord Dunsany: A Bibliography* (Metuchen, NJ: Scarecrow Press, 1993), 10.

7. HPL to RK, 7 March 1920 (*SL* 1.110).

8. Poe, *Collected Works,* 2.204.

9. HPL to FBL, 26 January 1924 (*SL* 1.287).

10. HPL to Arthur Harris, 1 May 1921 (ms., JHL).

11. HPL to Edwin Baird, [c. October 1923]; *Weird Tales* (March 1924).

12. "The Vivisector," *Wolverine* No. 11 (November 1921); rpt. in *The Vivisector* (West Warwick, RI: Necronomicon Press, 1990), 9.

13. Sam Moskowitz, *Under the Moons of Mars,* 339.

14. HPL to RHB, 28 July 1932; *O Fortunate Floridian,* 34.

15. Henry R. Chace, *Owners and Occupants of the Lots, Houses and Shops in the Town of Providence, Rhode Island in 1798* (Providence: Privately printed, 1914), plate III. I am grateful to Kenneth W. Faig, Jr, for pointing out this datum.

16. See further my article, "The Sources for 'From Beyond'" (*CoC,* Eastertide 1986), in *Primal Sources,* 167–71.

17. *SL* 1.160–62; the letter is misdated in *SL* as December 14, 1921.

18. George T. Wetzel's discussion of this historical connexion ("The Cthulhu Mythos: A Study" [1972], in Joshi, *Four Decades,* 82–83) is wildly erroneous.

19. Will Murray, "Behind the Mask of Nyarlathotep," *LS* No. 25 (Fall 1991): 25–29.

20. HPL to MWM, 18 September 1932 (*SL* 4.65).

21. Margaret Chaney, *Tesla: Man out of Time* (Englewood Cliffs, NJ: Prentice-Hall, 1981); quoted in Murray (n. 19 above).

22. HPL to RHB, [1 December 1934]; *O Fortunate Floridian,* 191.

23. HPL to RK, 21 May 1920 (*SL* 1.116).

24. Alfred Galpin, "Department of Public Criticism," *United Amateur* 21, No. 2 (November 1921): 21.

25. See Will Murray, "In Search of Arkham Country," *LS* No. 13 (Fall 1986): 54–67; Robert D. Marten, "Arkham Country: In Rescue of the Lost Searchers," *LS* No. 39 (Summer 1998): 1–20.

26. HPL to REH, 4 October 1930 (*SL* 3.175).

27. HPL to FBL, 11 December 1923 (*SL* 1.275).

28. Maurice Lévy, *Lovecraft: A Study in the Fantastic,* 15–16.

29. Colin Wilson, *The Strength to Dream* (Boston: Houghton Mifflin, 1962), 5.

30. HPL to E. Hoffmann Price, 24 March 1933 (*SL* 4.162).

31. See further my article, "Lovecraft and the *Regnum Congo*" (*CoC,* Yuletide 1983), in *Primal Sources,* 172–76.

32. HPL to Woodburn Harris, 25 February–1 March 1929 (*SL* 2.306).

33. See Jason C. Eckhardt, "The Cosmic Yankee," in *An Epicure in the Terrible,* ed. Schultz and Joshi, 89–90.

34. HPL to MWM, 29 August 1916 (AHT).

35. RHB to AD, 14 June 1944 (ms., SHSW).

36. George T. Wetzel, "The Research of a Biblio," in *Howard Phillips Lovecraft: Memoirs, Critiques, and Bibliographies* (North Tonawanda, NY: SSR Publications, 1955), 41.

37. HPL to FBL, 26 January 1921 (*SL* 1.122).

38. Ibid.

39. William Fulwiler, "Reflections on 'The Outsider,'" *LS* No. 2 (Spring 1980): 3–4.

40. Donald R. Burleson, "On Lovecraft's Themes: Touching the Glass," in *An Epicure in the Terrible,* ed. Schultz and Joshi, 135.

41. Colin Wilson, *The Strength to Dream,* 8.

42. Oscar Wilde, *Works* (London: Spring Books, 1963), 515, 526.

43. See note 18.

44. *Three Gothic Novels* (Harmondsworth: Penguin, 1968), 379. This passage was brought to my attention by Forrest Jackson.

45. Ibid., 371.

46. HPL to JVS, 19 June 1931 (*SL* 3.379).

47. RHB, *On Lovecraft and Life,* 16.

48. W. Paul Cook, "A Plea for Lovecraft," *Ghost* No. 3 (May 1945): 56.

49. HPL to LDC, 2 October 1925 (ms., JHL). In his memoir (*In Memoriam* [1993 ed.], 31) Cook claims that he had set "The Outsider" in type for the *Vagrant* but that he was not sure whether it had ever actually been published there; this seems, however, a lapse of memory.

Chapter 13: The High Tide of My Life

1. Winfield Townley Scott, "His Own Most Fantastic Creation," in *Lovecraft Remembered,* 17.

2. HPL to Anne Tillery Renshaw, 1 June 1921 (*SL* 1.133).

3. HPL to FBL, 4 June 1921 (*SL* 1.135).

4. *SL* 1.134 (note 2).

5. Faig, *Parents,* 40.

6. HPL to MWM, 5 April 1931 (*SL* 3.370).

7. HPL to RK, 12 June 1921 (*SL* 1.140).

8. HPL to AEPG, 27 August 1921 (ms., JHL).

9. HPL to AEPG, 19 August 1921 (*SL* 1.146–47).

10. Ibid. (ms., JHL; this portion not in *SL*).

11. HPL to RK, 21 August 1919 (*SL* 1.86).

12. HPL to MWM, 15 June 1925 (ms., JHL).

13. Quoted in [Horace L. Lawson], "Editorial," *Wolverine* No. 13 (December 1922): 13.

14. Anthony F. Moitoret, "Anent the United Amateur," *United Official Quarterly* (October 1922): 8.

15. HPL to John T. Dunn, 28 June 1916; *Books at Brown,* 184.

16. HPL to RK, 16 July 1919; *Letters to Reinhardt Kleiner,* 161,

17. See note 13 (14).

18. Paul J. Campbell, "The Official Organ as a Political Issue," *Liberal,* Special Issue (June 1922): 1–2.

19. "I suppose you received the card announcing United election results, with its astonishing and inexplicable mention of Mrs. Greene (who apparently knows nothing about it) as president." HPL to FBL, 18 September 1923 (AHT).

20. Sonia H. Lovecraft, "President's Message," *United Amateur* 23, No. 1 (May 1924): 11–14.

21. Found in AHT; also published in *Interesting Items* No. 540 (January 1924): [1–3].

22. All letters by Lawson to HPL are in JHL and NYPL.

23. R. Alain Everts ("Mrs. Howard Phillips Lovecraft," *Nyctalops* 2, No. 1 [April 1973]: 45), having interviewed Sonia in her old age, claims that she first met Lovecraft at a Hub Club meeting; but this seems to be an error. Everts writes: "Sonia stopped in Boston, and at one of the Hub Club meetings, Ed Cole, Edith Miniter and Michael White jokingly sat her down next to the reticent and shy Howard Lovecraft, never knowing that Sonia would set her sights on him as her next husband." But Lovecraft makes no mention of Sonia in any of his accounts of the Hub Club gatherings in early 1921, and he does not appear to have met Michael White until 1923. Sonia's remark—"I first met him at the Boston Convention when the amateur journalists gathered there for this conclave, in 1921" (*Private Life,* 15)—suggests the national convention rather than local or regional ones.

24. Sonia H. Davis, ["Autobiography"] (ms., JHL).

25. RK, "A Memoir of Lovecraft," in *Lovecraft Remembered,* 197.

26. HPL to RK, 11 August 1921 (*SL* 1.143).

27. See Faig, *Some of the Descendants,* 176–77, citing research conducted by R. Alain Everts.

28. Alfred Galpin, "Memories of a Friendship," in *Lovecraft Remembered,* 170–71.

29. Davis, *Private Life,* 10.

30. Sonia H. Davis, ["Autobiography"] (ms., JHL).

31. HPL to RK, 30 July 1921 (*SL* 1.142).

32. HPL to Winifred Virginia Jackson, 7 June 1921 (*SL* 1.137–38).

33. Faig, *Parents,* 22.

34. HPL to RK, 21 September 1921 (*SL* 1.152).

35. Ibid., 153.

36. HPL to RK, 21 September 1921; *Letters to Rheinhart Kleiner,* 216.

37. HPL to the Gallomo, 21 August 1921; *Letters to Alfred Galpin,* 104.

38. Davis, *Private Life,* 24.

39. Kleiner, "A Memoir of Lovecraft," in *Lovecraft Remembered,* 200.

40. HPL to Alfred Galpin, 29 August 1918; *Letters to Alfred Galpin,* 38.

41. The flyer is in JHL.

42. HPL to FBL and Alfred Galpin, 1 May 1923 (*SL* 1.225).

43. HPL to the Gallomo, [April 1920] (*SL* 1.103).

44. HPL to Anne Tillery Renshaw, 14 June 1922 (*SL* 1.185–86).

45. Davis, *Private Life,* 15.

46. David V. Bush, *Poems of Mastery and Love Verse* (St Louis: Lincoln Press, 1922), 41.

47. HPL to JFM, 17 May 1923 (AHT).

48. HPL's annotations to David Van Bush to The Symphony Literary Service, 28 February 1917 (ms., JHL).

49. David Van Bush to HPL, 24 July 1920 (ms., JHL).

50. HPL to LDC, 29 September 1922 (*SL* 1.199).

51. HPL to the Gallomo, [April 1920]; *Letters to Alfred Galpin,* 67.

52. HPL to RK, 23 January 1920 (*SL* 1.106).

53. HPL to Anne Tillery Renshaw, 3 October 1921 (*SL* 1.154).

54. HPL to RK, 7 October 1921 (*SL* 1.157).

55. HPL to FBL, 8 October 1921 (*SL* 1.158).

56. See note 53.

57. HPL to RK, 12 March 1922 (*SL* 1.167).

58. HPL to RK, 17 June 1922 (*SL* 1.188).

59. HPL to RK, 10 February 1920 (*SL* 1.108).

60. See note 58.

61. HPL to Samuel Loveman, 17 November [1922]; *Letters to Samuel Loveman and Vincent Starrett* (West Warwick, RI: Necronomicon Press, 1994), 9.

62. HPL to FBL, 8 February 1922 (*SL* 1.166).

63. HPL to Wilfred Blanch Talman, 10 November 1936 (*SL* 5.348).

64. Robert M. Price, "Erich Zann and the Rue d'Auseil," *LS* Nos. 22/23 (Fall 1990): 13–14.

65. HPL to Elizabeth Toldridge, 31 October 1931 (ms., JHL).

66. Jacques Bergier, "Lovecraft, ce grand génie venu d'ailleurs," *Planète* No. 1 (October–November 1961): 43–46.

67. See note 57.

68. Cf. HPL to MWM, 18 May 1922 (*SL* 1.176), noting that HPL read "Hypnos" to friends in New York in early April.

69. Steven J. Mariconda, "'Hypnos': Art, Philosophy, and Insanity," in *On the Emergence of "Cthulhu" and Other Observations* (West Warwick, RI: Necronomicon Press, 1995), 49–52.

70. HPL to Woodburn Harris, 25 February–1 March 1929 (*SL* 2.298–301).

71. *SL* 1.176 (note 68).

72. Davis, *Private Life,* 16.

73. *SL* 1.180 (note 68).

74. Davis, *Private Life,* 17.

75. *SL* 1.181 (note 68).

76. HPL to Anne Tillery Renshaw, 3 May 1922 (*SL* 1.174).

77. HPL to LDC, 25 May 1922 (postcard) (ms., JHL).

78. HPL to FBL, 9 June 1922 (*SL* 1.184).

79. HPL to Anne Tillery Renshaw, 14 June 1922 (*SL* 1.187).

80. HPL to FBL, 21 June 1922 (*SL* 1.189).

81. HPL to LDC, 29 June 1922 (postcard) (ms., JHL).

82. Davis, *Private Life,* 19.

83. Sonia H. Davis to Winfield Townley Scott, 11 December 1948 (ms., JHL).

84. See Everts, "Mrs. Howard Phillips Lovecraft," 45.

85. Davis, *Private Life,* 19.

86. HPL to LDC, 16 July 1922 (postcard) (ms., JHL).

87. HPL to LDC, 4 August 1922 (*SL* 1.191).

88. HPL to LDC, 9 August 1922 (ms., JHL).

89. Ibid.

90. HPL to FBL, 8 January 1924 (*SL* 1.281–82).

91. HPL to JFM, 8 January 1924 (*SL* 1.280).

92. HPL to CAS, 12 August 1922 (*SL* 1.193).

93. The publication of a three-volume edition of Smith's *Complete Poems and Translations* (Hippocampus Press, 2007–08) was the culmination of decades of work by my coeditor, David E. Schultz.

94. See *The Shadow of the Unattained: The Letters of George Sterling and Clark Ashton Smith* (New York: Hippocampus Press, 2005).

95. George Sterling's *Complete Poetry* is scheduled for publication in 2011 by Hippocampus Press.

96. HPL to CAS, 25 March 1923 (*SL* 1.213–14).

97. See Paul Livingston Keil, "I Met Lovecraft," *Phoenix* 3, No. 6 (July 1944): 149.

98. HPL to LDC, 29 September 1922 (ms., JHL).

99. Ibid.

100. The story is listed in Lovecraft's chronologies as written in 1922, prior to "The Lurking Fear," which was clearly written in November.

101. Steven J. Mariconda, "'The Hound'—A Dead Dog?" (*CoC,* Eastertide 1986), in *On the Emergence of "Cthulhu,"* 45–49.

102. HPL to FBL, February 1924 (*SL* 1.292–93).

103. HPL to MWM, [c. August 1922] (AHT).

104. HPL to Harry O. Fischer, [late February 1937] (*SL* 5.418).

105. HPL to RK, 30 July 1921; *Letters to Reinhardt Kleiner,* 209.

106. HPL to FBL, 9 June 1922 (*SL* 1.185).

107. HPL to Winifred V. Jackson, 7 October 1921 (ms., JHL).

108. HPL to FBL, 9 June 1922 (AHT).

109. In a letter to Samuel Loveman (17 November [1922]; *Letters to Samuel Loveman and Vincent Starrett,* 9) HPL announced not having started the story; by early December he had sent it to CAS (HPL to CAS, 2 December 1922 [*SL* 1.201]).

110. See "Observations on Several Parts of America" (1928).

111. HPL to JFM, 19 October 1929 (*SL* 3.31).

112. HPL to Samuel Loveman, 29 April [1923]; *Letters to Samuel Loveman and Vincent Starrett,* 16.

113. HPL to CAS, 14 May 1926 (*SL* 2.50).

114. HPL to F. Lee Baldwin, 16 May 1934 (ms., JHL).

115. HPL to REH, 25–29 March 1933 (*SL* 4.170).

116. In a letter to Kleiner (11 January 1923 [*SL* 1.203] he dates the trip to "Monday"; in a later letter (HPL to JFM, 12 March 1930 [*SL* 3.126]) he states it was December 17, which is a Sunday. In "Mrs. Miniter—Estimates and Recollections" he oddly states that Miniter and Cole accompanied him to Marblehead; but perhaps this refers to a later visit.

117. HPL to RK, 11 January 1923 (*SL* 1.204).

118. Ibid.

119. HPL to JFM, 12 March 1930 (*SL* 3.126–27).

Chapter 14: For My Own Amusement

1. Truman J. Spencer, *The History of Amateur Journalism* (New York: The Fossils, 1957), 70.

2. HPL to LDC, 27 July 1925; *Letters from New York,* 153.

3. RK, "Howard Phillips Lovecraft," *Californian* 5, No. 1 (Summer 1937): 6.

4. HPL to Ralph Babcock, [1930s]; published as "The Voice from the Grave," *Scarlet Cockerel* No. 15 (January 1941): 15–19.

5. HPL to LDC, 31 August 1922 (AHT).

6. See HPL to RK, 11 January 1923; *Letters to Reinhardt Kleiner,* 224.

7. HPL to Edward H. Cole, 23 and 24 February [1923] (mss., JHL).

8. HPL to Samuel Loveman, 24 March [1923]; *Letters to Samuel Loveman and Vincent Starrett,* 11–12.

9. HPL to Samuel Loveman, 29 April [1923]; *Letters to Samuel Loveman and Vincent Starrett,* 16.

10. Ibid.

11. HPL to RK, 29 April 192[3] (*SL* 1.131). The letter is misdated to 1921 in *SL.*

12. HPL to LDC, 14–19 November 1925 (ms., JHL).

13. "My card sent from Salem last month . . .": HPL to CAS, 25 March 1923 (*SL* 1.213). Cf. also HPL to LDC, [9 Feb. 1923] (postcard) (ms., JHL).

14. See note 8.

15. HPL to FBL and Alfred Galpin, 1 May 1923 (*SL* 1.219–20).

16. See note 9.

17. Ibid.

18. HPL to FBL, 3 June 1923 (*SL* 1.233).

19. Davis, *Private Life,* 18.

20. Cole, "Ave atque Vale!"(*Olympian,* Autumn 1940), in *Lovecraft Remembered,* 101.

21. HPL to Robert E. Moe, 13 February 1935 (ms., JHL).

22. HPL to MWM, 31 July [1923] (ms., JHL).

23. HPL to FBL, 4 September 1923 (*SL* 1.248).

24. HPL to LDC, [15 September 1923] (postcard) (ms., JHL).

25. HPL to FBL, 21 September 1923 (*SL* 1.251).

26. HPL to JFM, 29 March 1923 (AHT).

27. HPL to JFM, 3 May 1923 (*SL* 1.226).

28. See Robert E. Weinberg, *The Weird Tales Story* (West Linn, OR: FAX Collector's Editions, 1977), 3.

29. HPL to the Gallomo, [April 1920]; *Letters to Alfred Galpin,* 84.

30. See note 27.

31. HPL to JFM, 29 May 1923 (AHT).

32. HPL to MWM, 19 October 1924 (AHT).

33. HPL to Bernard Austin Dwyer, [1932] (*SL* 4.4).

34. HPL to FBL, 3 June 1923 (*SL* 1.233–34).

35. Ibid.

36. *SL* 1.250 (note 25).

37. Steven J. Mariconda, "Baring-Gould and the Ghouls: The Influence of *Curious Myths of the Middle Ages* on 'The Rats in the Walls'" (*CoC,* St John's Eve 1983), in *On the Emergence of "Cthulhu,"* 53–56.

40. HPL to JVS, 8–22 November 1933 (ms., JHL).

41. Irvin S. Cobb, "The Unbroken Chain," in *On an Island That Cost $24.00* (New York: George H. Doran Co., 1926), 66–67.

42. HPL to FBL, 8 November 1923 (*SL* 1.259).

43. See Sam Moskowitz, *A. Merritt: Reflections in the Moon Pool* (Philadelphia: Oswald Train, 1985), 50–52.

44. HPL to C. L. Moore, 2 July 1936 (*SL* 5.181).

45. See HPL to FBL, 7 October 123 (*SL* 1.255).

46. HPL to CAS, [3 October 1933] (ms., JHL).

47. HPL to REH, 2–5 November 1933 (*SL* 4.297).

48. HPL to REH, 4 October 1930 (*SL* 3.178, 182–83).

49. HPL to LDC, 30 March 1924; *Letters from New York,* 53.

50. *New Statesman* (9 September 1921): 611.

51. Muriel E. Eddy, "Howard Phillips Lovecraft," in *Rhode Island on Lovecraft,* ed. Donald M. Grant and Thomas Hadley (Providence: Grant-Hadley, 1945), 14. Not included in *Lovecraft Remembered.*

52. Muriel E. Eddy, *The Gentleman from Angell Street,* in *Lovecraft Remembered,* 49–50.

53. *SL* 1.254 (note 45).

54. HPL to JFM, 28 October 1923 (*SL* 1.257).

55. Quoted in AD's prefatory note to "Three Stories" by C. M. Eddy, Jr, in *The Dark Brotherhood and Other Pieces* (Sauk City, WI: Arkham House, 1966), 97.

56. See note 54.

57. Quoted in Derleth (n. 55).

58. See note 53.

59. *SL* 1.264 (note 42).

60. HPL to Edwin Baird, [c. November 1923]; *Weird Tales* (March 1924).

61. See note 54.

62. HPL to AD, [7 December 1929]; *Essential Solitude,* 1.234.

63. "In the Editor's Study" (*Conservative,* July 1923).

64. HPL to Anne Tillery Renshaw, 1 June 1921 (*SL* 1.134).

65. HPL to RK, 25 August 1918 (*SL* 1.73).

66. W. Jackson Bate, *The Burden of the Past and the English Poet* (Cambridge, MA: Harvard University Press, 1970), 21.

67. HPL to JFM, 1 April 1927 (*SL* 2.123).

68. Edward Hale Bierstadt, *Dunsany the Dramatist* (Boston: Little, Brown, rev. ed. 1919), 160.

69. T. S. Eliot, "The Metaphysical Poets" (1921), *Selected Essays* (New York: Harcourt, Brace, 1950), 248.

70. HPL to MWM, 18 May 1922 (*SL* 1.180).

71. HPL to FBL, 11 December 1923 (*SL* 1.275).

72. HPL to FBL, 13 May 1923 (*SL* 1.229).

73. HPL to FBL, 20 February 1924 (*SL* 1.315).

74. HPL to FBL, 8 January 1924 (*SL* 1.283).

75. Michael White, "Poets of Amateur Journalism: III. The Poetry of Samuel Loveman," *Oracle* 3, No. 4 (December 1922): 12–17.

76. Alfred Galpin, "A Critic of Poetry," *Oracle* 4, No. 2 (August 1923): 8–10.

77. HPL to Samuel Loveman, 24 March [1923]; *Letters to Samuel Loveman and Vincent Starrett,* 15.

78. HPL to FBL, 26 May 1923 (*SL* 1.230).

79. See Peter Ackroyd, *T. S. Eliot: A Life* (New York: Simon & Schuster, 1984), 127.

80. *Freeman* (17 January 1923): 453.

81. See note 78.

82. HPL to JVS, 24 March 1933 (*SL* 4.159).

83. Barton L. St Armand and John H. Stanley, "H. P. Lovecraft's *Waste Paper:* A Facsimile and Transcript of the Original Draft," *Books at Brown* 26 (1978): 40.

84. HPL to AD, 2 January 1927 (*SL* 2.96).

85. HPL to JVS, 5 February 1932 (*SL* 4.14).

86. HPL to CAS, 17 October 1930 (*SL* 3.195).

87. HPL to Myrta Alice Little, 17 May 1921; *LS* No. 26 (Spring 1992): 28.

88. HPL to CAS, 16 November 1926 (*SL* 2.90).

89. HPL to JFM, 26 May 1923 (*SL* 1.231).

90. HPL to the Gallomo, [April 1920]; *Letters to Alfred Galpin,* 75.

91. *New York Times* (12 April 1923): 1.

92. HPL to JFM, 23 September 1923 (*SL* 1.253).

93. HPL to JFM, 10 February 1923 (*SL* 1.207).

94. *Twilight of the Idols* [1888], in *Twilight of the Idols and The Anti-Christ,* tr. R. J. Hollingdale (Harmondsworth, UK: Penguin, 1968), 93.

95. *SL* 1.208 (note 93).

96. HPL to MWM, 24 November 1923 (*SL* 1.268–72).

97. HPL to Samuel Loveman, [5 June 1924] (*SL* 1.277).

98. HPL to Edwin Baird, 3 February 1924 (*SL* 1.294).

Chapter 15: Ball and Chain

1. HPL to MWM, 18 May 1922 (*SL* 1.179).

2. Lord Dunsany, "A City of Wonder," in *Tales of Three Hemispheres* (Boston: John W. Luce Co., 1919), 64.

3. HPL to Elizabeth Toldridge, 26 February 1932 (*SL* 4.21).

4. FBL, *Howard Phillips Lovecraft: Dreamer on the Nightside* (Sauk City, WI: Arkham House, 1975), p 46–47.

5. Kleiner, "A Memoir of Lovecraft," in *Lovecraft Remembered,* 197–98.

6. Muriel Eddy, "Howard Phillips Lovecraft," in *Rhode Island on Lovecraft,* 20.

7. HPL to JFM, 12 March 1924 (*SL* 1.326).

8. HPL to LDC, [4 March 1924] (postcard) (ms., JHL).

9. HPL to LDC, 9 March 1924 (*SL* 1.319–22).

10. Sonia H. Davis, *Private Life,* 18.

11. HPL to CAS, 25 January 1924 (*SL* 1.285).

12. HPL to Edwin Baird, 3 February 1924 (*SL* 1.298).

13. Davis, *Private Life,* 18.

14. Sonia H. Greene to LDC, 9 February 1924 (AHT).

15. *SL* 1.325 (note 7).

16. HPL to FBL, 21 March 1924 (*SL* 1.329).

17. Koki, 89.

18. Note to Sonia H. Davis, "The Psychic Phenomenon of Love" (ms., JHL).

19. "Lovecraft on Love," *Arkham Collector* No. 8 (Winter 1971): 244.

20. HPL to LDC, 29–30 September 1924 (ms., JHL).

21. HPL to E. Hoffmann Price, 18 November 1934 (ms., JHL).

22. HPL to FBL, 14 February 1924 (*SL* 1.311–12).

23. Davis, *Private Life,* 18.

24. See *SL* 1.331 (note 16).

25. HPL to MWM, 24 November 1923 (*SL* 1.269).

26. Davis, *Private Life,* 11–12.

27. *SL* 1.332 (note 16).

28. *SL* 1.333 (note 16).

29. HPL to JVS, 29 May 1933 (*SL* 4.191).

30. HPL to LDC, 22–23 December 1924 (ms., JHL).

31. *SL* 1.332 (note 16).

32. HPL to FBL, 7 February 1924 (*SL* 1.304).

33. *SL* 1.332 (note 16).

34. *SL* 1.304 (note 32).

35. Robert E. Weinberg, *The Weird Tales Story,* 4.

36. *SL* 1.304 (note 32).

37. HPL to LDC, 30 March 1924; *Letters from New York,* 52–53.

38. HPL and Sonia H. Greene to LDC, [5 March 1924] (postcard) (ms., JHL).

39. HPL to LDC, 9 March 1924; *Letters from New York,* 43.

40. See Long, *Dreamer on the Nightside,* 40.

41. HPL to LDC, 1 August 1924 (*SL* 1.341).

42. Kleiner, "A Memoir of Lovecraft," in *Lovecraft Remembered,* 201.

43. Koki (106) claims that Samuel Loveman told him that Florence actually did live with Sonia and Lovecraft for the first few months of their marriage, but I believe this to be a misremembrance on Loveman's part. He was, in any case, not in New York at this time, arriving only in September 1924.

44. See R. Alain Everts, *Lovecraft's Daughter* (a three-part article distributed through the Esoteric Order of Dagon amateur press association in mailings 38 [Roodmas 1982], 39 [Lammas 1982], and 41 [Candlemas 1983]).

45. Geoffrey Perrett, *America in the Twenties: A History* (New York: Simon & Schuster, 1982), 323.

46. Sonia H. Greene to LDC, 9 February 1924 (AHT).

47. Sonia H. Davis, ["Autobiography"] (ms., JHL).

48. *SL* 1.303 (note 12).

49. HPL to LDC, [10 March 1924] (postcard) (ms., JHL).

50. HPL to LDC, 9 March 1924; *Letters from New York,* 38.

51. *SL* 1.337 (note 41).

52. Cf. FBL to HPL, [20 December 1928] (ms., JHL): ". . . the Thompson [*sic*] whose *What Is Man* you reviewed for *The Reading Lamp* several years ago."

53. HPL to LDC, [28 May 1924] (postcard) (ms., JHL).

54. Sonia H. Davis, ["Autobiography"] (ms., JHL).

55. I am grateful to A. Langley Searles for some of this information on Yonkers.

56. HPL to RK, 16 November 1916 (*SL* 1.33).

57. *SL* 1.343 (note 41).

58. HPL to the Homeland Company, 29 July 1924 (ms., JHL).

59. See note 54.

60. Cashman, *America in the Age of the Titans,* 165; see also Geoffrey Moorhouse, *Imperial City: The Rise and Fall of New York* (London: Hodder & Stoughton, 1988), 84.

61. *SL* 1.337 (note 41).

62. *SL* 1.338 (note 41).

63. HPL to LDC, [10 September 1924] (postcard) (ms., JHL).

64. Letter of application, 1924 (*SL* 1.xxvii–xxviii).

65. Kleiner, "A Memoir of Lovecraft," in *Lovecraft Remembered,* 201–2.

66. Long, *Dreamer on the Nightside,* 67.

67. *New York Times* (10 August 1924): 10:6.

68. M. A. Katherman to HPL, 11 August 1924 (ms., JHL).

69. HPL to LDC, [19 March 1924] (postcard) (ms., JHL).

70. HPL to LDC, [18 September 1924] (postcard); *Letters from New York,* 62.

71. HPL to LDC, 29–30 September 1924; *Letters from New York,* 70.

72. See Robert E. Weinberg in *Science Fiction, Fantasy, and Weird Fiction Magazines,* ed. Marshall Tymn and Mike Ashley (Westport, CT: Greenwood Press, 1985), 727.

73. See note 71 (*Letters from New York,* 75).

74. Long, *Dreamer on the Nightside,* 80–82.

75. See note 71 (*Letters from New York,* 74).

76. HPL to LDC, 18 March 1924 (*SL* 1.328).

77. Harry Houdini to HPL, 28 September 1924; quoted in HPL to LDC, 29–30 September 1924; *Letters from New York,* 75.

78. HPL to LDC, 29–30 September 1924 (ms., JHL).

79. HPL to LDC, 4–6 November 1924; *Letters from New York,* 84.

80. See Sonia H. Greene Lovecraft, "President's Message," *United Amateur* 24, No. 1 (July 1925): 9.

81. HPL to MWM, 15 June 1925 (*SL* 2.15).

82. HPL to JFM, 3 February 1932 (*SL* 4.13).

83. *SL* 2.15 (note 81).

84. HPL to LDC, [11–12 November 1924]; *Letters from New York,* 88.

85. HPL to LDC, 17–18 November 1924; *Letters from New York,* 92.

86. Davis, *Private Life,* 10.

87. See note 71 (*Letters from New York,* 67).

88. See note 85 (*Letters from New York,* 94).

89. Ibid.

90. HPL to LDC, 17–18 November 1924 (ms., JHL).

91. *SL* 2.16 (note 81).

92. R. Alain Everts, "Howard Phillips Lovecraft and Sex; or, The Sex Life of a Gentleman," *Nyctalops* 2, No. 2 (July 1974): 19.

93. Sonia H. Davis, "Memories of Lovecraft: I," in *Lovecraft Remembered,* 275.

94. Ibid., 275–76.

95. See note 92.

96. Davis, *Private Life,* 15.

97. HPL to FBL, February 1924 (*SL* 1.292).

98. Davis, *Private Life,* 13.

99. See note 93.

100. *SL* 2.19 (note 81).

101. See Mara Kirk Hart, "Walkers in the City: George Willard Kirk and Howard Phillips Lovecraft in New York City, 1924–1926," *LS* No. 28 (Spring 1993): 3. Excerpts only reprinted in *Lovecraft Remembered.*

102. HPL to LDC, 29 November 1924; *Letters from New York,* 99–100.

103. Davis, *Private Life,* 12.

104. HPL to AD, 16 January 1931 (*SL* 3.262).

105. HPL to FBL, 21 March 1924 (*SL* 1.329).

106. HPL to JFM, 6 May 1924 (*SL* 1.337).

107. A complete list of his novels is as follows: *Dickon Bend the Bow and Other Wonder Tales* (Akron, OH: Saalfield Publishing Co., 1903); *The Hermit of the Culebra Mountains; or, The Adventures of Two Schoolboys in the Far West* (New York: Dutton, 1904); *The Lost Treasure Cave; or, Adventures with the Cowboys of Colorado* (New York: Dutton, 1905); *The Boy Forty-niners; or, Across the Plains and Mountains to the Goldmines of California in a Prairie-Schooner* (New York: McClure Co., 1908); *In Texas with Davy Crockett: A Story of the Texas War of Independence* (New York:

Dutton, 1908; rpt. 1937); *With Kit Carson in the Rockies: A Tale of the Beaver Country* (New York: Dutton, 1909); *Fighting with Fremont: A Tale of the Conquest of California* (New York: Dutton, 1910); *The Cave of Gold: A Tale of California in '49* (New York: Dutton, 1911); *The Totem of Black Hawk: A Tale of Pioneer Days in Northwestern Illinois and the Black Hawk War* (Chicago: A. C. McClurg & Co., 1914); *The Lost Nation* (New York: Dutton, 1918); *Buried Treasure: A Tale of an Old House* (New York: Duffield & Co., 1919); *Tonty of the Iron Hand* (New York: Dutton, 1925); *Daniel Du Luth; or, Adventuring on the Great Lakes* (New York: Dutton, 1926); *For the Glory of France* (New York: Dutton, 1927); *The Shadow of the Iroquois* (New York: Dutton, 1928); *The Shores of Adventure; or, Exploring in the New World with Jacques Cartier* (New York: Dutton, 1929).

108. Hart (note 101), 4.

109. HPL to LDC, 29–30 September 1924 (ms., JHL).

110. Long, *Dreamer on the Nightside,* 51.

111. Ibid., 157–58.

112. Davis, *Private Life,* 18–19.

113. Talman, *The Normal Lovecraft* (Saddle River, NJ: Gerry de la Ree, 1973), 16.

114. HPL to RHB, 10 April 1934; *O Fortunate Floridian,* 126.

115. See note 71 (*Letters from New York,* 65).

116. HPL to LDC, 1 August 1924 (AHT).

117. See note 71 (*Letters from New York,* 69).

118. Ibid. (*Letters from New York,* 70).

119. Ibid. (*Letters from New York,* 72).

120. Ibid. (ms., JHL; not published in *Letters from New York*).

121. John Unterecker, "Introduction" to *Poems of Hart Crane* (New York: Liveright, 1986), xxii.

122. Hart Crane, Letter to Grace Hart Crane and Elizabeth Belden Hart (14 September 1924), *Letters of Hart Crane and His Family,* ed. Thomas S. W. Lewis (New York: Columbia University Press, 1974), 342–43.

123. Kleiner, "A Memoir of Lovecraft," in *Lovecraft Remembered,* 200.

124. HPL and AEPG to LDC, [26 September 1924] (postcard) (ms., JHL).

125. HPL to LDC, 17–18 November 1924 (ms., JHL).

126. HPL to LDC, 4–6 November 1924 (ms., JHL).

127. Hart Crane, Letter to Grace Hart Crane and Elizabeth Belden Hart (14 October 1924), *Letters of Hart Crane and His Family,* 354.

128. See note 126 (*Letters from New York,* 82).

129. Ibid. (*Letters from New York,* 84).

130. Faye Ringel Hazel, "Some Strange New England Mortuary Practices: Lovecraft Was Right," *LS* No. 29 (Fall 1993): 13–18.

131. HPL to CAS, [11 February 1934] (ms.).

132. HPL to LDC, 17–18 November 1924; *Letters from New York,* 93.

133. HPL to LDC, 4–6 November 1924 (ms., JHL).

134. Hart, 5.

135. HPL to LDC, 4–6 November 1924; *Lettters from New York,* 79n.

136. See the reference to "my late visitor Sechrist": HPL to FBL, February 1924 (*SL* 1.292).

137. *SL* 1.341–42 (note 41).

138. HPL to LDC, [11 November 1924]; *Letters from New York,* 90.

139. HPL to LDC, [11 November 1924] (postcard) (ms., JHL).

140. HPL to LDC, [12 November 1924] (ms., JHL).

141. HPL to LDC, 17–18 November 1924 (ms., JHL).

142. Ibid.

143. Ibid. (*Letters from New York,* 92–93).

144. HPL to LDC, 29 November 1924; *Letters from New York,* 98.

145. Ibid. (*Letters from New York,* 98–99).

146. Hart, 6.

CPSIA information can be obtained
at www.ICGtesting.com
Printed in the USA
BVOW06s0548071217
501961BV00004B/10/P